Narcissism and the Self

Narcissism and the Self

Dynamics of Self-Preservation in Social Interaction, Personality Structure, Subjective Experience, and Psychopathology

Ralf-Peter Behrendt
Princess Elizabeth Hospital, Guernsey

palgrave
macmillan

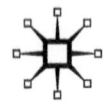

© Ralf-Peter Behrendt 2015

All rights reserved. No reproduction, copy or transmission of this publication may be made without written permission.

No portion of this publication may be reproduced, copied or transmitted save with written permission or in accordance with the provisions of the Copyright, Designs and Patents Act 1988, or under the terms of any licence permitting limited copying issued by the Copyright Licensing Agency, Saffron House, 6–10 Kirby Street, London EC1N 8TS.

Any person who does any unauthorized act in relation to this publication may be liable to criminal prosecution and civil claims for damages.

The author has asserted his right to be identified as the author of this work in accordance with the Copyright, Designs and Patents Act 1988.

First published 2015 by
PALGRAVE MACMILLAN

Palgrave Macmillan in the UK is an imprint of Macmillan Publishers Limited, registered in England, company number 785998, of Houndsmills, Basingstoke, Hampshire, RG21 6XS.

Palgrave Macmillan in the US is a division of St Martin's Press LLC, 175 Fifth Avenue, New York, NY 10010.

Palgrave is the global academic imprint of the above companies and has companies and representatives throughout the world.

Palgrave® and Macmillan® are registered trademarks in the United States, the United Kingdom, Europe and other countries.

ISBN 978–1–137–49147–3

This book is printed on paper suitable for recycling and made from fully managed and sustained forest sources. Logging, pulping and manufacturing processes are expected to conform to the environmental regulations of the country of origin.

A catalogue record for this book is available from the British Library.

Library of Congress Cataloging-in-Publication Data

Behrendt, Ralf-Peter.
  Narcissism and the self : dynamics of self-preservation in social interaction, personality structure, subjective experience, and psychopathology / Ralf-Peter Behrendt.
       pages cm
  ISBN 978–1–137–49147–3
  1. Narcissism.   2. Self.   3. Self-preservation.   I. Title.
  BF575.N35B445   2015
  155.2—dc23   2014049689

Typeset by MPS Limited, Chennai, India.

Contents

List of Figures   xiii

1 Introduction   1
2 Affective Expressions   11
    2.1 Aggression   14
       2.1.1 Phylogenetic ritualization   15
       2.1.2 Disdain and disgust   16
       2.1.3 Control of resources   17
       2.1.4 Enforcement of compliance and normality   18
       2.1.5 Neutralization   20
       2.1.6 Coercion and hatred   22
    2.2 Appeasement and submission   23
       2.2.1 Bonding and familiarity   24
       2.2.2 Infantilisms and alloparental behaviour   26
       2.2.3 Smile   27
       2.2.4 Bowing and nodding   28
       2.2.5 Greeting   29
       2.2.6 The imaginary plane   30
       2.2.7 Interaction with context and emotion   31
    2.3 Care seeking and giving   33
       2.3.1 Face-to-face interactions   34
       2.3.2 Infantile cries   35
       2.3.3 Distance-decreasing and contacting behaviours   36
       2.3.4 Infantile appeals to care   37
       2.3.5 Bonding and courtship   38
       2.3.6 Exhibitionism   39
       2.3.7 Social feeling   40
3 Affective States   42
    3.1 Anxiety   44
       3.1.1 Anxiety-related behaviours   45
       3.1.2 Gregariousness   46
       3.1.3 Attachment   48
       3.1.4 Loneliness   49
       3.1.5 Fear of strangers   50
       3.1.6 Anxiety as a contagion   50
       3.1.7 Basic anxiety   51
       3.1.8 Disintegration anxiety   52
       3.1.9 Fear of loss of love   53

	3.1.10	Fear of castration	55
	3.1.11	Shame	56
	3.1.12	Fear of exposure	57
	3.1.13	Conflict and defence	58
	3.1.14	Anticipation and risk assessment	59
3.2	Safety		60
	3.2.1	Self-satisfaction and self-esteem	61
	3.2.2	Ego instincts	62
	3.2.3	Attachment versus narcissism	63
	3.2.4	Functions of the object	64
	3.2.5	Responsiveness of the selfobject surround	65
	3.2.6	Introjection of the source of approval	66
	3.2.7	Replacement of the source of approval	66
	3.2.8	Desire and the symbolic	67
	3.2.9	Conversation	68
	3.2.10	Wishful fantasy and activity	70
	3.2.11	Subordination of instinctual drives	71
	3.2.12	Conflict with the idealized image	72
3.3	Habitual transfer from danger to safety		73
	3.3.1	Learning to escape from aversiveness	74
	3.3.2	Hedonic control	76
	3.3.3	Psychotaxis	77
	3.3.4	Compulsion to repeat	79
	3.3.5	Role relationships	80
	3.3.6	Goal-directedness of the personality	81
	3.3.7	Neurotic trends	83
	3.3.8	Reality principle and ego defences	84
3.4	Narcissism versus object love		85
	3.4.1	Narcissistic versus libidinal object relations	86
	3.4.2	Libido theory	88
	3.4.3	Primary narcissism and love	89
	3.4.4	Guilt and reparation	89
	3.4.5	Self-interest versus social interest	90
	3.4.6	Façade versus spontaneity	92
3.5	Pain and anger		93
	3.5.1	Separation and threat of abandonment	94
	3.5.2	Loss of object	95
	3.5.3	Narcissistic injury	97
	3.5.4	Retaliation	98
	3.5.5	Guilt and reparation	99
3.6	Depletion		100
4	**Development**		**102**
4.1	Symbiosis and attunement		103

			Contents vii
	4.1.1	Primary narcissism	104
	4.1.2	Primary identification	105
	4.1.3	Archaic narcissistic configurations	106
	4.1.4	Empathic responsiveness	107
	4.1.5	Maternal preoccupation	107
	4.1.6	Mirroring of the self	108
	4.1.7	Affectionate interactions	110
	4.1.8	Intersubjective relatedness	111
4.2	Individuation and attachment		112
	4.2.1	Separation	112
	4.2.2	Modification of omnipotence	114
	4.2.3	Mature dependence	115
	4.2.4	Depressive position	115
	4.2.5	Basic trust	116
	4.2.6	Attachment behaviour	117
	4.2.7	Internal working models	119
4.3	Exhibitionism and idealization		121
	4.3.1	Attention seeking	122
	4.3.2	Ambition and self-esteem	122
	4.3.3	Transmuting internalization	124
	4.3.4	Responsiveness of the selfobject milieu	125
	4.3.5	Merger with the idealized parent imago	125
	4.3.6	Attainable ideals	126
	4.3.7	Selfobject failures	128
	4.3.8	Overindulgence	130
4.4	Compliance and approvability		130
	4.4.1	Fear of punishment	131
	4.4.2	Conditionality of love	132
	4.4.3	Protomorality	133
	4.4.4	Turning aggression against the self	135
	4.4.5	Oedipus complex	136
	4.4.6	Ego identity	137
4.5	Compulsiveness versus spontaneity		138
	4.5.1	Inferiority and striving for superiority	139
	4.5.2	Formation of neurotic trends and loss of spontaneous initiative	141
	4.5.3	Playfulness and ego-syntonicity	141
5	**Superego**		**143**
5.1	Instinctual life and social reality		144
	5.1.1	Superego projection	146
5.2	Ego ideal		147
	5.2.1	Idealization and identification	148
	5.2.2	Infantile grandiosity and need for merger	150

	5.2.3	Ideal self	151
	5.2.4	Ideal object	152
	5.2.5	Self-satisfaction and -dissatisfaction	153
	5.2.6	Mechanisms of defence	154
	5.2.7	Superiority and perfectionism	155
	5.2.8	Self-actualization and inner dictates	157
	5.2.9	Moral masochism	159
5.3	Self-observing function		160
	5.3.1	Anticipatory affects	161
	5.3.2	Choice conflicts and decision-making	162
	5.3.3	Identification with the ideal self	163
	5.3.4	Oscillation between wishing and 'oughtness'	164
	5.3.5	Oscillating perspective	164
5.4	Drive modulation		166
	5.4.1	Deflection of aggression	167
	5.4.2	Momentary awareness of impulse	168
	5.4.3	Anticipation of punishment or reward	169
	5.4.4	Defence	171
5.5	Guilt		172
	5.5.1	Shame	173
	5.5.2	Fear of loss of love	175
	5.5.3	Conflict resolution	176
	5.5.4	Tension between ego states	177
	5.5.5	Need for absolution	177
	5.5.6	Need for punishment and its manifestations	178
	5.5.7	Unconscious guilt	180
	5.5.8	Love and reparation	181
6 Self-experience			**182**
6.1	Constitution of the self		183
	6.1.1	Satisfaction and desire	185
	6.1.2	Ego boundary	186
	6.1.3	Selfobjects	188
	6.1.4	Self as another	190
	6.1.5	Internalized object relations	191
	6.1.6	Façade and self-alienation	192
6.2	Sociological perspectives		193
	6.2.1	Me and I	194
	6.2.2	Role performance	195
	6.2.3	Duty	196
	6.2.4	Ego identity and collective consciousness	196
	6.2.5	Affirmation of identity	198
	6.2.6	Self as a narrative or theory	198
6.3	Vulnerability of the self		199
	6.3.1	Self-serving bias	200

		6.3.2	Self-system	201
		6.3.3	Repression	202
		6.3.4	Displaced action	203
		6.3.5	Projection	204
		6.3.6	Denial	205
		6.3.7	Rationalization	206
	6.4	Self-enhancement through identification		208
		6.4.1	Identification with an admired object	208
		6.4.2	Altruism	209
		6.4.3	Identification with the aggressor	210
		6.4.4	Omnipotent fantasy	211
	6.5	Paying attention to oneself		212
		6.5.1	Self-observation as a social phenomenon	213
		6.5.2	Self-consciousness	215
		6.5.3	Self-pity and inconsolability	216
7	**Character Defences**			**218**
	7.1	Primitive modes of attracting attention		219
		7.1.1	Craving and clinging	220
		7.1.2	Pseudovitality	222
		7.1.3	Regression	222
		7.1.4	Illness behaviour and appeal to pity	223
		7.1.5	Masochistic submission	224
	7.2	Identification		225
		7.2.1	Idealization and merger	225
		7.2.2	Love and subservience	226
		7.2.3	Acting a part	227
	7.3	Detachment		228
		7.3.1	Aloneness	229
		7.3.2	Fantasy	230
		7.3.3	Intellectualization	231
		7.3.4	Religiosity	232
		7.3.5	Gambling	233
		7.3.6	Self-sufficiency	234
		7.3.7	Infidelity	236
	7.4	Compliance		237
		7.4.1	Submissiveness	237
		7.4.2	Inconspicuousness	238
		7.4.3	Controlled self-definition	239
		7.4.4	Humour	240
	7.5	Enhancement of approvability		241
		7.5.1	Self-seeking	242
		7.5.2	Ego interests	243
		7.5.3	Sublimation	243
		7.5.4	Reaction formation	245

	7.5.5	Ego restriction	247
	7.5.6	Compensation	247
	7.5.7	Ambition	248
	7.5.8	Striving for superiority	249
	7.5.9	Achievements and possessions	250
	7.5.10	Search for glory	252
	7.5.11	Pretence and deception	253
7.6	Aggressive strategies of narcissistic control		254
	7.6.1	Defiance and stubbornness	254
	7.6.2	Jealousy	255
	7.6.3	Envy	256
	7.6.4	Prejudice	257
	7.6.5	Sense of entitlement	258
	7.6.6	Bossing attitude and rightness	259
	7.6.7	Depreciative and critical attitude	260
	7.6.8	Aggressive competitiveness	261
	7.6.9	Manipulativeness	262
	7.6.10	Criminal aggressiveness	263

8 Psychopathology — 264

8.1	Narcissistic personality disturbance		265
	8.1.1	Disturbed object relationships	266
	8.1.2	Methods of self-aggrandizement	267
	8.1.3	Grandiose self-image and unattainable ego ideal	269
	8.1.4	Vanity	270
	8.1.5	Screen character	271
	8.1.6	False self	273
	8.1.7	Shame and humiliation	274
	8.1.8	Envy	275
	8.1.9	Destructiveness	277
	8.1.10	Transference	278
	8.1.11	Resistance	280
8.2	Borderline personality disorder		282
	8.2.1	Fixation in the paranoid-schizoid position	282
	8.2.2	Idealization and identification	283
	8.2.3	Self-harm	285
8.3	Schizoid personality disorder		285
	8.3.1	Fear of rejection	286
	8.3.2	Withdrawal into fantasy	286
	8.3.3	Concealed hostility	287
8.4	Neurotic personality organization		287
	8.4.1	Superiority complex	288
	8.4.2	Inhibition and self-restraint	289
	8.4.3	Neurotic pride	290
	8.4.4	Idealized image	291

	8.4.5	Self-contempt and self-recriminations	293
	8.4.6	Neurotic claims	295
	8.4.7	Irresponsibility and undependability	296
	8.4.8	Vindictiveness	296
	8.4.9	Envy	298
	8.4.10	Fear of retaliation	299
	8.4.11	Timidity	300
	8.4.12	Perfectionism	301
	8.4.13	Obsessionality	303
8.5	Moral masochism	304
	8.5.1	Control through helplessness and suffering	305
	8.5.2	Inverted sadism	306
	8.5.3	Depressive-masochistic personality disorder	307
	8.5.4	Injustice collection	308
8.6	Symptom neuroses	309
	8.6.1	Superego conflict	311
	8.6.2	Inhibition and gigantic claims	312
	8.6.3	Defeat and disillusionment	313
	8.6.4	Social fears and social neurosis	315
	8.6.5	Compulsions	317
	8.6.6	Hypochondriasis	318
	8.6.7	Alexithymia and somatization	319
	8.6.8	Conversions and dissociations	320
8.7	Depression	321
	8.7.1	Loss of self-esteem	322
	8.7.2	Precarious self	323
	8.7.3	Concealed grandiosity	324
	8.7.4	Hopelessness	325
	8.7.5	Narcissistic object control	326
	8.7.6	Self-contempt	328
	8.7.7	Contrition and expiation	330
8.8	Mania	332
	8.8.1	Approximation of the ego ideal	333
	8.8.2	Release of inhibitions	334
	8.8.3	Lack of good internal objects	335
	8.8.4	Manic attitude and defence	336
8.9	Psychosis	337
	8.9.1	Inner self	338
	8.9.2	Ego weakness	339
	8.9.3	Psychoanalytic treatment of schizophrenia	339
	8.9.4	Depersonalization	341
	8.9.5	Obsessions and catatonia	341
	8.9.6	Paranoid delusions	342
	8.9.7	Delusions of grandeur	343

9 Interpersonal and Social Dynamics — 345
9.1 Safety in interactions and relationships — 346
- 9.1.1 Role relationships — 347
- 9.1.2 Projective identification — 347
- 9.1.3 Submission, ingratiation, and dominance — 349
- 9.1.4 Transference and transference neurosis — 350
- 9.1.5 Defining the situation — 353
- 9.1.6 Self-relevance of others — 354
- 9.1.7 Selection of friends — 356
- 9.1.8 Relationship with God — 357
- 9.1.9 Love — 358
- 9.1.10 Trust and identification — 359

9.2 Competition and conformity — 360
- 9.2.1 Ranking order — 361
- 9.2.2 Norms and rites — 362
- 9.2.3 Substitutes of taboo — 363
- 9.2.4 Possessions and prestige — 364
- 9.2.5 Enforcement of conformity — 365
- 9.2.6 Therapeutic groups — 366
- 9.2.7 Social monitoring and alliance formation — 368

9.3 Group cohesion — 368
- 9.3.1 Dependency — 370
- 9.3.2 Anxiety — 371
- 9.3.3 Identification with the leader — 372
- 9.3.4 Omnipotence of the leader — 373
- 9.3.5 Submission to the leader — 374
- 9.3.6 Identification with the group as a whole — 375
- 9.3.7 Joint aggression — 377
- 9.3.8 Enthusiasm — 379

9.4 Self-culture — 379
- 9.4.1 Self-evaluation — 380
- 9.4.2 Self-actualization — 381
- 9.4.3 Risk awareness — 383
- 9.4.4 Emotional emptiness — 383
- 9.4.5 Psychopathological vulnerability — 384

10 Conclusion — 385

References — 392

Index — 403

List of Figures

1.1	Relationship between the main branches of psychoanalytic theory	6
2.1	Relationship between appetitive and instinctive behaviour	13
2.2	Role of emotions in appetitive behaviour	21
2.3	Approval is derived from appeasement, assertiveness from offensive aggression	23
2.4	Affective interaction with mutual induction of expressions and emotions	32
3.1	Aversiveness of loneliness and unrelatedness	49
3.2	Two models of anxiety	78
3.3	Movements from anxiety to safety	82
3.4	Narcissistic and libidinal object relations	87
3.5	Spontaneity and assertiveness versus compliance in object relations	92
3.6	Affective states involved in control of the selfobject milieu	98
3.7	Guilt and reparation	100
4.1	Active solicitation and passive attraction of narcissistic supplies	140
5.1	The self in relation to the superego or one of its projections	147
5.2	Anticipation, anxiety, and inhibition	162
5.3	Ego feeling oscillates between ego and superego	165
5.4	Intrusion of drive impulses into awareness	169
5.5	The ego in relationship with the superego	170
6.1	The self is a defence against anxiety or a measure of safety	184
6.2	True self, false self, and self-image	213
7.1	Ambitions and exhibitionism	251
8.1	Dynamic and static functions of the idealized image	292
8.2	Regulation of self-esteem in neurosis	294
8.3	Two of the vicious circles afflicting the neurotic person	300
8.4	Schultz-Henke's (1951) model of neurosis	313
8.5	Adler's model of neurosis	314

8.6	Approximation of the ideal self in pursuit of approval from the superego	325
8.7	Self-reproaches in melancholia	329
9.1	Differentiation between self and other and their re-fusion	354
9.2	Aggression and conformity	366
9.3	Relationship between self and group	369
10.1	Others' submission and control of narcissistic resources	387
10.2	Self-actualization and control of narcissistic resources	390

1
Introduction

FREUD (1914) understood that the aim of narcissistic object choice is to *be* loved; the aim is to raise one's self-regard. Narcissistic object relations serve to maintain self-regard or self-esteem. Self-esteem can be defined simply as "confident conviction of being lovable" (STORR, 1968, p. 77). Narcissism, in turn, can be defined as a need – indeed an *automatic tendency* that is expressed in behaviour and cognition – to maintain self-esteem, that is, to be loved and to be *lovable*, to be approved and to be *approvable*, and to be generally accepted by and thus to feel connected to one's social surround. It is interesting to realize how much of human personality, social behaviour, social structure, and psychopathology are centred on this need to maintain self-esteem, even though the central importance of narcissism is often not immediately apparent. Narcissism, as a fundamental behavioural tendency, is often expressed in highly abstract forms; and much of the social complexity around us becomes translucent when considered in this way, as this book aims to show. 'Narcissistic' behaviour strategies unfolding in a particular social and cultural context not only aim to optimize the level of positive attention we can gather from fellow humans but also, more generally, to control *self*-referential patterns reflective of our acceptance by and safety within our social surround; and they do so on different levels of abstraction.

Healthy narcissism, that is, the set of adaptive behaviours and personality structures concerned with enhancing our acceptability and approvability in the eyes of others, is at work when we shape and define our self (and when we 'defend' our ego by repressing *unacceptable* instinctual wishes or expressing them egosyntonically), when we defend the social position and the system of rules and norms that define our self and identity (or even the beliefs and allegiances through which we define ourselves), and when we offensively aggress those who challenge our self or the means by which we define our self. Pathological narcissism refers to an excessive reliance on external (and concrete) 'narcissistic supplies' (displays of others' love, approval, respect, recognition, or admiration directed towards ourselves), supplies that are solicited by way of inappropriate, maladaptive, and hence ultimately self-defeating behaviours in an attempt to maintain a precarious self-esteem. Pathological narcissism covers over and defends against a 'basic anxiety' (HORNEY) or 'disintegration anxiety' (a sense of self-fragmentation) (KOHUT) and thereby steers the individual away from the abyss of 'annihilation' (FENICHEL). Pathological narcissism is a special case that illustrates the broader principle of self-preservation (need for safety), which is deeply embedded in a whole spectrum of social and psychopathological phenomena.

The self is an aggregate of self-representations, which are the various ideas a person has about himself (SCHAFER, 1967). The self is inseparable from the social environment, inseparable from others, inseparable also from one's representations of others (KERNBERG, 1982a). More particularly, the self is dependent on others' attitudes towards oneself; and it is dynamically constituted by way of influencing these attitudes, whether in an external social situation or in internal imagery (conscious fantasy). Others' attitudes that constitute the self, that provide the self with cohesion (KOHUT), are approving, respecting, accepting attitudes towards oneself; hence, the self can be said to be narcissistically cathected (HARTMANN, 1964; JACOBSON, 1964).[1] The self is not an agent but the core of a social monitoring mechanism (DANZIGER, 1997). Feedback control of social behaviour involves the perception of approving or acknowledging self-referential patterns in the social environment, patterns that are abstracted and integrated in form of a self-image or the sense of self or identity. Behaviour that regulates the sense of self with the aim of enhancing self-esteem (maintaining the narcissistic balance) is conveniently termed narcissistic. Narcissism automatically (and unconsciously) constitutes the self and thereby moves the individual from anxiety and insecurity to a feeling state of 'safety' (SANDLER), a feeling of self-worth or pride. In the absence of external approvals, the self disintegrates, especially when internal self-esteem regulating mechanisms are insufficiently developed (KOHUT). Self-experience and its regulation are explored in Chapter 6.

The need to maintain coherence of the self as a proxy for the individual's approval, recognition, or acceptance by the social surround – by way of behaviours and psychological mechanisms that can be subsumed under the

---

[1] In keeping with FEDERN and with FREUD's earlier work, the terms 'ego' and 'self' are treated synonymously in this book. 'Ego' should be read in most contexts as 'self', unless the term 'ego' is used specifically to denote part of the 'mental apparatus'. HARTMANN, JACOBSON, and KOHUT distinguished between the ego as a structure (part of the mental apparatus) or set of functions, on the one hand, and the self as an experiential (experience-near) entity, on the other. The self is one's image or concept of one's person. Self-representations are mental contents, contents of the ego. Self or self-representations, defined as mental contents, are narcissistically-libidinally cathected (HARTMANN, 1964; JACOBSON, 1964).

term 'narcissism' – has a precise evolutionary significance, as is argued in the book. The importance of intraspecific aggression in structuring interpersonal relations has been highlighted by ethologists (EIBL-EIBESFELDT, HASS, LORENZ, MOYNIHAN). Narcissism, it is proposed, is phylogenetically based on mutual appeasement of intraspecific aggression in group-living primates. Individuals acquire, in the course of their development, behaviours that ensure that they are accepted or recognized by others, which are behaviours that fundamentally have an appeasing function on others' aggressive potential. These culturally evolved behaviour patterns are superimposed on phylogenetically evolved appeasement gestures (Chapter 2). By behaving in accordance with cultural norms (internalized in form of the 'ego ideal') and by thus presenting the self as compliant and approvable, the individual counters the risk, deeply embedded in primate evolution, of becoming the target of the group's joint aggression (HASS) and of thus being *annihilated*. It is this risk that is signalled by social or paranoid anxiety (or 'basic anxiety' [HORNEY]); and it is to the extent that this risk has to be minimized (and related anxiety has to be reduced or prevented) that the 'ego' (in the sense of a structure) employs its defensive operations ('mechanisms of defence').

The context in which the infant is protected not only against interspecific (predatory) but also intraspecific aggression is the presence and devoted care of the mother. The mother's love and caring attention also signals that the infant is protected against the mother's own aggression. The self first emerges in the matrix of the mother's appreciating and loving relation to the infant, which is why the self-representation is bound to a representation of the good (caring) mother. Unconsciously, the self remains bound to the internalized omnipotent object or superego, which is a derivative of the primary maternal object. The superego as the counterpart of the self (and of the ego in its ideal form) is discussed in Chapter 5. As the self develops, it remains dependent on external appreciation and approval, although internalized self-esteem regulating structures (KOHUT), the superego in particular, play an increasing role in the maintenance of narcissistic balance or safety feeling (SANDLER).

Culturally, self-definition and self-actualization have become prevalent concerns (and the self has become a matter for theorizing), inasmuch as social structure has become less stable and cohesive (Chapter 9). The self acts as a defensive structure whenever the individual is exposed to an uncertain social situation or included in a fluid social structure; and, to ensure the individual's safety under these circumstances, the self has to be defined and actualized; the self has to be concerned with its own esteem or value. The self, as is argued in Chapter 9, contains (holds) the individual's culturally imposed separateness and vulnerability, in the same way that the cohesive group contains its members. In primitive groups or groups that have a high degree of cohesiveness, the safety-procuring infant–mother duality is replaced with the relationship between the group member and the group as a whole or its leader (so that the group, too, can be regarded as a developmental derivative of the primary maternal object [SCHEIDLINGER]). The self can then be said to merge with the group or with the collective consciousness (DURKHEIM), much as the ego can fuse with the superego in states of mania or love (FREUD) (whereby in each case the state of primary narcissism would be approximated).

FREUD (1914) was aware of a fundamental connection of narcissism with self-preservation, that is, with the organism's need to avoid danger and steer away from annihilation. Narcissistic mechanisms, while maintaining or restoring self-regard or self-esteem (a developmental derivative of the blissful state of primary narcissism, the state of union with the mother [FREUD, 1914]), ensure the organism's safety. Character, according to WILHELM REICH (1928, 1929), is a 'narcissistic protection mechanism', a mechanism that protects against dangers emanating from an inherently dangerous outer world. Manoeuvres coordinated by one's character (personality) take place along one axis: they overcome or decrease anxiety or psychic pain[2] and restore, more or less successfully, the narcissistic equilibrium, that is, the feeling of safety (Chapter 7). Defence mechanisms, *in preserving the self* ('ego defences'), serve the same purpose, although movements from dangerousness to safety can be maladaptive and self-defeating, leading to conflicts and necessitating secondary defences. The 'principle of self-preservation', posited by self psychology as a fundamental principle of social behaviour (BRANDCHAFT, 1985), is likely to be an expression of a more fundamental tendency underpinning animal behaviour: the tendency to move from situations of danger to situations of safety. The organism's behaviour is so organized that it tends to decrease dangerousness and increase safety; and it is shaped (in the process of learning) according to whether or not it has this effect. Crucially, in humans, safety is signalled by the receipt (or *confident expectation*) of accepting, acknowledging, approving, affirming, or praising signals from others. Safety is experienced by the individual in terms of these reflections of himself in others' responses and attitudes, reflections that constitute or sustain the sense of self.

Object-relations theorists (KLEIN, BALINT, WINNICOTT, BION, FAIRBAIRN, KERNBERG) emphasized the importance of our dependence on objects, of our need for them. Object-relations theory does not explicitly address the question wherein this dependence on objects consists. Self psychology elucidates the nature of our dependence on objects and thereby brings into sharper relief many of the insights that have germinated on the fertile grounds of object-relations theory (BRANDCHAFT, 1986). Objects have different functions; they serve as targets for libidinal and aggressive impulses ('drives') and as sources of narcissistic supplies (GOODMAN, 2002). It is their role in maintaining the narcissistic balance (self-esteem), their

---

[2] Imminent danger is signalled by pain, and dangerousness is signalled by anxiety.

'selfobject' function (KOHUT), that is of greatest relevance to gaining a better understanding of personality development, psychopathology, and social processes, as this book aims to demonstrate (Chapters 4 to 9). Object-relations theorists speak of 'depressive anxiety', which relates to the infant's insight into his dependence on the maternal object (and, correspondingly, the adult's dependence on a derivative of the primary object, including the superego or omnipotent object internally). Failure to work through (resolve) the 'depressive position' in infanthood – that is, an inability to save and repair internal loved objects (who, in their external incarnation, are the targets of the infant's hostility in the 'paranoid-schizoid position') – renders the individual vulnerable to psychological suffering later in life (KLEIN, 1940, 1946). Failure to securely establish good inner objects leaves the developing child with an inner insecurity that is coupled with heightened narcissistic needs vis-à-vis external objects. The critical insight is that the lack of secure internal objects, as conceptualized in object-relations theory, is equivalent to an insecure self (internal objects and self being inseparable [KERNBERG, 1982a; CASHDAN, 1988]). Individuals who lack secure internal objects and who hence have an insecure self are engaged in life-long attempts to overcome anxieties resulting from the loss of the primary object ('depressive anxieties').[3]

Lack of close and happy relationships confirms (perpetuates) 'fears of annihilation' from inside and fears of persecution from outside (whereby fears of persecution manifest a regression to the paranoid-schizoid position) (KLEIN, 1940). External reality under these circumstances cannot provide proof for the groundlessness of the individual's insecurities and of his worries about his 'internal world'. As KLEIN (1940) argued, insecurity constantly incites a need to observe the world of external objects. There is a deep evolutionary meaning to KLEIN's paranoid-schizoid position. The danger to which primitive humans were exposed early on in their phylogenesis was that of persecution and *annihilation* by the primal group. The need therefore arose to be constantly watchful of others' intentions and to guard against the possibility of persecution and annihilation by the group, and this had to be done by way of soliciting others' good will (especially that of the leader), that is, by drawing on their selfobject function.[4] It is for reasons of security and self-preservation that we depend on others' approval and recognition. This dependence is particularly obvious in those with a 'neurotic personality' (HORNEY) or a 'disorder of the self' (KOHUT, WOLF), whose self-esteem is fragile (and who lack secure internal objects). Fragility of self-esteem is the

---

[3] Defensive means of reducing the suffering of the depressive position include an excessive turning to *external* 'good objects' (those that meet narcissistic needs), which can manifest as neurosis (KLEIN, 1940).
[4] Again, the fear of annihilation (equivalent to 'disintegration anxiety' or 'paranoid anxiety') is the opposite of the feeling of safety (SANDLER), of a secure sense of self.

origin of "the compulsive drive for worldly glory through success, power, and triumph" (HORNEY, 1950, p. 368). Compensating for 'inferiority' (inner insecurity, corresponding to week self-esteem), the neurotic person strives for power and 'superiority' (ADLER, 1965). Even those who have securely established good internal objects and who benefit from internal self-esteem-regulating structures pursue power, prestige, and possessions for the same reason, namely narcissistic gratification (Chapter 7), although they do so less compulsively.

In self psychology, we have a convergence of object-relational theories and theories that emphasize the central role of self-esteem (or safety) and of its regulation in social behaviour, personality, and psychopathology (ADLER, HORNEY, SANDLER). Both of these branches of psychoanalytic thinking – the one that is primarily concerned with object relations and the one that places self-esteem at the heart of its theoretical investigations – have sprung from 'classical' psychoanalysis (which, in itself, underwent further theoretical development in the form of ego psychology [HARTMANN]) (Figure 1.1). KOHUT (1977) suggested that self psychology and traditional psychoanalysis constitute alternative theoretical frameworks that should coexist. In fact, most of the statements of classical psychoanalysis can be translated into the language of self psychology. For instance, conflict between drives, as it is understood classically, is associated with *intolerable* feelings, which refer to the social *unacceptability* of certain impulses. Impulses are intolerable or inacceptable, and hence need to be repressed or otherwise defended against, if they risk eliciting *disapproval* from others and hence causing disruption of the subject's narcissistic balance (which is maintained by others' approval or the confident expectation thereof). Impulses or thoughts are *ego*dystonic insofar as they are subjectively intolerable *and socially inacceptable*, insofar as they are, or tend to be, disapproved by others, and insofar as they would therefore threaten the subject's narcissistic balance. Thoughts are

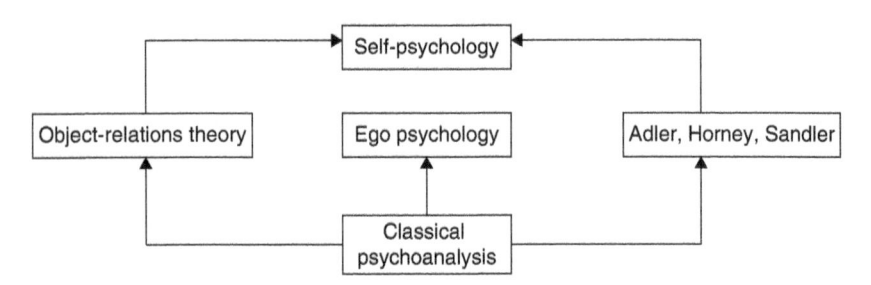

Figure 1.1 Relationship between the main branches of psychoanalytic theory. SANDLER's work, unlike that of ADLER and HORNEY, is firmly rooted in traditional psychoanalysis and unifies traditional psychoanalysis and self psychology in many ways

experienced as visible to internal objects, on whose approval the internal image of the self depends (Chapter 5), much as impulses that translate into actions or attitudes are evident to external objects. The internal image of the self, created in states of introspection and fantasy, and the world of internal objects to which it relates are two sides of the same coin, much as the 'ego' (insofar as it denotes the self) and the subject's selfobject surround are two sides of the same coin.

Rather than arranging psychoanalytic insights related to questions of narcissism, self, and the regulation of self-esteem according to theoretical schools (classical Freudian, ego psychology, self psychology, object-relations theory, etc.), the book takes a somewhat integrative approach, exploring how insights, formulated in whichever psychoanalytic framework, help us to understand the role of narcissism and self-esteem regulation in personality development, character structure, superego, self-experience, psychopathology,[5] and sociology (Chapters 4 to 9). Much can be gained by blurring theoretical boundaries and considering within the same context the works of FREUD, FEDERN, RADO, FENICHEL, BERGLER, HARTMANN, SANDLER, KLEIN, KERNBERG, KOHUT, and many others, a lot more perhaps than by focusing on and amplifying differences. ADLER's, HORNEY's, SULLIVAN's, and LACAN's contributions to understanding character structure, superego, self, and psychopathology are discussed alongside those of classical analysts, ego psychologists, object-relations theorists, and self psychologists. All of these theoreticians were concerned with the same product of primate and cultural evolution; they all tried to disentangle innate human potentialities and their complex manifestations in culture. Despite differences in emphasis and terminology and despite the pursuit of some blind alleys (e.g., the death instinct), they all contributed to a body of knowledge within which we can discern the principles that govern the individual's development, social behaviour, and seemingly private thought. By taking an integrative approach, it will be appreciated how different schools approach and approximate the same fundamental process from different angles. What transpires through layers

---

[5] The book is primarily about healthy narcissism, defined as adaptive behaviours and personality structures that serve to maintain one's connectedness to the selfobject milieu, that is, one's recognition and acceptance by the social surround (thereby maintaining one's self-esteem or narcissistic balance). It is not in the first place concerned with pathological narcissism and narcissistic personality disorder; pathological narcissism and other disorders of the self are discussed insofar as they demonstrate the malfunctioning of mechanisms evolved for maintaining one's connectedness to the group and acceptance by others. Other mental disorders are discussed insofar as concerns with the self and one's reflection in the social environment are central to their dynamics. The book does not discuss treatments and other clinical aspects (except where these matters provide an opportunity for illuminating theoretical points).

of different theories superimposed upon each other is a core dynamic model of human social behaviour and personality.[6]

The purpose of the book is to show that different psychoanalytic theories or paradigms complement each other and jointly give shape to and provide support for an evolutionarily sensible model of social behaviour and personality. The book is decidedly not an effort to critically appraise past psychoanalytic writers or contrast their theories with each other, but attempts to offer a synthesis of psychoanalytic thought that will impress the sympathetic reader as compelling once he or she adopts the position that self-esteem regulation (maintenance of the narcissistic balance) – being a proxy for regulation of interpersonal safety (self-preservation) – is of central importance for intrapsychic and behavioural phenomena in both mental health and illness. Differences between schools of thought, as stark and divisive as they can be made to appear,[7] should not distract us from their common insight, expressed more or less explicitly and shared to a greater or lesser degree, that as humans we need to establish and maintain safety – to protect ourselves from latent but pervasive intraspecific aggression (LORENZ) – by appeasing others and making others acknowledge, approve of, or respect our*selves* (and thus making others constitute our self). If, having read Chapters 2 and 3, dealing with affective expressions and affective states, the reader bears in mind that social behaviour and personality structure are predominantly organized according to the principle of 'movement' (ADLER) from insecurity or 'basic anxiety' (HORNEY) to safety (SANDLER), that is, from separateness (ROTHSTEIN, 1979) to self-cohesion (KOHUT) and to a sense of social inclusion and identity (ERIKSON), that is, in a neurotic context, from inferiority (associated with vulnerability and insecurity) to

---

[6] The book does not offer a critical review of psychoanalytic theory and does not discuss aspects of the evolution of psychoanalytic thought, its historical context and significance, or the differences between schools of thought. Much has been written about these differences. Less perhaps has been said about the convergence of theoretical schools; yet it is likely to be at points of convergence where these schools approximate more closely the essence of what is their joint concern: the motivational structure and dynamics of social behaviour and subjective experience, in both mental health and illness. Psychoanalytic schools are not challenged in the book; they have their different areas of clinical application and different strengths with regard to interpretation of clinical material and guidance for psychotherapeutic endeavours. All the book tries to do is to show that, when looked at from a certain angle, the various theoretical schools substantially overlap and merge into a common shape. One can revert the perspective, without loss, to one that suits a particular clinical problem and treatment paradigm.

[7] FREUD refused to pay serious attention to ADLER's work; and ego psychology and object-relations theory ignored HORNEY and SULLIVAN as well as each other. HORNEY's theories are perhaps the most underrated in the history of psychoanalysis, which has been a history to some extent of fractionism and ignorance, if not hostility, towards rival schools, the same hostility that is at work when we defend our narcissistically invested belief systems in professional, political, or other arenas.

superiority (ADLER), status, power, and possessions (HORNEY) (and the sense of security that they afford), then discussions (from different psychoanalytic or depth-psychological perspectives) of intrapsychic, interpersonal, social, and psychopathological phenomena and dynamics in subsequent chapters will hang together seamlessly.[8]

KOHUT himself felt that the task of showing how his insights can be related to the works of psychoanalytic theoreticians before him still had to be tackled. The book uncovers the extent to which KOHUT's ideas were anticipated in the works of ADLER, HORNEY, FEDERN, and of course FREUD, and also the extent to which they resonate with SANDLER's work. Looking back over the history of psychoanalytic theory from the platform erected by KOHUT, one could argue that ADLER's and HORNEY's oeuvres were closer to grasping the main unconscious current in human social behaviour and personality – and understanding it in a way that makes evolutionary sense – than was FREUD's work with his overemphasis of libido and belated recognition of aggression, although his work 'On Narcissism' (1914) remains a towering landmark in the field. By showing how themes of self-esteem and self-preservation more or less explicitly pervaded other psychoanalytic schools and were addressed in a wide range of theoretical writings, powerful support is provided for central notions of self psychology. Manifold evidence, harnessed from a wide range of theoretical approaches and paradigms, is marshalled for a model of the mind that makes evolutionary sense, that recognizes the central importance, in the phylogenesis of social behaviour and in cultural evolution, of latent fears of intraspecific aggression from the group (paranoid fears) and the overriding need for soliciting and receiving appeasing signals (expressed in culturally and phylogenetically ritualized forms) from the social surround. The need to feel safe by virtue of being recognized, accepted, approved by others is the central theme underpinning man's social behaviour, as recognized explicitly by SANDLER and KOHUT and implicitly by many others. The self, as an intrapsychic measure for safety, is the product of others' approval and recognition, whether real or fantasized; and it is constituted

---

[8] In the book, psychoanalytic authorities are invoked rather than critically engaged. Their insights and formulations, when left to speak for themselves, have the power to substantiate a model of social behaviour that affords central importance to narcissistic sustenance and to mechanisms concerned with its attainment; by bringing into focus often forgotten insights and formulations, we can appreciate how the concept of narcissism illuminates a wide range of normal psychological and psychopathological phenomena. The most relevant theoretical insights are selected and placed side by side, regardless of their origin in one or another theoretical school. The selected material is arranged in a way that shows how authorities, of whatever allegiance, intuitively and often implicitly grasped the central point of crystallization in psychological, psychopathological, and social processes. Theoretical insights are not generally rephrased or knitted together; it is often the context of their placement and the sequence of their arrangement that will support arguments that are woven through the chapters.

increasingly, in normal development, by the confident expectation of approval and recognition within the specific cultural context to which the individual becomes adapted. This is a simple notion but its implications are vast and its potential for appreciating, bringing to life, and integrating a now often neglected body of psychoanalytic theories is impressive.

Can a reduction and synthesis of psychoanalytic theory advance our understanding of how human social behaviour has evolved and how it came to provide the substrate for cultural evolution? In order to understand how the balance between intraspecific aggression and phylogenetically and culturally evolved appeasement gestures, when played out among humans, can give rise to complex social and cultural as well as psychopathological phenomena, we need psychoanalysis or, more precisely, a form of psychoanalysis that places narcissism at its conceptual centre. The book aims to show how the concept of narcissism helps us to relate a range of phenomena that we consider to be specifically human to principles of sociality that were elicited by ethologists (LORENZ, HASS, EIBL-EIBESFELDT, MOYNIHAN). If we were able to deduce from the basic premise – that humans, when finding themselves in a social context, solicit and actively maintain the good will or respect of others and thereby inhibit others' intraspecific aggression – an internally consistent framework within which we can parsimoniously understand much of individual social behaviour and experience, personality structure and its development, and social processes on different levels of organization, then we could place social psychology and sociology on deterministic grounds in continuity with the natural sciences. If we were to accept that the equations that map the complexities of human social behaviour and experience on to phylogenetically more primitive group processes can only be provided by, or have to be derived from, psychoanalytic theory, then the book should be of interest to philosophers and sociologists who wish to understand human social behaviour and wider social processes deterministically as natural phenomena. In addition, psychoanalytic theory, when distilled into a philosophy of the self, can address and help to answer some of the fundamental questions debated in the behavioural and social sciences, that is, questions about the nature of selfhood, about the motivational processes at work in individual social behaviour and in collective and cultural processes, about the factors that govern our experience of the social world, and about the undercurrents that are responsible for the formation and stabilization of various psychopathological constellations and clinical syndromes.[9]

---

[9] The dynamics of depression, for instance, can be shown to centre on the disruption and compensation of the narcissistic equilibrium, that is, around frustrations and circuitous attempts at satisfaction of the need for approval, recognition, and hence safety. Such formulations in the field of psychopathology will eventually allow us to make sense of the neurobiology of mental illness, to understand how the neural system that has evolved for the purpose of regulating social relatedness and individual safety can fail.

2
Affective Expressions

Instincts (innate actions), according to LORENZ (1935, 1952), are rigid and stereotypical, genetically determined and species-specific behaviour patterns. A releasing stimulus or stimulus configuration ('releasing stimulus situation') is required to elicit an innate behaviour sequence. If the naturally occurring releasing stimulus configuration remains absent, the threshold at which the releasing stimulus elicits the instinctive pattern is progressively lowered until the animal produces the innate behaviour spontaneously. The stimulus configuration that selectively activates an innate behaviour, or the 'device' that emits this stimulus configuration, is called 'releaser'. The 'releaser' evokes an instinctive behaviour sequence via activation of an 'innate releasing mechanism', that is, the perceptual correlate of the releaser. Each releaser activates a specific 'innate releasing mechanism' in the recipient and, thereby, sets off the innate behaviour sequence (LORENZ, 1935, 1952).

Fellow members of the species are the target (object) of various instinctive actions performed by the individual in social situations. Fellow members are also the *releasers* of (emit stimulation for) instinctive actions that the individual is programmed to perform in social situations. 'Social releasers' include conspicuous morphologic features and conspicuous (ritualized) behaviour patterns of fellow members of the species. Social releasers, their perceptual correlates (innate releasing mechanisms), and the responses elicited by them "constitute a sort of 'understanding' within a species" (LORENZ, 1937, p. 148). Once a social releaser, such as an individual's ritualized performance, has activated an innate releasing mechanism and evoked an innate behaviour pattern in another individual, that individual comes to act as a social releaser in its own right and elicits a matching social response in the former individual (feedback). LORENZ (1935) envisaged that, in social species, "the interlocking performances of individuals, the releaser in one animal and the released reaction in the other, make up the complex function of society" (p. 125).

The entire sociology of many animals, and particularly of birds, is based on complex systems of releasers and innate mechanisms, which guarantee consistent and biologically adequate handling of the sex partner, the young, in brief, of all the fellow members of the species.

(LORENZ, 1937, p. 141)

The entire sociology of higher animals is built up on social releasers and corresponding innate mechanisms. They should be the main building stones of all sociological research, because the thin coating of acquired behavior amounts to very little in proportion.

(LORENZ, 1939, p. 257)

'Drive', "which is a psychological concept with clinical referrents such as impulses toward goal-directed behavior, persistence and plasticity", is distinguished from 'instincts', "referring to inherited, unchangeable patterns of behavior" (CURTIS, 1986, p. 50). Drive ('instinctive drive'), as an organizing principle of appetitive (goal-directed) behaviour, is correlated with experiences of wanting and striving. What the organism wants, or strives for, is what acts as a reward under certain physiological (motivational) conditions. What is the relationship between drive and instinct?[1]

Drive is a property of appetitive (learned) behaviour, which moves the organism from one location to another on a multidimensional map representing contingencies of the external world, usually away from locations in which punishments are likely to be encountered to locations in which rewards of one kind or another are likely to be found. Drive is associated with emotional feeling, which represents the organism's specific autonomic preparedness and its readiness to express one or another instinctive motor pattern (hence drive can be called 'instinctive'). Emotional feeling may be regarded as an aspect of the releasing stimulus constellation for a particular instinctive motor pattern. In the context of a drive and hence of a feeling state, an external stimulus constellation ('releasing stimulus situation') triggers a suitable instinctive motor display, which, in turn, effects a change in the external world that translates into the satisfaction of a physiological

---

[1] WAELDER (1960) reminded his readers that FREUD'S notion 'Trieb' is often confused (due to inaccurate translation) with the concept of 'instinct'. FREUD was not concerned with 'instincts' (in the sense of inherited dispositions to unlearned behaviour patterns that are useful for the survival of the species) but with 'Triebe', that is, 'instinctual drives' (or simply 'drives'). FREUD regarded drive (or what is often wrongly translated as 'instinct') as an endogenous source of continually flowing stimulation that compels the mind to do some adaptive work (i.e., to engage in learned, goal-directed behaviour). Instinctual drive (or 'instinct' in the psychoanalytic sense) and instinct (in the ethological sense) may be linked nonetheless. WAELDER (1960) speculated that instinctual drives (as well as intelligence) "may be the *differentiation products of animal instincts*" (p. 102).

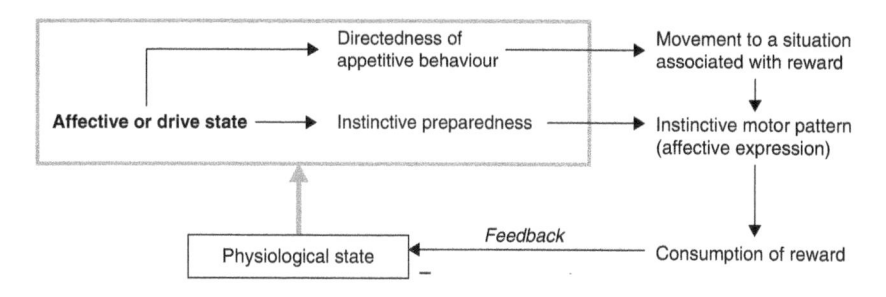

Figure 2.1 Appetitive behaviour navigates a landscape representing external contingencies with regard to the availability of rewards, while instinctive behaviour may be more directly involved in attaining a reward and thus resolving the drive state

need (reward) and hence the resolution of the drive state (Figure 2.1). Reward consumption is generally an instinctive behaviour, according to LORENZ. The likelihood of exposure to a motivationally relevant releasing stimulus constellation (i.e., the likelihood of consuming a reward and satisfying a need) is correlated with the attractiveness of the animal's location in the external landscape across which it manoeuvres by way of appetitive behaviour.

How does this model relate to narcissism? The receipt from others of signals of reassurance, acceptance, acknowledgement, approval, or tenderness acts as social reward (narcissistic nourishment). Appetitive behaviour manoeuvres the organism across a landscape consisting of social situations (abstract locations), each of which is characterized by a certain availability of or accessibility to social reward and a certain risk of exposure to social punishment (disapproval, rejection, hostility). Time and again, the organism is driven away from an anxiogenic situation (characterized by an increased risk of punishment) and towards a situation associated with an increased probability of receiving social reward. Exposure to social reward renders the present situation safe, concludes the train of appetitive behaviour that has moved the organism to that situation, and acts as reinforcement for this train of behaviour. Furthermore, in the context of any particular social situation, others act as releasers for our own instinctively submissive gestures, care-seeking expressions (derivatives of separation cries), assertive and exhibitionistic displays, or caring gestures. Our own feeling state codetermines the readiness with which we engage in these innate patterns of behaviour vis-à-vis others.

In safe situations, as judged by contextual cues and reflected in our feeling state, social releasers induce within us affectionate and playful expressions. If these are consistently not reciprocated by others, the attractiveness of the type of social situation in which affective exchange takes place is weakened.

Social punishment (rejection, disapproval, or disrespect) renders a situation aversive and may switch us into an affective (drive) state that entails an unpleasurable emotional tone (anxiety, pain, or anger), heightened defensive preparedness, and a disposition to display care-seeking, submissive, or offensively aggressive motor patterns vis-à-vis further social stimuli. Aversiveness needs to be overcome by appetitive retreat to safety. Appetitive aspects of submissive (compliant) and care-seeking (attention-seeking) behaviours are implemented, so as to move the individual to a safe situation. Thus, social behaviour is organized on two levels: it is appetitive behaviour, driven from anxiety to safety, that sets the framework within which affective exchange takes place; and it is affective exchange that, acting as reward or punishment, reshapes the navigationable social landscape.

For Kohut there is clearly an innate, drive-like, peremptory, requirement for experiences with objects, more specifically selfobjects, for responses from human caretakers who guide psychological development; and it is the adequacy or inadequacy of these self-selfobject experiences that crucially organize and shape the infant, the child, and the adult in health and disease.

(P. TOLPIN, 1986, p. 102)

2.1 Aggression

The 'instinct of combat', as described by MCDOUGALL (1924), is "evoked by the behavior of any other creature that tends to thwart or obstruct him in the pursuit of any natural goal, that is, in the working out of any instinctive train of behavior" (p. 140) (i.e., appetitive pursuit of a goal). Combative behaviour (expression of the 'instinct of combat') is accompanied by an emotional excitement of anger, rage, or fury (representing degrees of intensity of this emotion). The instinct of combat operates in two successive phases: the phase of threatening and the phase of attack. The most widely used behavioural expressions of the threatening phase are "sounds produced by the voice or other means" (MCDOUGALL, 1924, p. 141). Strictly speaking, aggression has a drive component in the form of anger; and it is within this drive state that instinctive motor patterns associated with aggression readily find their expression. MCDOUGALL (1924) also discerned 'instincts' of self-assertion and submission, which he thought are crucial for the maintenance of social order, arguing that combat, fear, and punishment alone would be "wasteful of energy" and "little conducive to harmonious social existence" (p. 158).

FREUD (1930) gave credit to the "fundamental hostility of human beings to one another" (p. 49); he appreciated that "the tendency to aggression is an original, autonomous disposition in man" (p. 58) and acknowledged that he could "no longer understand how we could have ignored the ubiquity of non-erotic aggression and destruction and failed to accord it its due place in the interpretation of life" (pp. 56–7). Human beings are endowed with instinctive aggression,[2] which, like any other instinctive mechanism, "waits for some provocation"; or it "manifests itself spontaneously", if, under favourable circumstances, "the psychical counter-forces that would otherwise inhibit it have ceased to operate" (FREUD, 1930, p. 48). Then, "cruel aggression" can reveal "man as a savage beast that has no thought of sparing its own kind" (p. 48). When aggression is restricted by external circumstances and controlled by "psychical counter-forces", it "puts itself at the service of a different aim, which could be attained by milder means" (p. 48). If man's aggression finds no acceptable external aim, and if it is prevented by circumstances from expressing itself spontaneously, then "this outward-directed aggression would be bound to increase the degree of self-destruction" (FREUD, 1930, p. 56).

2.1.1 Phylogenetic ritualization

Interspecific (predatory and defensive) aggression (behaviour aimed at killing prey or protecting against predation) is the evolutionary precursor of *intraspecific* aggression (offensive aggression or hostility), which serves to control competition between conspecifics for resources. Interspecific aggression is dangerous, whereas intraspecific aggression, given its role in controlling competition, has to be safe; it has to be controlled in its turn (LORENZ, 1963; MOYNIHAN, 1998). Under selection pressures that favoured "the development of precautionary measures" (MOYNIHAN, 1998, p. 96), "the weapons and behaviour patterns for killing a prey or for defence against predators" were curtailed in their effectiveness, for they "are far too powerful, cruel and effective for rival fighting" (LORENZ, 1973, p. 211). This curtailment is attributed to phylogenetic ritualization. Hostile (offensive) performances are aggressive behaviour patterns that have become 'ritualized' in the course of evolution (LORENZ, 1963; MOYNIHAN, 1998).

'Unritualized' behaviour refers to sequences of postures and movements that are employed in the course of purposeful activities, such as feeding or hunting (interspecific aggression). 'Ritualized' performances ('displays') are behaviour patterns that are derived from unritualized forms of behaviour and that are specialized to convey information (serving the purpose of intraspecific communication) (MOYNIHAN, 1998). Ritualized displays of antagonistic behaviour "evolved from intention movements and ambivalent behaviour patterns derived from instinctive conflicts" (LORENZ, 1973, pp. 211–12). Unritualized patterns of advance or retreat performed in hostile contexts became, in the course of evolution, ritualized *movements of intent* (displays), the performance of which came to serve only the purpose of communication. In mammals, hostile performances are traceable to intention

---

[2] Here the term 'instinctive' refers to affective displays in LORENZ's sense.

movements of attack, defence, and withdrawal (and much less to 'displacement patterns', as is the case in birds) (MOYNIHAN, 1998). Communication is based on innate 'expressive movements' (phylogenetically ritualized patterns) as well as coevolved innate recognition mechanisms (HASS, 1968). Humans have an innate capacity to recognize "the most fundamental and important facial movements" (p. 119). The raising or lowering of the corners of the mouth, for instance, is an innate movement that acts "as an indication of mood" (p. 117), an indication that, owing to innate perceptual schemas, is understood by conspecifics. HASS (1968), too, recognized that many ritualized behaviour patterns with a communicative function are based on 'movements of intent' ("which convey an appetency toward specific modes of behavior" [p. 112]). Our ancestors defended themselves by biting. Teeth grinding is a "movement of intent which conveys a readiness to bite"; it is a phylogenetically ritualized "forewarning of the intention to bite" (p. 112). Acting as a signal, teeth grinding "may alone be sufficient to intimidate an opponent and provoke a withdrawal" (p. 112). For the communicative effect to occur, a 'receptive mechanism' (innate recognition mechanism) had to have evolved, which, at the sight of teeth grinding, prompts the appropriate behavioural response in the opponent. Our ancestors also possessed well-developed canines, and, in humans, the lowering of the corners of the mouth, originally to reveal these canines, is still part of the expressive movement of anger evolved from teeth grinding (HASS, 1968).

> Baboons, which are equipped with particularly long upper canines, pull their lower lips down at the far corners when threatening, so that the canines are exposed to their full extent. We do just the same, although we do not possess long upper canines. Thus the motor pattern has outlived the reduction in size of the organ that was originally displayed.
> (EIBL-EIBESFELDT, 1970, p. 19)

2.1.2 Disdain and disgust

Distrust, "as we call interest which is overlaid with fear", is communicated by subtle ritualized movements of head, body, and eyes that have evolved from "movements of intent denoting a readiness to turn away and flee" and a concurrent narrowing of the eyes (in order to protect the eyes) (HASS, 1968, p. 113). HASS (1968) established, in correspondence with DARWIN's views, that "a raising and half-turning of the head, a narrowing of the eyes, and a simultaneous expulsion of air through the nose" – reflecting a combination of "turning away from someone", rejecting his smell, and "the wish to impress", or assume a dominant position towards, him – became ritualized into a special signal conveying disdain (HASS, 1968, p. 114). Contempt, in MCDOUGALL's system, is a compound conative attitude, representing a fusion of conative attitudes of self-assertion (positive self-feeling) and disgust. Disgust is a feeling of aversion; it is related to nausea (ADLER, 1927, p. 217). Disgust – "an archaic physiological defense syndrome which is automatically produced as soon as something repulsive reaches the digestive tract" – has evolved into "an expression of negation in general" (and "a defence against certain sexual, especially oral and anal, drives") (FENICHEL, 1946, p. 139). Disgust contains an impulse of rejection. Grimaces that accompany disgust "signify contempt for everything and everyone, and an attempt to solve a problem by gesture of rejection" (ADLER, 1927, p. 217). Others' expressions of contempt or disgust towards ourselves are powerful aversive stimuli that reveal our deepest anxiety, that related to the threat of annihilation.

2.1.3 Control of resources

Offensive (intraspecific) aggression serves the purpose of establishing a ranking position or defining a territory. Territorial aggression spaces out members of a species in order to optimize the utilization of resources (LORENZ, 1963). Situations that elicit offensive aggression in rats and other animals typically involve *dominance claims* or *resource disputes* (BLANCHARD & BLANCHARD, 1989). These situational elicitors are linked, in that dominance status influences access to resources. In these situations, "a challenge from a conspecific" serves "as an immediate elicitor of offence ... regardless of the resource/dominance focus of any actual dispute" (p. 102).[3] Resource disputes (including disputes over property) and disputes over 'rights' are sources of offensive (angry) aggression in humans. Violations by others of "one's own personal views of 'how things should be'" are another, and possibly related, source of anger and angry (intraspecific) aggression in humans (BLANCHARD & BLANCHARD, 1989).

Implicit challenges (to one's status, rights, or access to resources) may be reciprocated by explicit challenges and insults, which, in themselves, elicit angry (offensive) aggression. Explicit challenges and insults, expressed verbally and through gesture, prompt opponents to display their agonistic capabilities.[4] Disputes are usually limited to the exchange of verbal threats and the display of fighting abilities, given that actual attack behaviour tends to be "inhibited by fear of the physical or social consequences of the attack" (p. 113). Fear predicated on an assessment of the opponent's fighting ability restrains offensive aggression, much as anticipation of social punishment inhibits aggression. Through offensive aggression, one aims "to gain access

---

[3] Even in the absence of resource/dominance disputes, "some highly aggressive animals seek out opponents to attack" (BLANCHARD & BLANCHARD, 1989, p. 103), consistent with the instinctive nature of offensive aggression (in LORENZ's sense).

[4] Unlike other states of emotional arousal, anger is usually accompanied by vocalizations (BLANCHARD & BLANCHARD, 1989). In other words, the drive-related, affective state of anger predisposes to the release of innate (instinctive) vocal patterns (displays).

to, control of, or possession of, the disputed property" or "to assert one's right vis-à-vis the other" (p. 111). If the aim is achieved, offensive aggression is reinforced and becomes a more likely response to similar situations (BLANCHARD & BLANCHARD, 1989).[5]

STORR (1968) had "no doubt that man, too, is a territorial animal" (p. 33). Hence, man "possesses a great deal of innate hostility towards his neighbour" (p. 36), be it in the form of a neighbouring tribe or clan or another nation. Both territoriality and ranking order define our identity (and ultimately self-esteem). STORR (1968) thought that "there exists within us an aggressive component which serves to define the territorial boundaries of each individual personality" (p. 77), that is, the boundaries of our identity and self. Insofar as self-esteem, the sense of being accepted by or acceptable to others, is evolutionarily related to holding an eminent or stable position in the group's ranking system, an injury to self-esteem will evoke within us a reaction of offensive or 'territorial' aggression, much as infringements upon our territory or rights (which define an abstract territory we occupy in society) can have this effect. Mental pain, having been inflicted by another's disrespectful or subordinating action, activates offensive aggression, which evolutionarily has the objective of inducing submission in whoever poses the challenge. Successful induction of submission in the challenger not only reaffirms our social position (and makes further challenges unlikely) but also allows us to receive *appeasing signals* from the challenger, signals that are evolutionarily related to approving and praising signals, the very signals that we are likely to receive when we occupy a state of 'safety' (SANDLER), as opposed to anxiety.

2.1.4 Enforcement of compliance and normality

Offensive (intraspecific) aggression is inhibited in most situations. The expression of animosity is inhibited by "consideration of the circumstances as they are in a given situation" (HORNEY, 1937, p. 67). Circumstances show the individual "what he can and what he cannot do toward an enemy or alleged enemy" (p. 67). Behavioural inhibition is linked to anxiety, which in itself roots in an assessment of the situation. Anxiety is "the promoting factor behind inhibitions" (HORNEY, 1937, p. 59). Our compliance, motivated in part by anxiety, is a powerful inhibitor of intraspecific aggression in fellow humans. Our compliance helps to create the situational context within which others' aggression is inhibited. We can become quite readily the target of others' expressions of distrust and contempt, unless we inhibit these reactions through our compliance and normality (LAING, 1960).

With respect to 'normality', people may feel "some distaste or even hostility" for individuals who are handicapped or unattractive (BERKOWITZ,

---

[5] This refers to the appetitive dimension of offensive aggression, the one that involves angry feeling and drive.

1989, p. 51). These "unfortunate individuals are basically aversive stimuli for others" (p. 51). There is evidence to suggest that an unattractive or handicapped individual is more likely "to draw aggressive reactions from those who are disposed to be aggressive for some reason and do not restrain themselves" (BERKOWITZ, 1989, pp. 52–3). Laughter is evolutionarily a form of joint aggression (HASS, 1968; EIBL-EIBESFELDT, 1970). Some children grow up in constant fear of appearing ridiculous and "being laughed at" (ADLER, 1927, p. 68). Ridicule "leaves a permanent mark on the psyche of children which resurfaces in the habits and actions of their adult lives" (ADLER, 1927, p. 68).

Many, perhaps most, disorders of social conduct, whether this conduct be innate or the product of cultural norms, induce in normal men strong feelings of aversion and rejection.

(LORENZ, 1973, pp. 243–4)

What we are afraid of is becoming the target of the group's joint aggression, as it unconsciously carries with it the threat of our annihilation or elimination ('expulsion reaction' [HASS]). Instinctive aggression discharged jointly against outsiders and those who are unable to conform would have served an adaptive purpose in the evolution of primates as well as in early cultural evolution. Nonconformity was selected against, as was the inability to inhibit anger and aggression in accordance with social restraints and standards that pertain to a particular situation. MONEY-KYRLE (1961) spoke of "the elimination since the dawn of civilisation of those whose undisciplined aggression rendered them least adapted to it", which "may have reinstated innate inhibitions, or developed in us an innate disposition to acquire them" (p. 41).

'Knowing' when to inhibit aggression against others and how to avoid becoming a target for others' aggression is essential to the maintenance of social complexity; and it draws particularly heavily on higher cognitive functions. Complex assessments have to be made automatically, as illustrated by macaques. Macaque infants – when maternal protection disappears between the sixth and seventh month of their life – come to be punished more severely by others (reviewed in MACHADO & BACHEVALIER, 2003). Infants learn to judge aggressive signals from others. Around the same time, infants themselves start to show more aggression to control the behaviour of others. Between the sixth and eighth months, infants also start to initiate more grooming with others, especially with peers. In the first year of life, interactions with other individuals thus become increasingly more complex, and macaque infants have to learn that each individual has a "unique set of intensions determined by the combination of kinship, dominance, gender, environmental conditions and the current social context". As MACHADO and BACHEVALIER (2003) pointed out, "macaques must learn to accurately assess the emotional state and intentions of others and choose the most appropriate behavioural reactions for that situation".

During the second year of their lives, macaques acquire their dominance rank in the troop (reviewed in MACHADO & BACHEVALIER, 2003). Punishment, or 'retaliatory aggression', is used to *discipline* offspring and maintain dominance relationships (MOYNIHAN, 1998). While an individual's offensive aggression (in the form of punishment or retaliatory aggression) induces conformity in others, others' nonconformity releases the individual's aggressive potential. Punishment provides "a convenient outlet ... for the residual aggressive tendencies that may be supposed to lurk underneath the placid surfaces of even the most friendly associations" (MOYNIHAN, 1998, p. 54).

The shrine of normality at which all of us devoutly worship must on no account be examined into. ... The least infringement upon it calls forth a reflex defence-reaction in individual and community.

(BURROW, 1949, p. 50)

We help to enforce social and cultural norms by displaying anger (offensive aggression) and 'punishing' those who deviate from theses norms. Normality, as recognized by BURROW (1949), "is the measure by which we judge all behaviour and indict as subversive or pathological whatever behaviour deviates from this popularly cherished 'norm'" (p. 50). Others' socially deviant behaviour automatically induces anger within ourselves and disposes us to display offensively aggressive signals towards them. We show "automatic defence-reactions in support of the accustomed habits and mores characteristic of the normal level of adaptation" (BURROW, 1949, p. 51).

To reemphasize, offensive aggression evolutionarily has the objective of inducing submission in an opponent (unless aggression turns into hatred and vindictiveness, as can be seen in neurosis [HORNEY]). In animals, offensive aggression stabilizes dominance hierarchies (much as its forerunner, territorial aggression, stabilizes the distribution of the species across its habitat). In humans, others' submission is signalled by their reaffirmation of shared social norms, which entails an affirmation of our own position in society (and hence affirmation of our identity and restoration of our self-esteem). Others' expressions of 'respect' or conformity have an appeasing function, in that they remove the trigger for our anger and aggression (Figure 2.2).

2.1.5 Neutralization

When maintaining and defending one's 'self' (an abstract territory demarcating one's access to narcissistic resources), one can aggressively restore others' respect for oneself or work to obtain it by seemingly nonaggressive means. 'Neutralization' (sublimation) refers to "a change in the mode of energy,

Provoking situation

Frustration of access to resources; intrusion into one's territory; challenge to one' social position; violation by others of social norms

Offensive (territorial) aggression

Emotional arousal → Recruitment of appetitive behaviour mechanisms (emotional feeling of anger)

Affective expressions

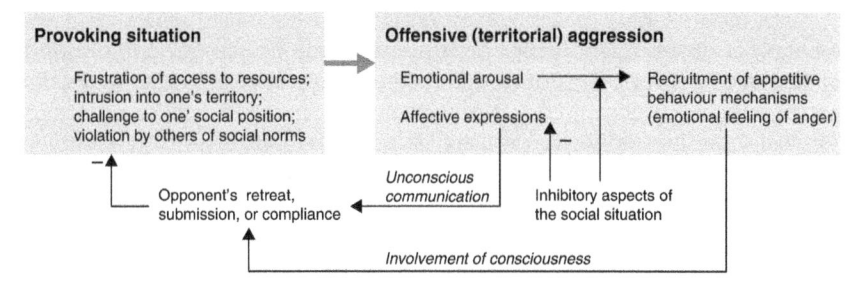

Opponent's retreat, submission, or compliance ← Unconscious communication

Inhibitory aspects of the social situation

Involvement of consciousness

Figure 2.2 Appetitive behaviour, which is accompanied by emotional feelings, may be a derivative of the arousal component of instinctive reactions. Social circumstances may effect a delay in the enactment of instinctive displays, allowing for the recruitment of appetitive (goal-directed) behaviour. Recruitment of an emotional appetitive behaviour mode may also be due to a persistence of provoking circumstances

away from instinctual and toward a noninstinctual mode" (HARTMANN, 1964, p. 223); neutralization concerns the "deinstinctualization of both aggression and libido" (p. 227). Instinctual drives are deflected "from instinctual aims to aims which are socially or culturally more acceptable or valued" (HARTMANN, 1964, p. 217). Indeed, activities fed by neutralized instinctual energy often aim to elicit *acceptance* and valuation of the self by the social surround. Social acceptance and approval is what the self or ego is concerned with.

Attraction of narcissistic supplies (and regulation of narcissistic homeostasis on more abstract levels) would count among what HARTMANN called 'ego aims' (ego functions). Energies that "the ego uses for its specific functions are as a rule not instinctual", they are 'desexualized' and 'deaggressivized' (p. 226). Ego aims are usually "fed by neutralized energy", although they "may, under certain conditions, also be cathected with instinctual energy", especially when "ego aims lie in the direction of id tendencies" (p. 230). By way of neutralization, "the ego allows a certain amount of discharge of the original tendencies, provided that their mode (and, often, their aims) have been modified" (HARTMANN, 1964, p. 231). For example, aggression can be woven into healthy assertiveness that is used to control selfobjects, that is applied, in other words, to an ego aim and used for the benefit of the ego (*self*-assertion). Thus, "the ego accepts some instinctual tendencies and helps them toward gratification", while, at the same time, substituting "ego aims for the aims of the id" (HARTMANN, 1964, pp. 229–30).

Ego functions (corresponding to psychic structures) provide aggressive and other instincts (instinctual *drives*, to be precise) with "specific modes of expression" (HARTMANN, 1964, p. 87). Defence mechanisms ('ego defences'), for example, are ego functions that have at their disposal "a neutralized form of aggressive energy" (p. 87). Some defence mechanisms retain "an element (fight) that allows of their description as being mostly fed by one mode of aggressive energy" (p. 232). Furthermore, the establishment and maintenance of object relationships presupposes some degree of neutralization of instinctive drives, including aggression. Adaptation to reality generally presupposes neutralization of aggressive energy; however, reality situations "appeal sometimes to the unmitigated expression of aggression" (HARTMANN, 1964, p. 87). Aggression can be expressed in unmodified form under 'favourable' circumstances, such as when "psychical counter-forces" (FREUD, 1930) are suspended by a sense of injustice or righteousness.

2.1.6 Coercion and hatred

Normal, primary, nondestructive aggression, in its primitive as well as in its developed form, subsides as soon as the goals that had been striven for are reached (whether these goals are related in the main to objects that are experienced as separate from the self – as independent centres of initiative – or to the self and to self-objects). If, however, the phase-appropriate need for omnipotent control over the self-object had been chronically and traumatically frustrated in childhood, then chronic narcissistic rage, with all its deleterious consequences, will be established.
(KOHUT, 1977, p. 121)

Aggression, according to KOHUT (1977), "is, from the beginning, a constituent of the child's assertiveness, and under normal circumstances it remains alloyed to the assertiveness of the adult's mature self" (p. 116). Destructiveness, being a nonadaptive manifestation of aggression, emerges as a 'disintegration product' when the 'psychological configuration' of assertiveness breaks down vis-à-vis 'empathy failures' of selfobjects (pp. 114–15). Destructiveness is "the result of the failure of the self-object environment to meet the child's need for optimal ... empathic responses" (p. 116). Empathy failures result in an injury to the self (narcissistic injury). Destructive, narcissistic rage "is always motivated by an injury to the self" (KOHUT, 1977, p. 116). An individual's disposition to react with narcissistic rage is predicated on a 'vulnerable self-structure'. Destructive rage is viewed by self psychology "as a secondary reaction to the traumatic empathy failures of caregivers that have menaced the cohesion of a vulnerable self-structure" (STOLOROW, 1983, p. 288).

KERNBERG (1992) regarded hatred as an affective response to danger felt to be emanating from an object. The aim of hatred is to destroy or devalue (dehumanize) the "object, a specific object of unconscious fantasy, and this object's conscious derivatives" (p. 23). In milder forms of hatred, the person desires to dominate the object and exert power over it, so that "attacks on the object tend to be self-limited by the object's submission" (KERNBERG, 1992, p. 24). The aim of offensive aggression is to induce submission in a challenger; the other's submission, in turn, allows for the receipt from the other of appeasing signals, which are evolutionarily related to affectionate

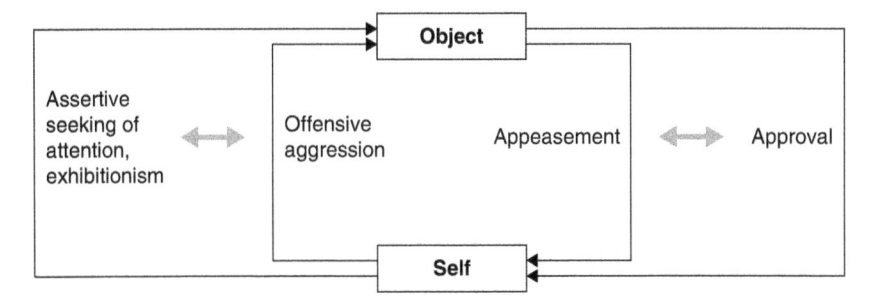

```
┌─────────────────┬──────────────▶ Object ◀────────────────────┐
│   Assertive     │                                             │
│   seeking of    │◀──▶ Offensive        Appeasement    ◀──▶ Approval
│   attention,    │     aggression                              │
│   exhibitionism │                                             │
└─────────────────┴──────────────────▶ Self ◀─────────────────┘
```

Figure 2.3 Signals of approval (and affirmation) are evolutionarily related to signals of appeasement (and submission). Assertiveness can turn into coercion and hatred, all of which are related to offensive aggression and efforts to control resources (in territorial or status disputes with conspecifics)

signals (providing narcissistic sustenance). Aggressively inducing submission is therefore related to coercion of the love object (Figure 2.3). BOWLBY (1973) recognized that angry behaviour "has coercion as its function" (p. 248). Angry coercive behaviour expressed towards a parent or partner "acts to promote, not to disrupt, the bond" (p. 248). Anger is dysfunctional "whenever a person, child or adult, becomes so intensely and/or persistently angry with his partner that the bond between them is weakened, instead of strengthened" (pp. 248–9). Anger becomes hatred "whenever aggressive thoughts or acts cross the narrow boundary between being deterrent and being revengeful" (BOWLBY, 1973, p. 249).[6]

2.2 Appeasement and submission

The majority of fights between members of a species for territory or ranking position are ritualized tests of strength; they rarely have a lethal outcome (LORENZ, 1963). The victor in an agonistic confrontation is usually satisfied with the defeated animal's retreat (from the disputed territory or contested status). The defeated animal displays appeasement (submissive) gestures to *signal* that it concedes victory to its opponent. Gestures of submission displayed in the course of an agonistic confrontation are innately 'understood' by the opponent. Signalling admission of defeat, they inhibit any further attack from the opponent (EIBL-EIBESFELDT, 1970). Appeasement gestures are ritualized escape behaviours; their purpose is to attain safety. Submission to authority, visually communicated by submissive gestures, can be regarded

---

[6] In BALINT's view, hate and aggression are remnants of archaic object love; they are derivatives of *frustrated* archaic object love. BALINT stated that behind the rage of a narcissistically injured patient lies his love (reviewed in BRANDCHAFT, 1986).

as a derivative of escape behaviour, too (RADO, 1956). Submission is a ritualized escape behaviour that is employed in "social dependency relationships" (pp. 219, 245). Submission to authority would have the same motivational origin as the infant's cry for help, namely fear prompting escape to safety (RADO, 1956). It is this safety – attained by displaying submissive gestures and witnessing the opponent's or authority's pacification (appeasement) – that constitutes the essence of the narcissistic equilibrium we try to maintain by more complex social behaviours or intrapsychic manoeuvres.

Appeasement behaviour, according to MOYNIHAN (1998), refers to "any behavior pattern that reduces an opponent's tendency to attack" (p. 51). Appeasement gestures often involve the turning away from the victor of the animal's natural weapon or the presentation to the victor of the animal's vulnerable part (STORR, 1968). Looking away is an effective signal of submission. Removing the face, eyes, and beak from the view of the opponent may terminate a hostile encounter between birds "by virtually hiding the releasing stimuli" (MOYNIHAN, 1998, p. 44). Presenting to an opponent a vulnerable part of the body, and thereby exposing it to possible attack, also inhibits the opponent's aggression. 'Advertisement of vulnerability' is a common method (message) used to control conspecific aggression (MOYNIHAN, 1998, p. 44). Vulnerability is also expressed by making oneself appear small. Lying flat on the belly in front of the victor, as can be seen in marine iguanas, is designed to make the losing animal appear smaller, which, according to EIBL-EIBESFELDT (1970), actively inhibits the opponent's aggression or removes the releasing stimulus for the opponent's aggression. By contrast, gestures that enlarge the animal's physical stature are ritualized displays of aggressive intent that serve to challenge or threaten a conspecific. The submissive gesture of making oneself appear small is "the precise opposite of threatening behaviour" (EIBL-EIBESFELDT, 1970, p. 172).

2.2.1 Bonding and familiarity

Appeasement gestures contribute to bond formation by inhibiting intraspecific aggression and the potential thereof. What is more, personal bonds (partner bonds) are in their nature "aggression-inhibiting, appeasing behaviour mechanisms" (p. 133); they evolved on the basis of appeasement gestures (LORENZ, 1963). As stated by STORR (1968), "aggression was antecedent to brotherly love" (p. 35). Bonding behaviour was shown by LORENZ (1963) to be more pronounced in species with notable intraspecific aggression (even when aggressiveness is heightened only under certain conditions or at certain times, such as during breeding seasons). STORR (1968) agreed that "it is only when intense aggressiveness exists between two individuals that love can arise" (p. 36). Bonding takes place between sexual or breeding partners and between parents and offspring. Care-seeking and care-giving gestures inherently inhibit aggression between mother and offspring, similarly to appeasement gestures exchanged in resource disputes. Familiarity further inhibits aggression between mother and offspring. Nevertheless, "aggression between mother and child is inevitable" (STORR, 1968, p. 41).

In most mammals and birds, the mother's bond with her young is individualized. Mothers recognize their own offspring and "often drive strange youngsters away fiercely" (EIBL-EIBESFELDT, 1970, p. 121). Acquaintanceship inhibits the mother's aggression towards her own offspring. The bond between partners in parental care, too, is based on acquaintanceship. In birds, at the beginning of bond formation, courtship ceremonies serve to inhibit aggression. Once the bond has been formed, and partners recognize each other, acquaintanceship takes over the function of inhibiting aggression between partners, so that appeasing behaviours are no longer necessary (EIBL-EIBESFELDT, 1970). Familiarity also reduces the aversiveness of relatives, peers, and others. We are, as a rule, friendly towards those who are familiar to us. Others' familiarity (a complex contextual stimulus) has the same effect as their appeasement gestures on our innate aggressiveness. The exchange of appeasement gestures is the only way of inhibiting aggression between *unfamiliar* individuals (strangers), but, through the exchange of appeasement gestures, individuals become familiar with each other. Appeasement gestures have the "side effect ... that different individuals become accustomed to one another" (MOYNIHAN, 1998, p. 47).

Familiarity reduces hostility between territorial rivals; territorial rivals that have become familiar with one another fight less frequently and less vigorously (MOYNIHAN, 1998). Familiarity also reinforces the cohesion in family units, herds, flocks, groups, and dominance hierarchies (p. 14). Familiarity between individuals (based upon individual recognition) is a mechanism that establishes "relatively peaceful social bonds" among members of a group (MOYNIHAN, 1998, p. 85). The need to be *recognized* (as familiar) and *accepted* (into a bond) may have arisen in evolution insofar as the state of not being recognized or accepted in the company of conspecifics became aversive (and dangerous), while the state of loneliness (of not being in the company of conspecifics) remained aversive, too (and dangerous for other reasons). *Being recognized or accepted instils feelings of safety precisely because it signifies that others' aggressiveness is inhibited.* Trust in another person is a conviction in the absence of the other person's aggressive inclinations towards oneself. Trust, too, instils safety. Sudden loss of trust in a person upon whom one relies generates 'basic insecurity' (STORR, 1968, p. 40).

The perception of cues related to others' aggressive potential or their aggressive readiness is associated with anxiety. Instinctively, the individual overcomes anxiety and attains safety by displaying appeasement gestures and thus inhibiting others' aggressive potential. Others' aggressive potential can be inhibited also contextually, that is, by a complex context that is established and recreated by way of appetitive behaviour. The bond can be regarded as a context of safety. Attainment of safety is reinforcing, and appetitive behaviour becomes so organized that it repeatedly moves the individual away from an anxiogenic and towards a safe situation, and thereby renews the bond. We form bonds or friendships partly *in order to feel safe* (and partly to satisfy our libidinal needs).

2.2.2 Infantilisms and alloparental behaviour

Appeasement (pacification) of an opponent in a potentially hostile situation can be achieved by displaying gregarious patterns of behaviour (MOYNIHAN, 1998, p. 100). Appeasement behaviours are often derivatives of infantile behaviours (although infantile behaviours may have originally evolved from more primitive submissive gestures). The mother reacts to signals emitted by her infant (signals advertising the infant's vulnerability) by looking after it. Parental care behaviour is associated with inhibition of aggression. Appeasement rituals capitalize on this mechanism (EIBL-EIBESFELDT, 1970). Alloinfantile behaviour, which is "reminiscent of the behavior of young animals seeking comfort or protection from a parent", reduces the probability of fighting between bonding partners (and may, at the same time, help soliciting in sexual encounters) (MOYNIHAN, 1998, p. 48).

Infantile behaviours inhibiting an opponent's aggression include lying on the back.[7] Begging and mutual feeding are common behaviours among social canines. Dogs and wolves feed other animals in the pack with the prey they catch. Begging behaviour induces this feeding response in a conspecific (or, insofar as domestic dogs are concerned, in a human) (LORENZ, 1973). In wolves and dogs, ritualized behaviour patterns that derived from the young animal's begging for food have an appeasing function. The ritualistic display of begging to be fed arouses a friendly mood in an opponent (EIBL-EIBESFELDT, 1970). Similarly, a dog can use puppyish behaviour to induce a friendly mood in the opponent. Humans, too, display helplessness, weakness, and infantile behaviours in order to arouse pity in an opponent and thereby curtail or prevent the opponent's aggression (EIBL-EIBESFELDT, 1970).

Alloparental behaviour in gregarious mammals and birds (in which one individual reacts to another, potentially aggressive individual as if it was its own infant) similarly inhibits intraspecific aggression. Allopreening and allogrooming (preening or grooming *another instead of oneself*) in birds and mammals, respectively, are ritualized behaviour patterns that are related to alloparental behaviour. Allopreening and allogrooming, which involve tactile contact, seem to prevent hostile encounters, but cannot be used to curtail an opponent's aggression. Tactile signals "are both particularly risky and perhaps unusually effective in reducing social tensions" (MOYNIHAN, 1998, p. 98).

---

[7] A dog or wolf can break off a fight by rolling on to his back and urinating a little. This ritual replicates the behaviour of "a cub offering itself to its mother to be cleaned" (EIBL-EIBESFELDT, 1970, p. 65).

In species with parental care, birds and mammals, all or most of the numerous friendly and gregarious patterns, so often used to control or canalize aggression, seem to be derived from familial reactions. They include joining, following, and helping, at the nest and elsewhere. These patterns can be shown, by extension, to all sorts of potential cooperators, competitors, rivals, opponents. The results include the formation of groups of different sizes ... of different levels of structural complexity ...

(MOYNIHAN, 1998, p. 100)

2.2.3 Smile

The suspicious or surly face is an unmistakeable warning which arouses uneasiness in the person approaching – not only because of past experience but because of an innate recognitive reaction situated far deeper within us.

(HASS, 1968, p. 123)

Humans are innately aggressive and possibly aggressive by default, so that being among them is innately aversive and dangerous, as illustrated by developmentally normal stranger anxiety as well as perhaps by paranoia. Normally, this is not apparent to us because of a multitude of appeasement behaviours that are subliminally exchanged in social contexts. Familiarity and appeasement gestures counteract the aversiveness of conspecifics and inhibit their inherent aggressiveness. The smile is an effective appeasement gesture. Smiling powerfully inhibits others' aggressive potential or dissolves their anger ('smile disarms') (EIBL-EIBESFELDT, 1970). We depend for our safety on others' friendly expressions (which we induce by our own friendly expressions) as well as on their adherence to common norms (which we foster by our own compliance). It is because of our thorough dependence on others' friendliness that narcissism (the attitudes and behaviours that regulate others' friendliness towards us) plays such a central role in social behaviour and psychopathology.

In our primitive forebears' communities it must have been extremely important to a child to know when it was permissible or inadvisable to approach an adult. The same applied equally to adults encountering strangers. The angry, ill-tempered, sick individual could be dangerous if approached too closely by those who encroached on his private territory. In this context, it was extremely important for man to develop an innate recognition mechanism which would give him suitable warning on sighting such a face. It was just as important for man to develop an appropriate signal for the contrary mood – a sign of approachability. And this ... became further strengthened into a means of inhibiting aggression and actively enlisting fellow feeling.

(HASS, 1968, pp. 130–1)

HASS (1968) spoke of an "instinctive tendency to remain aloof from members of the same species", a tendency that "constitutes a disruptive factor" in processes of mating and bond formation (p. 121). Human smile, expressing a friendly and accommodating attitude, became "an arrow which pierced these invisible barriers", fulfilling "the important function of bringing us aggressive creatures closer together" (p. 131). Smiling became "a means of eliciting contact readiness in others and of conveying our own accessibility to contact" (p. 123). By smiling, "we ingratiate ourselves with other people and bind them to us" (p. 131). Civilization "can be said to owe its cohesion to a myriad-and-one such smiles" (HASS, 1968, p. 131).

Smile probably evolved as the 'antithesis' (DARWIN), that is, the direct opposite, of threatening expressive movements. This is to say that the facial expression communicating "friendliness and accessibility to contact" evolved to be as dissimilar as possible from the expressive movement signalling an aggressive stance (HASS, 1968, p. 130). Smile, thus, is the opposite of "the human facial expression which conveys ill humour", the latter being characterized by "a mouth drawn downward at the corners, vertical furrows in the forehead, and a slight jutting of the lips" (p. 130).[8] Smiling is fundamentally different from laughter, "both in significance and origin" (p. 126). Unlike laughter, smiling does not involve the opening of the mouth or emission of sounds. Both signals, however, possess "a strongly infectious quality" (HASS, 1968, p. 127).

If we encounter a stranger and laugh at him on sight, he will probably interpret it as a sign of derision and disparagement rather than as a greeting. If we smile at him, all misunderstanding is precluded.

(HASS, 1968, p. 127)

2.2.4 Bowing and nodding

Phylogenetic ritualization can be distinguished from ontogenetic and traditional (cultural) ritualization (EIBL-EIBESFELDT, 1970). Traditional (cultural) ritualization is transmitted in the course of cultural evolution from one generation to the next, impacting on the ontogenesis of behaviour in each generation. Ontogenetic and traditional ritualization plays a particular role in humans. Unlike phylogenetic rituals, ontogenetic and traditional rituals are acquired through learning; however, similarly to phylogenetic ritualization, behaviour patterns that become ritualized in ontogenesis or cultural evolution "are exaggerated in pantomime and accentuated through additional equipment" but also simplified and rhythmically repeated (p. 50). Modifications that original behaviour patterns undergo in the process of

---

[8] Smile can be "embarrassed, shamefaced, or nervous", in which case "the friendship signal is superimposed upon the expression of fear or shame appropriate to the circumstances" (HASS, 1968, p. 128).

ritualization are "designed to make the signal striking and unmistakable" (EIBL-EIBESFELDT, 1970, p. 54). Cultural, ontogenetic, and phylogenetic forms of ritualization are interwoven in the evolution of human appeasement gestures. Appeasement and submissive gestures that are culturally developed often have an innate (phylogenetically evolved) element (EIBL-EIBESFELDT, 1970). In humans, bowing is an appeasement gesture; it inhibits another person's potential aggression (STORR, 1968). It is related to the defeated animal's diminutive behaviour and its aversion, from the victor, of its offensive weapons. One submits to another person by making oneself appear smaller, which culturally developed not only into bowing but also kneeling or lying flat in front of the ruler (EIBL-EIBESFELDT, 1970). Bowing, being a gesture of submission, is used in greetings. Greeting behaviours, observed in humans and other species, "are ritualized forms of submission that confirm asymmetries of status between the participants or partners" (MOYNIHAN, 1998, p. 50). Greetings are usually initiated by subordinate individuals. Formal expressions of status "often obviate the need for actual attacks or fighting" as a means of organizing dominance hierarchies (MOYNIHAN, 1998, p. 97).

Nodding is a ritualized bowing gesture and signals submission. Nodding is used as a gesture of affirmation and as a greeting gesture. Nodding is more ritualized than bowing or falling to one's knees (EIBL-EIBESFELDT, 1970). The nod is "a curtailed inclination of the head – that is to say, a ritualized appeasement gesture", whereby ritualization involved not only curtailment but also acceleration and reiteration (HASS, 1968, p. 147).[9] Nodding means that "one accepts the views, suggestions, or commands of another" (HASS, 1968, p. 147). When nodding towards a speaker, "we are submitting, as listeners, to the ideas of the speaker" (EIBL-EIBESFELDT, 1970, p. 169). If the speaker feels unsure of himself, he "will look enquiringly at his friends and wait for a sign of encouragement: a nod or a wink will suffice" (EIBL-EIBESFELDT, 1970, p. 177). The speaker feels less anxious because nodding in the audience signals to him that their aggressiveness is inhibited.

> We are dependent to an enormous degree upon others for the minute nods of agreement and approval, for signs that friendliness rather than hostility is present, for safety signs.
> (SANDLER, 1989a, p. 81)

2.2.5 Greeting

In the "most differing peoples in the world", greeting takes the form of "a rapid raising and lowering of the eyebrows, accompanied by a smile and

---

[9] Correspondingly, our expression for 'no' is a "curtailed, accelerated, and reiterated" (i.e., ritualized) movement of aversion (HASS, 1968, p. 147).

often also a nod" (EBIL-EIBESFELDT, 1970, p. 16). Greeting with the eyes is a phylogenetically ritualized expression of pleasant surprise. Phylogenetic ritualization "is often accompanied by the development of special physical structures" (p. 54), of which the eyebrows are an example. EBIL-EIBESFELDT thought that, in our phylogenesis, eyebrows have survived the otherwise widespread loss of facial hair because they evolved into "a means of emphasizing the optical greeting" (HASS, 1968, p. 116). It is not a coincidence that "girls spend so much time on their eyebrows", "painting them and tracing their outlines" (HASS, 1968, p. 116). Although many greetings have an innate basis, greetings are often culturally emphasized in humans (EBIL-EIBESFELDT, 1970). Culturally developed greeting rites include the raising of a hand, the touch to the side of one's head, or the shaking of hands. The raising of the open hand in greeting demonstrates peaceful intent and "that one is not holding a weapon in the right hand" (p. 181). Leave taking in humans is also a form of greeting behaviour. When a person walks away from another, he enters a *dangerous situation* (EIBL-EIBESFELDT, 1970). The person – when leaving the aggression-inhibiting context of the interaction and turning his back to the other – has to assure himself of the other's peaceful intentions.

In birds, the passing over of nesting material is a common greeting gesture with a clear appeasing function (EIBL-EIBESFELDT, 1970). In some species of birds, the sight of a conspecific "releases strong aggressive feelings which can only be appeased by the offer of nesting material" (p. 105). Gifts have a similar function in humans. Gifts and food are offered in greeting to guests in various peoples and cultures (EIBL-EIBESFELDT, 1970). While familiarity powerfully inhibits intraspecific aggression, aggression is less inhibited when meeting strangers. The aggression-inhibiting effect of greeting gestures has to be relied on when meeting strangers or people with whom one is less familiar. Humans greet each other after a period of separation, often repeatedly during the day and after only short separations. We feel an urge to greet as soon as "we step out of the anonymous crowd" (p. 167). We greet a stranger "when we enter a shop or a strange house" or "if we meet him alone somewhere out in the open" (p. 167). If we fail to offer greetings in these situations, "we experience an unpleasant feeling of tension" (p. 167). Omission of a greeting releases others' aggression and undermines our safety. Conversely, a greeting "can relax the tension in a situation" (p. 166). The return of a greeting "is generally a guarantee of security" (EIBL-EIBESFELDT, 1970, p. 166).

2.2.6 The imaginary plane

Being familiar with the work of LORENZ and TINBERGEN, LACAN (1966) understood that instinctive behaviour patterns are released in response to particular visual images (imagos). Recognition (unconscious, in accordance with a 'mental schema') of a visual image ('imago' or perceptual gestalt) of another member of the species mobilizes a primitive impulse towards that member of the species (whereby the impulse may be related to attack, territoriality, courtship, or mating). LACAN (1966) assigned the visual image ('imago') and the reflexive response to it to a fundamental plane or dimension of behaviour, which he called 'the imaginary' ('the register of the imaginary'). On the imaginary plane, the gestalt provides the stimulus for behaviour. The 'logic' of the imaginary plane is one of acting and being acted upon (LACAN, 1966). The individual is manipulated, in a sense, by an other; and it is through these manipulations that the infant's first attitudes take shape. The power of looking at others or being looked at by others can be ascribed to the power of 'the imaginary'. The imaginary is the seat of primitive 'drives' (or instincts, strictly speaking), such as the libidinal 'drive'. Attunements or communications unfolding on 'the imaginary' plane can be libidinal (referring to the induction, giving, and receipt of care or love) or aggressive-submissive in nature. The cycle of sexual behaviour, too, is centred on the imaginary. By fixing libidinal and other 'drives' (instincts) to visual images (perceptual registrations), the imaginary establishes the initial conditions under which objects in the world can be predictably experienced. Our relation to 'the other' (another individual) is ultimately rooted in 'the imaginary' plane (LACAN, 1966).

2.2.7 Interaction with context and emotion

In higher social animals, including humans, "the great majority of expressive actions and gestures reflect an urge to threaten or appease" (LORENZ, 1973, p. 213). An individual's aggressive display in the *context* of evidence for his aggressive potential (related to dominance status) automatically induces a disposition towards submissive displays (an urge to appease) in the opponent; and displays of submission, in turn, tend to inhibit aggressive displays in those who are the recipient of submissive signals. Expressive actions and gestures not only reflect one's own mood but also tend to induce an emotional state in the other, which, in turn, controls the likelihood of the other's expressive actions and gestures. Contextual factors, too, control emotional responses and hence the disposition to emit certain gestures. In conversations, we automatically assume postures of submission when talking to somebody in authority, while our conversation partner unknowingly emits signals of dominance (reviewed in FERGUSON & BARGH, 2004).

Many social behaviours in humans are automatically triggered by the perception of others' actions (FERGUSON & BARGH, 2004). Insofar as others' actions have an innate component, the triggering involves activation of an innate releasing mechanism (LORENZ). In a conversation, verbal and gestural expressions are elicited *more or less* automatically by perception of the other's linguistic and affective motor patterns. Perception of the other's affective or linguistic expressions may elicit one's affective or linguistic expressions *less* automatically if they trigger instead an emotional response (an evolutionary derivative perhaps of the instinctual response), which, in

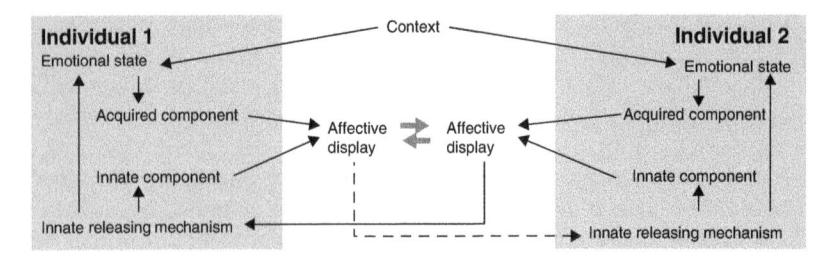

Figure 2.4 Affective interaction with mutual induction of expressions and emotions

turn, controls acquired (and cortically represented) components of one's affective or linguistic expressions. Individuals involved in a conversation 'prime' each others' linguistic representations, bringing them close to the threshold at which they produce the encoded motor pattern, thus making it *likely* that "each partner generates his utterances on the basis of what he has just heard from the other" (GARROD & PICKERING, 2004, p. 9). The priming effect – the increase in probability of the release of culturally and ontogenetically ritualized linguistic and affective motor patterns (the disposition towards the display of these patterns) – is a function of the emotional state within which the conversation takes place (Figure 2.4).

Although drives, in the sense of affective states, need to be distinguished from instincts, in the sense of innate motor patterns (LORENZ), affects and instincts are nevertheless likely to be related (and hence it is not insensible to speak of 'instinctual drives'). Affects, as understood by KERNBERG (1996), "always include a cognitive component, a subjective experience of a highly pleasurable or unpleasurable nature, neurovegetative discharge phenomena, psychomotor activation, and, very crucially, a distinctive pattern of facial expression" (p. 127). Patterns of facial expression associated with affects originally served "a communicative function directed to the caregiver" (KERNBERG, 1996, p. 127). Affective states (drives) and affective expressions (ritualized instinctive displays) may well have coevolved from unritualized instinctive motor patterns. Unritualized instincts may have become ritualized displays (with a communicative function) once they could be partially inhibited (by a contradictory instinct or action tendency). Partial inhibition (implicit in so-called intention movements) helped to make the expression of instinctive patterns conditional on the context (a prerequisite for their effective communicative function), while the state of tension concomitant to partial neurovegetative and psychomotor activation (the partial activation of neurovegetative and general psychomotor components of instincts) evolved into affective or drive states. With further evolution, the conditionality of instinct inhibition upon context (sensitivity to context) could have combined with neurovegetative discharge phenomena to give rise to emotional feelings (subjective experience of a pleasurable or unpleasurable nature).

2.3 Care seeking and giving

'Instinctual responses', according to BOWLBY (1958), denote observable patterns of behaviour, patterns that often have the function of safeguarding the individual or mediating reproduction. These instinctual responses are often directed towards one particular individual ('monotropy'). Mating responses, for instance, tend to be directed towards a particular member of the opposite sex. The mother figure plays an integrative function for the child's instinctual responses. The repertoire of 'positively directed mother-oriented instinctual responses' (sucking, clinging, following, crying, smiling) ensures that the infant evokes maternal care and remains in close proximity to the mother (BOWLBY, 1958). BOWLBY (1958) proposed that each of the child's mother-oriented instinctual responses (sucking, clinging, following, crying, smiling) makes a distinct contribution to the formation of the child's tie to his mother. Component instinctual responses become integrated into 'attachment behaviour' in the course of the first year of life. For an emotional attachment to form, the mother has to permit the child to display clinging and following behaviours towards her. Rejection of clinging and following causes emotional and psychological disturbances (BOWLBY, 1958).

Libido (love) is, as FAIRBAIRN (1952) emphasized, object-seeking rather than pleasure-seeking. The real libidinal aim is not pleasure, as FREUD had proposed, but to establish satisfactory relationships with objects. Libidinal tendencies urge the individual to *make emotional contact* with others (FAIRBAIRN, 1952). Expressions of libido can be considered as caring or care-giving behaviours, but they also provide narcissistic nourishment, whereas care-seeking behaviours express narcissistic needs. Care-seeking and care-giving displays coevolved (BOWLBY, 1977). They act as releasing stimuli for each other and are linked in processes of 'affective attunement' (FELDMAN et al., 1999) or 'mutual cueing' (MAHLER, 1967, 1968).

Care-seeking and care-giving interactions (affectionate interactions) are both soothing and rewarding (pleasurable); they assuage anxiety and gratify narcissistic needs. Narcissistic supplies in the form of others' caring and affectionate signals are needed in order to maintain self-esteem (FENICHEL, 1946). Failure to elicit care-giving responses from an other is injurious to self-esteem. If care-seeking behaviour fails, that is, if the care-seeker fails to induce care-giving or affectionate behaviour in the partner, then pain or anxiety arises, which, in turn, may lead to a switch to anxious care-seeking behaviour ('attention-seeking behaviour') (MCCLUSKEY, 2002). The pain or distress experienced when care-seeking behaviour fails (narcissistic pain) is likely related to infantile separation distress. Failure to effectively solicit care or 'attention' promotes 'self-defensive' behaviours and interactions (MCCLUSKEY, 2002).

If the careseeker fails to have his or her careseeking needs met, the behavioral patterns that accompany careseeking cannot shut down and the system for careseeking is infiltrated by the activation of the personal defense system. In this way careseeking is then expressed by whatever behaviors have been found to evoke in the caregiver responses that assuage the pain of not reaching careseeking goals.

(McCluskey, 2002, p. 133)

Narcissistic needs "compel the child to ask for affection" (Fenichel, 1946, p. 41). The child may solicit and procure essential narcissistic supplies, that is, supplies of affection and approval, by way of exhibitionistic behaviours or "by force"; or he may seek to attain them "by submissiveness and demonstration of suffering"[10] (Fenichel, 1946, p. 41). The feeling state of wellbeing or 'safety' is a state of narcissistic balance, which the individual strives to attain in compliance with external standards, often through situationally *appropriate* forms of attention-seeking or exhibitionistic behaviour. The state of well-being or safety is "the polar opposite of feelings of pain, anxiety, or discomfort" (Joffe & Sandler, 1965, p. 157), that is, the opposite of feelings that may arise in consequence of failed care-seeking behaviour, failures that are often predicated on parental or wider social attitudes towards *inappropriate* 'drive' satisfaction, including inappropriate exhibitionistic displays and inappropriate attention-seeking behaviours. It is the maintenance of this feeling state of wellbeing or safety with which the ego is ultimately concerned and for which it enlists the help of the superego (Joffe & Sandler, 1965).

2.3.1 Face-to-face interactions

Newborns are predisposed to express certain emotional states (affects) by facial expressions, vocalizations, and gestures (Izard, 1994). These expressions evoke complimentary affective responses from the mother. Short face-to-face interactions between mother and infant emerge when the infant is approximately two months of age. During face-to-face interactions, infant and mother attune to each other's affective expressions, that is, they synchronize their affective behaviour (Feldman et al., 1999). Mutually attuned, synchronized face-to-face interactions have a soothing effect. Asynchrony in reciprocal facial communication causes the infant to experience distress. Synchrony will be disrupted at times, and the infant will be in distress; however, the mother usually reattunes her affective expressions to allow the infant to recover from distress (Feldman et al., 1999). Face-to-face interactions have a soothing effect, perhaps insofar as they reaffirm contact and

---

[10] This is also the mechanism of masochism.

safety. The infant synchronizes his affective expressions with his mother's "in order for him to feel secure" (SANDLER, 1989a, p. 81).

Similarly, macaque infants remain in close physical contact and establish frequent face-to-face interactions (mostly lip-smacking) with their mothers in the first few postnatal weeks (reviewed in MACHADO & BACHEVALIER, 2003). In humans, smiling plays a particular role in face-to-face interactions between mother and infant. It is clear that "the infant is equipped innately with the capacity for a smiling response, a capacity that is evoked by a set of key releaser stimulus configurations, such as the human face gestalt, which become effective at certain phases of development" (SCHECTER, 1973, p. 22). For the mother, eye-to-eye contact with her infant and perception of his smile are innately rewarding (EIBL-EIBESFELDT, 1970).

KOHUT recognized the exhibitionistic (*attention-seeking*) nature of the child's expressions towards his mother. The child's exhibitionism, much as the adult's ambitiousness, expresses the need to be seen, to be acknowledged and accepted, and thus to feel safe (and, from evolutionary point of view, to *be* safe). Care-seeking displays (related to separation cries), aiming to *attract* the mother's *attention*, find expression in the context of anxiety (the polar opposite of safety). On the other hand, affective exchange, especially *affectionate* interaction, often develops spontaneously on the background of safety; safety may even be a precondition for affectionate interaction. Thus, the child's or adult's narcissistic needs (expressed by way of attention-seeking and exhibitionistic behaviours) may have to be satisfied – and safety may have to be attained – before his libidinal needs can be expressed (by way of affectionate or care-*giving* behaviours, which would then induce reciprocal affectionate and care-giving responses from the other).

2.3.2 Infantile cries

As already pointed out, parental (care-giving) behaviour has evolved to be complementary to the child's care-seeking behaviour (BOWLBY, 1977). The 'parental instinct', according to MCDOUGALL (1924), is evoked by distress cries of the young; but it can also be evoked by the sight of any young and helpless creature. Emission by the infant of the cry of distress is an expression of what MCDOUGALL (1924) called the 'instinct of appeal'. Many young mammals or birds emit cries when they have lost contact with their mother or fallen out of their nest. A newborn child frequently cries and only "calms down when it is caressed, picked up or spoken to" (EIBL-EIBESFELDT, 1970, p. 206). Infants tend to cry when they are put down, not when they are carried.

> This is a natural and probably innate reaction which has its roots in our remote past. If the child of primitive man lost contact with its mother, it was exposed to attack by predators. Cries, which functioned as a request to the mother to reestablish contact, were thus of species-preserving importance.
> (HASS, 1968, p. 164)

Crying behaviour serves the function of bringing the mother to the infant's side. Presence of the mother provides the 'terminating stimulus' for the infant's crying (BOWLBY, 1958).[11] In primate infants, being prevented from clinging to the mother provokes the crying response. In humans, crying behaviour, but not clinging or following, is effective at birth, consistent with the greater extent to which human infants are dependent on the exertions of their mother (BOWLBY, 1958). Smiling is present in human infants when they are six weeks old. The instinctual smiling response, which is elicited by perception of a face gestalt, acts as another powerful releaser for maternal behaviour, especially for maternal affection (love). Thus, infantile crying and smiling influence maternal behaviour; they act as social releasers for instinctual responses in the mother (BOWLBY, 1958).

2.3.3 Distance-decreasing and contacting behaviours

Mammals are "equipped with appetitive behaviour for restoring contact – to begin with by crying out and later through active seeking" (EIBL-EIBESFELDT, 1970, p. 205). The mother is the 'goal-in-flight' for the infant (EIBL-EIBESFELDT, 1970). The appetitive urge to establish contact with conspecifics persists into adulthood in many species. In many species of mammals and birds, animals readily approach, join, and follow their conspecifics (MOYNIHAN, 1998). These movements are called friendly, gregarious, affiliative, or 'distance-decreasing'. Joining and following patterns in gregarious mammals and birds are evolutionary extensions of familial reactions between parents and offspring. Friendly or gregarious patterns of behaviour are derived from patterns preexisting within the behavioural repertoire of the species, "patterns that were originally evolved to regulate and encourage family (possibly including sexual) relations" (MOYNIHAN, 1998, p. 89).

Following behaviour that is focused on a parent has the function of keeping the infant in close proximity to the parent. The same can be said about clinging behaviour. While infants can be observed to follow their mother in a great variety of species of mammals and birds, clinging behaviour is virtually confined to primates (BOWLBY, 1958). Primate infants cling with hands and feet to their mother's belly or back. Infants often cling to their mother both day and night during the early weeks of their life. Although the clinging response is predominantly directed towards the mother, it can be directed, according to BOWLBY (1958), towards 'transitional objects' (WINNICOTT, 1953). BOWLBY (1958) cited evidence suggesting that even chimpanzee infants cling to transitional objects, objects that are plainly identified with an absent parent. In humans, the clinging response appears to

---

[11] Infants readily cry when they experience cold, hunger, fear, or loneliness. The infant's crying not only brings about maternal presence but also elicits maternal aid; and if the infant's hunger has brought forth his crying, then the maternal feeding response may act as the 'terminating stimulus' for the crying (BOWLBY, 1958).

have become ritualized into an intention movement that signals the intention to cling to the parent (arm extensions towards the parent) and that (acting as a social releaser) has the effect of activating the parental response of picking up the infant (BOWLBY, 1958).

Many innately friendly social interactions between humans are derived from the seeking and granting of contact in interactions between mother and infant. Extending the hand or placing it on another person's outstretched hand are gestures of seeking and granting contact, respectively, gestures that are derived from parent–infant interactions (EIBL-EIBESFELDT, 1970). Importantly, seeking and granting contact have the function of seeking and granting reassurance, respectively. Other gestures of granting contact are patting and embracing. The embrace, originally a protective action on part of the mother towards her infant, has been ritualized into a social gesture of *comforting* and greeting (EIBL-EIBESFELDT, 1970).

Nonhuman primates have a fully developed clinging response at birth and develop a following response later (BOWLBY, 1958). In humans, neither the clinging response nor the following response are effective at birth. The clinging response is present in rudimentary form from the earliest days and remains ineffective in the early months of life. Once the clinging response has become effective, infants cling to their mother with great tenacity at times of anxiety or after a separation experience. The clinging response is at its peak in the second year of life. Human infants follow their mother as soon as they have become mobile.[12] The zenith, with regard to the intensity of the following response, is reached in the period of 18 to 30 months of age (BOWLBY, 1958).

2.3.4 Infantile appeals to care

The infant's cries attract the mother, but may not always in themselves release the mother's cherishing behaviour. There are behaviours displayed by the young animal that are designed to elicit the mother's caring behaviour. In mammals and birds, "the young of the species transmit signals which release cherishing behaviour" in their parents, whereby the parents' response to their infant is "motivated by the parental care drive" (EIBL-EIBESFELDT, 1970, p. 120). The infant's display of helplessness is one of the factors that evokes the 'parental instinct' in the mother (MCDOUGALL, 1924).

> The cherishing behaviour patterns of parental care have their natural counterpart in the signals which release them, which have been taken over into the repertoire of contact-making and aggression-inhibiting behaviour patterns as 'infantile appeals'.
> (EIBL-EIBESFELDT, 1970, p. 148)

---

[12] Infants are more likely to remain within their mothers' sight or earshot when they are tired, hungry, in pain, or anxious (BOWLBY, 1958).

Adult animals display infantile behaviour patterns whenever the aim is appeasement or to release cherishing behaviour in a conspecific (EIBL-EIBESFELDT, 1970, p. 113). Humans who seek to elicit affectionate behaviour "relapse quite involuntarily into the role of a small child" (p. 148). Culturally or phylogenetically ritualized displays of helplessness release in others the impulse to cherish the person displaying these patterns, much as an infant's display of helplessness releases the mother's care-giving behaviour. Care-seeking signals (infantilisms) and care-giving (cherishing) behaviours not only unite parents with their offspring but are also "excellently suited to reinforcing the bond between adults" (p. 124). Owing to their aggression-inhibiting effects, care-seeking and care-giving behaviours are innately understood as friendly (EIBL-EIBESFELDT, 1970).

2.3.5 Bonding and courtship

Distance-decreasing and contact-seeking behaviours need to be somewhat distinguished from attachment behaviour. Attachment is defined ethologically as a set of behaviours that help to maintain contact with a *specific* individual (BOWLBY, 1973; SCHECTER, 1978). Parent and infant are equipped with behavioural modes that enable the formation of a bond; contact seeking is one of them. According to EIBL-EIBESFELDT (1970), appetitive behaviour for contact "is the true root of the bond between mother and child" (p. 205). Contact-seeking behaviour is an attachment behaviour when it is directed at the attachment object. Attachment behaviours also include affectionate displays towards the attachment object. Affectionate interactions are rewarding (pleasurable) and may thus serve to reinforce appetitive mechanisms involved in bond formation. The bond between parent and infant is formed and strengthened in processes of mutual smiling and playful interaction. These early reciprocal interactions are important precursors of all human communication (SCHECTER, 1978).

Most bond-establishing rites are derived from the field of parental care. In courtship, animals display phylogenetically ritualized behaviour patterns that are modified infantilisms or actions derived from parental behaviour, especially parental cherishing behaviour (EIBL-EIBESFELDT, 1970). Parental behaviour includes protective actions towards the infant, such as fetching back the infant if it goes too far away during its explorative forays. Coy behaviour is ritualized flight behaviour signalling an invitation to pursuit in mating foreplay (EIBL-EIBESFELDT, 1970). Young animals use contact calls to call their mothers; and adults in some species emit the contact call of the young when pursuing a prospective partner. Begging behaviour of the young animal elicits a feeding response from its parents. Begging behaviours of young animals have, in many species of birds, evolved into ritualized appeasement gestures and expressions of affection. Many courtship behaviours in birds are derived from the begging of the young animal (EIBL-EIBESFELDT, 1970).

Ritualized feeding behaviour, too, has an appeasing and bond-strengthening effect. Kissing is a ritualized feeding gesture[13] that is used by humans and chimpanzees during courtship or when greeting each other (EIBL-EIBESFELDT, 1970). Offerings of food or drink are also ritualized feeding behaviours. Sharing food and eating together form part of many bond-forming cultural rituals. Social grooming is another affiliative behaviour derived from parental care. Caressing is a ritualized derivative of the mother's grooming of her infant. Like ritualized feeding behaviour, social grooming has an appeasing and bond-strengthening effect (EIBL-EIBESFELDT, 1970).

> Even the individualized relationship – love – evolved primarily from the parental care relationship. ... The roots of love are not in sexuality, although love makes use of it for the secondary strengthening of the bond.
> (EIBL-EIBESFELDT, 1970, pp. 124–5)

2.3.6 Exhibitionism

Exhibitionistic behaviour seeks to gratify narcissistic needs, given that exhibitionism is "always connected with an increase in self-esteem, anticipated or actually gained through the fact that others look at the subject" (FENICHEL, 1946, p. 72). Infantile exhibitionism and its developmental derivatives play an important role in the maintenance of narcissistic homeostasis (as reflected in self-esteem and feelings of 'safety' [SANDLER, 1960a]). Exhibitionistic means of attracting others' positive attention (and, thereby, of regulating the narcissistic homeostasis) have to be reality-syntonic (and hence egosyntonic). This is to say that exhibitionistic impulses (seeking to gratify narcissistic needs, i.e., needs for safety) have to be sublimated. Actors, for instance, are "attempting to sublimate their exhibitionistic impulses in their work" (JOFFE & SANDLER, 1967, p. 181), whereby sublimation, an adaptive ego activity (HARTMANN), ensures that the safety-enhancing effect of being in the focus of others' attention is not offset by greater vulnerability of becoming the target of others' aggression (and ridicule), a vulnerability that is signalled to the ego (self) by feelings of anxiety (and shame). Schizoid individuals engage in artistic activities as a way of expressing their exhibitionism without exposing themselves directly to potentially dangerous social contact (FAIRBAIRN, 1952).

Exhibitionism is allied with vanity (ADLER, 1927). Vanity can be seen "in those people who dress conspicuously, or with self-importance, who deck themselves out for a brave show, in the same way that primitive peoples made an exhibition of themselves by wearing an especially long feather in their hair when they have reached a certain degree of pride and honour" (p. 172). Body ornaments and tattoos are exhibitionistic expressions of

---

[13] In anthropoid apes (gorilla, chimpanzee, orang-utan) and some human cultures, mothers feed their children with premasticated food (EIBL-EIBESFELDT, 1970).

vanity. People's striving to make an impression can be shameless, as ADLER (1927) pointed out (p. 172), and, indeed, shame is the counterpart and inhibitor of exhibitionism.

Exhibitionistic impulses, with which humans are endowed, can be discharged spontaneously or are used in the service of defence ("the question of defensive exhibitionism versus instinctual exhibitionism" [SANDLER, 1985, p. 348]). Children age-appropriately perform actions of 'showing off' or clowning in order to attract attention (REDDY, 2003). Positive attention (communicating interest or praise), if it can be attracted, is innately rewarding (SCHECTER, 1973). Inappropriate exhibitionism, borne out of a heightened need for attention and reassurance, often has the opposite effect, attracting negative attention and further increasing anxiety. SANDLER (1985) pointed out that "children become exhibitionistic when they lose the parent's attention (when a sibling arrives, for example)" (p. 348). Clowning or joking then constitute defensive manoeuvres "directed toward restoring self-esteem" (p. 105). In adults, defensive exhibitionism is linked to disturbances of narcissism (SANDLER, 1985, p. 105). Exhibitionism, when used defensively, is "a technique for gaining admiration and praise in order to do away with underlying feelings of unworthiness, inadequacy, or guilt" (JOFFE & SANDLER, 1967, p. 181).

Exhibitionism is often not evident as such; in sublimated forms, it underpins a great deal of adaptive social behaviour, as already pointed out. Moreover, in the normal personality, exhibitionistic means for regulating safety are in a balance with object love. Libidinal investment in objects (establishment of love relationships) provides an alternative way of securing narcissistic supplies, one that lowers the individual's reliance on exhibitionistic techniques. FENICHEL (1946) pointed out that the capacity for object love makes available a "higher, postnarcissistic type of self-respect" (p. 85).

2.3.7 Social feeling

ADLER (1927) proposed that 'social feeling', that is, the ability to feel affectionate towards another human being, is inborn and developmentally "unfolds in an early search for affection" (p. 46). 'Social feeling' changes and broadens in development, "until it touches not only on the members of the immediate family, but also the extended family, the nation and finally, the whole of humanity" (p. 46). Social feeling is what "binds humanity together" (p. 156).[14] ADLER (1927) thought that "cheerful temperament, when not taken to extremes, is an indicator of a highly developed social feeling" (p. 203). Laughter is associated with cheerful temperament and strengthens "the natural bond that links all human beings", although the "laughter of those who find humour in other people's misfortune" is an

---

[14] ADLER's concept of 'social feeling' or 'social interest' is thus closely related to FREUD's concept of libido.

aggressive one (p. 203). Social feeling underlies our tendency to take interest in others, to be caring towards them. Our willingness to respond to others' care-seeking behaviour (and our capacity to be influenced to this effect) can be regarded as evidence for "natural social feeling" (p. 61). Caring gestures towards others and attendance to their wellbeing are evoked by signs of their helplessness or sickness; "sickness of fellow human beings calls on the social feeling of every normal person" (p. 165); "sickness is a danger sign that says, 'Take care!'" (p. 166). Our "willingness to give, serve, or help, brings with it a certain compensation and psychological harmony" (ADLER, 1927, p. 172).[15]

---

[15] It is likely that commitment to and genuine interest in fellow human beings fosters the sense of connectedness with the social surround (and thus increases inner harmony and the sense of safety). Others' gratitude has an additional self-esteem-enhancing effect, much as libidinal (as opposed to narcissistic) investment in objects provides a 'postnarcissistic' source of self-esteem (FENICHEL).

3
Affective States

An instinctive act (such as an affective display) is released by a 'stimulus situation' (a simple set of stimuli) that is recognized by an 'innate releasing mechanism' (the perceptual equivalent of the releasing stimulus situation) (LORENZ, 1935). Certain internal (physiological) and external (environmental) *conditions* are necessary to evoke an instinctual response (BOWLBY, 1958). Conditions in the presence of which an instinctual response can be released may also include thoughts and wishes (BOWLBY, 1958). These conditions need to be distinguished from the releasing 'stimulus situations', that is, the configurations of stimuli that evoke an instinctual response, which are likely to operate exclusively unconsciously. BOWLBY (1958) proposed that conditions operate by putting the organism into a 'responsive mood', which may (or may not) be accompanied by engagement of seeking (appetitive) behaviour. When an 'instinctual response system' is activated and free to reach termination (BOWLBY, 1958), we experience, as LORENZ suggested, (i) an emotional state that is peculiar to the type of instinctual response and (ii) possibly an urge to action (of an appetitive nature). For instance, smiling, laughing, weeping, and temper are instinctual responses that are each associated with a peculiar emotional state (BOWLBY, 1958) however, they may not be accompanied by an urge to action (an experience of drive). The emotional state that is associated with activation of an instinctual response system could be regarded as a conscious representation of conditions necessary to activate the instinctual response system. *Emotional states may signify a preparedness to emit one or another type of instinctual response*, whereas the urge to action may indicate a preparedness to engage in seeking (appetitive) behaviour.

Goal-directed, purposive, seeking, or appetitive behaviour refers to the organism's striving to gain exposure to a stimulus situation in response to which an instinctive act can be discharged. *The goal of appetitive behaviour is the attainment of a stimulus situation needed to release an instinctive act* (LORENZ, 1937). Appetitive, purposive, or goal-directed behaviour employs subordinate locomotor patterns ('tool reactions') and orienting reactions, both of which help the organism to reach and confront a releasing stimulus situation that triggers an innate releasing mechanism (LORENZ, 1937). 'Drive' refers to the process that "spurs the animal to search, directedly or at random, for a specific stimulus situation (the only one in which the innate releasing mechanism of the craved reaction will respond)" (LORENZ, 1937, p. 171). Appetitive behaviour is organized hierarchically. Appetitive behaviour of a more general nature, spurred on by a more general drive, does not lead directly to an innately recognized releasing stimulus situation and an instinctive (usually consummatory) act but exposes the organism to a complex stimulus that elicits appetitive behaviour of a subordinate (more specialized) type (LORENZ, 1952).[1] Drives do not motivate instinctive actions; instead, by motivating and coordinating appetitive behaviour aimed at obtaining a motivationally relevant object or stimulus situations, drives *prepare* the ground for instinctive action.

Emotional (affective) states involve patterned autonomic activation, cortical arousal, emotional feeling, and a disposition to release certain instinctive affective displays or consummatory actions in response to innately recognized stimulus patterns. Anxiety, as an emotional state, involves increased attentiveness to threat stimuli and a preparedness to emit instinctive actions of flight or fight. Drives (drive states) additionally comprise general psychomotor activation and an impulse (urge) to preparatory or appetitive action (conative experience, i.e., experience of drive or tension). We can regard drives as states of being driven away from some need towards some object or external stimulus constellation (the releasing pattern for an instinctive motor act). We may be driven away from adversity and towards safety, away from a state that favours one set of instinctive affective responses and towards a state that favours another set.

Regarding the function of emotional feelings, SANDLER (1972) thought that "feeling states aroused by drive stimuli ... bring about the regulation of drives" (i.e., of needs) (p. 295); he suggested that "drives, needs, emotional forces ... exert their effect *through changes in feelings*" (p. 296). Changes in feelings, often actively brought about by appetitive behaviour, mean

---

[1] The response to complex stimulus qualities in form of appetitive behaviour must be acquired through conditioning; what is acquired are releasing mechanisms that respond to complex sets of stimuli (LORENZ, 1935). Objects, perceived within a particular emotional and situational context, can be regarded as acquired releasing stimulus constellations that allow switching from a more general to a more specialized appetitive behaviour mode. According to McDOUGALL (1924), 'conative' experience, being the "felt impulse to action", is integral to all (conscious) 'sense impressions'; an 'object recognised or thought about' "evokes in [the subject] an impulse to effect some change" (p. 265). Not only perception of an external object but also an internal image thereof can evoke a "longing or appetite for the corresponding external object"; in response to imagery, "the individual becomes capable of wishing something that is not present and is motivated toward the fulfilment of his wishes" (ARIETI, 1970, p. 25).

changes in probabilities of instinctive actions; and it is ultimately through these instinctive actions that needs are satisfied. Changes in emotional *tensions* may play a role in reinforcement learning. For instance, a reduction in feelings of pain or hunger may reinforce an appetitive behaviour sequence that has led to the tension reduction. Drive states (appetitive behaviour modes) are thus shaped and linked to a complex stimulus constellation (Pavlovian stimulus) preceding the tension-reducing behaviour sequence. The emotional feeling of anxiety is often tinged with pain or tension, indicating a drive or impulse to attain safety; and it may be a reduction in this tension that reinforces safety-directed appetitive behaviour.

3.1 Anxiety

Anxiety serves "the aim of self-preservation" (p. 192), an objective shared with narcissism; and, just like narcissism, anxiety is regulated within and by the ego (NUNBERG, 1955).[2] Anxiety originally evolved as a signal of danger of *interspecific* (predatory) attack, but it then became a signal of danger of *intraspecific* attack. Inasmuch as protection against intraspecific attack (intraspecific safety) became associated with connectedness or relatedness to conspecifics, anxiety became associated with the absence of, or inability to obtain, narcissistic supplies from the social surround. Thus, safety does not simply denote the absence of anxiety; it is indeed more properly regarded as the polar opposite of anxiety. Safety entails feelings of being accepted, approved of, loved, or cared for and hence of being protected. Safety or wellbeing "results from social recognition and approval", that is, from narcissistic supplies or their *availability* (JOFFE & SANDLER, 1968, p. 231).

Anxiety recruits behaviour that actively changes the situation in the direction of safety. Anxiety also calls into play mechanisms of defence that merely alter the perception of the situation, that *"alter* the content of experience before the content is allowed access to consciousness" (SANDLER, 1972, p. 296). Anxiety entails inhibition of drives ('behavioural inhibition'), although the organism's preparedness to engage in *emergency* fight-or-flight behaviour (including defensive aggression) is increased. Anxiety suppresses 'instinctual drives', whereas safety promotes the expression of drives such as intraspecific aggression (aggression of an offensive or competitive nature) or sexuality, generally of drives that propel the organism towards objects in the world. Anxiety arises not only in consequence of external changes that render the individual's situation unsafe but also when the expression of drives does – or when drives pressing for discharge *would* (if they were to be enacted) – undermine the individual's connectedness to his social milieu. Restoration of the feeling of safety would involve the suppression of 'drive discharge'. Preservation or restoration of the feeling of safety is the

---

[2] FREUD regarded the ego as "the only seat of anxiety" (HARTMANN, 1964, p. 292).

overriding concern of the ego, and its various defensive mechanisms are used to this end.

> Mental conflict may, for example, cause the mental apparatus to find an adaptive solution that restores a feeling of safety, at the same time ... preventing so-called drive discharge. If we assume that an aggressive impulse causes affective changes in the body, ... the mental apparatus may (because of, say, guilt feelings) prevent the activity that would normally restore physiological affective homeostasis. The body may, as a consequence, remain in a state of chronic physiological imbalance because of the defensive activity of the mental apparatus. ... The body is thrown out of balance, so to speak, because the normal behavioral processes that lead to the disappearance of temporary and normal affective states are not permitted to take place.
> (SANDLER, 1972, p. 297)

What is the relationship between anxiety and pain, either of which can be regarded as the polar opposite of the feeling of safety (wellbeing) (SANDLER, 1960a; JOFFE & SANDLER, 1968)? JOFFE and SANDLER (1968) proposed that pain is "a fundamental component of all forms of unpleasure, including that of instinctual tension and anxiety" (p. 229). Perhaps, anxiety is a mild form of pain (and probably anxiety has evolved from pain). Perhaps, anxiety signals a *lack* of safety (protection), whereas pain arises when safety is suddenly *lost*, especially when an environmental factor can be implicated in this loss. Pain calls forth emergency defences, "the normal response to pain" being "aggression directed at whatever is considered to be the source of the pain" (JOFFE & SANDLER, 1968, p. 231) (defensive aggression), whereas anxiety (in the absence of pain) may engender more adaptive, that is, reality-oriented, safety-directed behaviour.

Anxiety can be distinguished more easily from fear. Fears, according to ERIKSON (1950), "are states of apprehension which focus on isolated and recognizable dangers" (p. 366). Anxieties, on the other hand, "are states of tension ... which magnify and even cause the illusion of an outer danger, without pointing to appropriate avenues of defence or mastery" (p. 366). Anxiety "drives us into irrational *action*, irrational *flight* – or, indeed, irrational *denial* of danger" (ERIKSON, 1950, p. 367). Perhaps, anxiety is maladaptive when it is intense and has a quality of tension or pain, because then it may cut off foresight and hinder the identification of safe retreats. Perhaps, the inhibitory function of anxiety applies not only to the 'instinctual drives' but extends to safety-directed behaviour when anxiety is intense.

3.1.1 Anxiety-related behaviours

BOWLBY (1973) established that separation from loved figures, or the threat of separation, is a principal source of anxiety. However, anxiety can be aroused under many different conditions; "missing someone who is loved and longed for" is only one of them (p. 31). Other conditions that elicit alarm and retreat are "mere strangeness", noise, "objects that rapidly expand or approach", darkness, and isolation (p. 85). All of these conditions are "statistically associated with an increased risk of danger" (Bowlby, 1973, p. 85). Under any of these conditions, animals "behave in fact as though danger were actually present" (p. 85). Animals may take avoiding action, run away, cower, hide in a shelter, or *seek others' company*. They also display "a preparedness to meet real dangers" (p. 86). Behaviours indicative of anxiety include "wary watching combined with inhibition of action" and "a frightened facial expression accompanied perhaps by trembling or crying" (p. 88). 'Freezing' refers to "behaviour that results in immobility" (p. 90). The 'biological function' of all of these behaviours is the protection against potential danger (Bowlby, 1973).

Different types of anxiogenic, that is, potentially dangerous, conditions may activate different and somewhat separate anxiety-related 'systems of behaviour', such as freezing or withdrawal, which "may even be mutually inhibiting" (Bowlby, 1973, p. 88). Other types of behaviour act in concert, such as running away from a dangerous situation and running towards cover or company. An animal or person may, not infrequently, try "simultaneously to escape from one situation" and "gain proximity to another" (p. 95). Behaviour that brings about escape from a situation of maternal separation or social isolation and that, at the same time, reduces the distance to a person that provides protection "is nothing other than attachment behaviour" (Bowlby, 1973, p. 89).

Bowlby (1973) pointed out that "small changes in a situation can have great influence on the form of behaviour shown" (p. 137). A strange or novel situation "can elicit either withdrawal or exploration or both together", whereby often "an interested approach and an alarmed withdrawal are shown either simultaneously or in rapid succession" (p. 137). Encountering stimuli in an anxiogenic situation, the animal or person may engage in either attack or withdrawal (flight) behaviour, depending on species-related, individual organismic, and situational factors. Whether, in an anxiogenic situation, "an animal responds with attack or withdrawal, or with a combination of both, depends on a variety of factors that have the effect of tipping the balance either one way or another" (Bowlby, 1973, p. 253).

3.1.2 Gregariousness

The 'instinct of escape', according to McDougall (1924), ensures avoidance of danger and self-preservation. Fear (in form of timidity or terror, representing fainter or most intense expressions of fear) is the instinct's 'characteristic emotional accompaniment'. A loud and sudden noise "is perhaps the most nearly universal key" to the "gates of fear", others being "the sudden move of a large object", certain odours of predators and pain (p. 152). The 'instinct of escape' is a two-phased 'instinct', comprising, firstly, "a running to shelter" and, secondly, "a lying hid when the shelter has been attained" (pp. 150–1). Importantly, for gregarious species, shelter may be represented by "the mass of the congregated herd" (MCDOUGALL, 1924, p. 151).

The impulse of the 'gregarious instinct' is to approach other members of the species, its goal being "merely the near presence" of others (MCDOUGALL, 1924, p. 154). Thus, the 'instinct of escape' converges with the 'gregarious instinct'. The emotional accompaniment of the gregarious instinct may be similar to that of the instinct of escape, further suggesting that the gregarious instinct (and ultimately also the human need for relatedness to and acceptance by others) evolved from the 'instinct of escape', that is, from anxiety-related behaviour. As MCDOUGALL (1924) pointed out, *uneasiness* and restlessness, and a craving to be back in the company of others, afflict the gregarious animal on its absence from the herd or group. Anxiety associated with absence from the group may drive the individual back into the company of others.[3]

In many species, anxiety is innately linked to situations of relative isolation from conspecifics. Anxiety can be measured by an animal's defensive readiness, such as readiness to take flight. Animals, including shoaling fish, are much more inclined to take flight when alone (EIBL-EIBESFELDT, 1970). Primate infants take flight from unfamiliar objects when alone but watch them with interest when they are in the presence of their mother. The presence of the mother or inclusion into a group, flock, herd, or shoal has a calming (anxiolytic) effect. A primate infant takes flight towards his mother and clings to her when frightened (attachment behaviour). Later in life, the animal seeks refuge with a high-ranking member of the group, whereby the highest-ranking male is the most common 'goal-in-flight'. EIBL-EIBESFELDT (1970) spoke of "appetitive behaviour for security which is activated by flight motivation" (p. 118). In the case of gregarious animals, "the conspecific becomes what the mousehole is to the mouse or the hiding place in the reef is to the coral fish" (p. 118). The conspecific adopts 'home valency', inasmuch as this can be said about hiding places (EIBL-EIBESFELDT, 1970).

> The conspecific becomes the 'goal-in-flight', its proximity means security. That is why the bond with a member of the group can be cemented by means of a fear motivation.
> (EIBL-EIBESFELDT, 1970, p. 118)

---

[3] Alternatively, contact seeking may be motivated by 'loneliness' (SULLIVAN, 1953), insofar as loneliness is aversive for a particular species. Loneliness would give way to anxiety secondarily, if the company of others cannot be attained.

3.1.3 Attachment

Separation anxiety is "an instinctive response to one of the naturally occurring clues to an increased danger" (p. 86); being alone and separated from the mother "carries an increased risk of danger" (BOWLBY, 1973, p. 178). Separation anxiety occurs when "either mother leaves child or child is removed more or less unwillingly from mother" (p. 32), not when the child takes the initiative.[4] Separation anxiety enhances the child's responding with fear or anxiety to other threatening stimuli. In the mother's absence, the child "responds to all sorts of slightly strange and unexpected situations with acute alarm" (p. 31). Moreover, upon separation from his mother, the child "is likely to take action aimed at detaining her or finding her; and he is anxious until he has achieved this goal" (p. 31). Attachment behaviour is "directed as least as much to regaining the familiar figure as it is to escaping from the strange people and situation" (p. 96). Attachment behaviour serves, not only in humans but also in other species, to "maintain a younger or weaker individual in more or less close proximity to another discriminated and stronger individual", usually the mother (BOWLBY, 1973, p. 148).

Attachment behaviour "serves the functions of protecting the mobile infant and growing child from a number of dangers, amongst which in man's environment of evolutionary adaptedness the danger of predation is likely to have been paramount" (BOWLBY, 1989, p. 105). Generally, separation anxiety and attachment behaviour maintain the individual within a defined context of safety, which, in 'man's environment of evolutionary adaptedness', offers protection not only against predation but, crucially, also against intraspecific aggression (from *innately* dangerous 'strangers'). Safety is initially signalled by maternal proximity; but it is then linked to the receipt of maternal care and love or, later in life, to the receipt of narcissistic supplies or to access to resources of narcissistic supplies (whereby these resources are themselves unconsciously equated with the mother). However, behaviour that solicits, or ensures the receipt of, maternal love and, more generally, of narcissistic nourishment cannot be described as 'attachment behaviour', but is more properly termed 'narcissistic behaviour'.

Exploration and anxiety are antithetical. In the presence of the mother, the infant employs exploratory behaviour, which is a form of appetitive behaviour. The attachment figure acts as a 'secure base' from which the infant ventures out and explores his environment (BOWLBY, 1989). If sight of the mothers is lost, the infant experiences separation anxiety and employs behaviours aimed at reestablishing contact with her. Separation anxiety inhibits exploratory behaviour but predisposes the child to respond to strange or unexpected stimuli by way of risk assessment. Attachment

---

[4] The intensity of attachment to the mother can be measured by the infant's protest response to her leaving (separation distress).

behaviour, which in humans remains evident throughout life, is strictly speaking not 'instinctive', even though BOWLBY (1973) described it as such (p. 179). It is a form of appetitive behaviour, an 'appetitive behaviour for security' (EIBL-EIBESFELDT, 1970), as it is adaptable and subject to learning.

3.1.4 Loneliness

SULLIVAN (1953) argued that we have a need for more or less continuous interpersonal contact. We avoid, or escape from, isolation. Isolation is tantamount to mental illness, although "a conspicuous indifference to other people's approbation constitutes a disorder in itself" (CHRZANOWSKI, 1973, p. 142). We also have a need for 'tenderness'. Needs for contact and for tenderness are resolved in interpersonal relations. While isolation is aversive (and can be anxiety-provoking), interpersonal contact without affectionate (tender) or reassuring interchange (being among strangers) is anxiety-provoking (and perhaps also aversive) (Figure 3.1). Denial of tenderness during interpersonal contact (rebuff) can bring about "frank anxiety, which aggravates the need for tenderness" (SULLIVAN, 1953, p. 198). Similarly, the 'foresight of rebuff' or anticipation of 'forbidding gestures' can induce anxiety (SULLIVAN, 1953, p. 198).

Separation anxiety may not be in itself what drives us into the company of others. The felt component of the need for contact is, according to SULLIVAN (1953), 'loneliness'. The experience of loneliness is integral to the need for compeers in the juvenile era and the need for acceptance, which arises in the later phases of juvenility. Loneliness also accompanies the need for intimate exchange in adolescence. Anxiety that may be felt upon rejection or in anticipation of rejection does not normally prompt us to withdraw into social isolation (and indeed increases our need for acceptance).

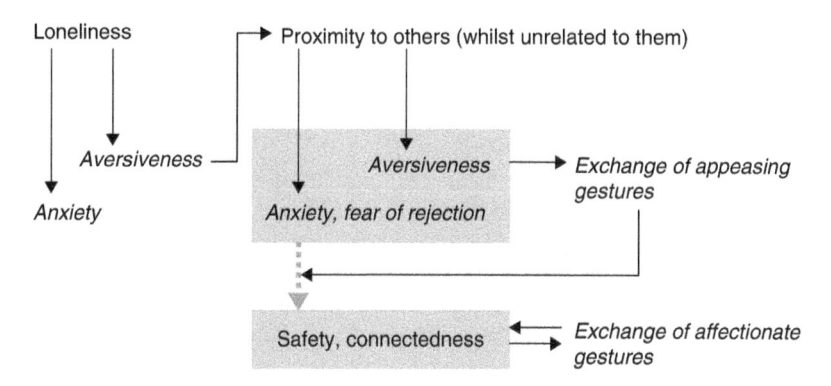

Figure 3.1 The exchange of *appeasing* signals creates safety. The exchange of *affectionate* gestures can take place only in the context of safety, but it also reinforces safety. States of loneliness and unrelatedness are perhaps primarily aversive and secondarily – if these states persist or cannot be overcome immediately – anxiety-provoking. Alternatively, aversiveness is integral to anxiety

Intense social anxiety does not distract the person from trying to overcome loneliness and seeking companionship, which means that "loneliness in itself is more terrible than anxiety" (p. 262). Anxiety does not stop the person from "stumbling out of restlessness into situations which constitute, in some measure, a relief from loneliness" (SULLIVAN, 1953, p. 262).

3.1.5 Fear of strangers

EIBL-EIBESFELDT (1970) suggested that children's fear of strangers is more significant than that of separation. Attachment to a familiar figure counteracts the fear of strangers. The child's bond with the attachment object increases as the fear of strangers matures in the second year of life (p. 211). Adults never outgrow the fear of strangers (just as attachment behaviour remains evident throughout life). In primitive peoples or isolated communities, strangers "are rejected, often attacked, or at best tolerated with reserved curiosity" (EIBL-EIBESFELDT, 1970, p. 217).

Fear of strangers can be seen in other primates. In the third month of macaque development, mothers start to reject their infants' nursing attempts so that infants are now forced to search for food independently (reviewed in MACHADO & BACHEVALIER, 2003). Between the sixth and seventh month, maternal protection disappears completely. As their independence increases, infants become more fearful of objects. New stimuli that would previously have provoked curiosity with explorative and play behaviour now come to evoke anxiety and defensive reactions. Infants also develop a fear of strangers, which is conveyed by fear grimace and other behaviours such as withdrawal, rocking, and screaming (reviewed in MACHADO & BACHEVALIER, 2003). In human infants, by comparison, fear of strangers and shyness emerge only around the age of one year. Then, the infant's response to a stranger ranges from mild apprehension and wide-eyed staring to "outright terrified screaming and panic behaviour" (SCHECTER, 1973, p. 29). Often, the infant's response consists in "a freezing (inhibition) of motor and expressive behaviour" (SCHECTER, 1973, p. 29).

3.1.6 Anxiety as a contagion

SCHECTER (1973) distinguished three forms of infantile anxiety. Separation anxiety, evident at around eight months of age, was suggested to have its dynamic root in the 'fear of object loss', whereas stranger anxiety, arsing by the age of one year, may be a manifestation of the infant's general 'fear of the strange'.[5] Indeed, any unfamiliar configuration of stimuli that conflicts with an anticipated pattern can provoke fear (neophobia). The fear of the

---

[5] Although stranger anxiety seems more likely to be an evolutionary corollary of intraspecific aggression. The developmental sequence of separation anxiety followed by stranger anxiety would repeat the phylogenetic sequence of interspecific (predatory and defensive) aggression followed by intraspecific (offensive or hostile) aggression.

strange can also arise in a social situation that contains strange elements in conjunction with familiar elements. SCHECTER (1973) thought that stranger anxiety contributes to the third form of infantile anxiety: the anxiety that is induced in the infant by anxiety of the mother (anxiety as a contagion, empathically induced anxiety). Automatic imitation of the mother's fearful expressions may contribute to this type of anxiety. Importantly, "the mother has the power to neutralize certain forms of anxiety in her infant, if she is not too anxious, by ... reassuring behavior, such as the playful interchange, the calm smile or embrace" (p. 32). By calming the infant's anxiety, the mother can render that which is strange into that which is engagingly novel (SCHECTER, 1973).

3.1.7 Basic anxiety

Anxiety, as understood by HORNEY (1939), "is an emotional response to danger", danger that ("in contradistinction to fear") is characterized by "diffuseness and uncertainty" (p. 194). Anxiety is also characterized (again "in contradistinction to fear") "by a feeling of helplessness" (p. 195). This helplessness is conditioned "by internal factors such as weakness, cowardice, lack of initiative" (p. 195). HORNEY (1939) distinguished between manifest and basic anxiety. While 'manifest anxiety' "is the response to a *manifest* danger", 'basic anxiety' "is the response to a *potential* danger" (HORNEY, 1939, p. 202). It has to be said though that any danger that is diffuse and uncertain is also a potential danger.

Importantly, helplessness is implicit in basic anxiety (HORNEY, 1939). Basic anxiety ('basic insecurity') is "a feeling of helplessness toward a potentially hostile world" (pp. 74–5), "a basic feeling of helplessness toward a world conceived as potentially dangerous" (p. 173). In a state of basic anxiety, the environment is felt as a menace, "the environment is dreaded as a whole" (HORNEY, 1939, p. 75). Basic anxiety is a feeling of "impending punishment, retaliation, desertion" (HORNEY, 1937, p. 235). The danger for the individual consists, in part, in the possibility of being 'obliterated' (HORNEY, 1939, p. 75), that is, of being annihilated by conspecifics or the whole group. Basic anxiety, it can be added, is the opposite of the feeling of safety implicit in connectedness to and acceptance by the group.

> The general feeling of insecurity is increased by the fact that for the most part neither tradition nor religion is strong enough today to give the individual a feeling of being an integral part of a more powerful unity, providing shelter and directing his strivings.
>
> (HORNEY, 1939, p. 174)

The social surround is felt to be menacing when the individual is unrelated or disconnected to it, that is, when the individual is not acknowledged, accepted, or approved by those about him. Basic anxiety is "a feeling of being isolated and helpless toward a world potentially hostile" (HORNEY, 1950, p. 366). Basic anxiety, arising when "one feels fundamentally helpless toward a world which is invariably menacing and hostile" (HORNEY, 1937, p. 106), motivates the pursuit of reassurance, approval, and love (i.e., narcissistic sustenance). Receiving others' reassurance, approval, or affection serves "as a powerful protection against anxiety" (p. 96). In soliciting others' approval or affection, we inhibit their innate hostility towards us and counteract our sense of being helplessly exposed to a menacing world. We thus reduce our basic anxiety; and others, in return, inhibit our own basic hostility towards them. HORNEY (1937) spoke of "the dilemma of feeling at once basically hostile toward people and nevertheless wanting their affection" (p. 111), a dilemma that is faced particularly by neurotic persons.

The self – one's sense of connectedness or relatedness to the social surround (and thus of accessibility of narcissistic supplies) – is the antithesis of anxiety. Self-control (control of one's 'instinctual impulses') is, at the same time, control of basic anxiety. HORNEY (1937) understood that "an imperative impulse, if yielded to, would mean a catastrophe for the self" (p. 64); giving in to a hostile impulse can cause anxiety and thereby undermine "the purpose of the self" (p. 63), which is to maintain or establish connectedness (to the social surround) and thereby to avoid or escape basic anxiety. Contrariwise, anxiety, "when based on a feeling of being menaced, easily provokes a reactive hostility in defense" (p. 74). One's aggression is easily provoked whenever one's safety and the cohesiveness of the self are undermined. Basic anxiety "concurs with a feeling of intrinsic weakness of the self" (HORNEY, 1937, p. 96). This intrinsic weakness causes "a desire to put all responsibility upon others, to be protected and taken care of" (p. 96). Submissiveness is another strategy for countering basic anxiety and strengthening the self. Thus, there are, according to HORNEY (1937), "four principal ways in which a person tries to protect himself against the basic anxiety: affection, submissiveness, power, withdrawal" (p. 96). These four principal ways lie at the heart of different types of personality structure.

> In order to keep this basic anxiety at a minimum the spontaneous moves toward, against, and away from others became compulsive.
> (HORNEY, 1950, p. 366)

3.1.8 Disintegration anxiety

KOHUT (1977) distinguished between two "classes of anxiety experiences" (p. 102). There are "fears of specific danger situations", which are "the anxieties experienced by a person whose self is more or less cohesive"; and there are "the anxieties experienced by a person who is becoming aware that his self is beginning to disintegrate" (p. 102). The latter anxieties emphasize "the precarious state of the self" and correlate with a "profound drop in self-esteem" (p. 103); whereas the former anxieties are an "expression of circumscribed fears vis-à-vis the threat of abandonment, or disapproval, or physical attack (fear of loss of the love-object, fear of loss of the love of the love-object, castration fear)" (p. 102), they "relate to specific verbalized fears" (p. 105). 'Disintegration anxiety', reflecting "the danger of the dissolution of the self", is a diffuse, indescribable anxiety ('nameless tension') that often has a hypochondriacal cast (KOHUT, 1977, pp. 104–6).

Disintegration anxiety can be provoked by loss of selfobjects or 'empathy failures' of selfobjects; or it can arise when an unfamiliar environment is "not empathically in tune" with the individual (KOHUT, 1977, p. 163). Cohesive self-experience is the antithesis of disintegration anxiety. Failure to build and maintain a cohesive self is correlated with "nameless mortification" (p. 224). As KOHUT (1977) remarked, "a self struggling to maintain its cohesion" is "a self motivated by disintegration anxiety" (p. 222).

There is also a distinction between anxiety felt in states of disconnectedness from the selfobject milieu and hence dissolution of the self, on the one hand, and anxiety concerning the *possibility* of being disconnected, rejected, and abandoned. Narcissistic injuries activate the former anxiety (disintegration anxiety); and those prone to suffering narcissistic injuries may experience an anxiety about incurring narcissistic injuries. Anxiety associated with narcissistic disturbances relates to the patient's awareness of his vulnerability to narcissistic injury (KOHUT, 1971). This again would be an anxiety about a specific type of 'danger situation'.

3.1.9 Fear of loss of love

> Fear is felt ... lest there be a loss of certain pleasurable feelings, such as well-being, protection, and security, which were hitherto present. This feared loss may be characterized as a loss of self-esteem, the most extreme degree of which is a feeling of annihilation.
>
> (FENICHEL, 1946, p. 134)

Evolutionarily, the subject's protection is linked to the receipt or availability of narcissistic supplies (love and recognition). The receipt or availability of narcissistic supplies is experienced by the subject as wellbeing or intact self-esteem. Anxiety arises "out of loss of narcissistic supplies" (FENICHEL, 1946, p. 136). The anxiety that signals an increased probability of coming to harm as a consequence of lack of help and protection is equivalent to a loss of self-esteem, "so that a loss of help and protection means also a loss of self-esteem" (p. 44). Anxiety may be concerned with an immediate risk of coming to harm and being annihilated; or it may be concerned with the risk of *losing conditions* that ensure the absence of harm (consistent with KOHUT's and HORNEY's distinction between two types of anxiety). The former type of anxiety (a 'feeling of annihilation', 'basic anxiety', or 'disintegration anxiety') arises when help and protection *have been lost* (when the self 'senses' that narcissistic supplies, in the form of being loved or acknowledged, have been lost). The latter type of anxiety represents a fear over "loss of help and protection" and a "fear over loss of love" (p. 44). Anxiety, as a warning signal, would then indicate "that there is a danger of a cessation of essential narcissistic supplies"; and the behavioural effect of this signal "must be to influence objects to furnish these supplies" (Fenichel, 1946, pp. 135–6) (to fulfil their 'selfobject function').

Birth anxiety, "the prototype of psychic anxiety", is developmentally continuous with anxiety felt upon "separation from a narcissistically highly valued object" (from a 'selfobject') or in relation to the *danger of losing* such object (Nunberg, 1955, pp. 197–8). Bowlby (1973), too, saw that separation anxiety may arise in response to, or be exacerbated by, *threats* of separation (abandonment). Thus, anxiety experienced upon separation becomes anxiety over the possibility of separation, that is, anxiety over the possibility of losing the object, which, in turn, becomes anxiety over the loss of conditions that signal the devotion of the object, that is, a fear of the loss of the object's love. Once the child has started "to develop affectionate feelings, a mere turning away by the mother, a threat, a reproach, is sufficient to cause fear of object loss, which soon changes into a fear of the loss of love" (Nunberg, 1955, p. 199) (of the loss of narcissistic supplies).

Thus, superimposed on separation anxiety and anxiety concerning possible separation is "the anxiety caused by disapproval, loss of love and praise" (Flugel, 1945, p. 56). More particularly, this latter anxiety can be regarded as a continuation or renewal of "the more primitive fears of loneliness or separation from the parents" (Flugel, 1945, p. 56). The fear of the loss of the object's love is developmentally followed by the fear of castration. Conversely, the "threat of castration, of the loss of the object's love, and of the loss of the object itself" form a regressive sequence (Lebovici, 1989, p. 429).

Fear of loss of others' love or approval is intimately linked with the fear of aggression from without, because, again, others' love, recognition, and approval signal that their aggressive potential is inhibited. Social anxiety captures "dangers which can be attributed to aggression from without" (Glover, 1931, p. 150). In the course of time, "anxiety about actual aggression" becomes an "anxiety regarding external criticism", "which is identical with anxiety regarding loss of love" (p. 150). With the formation of the superego, social anxiety becomes "an anxiety of internal criticism" (p. 150). This would be identical with anxiety regarding loss of love from the superego (or from the unconscious omnipotent object). Guilt refers to the "fear of loss of love on part of the super-ego" (p. 150). Anxiety regarding internal criticism can be changed, by way of projection, back into a fear of aggression from an external authority; or it can be displaced "in the form of social anxiety" (Glover, 1931, p. 150).

3.1.10 Fear of castration

Anxiety signalling an increased risk of being punished or aggressed by a dominant conspecific is psychoanalytically known as 'fear of castration' ('castration anxiety'). The term reflects the fact that anxiety often arises as a result of a conflict between the need to maintain one's cloak of protection against conspecific attack and the resurgence of drive impulses, including sexual impulses. For KOHUT (1971), castration anxiety (neurotic anxiety) reflects retribution fears arising in consequence of "competition with superior rivals" (p. 154). Castration anxiety is a fear – originating in the oedipal developmental phase – "of being killed or mutilated by a circumscribed adversary of superior strength" (p. 153). In castration anxiety, compared to narcissistic anxiety (disintegration anxiety), there is "a greater degree of elaboration of the source of the danger (a personal adversary)" and "a greater elaboration of the nature of the danger (i.e., the punishment)" (KOHUT, 1971, pp. 153–4). Anxieties encountered in the analyses of 'transference neuroses' may be concerned not only with the possibility of "punishment by an object which is cathected with object-instinctual energies" but also with "the possibility of a lonely longing for an absent object" (p. 21). Self-esteem, in cases of castration anxiety or anxiety related to the longing for an absent object, decreases only secondarily (KOHUT, 1971, p. 21), whereas disintegration anxiety entails a primary decrease in self-esteem.

Both disintegration and castration anxiety may be related to an increased risk of conspecific attack; however, in the case of disintegration anxiety, the attack is potentially fatal (and so it would have been earlier in our phylogenesis), whereas, in the case of castration anxiety, exposure to competitive attack potentially leads to loss of status and of access to sources of 'instinctual' gratification. It could also be argued that, while disintegration anxiety reflects disconnectedness from the social surround and signals an imminent risk of being ridiculed, humiliated, rejected, or attacked by the group as a whole (with fatal consequences, from the point of view of primate phylogenesis), paranoid or castration anxiety presupposes a degree of connectedness for the time being; it signals a threat of being attacked by a rival or dominant other, without there being, at the same time, an imminent risk of annihilation.

While the deeper and more profound disintegration anxiety may be hidden, paranoid or castration anxiety may lie closer to the surface. Narcissistic patients are prone to experiencing both. ANNIE REICH (1960) thought that the need for narcissistic self-inflation is a response to both paranoid and castration anxieties. Narcissistic patients are continually preoccupied with efforts to feel great and important because they are constantly anticipating attack from others. ANNIE REICH (1960) regarded narcissistic preoccupations and narcissistic object relations as attempts to compensate for unbearable castration fears. Beneath the surface of self-inflation and grandiosity, narcissistic patients feel unloved and unappreciated (disconnected), so that they readily feel slighted and take offence at the least provocation. Narcissistic injuries reveal the *helplessness* and *uncontrollable* anxiety against which narcissistic patients (ultimately) have to defend themselves (A. REICH, 1960). Narcissistic injuries reveal the disintegration anxiety underneath paranoid anxiety and castration fears.

3.1.11 Shame

Insight into one's deficiency or inferiority produces feelings of shame, particularly when such realization is associated with the collapse of an essential belief about one's omnipotence or grandiosity. Shame is experienced when one's efforts to obtain narcissistic sustenance (to receive appeasing and approving signals) are frustrated. Shame is linked with exhibitionism and arises, according to KOHUT, when the expression of exhibitionistic demands (of the 'narcissistic self') is blocked. Shame (or "disappointment tinged with shame") is felt when exhibitionistic efforts are thwarted, when attempts to enlist others' participation in one's exhibitionism (or in the realization of one's ambitions) are not met with their approval (KOHUT, 1966). KOHUT's (1977) 'bipolar self' contains a pole of goals and ideals, which – by way of ambitions (a developmental derivative of infantile exhibitionistic urges) – we strive to reach or realize. Life aims (goals and ideals) and ambitions (the two poles of the 'bipolar self') cooperate with each other, with talents and skills playing a mediating role. Subliminal signals of shame arise whenever, in our ambitious striving, we fall short of an ideal or goal, of a standard expected by the external world or superego. Minute shame signals alert the ego about potential experiences of painful shame (KOHUT, 1966). If the ideal that is pursued is inspired by a grandiose self, then shame is felt readily and intensely; painful shame is felt whenever *overambitious* pursuit of a *grandiose* goal – the endeavour to actualize a 'grandiose self' and meet the standard of an 'omnipotent object' – is thwarted.

Shame is closely related to experiences of humiliation and embarrassment. Embarrassment in humans is a ritualized hiding movement (EIBL-EIBESFELDT, 1970). Shame is a form of anxiety and constitutes one of the 'motives of defence'; shame is "mainly directed against exhibitionism and scoptophilia" (FENICHEL, 1946, p. 139). Shame counteracts exhibitionism, in that it leads to concealment of oneself or of part of oneself (MORRISON, 1983). The individual seeks to hide or run away when he feels ashamed. By hiding, the individual tries to avoid becoming the target of others' disgust or ridicule. Feeling ashamed means not wanting to be seen or looked at, because being looked at "is automatically equated with being despised" (FENICHEL, 1946, p. 139). Shame is closely related to 'social anxiety', in which there is a "constant fear of being criticized, ostracized, or punished" (FENICHEL, 1946, p. 518). Perhaps, shame implies a feeling of *being* despised or ostracized and of *being* considered unworthy of others' companionship. Shame reflects the deeper dangers that are inherent in the subject's exposure to others

(MORRISON, 1983). The dangers are those that arise when one is not connected with, unrelated to, or estranged from the social milieu (the selfobject surround). The ultimate danger, implicit in the experience of shame, is that of annihilation. Shame about a perceived deficiency may imply an expectation of becoming the target of others' disgust or their aggressive laughter ('expulsion reaction' [HASS, 1968]), inasmuch as one's own disgust may be an innate response to others' deficiency (feelings of disgust, in turn, being related to acts of expulsion).

3.1.12 Fear of exposure

The neurotic person, according to HORNEY (1945), has an 'idealized image' of himself; he "wants to appear, both to himself and others, different from what he really is – more harmonious, more rational, more generous or powerful" (p. 148). He is therefore "afraid of being exposed to himself or to others"; he is anxious that "others should find him out", find out that he "is a bluff" (p. 148). The neurotic person is "convinced that he has always been a bluff" and that he will be caught (p. 150). The person's fear of exposure is provoked by any situation "that might make him conspicuous" (such as social gatherings or examinations or "any kind of performance", "even if it is no more than taking part in a discussion") (HORNEY, 1945, p. 149). The fear of exposure is ultimately a "fear of *disregard, humiliation,* and *ridicule*" (p. 151). It is the person's "unconscious fraudulence" – involved in "the creation of an idealized image" that compensates for an injured self-esteem – that "breeds fear of exposure" or humiliation (although the fear of exposure or humiliation also "comes from an injured self-esteem" directly) (p. 151). The fear of exposure is related to "blushing or a fear of blushing" (HORNEY, 1945, p. 149), suggesting that presentation to others of an 'idealized image' is, in part, a derivative of instinctual exhibitionism.

Defences against the fear of exposure include avoidance of 'test situations' or adoption of a reserved and self-controlled attitude when such situation cannot be avoided (HORNEY, 1945, p. 150). The fear of exposure can manifest as shyness ("particularly in any new situation") or a "weariness in the face of being liked or appreciated" (HORNEY, 1945, p. 150). An attitude of humility or modesty can prevent experiences of humiliation or embarrassment; exhibitionistic self-exposure, which entails a risk of being humiliated or feeling embarrassed, is avoided (while concurrently self-esteem is maintained by living up to the standards of the ego ideal). Humility, as ADLER (1927) saw it, arises "whenever it seems that the value of one's personal qualities is about to be questioned, or where one's conscious self-esteem might be lost" (p. 222). Humility "can be an attitude of withdrawal": downcast eyes and coyness betray preparation for flight, "a readiness to flee from a threatening situation" (ADLER, 1927, p. 222). Humility as an attitude, it seems, is planted on the emotional reaction of shame.

3.1.13 Conflict and defence

Man seeks to avoid anxiety in every possible way. One major avenue for this defensively-intended avoidance is via the unconscious evolution of various of the ego defenses. Their hypertrophy, misdirection, inadequacy or failure contributes to psychopathology. This is a central formulation in our conceptions of the origin of the emotional illnesses, whether these are neuroses, character neuroses, or functional psychoses.

(LAUGHLIN, 1970, p. 211)

Anxiety, signalling the presence of a danger situation, prompts the engagement of protective or defensive mechanisms (FREUD, 1933). Ego defences (defence mechanisms) are unconscious attempts to deal with anxiety arising in response to 'unconscious dangers' or from "conflicts which would otherwise prove intolerable" (LAUGHLIN, 1970, p. 211). By eliminating an unconscious danger or resolving an emotional conflict, defence mechanisms reduce anxiety and produce an "increase of personal security" (LAUGHLIN, 1970, p. 214) (as reflected in a sense of 'safety'). Essentially, defence mechanisms eliminate elements (one's attributes or wishes or impulses) from internal imagery or perceived reality that are threatening to the ego (self), which is to say that they would, if they remained in place (i.e., in the sight of consciousness), undermine self-esteem and cause anxiety. These elements are wishes or impulses that are socially unacceptable (as they would invite criticism or ostracism), or they are tentative self-critical insights into qualities, attitudes, or past behaviours: insights that are equivalent to others' criticisms of oneself, that is, to others' devaluations or depreciations of one's self or ego. Defence mechanisms, by avoiding or reducing anxiety, also serve the "preservation and enhancement of self-esteem" (p. 214); they foster 'ego integration' (self-cohesion) by combating "the disruptive effects of anxiety, conflict, and stress" (LAUGHLIN, 1970, p. 213).

Anxiety, shame, guilt, and disgust are 'motives of defence' (FENICHEL, 1946). Helplessness and the signal of anxiety define "the most general condition for all of the defence mechanisms" (NUNBERG, 1955, p. 226). What is also common to all the defence mechanisms at the disposal of the ego (i.e., the ego as a structure) is that they increase (by whatever means) narcissistic investment in the self (i.e., they enhance self-esteem). Defences, as pointed out by NUNBERG (1955), are "in the service of narcissistic protective tendencies of the ego" (p. 226). Assurance of 'narcissistic rest' or equilibrium corresponds to protection of the ego (p. 229) (i.e., of the self). Narcissistic tendencies serve to protect the ego from narcissistic injuries and maintain the integrity of the personality (NUNBERG, 1955, p. 63). Ultimately, by way of satisfaction of narcissistic needs, the individual maintains his relatedness to his objects and his social milieu. In the social realm, relatedness to others is evolutionarily the most important condition for the protection of the individual, that is, for self-preservation. Social relatedness is the polar opposite of (persecutory) anxiety and vulnerability to attack (helplessness [HORNEY]); and the ultimate purpose of defences and narcissistic strivings is to maintain connectedness.

Objective versus neurotic anxiety

Historically, FREUD (1916–17) suggested that 'objective anxiety' (*Realangst*), the response to external danger, is an expression of the instinct of self-preservation (*Selbsterhaltungstrieb*). He ascribed the emotional aspect of 'objective anxiety' to 'ego libido' (i.e., narcissism), while its behavioural aspect was ascribed to the ego-preservative (self-preservative) instinct (reviewed in WAELDER, 1960). FREUD (1916–17) distinguished 'objective anxiety' from 'neurotic anxiety', which he thought of as a transformation product of overflowing 'object libido' (sexual instinctual energy) and which gives rise to a need for tension reduction. Psychoanalytic theory later abandoned the idea that anxiety can be produced by overflowing object libido, regarding neurotic anxiety instead as an anxiety that is caused by an *internal* danger (WAELDER, 1960, pp. 155–8).

In fact, neurotic anxiety partly arises from *libidinal* and other instinctual impulses pressing for discharge *in spite of cultural taboos and restrictive social norms* and thereby threatening the approvability and hence the safety of the self. Here, the danger is an external one again, in that the individual (in his 'unconscious fantasy') is threatened with social punishment or exclusion or even annihilation. Narcissism, too, was conceptualized by FREUD in terms of the libido theory (as sexual energy concentrated upon the ego or self), but if we regard narcissism as synonymous with the self-preservative instinct (ego instinct), that is, as an expression of self-preservative needs (as the striving for self-coherence or ego integrity), then narcissism aligns itself more easily with anxiety. Narcissism is the opposite of anxiety, but not of any anxiety; it is the striving away from feelings that signify one's vulnerability in the social realm, it is the striving towards safety in one's social affairs (and it is this striving that can adopt healthy or neurotic forms).

3.1.14 Anticipation and risk assessment

Defence mechanisms are 'ego functions' that are derived from "reflectory defenses against unpleasant stimuli" (HARTMANN, 1964, p. 170). Moreover, defence mechanisms ('ego defences') are "a specific expression of [the ego's] inhibiting nature" (p. 115); they often have "a definitely inhibitory aspect so far as the discharge of instinctual energy is concerned" (HARTMANN, 1964, p. 124). Anxiety, in the face of which defences operate, is, according to FREUD, seated in the ego,[6] too, and similarly facilitates defensive (fight

---

[6] The 'ego' here referring to part of the mental apparatus.

or flight) responses and has an inhibitory effect on drive-related activity ('behavioural inhibition'). Moreover, when anxiety is felt in association with an imagined goal or anticipated outcome, then the drive-related action that would lead to the anticipated outcome is inhibited. Anxiety, in itself, has a predictive or anticipatory function, in that it signals the likelihood of upcoming discrete threats and prepares the organism accordingly. HARTMANN (1964) regarded anxiety as a "special form of anticipation", one that is "paramount among those forms of anticipation that make organized action possible" (p. 40). He saw parallels between "the anxiety signal, which from a certain level of development on is used by the individual in danger situations" and the "anticipating activities of the ego" (p. 40), the capacity for anticipation being a "most important" and "a very general feature of the ego" (HARTMANN, 1964, p. 292).

Thoughts about past experiences and future possibilities may be entertained as part of risk assessment. Risk assessment is a function of anxiety. Anxiety, that is, "apprehension of the possibility of any painful event" happening (p. 207), contains within it "an impulse to consider over and over again unpleasant possibilities" (p. 198), "to think over a situation and its dangers" (MOORE, 1926, p. 207). Anxiety is associated with a tendency to go "over and over again the possibility that the worst will some day come true" (p. 199), a "tendency to picture the anticipated evil", "*to bring up again and again to the mind the anticipated evil*" (MOORE, 1926, p. 198).

If anxiety is severe, foresight is cut off. As SULLIVAN (1953) saw it, "the more anxious one is, the less the distinguished function of foresight is free to work effectively in the choice, as we call it, of action appropriate to the tensions that one is experiencing" (p. 44). When anxiety is a mere signal, adverse consequences can be foreseen and avoided. When anxiety is not associated with overwhelming stress, safe goals can be anticipated and appetitive behaviour can be employed to move away from anxiogenic circumstances, by approaching or creating secure circumstances. Anxiety that is not overwhelming may also prompt the constructive employment of mechanisms of defence, aimed at improving others' regard for us and enhancing our self-esteem.

> The more the development of anxiety can be restricted to a mere signal, the more the ego can make use of defensive acts ...
> (FREUD, 1933, p. 119)

3.2 Safety

SANDLER (1960a) understood that humans are engaged in a more or less continuous search for conditions of safety; they strive to maintain a background of safety ('principle of safety'), while escaping the pressure of anxiety (which signals the presence of danger). He regarded "much of the ordinary everyday behavior as a means of maintaining a minimum level of safety feeling", that is, as "the ego's attempts to *preserve* this level of safety" (p. 2). The feeling of safety or security "bears the same relation to anxiety as the positive body state of satiation and contentment bears to instinctual tension";[7] safety, in other words, is the "polar opposite" of anxiety (SANDLER, 1960a, p. 4). Safety experienced in a social context is the opposite of a deep anxiety that signals an increased danger of being aggressed and abandoned by others, so that social behaviour, according to the 'principle of safety', is organized in such a way that it moves the individual, time and again, from an anxiogenic situation (which arises, time and again, due to inevitable perturbations in the social surround) to a situation of safety. Anxiety (the anxiety signal) initiates *adaptive* activity that aims to attain a state of safety. *Defensive* activity, likewise, is aimed not only "at the reduction of anxiety" but also at "heightening the safety level" (SANDLER, 1960a, p. 5). Homeostatic maintenance of feelings of wellbeing or safety and reduction of anxiety or, more generally, of feelings of unpleasure were considered by SANDLER (1960a) to be functions of the ego. Techniques at the disposal of the ego "involve modification of the perceptual processes" (p. 5); or they "involve deliberate and purposive behavioral manipulation of the external world so that the sense organs are subjected to altered and different stimulation" (p. 6). Defence mechanisms of repression, denial, and 'ego restriction' (as described by ANNA FREUD) are examples of how the ego lowers anxiety and "reinforces its feelings of safety" by way of controlling perception or behaviour (SANDLER, 1960a, p. 6).

3.2.1 Self-satisfaction and self-esteem

JAMES (1890) proposed that instincts drive us not only to be in sight of our fellows but also to be recognized by them favourably. He noted that "we have an innate propensity to get ourselves noticed, and noticed favourably, by our kind" (p. 293). 'Social self-seeking' – the behaviour that is concerned with attracting other's positive notice and admiration – involves "fundamental instinctive impulses" (pp. 307–8). What underpins the "desire to be recognised", and the need for self-preservation more generally, "are probably pure instincts" (JAMES, 1890, p. 308). Being recognized engenders self-satisfaction, which, on an evolutionarily deeper level, is linked with self-preservation. Self-satisfaction, as it expresses itself in "its own peculiar physiognomical expression", can be seen "in an exquisite way in lunatic asylums", in patients "whose fatuous expression and absurdly strutting or swaggering gait is in tragic contrast with their lack of any valuable personal quality" (JAMES, 1890, p. 307).

Instinctual impulses aim for satisfaction (and the self-seeking impulse can be said to aim for self-satisfaction); however, strivings to be noticed

---

[7] See also RADO's (1956) notion of 'alimentary orgasm'.

and admired (expressing narcissistic needs) likely unfold on the preparatory (appetitive) rather than instinctive level of behaviour. SULLIVAN (1953) thought that "anxiety appertains to the infant's, as also to the mother's, communal existence" (p. 42) and that "the relaxation of the tension of anxiety ... is the experience, not of satisfaction, but of interpersonal *security*" (p. 42). Even if security is not in itself satisfying or rewarding (although it does, once it has been attained, relax 'the tension of anxiety'), it prepares for the receipt of reward; it is an important condition for affective attunements and rewarding interpersonal experiences. The receipt of love, praise, or approval from another person is inherently rewarding (ARIETI, 1973). We learn to control others so as to receive *gratifying* narcissistic supplies; and our acquired capacity to obtain approving signals from others (and our confidence in this capacity) is reflected in our self-esteem (SCHECTER, 1973).

Safety is closely aligned with narcissism, the feeling of being liked (of being the object of loving care), as recognized by SANDLER (1960a). The need to preserve one's safety is equivalent to the need to maintain one's narcissistic equilibrium. FREUD (1914) thought that narcissism is an expression of the 'instinct of self-preservation', and that the ego (the mental structure that is concerned with homeostatic regulation) develops as a result of disturbances in the primary state of narcissism. Self-esteem is a sense of being accepted by others and of being worthy of approving recognition from others; it is, therefore, also a sense of being protected against rejection by others and against their innate hostility. Self-esteem reflects a "confident conviction of being lovable", a conviction that is based on the infant's earliest experience of his mother, namely the experience of receipt of "sufficient loving care" (STORR, 1968, p. 77). Self-esteem can be regarded as a *derivative* of the earliest narcissistic state (primary narcissism) (RADO, 1928; BURSTEN, 1973). FENICHEL (1946) recognized that self-love, or self-esteem, is closely related to infantile feelings of omnipotence, that is, feelings of *invulnerability*, of being *protected* against harm. The feeling of safety, according to SANDLER (1960a), is a developmental extension of "the awareness of being protected ... by the reassuring presence of the mother"; it "develops from an integral part of primary narcissistic experience" (p. 4).

3.2.2 Ego instincts

'Ego instincts', a concept from FREUD's earlier theoretical work, are 'dynamic forces'[8] that serve the function of self-preservation (HENDRICK, 1958). They were thought to work in opposition to sexual and aggressive drives (although FREUD, who recognized the significance of aggression only later in his life,

---

[8] 'Instincts' or 'drives', in Freudian theory, are hypothetical 'dynamic forces' that organize behaviour and thought and determine "unconscious as well as conscious phantasies" (HENDRICK, 1958, p. 139). Freudian 'instincts' (*Triebe*) are not to be confused with animal instincts, as defined, for instance, by LORENZ.

initially opposed ego instincts to sexual instincts alone). Ego instincts (the instinct of self-preservation) are the forces that "demand we heed the restrictions society imposes on adult sexuality" and that "compel the intra-psychic repression of 'dangerous' (conflict-threatening) impulses" (HENDRICK, 1958, p. 115), that is, of sexual and aggressive impulses. Ego instincts "serve the individual's need for survival, both by mastering the environment and by repressing the sexual impulses whenever the aims of self-preservation are in conflict with them" (HENDRICK, 1958, p. 139). Literally, the aim is the preservation of the *self*, hence the concept of 'ego instincts' may be considered as synonymous with narcissism (defined here as the dynamic force that protects and regenerates the self). As NUNBERG (1955) pointed out, the instinct of self-preservation "is a 'narcissistic' instinct whose function it is to maintain the integrity of the personality and to protect the ego from injuries" (p. 63). Narcissism, which was originally thought to be the libidinal component of egotism,[9] serves "one's self-preservative needs" (HENDRICK, 1958, p. 117).

3.2.3 Attachment versus narcissism

Attachment behaviour is activated by perceived danger in the environment and deactivated when the environment signals safety (BOWLBY, 1973). The presence of a stranger, for instance, is perceived as danger and causes the infant to seek proximity to the primary caregiver. Separation from the primary caregiver constitutes another danger situation (reflected in separation anxiety) that activates attachment (i.e., safety-seeking) behaviour. BOWLBY (1973) felt that separation anxiety and attachment play a much greater role in human social behaviour and psychopathology than libido (object-libidinal impulses). In his early theoretical work, FREUD (1905) recognized the self-preservative drive ('ego instinct') as an independent motivational force; and he thought that the self-preservative drive phylogenetically antedates libido. Attachment behaviour can be regarded as an expression of this very self-preservative drive (SILVERMAN, 1991). Attachment behaviour can also be regarded as an aspect of narcissism or, at least, as being phylogenetically and developmentally continuous with narcissism, which, in its own right, has been equated with the self-preservative drive (FREUD, 1914). Attachment behaviour attains safety via establishment of proximity to and maintenance of contact with the primary caregiver (or a derivative of the primary object), whereas normal narcissism is the striving for safety via solicitation of *attention* and approval from the social surround (or, more abstractly, via maintenance of recognition and acceptance by the social surround). Importantly, attachment behaviour itself involves the attraction of *attention* from the primary caregiver. If attachment to the primary caregiver were to be a special case of relatedness to the social surround, then

---

[9] The concern with one's self-interest.

attachment behaviour would be a special form of narcissism. Attachment behaviour protects the self against environmental and predatory threats, whereas behaviours and personality structures that can be subsumed under the term of narcissism protect the self against intraspecific aggression and expulsion from the community (with subsequent exposure to environmental and predatory harms).[10]

3.2.4 Functions of the object

The object, from a narcissistic point of view, is "a vehicle for the attainment of the ideal state of well-being" (JOFFE & SANDLER, 1965, p. 158). The object's approving responses as well as the object's responsiveness at any one time and its presence "when its presence is expected" (p. 158) enhance feelings of wellbeing or safety; they are the sources from which the ego obtains its narcissistic sustenance. Narcissistic sustenance (acceptance and approval) obtainable from others and hence the subject's wellbeing are dependent on whether or not cultural standards have been met and respected ideals have been realized. Insofar as the mere "presence of the object is a condition for a state of well-being", "loss of the object signifies the loss of an aspect of the self" (JOFFE & SANDLER, 1965, p. 158). Loss of the object's responsiveness or failure to reliably obtain approving responses from the object, too, would amount to a loss of a part of the self. What JOFFE and SANDLER (1965) considered to be "the object-complementary aspect of the self-representation" depends on the object's approving responses and empathic responsiveness, in keeping with KOHUT's notion of selfobject functions of the object. Their statement that "the object is ultimately the means whereby a desired state of the self may be attained" (JOFFE & SANDLER, 1965, p. 158) precisely anticipated a key position of self psychology.

KOHUT (1971) maintained that self-esteem is controlled via the creation and manipulation of selfobjects or via libidinal ('selfless') investments in 'mature object relations' (but generally through both). Selfobjects can be manipulated (i.e., the selfobject function of objects can be activated) by way of exhibitionistic displays or the emulation of ideals (thereby manoeuvring objects into a position in which they are likely to supply narcissistic nourishment). Objects that are experienced *only* narcissistically (objects of 'narcissistic love') tend to feel "oppressed and enslaved by the subject's expectations and demands" (p. 33) for approval or admiration. A 'narcissistic imbalance' (decrease in self-esteem) arises when selfobjects withdraw

---

[10] The anxiety that is paired with attachment behaviour is separation anxiety, whereas the anxiety that is paired with narcissism is basic anxiety or stranger anxiety. Stranger anxiety can be said to activate attachment behaviour, but the danger situation to which it refers is an intraspecific or social one. Strangers are not predators but potentially hostile conspecifics.

their love or bring about their "temporary absence or permanent disappearance" (KOHUT, 1971, p. 21).[11]

Selfobjects, which serve the regulation of self-esteem (providing reassurance and approval), have to be distinguished from 'mature objects' (KOHUT, 1971). 'Mature objects' are cathected with 'object libido' (as opposed to 'narcissistic libido'), although, in most cases, objects are cathected both narcissistically and libidinally. Mature objects respond to the subject's care, affection, or love with reciprocal care, affection, or love and thereby enhance or maintain the subject's self-esteem (KOHUT, 1971). Thus, mature objects contribute to the regulation of self-esteem; they are responsible for a 'postnarcissistic source' of self-respect (FENICHEL, 1946).

3.2.5 Responsiveness of the selfobject surround

A person's wellbeing and sense of self depend on selfobject experiences, that is, on experiences of *self-sustaining* responses (selfobject responses) "performed for the self by objects" (WOLF, 1988, p. 26). Being heard, acknowledged, and responded to is what enhances the person's self-esteem and makes him surer of himself. The template for all selfobject experiences is that of the child "sensing the mother's active and benevolent interest in him or her" (pp. 14–15). As the infant develops psychologically, "the sustaining effects of the selfobject experience on the self last longer", so that the infant becomes better able to tolerate the caregiver's absence for periods of time. In adulthood, symbolic selfobject experiences replace the more concrete selfobject experiences of childhood (WOLF, 1988). One's wellbeing, sense of self, and self-esteem now depend on the selfobject *responsiveness* of the environment. One's connectedness to the selfobject surround (i.e., the responsiveness of this surround) – being maintained by oneself on whatever level of abstraction – is reassuring, whereas an emotional "state that is most unpleasant" arises if one feels "unresponded to, disconnected from one's surroundings" (WOLF, 1988, p. 27).

> If a person is to feel well – to feel good about himself, with a secure sense of self, enjoying good self-esteem and functioning smoothly and harmoniously without undue anxiety and depression – he must experience himself consciously or unconsciously as surrounded by the responsiveness of others. The mode of this responsiveness varies from simple to complex and changes age-appropriately. Archaic modes are characterised by the need for the ministering physical presence of caregiving others; in maturely ripened modes, the needs for selfobject responsiveness are often highly complex and can be met by symbolic representatives supplied by and characteristic of the general culture.
> (WOLF, 1988, p. 39)

---

[11] 'Narcissistic rage' may then be precipitated, proximally with the aim of restoring the narcissistic balance.

3.2.6 Introjection of the source of approval

The need for approval from those about us, "for the feeling that we are accepted by society", is "a continuation into adolescent and adult life of the young child's need for the approval of his parents, while the anxiety and despondency caused by the sense of being outcasts from society corresponds similarly to the infant's distress at losing their love and support" (FLUGEL, 1945, pp. 55–6). Man's need for the approval and support of his fellow human beings is, as FLUGEL (1945) concluded with reference to KAREN HORNEY and ERICH FROMM, "due at bottom to an attitude that he inevitably acquires during his long defenceless infancy in which he is dependent on parental love and care" (p. 57). As the child develops, he must learn to anticipate others' expressions of "approval or disapproval, praise or blame", so as "to win praise and escape blame", "since these attitudes have such an intimate bearing upon his own weal or woe" (FLUGEL, 1945, p. 40). The developing child gradually frees himself from the more infantile dependence on others' approving attitudes and supportive emotional expressions by introjecting the image of his parents and thus forming the superego. The superego is an introjected source of approval and disapproval, and as such would "take over the functions of parents or other moral authorities", but "we can never – at any rate within the range of normal mental life – become entirely independent of the approval or disapproval of our social environment" (FLUGEL, 1945, p. 55).

> As McDougall and others have stressed, even those of us who, relying on our own inner strength or moral conviction, are ready to face the displeasure of the vast majority of our contemporaries ... tend to find consolation in the idea that we shall be admired as farsighted pioneers by generations yet unborn, or that at least we shall be pleasing in the sight of God, whose judgement and rewards are above those of men. Permanent and universal disapproval is a condition that is well-nigh unthinkable and unendurable, and no more appalling calamity can befall a human being than to feel himself utterly outcast and alone.
> (FLUGEL, 1945, p. 55)

3.2.7 Replacement of the source of approval

> In the last analysis the image of the loved parents is preserved in the unconscious mind as the most precious possession, for it guards its possessor against the pain of utter desolation.
> (KLEIN, 1937, p. 98)

The mother, in loving her children, "affords them security" (p. 80); "she is therefore felt as the source of all goodness and of life, in unconscious phantasy she becomes an inseparable part of oneself; her death would therefore imply one's own death" (KLEIN, 1937, p. 84). The term 'omnipotent object' denotes an abstract (internal) representative of the mother who, in unconscious fantasy, remains an inseparable part of one's self. The term 'superego' can be used in the same sense.

Dependence on the primary object or a later representative of the primary maternal object is coupled with ongoing fear of losing this object, which, in turn, can manifest as a *fear of dependence* on the object or as *guilt* about having harmed or even destroyed (in fantasy) the object (KLEIN, 1937). Guilt about having harmed one's good object in fantasy and the related fear of losing the object ("the unconscious fear that the loved one will die") can lead to an overdependence on the attachment object or, if guilt and fear are not too great, to "displacement of love to things and interests" (p. 84). The child's fear of dependence is an incentive to detach himself from his mother, thereby "turning to other people and things and thus enlarging the range of interests" (p. 117). The developing child learns to take in 'goodness' and gain security from other sources (KLEIN, 1937, p. 116).

> If in our earliest development we have been able to transfer our interest and love from our mother to other people and other sources of gratification, then, and only then, are we able in later life to derive enjoyment from other sources. ... there are innumerable ways of taking in beauty, goodness and love from without. By doing this we continuously add to our happy memories and gradually build up a store of values by which we gain a security that cannot easily be shaken, and contentment which prevents bitterness of feeling.
> (KLEIN, 1937, p. 118)

Through work and the pursuit of interests, the individual gains the approval of the internalized omnipotent object (or one of its many external representatives) and thereby assuages his fear of abandonment and the related unconscious sense of guilt. The striving for power, possessions, and prestige (HORNEY) reflects the individual's dependence on his omnipotent object (benevolent aspect of the superego), which contrasts with dependency behaviour (overdependence) in relation to a single external object acting as a representative of the primary maternal object.

3.2.8 Desire and the symbolic

Humans have a basic 'desire' for recognition. KOJÉVE (1947) understood that mutual desire for recognition plays a fundamental role in structuring human relationships. The human subject, according to KOJÉVE (1947), is constantly struggling for acknowledgment and recognition by the other, wishing to become the object of the other's love or desire (or simply to attract the other's gaze). Desire is for something that is lacking; desire is driven by *lack*. In LACAN's (1966) psychology, frustrated libido (or rather frustrated narcissism, the unsatisfied need for love and recognition) gives rise to desire, the desire for the other's love and recognition. The formula is: the object of human desire is the other's desire. However, human desire can also be directed at another person's *object of* desire. An object (usually one with symbolic significance relating to status) can be desired simply because it is an object of desire for others. This, according to KOJÉVE (1947), is true only for human desire. This also makes the point that what is desired is social recognition (others' approval), which can be solicited and attained directly, as well as indirectly via the acquisition of status symbols or possessions.

The infant, according to LACAN (1966), not only has a desire for his mother (expressing his love for his mother) but also positions himself as the object of his mother's desire. If the early desire for recognition and love is not fulfilled, the search for such fulfilment becomes desperate later in life. With the resolution of the Oedipus complex, the desire for the other's desire expresses itself in accordance with 'the law of the father'. Desire (*for love and recognition*) comes to be expressed symbolically, to be passed along the linguistic 'chain of signifiers', meaning that desire (for love and recognition) is expressed symbolically through language.[12] Not only the signifying chain of language but also memory recollection and anticipation of the future are at the service of desire. In LACAN's (1966) psychology, the plane of 'the symbolic', which is the register of language and linguistically mediated cognitions, extends over time, unlike the plane of 'the imaginary', which is concerned only with the present.[13] The symbolic plane is characterized by temporality and intentionality. We can conceive of 'the symbolic' as the linguistically created context of safety within which *affective attunement* (the exchange of innately appeasing and affectionate displays) can take place (on the plane of the imaginary).

3.2.9 Conversation

Stereotypes conveying protective assurances and soothing remarks are part of affectionate conversations (EIBL-EIBESFELDT, 1970). Gestures of feeding or granting contact can be expressed verbally in a highly ritualized form, such as the giving of good wishes or the declaration of interest and sympathy. Conversation is part of the bond-forming ritual in humans (EIBL-EIBESFELDT, 1970). Conversations seem to take place on two levels, one that involves ritualized affective expressions and another that involves the pursuit of goals,

---

[12] Language is not only at the service of desire. Routinized, empty speech, flattened out in day-to-day use, draws resources of 'the symbolic' onto the plane of the imaginary. Routinized speech allows for unthinking reflexes in conversations (LACAN, 1966).
[13] Levels of imaginary and symbolic functioning are related to FREUD's concepts of primary and secondary processes, respectively. Secondary processes, including thought and expectation, obey the reality principle. Primary processes, obeying the pleasure principle, ignore time and do not tolerate delay.

often hierarchically structured goals that encapsulate, in one w
the favourable disposition of others towards oneself. NUNBER
nized that the task of language "is to influence others" (p.
speaking, the subject often seems to "cling to other people with words,
hold on to them", to bind himself to them (p. 121). NUNBERG (1955) thought
that "speech is set in motion ... through aim-inhibited sexual strivings,
desexualized libido" (p. 122). Conversation clearly has a narcissistic, self-
preserving function. By way of conversation, partners bind each other into
a mode that facilitates the exchange of appeasing or affectionate signals.
Conversation partners look for the gleam in each other's eyes (akin to the
gleam in the mother's eyes [KOHUT]).

> Sometimes the speaker looks directly and searchingly at the listener's
> eyes. The response he sees, or thinks he sees, in the listener's eyes has a
> special importance to him; he is remarkable sensitive to it. A confirming
> response from the listener produces visible relief, while the slightest hesi-
> tation is quite discomforting and often prompts the speaker to renewed
> efforts. Despite his apparent concentration on the listener, however, the
> speaker, here, is actually addressing and listening to himself. His con-
> centration on the listener's expression is misleading; he is watching the
> listener in a way one looks carefully in a mirror for signs of a blemish,
> losing awareness of the mirror itself. He is addressing himself through
> the listener.
>
> (SHAPIRO, 2000, p. 37)

Speech is partly derived from distress vocalizations and separation calls;
and it is – insofar as it serves to attract and bind a conversation partner –
an appetitive (preparatory) behaviour. The purpose of speech is to create
a situation (and to bind the conversation partner into this situation) that
facilitates the exchange of appeasing or affectionate signals. Conversation
partners interactively align their 'situation models', which are "multidimensional representations containing information about space, time,
causality, intentionality and currently relevant individuals" (GARROD &
PICKERING, 2004, p. 8). Conversation partners may, for instance, align
situation models derived from early object relations. When relating to each
other, we recreate aspects of early object relations, especially with regard to
the context they provided for the interplay of infantile care-soliciting and
maternal care-giving signals. In conversations, we unconsciously solicit the
other's caring attitude and benevolent interest by recreating conditions
under which we received affectionate and soothing maternal signals early
in life (or under which we assured ourselves of our potential to receive narcissistic supplies). Conversation is an important means for establishing and
confirming connectedness to the selfobject surround and thereby preventing basic or disintegration anxiety.

[margin note: Compromised ↓ Social Situations with new social]

The façade we show when interacting with others, especially in novel or less familiar situations, is a safety device par excellence. Poise is a state of anticipation or readiness that "comes into play only in a social or interpersonal situation" (RANGELL, 1954, p. 331). Poise is an ego function that is implemented by the postural system, the hand, and "the perioral or snout region", and that has the aim "to hold on to and maintain the source of narcissistic supply, to belong, to be anchored to a larger and firm unit (person or group)" (p. 331). Poise is coupled with a fear concerning the possibility of "the cutting off of the stream of narcissistic supplies and the substitution for it of a state of shame" (RANGELL, 1954, p. 331). Poise is related to self-control, renunciation of 'instinctual drives', and actualization of an idealized image of the self.

[margin note: → Vulnerable narcissism?]

3.2.10 Wishful fantasy and activity

SANDLER (1989a) confirmed that "the individual constantly obtains a special form of *gratification* through his interaction with others ... in real life or in fantasy" (p. 80). Interacting with others, the individual "provides himself with a variety of reassuring feelings" (p. 80). The level of safety feelings "has to be constantly maintained, because if it drops below a certain value, wishes will be aroused connected with restoring the necessary level of basic comfort" (SANDLER, 1989a, p. 80). Wishes or *wishful fantasies* (fantasy elaborations of 'unconscious wishes') concerning objects are often shaped not by sexual or aggressive instinctual drives but by the need to restore safety or preserve self-esteem. Anxiety, the pain of loss, narcissistic injury, or threatened self-esteem stimulates wishful fantasy and "wishful activity, the aim of the wish being to restore feelings of well-being" (p. 73). A lessening of the background feeling of safety evokes "appropriate wishes to do something that would restore that feeling of security" (p. 73). Safety is restored by way of *restoring relationships*; and, for this reason, wishes and wishful fantasies profoundly affect relationships with others. SANDLER (1989a) stressed that "wishes to establish and re-establish certain types of relationships ... represent attempts to restore or maintain feelings of well-being and security" (p. 74).

Homeostatic regulation of safety feelings (of the narcissistic cathexis of the self) involves interaction with others "in real life or in fantasy" (SANDLER, 1989a, p. 80). The *perception* of others' concern for or interest in ourselves or of others' approval or appreciation of ourselves – or our *awareness* of the *responsiveness* of the social milieu and of our *potential* to induce our surround into furnishing narcissistic supplies – provides a sense of safety, alleviates or prevents anxiety, and arrests or tempers our approval- or attention-seeking behaviour or our more mature ambitiousness. *Imagery* of or thinking about others' care and attention towards us has a similarly calming effect. When, in states of dreaming, daydreaming, or thinking, our mind is occupied with images of appreciation or admiration by others, these images provide an *illusion* of safety. An attitude of (schizoid) detachment allows this mechanism to be carried to the extreme of megalomanic self-preoccupation.

Omnipotence

Feelings of omnipotence, megalomania, and delusions of grandeur represent an increase in the narcissistic cathexis of the self, which, in turn, compensates for a lack of object-libidinal cathexes, reflecting a situation "when real objects are lacking" (NUNBERG, 1955, p. 123) (and the self is insecure). Lack of object-libidinal investments causes insecurity and is, for this reason, associated with measures aimed at increasing the narcissistic cathexis of the self. NUNBERG (1955) recognized that a patient can counter his "feelings of inferiority" by striving to return to the 'narcissistic ideal' (the 'ideal ego', as opposed to the 'ego ideal'), "an ideal condition, in which he grants himself everything pleasurable and rejects everything unpleasurable" (p. 126). The more or less conscious "faith in one's own omnipotence" is ubiquitous, "because man is not willing to renounce his narcissistic ideal ego completely" (NUNBERG, 1955, p. 127). Children hope to regain their omnipotence when they grow up (p. 127). Psychopathologically, feelings of omnipotence and the magic of thought play an important role not only in schizophrenia but also in compulsion neurosis and other conditions. In psychoanalytic treatment, the patient's feelings of omnipotence become apparent when they are "displaced onto the analyst" (NUNBERG, 1955, p. 127). Idealization of the analyst needs to be distinguished from the patient reinvesting his object with libido and hence relinquishing his omnipotence.

3.2.11 Subordination of instinctual drives

HARTMANN (1964) observed that "the child renouncing an instinctual desire expects, and often gets, a recompense in the form of love or approval by the parents" (pp. 251–2). One form of gratification is forgone in order to attain another, a narcissistic one. The need to sustain or restore feelings of safety is the overarching principle of mental functioning; drive-related ('instinctual') activity is subordinated, so that, for instance, sexual strivings are "readily sacrificed in the interest of preserving feelings of safety" (JOFFE & SANDLER, 1967, p. 188). A pleasurable activity is "inhibited if it lowers the level of safety feeling" (SANDLER & JOFFE, 1968, p. 262). A drive impulse (or a sensori*motor* representation activated by an external stimulus) "is normally only permitted discharge if the feeling state that accompanies it is not too disruptive of safety and well-being" (p. 263). If there is "an ongoing conflict between an instinctual wish" and the need to maintain safety in accordance with "the internal (superego) standards of the individual", then a compromise solution may be found in form of a neurotic symptom (SANDLER & JOFFE, 1968, p. 263).

The need to maintain safety gains dominance over the need to gain pleasure, and indeed the conflict between these different needs is probably the forerunner of neurotic conflict in general. ... From the point of view of learning, it would seem that the maintenance of safety feeling is the most potent reinforcing agent after a certain level of development has been reached.

(SANDLER & JOFFE, 1968, p. 262)

Gaining pleasure leads to reinforcement, as does the avoidance of pain or unpleasure, but dominant over this is the process of increasing or maintaining safety feeling.

(SANDLER & JOFFE, 1968, p. 262)

Self psychology posits that selfobject experiences (narcissistic experiences) and the self are in a supraordinate position with respect to the 'traditional drives' and their vicissitudes (KOHUT, 1977). The "overriding urge for a selfobject connection" channels the expression of the 'traditional drives' (P. TOLPIN, 1986, p. 102). In being channelled, "the traditional drives" express "the needs of the self" (p. 102). Once it is appreciated that self–selfobject experiences are "the primary force in human psychology", "sex and aggression fall into place", as they can be understood "to shape and intensify self experiences" or to "be used defensively to stabilize the disintegrating self" (P. TOLPIN, 1986, pp. 102–3). Furthermore, pain and suffering can be used defensively to prevent self-fragmentation; they may be the price the individual is willing to pay for feelings of safety, for reassurances against loneliness and separation, against states that are in themselves associated with pain and suffering.

3.2.12 Conflict with the idealized image

A person's needs to belong to and be liked by others and to feel safe may be in conflict, time and again, with his aggressive and self-assertive tendencies. Feelings of hostility towards others, in particular, may endanger the person's need to be liked, partly insofar their expression would disrupt the agreeable image of himself that he wants to present to them. Aggressive and self-assertive behaviours may be regarded by him as selfish; and he understands that a selfish person will not be liked. To the extent that his popularity and his safety depend on an 'idealized image' of himself, he will be concerned unconsciously with maintaining this image and with redirecting or repressing impulses that would be in conflict with it. The more neurotic the person is, the more his self-esteem and safety depend on his idealized image, on an image of himself that he expects others will approve or like (HORNEY, 1945). The neurotic person's "self-esteem is all too dependent on their approval" (p. 56), which he cannot solicit actively but has to attain passively: by presenting to them an image that they will approve. For a person who lacks *confidence* in his affectionate and assertive capacities (due to deep-seated a fear of rejection) and who therefore lacks a *spontaneous sense of self* (reflecting a lack of spontaneity or, in other words, a diffuse inhibition), the idealized image may be "the only element that provides him with a kind of self-esteem" (HORNEY, 1945, pp. 223–224).

The conflict between spontaneous self-expressive tendencies, on the one hand, and the idealized image and need for approval, on the other hand, may be the cardinal conflict in neuroses. Neurotic conflicts always involve inhibition; and their elusive solution is centred on the goal of safety, the safety that is associated with being loved or recognized by others. *Neurotic conflicts*, as discussed by HORNEY (1945), are always unconscious and compulsive. Neurotic conflicts counteract the person's hopelessness (arising from deep-seated feelings of unworthiness) in offering him the prospect of *love* (relevant especially for the 'compliant type' of neurotic personality) or of *recognition* and respect (relevant especially for the 'aggressive type' of neurotic personality [p. 70]). The prospect of love or recognition acts as the 'saving mirage' that offers a solution to the person's conflicts (HORNEY, 1945).

For the neurotic person, the prospect of recognition not only promises "affirmation of himself"; it also "holds out the additional lure of being liked by others and of being able in turn to like them" (HORNEY, 1945, p. 70). Being liked or accepted by others is associated with safety precisely insofar as, under these conditions, others' innate hostile tendencies are inhibited and aggressive rejection or humiliation by them does not have to be feared. Safety, in turn, enables the expression of libidinal strivings towards others (the liking of others).

This dependence on approval may not be all that evident in nonneurotic persons, as it is often focused on the superego (acting as an internal self-esteem-regulating structure). The superego can, however, be projected back onto an external authority figure on whose approval the person then depends (FLUGEL, 1945). What needs to be emphasized is that we are dealing with a universal human need, which, in most people, most of the time, expresses itself in harmony with spontaneous assertiveness and other drive-related activity, and which manifests in constructive ambitiousness and the pursuit of attainable and socially valuable ideals (KOHUT).

3.3 Habitual transfer from danger to safety

> We all underestimate, I think, the extent to which we are constantly haunted by anxiety and equally long for security.
> (LORENZ, 1973, p. 200)

One of the most familiar tenets of psychoanalysis is that "unpleasure in the form of anxiety" – which can be caused not only by resurgence of drives but also by "happenings in the external world" – is a motivator for defence

(SANDLER, 1985, p. 532). Anxiety, being a painful affect, is a motive for defence, but any 'unpleasurable' affect or painful signal can act as an instigator of defence. Defences operate "to do away with" or avoid unpleasure or pain of any type (SANDLER, 1985, p. 530). The 'ego' (considered here as part of the 'mental apparatus') attempts "to deal with the external danger by actively intervening to change the conditions of the world around it" (ANNA FREUD, 1937, p. 174). In an effort *to move from an unpleasant state to a pleasant one*, the ego tries "to modify the representation to itself either of an unconscious wish, or of something coming from the external world" (SANDLER, 1985, p. 533).[14] Defences can thus be defined as operations that move the organism from a state of unpleasure to a state of pleasure (essentially from a state of vulnerability or unrelatedness to a state of safety); they are, as such, perhaps not dissimilar from the navigation of an animal across its territory from a dangerous or unpleasant location to a safe or resourceful location.

Furthermore, disruptions or "changes in feeling states can be considered to be the motivators for ego development as a whole" (SANDLER, 1985, p. 532). Having been forced, in early childhood, to depart from a state of 'primary narcissism', the ego makes "a strenuous attempt to regain that state", to escape anxiety and regain "a feeling state of well-being" ('safety') (SANDLER, 1985, p. 532), which is the state of connectedness to the selfobject milieu. The ego acquires structure in the course of development as it has to repeat the manoeuvre from anxiety to interpersonal connectedness many times. The building of 'psychic structure' in relation to affective processes touches on insights provided by learning theory.

3.3.1 Learning to escape from aversiveness

Affective processes play an essential role in organizing, activating, regulating, and sustaining behaviour patterns (YOUNG, 1959). Affective processes are elicited by physiological events, but they can also be anchored to events within the physical environment. Environmental situations can have an *innate* capacity to arouse an affective process; or they *acquire*, through conditioning, the capacity to arouse an affective process. A situation may produce positive or negative affective arousal (YOUNG, 1959). Affective arousal orientates the animal towards or away from stimulus cues and objects. If a situation produces positive affective arousal, the animal reacts positively to stimulus cues in the environment. Positive affective arousal is associated with approach patterns of behaviour (exploration), whereas negative affective arousal (pain, fear, or anxiety) is associated with avoidance or

---

[14] A threat "must be experienced by the ego at some level", whereupon a defensive manoeuvre allows a "new image" of something being acceptable and nonthreatening "to come to consciousness" (SANDLER, 1985, p. 533).

terminating patterns of behaviour (YOUNG, 1959). When positive affectivity is present, the animal tries to increase it, such as by employing approach patterns of behaviour. When negative affectivity is present, the animal tries to reduce it by employing behaviour that aims to terminate an aversive condition or escape from it (YOUNG, 1959).

When a noxious stimulus (unconditioned stimulus) impinges upon an organism, the organism will engage in behaviour designed to eliminate that stimulus (unconditioned response) (MOWRER & LAMOREAUX, 1946). In fear conditioning, an affectively neutral stimulus that is paired with a noxious stimulus (traumatic event) acquires the capacity to elicit fear. A stimulus that has acquired the capacity to elicit fear (and has thus become a fear-conditioned stimulus) serves as a warning signal with regard to the original traumatic event (unconditioned stimulus). Fear, not unlike pain, motivates the organism to engage in whatever behaviour is best calculated to remove this 'painful emotion' (MOWRER & LAMOREAUX, 1946). By removing fear (and moving away from a fear-inducing, conditioned stimulus), the organism averts reexposure to the traumatic (noxious) stimulus. The actual response required to eliminate the *fear-conditioned* stimulus and, at the same time, overcome the attendant fear is different from the response required to eliminate a *noxious* stimulus and the attendant pain (MOWRER & LAMOREAUX, 1946). When the timing, source, and severity of noxious events or punishment are uncertain, fear is experienced as anxiety. Anxiety is an unconditioned or conditioned response to *situations*; it signals dangerousness of a situation or context, rather than that of a discrete stimulus. Anxiety, too, may have the effect of motivating the animal to remove itself from the anxiety-producing situation.

MOWRER and LAMOREAUX (1946) proposed that reduction in fear (elimination of this 'painful emotion') constitutes a rewarding state, which can reinforce the link between fear (or, rather, the fear-conditioned stimulus) and the behaviour that immediately preceded the reduction in fear. MILLER (1948), too, argued that fear reduction serves as a reinforcer to produce learning of the immediately preceding response. A new response is learned when it allows the animal to *remove* itself from a fear-producing cue or to eliminate the fear-producing cue in other ways (e.g., by turning a wheel or pressing a bar). Fear reduction, as MILLER (1948) thought, plays a crucial role, similar to that of primary rewards, in the acquisition and maintenance of new habits. Fear is an intermediate *step* ('intervening variable') in *avoidance learning*: a conditioned stimulus produces fear, which then calls for a fear-reducing response, which, once reinforced, becomes an avoidance response (MOWRER & LAMOREAUX, 1946).

We may similarly learn to escape from fear-inducing or anxiogenic *situations* or to avoid exposure to anxiogenic situations. At the same time, the reward associated with attainment of safety (narcissistic gratification) would reinforce the link between situations and the behaviour that produced the reward, in accordance with THORNDIKE's (1911) 'law of effect'. Indeed, THORNDIKE (1911) proposed that, in the process of learning, connections are formed between *situations* and actions. Taken together, goal-directed (appetitive) behaviour that moves us from situation to situation (through social space) becomes so organized that it reduces or avoids anxiety (i.e., minimizes negative affectivity) and, at the same time, maximizes safety (associated with positive affectivity).

3.3.2 Hedonic control

RADO (1956) discerned similar principles, arguing that activities of 'moving toward' and 'moving away from' are the basic operations of hedonic control and self-regulation. At the level of hedonic control, the organism is designed to "move *toward* the source of *pleasure*, and *away* from the cause of *pain*" (p. 290). At this level of control, "the organism relies on the expectation that pleasure signals the presence of needed supplies or of conditions otherwise favourable to its survival; and pain the presence of a threat to its organic integrity" (RADO, 1956, p. 290). Thus, movements from pain to pleasure are, at the same time, movements from a source of pain to a source of pleasure, that is, from anxiety and danger to subjective wellbeing and objective security; much as movements from hunger or craving to subjective satiety are, at the same time, movements from unmet need to the reestablishment of physiological homeostasis. These movements are a form of appetitive behaviour, which may be derived evolutionarily from navigational behaviour. In general terms, appetitive behaviour acts to decrease negative affect (negative emotional tone) and to attain or prolong a positive affective state (positive feeling state); it always moves the organism from a situation associated with a negative feeling tone to a situation associated with a positive feeling tone, corresponding to a movement from a dangerous or deprived to a safe or resourceful situation.

The organism seeks "to repeat pleasurable experiences and to avoid painful ones" (RADO, 1956, p. 333). For a pleasurable experience to be repeated, or a painful one to be avoided, learning has to take place (reinforcement learning). If "pleasure is the reward for successful performance", then "memory of pleasure invites repetition of the beneficial activity" (p. 291) (acting as an incentive stimulus). Likewise, if pain is "punishment for failure", then "memory of pain deters the organism from repeating the self-harming activity" (RADO, 1956, p. 291). The recall in imagery of memories of pleasure or pain corresponds to the simulation of action outcomes (in imagery), identifying goals to be pursued or warning against consequences to be avoided. Anticipation of adverse consequences reorientates behaviour or prolongs the process of decision making. During decision making, the principle of hedonic control appears to operate on a psychic level, in that "whenever possible, the organism intentionally suppresses painful or pain-connected tensions, feelings, and thoughts", removing them automatically from consciousness (RADO, 1956, p. 292).

> Nature has placed massive pleasure rewards on the operations which supply the organism's aboriginal needs; such as, intake of food, evacuation of waste and reproduction. The perennial problem of cultural development is to extend this system of pleasure rewards to the operations that will supply the organism's acculturated needs, i.e., where it will have adaptive utility, in a given culture. At the same time, pleasure-yielding yet socially undesirable activity must be vigorously combatted by the threat of punishment or, in other words, the infliction of pain. The reward and punishment system of society is based upon, and is but an extension of, the hedonic self-regulation of the biologic organism.
>
> (RADO, 1956, p. 291)

3.3.3 Psychotaxis

Persons *avoid* or *escape* unpleasant emotions; they "may attempt to avoid thoughts, memories, or situations that they expect to elicit the emotion"; or they "may seek to escape from experiencing the emotion as quickly as possible" (PRETZER & BECK, 1996, p. 52). Unpleasant emotions are linked to unpleasant (and inherently dangerous) situations. Unpleasant situations evoke an impulse to escape (MOORE, 1926).

Perhaps, defence mechanisms are not so much concerned with escaping an anxiety-provoking situation as they are concerned with escaping an unpleasant or aversive situation. Primarily, defence mechanisms would ensure escape from or avoidance of unpleasant situations; secondarily, they would resolve or avoid anxiety (Figure 3.2). It would be "an unpleasant situation" that constitutes the "fundamental condition which calls forth a defense reaction" (MOORE, 1926, p. 231). Defence reactions not only represent "spontaneous tendencies to get out of an unpleasant situation" or to avoid it (p. 230), but also aim to instate a pleasant situation. Human beings have "very strong innate tendencies" to make use of, and enjoy, "all pleasant situations, and to get out of or avoid to the uttermost all unpleasant ones" (p. 183). These tendencies, called positive and negative psychotaxes, respectively, "are almost reflex in character" (MOORE, 1926, p. 183). Unpleasant situations we escape include those that are conjured up in imagination.

> We all dislike to remember certain unpleasant situations of the past, and to consider various disagreeable eventualities of the future. ... Most men have a spontaneous tendency to put this eventuality out of mind, and they just as spontaneously avoid anything that brings it up. Natural and spontaneous tendencies to make use of any ability in our mind to avoid an unpleasant thing, or a disagreeable situation, have every right

78 *Narcissism and the Self*

> to be considered impulses; and because they are impulses which have to do with the problems which arise in unpleasant situations, they belong to that group of mental reactions that we have termed the psychotaxes or parataxes.
>
> (MOORE, 1926, pp. 230–1)

> The mode of avoidance is indeed mental, but it is no less impulsive than the motor impulses that one experiences to get out of a cold bath, or to get in out of the rain, or to go from the sun to the shade on a hot day, etc.
>
> (MOORE, 1926, p. 230)

Defences thus are negative, but ultimately also positive, psychotaxes that can be applied to situations encountered or recalled. We may be prevented from escaping an unpleasant (and implicitly dangerous) situation by a conflicting impulse, such as by a need for resources (such as narcissistic supplies) that are only available in this situation or by fear of punishment for escaping this situation. Anxiety may arise only insofar as we cannot give in to the impulse to escape an unpleasant situation (Figure 3.2). MOORE (1926) thought that the "conflict of incompatible desires ... is the main factor in producing a state of anxiety" (p. 209).

> Whenever it is possible for us to avoid or escape an unpleasant situation, we experience a strong tendency to do so. ... In some, this tendency may be obscured by ideals of conduct, ...
>
> (MOORE, 1926, p. 211)

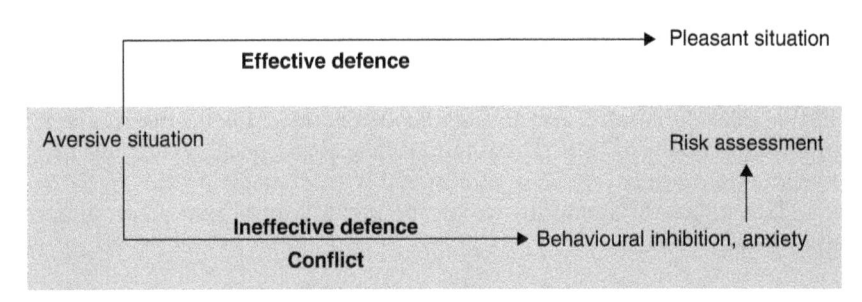

Figure 3.2 There are two models of anxiety: one in which anxiety prompts escape behaviour and one (depicted) in which anxiety is the consequence of an inability to escape from aversiveness, usually due to conflict between contradictory response tendencies. Anxiety would then serve to engender risk assessment behaviour and defensive preparedness, rather than escape to safety

3.3.4 Compulsion to repeat

Aspects of infantile relationships are reproduced in the present because these relationships provide enduring templates for safety. People feel indeed *compelled* to reenact in the present an early pattern of relating. The 'compulsion to repeat' may be an expression of a fundamental tendency to reduce tension that has been raised in the organism. The same fundamental tendency may also find expression in the 'pleasure principle' (FREUD, 1920, p. 56). In interpersonal situations, the individual's behaviour is designed to escape from, or avoid, an aversive or painful situation and reinstate a previously gratifying interpersonal situation (object relation). Feeling states may mediate in this process (SANDLER, 1972). Seeking to instate a desired state or avoid a painful situation, the individual is motivated "to respectively reinstate or avoid similar affective experiences" (KERNBERG, 1992, p. 13).

The compulsion to effect the transformation of the presently aversive into a desired (and safe) interpersonal situation may be incentivized by an awareness of the discrepancy between the two. It may be, as KERNBERG (1992) thought, "the juxtaposition of an evoked remembered state with a future desired state in the context of a current perception that activates the desire for change" (p. 13). Thus, either an aversive situation or images of a desirable situation initiate patterns of behaviour that allow the individual to reexperience, in unconscious fantasy, aspects of his primary object relation (particularly the mother's approving and reassuring gestures). Perhaps, the goal of securing relatedness, if it is fleetingly experienced in imagery, imbues the individual's agitation and urge to leave an unpleasant situations with the necessary directedness.

The compulsion to repeat, a manifestation of the need for safety, can have a truly compulsory quality, the quality of an urge, especially if the repetition of an early pattern of relating is resisted at the same time. When the need to maintain safety takes the form of a peremptory urge, it operates like an instinctual ('traditional') drive, even though it does not arise from the 'id' (SANDLER, 1989b). Different modes of attaining safety can be in conflict with each other, so that 'mental conflict', in general, does not depend on 'instinctual drives' (in the traditional sense of the term) arising from the 'id' and pressing for discharge. For instance, an impulse to cling to someone or to 'regress' to a level of functioning characteristic of childhood can have a peremptory quality (SANDLER, 1989b) and be in conflict with a wish to maintain safety by more appropriate means.

> The pressure to re-establish our relations with internal or internalized objects by setting them up outside is all the greater the more anxious we are, the more we are threatened, and the less in control of ourselves or our environment we feel. Indeed, we could not exist with any degree of sanity at all if we did not succeed in brining our inner and outer worlds

into some sort of harmony, and the pressure to do this has as peremptory a quality as any instinctual drive.

(SANDLER, 1989b, p. 237)

3.3.5 Role relationships

Through interaction with objects, the individual satisfies his need for a special form of gratification, namely 'affirmation' and reassurance (SANDLER & SANDLER, 1978). The need for affirmation and reassurance has to be constantly satisfied. By continually satisfying the need for this type of 'nourishment', the individual maintains a background of feelings of 'safety' or wellbeing. It was the interchange of affectionate signals with the mother that provided the original source of feelings of safety (SANDLER & SANDLER, 1978). FREUD's (1914) concept of primary narcissism, as implicated in the earliest relationship between mother and infant, was considered by SANDLER and SANDLER (1978) to be equivalent to the state of safety or wellbeing that the individual attempts to regain, throughout his life, by way of relating to objects. It is the developmental departure from primary narcissism that gives rise to vigorous attempts, throughout life, to reexperience feelings of safety by approximating aspects of the primary relationship with the mother (SANDLER & SANDLER, 1978). Aspects of the primary relationship that are pertinent concern conditions for the exchange between mother and infant of affectionate and affirmative signals. The need to relate to others is equivalent to the need for affirmation (narcissistic supplies) from others and the need for reexperiencing the safety implicit in the symbiotic union with the mother.

Object relationships develop in the early years of life as a means for attaining safety; and patterns around which early object relationships are organized endure throughout life. In other words, we relate to others in ways that were shaped by early object relationships, although what we try to recapture (or at least approximate) in our relationships is a characteristic of the very *earliest* object relation. There is, throughout life, a constantly recurring urge to reenact aspects of object relationships maintained during the first years of life and thus to reexperience the safety that was associated with early and the *earliest* relationships. This urge arises particularly "when our feelings of security or safety are threatened, as they constantly are" (SANDLER & SANDLER, 1978).

SANDLER and SANDLER (1978) explained that "a great deal of life is involved in the concealed repetition of early object relationships", especially of relationship *patterns* that have from the first years of life operated as "safety-giving or anxiety-reducing manoeuvres". For this reason, object relationships have to be regarded as 'role relationships'; they always involve the *reenactment of roles* played by self and object in early object relationships. Thus, interpersonal behaviour is motivated by the need for affirmation and for replenishment of feelings of safety; and it is given shape by early patterns of gratifying object relationships (SANDLER & SANDLER, 1978).[15]

3.3.6 Goal-directedness of the personality

ADLER (1927) thought that "the psyche is intimately related to mobility" (p. 50) (i.e., to goal-directed navigation). Our imagination and sentiments and our very perceptions "are influenced by our striving for a definite goal" (p. 68); they "are chosen, so to speak, with a hidden reference to the final goal towards which the personality is striving" (pp. 68–9). Our actions are directed towards a psychological goal "that is constantly present, more or less consciously" (p. 229) and that represents an 'ideal state' of being *recognized* or *favoured* by others, a goal that promises 'security', not only "security from danger, but that further element of safety that guarantees our continued existence under optimum circumstances" (ADLER, 1927, p. 32).

Every memory recollected "is dominated by the unifying theme or goal that directs the personality as a whole" (ADLER, 1927, p. 51). Every recollection of memory serves to "further an important underlying movement" (p. 50) towards the *goal of the personality*, whereby "in our civilization, this goal involves social recognition and significance" (p. 57) (i.e., narcissistic gratification). The goal that is conjured up may express "the desire for superiority and the hope of success in competition" (p. 57); and it may thereby aid the personality's underlying 'movement' towards recognition and significance (and ultimately towards security) (ADLER, 1927). Fantasy, too, "is bound up with the mobility of the human organism and is indeed nothing more than a method of foresight" (p. 57).[16] Every daydream and even every hallucination (based, as it is, on episodic memory recall and recombination) is "designed and fashioned according to the goals and purposes of the particular individual who creates it" (p. 51). Daydreams (as well as sleep dreams) can be understood as attempts "to map, plan and direct the future life towards a goal of security" (ADLER, 1927, p. 59) (SANDLER's 'safety').

The 'sense of inferiority' is a feeling of insufficiency or insecurity; it "is a positive pain", a state that is "comparable to a painful tension that seeks

---

[15] The patient in psychoanalytic therapy, for instance, tries to tempt the analyst to play the role of the comforting mother so that he, the patient, can reexperience gratifying feelings associated with her presence. The analyst may or may not be responsive to the role the patient attempts to impose on him ('role responsiveness'). It is the analyst's compliance with the role the patient wants him to play that allows the 'transference' to emerge in therapy (SANDLER & SANDLER, 1978).
[16] Fantasy can have an incentive effect. When the person faces difficulty in his pursuit of the goal of superiority (as a means to achieving security), fantasy provides "an illusionary picture of increased personal worth" that has the effect of "spurring him on" (ADLER, 1938, p. 182). Fantasy that lacks this incentive effect "is entirely a matter of compensation" (p. 182) for inescapable inferiority and insecurity (ADLER, 1938).

82 Narcissism and the Self

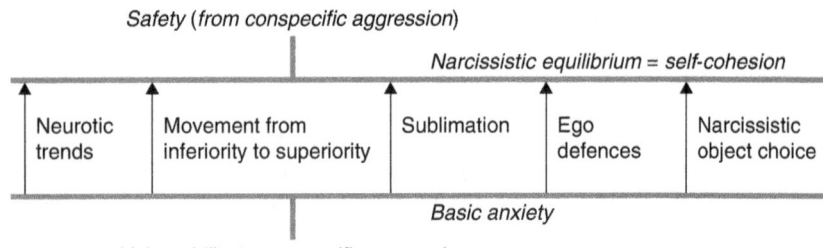

```
                    Safety (from conspecific aggression)
                                    │
                                    │      Narcissistic equilibrium = self-cohesion
─────────────────────────────────────────────────────────────────────────
  ▲              ▲                  ▲              ▲              ▲
┌─────────┐ ┌──────────────────┐ ┌────────────┐ ┌──────────┐ ┌──────────────┐
│ Neurotic│ │ Movement from    │ │ Sublimation│ │ Ego      │ │ Narcissistic │
│ trends  │ │ inferiority to   │ │            │ │ defences │ │ object choice│
│         │ │ superiority      │ │            │ │          │ │              │
└─────────┘ └──────────────────┘ └────────────┘ └──────────┘ └──────────────┘
─────────────────────────────────────────────────────────────────────────
                                    │      Basic anxiety
                                    │
                    Vulnerability to conspecific aggression
```

Figure 3.3 Patterns of habitual movement (ADLER) from anxiety to safety constitute the personality or character of an individual. Safety, experienced as ego feeling (FEDERN), self-cohesion (KOHUT), or self-esteem, is linked to acceptance by the primary maternal object (or its later derivatives), the superego (or its external representatives), or the group (being another derivative of the primary maternal object), much as the self, whenever it is a consciously experienced phenomenon, remains unconsciously dependent on the superego

relief" (ADLER's, 1938, p. 77). The "finding of a path that leads from a feeling of inferiority to one of superiority" is associated with the "release of tension" (p. 75). According to the 'law of movement', life is "constantly bent on reaching a positive situation from a negative one" (pp. 77–8). The sense of inferiority – a negative situation – urges the individual "towards a 'plus' situation, towards security" (p. 79). The 'law of movement' that governs social behaviour and psychic phenomena is an expression of the more fundamental 'principle of security', the 'law of self-preservation' (p. 78) (Figure 3.3). In their social and cultural context, "human beings are in a permanent state of feeling their inferiority, which constantly spurs them on to further action in order to attain greater security" (p. 78). Security, in turn, is associated with eminent or dominant status, that is, with superiority (ADLER, 1938).

The striving for superiority or power is manifested in ambition and vanity. ADLER (1927) acknowledged that "a degree of ambition and vanity appears in all human beings, according to their individual method of striving for power" (p. 229) (whereby "exaggerated ambition and vanity prevent a person's orderly development" [p. 230]). The individual's 'life style'[17] is "formed by the compelling goal of superiority and spurred on by the sense of inferiority" (ADLER, 1938, p. 86). Being "drawn on by an ever-increasing longing for a final goal: superiority" (p. 79), the individual reaches for intermediate and more concrete goals along the way, goals that accord with his 'life style'; "the goal of conquest, as soon as it assumes concrete form in the world, prescribes a different direction for each individual" (ADLER, 1938, p. 80).

---

[17] 'Life style' in ADLER's psychology refers to a person's character structure, as it is established in early childhood, and as it determines choices and structures relationships across the person's life.

The amount of security that human beings "demand in relation to the everyday realities of our society" is determined early in their lives (ADLER, 1927, p. 32). Children generally demand "a safety margin greater than is strictly necessary for the satisfaction of their basic needs" (p. 32). Children learn that what "will guarantee them the security" is their surpassing of "all their rivals"; so they learn to strive for 'superiority', a striving that becomes a "thirst for glory" (p. 32). They also learn to strive for 'power' over others, that is, for control over others' attitudes towards themselves, over others' willingness to recognize or favour them. Habitual ways in which conditions that afford superiority or power are recreated – and in which the goal that promises security is approached – constitute the individual's personality. However, the demand for security (as manifested in the demand for superiority or power) also depends on the second force that works "on each person's psyche", namely 'social feeling' (ADLER, 1927, p. 229). The degree to which the sense of inferiority and the striving for superiority dominate the personality and 'life style' depends on the relative presence or absence of social feeling ('social interest'). Lack of social feeling gives rise to greater insecurity and a pervasive sense of inferiority and, hence, to a preeminent need to attain security through superiority (ADLER, 1938).

3.3.7 Neurotic trends

Anxiety (or the aversiveness that is implicit in it) engenders strivings for safety. Attainment of safety, that is, of "reassurance against a lurking anxiety", is a guiding principle of social behaviour (HORNEY, 1939, p. 73). 'Basic anxiety' (basic insecurity) "necessitates the rigid pursuit of certain strivings for safety" (p. 173). Strivings that are "determined mainly by a search for safety" were designated by HORNEY (1939) as 'neurotic trends' (p. 77). HORNEY (1939) described narcissistic, perfectionist, and masochistic neurotic trends, in particular. Neurotic trends "are conditioned by an underlying 'basic anxiety' and develop in the personality 'for the sake of safety'" (HORNEY, 1939, p. 202) (Figure 3.3).

The neurotic person "has more anxiety" and "has to put an infinitely greater amount of energy into maintaining his security" (HORNEY, 1939, p. 73). The greater the person's anxiety, the more stringent is the striving for safety. Safety then rests on the unhampered operation of neurotic trends (p. 202). Anxiety arises as soon as neurotic trends, that is, the safety devices that constitute the individual's character structure, fail to operate. If a person's "safety rests on infallibility", then anxiety can arise "from a mistake or error in judgment of a kind that may happen to anyone"; or "in a person bent on presenting a façade of unselfishness, a legitimate modest wish for himself may provoke anxiety" (p. 199). Whatever jeopardizes the neurotic person's "specific protective pursuits, his specific neurotic trends" (p. 199) (whatever endangers "those trends on the pursuit of which his safety rests" [p. 198]) is likely to "provoke anxiety" (HORNEY, 1939, p. 199).

3.3.8 Reality principle and ego defences

One of the 'ego functions' is the defence against unpleasant affects (HARTMANN, 1964). The immediate concern of the ego (the part of the mental apparatus) is to regulate its feeling state, particularly to reduce painful or unpleasurable affects (SANDLER, 1985). Drive impulses evoke painful affects or anxiety insofar as their unrestrained expression (in accordance with the 'pleasure principle') would be in conflict with social reality (would be disapproved of by others). Reduction and avoidance, through ego defences, of painful or unpleasurable affects (anxiety in particular) would have the adaptive effect of stabilizing the person's selfobject milieu and minimizing his vulnerability to conspecific attack (in the form of criticisms or ridicule). Some defence mechanisms, such as repression and projection, seem to be concerned mostly with the reduction or avoidance of anxiety, whereas others, such as sublimation and regression, have clearly narcissistic aims (and hence have 'pleasurable potentialities'). In general, we defend not only against anxiety but also "in order to gain or maintain a good feeling of security or safety" (SANDLER, 1985, p. 19).[18]

SANDLER and JOFFE (1966) pointed out that "an activity that is used for purposes of sublimation", that is, an activity that changes the expression of an 'instinctual drive' in such a way that its expression becomes acceptable to others, "may provide an excellent source of narcissistic supplies" (p. 203). Such activity, in other words, is "invested with narcissistic cathexis" (p. 203). Sublimation provides, at the same time, "a means of avoiding or reducing areas of conflict and anxiety" (SANDLER & JOFFE, 1966, p. 200) (Figure 3.3).

Approach-avoidance conflict is associated with anxiety; 'signal anxiety' arises and persists insofar as conflict cannot be resolved, insofar as approach and avoidance tendencies simultaneously seek expression. Approach-avoidance conflicts in the social realm are conflicts between the desire for approval (narcissistic supplies) and the fear of disapproval (criticism), that is, between the need to be seen (exhibitionistic need) and the need not to be seen (or not to be conspicuous and hence vulnerable) (LAING, 1960). In situations of conflict, a compromise solution has to be found: a manoeuvre that allows approach to a source of reward (source of approval) while minimizing the risk of punishment (disapproval). Henceforth, an acquired (appetitive) behaviour can be engaged in similar situations, allowing for the receipt of

---

[18] The reality principle "represents a tendency to wrest our activities from the immediate need for discharge inherent in the pleasure principle" (HARTMANN, 1964, p. 244). The reality principle has a dual function: to ensure that instinctual drives are satisfied in a manner that is adapted to reality, and to preserve or even enhance the person's access to narcissistic supplies and hence his safety or 'wellbeing' (SANDLER). This would be why "functions that constitute the reality principle can be pleasurable in themselves" (p. 244), why sublimated activities, in particular, have 'pleasurable potentialities' (HARTMANN, 1964, p. 244).

approval while minimizing the risk of punishment. If the conflict between these behaviour tendencies (needs) does not recur, anxiety will not be felt, and hence the behaviour can be described as habitual (habitually defensive). Exhibitionistic or care-seeking impulses can be expressed spontaneously and induce in others automatic responses of approval or reassurance, although when used inappropriately (out of the situational context in which they are sanctioned), they can be met with rejection or social punishment. The risk of disapproval can be minimized by merging exhibitionistic or care-seeking behaviours with expressions of conformity and with displays that effect appeasement of others (expressions that take 'reality' into account). Avoidance of disapproval (punishment) is an integral part of appetitive behaviour that more or less habitually creates conditions (moves the organism towards situations) in which approval can be received. Similarly, there are defence mechanisms that enable the safe (socially acceptable) expression of aggression, whereby modified aggression (aggression in its neutralized form of assertiveness or leadership behaviour) can itself be used to control access to sources of approval (as in sublimation).

Unless exhibitionistic, care-seeking, or aggressive impulses are coupled with normative or submissive behaviours, they would *invite* an aggressive response from others and therefore would be accompanied by signal anxiety. Even to give these impulses expression in thought[19] can raise anxiety (since, in thought, they are subjected to an 'imaginary audience' [CASHDAN, 1988] or the superego). Exhibitionistic, care-seeking, or aggressive impulses have to be defensively modulated; or else they need to be 'repressed' (as soon as signal anxiety arises) or completely inhibited, so as to avoid, with greater certainty, exposure to others' criticism and disapproval (or exposure to the superego and its disapproving attitude in imagination).[20]

3.4 Narcissism versus object love

Love of objects, which draws on libidinal capacities, must not be confused with the struggle to gain the love of objects and the need for self-enhancing reflections (KOHUT, 1984). Object choice and object relatedness can be narcissistic or anaclitic (object-libidinal) in nature. Libidinal object cathexis expresses the *desire to love*; the aim of narcissistic object choice is *to be loved* (FREUD, 1914). Self-regard depends on the narcissistic element in love; it is not raised directly by libidinal object cathexis, although satisfaction of libidinal striving for an object ('object libido'), that is, of the libidinal element in

---

[19] FREUD regarded thought as 'trial activity'.
[20] Inhibition of exhibitionistic, care-seeking, or aggressive impulses can be coupled with (schizoid) withdrawal into a fantasy world in which conditions conducive to the receipt of approving signals would be created fleetingly (the simulation, rather than creation, of a safe situation).

love, makes it likely that love will be returned and self-regard can be maintained. Self-regard, the narcissistic cathexis of the self, is increased, as FREUD (1914) realized, by being loved or having one's love returned (such as in love relations); it is lowered when one is not loved. Being loved is one way of raising self-esteem; being admired or approved by others (as a reflection of one's conduct) is yet another way of narcissistic gratification. Conduct in accordance with familial or cultural expectations, that is, living up to one's 'ego ideal', ensures that one is accepted, approved, or admired by others. The ego ideal also imposes limiting conditions on the satisfaction of object libido, causing libidinal impulses that are not ego-syntonic to be rejected (FREUD, 1914). Thus, narcissistic strivings can antagonize libidinal strivings, and libidinal strivings can be an aid to the satisfaction of narcissistic needs.[21]

FEDERN (1952) (like FREUD) thought that narcissism ('ego libido') is antithetic to 'object libido', much as "narcissistic injury is antithetic to the suffering resulting from frustrated object libido" (p. 325). Narcissism is not only self-love (even though pathological narcissism impresses as such); narcissism (i.e., secondary narcissism) can have an object other than the ego. Narcissism with object cathexis, that is, 'narcissistic object choice', establishes a form of relatedness to an object that is fundamentally different from investment of 'object libido' in the same object (p. 325). Narcissistic investment in an object turns it into part of the self. Narcissism (secondary) has as its object "what has been incorporated into or enclosed by the ego" (p. 325), a selfobject, in other words. In the healthy personality, "a narcissistic process of cathexis" is "added to the object libidinal one" (p. 333); however, pathologically increased narcissistic investment (in objects and the self) "consumes libido which should benefit reality adjustment and the objects; it prevents relationships with other persons" (FEDERN, 1952, p. 342).

3.4.1 Narcissistic versus libidinal object relations

The association, observed by FREUD (1914), FEDERN (1952), and HARTMANN, between heightened narcissistic cathexis of the self (ego) and lack of libidinal cathexes of objects probably only applies to pathological narcissists, to persons who, because of their inability to genuinely care for or love their objects, treat them exclusively as selfobjects (rather than love objects). The less a person is able to make libidinal investments in his objects, the more his narcissistic balance depends on his ability to induce his selfobjects (actively or passively) to reflect his self back to him in an acknowledging, approving, or praising manner. Moreover, the more incapable of genuine

---

[21] Narcissistic satisfaction is often "conditional on real object libidinal discharges" (FEDERN, 1952, p. 361). Conversely, "the satisfaction of the object libido is often conditional upon the simultaneous satisfaction of the preformed narcissistic phantasies" (p. 359), even though "the narcissistic premium is not conscious in many object-libidinally cathected actions" (FEDERN, 1952, p. 359).

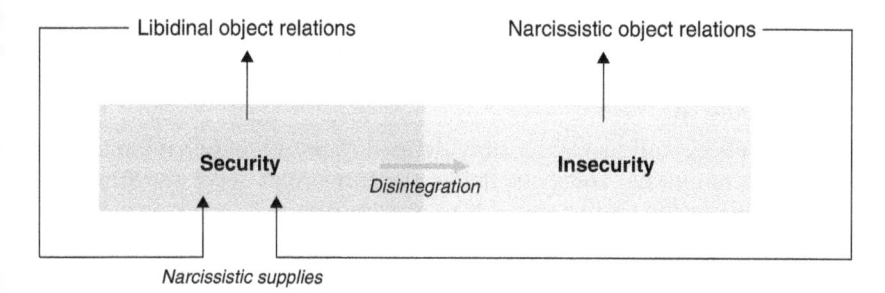

Figure 3.4 Narcissistic object relations aim to protect against insecurity, whereas libidinal relations are born out of security. Security (self-experience) disintegrates unless a constant effort is made to attain narcissistic supplies from the selfobject surround. Such disintegration is less likely to happen if the self is supported by libidinal as well as narcissistic object relations

love he is, the more insecure he feels. The person with "intense feelings of inferiority", who may "appear to be very insecure", shows "marked dependence on the attitude of his objects for his well-being" (JOFFE & SANDLER, 1967, p. 181). He pays constant attention to his objects "in relation to the use he makes of them to gratify his need for admiration, support, or praise" (JOFFE & SANDLER, 1967, p. 181), that is, in relation to their selfobject function. A person, on the other hand, who is capable, to a high degree, of libidinal investments in objects (libidinal object cathexes), who can show genuine love and concern for his objects, is less concerned about, and invests less effort in, controlling the selfobject function of his objects (Figure 3.4). In the latter case, the narcissistic cathexis of the self *seems* to be reduced, but it is not. Narcissistic homeostasis is maintained effortlessly inasmuch as the person loves his objects. The capacity for love protects him against narcissistic disorders (disturbances in the regulation of self-esteem).

In relationships founded on narcissistic object choice, the "need for self-love (self-esteem) … overshadows object love"; however, when capacity for genuine object love is intact, "another, higher, postnarcissistic type of self-respect becomes available" (FENICHEL, 1946, p. 85). Object love helps to satisfy narcissistic needs (needs for safety). The capacity for object love obviates the need to resort to narcissistic object choice and tempers the compulsion to draw on the selfobject function of objects. Conversely, as KOHUT (1984) observed, security (self-preservation) – maintained by way of intuneness with the selfobject surround (allowing for an intact narcissistic homeostasis) – is a precondition for object love (Figure 3.5). An excessive reliance on the narcissistic mode of relating is incompatible with (or antithetical to) libidinal investments in objects, either because an overtly narcissistic style of relating is associated with anxiety (insecurity), which inhibits libidinal impulses, or because a narcissistic personality structure compensates for a primarily inhibited capacity to libidinally connect to objects.

3.4.2 Libido theory

Narcissism is evolutionarily sensibly defined as the set of behaviours, psychological functions, and personality structures that serve the function of self-preservation. Narcissism, in preserving the self (one's own being) *on the level of psychological functioning and social interactions*, creates the 'ego' (in FEDERN's sense) or 'self' (in HARTMANN's [1964] or JACOBSON's [1964] sense) as a psychological and social experience. Classical psychoanalytic theory, on the other hand, embedded the concept of narcissism in 'libido theory'. Narcissism was regarded as self-love, "as any phenomenon in which one's person, one's body, or one's psychic attributes are the object of the libido" (HENDRICK, 1958, p. 117). However, taking the matter outside libido theory, we can appreciate that self-love is merely a special case of narcissism. The self-preservative, egotistic function of narcissism is not easily apparent from within the libido theory. Narcissism was considered by FREUD as the libidinal *complement* of egotism, of self-interest, so could operate in the "service of one's self-preservative needs" (HENDRICK, 1958, p. 117), seemingly by virtue of its association with egotism. It was in the context of FREUD's libido theory that narcissism (libido invested in the ego or self) and object libido were considered as being alternative expressions of a more general life force ('Eros'), as being transformable into each other, and as jointly operating in opposition to the 'death instinct' (FREUD, 1920; HENDRICK, 1958).

The close relationship between object libido and narcissism is supported by the observation that narcissism is "always mingled with variable degrees of object-love" (p. 118); their cooperation can be seen in "a great variety of psychological conditions, both normal and pathological" (HENDRICK, 1958, p. 117). Narcissism (ego libido) is the *passive* counterpart of object libido. Narcissism entails a preparedness "to derive pleasure passively and receptively" and an attitude of valuing others for what they can *give* to oneself (p. 117). The narcissistic component in love concerns the requirement "to be adored and cared for" (HENDRICK, 1958, p. 118). In neuroses, a predominantly passive attitude concerned with attracting adoration or care develops on the background of inhibition of object libido. In narcissistic disorders ('disorders of the self' [KOHUT]), this passive attitude is expressed in form of frank and unrealistic overvaluation of the self, and it combines with almost complete inability to make object-libidinal investments. Overvaluation of the self is not only unrealistic but delusional in megalomania.

One loves oneself and cherishes one's attributes, yet one's self and one's attributes are based on identifications with others, on the accrual of safety (to the effect of self-preservation) by way of identifications with parents, the leader of a group, or any successful and *attractive* person. The person with

3.4.3 Primary narcissism and love

BERGLER (1949) discussed the (primary) narcissistic character of tender love and sexual intercourse (p. 45). Object relatedness, more generally, has a narcissistic quality; "it represents ... a narcissistic attempt at restitution", "since through identification with the object the infant situation is found again" (p. 45) (i.e., primary narcissistic fusion with the primary maternal object is recreated to some extent). Object relationships, insofar as they involve "the wish to be loved", "can be traced back to the wish *not to be separated from the 'unending stream' which pours from the mother's breast*" (p. 45). This is the wish to be identified (re-fused) with the breast, to return to the state in which the breast "was *conceived as a part of one's own ego*" (BERGLER, 1949, p. 45) (primary narcissism). The experience of love is based on re-fusion of the ego with the object, that is, on reintrojection of the object into the ego.

> That grotesque mistake of the infant – assumption that the breast belongs to him – has far-reaching consequences in love. It leads directly to object-relations in love with the purpose of helping to restore the lost narcissistic unity.
>
> (BERGLER, 1949, pp. 45–6)

An approximation of primary narcissism can be achieved in states of love and mania by way of identification with the ego ideal and, through this identification, fusion with the superego. In addition, as already outlined, there is a secondary narcissistic element in object relationships: the object (selfobject) is recognized as separate but provoked and used to replenish self-esteem. Primary and secondary narcissistic elements in object relationships are complemented by libidinal investments in objects, that is, by feelings of tenderness towards the object and the desire to nurture the object. That latter aspect of object relationships is derived evolutionarily from true parental care, too. Thus, true parental care contributed to the evolution of object relations via both of its branches: care-seeking and infantile behaviour, on the one hand, and care-giving and maternal behaviour, on the other.

3.4.4 Guilt and reparation

KLEIN (1937) remarked that lack of appreciation from others causes distress, especially when it confirms one's suspicion of being inferior, unworthy of others' regard (p. 62). People's strong "need for general praise and approval" and "for evidence that they are lovable, worthy of love" "arises from the unconscious fear of being incapable of loving others sufficiently and truly" (pp. 62–3). In other words, incapacity to love causes excessive reliance on narcissistic supplies (selfishness). For KLEIN (1937), feelings of unworthiness "are always connected with unconscious feelings of guilt" (p. 62). Unconscious feelings of guilt, in turn, can be linked to the incapacity to love. KLEIN (1937) thought that the incapacity to love and to be considerate to someone "is, to a certain extent, a cover for over-strong feelings of guilt" (p. 79). However, the incapacity to love, likely due to fear of rejection, may be the primary problem, which leads to excessive reliance on others' love and approval and a strong fear of losing others' love and approval as a consequence of one's ambivalently aggressive (controlling) impulses, which is what could be conceptualized as unconscious guilt.

KLEIN (1937) stressed that unconscious feelings of guilt arise in connection with fantasized destruction of a loved object. These "feelings of guilt give rise to the fear of being dependent upon this loved person whom the child is afraid of losing, since as soon as aggression wells up he feels he is injuring her" (p. 117). The capacity to love and the ability to keep "loved people safe and undamaged" (and to keep their internal representatives undamaged) engender feelings of security (KLEIN, 1937, p. 98). *Being able to love means being able to repair damaged objects*, which ensures that the object is not lost and hence narcissistic supplies and safety are retained.

KLEIN (1937) thought that a "satisfactory balance between 'give' and 'take' is the primary condition for further happiness" (p. 118). The capacity for 'give' and 'take' has to be "developed in us in a way that ensures our own contentment, and contributes to the pleasure, comfort or happiness of other people" (KLEIN, 1937, p. 118). The capacity to 'give' is the capacity for love and reparation, whereas 'take' refers to our dependence on narcissistic gratification. Capacities to 'give' and 'take', that is, to love and be loved, evolved from, and are developmentally first expressed in, the bond between mother and child.

> The satisfaction of our self-preservative needs and the gratification of our desire for love are forever linked up with each other, because they are first derived from one and the same source. Security was first of all afforded to us by our mother, who not only stilled the pangs of hunger, but also satisfied our emotional needs and relieved anxiety. Security attained by satisfaction of our essential requirements is therefore linked up with emotional security, and both are all the more needed because they counteract the early fears of losing the loved mother. To be sure of our livelihood also implies, in the unconscious phantasy, not being deprived of love and not losing our mother altogether.
> (KLEIN, 1937, p. 108)

3.4.5 Self-interest versus social interest

'Social interest' ('social feeling') refers to "an ability to co-operate and mix with other people" (ADLER, 1938, p. 37). Evolutionarily, the largest part of social feeling probably stems from "the maternal sense of contact" with her offspring (p. 163). Social interest is indispensible for the care of offspring and the choice of a partner and for companionship (pp. 40–1). Social interest also underpins the "compulsion to co-operate" with fellow human beings (ADLER, 1938, p. 93). The concept of 'social interest' corresponds to the concept of libidinal investment in objects (or to the ability to make such investments). Investment of libido in and devotion to objects is contrasted with narcissistic investment in and *concern with* the self (i.e., with the way the self is seen by others). As ADLER (1938) put it, when two people love each other, "each of these two people must forget their own self entirely and give complete devotion to the other" (p. 51).

Social interest involves 'courage', the courage to establish contact with other human beings. Courage refers to the ability "to find straightforward solutions" to the tasks of life (ADLER, 1938, p. 121). Underdeveloped courage, which is associated with lack of social feeling ("a lack of interest in other people" [p. 121]), instils a "hesitant attitude towards the tasks of life" (ADLER, 1938, p. 122). Lack of social interest (lack of social feeling), apart from denoting an inability to love, means that the courage or assertiveness that comes to bear in interactions with others is inhibited. The individual lacks social feeling (and self-esteem) insofar as he lacks confidence in his ability to *actively solicit* others' affection and approval. He has to rely instead on measures of *passive attraction* of attention or approval. It is through the striving for 'superiority' that the individual tries to bolster his attractiveness, his potential to passively attract others' attention and approval.

To the extent that the individual is handicapped by a lack of social interest ("a lack of ability to make contact with other people" [p. 38] and lack in the 'capacity for devotion' to others [p. 52]), he is also burdened, according to ADLER (1938), with a pervasive sense of inferiority. Lack of social interest and a deep sense of inferiority are "intimately linked with one another" (p. 85). It is a "relatively greater deficiency of social interest" that gives rise to persistent feelings of inferiority ('inferiority complex') (p. 90). In the relative absence of social interest (and under the influence of pervasive inferiority), the person develops a compensatory 'superiority complex', which "always aims for the glitter of personal conquest" (p. 38) (and which "stands in opposition to co-operation" [p. 92]) (ADLER, 1938). Thus, what underlies "both the inferiority and the superiority complex" is a "deficiency of social interest" (p. 38). The strength of narcissistic neediness, that is, the extent to which the personality is dominated by the need to move from inferiority to superiority, is inversely proportional to the individual's social feeling (ADLER, 1938).[22]

---

[22] Inferiority and the striving for superiority are also intimately linked with self-concern and self-preoccupation. Those who are struggling for superiority, due to their deficient social feeling, have been "preoccupied from childhood with themselves and their own pleasure and pain" (ADLER, 1938, p. 91).

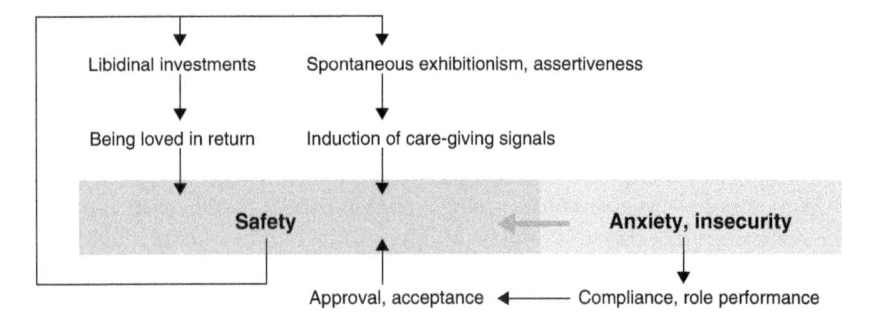

Figure 3.5 Modes of narcissistic homeostatic regulation. Social feeling (ADLER) and genuine spontaneity (HORNEY) help to maintain safety (postnarcissistically [FENICHEL]), but their expression presupposes safety. Neurotic mechanisms of attaining safety and normative and compliant behaviours in general work on a background of anxiety; they move the organism from anxiety to safety

3.4.6 Façade versus spontaneity

A person feels safe or secure if his 'centre of gravity' lies *within* himself, that is, if he is capable of spontaneous *outward*-directed actions (HORNEY, 1939) (i.e., actions of a libidinal nature, affective expressions of 'social feeling', and even spontaneous expressions of assertiveness and exhibitionism in the service of narcissistic homeostatic regulation [Figure 3.5]). In the neurotic person, however, "[s]pontaneous positive feelings for others are choked" (p. 222). The neurotic person's safety is built not upon "being himself" (p. 227) ('true self') but on his ability to *attract* recognition and approval from others towards himself, towards a façade that represents himself ('false self') (HORNEY, 1939). His actions are directed, so to say, *inwards* (via others to his self) and hence impress as narcissistic (self-centred).

A person's safety rests on a socially acceptable and hence *approvable* façade, inasmuch as his spontaneous individual self has been suffocated or stunted in development (HORNEY, 1939). The maintenance of an acceptable and approvable façade is an important strategy by way of which any person, neurotic or nonneurotic, establishes and controls his safety (narcissistic homeostasis); however, this strategy can dominate the personality and have a compulsive character. The neurotic person, especially when he is perfectionistic, "is superficially friendly to people", yet his friendliness has a compulsory character (p. 231). Whatever the composition of the façade (compliant, self-assured, or domineering), it has to be upheld *at all cost*. Whatever is in conflict with the person's style of striving for safety, that is, with his 'neurotic trends', has to be *repressed*.[23] The person's façade coincides

---

[23] As HORNEY (1939) emphasized, "what is repressed depends on the kind of façade an individual feels forced to present; everything is repressed which does not fit into the façade" (p. 228).

"with what is regarded as 'good'", whereas "what is repressed on its behalf will mostly coincide with what is regarded as 'bad' or 'inferior'" (Horney, 1939, p. 228).

For instance, either a "necessity to keep up an altruistic façade" (p. 227) or a need to "hang on to others in a masochistic way" (p. 228) may bring about the repression of *destructive impulses* (Horney, 1939). The person's traits of "pronounced egoism, vindictiveness, distrust, disregard for others if they do not serve his glory" are regarded "as morally objectionable" and hence "must be covered up", that is, they must be repressed; "or they are simply denied" (p. 96). The problem is that "the necessity to maintain a certain façade leads not only to repressing 'bad', anti-social, egocentric, 'instinctual' drives, but also to repressing ... spontaneous wishes, spontaneous feelings" (p. 229). Thus, "people may repress not only greediness but also their legitimate wishes" (Horney, 1939, p. 229). For the perfectionistic neurotic person, the "need to appear perfect" and maintain a perfect façade (the "imperative to be infallible") is of overriding importance and is pursued despite "painful consequences" (p. 229). The person's perfectionistic and "pseudo-moral aims" (p. 230) "interfere with a good relationship with others" and "prevent his best possible development" (p. 231). Again, in the interest of the need to appear perfect, "everything that does not fit into his ... façade" and "that would render it impossible for him to maintain that façade" is repressed (p. 229). Valuable human qualities, such as spontaneous wishes and feelings, are repressed "because they would endanger the façade" (Horney, 1939, p. 229).

3.5 Pain and anger

Pain promotes behaviour that aims to rid the organism "of the source of suffering" (Rado, 1956, p. 243). Pain, acting as a signal of actual damage, "is the very basis upon which the entire organization of emergency behavior has evolved" (p. 243). The 'emergency emotions' of fear and rage work "in the same adaptive direction as pain" (p. 219). Pain is tightly coupled with rage, perhaps less so with fear. Anticipation of pain (threat of pain, expectancy of impending damage), on the other hand, is more closely linked to fear. The aim of fear is "to escape from the threat", while the aim of rage is "to eliminate it by combat" (Rado, 1956, p. 219).[24] Anxiety is related to fear; and it is also continuous with the feeling of panic, the latter predisposing to vigorous flight or fight responses to any provocation or obstacle (Nunberg, 1955, p. 194). Anxiety and pain, too, "must have a common root"; and it can be

---

[24] Foresight of damage may elicit rage indirectly; rage, unlike fear, is not "an immediate response to the threat of pain from damage" (Rado, 1956, p. 244). To Rado it seemed "as if the organism has to be primed to rage by a shot of fear" (p. 244). Fear can be converted into rage, and vice versa; and "the organism is often seen to oscillate between fear and rage until one or the other prevails" (Rado, 1956, p. 244).

supposed "that, in the infant, pain cannot be distinguished from anxiety" (p. 200). Separation and separateness is anxiogenic. Separation from or loss of an object can also be painful; separation or loss can cause psychic pain in association with longing for the object ("which is highly cathected with libido") (p. 201). However, anxiety, not pain, is felt in relation to the *danger* of object loss. NUNBERG (1955) thought that "psychic pain is the reaction to the trauma of real object loss" (arising "when a highly cathected libidinal tie between object and subject is broken"), whereas "anxiety is the reaction to the *danger* of object loss" ("when such a break is merely threatened") (p. 202).

3.5.1 Separation and threat of abandonment

Separation from the mother is a source of pain for the child. Mental pain caused by separation is associated with angry efforts to recover the lost object. Upon reunion, the child's hostility is "directed towards a parent or parent-substitute"; and it may take "the form of a reproach for his having been absent when wanted" (BOWLBY, 1973, p. 246). When the mother (attachment figure) is unresponsive or dismissive or otherwise preoccupied, the child may perceive a threat of separation or abandonment. Both actual abandonment and the *threat* thereof can cause intense distress and pain. In consequence of such pain, the person can feel "furiously angry with the person who inflicts it" (p. 249). Anger that is engendered by the threat of separation tends to be directed at the attachment figure. The threat of separation causes anxiety, too; and anxiety tends to aggravate hostility (p. 256). Hostility may increase when the child is anxious "that an attachment figure may be inaccessible or unresponsive when needed" (p. 255). An anxious child may be "furiously angry with a parent", at one moment, and "seeking reassurance and comfort from that same parent", at the next (BOWLBY, 1973, p. 253).

> In the schema proposed, a period of separation, and also threats of separation and other forms of rejection, are seen as arousing, in a child or adult, both anxious and angry behaviour. Each is directed towards the attachment figure: anxious attachment is to retain maximum accessibility to the attachment figure; anger is both a reproach at what has happened and a deterrent against it happening again.
> (BOWLBY, 1973, p. 253)

As emphasized by BOWLBY (1973), anger arising in situations of temporary separation has two functions: "first, it may assist in overcoming such obstacles as there may be to reunion; second, it may discourage the loved person from going away again" (p. 247). In other words, whenever separation is temporary, "anger is expressed as reproachful and punishing behaviour that has as its set-goals assisting a reunion and discouraging further separation" (p. 248). Similarly, when anger arises due to frustration of the child's attempts to induce the object to display affectionate or attentive behaviour (when the selfobject is temporarily unresponsive), anger has again both a coercive and punishing effect on the object. In either case (concerning the object's absence or unresponsiveness), the child's aggression can act as a "forceful reminder", aiming to ensure that the parent or parent-substitute "would not err again" (BOWLBY, 1973, p. 247).

Insecure attachment
Attachment behaviour, in its most primitive form, consists in approach locomotion towards the attachment object, which (like any goal-directed behaviour) can be combined, in the face of obstacles, with aggression. In humans, aggressive and coercive behaviour is used to control the attachment object (with the aim of preventing separation anxiety). BOWLBY (1973) pointed out that "hostile impulses, whether conscious or unconscious, directed towards a loved figure can greatly increase anxiety" (p. 255).[25] Renewed anxiety may cause renewed seeking of reassurance; and a balance may establish itself between 'anxious attachment' and 'angry attachment' (p. 253). Alternatively, a vicious cycle may develop, wherein "separation or rejection arouses a person's hostility and leads to hostile thoughts and acts; while hostile thoughts and acts directed towards his attachment figure greatly increase his fear of being further rejected or even of losing his loved figure altogether" (BOWLBY, 1973, p. 254).

> Thus not only may angry discontented behaviour alienate the attachment figure but, within the attached, a shift can occur in the balance of feeling. Instead of a strongly rooted affection laced occasionally with 'hot displeasure', such as develops in a child brought up by affectionate parents, there grows a deep running resentment, held in check only partially by an anxious uncertain affection.
> (BOWLBY, 1973, p. 249)

3.5.2 Loss of object

Separation can be permanent, rather than temporary, in which case it is designated as 'loss' (BOWLBY, 1973, p. 178). Object loss, too, causes mental pain. The individual may react with sadness, which "is the painful ego state created by ceasing to love", or with hate, which "can give some satisfaction and diminish the sadness through the pleasure in seeking revenge" (FEDERN, 1952, p. 262). In the latter case, instead of *suffering* the pain, the individual reacts with anger and aggression. BOWLBY (1973) thought that, following a bereavement, "anger and aggressive behaviour are necessarily without function" (p. 247). Nevertheless, anger aroused

---

[25] Whereby this anxiety could take the form of guilt, albeit an unconscious guilt (M. KLEIN).

by object loss appears to be linked to the individual's hopes of recovering or attempts to recover the lost object. During early phases of grieving, "a bereaved person usually does not believe that the loss can really be permanent; he therefore continues to act as though it were still possible not only to find and recover the lost person but to reproach him for his actions" (BOWLBY, 1973, p. 247).

> For the lost person is not infrequently held to be at least in part responsible for what has happened, in fact to have deserted. As a result, anger comes to be directed against the lost person, as well as, of course, against any others thought to have played a part in the loss or in some way to be obstructing reunion.
> (BOWLBY, 1973, pp. 247–8)

When a love object is lost and, hence, mental pain arises, "the affective value cathexis of the object is greatly increased, and attention is focused almost exclusively on the object because it is the key to the reattainment of the lost state of the self" (JOFFE & SANDLER, 1965, p. 159).[26] Mental pain arising from frustration of an object relation can be reduced by shifting the libido to a new object or by occupying "the mind with familiar objects which are known, either in reality or in fantasy, as pleasant; this form of reaction is called self-consolation" (FEDERN, 1952, p. 262), which may succeed in partly restoring the narcissistic cathexis of the self. Other ways of dealing with the pain of loss include 'repression' (which is the "easiest way to avoid any state of pain"), 'scotomization' ("which means unawareness of the entire sector of the world to which a frustrating object belongs"), 'denial' (in which the "individual sacrifices knowledge in order to gain quietude of mind"), and 'negation' (which "is the voluntary decision to refrain from any further investment of libido in the negated object") (FEDERN, 1952, pp. 263–4).

> From the point of view of the drives, the normal response to pain is aggression, directed at whatever is considered to be the source of the pain. ... Although clinically we may deal with states of object loss, we would stress again that what is lost in object loss is ultimately a state of the self for which the object is a vehicle. A failure to defend against pain, to discharge aggression adequately, or to reduce an intolerable 'cathexis of longing' may be followed by a depressive response.
> (JOFFE & SANDLER, 1965, p. 178)

---

[26] Similarly, the distress that a child experiences upon separation from his mother causes him to direct all "attention and activity ... toward restoring her presence" (JOFFE & SANDLER, 1965, p. 159).

3.5.3 Narcissistic injury

Narcissistic injury, a wound to self-esteem, causes pain and brings about an aggressive response directed at the person who is perceived to have inflicted the injury. Individuals with a narcissistic personality disorder readily respond with aggression to an injury inflicted upon their vulnerable self (KOHUT & WOLF, 1978). Narcissistic patients react offensively with anger and revengeful fantasies when they are frustrated in their need for constant admiration (REICH, 1960), given especially that constant admiration is of vital importance for maintaining the coherence and preventing the disintegration of their vulnerable self. *Aggressive rage* borne out of narcissistic injury is ostensibly aimed at restoring the empathic responsiveness of the selfobject surround and thereby restoring the cohesiveness of the self (KOHUT), but it is unlikely to be effective in this way.

> The offending selfobject or the totally ashamed self must be made to disappear, violently if necessary, even if the whole world will go up in flames.
>
> (WOLF, 1988, p. 79)

Aggressive responses to narcissistic injury may in some circumstances – when the cohesiveness of the self is not vitally threatened (i.e., when the self is not "injured in its very core" [WOLF, 1988, p. 79]) – succeed in reestablishing the respect and approbation of selfobjects, especially if aggressive impulses can be aim-inhibited (neutralized) to some extent and intertwined with exhibitionistic (attention-seeking) impulses.

> It is the loss of control of the self over the self-object that leads to the fragmentation of joyful assertiveness and, in further development, to the ascendancy and entrenchment of chronic narcissistic rage.
>
> (KOHUT, 1977, p. 130)

KOHUT (1971) considered that narcissistic rage may be a consequence of feelings of helplessness. Helplessness concerns the lack or loss of *control* over others (over the selfobject milieu). Others need to be controlled, so that the narcissistic individual can maintain his precarious self-esteem (narcissistic homeostasis) and save himself from *annihilation* (the imminent risk of which is signalled by 'disintegration anxiety'). Safety from annihilation depends on the individual's ability to control others in a manner that is not dissimilar to how he controls his movements (hence these others are termed 'selfobjects'[27]). If control is disrupted, that is, if the object does not behave

---

[27] A narcissistically cathected object (selfobject) is experienced by the subject as being under his control and constituting a part or function of himself.

98 Narcissism and the Self

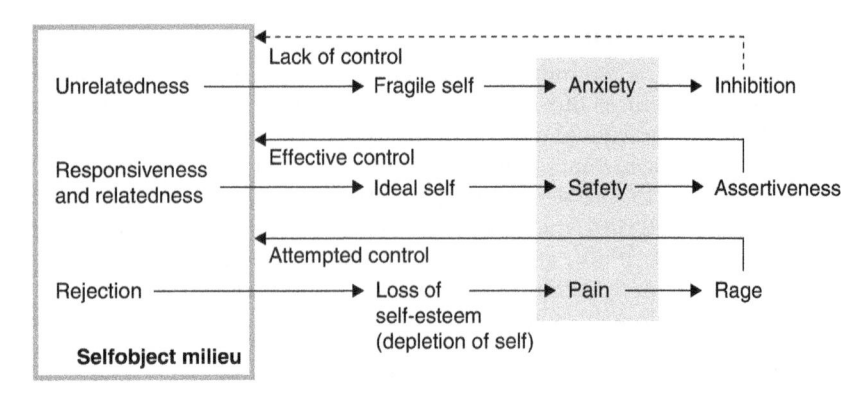

```
Unrelatedness ─────┬──── Lack of control ───────────────────────────────┐
                   │      Fragile self ────► Anxiety ────► Inhibition   │
                   │                                                     │
Responsiveness     ├──── Effective control                               │
and relatedness    │      Ideal self ─────► Safety ─────► Assertiveness  │
                   │                                                     │
                   ├──── Attempted control                               │
Rejection ─────────┘      Loss of ──────► Pain ──────► Rage
                          self-esteem
Selfobject milieu         (depletion of self)
```

Figure 3.6 Failure to control the selfobject milieu, perhaps due to neurotic inhibition, causes anxiety, whereas sudden loss of control causes pain and rage, the latter being an attempt to reestablish control

in expected ways (if the object does not provide the expected narcissistic supplies), disappointment arises; and if control is lost suddenly, narcissistic rage can ensue (MILLER, 1979). Loss of control over selfobjects, experienced as fragmentation of the self (disintegration anxiety), causes pain, which is rationalized as 'disappointment' or (if it cannot be rationalized) precipitates anger and aggression (Figure 3.6).

Narcissistic injury may be incurred and pain be suffered when one gains insight into a "discrepancy between an ego created in fantasy and the actual person" (FEDERN, 1952, p. 313) – "a discrepancy between the actual state of the self on the one hand and an ideal state of well-being on the other" (JOFFE & SANDLER, 1965, p. 156). Such discrepancy cuts off narcissistic supplies from the benevolent aspect of the superego (the unconscious omnipotent object acting in the role of the primary selfobject) or from one of its external representatives; but it does not necessarily cause disintegration of the self. An individual may "react to a painful discrepancy between the ideal self and his actual self by a response of angry resentment" (JOFFE & SANDLER, 1965, p. 171), as opposed to narcissistic rage. If, however, his angry and resentful efforts to *reassert himself* and regain the approval of his superego or one of its external representatives are repeatedly frustrated, depression may ensue.

3.5.4 Retaliation

Self-esteem or pride is linked, more or less securely, to an abstract territory or position we occupy in a landscape featuring limited narcissistic resources, a territory or position that is defined with reference to norms and laws that are applicable in this landscape. An insult to our self-esteem or pride – being humiliated or disrespected by others or having our legal rights infringed or position challenged – causes pain and mobilizes offensive aggression (territorial aggression). *Insults* directed at us represent infringements upon our territory to which we cannot but respond in an offensively aggressive way. Neurotic pride, as opposed to healthy self-esteem, renders us more vulnerable to humiliation, and "any hurt to our pride may provoke vindictive hostility" (HORNEY, 1950, p. 99). Thus, if pride (or self-esteem) is hurt, if a humiliation is experienced, "irrational hostility" ensues (p. 99). Importantly, vindictive or irrational hostility "has ingredients of derogation, contempt, or intent to humiliate", suggesting that what "operates here is the straight law of retaliation" (HORNEY, 1950, p. 99). Offensive behaviour, stemming from hurt pride, endeavours to restore pride, that is, to reclaim the lost territory or position, and to put the offender back into its former place *or below*.

> The need to save face is urgent, and there is more than one way of effecting it. ... The most effective and, it seems, almost ubiquitous one is interlinked with the impulse to take revenge for what is felt as humiliation. ... vindictiveness may ... be a means toward self-vindication. It involves the belief that by getting back at the offender one's own pride will be restored. This belief is based on the feeling that the offender, by his very power to hurt our pride, has put himself above us and has defeated us. By our taking revenge and hurting him more than he did us, the situation will be reversed. We will be triumphant and will have defeated him. The aim of the neurotic vindictive revenge is not 'getting even' but triumphing by hitting back harder. Nothing short of triumph *can* restore the imaginary grandeur in which pride is invested.
> (HORNEY, 1950, p. 103)

The power to retaliate "can itself be invested with pride" (HORNEY, 1950, p. 103), as illustrated by patients with antisocial or paranoid personality disorder. Conversely, an inability to retaliate can in itself constitute a humiliation. The neurotic person "suffers a double injury: the original 'insult' and the 'defeat', as opposed to the vindictive triumph", if "the situation or something within him does not allow him to retaliate" (p. 104). The particular situation may favour a fearful or submissive response over an offensively aggressive one, such as when the challenger is endowed with greater power or has the law of the land on his side.

3.5.5 Guilt and reparation

Frustration leads to hostile impulses against the frustrating object (which is then regarded as 'bad'). Hostility felt or expressed against the object is followed by *guilt*, which, in turn, arouses a 'need for punishment' and prompts repentance (FLUGEL, 1945). *Reparation*, the making good of the damage the individual has done to the object, is an alternative way of assuaging guilt, one that was stressed by MELANIE KLEIN (1937). Ultimately, reparation, like

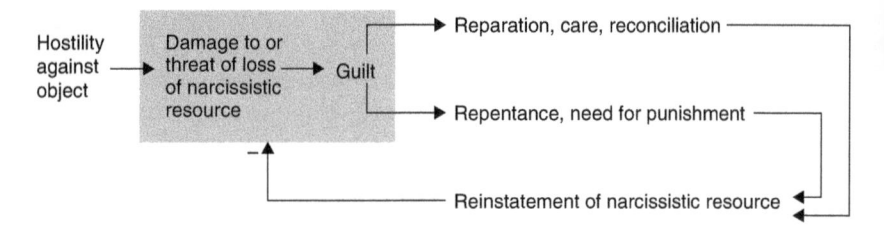

Figure 3.7 It may be through the reinstatement of a reliable source of narcissistic gratification that reparation of the object reassures the individual and assuages his guilt

repentance, is an attempt to reestablish the object's good will, that is, to reinstate the object as a source of narcissistic gratification (Figure 3.7).

Reparation involves the showing of love or care towards the object; or it requires work towards regaining the object's approval. FLUGEL (1945) observed that "creative and constructive work" is a "most satisfactory means of reassurance and of assuaging guilt" (p. 119); possibly insofar as constructive work involves cooperation (founded on 'social interest') and earns approval from colleagues and especially from authority figures onto whom the internal representative of the primary object (superego) is projected. KLEIN emphasized the role of useful work in assuaging unconscious feelings of guilt. The 'impulse of reparation' also comes to bear in many obsessional symptoms ("in which indeed there may be an alternation of symbolically destructive and symbolically restitutive thoughts and actions") (FLUGEL, 1945, p. 119).

3.6 Depletion

Relationships are central to efforts to maintain the 'feeling of safety' (and self-esteem) (SANDLER, 1960a). When the object is lost, the feeling of safety is lost, too, and psychic pain arises. Psychic pain (reflecting a lowering of self-esteem or a discrepancy between the actual state of the self and the ideal state of wellbeing) also ensues when sources of narcissistic supplies become inaccessible for other reasons (e.g., loss of status or prestige). The individual may react in a variety of ways to psychic pain, such as by acting out or consumption of drugs or alcohol. If these or other defensive measures fail, if the feeling of safety cannot be restored and psychic pain persists, a state of helplessness and depression[28] arises. 'Self states' of depletion (depression) or fragmentation arise from the *unavailability* of needed mirroring or ideal-

---

[28] Depression needs to be distinguished from sadness. Sadness seeks to procure sympathy; it contains a "craving for sympathy", an impulse to solicit "tender caresses" (MOORE, 1926, p. 189).

izable selfobjects, that is, from persistent failures by selfobjects to maintain the subject's previously cohesive self-experience. Self states of depletion may also arise from persistent failure to live up to the demands of the ego ideal, which implies that approval cannot be obtained internally from the superego (or externally from an authority figure onto whom the superego is projected). If narcissistic satisfaction fails to materialize time and again, as one's 'ego ideal' cannot be reached and "the claims on one's ego" cannot be fulfilled, then the ego will be "injured to the point of loss of ego libidinal cathexis" (FEDERN, 1952, p. 353) (loss of narcissistic cathexis of the self).

The ego uses objects for the maintenance of states of safety and wellbeing (narcissistic homeostasis); however, objects are, at the same time, from the point of view of the id, "the means whereby the drives attain discharge" (JOFFE & SANDLER, 1965, footnote on p. 158). This conflict as well as one's competition with others for the love and attention attainable from an admired object (a representative of the primary object, i.e., a projection of the superego) bear the potential for repeated narcissistic injuries. Repeated narcissistic injuries can produce persistent mental pain and lead to a 'depressive response' (JOFFE & SANDLER, 1965).

JOFFE and SANDLER (1965) considered the basic 'depressive response' to be "a state of helplessness, hopelessness, and resignation in the face of mental pain" (p. 155), "in which there is a feeling of being unable to restore a wished-for state" (the 'ideal self') (p. 156) (the state on which one's hopes of being lovable are pinned). Depression entails deeply held beliefs about being *worthless* (in the eyes of others or the superego) and unlovable, leaving the self in a state of utter narcissistic depletion. As the severity of depression fluctuates, a range of defence mechanisms directed against experiencing mental pain or a painful sense of depletion allow the temporary reestablishment of a fragile sense of safety (a transient restoration of self-esteem) (JOFFE & SANDLER, 1965). It is usually the maladaptive nature of these defences that perpetuates the depression (or that was responsible for its emergence in the first place).

4
Development

FREUD (1914) argued that libido, which is contained within the ego very early in life (primary narcissism), is invested in objects (object love) as the child develops but can be withdrawn from objects back into the ego (secondary narcissism). According to self psychology, narcissism and object love follow separate developmental lines (KOHUT, 1971, 1983). Narcissism does "not mature by turning into object love"; instead, it matures into "realistic self-esteem, the ability to be guided and sustained by realizable ideals", and the self's "ability to seek and find realistically available other selves who will sustain it by functioning as mirrors and ideals" (KOHUT, 1983, p. 396). Self psychology posits: that selfobject experiences (narcissistic experiences provided by objects) and the self are "the primary organizers of psychological development" (p. 101); that "the guiding force in human development is the need for connections to ... selfobjects" (p. 102); and that "the development of the self in relation to its selfobjects" provides "the supraordinate framework" for "the traditional drive-conflict-structural model of the mind" (P. TOLPIN, 1986, p. 102).

The child's 'nuclear self' comprises the 'grandiose-exhibitionistic self' ('narcissistic self') and the 'idealizing self'. The 'grandiose-exhibitionistic self' looks for the caregiver's *gleam* and *smile*, whereas the 'idealizing self' wants to be picked up and calmed down by the caregiver. The child acts "to elicit the needed responses of parents", whereupon "parents dispense selfobject functions that either consolidate or weaken the self of the child" (KOHUT, 1983, p. 392). The early maternal selfobject fulfils a *mirroring* function, whereas the early paternal selfobject serves as an *idealizable* target. In serving these functions, parental selfobjects enhance the child's self-esteem and support the development of a cohesive self (KOHUT, 1983). The cohesive self matrix that develops has two poles: the pole of ambitions and the pole of guiding ideals ('bipolar self') (KOHUT, 1977). Firstly, the approving and mirroring relationship with the usually maternal selfobject crystallizes into the pole of self-assertive ambitions, which becomes responsible for strivings for power and success later in life. Secondly, the pole of values and guiding ideals (reminiscent of FREUD's ego ideal) is consolidated by the relationship with the admired and idealized, usually paternal selfobject. As the child's needs to be mirrored and to idealize advance the development of the self, an intermediate area concerned with 'talents and skills' establishes itself between the two poles (the 'tension arc').

'Structure building', that is, the generation of a growth-facilitating matrix for the self, depends on optimal frustrations of the child's needs to be mirrored (approved) and to merge with the object of his idealizations. *Traumatic* disruptions in the links between self and early selfobjects "lead to defects or deficits in structure building, which, in turn, lead to *secondary* conflicts" (ORNSTEIN, 1983, p. 358). Relationships to archaic selfobjects in early childhood develop – through optimal frustrations and 'transmuting internalizations' – into mature self-selfobject relationships (KOHUT, 1983). Our need for selfobjects is enduring. Throughout life, we seek out, in our social surround, available mature selfobjects in order to establish empathically resonant relationships with them. Although "our selfobject experiences mature", "the archaic selfobject continues to exist in the depth of our psyche; it reverberates as an experiential undertone every time we feel sustained by the wholesome effect of a mature selfobject" (KOHUT, 1983, p. 398).

4.1 Symbiosis and attunement

Relatedness to others is a goal in itself, a need that exists for its own sake (FAIRBAIRN, 1952; SULLIVAN, 1953). Early relatedness is not secondary to some more primary physiological goal; it does not depend on the satisfaction of physiological needs (BOWLBY, 1973; STERN, 1985). There is a primal human wish to remain connected with the maternal object (ROTHSTEIN, 1979). The infant's wish to remain connected with the maternal object is developmentally continuous with the need to feel related to, and be included in, the family or group (SCHEIDLINGER, 1964). As the child develops, the need arises "for human-group-psychic-membership – that is, inclusion into the human group as a member with potentially sharable subjective experiences" (STERN, 1985).

KOHUT (1983) explained that to be "in the center of another individual's attention" and "in someone else's mind – to be listened to, watched, understood, thought about, remembered – is not 'neutral'; rather, it is one of the most subjectively meaningful experiences that a human being can have" (pp. 394–5). He went on to say that "the feeling of being within the compass of human empathy may indeed exert a beneficial, wholesome, and, under certain circumstances, 'therapeutic' effect" (KOHUT, 1983, p. 398). To be acknowledged, accepted, or approved is an experience that enhances self-esteem and maintains self-cohesion. A stable representation of the self signifies relatedness to others and connectedness to the selfobject milieu. Humans strive to establish and maintain conditions under which they feel related and accepted and under which they can reliably obtain narcissistic nourishment from selfobjects. The self is a measure of the effectiveness of control that is exerted over the selfobject milieu (on increasingly abstract levels as the personality develops). From the perspective of self psychology, "the primary psychological task from infancy on is the maintenance of the self" (M. TOLPIN, 1986, p. 124), a task that is rooted in the infant's needs for support, recognition, and confirmation. Psychopathology, especially pathology of the self, can become established later in life "when basic needs for support, recognition, and/or confirmation are not adequately met" in "childhood or even in adolescence" (M. TOLPIN, 1986, p. 125).

4.1.1 Primary narcissism

Primary narcissism is associated with the earliest developmental phases of 'normal autism' (lasting the first few weeks of life) and 'normal symbiosis' (from approximately the second to the forth or fifth month of life) (MAHLER, 1967, 1968; MAHLER et al., 1975). As the infant emerges from the phase of 'normal autism' (an initial phase of unrelatedness to the maternal object), he becomes dimly aware of the object. During the phase of 'normal symbiosis', the infant perceives gestalts of the mother's face and breast during hungry wakeful periods, but he does not yet differentiate between self and other. Despite having a dim awareness of the maternal object, he remains in a state of *union* with the object. The infant behaves as though he and his mother form a symbiotic 'dual unity' that has a common boundary; as though he and his mother were part of the same omnipotent, need-satisfying system. The infant at the stage of 'normal symbiosis' has a sense of omnipotence (MAHLER, 1967, 1968; MAHLER et al., 1975). The infant's experiences of his still poorly differentiated world is infused with a blissful sense of omnipotence, a sense that, later in life, can be approximated by extracting narcissistic supplies from selfobjects.

JACOBSON (1964) linked primary narcissism with undifferentiated self and object representations of the earliest infantile period. *Secondary narcissism*, the investment of 'libidinal energy' in the self-representation, presupposes that self and object representations have differentiated out of a previously fused representation. Infusion of the self-representation with good, libidinal energy is experienced as self-esteem (JACOBSON, 1964). Secondary narcissism also refers to the supportive, self-esteem-enhancing function *assigned* to objects (secondary narcissistic investment in objects). Thus, objects can be cathected (and used) narcissistically (insofar as they act as 'selfobjects') or libidinally (insofar as they are treated affectionately). In MAHLER's developmental phase of 'separation and individuation', the maternal object is narcissistically cathected (invested with 'narcissistic libido') but also invested with 'object love' (KOHUT, 1971).[1] Secondary narcissism emerges from primary narcissism as the infant, emerging from the symbiotic phase, enters the phase of separation and individuation (MAHLER, 1967). FREUD (1914) stated that the aim of narcissism is to *be* loved. By way of receiving love from objects, the individual approximates the lost state of primary narcissism. Secondary narcissism is a principal motivator for object relations. It aims at restoring feelings associated with primary narcissism via 'detours' involving object relatedness (FREUD, 1914) and connectedness to the social milieu, at large. For SANDLER and SANDLER (1978), object relationships serve the need for affirmation (narcissistic nourishment) and are a vehicle for attainment of the state of safety or wellbeing and ultimately for approximation of the feeling state of primary narcissism.

Self-esteem

RADO (1928) understood that the infant's enjoyment of the 'alimentary orgasm', which "satisfies the egoistic cravings of the little human being for nourishment, security and warmth", has a lasting influence that "radiates out into the whole of his later life" (pp. 53–4). Narcissistic gratification, being derived from 'alimentary orgasm', becomes a principle stimulus for "the ego's development in the direction of power and all the forms of activity by which it obtains gratification" (p. 54). It is "the peculiar quality of the experience" of 'alimentary orgasm' (primary narcissism) that persists in feelings of self-esteem, exaltation, and triumph (RADO, 1928). Self-esteem, according to FENICHEL (1946), is "the awareness of how close the individual is to the original omnipotence", to "the oceanic feeling of primary narcissism" (p. 40).

4.1.2 Primary identification

In the state of 'infantile dependence' (corresponding to the early *oral* phase of development), the infant's relationship with his object is characterized by 'primary identification' with the object (FAIRBAIRN, 1952, p. 47). Primary identification refers to "the cathexis of an object which has not yet been differentiated (or has been only partly differentiated)" from the self (p. 145). Primary identification with the object is equivalent to 'oral incorporation' of the object (p. 42). FAIRBAIRN (1952) stated that infantile dependence "is chiefly manifested in an attitude of oral incorporation towards, and an attitude of primary emotional identification with the object" (p. 145). In the state of infantile dependence, "separation from the object becomes the child's greatest source of anxiety" (p. 145); and primary identification ('oral

---

[1] Primary narcissism gives rise to a developmental line that is independent from the development of 'object libido'; secondary narcissism, developing in parallel with object libido, proceeds from archaic forms (exhibitionism and idealization) to higher forms and transformations (healthy ambition and idealism) (KOHUT, 1971).

incorporation') alleviates the anxiety of separation. For FAIRBAIRN (1952), narcissism was "a state in which the ego is identified with objects" (p. 83). While primary narcissism is a state of *identification* with the object (a state wherein self and object are fused or identical), in secondary narcissism there is an identification with an object that has been *internalized* (FAIRBAIRN, 1952, p. 48). Secondary narcissism, in other words, is the *relationship* with an object that has become *part* of the self.

MAHLER (1967, 1968), too, argued that, during the symbiotic phase of development, when primary narcissism prevails, the infant's relationship to his mother is characterized by 'primary identification'. In later phases, too, the infant restores his narcissistic balance by way of identification with the maternal object (A. REICH, 1953). Fusion with the powerful maternal object instils feelings of omnipotence in the infant. Identification involves *superficial* imitation of the object (A. REICH, 1953). Whatever is impressive is imitated. Identifications associated with superficial imitation are readily given up again. *Stable* identifications are required for the formation of the ego and the acquisition of new skills. For identifications to be lasting, long exposure to the imitated object is necessary, which presupposes stable attachment to the object (A. REICH, 1953).

4.1.3 Archaic narcissistic configurations

KOHUT (1971) initially proposed that early personality development proceeds from primary narcissism to "the two branches of narcissism itself" (p. 219). These two branches – the two 'archaic narcissistic configurations' establishing themselves in early childhood – are the 'grandiose self' and the 'idealized parent imago'. The 'grandiose self' has "subject quality", whereas the 'idealized parent imago' is an archaic selfobject (p. 33). 'Grandiose self' (the narcissistic subject) and 'idealized parent imago' (the narcissistic object) are cathected with 'narcissistic libido' (in form of 'grandiose-exhibitionistic libido' and 'idealizing libido', respectively). Having been exposed to unavoidable disturbances in "the psychological equilibrium of primary narcissism", the child assigns "all bliss and power" to the object and attempts "to maintain a continuous union with it" (p. 37). The grandiose self and the idealized parent imago are mechanisms that come into being in order to regain and approximate the primary narcissistic experience, the sense of omnipotence and perfection that the infant derived from being merged with the mother (KOHUT, 1971).

> The equilibrium of primary narcissism is disturbed by the unavoidable shortcomings of maternal care, but the child replaces the previous perfection (a) by establishing a grandiose and exhibitionistic image of the self: *the grandiose self*; and (b) by giving over the previous perfection to an admired, omnipotent (transitional) self-object: *the idealized parent imago*.
> (KOHUT, 1971, p. 25)

4.1.4 Empathic responsiveness

Tensions in the child's psychological balance "are, under normal circumstances, empathically perceived and responded to by the self-object" (KOHUT, 1977, p. 85). The selfobject (mother) senses the child's anxiety, distress, or rage (processing an 'affect signal', "not panic"), whereupon she establishes vocal and tactile contact with the child, which "the child phase-appropriately experiences as a merger with the omnipotent self-object" (p. 86). The child undergoes an "empathic merger with the self-object's mature psychic organization", allowing him to participate "in the self-object's experience of an affect signal instead of affect spread" (p. 87). The next step consists in "need-satisfying actions performed by the self-object" accompanied by the return of a shared sense of calmness (p. 87). At the preverbal stage of development, "parental in-tuneness with the content of the baby's mind (the baby's needs and wishes) is indeed the prerequisite for the formation of the baby's rudimentary self" (KOHUT, 1977, p. 150).

The self of the child (or that of a narcissistically disturbed patient) is "precariously established", so that the self "depends for the maintenance of its cohesion on the near-perfect empathic responses of the self-object" (KOHUT, 1977, p. 91). The child phase-appropriately (or the narcissistic patient pathologically) "demands perfect empathy" and "total control over the self-object's responses" (p. 91). A "faulty, nonempathic response of the self-object" causes the child (or patient) to respond with rage (KOHUT, 1977, p. 90). A defective, precariously established self is readily "endangered by the flawed responses of selfobjects throughout life"; it defends itself against a threat to its continued existence that arises "when the gap between the need for sustenance from selfobjects and the actual performance with which they respond becomes too great" (KOHUT, 1983, p. 413).

Normally, the child's "archaic needs for the responses of archaic selfobjects" (p. 77), for perfect mirroring and merger responses, develops into an "an empathic intuneness between self and selfobject on mature adult levels" (p. 66) and an "ability to identify and seek out appropriate self-objects" that present themselves in the person's "realistic surroundings" (KOHUT, 1984, p. 77).

4.1.5 Maternal preoccupation

'Primary maternal preoccupation' refers to the preoccupation of the mother with the needs of her infant in the first few weeks of the infant's life (WINNICOTT, 1963). At this time, the infant is in a state of 'absolute dependence', he seems to be a part of the mother; and even the mother can be said to be in a dependent state, as she has suspended her own life, being fully devoted to the care of her infant. Being closely protected and cared for by his mother, the infant lives in a 'subjective world' on to which external reality does not impinge. Living in a 'dream world while awake', he experiences feelings of omnipotence (WINNICOTT, 1989). By way of 'primary maternal preoccupation', the mother provides a 'facilitating environment' for her infant's emotional development (WINNICOTT, 1963). As recognized by MAHLER and WINNICOTT, a libidinally available mother at the earliest stages of development allows for the further unfolding of the infant's innate potentials.

To be 'good enough', the mother has to intermittently identify herself with her infant, to make the infant the object of her preoccupation. If there is unreliability on part of the mother or on part of the 'environmental provision' to meet the infant's need for identification, for being the object of her preoccupation, then the infant will feel 'unthinkable anxiety' (WINNICOTT, 1989). Availability of the mother for intermittent identification with her infant (her reliability in this regard) is a prerequisite for the infant's growing up with a sense of never having been significantly let down. If the mother fulfils this vital function, her infant can develop a capacity to rely on her, on the world in general, and, ultimately, on himself (WINNICOTT, 1989).[2]

Reverie

The distressed infant needs to feel that the mother understands and can make sense of his experiences (BION, 1962). The mother's reverie allows the infant to transform his distress, which is accompanied by an urge to act out, into a sense of being understood and knowing of himself. If the mother has capacity for reverie then she can make sense of the infant's distress by means of 'correlation'. The infant reintrojects a sense of being understood, which allows him to integrate his anxieties and give them meaning. If the mother's capacity for reverie breaks down and she does not accept the infant's projections, the infant cannot gain an understanding of himself and his distress, and he is left with a 'nameless dread' (BION, 1962). WINNICOTT's 'unthinkable anxiety' and BION's 'nameless dread' are related to KOHUT's 'disintegration anxiety'.

4.1.6 Mirroring of the self

In the state of 'relative dependence' (lasting from about the sixth month to the second year of life), according to WINNICOTT (1963), the child experiences anxiety in relation to his growing awareness of his dependence on the mother. The state of 'relative dependence' is associated with the process of 'mirroring'. The child at this time needs to be recognized as a being; he needs to be seen or understood (WINNICOTT, 1962). When the mother looks

---

[2] If the mother is not 'good enough' in this regard, the child has to defend against this 'unthinkable anxiety'; he may develop a schizoid personality structure (and even be at risk of developing schizophrenia later in life). His personality organizes 'towards invulnerability', so that the child, and later the adolescent and adult, must never experience the 'unthinkable anxiety' again (WINNICOTT, 1989).

at her infant, her appearance is related to what she sees in him. Her pleasure in her infant is reflected in her face. The infant, in turn, sees the mother's joy and feels good about himself. It is as if the infant – in looking at the mother's face – is looking at *himself*, like in a mirror. What the infant sees when looking at his mother's face is him*self*; and he thus arrives at a first sense of his self (WINNICOTT, 1962).

The process of 'mirroring', as conceptualized by WINNICOTT, involves mutual relatedness and shared empathy. Mirroring plays an important role in the early formation of the self. The mother, tolerating and containing the infant's feeling states, communicates to him an acceptance of his feelings and hence an acceptance of himself; the infant not only experiences a sense of containment of his distress but also a sense of *being accepted*. Winnicott thought that the better the process of mirroring (and the more the mother gives her infant opportunities to experiment), the more the infant's developing sense of self becomes imbued with aliveness and spontaneity, with a willingness to express himself spontaneously. The infant develops a 'true sense of self', a sense of the potentiality of his spontaneous expressions. Conversely, if maternal mirroring is insufficient, a false sense of self develops and the infant's potentialities for spontaneity and experimentation are choked.

The mother's successful adaptation to the infant's gestures and her consistently meeting the infant's spontaneous gestures gives the infant a sense of omnipotence; the infant begins to believe in an external reality that behaves as if it were under his control (WINNICOTT, 1960b). If the mother consistently fails to meet the infant's gestures, then the infant does not develop a sense of omnipotence; instead, he develops excessive compliance with the mother's behaviour and thereby adopts a 'false self', a state of isolation from his spontaneous core. The 'false self' hides the 'true self', that is, the infant's ability to act spontaneously and genuinely (WINNICOTT, 1960b). The person becomes unable to be genuine in relationships later in life.

Mutual cueing

'Mutual cueing' is a form of mother–infant interaction wherein the infant gives cues as to his needs and tensions, and the mother responds to these cues selectively (MAHLER, 1968). In the process of mutual cueing, the mother provides a 'mirroring frame of reference', to which the primitive self of the infant adjusts. The infant gradually alters his cueing behaviour in accordance with the mother's responses (MAHLER, 1968). Outside needs and tensions, beginning in the symbiotic phase, mother and infant engage in 'mutual libidinal cueing' (MAHLER, 1967). The libidinal signals the infant *receives* provide a narcissistic mirror in which he can see himself reflected, in which his identity is beginning to be delineated. If the mother's responses are hostile or unpredictable and the mirroring frame of reference is unreliable, then the infant develops weak self-esteem (MAHLER, 1968).

Mirror stage

In LACAN's (1966) 'mirror stage' of development, the infant's relationship to 'the other' is one of 'primary identification', a relationship in which self and other are indistinguishable (and notions of self and other are meaningless). Primary identification is based on recognition of primitive imagos (gestalts), recognition that gives rise to *reflexive* (instinctive) transformations in the infant (on 'the imaginary' plane). In the mirror stage, the infant is presented, for the first time, with an image of his own unity and coherence, an image that is reflected back to him by his parent (LACAN, 1966). This 'mirror image', reflected back to the infant, consists of the parent's *approving* gestures and her *recognition* and *acknowledgement* of the child. The mirror image is invested with libido and becomes the core of the child's ego and the later sense of self (LACAN, 1966; FINK, 1997).

4.1.7 Affectionate interactions

BALINT (1952) emphasized the concept of 'primary object love' over that of primary narcissism. The infant has intimacy needs (wishes for intimate association) and is object-seeking in the earliest phase of life. However, satisfaction of intimacy needs (wishes to love) implies that narcissistic needs (wishes to be loved and accepted) are met, too. BALINT (1968) spoke of a striving "to establish or re-establish an all-embracing harmony with one's environment, to be able to love in peace" (p. 69).

SULLIVAN (1953) similarly stressed the infant's need for 'tenderness'. The human infant engages in affectionate (tender) interactions with his mother from an early age. As human beings, we are innately disposed to express tenderness and engage in tender and affectionate interactions, although we can do so only in "a relatively anxiety-low atmosphere" (CHRZANOWSKI, 1973, p. 140). Affectionate interactions are rewarding; tenderness between mother and child "facilitates mutual satisfaction" (p. 140). Similarly, exchange of affectionate displays in adult dyadic encounters is satisfying (rewarding); and it is securing, too. Indeed, the "pursuit of satisfaction and security" is one of the "basic motivational forces in interpersonal situations" (CHRZANOWSKI, 1973, p. 142).

SCHECTER (1973) argued that reciprocal social stimulation during early social play provides a basis for the formation of the infant's emotional attachment to his mother. Moreover, reciprocal social stimulation and responsiveness during early social play have important consequences for the adult's capacity to form mutually satisfying relationships. Early reciprocal stimulation is one of "the precursors to all human communication"; mutual playfulness "prepares the individual and group for communication, language, and collaboration" (SCHECTER, 1973, p. 25).[3]

---

[3] Consistent with ADLER's conceptualization of 'social feeling'.

Playfulness, according to SCHECTER (1973), "constitutes a remarkably easy vehicle for the mutual exchange of affectionate and exuberant affects" (p. 24). Playful interactions (playful social reciprocity) allow the infant to learn that he can evoke a social response at times when his physiological needs are satisfied. The infant's realization that he can evoke playful patterns of response from significant others leads to the development of a 'sense of social potency' (SCHECTER, 1973). The infant's confidence that he can produce a social response is internalized as self-esteem. The initially omnipotent sense of potency has to be frequently frustrated, so that the child can acquire a "sense of the realistic limits of his powers" and learn about "the differentiation of his self and the other" (SCHECTER, 1973, p. 26).

4.1.8 Intersubjective relatedness

The capacity for 'intersubjective relatedness', arising after the seventh month of life, allows for the sharing of inner and subjective psychic experiences with an other (STERN, 1985). Intersubjective relatedness entails "the creation of mutually held mental states", "the joining of subjective psychic experience" (p. 127), a joining that is deliberately sought. Intersubjective relatedness between self and an other rests on capacities for sharing a focus of attention, attributing intentions and motives to the other, and sharing affective states (STERN, 1985). The sharing of affective states ('affect attunement') "is the most pervasive and clinically germane feature of intersubjective relatedness" (p. 138).[4] Attunements "occur largely out of awareness and almost automatically" (p. 145). Affect attunement involves "the performance of behaviors that express the quality of a shared affect state without imitating the exact behavioral expression of the inner state" (STERN, 1985, p. 142). Affect attunement is brought about less by imitation and more by mutual induction of innate 'expressive movements' (which act as releasing 'stimulus situations' for the other's affective displays).

As the infant experiences 'intersubjective relatedness' to the mother, he develops a subjective sense of self (STERN, 1985). The 'subjective self' is predicated on experiences of shared feelings, shared attention, and joint intentions with an other (the mother). The 'subjective self' is, in other words, organized by inner and subjective experiences shared with others. The self is also indissolubly linked with safety, the safety implicit in being *affectively attuned* to others. STERN (1985) regarded intersubjective relatedness as a basic psychological need; and it may be equivalent to the need for security. Intersubjective relatedness is reinforcing because it meets security

---

[4] Establishment of affect attunement allows infants to recast their situation and shift the focus of attention to what is important. When infants encounter a novel or uncertain situation, "they look towards mother to read her face for its affective content, essentially to see what they should feel, to get a second appraisal to help resolve their uncertainty" (STERN, 1985, p. 132).

needs; "intersubjective success can result in enhanced feelings of security", whereas "minor failures in intersubjectivity can be interpreted, experienced, and acted upon as total ruptures in a relationship" (STERN, 1985, p. 136).

> The more one conceives of intersubjective relatedness as a basic psychological need, the closer one refashions clinical theory toward the configurations suggested by Self psychologists and some existential psychologists.
>
> (STERN, 1985, p. 136)

4.2 Individuation and attachment

Once the developmental period of symbiosis, during which the gratifying aspects of the mother were experienced by the infant as a part of himself, has come to an end, the infant becomes aware of his mother's separateness and perceives separations from his mother. Separation from the mother stimulates the development of attachment behaviour. Attachment behaviour aims at establishing not only proximity but also relatedness to others ('intersubjective relatedness'). Formation of the sense of self, too, can be regarded as an expression of attachment behaviour.

Separation anxiety (being associated with feelings of helplessness and vulnerability) is implicit in the perception of a separate self and in the awareness of the mother's separateness (ROTHSTEIN, 1979). The self as a psychological structure, *a manifestation of secondary narcissism*, compensates for anxieties experienced in association with either separation from the mother or unrelatedness to the social milieu. Separation anxiety is the motivating force for secondary narcissistic investments in the self and its objects; it is a developmental spur for the formation of the sense of self (ROTHSTEIN, 1979). *Separateness and self are necessarily related, because the self compensates the insecurity (helplessness) that is implicit in separateness.*[5] Connectedness to objects and the social milieu, established and maintained by way of secondary narcissistic investments in, and extraction of narcissistic supplies from, objects and the selfobject milieu, remains liable to disruptions, giving rise to recurrent, partially subliminal experiences of separation anxiety throughout life.

4.2.1 Separation

The symbiotic phase of development is followed, around the age of four or five months, by the phase of 'separation-individuation', during which the infant establishes a sense of separateness from (and relatedness to) the

---

[5] As WINNICOTT (1969) saw it, the maternal ego at first implements the infant ego and makes it powerful and stable; and, as the infant's ego becomes free of the mother's ego support, the infant achieves differentiation into a separate self.

external world, ultimately leading to the development of a sense of identity (MAHLER, 1972; MAHLER et al., 1975). The experience of being basically separate from the world is taken for granted but has profound psychological implications. Awareness of separateness dawns, and the process of the 'psychological birth of the individual' starts to unfold, as the symbiotic phase of development – the 'blissful state of wellbeing' during which the mother is part of the self – comes to an end. The child gradually exchanges the omnipotence (and 'oceanic feeling') associated with the symbiotic 'dual unity' for the pleasure to be found in separateness and autonomy. The child becomes able to function separately from the mother, although still having to do so in her presence and with her emotional availability. The process of separation and individuation extends to the age of about 2½ to 3 years. Successful separation (achievement of a sense of separateness from the mother) and individuation (an early awareness of being oneself, of being one's own individual) imply that a clearly differentiated representation of the self, as distinct from object representations, has been formed (MAHLER, 1972; MAHLER et al., 1975).

During the phase of separation-individuation, the infant is confronted, time and again, with minimal frustrations and threats of object loss, while also developing pleasures in independent functioning. As the child becomes aware of his limitations and dependence, his self is gradually divested of omnipotence and overestimation (MAHLER et al., 1975). The child's self-esteem may suffer critical deflation, but identification with an emotionally available mother and internalization of a good child–mother relationship restore self-esteem and allow for further reduction of feelings of omnipotence. Nevertheless, the child's longing for the lost 'ideal state of the self' (JOFFE & SANDLER, 1965), in which the child was merged with the mother, remains a spur for development. The individual, in consequence of his psychological birth, becomes engaged in a life-long struggle against isolation, an eternal struggle that involves a longing for the 'ideal state of self', representing the state of fusion with the symbiotic mother (MAHLER, 1967, 1968, 1972).

Rapprochement

In the rapprochement subphase (18 to 24 months) of the separation-individuation process, the child has to gradually realize that he can no longer participate in the perceived omnipotence of the parents, that the parents are separate individuals with their own interests. He must also gradually and painfully give up the delusion of his own grandeur (MAHLER, 1967, 1972). The giving up of feelings of grandiosity and omnipotence during the second half of the second year goes along with an increased sense of dependency, increased suffering of separation anxiety, and employment of clinging behaviours, which conflict with, and thus balance, the child's strivings for separateness and autonomy. Having become accepting of his physical separateness from his mother, the child turns back to her. He may be constantly concerned with her whereabouts.[6] During the rapprochement subphase, the child alternates between demanding or protecting his autonomy and demanding or seeking the mother's closeness. MAHLER (1972) saw in the rapprochement subphase the origin of man's eternal struggle against fusion and isolation.

> One could regard the entire life cycle as constituting a more or less successful process of distancing from and introjection of the lost symbiotic mother, an eternal longing for the actual or fantasised 'ideal state of self', with the latter standing for a symbiotic fusion with the 'all good' symbiotic mother, who was at one time part of the self in a blissful state of well-being.
>
> (MAHLER, 1972)

4.2.2 Modification of omnipotence

When the child, in the course of his development, loses the belief in his omnipotence, he starts to believe that his parents are omnipotent instead. Realizing "that his actual powers are limited", "he delegates his secret omnipotence to his parents" (RADO, 1956, p. 301). Having had "to renounce his belief in his omnipotence", the child "considers the adults who have now become independent objects to be omnipotent, and he tries by introjection to share their omnipotence again" (FENICHEL, 1946, p. 40). The child participates in their omnipotence whenever he feels loved by them. Narcissistic feelings of wellbeing, revived in this way, "are felt as a reunion with an omnipotent force in the external world" (FENICHEL, 1946, p. 40).

For the child to gradually modify his feelings of omnipotence, maternal availability and responsiveness need to be 'optimal', which means that narcissistic injuries have to be experienced by the child in the context of maternal love, empathy, and understanding (ROTHSTEIN, 1979). Assignment of omnipotence to the parents is a normal phenomenon; reversal of the process and assignment of omnipotence back to the self is defensive. If the infant's capacity to tolerate frustration is low (but not too low), then he may use omnipotence as a mechanism of tolerating frustration (BION, 1962). The omnipotent infant is self-sufficient and independent in his phantasy. Omnipotence provides a substitute for negative realization; instead of realizing the 'no breast', the infant feels he does not need the object (BION, 1962).

---

[6] Anxious reactions to strangers are pronounced during the rapprochement subphase. Moreover, the child feels an increased need to share with his mother every new experience, skill, and acquisition (MAHLER, 1972; MAHLER et al., 1975).

4.2.3 Mature dependence

Infantile dependence on an object entails primary identification with the object, whereas 'mature dependence' means relating to an object that is independent and differentiated from the self (FAIRBAIRN, 1952). As infantile dependence gradually gives way to mature dependence, the original object relationship based upon identification is gradually abandoned, and an object relationship based on differentiation from the object is adopted. The original 'incorporating' or 'taking' attitude is replaced by the 'giving' attitude characteristic of mature dependence. FAIRBAIRN (1952) suggested that the distinction between infantile dependence and mature dependence corresponds to FREUD's (1914) distinction between narcissistic object choice and anaclitic object choice.

The transition from infantile dependence to mature dependence is gradual and may remain incomplete (FAIRBAIRN, 1952). There is, to a greater or lesser degree, a reluctance on part of the child to abandon the state of infantile dependence and the attitude of taking. The child experiences a conflict between separation from the object and progression to mature dependence, on the one hand, and a regressive urge "to achieve reunion with the object", on the other (FAIRBAIRN, 1952). Renunciation of infantile dependence and separation from the object raise anxiety, specifically "a fear of isolation". For the child to be able to "gradually to renounce infantile dependence without misgiving" (p. 39), he has to obtain conclusive assurance that he is genuinely loved by his parents. Such assurance enables the child "to depend safely upon his real objects" (p. 39). In the absence of such assurance, renunciation of infantile dependence would be fraught with too much anxiety. The child would be compelled to maintain relationships with *internalized* (incorporated) objects, as his relationship with external objects (objects that are well differentiated from the self) would be "fraught with too much *anxiety over separation*" (FAIRBAIRN, 1952, p. 39).[7]

4.2.4 Depressive position

MELANIE KLEIN (1932, 1946) observed that, from the beginning of life, the infant experiences love and hate towards the breast. The infant defensively creates an image of a 'bad breast' (using 'projection') that allows him to focus his destructive impulses. Attacks on the frustrating breast lead to fears of persecutory counterattacks. The stronger the infant's hostile feelings, the greater is the extent of paranoid fear during this early phase of development

---

[7] Frustration of the "desire to be loved as a person and to have his love accepted is the greatest trauma that a child can experience" (FAIRBAIRN, 1952, pp. 39–40). The child who experiences such a trauma is extremely reluctant to abandon infantile dependence. Persistence of identification *at the expense of differentiation* engenders "a markedly compulsive element" in his attitude towards objects (FAIRBAIRN, 1952) (due to the fact that objects then constitute a vital part of his self).

(ROSENFELD, 1965, p. 203). The bad breast becomes the prototype of all later persecuting objects. The 'good breast', the recipient of the infant's libidinal impulses, is kept separate from the bad breast. The state in which libidinal and destructive impulses are confused is "associated with extreme anxiety" (p. 53), consistent with the defensive nature of splitting and projection. The infant remains in the 'paranoid-schizoid position' for the first three to five months of his life. The 'depressive position' is introduced through a lessening of splitting "so that libidinal and aggressive impulses can be brought closer together" (p. 62) (and guilt and depression can be experienced [p. 203]). The depressive position extends over the remaining months of the first year (ROSENFELD, 1965).

In the depressive position, the infant integrates split representations (and introjects them securely). He recognizes that the object on which he depends is a *whole* object; and, along with the integration of his ego, he develops concern for his object (KLEIN, 1946; SEGAL, 1989a). The infant learns to withhold aggressive impulses towards his mother so as to not be abandoned by her. Although he fears the aggression of his objects, his greatest fear in the depressive position is that his destructive impulses could destroy the object ('depressive anxiety'). His anxiety is ultimately concerned with the possibility of loss of the object, consistent with the profound dependence of the immature human infant on his mother. Thus, the emphasis shifts from the fear of being destroyed by a persecuting object to the fear of losing or destroying the good object on whom the infant depends (KLEIN, 1932, 1946; ROSENFELD, 1965, pp. 70–1).

In the paranoid-schizoid position, the infant deals with disturbing feelings and destructive impulses by projecting them into a split-off aspect of the object. The mother receives the infant's projections and alleviates the infant's anxieties through her reactions towards him, especially through her emotional 'understanding' of him. As a result, the infant introjects an object that can contain and modify his distress (BION, 1959, 1962). Introjection of a containing object, in turn, leads to the development of the infant's own ability to contain and work through his distress. Even though the infant overcomes paranoid-schizoid mechanisms of defence, these mechanisms remain latent and can reemerge at times of heightened 'depressive anxiety' concerned with dependence on a whole object (SEGAL, 1989a). *It can be supposed that the whole of man's psychic structure is based on the tension between paranoid fear (the fear of others' aggression) and the need to be accepted and thus protected by others, the latter developing from a need to be in the presence of the mother via a need for her love to a need for approval and social recognition. This tension is played out in the depressive position.*

4.2.5 Basic trust

The infant externalizes pain and internalizes pleasure, including the pleasure of being the object of the mother's sensitive care and being in the focus of her devoted attention. Introjection of 'outer goodness' turns this into an 'inner certainty' (ERIKSON, 1950, p. 223), a sense of 'basic trust', which is an important foundation for the child's further psychosocial development. The infant's sense of basic trust establishes itself against a background of "a sense of having been deprived", "of having been abandoned", of a "universal nostalgia for a paradise forfeited";[8] and it has to be maintained against this background throughout life (ERIKSON, 1950, p. 224).

Basic trust – the ultimate foundation for the evolvement of 'ego identity' (ERIKSON, 1950) – is a minimum condition for *survival*, a condition that is lacking in those who are predisposed to psychotic illness. ERIKSON (1950) saw that "the bizarreness and withdrawal in the behaviour" of those who suffered a psychotic break "hides an attempt to recover social mutuality" (p. 223), the mutuality of trust. Those who habitually withdraw into schizoid and depressive states are afflicted with a life-long weakness of basic trust; and reestablishment of a state of trust is "the basic requirement for therapy in these cases" (ERIKSON, 1950, p. 223).

4.2.6 Attachment behaviour

The infant is biologically programmed to respond to separation from the mother with anxiety and searching behaviours (BOWLBY, 1977, 1988). Attachment refers to the infant's tendency to maintain proximity to the caregiver, to keep her available or in sight. Importantly, attachment behaviour establishes or maintains proximity to the caregiver *selectively*. Being attached to the cargiver, the infant becomes upset when she leaves, seeks her comfort when feeling threatened, and becomes fearful in the presence of strangers. Anxiety, associated with insecurity, causes renewed seeking of contact with the attachment object, which, if successful, renews the infant's security. Reunion with the caregiver after separation is reassuring, resolves anxiety, and invokes a pleasant affect. Emotional attachment to a caregiver allows the infant not only to obtain nourishment and protection but also to receive stimulation for further cognitive and social development (BOWLBY, 1977, 1988).

Emotional attachment to the mother figure is evident when the infant, by the seventh or eighth month, shows "clear differential responses to mother as against others in being held or soothed, in being played with or simply approached" (SCHECTER, 1973, p. 25). By seven or eight months of age, the infant's protesting at the disappearance of social stimulation ceases to be related to any social partner but "appears to be related to a specific attachment to one or more persons" (p. 28). The constancy of the attachment to the mother is revealed by the fact "that she usually continues to be preferred and sought after though she may be a source of frustration, disappointment,

---

[8] This is the first 'epigenetic crisis' in the lifecycle (ERIKSON, 1950).

and even cruelty" (Schecter, 1973, p. 26). Thus, during the latter half of the first year, the infant's "attachment to a mother figure is becoming steadily better organized", and so is his "withdrawal from a fear-arousing situation" (Bowlby, 1973, p. 122). By 12 months of age, a clear-cut attachment has been formed, and the infant "has become able so to organize his behaviour that he moves simultaneously both away from one type of situation and towards another type" (Bowlby, 1973, p. 122), from anxiety implicit in exposure to strangers (or strange situations) to the safety provided by the attachment object.

Secure attachment

By the age of two to three years, the child becomes less dependent on the physical presence of his attachment figure, who can now be *trusted* to provide protection when needed. The child has a need for independence that gets stronger as he gets older. Secure attachment to the caregiver is a prerequisite for the child's ability to periodically separate from her and find opportunities to develop his competence and independence. Secure attachment arises in the context of responsive and sensitive parenting, and provides the basis for successful social and intimate relationships in later life. Attachment behaviour remains evident throughout life, yet the manner in which attachment is brought about differs between individuals in accordance with their early life experiences.

> ... because models of attachment figures and expectations about their behaviour are built up during the years of childhood and tend thenceforward to remain unchanged, the behaviour of a person today may be explicable in terms, not of his present situation, but of his experiences many years earlier.
> (Bowlby, 1973, p. 256)

There are several aspects of parental behaviour that critically contribute to the infant's secure attachment and normal personality development. Firstly, the mother is innately responsive to the infant's care-seeking behaviour and separation distress. Secondly, "a certain amount of hostile control", exerted by the caregiver, is required to "assure normal socialization" of the child (Benjamin, 1996, p. 188). Hostile control in the form of blaming or ignoring is highly aversive to the child, ensuring that the child learns to "behave in ways that will help avoid" experiences of being blamed or ignored (Benjamin, 1996, p. 188). Thirdly, the caregiver provides the child with a secure base from which to explore his environment. The child's innate exploratory behaviour alternates with attachment behaviour. The task of the caregiver is to permit or encourage the child's exploratory behaviour and to actively intervene whenever the child 'heads for trouble' (Bowlby, 1977).

4.2.7 Internal working models

Object relations theory emphasizes the role of libidinal and aggressive drives in the formation of (intertwined) self- and object representations (KERNBERG, 1976). However, self- and object representations also contain and organize attachment (self-preservative) behaviours played out between self and object (GOODMAN, 2002). In other words, objects can be considered as targets not only for libidinal and aggressive drives but also for the self-preservative drive (SILVERMAN, 1991). 'Internal working models' refer, according to GOODMAN (2002), to the organization of self- and object representations as well as affective (drive-related) and defensive processes invoked during interactions between self and object (p. 145). Attachment theory locates internal working models in close vicinity of safety needs (BOWLBY, 1973, 1988), and thus of the self-preservative drive (SILVERMAN, 1991). Attachment or safety needs operate in tandem with libido and aggression to shape internal working models and thus the child's capacity to make accurate appraisals of interpersonal situations (GOODMAN, 2002).

Secure attachment to the caregiver enables the child to form an internal working model of a responsive caregiver and a *secure self* (BOWLBY, 1973, 1988). Internal working models formed in normal development operate as safety devices; they are models that children form "of their parents as sources of comfort and security and of themselves as worthy of love" (GOODMAN, 2002, p. 199). More generally, internal working models (or internal object relations) support connectedness to the social surround by encoding representations of others as *being related to the self*. A stable self structure is always also a representation of others who are responsive and caring to the self and who can be *trusted*.

Psychic proximity

The infant's propensity to form attachments provides the organizing template for personality development (BENJAMIN, 1996, p. 213). Personality development involves the formation of "internal working models of the attachment relationships" (p. 213). The child develops an internal working model or 'internalized representation' of the primary caregiver (attachment object) in three different ways: (i) imitation of the caregiver's behaviour, (ii) recapitulation of the caregiver's behaviour when the caregiver is absent, and (iii) 'introjection'. 'Introjection' is evident "when the child treats him/herself as did the attachment object" (BENJAMIN, 1996, p. 185).

The 'internalized representation' of the attachment object (or, rather, of the attachment relationship) allows the child to establish 'psychic proximity' to the attachment object at times of anxiety. BENJAMIN (1996) thought that the child, and later the adult, can bring about 'psychic proximity' by activating this internalized representation, that is, by (i) acting like the internalized attachment object, (ii) acting as if the internalized attachment object were present, or (iii) treating the self as would the internalized attachment object. Similarly to the effects of physical reunion with the mother, "psychic proximity is reassuring and invokes pleasant affects and cognitions" (p. 189). Through 'psychic proximity', the child, and later the adult, can simulate *conditions for receiving love* from attachment objects or from their derivatives later in life (BENJAMIN, 1996).

> By conjuring up a mental picture of the mother, the child internally 'captures her' and in so doing invests her with a psychic permanence of sorts. The inner image acts as a substitute while the mother is gone and mitigates the panicky feelings her absence might otherwise produce. Much of the child's attempt to 'preserve' the mother are wrapped up in efforts to create an inner maternal presence.
> (CASHDAN, 1988, p. 40)

The self-regulating other

STERN (1985) argued that the infant forms a representation of the 'self-regulating other' (a concept similar to 'selfobject'), the counterpart of "the forming sense of self" (p. 241). Episodes of *being with* the 'self-regulating other' (and episodes of 'lived experience', in general) become episodes for memory (episodic memories). Episodes of interactive experience (with the 'self-regulating other') generalize across several instances and are consolidated into a mnemonic representation that STERN (1985) called 'representation of interactions that have been generalized' (a concept similar to BOWLBY's [1973, 1988] 'working models'). The 'representation of interactions that have been generalized' is retrieved whenever one of the key attributes of the encoded type of interpersonal interaction is encountered (and acts as a retrieval cue) (STERN, 1985). Consequently, the currently unfolding interactive episode is apprehended in the light of this memory, and so the infant encounters an 'evoked companion'. The 'evoked companion' is an actual experience of being with the 'self-regulating other'.[9] Evoked companions "represent the accumulated past history of a type of interaction with an other";[10] and "they serve a guiding function in the sense of the past creating expectations of the present and future" (p. 115). When the infant engages with an evoked companion, "the memory of past experiences with

---

[9] 'Lived experience' (current experience) is, to a large extent, an instantiation in the form of an activated memory, although each 'lived experience', being different in some way from similar past experiences, also serves to update the memory (the 'representation of interactions that have been generalized').

[10] Similarly, 'internal object relations' (comprising self- and object representations in the context of affective interactions) are structures in the mind that *organize interpersonal experience*. We enact object relations by treating others as replicas or instances of internal objects, and treating them in a way that corresponds to an internal object relation (KERNBERG, 1996, p. 115).

self and other in exploratory contexts" creates trust and *security*, allowing the infant to feel trustful and *secure* in his explorations (STERN, 1985, p. 118).[11]

4.3 Exhibitionism and idealization

The need to be noticed and admired is an expression of secondary narcissism. The 'narcissistic self', differentiating out of the child's primary narcissism, represents the child's desire to be looked at and admired (KOHUT, 1966). The notion of 'narcissistic self' refers to the child's grandiosity and encapsulates his exhibitionistic tendencies. Expressing exhibitionistic urges, the child seeks to elicit "the gleam in the mothers' eye" and to thereby maintain his own 'narcissistic libidinal suffusion' (KOHUT, 1966). The child's exhibitionism is the origin of the adult's ambitions. The adult's enjoyment of his successes signifies satisfaction of narcissistic-exhibitionistic tendencies. The adult's disappointments about his failures are tinged with shame and anger. If narcissistic-exhibitionistic urges, that is, impulses to attract others' attention and admiration, are thwarted, shame arises. The 'ego ideal' offsets narcissistic vulnerability and offers protection against shame arising from the inevitable thwarting, in the absence of the ego ideal, of exhibitionistic urges (KOHUT, 1966). Failure to live up to or identify with the ego ideal, that is, failure to meet the expectations of the superego (the internalized parent imago), means that the individual's exhibitionistic or ambitious efforts or pursuits are inappropriate and cannot be met with approval or admiration.

The 'nuclear self', according to KOHUT (1971), is formed by the responsiveness of selfobjects, the mother in particular. The 'nuclear self' has aspects of both self and object, namely the 'grandiose self' (which KOHUT [1966] formerly called the 'narcissistic self') and the 'idealized parent imago'. The 'grandiose self' ('grandiose-exhibitionistic self') arises from relating to a selfobject that empathically mirrors the child's grandiose-exhibitionistic displays. The mother approves or admires the child's displays (the expressions of his grandiose self); and the child delights in being approved or admired. By relating to a responsive mirroring selfobject, the child's grandiose self is established and strengthened (KOHUT, 1977). The 'idealized parent imago' is established by relating to a selfobject that is the target of, and as such permits, the child's idealizations. The child delights in *being part of* his idealized (perfect and omnipotent) mother or father. The idealized parent

---

[11] STERN (1985) thought that, in the actual presence of the other, "the infant needs only recognition memory to call to mind the evoked companion that is stored in memory, since the actual episode is happening now before the infant" (p. 116). When a lived episode of being with an other is recalled in the other's absence, cued *recall memory* (evocative memory) is required, of which infants are capable from the third month of life and which "improves greatly toward the end of the first year of life" (STERN, 1985, p. 117).

imago is established as a cohesive psychic configuration by the selfobject that responds empathically and with enjoyment to the child's idealization and merger (KOHUT, 1971, 1977). Thus, selfobjects respond to and meet the child's mirroring and idealizing needs and thereby confirm the child's self. As the self matures, the grandiosity and exhibitionism of the grandiose self are tamed and transformed into healthy ambition, while the idealized parent imago is transformed into an internal structure that supplies healthy ideals and idealism ('ego ideal' [KOHUT, 1966] or 'idealized superego' [KOHUT, 1971]). The grandiose self and idealized parent imago are somewhat antithetical psychic configurations, but together they form a 'tension arc' that propels the individual to action: the individual is *driven* by his ambitions while being *led* by his ideals (KOHUT, 1977).

4.3.1 Attention seeking

Infants, by the age of around four months, make attempts to attract others' attention; they call out when they are not in the focus of attention (reviewed in REDDY, 2003). After the middle of their first year, infants perform actions such as 'showing off', 'clever actions', 'clowning', and 'teasing' in order to attract others' positive attention in the form of *praise* or laughter. Having become able to follow others' attention to objects or events in the world, infants from about the age of 12 to 14 months attempt to actively direct others' attention to the world (reviewed in REDDY, 2003). REDDY (2003) concluded that "what appears to be developing is an awareness of the objects to which others' attention can be directed: the first of these is the self, followed by what the self does, then what the self perceives, and then what the self remembers". Being an object of others' attention is what lies at the heart of self-awareness. REDDY (2003) pointed out that "the self is emotionally aware of being an object to others before it is an object to itself"; "before the infant has a conception of him or herself, he or she is aware of being an object to others".

4.3.2 Ambition and self-esteem

The child's exhibitionism and grandiosity are coupled with his "undisguised pleasure in being admired" (KOHUT, 1971, p. 25). The child's 'grandiose-exhibitionistic urges' obtain satisfaction by inducing maternal mirroring responses (KOHUT, 1977, p. 14). The mother's mirroring responses to the child's narcissistic-exhibitionistic displays ("the gleam in the mother's eye"), her 'intuneness' with the child, confirm the child's 'sense of worthwhileness' (p. 9). The mother's mirroring responses and her empathic responsiveness (in context of her relation to the child) form and strengthen "the child's cohesive grandiose-exhibitionistic self" (p. 185). The 'grandiose-exhibitionistic self' (narcissistic self) – one of the two polar areas of the self (the other one being the 'idealized parent imago') (p. 49) – is the seat of 'grandiose-exhibitionistic urges'. Mirroring responses that signal acceptance and approval gradually transform the child's 'nuclear grandiosity' into 'nuclear ambitions' in the second to the fourth year of life (p. 179). The grandiose-exhibitionistic self is the area of the bipolar self where basic ambitions, originating in the child's 'grandiose-exhibitionistic urges', are laid down (KOHUT, 1977, p. 49).

Appropriate responses by the mirroring selfobject to the child's grandiose-exhibitionistic displays channel these displays into *realistic* directions (KOHUT, 1977). Appropriate mirroring responses coupled with 'optimal frustration' of the child's narcissistic needs consolidate the self into a "storehouse of self-confidence and basic self-esteem that sustains a person throughout life" (KOHUT, 1977, p. 188). 'Optimal maternal acceptance' is a precondition for the transformation of the child's "crude exhibitionism and grandiosity into adaptively useful self-esteem and self-enjoyment" (KOHUT, 1971, p. 284).

Inasmuch as the child comes "to recognize that the claims of the grandiose self are unrealistic" (KOHUT, 1971, p. 229), "the exhibitionism and grandiosity of the archaic grandiose self are gradually tamed" (p. 27). Tamed exhibitionism and grandiosity become the "instinctual fuel for our ego-syntonic ambitions and purposes" (p. 27), while the infantile pleasure in being admired becomes a 'nonerotic satisfaction' with ourselves and our achievements. The child's "need for omnipotent certainty concerning the results of his efforts and for unlimited success and acclaim" is transformed into "ego-syntonic attitudes of persistence, optimism, and reliable self-esteem" (p. 151). Self-esteem carries "the earmark of the original narcissism" (p. 108). The original narcissism, which pervades early childhood, "infuses into the central purposes of our life and into our healthy self-esteem that absoluteness of persistence and of conviction of the right to success" (KOHUT, 1971, p. 108).

Assertiveness

The preoedipal child learns to overcome separation anxiety, which is implicit in the perception of the mother's separateness, by *eliciting* her smiling response (ROTHSTEIN, 1979) and generally by *controlling* her affectionate responses through his exhibitionistic displays. The child's healthy exhibitionism is complemented by healthy assertiveness vis-à-vis the mirroring selfobject (KOHUT, 1977, p. 171), so that the child can control the selfobject's mirroring responses. Aggression is an integral part of normal, socially adaptive, nondestructive assertiveness, an assertiveness that is brought to bear when controlling the emotional responsiveness of the selfobject, "whenever optimal frustrations (nontraumatic delays of the empathic responses of the self-object) are experienced" (p. 121). Aggression is "a constituent of the firmness and security with which [the child] makes his demands vis-à-vis self-objects who provide for him a milieu of (average) empathic responsiveness" (KOHUT, 1977, p. 118).

In the oedipal phase, the child's assertiveness becomes competitive aggressiveness in pursuit of healthy goals. Competitive aggressiveness is "directed at objects that stand in the way of cherished goals"; it is "a normal healthy reaction to obstacles that hinder the attainment of the person's aims in the world" (WOLF, 1988, p. 78).

4.3.3 Transmuting internalization

An eight-months-old infant, seeking to reconnect with his mother, that is, with his mirroring selfobject, expects her "to light up and applaud" in response to his "playful overtures" (M. TOLPIN, 1986, p. 123). The infant expects the selfobject to be magically in tune with him; however, the mother's attentions to the child are often imperfect or delayed. If the infant initially fails to reestablish the self–selfobject tie, he experiences, at first, surprise and puzzlement (p. 121) and, with repeated and protracted failure, "anger, anxiety, and/or depletion" (p. 126). Inevitable disruptions in the self–selfobject tie activate the infant's 'self-righting tendencies'; the infant "visibly recovers resolve and approaches the mother anew" (p. 121). The infant is engaged in a "repetitive cycle of establishment, disruption, and subsequent reestablishment of the self–selfobject tie that provides the developmental context for the silently working process of transmuting internalization" (p. 124). The early self, emerging in relation to its selfobject environment, is "a baseline of cohesion that is repeatedly disturbed, only to be restored and thereby transformed as development proceeds" (M. TOLPIN, 1986, p. 124).

'Optimal frustrations' compel the child to internalize aspects of his selfobjects (KOHUT, 1971, 1977). Narcissistic expectations are withdrawn from selfobjects and transformed into inner structures that perform mirroring functions for the self (KOHUT, 1971, 1977). In the process of 'transmuting internalization', the mother's soothing and comforting ministrations are gradually *internalized*. Transmuting internalization allows the child (or the narcissistic patient in psychoanalysis) to acquire functional capacities "involved in the maintenance of self-cohesion, self-continuity, and self-esteem – capacities which the [child] had formerly relied upon the selfobject to provide" (STOLOROW, 1983, p. 293). As functions performed by selfobjects are assimilated into the child's 'self-structure', self-esteem can be regulated, to some extent, independently of selfobjects. Developmental achievements acquired through transmuting internalization include self-regulatory capacities, such as capacities for empathetic self-observation and self-understanding (STOLOROW, 1983, p. 295).

The self can now be considered, by an 'observing ego', as an object, whereby the 'observing ego' may perform a function previously performed by selfobjects. The developmental achievement is a capacity to momentarily "consider oneself as if you were someone else", "to see oneself or to stand apart and scrutinize *as if* one were two individuals" (GOLDBERG, 1983, p. 300). Consideration of one's self-image in fantasy, coupled with an *appreciation* of this image, implies that the self is being looked at *and smiled at* by the self-identified-with-the-mother. Separation anxiety stimulates identification with the maternal object and internalization of the maternal smile (ROTHSTEIN, 1979). The maternal smile is transformed into 'the self smiling at itself', which can be regarded as the 'prototypical secondary narcissistic representational relationship' (libido flowing into the ego). The 'state of the self smiling at itself', in which the child's self is identified with the mother, calms the terror inherent in the perception of separateness (separation anxiety) (ROTHSTEIN, 1979).

The self-image entails a sense of worthwhileness, that is, a narcissistic expectation, the expectation of approving or comforting responses; or it may entail a memory of narcissistic gratification, a memory of the effect of such gratification on the self. In either case, the source of expected or attained narcissistic gratification is hidden from consciousness (and can be conceptualized as the unconscious 'omnipotent object').

4.3.4 Responsiveness of the selfobject milieu

As development proceeds, dependence of feelings of security on the actual experience of mirroring selfobject responses decreases, and sources of narcissistic supplies are controlled on increasingly abstract levels. On an archaic level, there is an "anxious clinging to the archaic selfobject" (KOHUT, 1984, p. 209) (attachment motivated by separation anxiety). On the archaic level, the need for security cannot be satisfied unless empathic selfobject responses can be elicited, whereas, on a mature level, "the experience of the availability of empathic resonance" is "the major constituent of the sense of security" (KOHUT, 1984, p. 77). On the mature level, 'cohesion of the self' and the sense of security do not depend on the actual experience of approving or accepting signals from the selfobjects milieu; instead, they depend on the *availability* of such responses, that is, on the *responsiveness* of the selfobject milieu.

As STOLOROW (1986a) put it, "the responsiveness of the surround, whether in childhood or in analysis, is experienced subjectively as a vital, functional component of a person's self organization" (pp. 47–8). Furthermore, while "in the more archaic states the tie to the object is required for the maintenance of fundamental self-regulatory capacities – that is, for sustaining the basic structural integrity and stability of self experience" (p. 277), in mature states, "the tie to the object is required primarily for the affective quality of self experience, not for its essential coherence", which means that disturbances in the tie of the self to its selfobject "produce only fluctuations in self-esteem" (STOLOROW, 1986b, p. 277).

4.3.5 Merger with the idealized parent imago

Children have an innate desire to admire, to idealize, and to merge (identify) with a selfobject. Early in the child's life, the mother's "holding and carrying allows merger-experiences with the self-object's idealized omnipotence" (Kohut, 1977, p. 179). Merger can take place with an "empathic omnipotent idealized self-object" (p. 85), a role played usually first by the mother and then by the father. The responsive father has to "allow himself to enjoy being idealized by his son" (p. 12). Idealization results in an enhancement of self-esteem "via the temporary participation in the omnipotence of the idealized self-object" (p. 13). The child's "relation to the empathically responding self-object parent who permits and indeed enjoys the child's idealization of him and merger with him" establishes "the child's cohesive idealized parent-imago" (p. 185). The 'idealized parent imago', representing the wish to merge with an idealized selfobject, is one of the two polar areas of the 'nuclear self', the other one being the 'grandiose-exhibitionistic self' (Kohut, 1977, p. 49) ('narcissistic self' [Kohut, 1966]).

Earlier, Kohut (1966) had argued that, in consequence of disturbances in the infant's primary narcissism (due to delays or imperfections of the mother's ministrations), primary narcissism differentiates into the 'narcissistic self' and 'idealized parent imago'. The 'narcissistic self' represents the child's desire to be looked at and admired, whereas the 'idealized parent imago' is what the child looks at and admires. The child admires and looks up to his parent. The rudimentary representation of the parent is imbued with power and perfection; the parent is idealized (Kohut, 1966).

The idealized parent imago and its cognitive elaborations later in life are "objects that are experienced narcissistically" (p. 33); they are not 'objects' in the strict psychoanalytic sense (Kohut, 1971). Objects in the strict psychoanalytic sense are those 'childhood images' that are invested with object-instinctual cathexes, namely love ('object love' or 'object libido') and hate, yet the idealized parent imago and its derivatives are cathected with 'narcissistic libido'. Under optimal developmental conditions, the child's idealizations, which retain their narcissistic character, will coexist and become integrated with object-instinctual cathexes. 'Idealizing narcissistic libido' (which is invested in selfobjects) "plays a significant role in mature object relationships, where it is amalgamated with true object libido" (Kohut, 1971, p. 40).[12]

4.3.6 Attainable ideals

The child's "archaic wish to merge with an omnipotent self-object" is transformed, in the course of development, into 'attainable ideals', which, along with 'realistic ambitions', underpin the individual's capacities to obtain narcissistic sustenance and maintain self-esteem (Kohut, 1977, p. 82).

---

[12] The normal state of being in love not only involves investment of 'object libido' into the object but also has a narcissistic component, which "does not detach itself from the object cathexes but remains subordinated to them" (Kohut, 1971, p. 76).

Transformation of the archaic wish for merger (with the omnipotent selfobject) into a healthy devotion to ideals (i.e., the formation of 'nuclear idealized goal structures' [p. 179]) takes place from the fourth to the sixth year of life (Kohut, 1977).

The child's archaic idealization of his parent (the 'idealized parent imago') is developmentally continuous with the "idealization of the parental objects of the late preoedipal and of the oedipal periods" (Kohut, 1971, p. 40). By identifying with an idealized object, the child can participate in narcissistic supplies available to that object. During the oedipal period, the child tends to identify with the parent of its own sex; although the oedipal girl may identify with mother or father. Idealization by the child of the paternal selfobject allows the child "to acquire (i.e., to integrate into his own self) certain of his father's abilities" (Kohut, 1977, p. 11). The child acquires the ability to act out "derivatives of his grandiose and exhibitionistic strivings" "in an aim-inhibited, socially acceptable way" (p. 11). Identification with and enactment of culturally cherished ideals ensures that the child receives parental approval, that is, narcissistic supplies. Indeed, "the acquisition of civilized habits bestows a feeling of heightened self-esteem" (Kohut, 1977, p. 112).

Frustration of the child's idealizing needs plays a role in this process. Disappointment in the parental imago, which may be due to the parent's absence, leads to decathexis of the parental imago, which, in turn, promotes its internalization (Kohut, 1966). The object alternatingly emerges from the child's rudimentary self and submerges again into the self, whereby such alternation correlates with intermittent, nontraumatic frustrations of the child's narcissistic demands (Kohut, 1966). The 'idealized parent imago', when taken into the self, is the point around which the 'ego ideal' crystallizes. Decathexis of the parental object representation, which increases most notably during the oedipal period, is coupled with introjection of idealized qualities of the object, gradually leading to the formation of the ego ideal. The ego ideal, once acquired, guides and controls exhibitionistic impulses pursued by the 'narcissistic self' (Kohut, 1966).

The ego ideal can be regarded as the counterpart of the superego, insofar as the 'superego' stands for the internalized omnipotent object. The 'idealized superego' (which is contrasted with the more primitive 'persecutory superego') represents a "massively introjected internal replica of the oedipal object" (Kohut, 1971, p. 47). The oedipal object's "loving-approving and angry-frustrating aspects" are internalized and "become the approving functions and positive goals of the superego, on the one hand, and its punitive functions and prohibitions, on the other" (pp. 47–8). The superego is "invested with narcissistic instinctual cathexes" (p. 40); and, as a result of "oedipal disappointment in the parent" (p. 41), it is idealized (and rendered omnipotent). If idealization of the superego remains incomplete, the person "will forever search for external ideal figures from whom he wants to obtain the approval and the leadership which his insufficiently idealized superego cannot provide" (KOHUT, 1971, p. 49).[13]

4.3.7 Selfobject failures

Persistent failure of selfobjects to empathically respond to the child's mirroring and idealizing needs, that is, failure to mirror the child's grandiose self or to foster the child's idealizations, can cause developmental fixation on an immature self. KOHUT (1971) suggested that "early disturbances in the mother–child relationship (due to emotional coldness of the mother, the absence of consistent contact with the mother, the baby's congenital emotional coldness, the mother's withdrawal from an unresponsive baby, etc.)" can result in a fixation on "the archaic (pre) stages of the grandiose self" or "a failure in the establishment of an idealized parent imago" (p. 301). Healthy ambitions and attainable ideals would not become established in the personality. Moreover, narcissistic needs would remain immoderate (and the self precarious) if internal self-esteem-regulating and anxiety-reducing structures did not develop. Persistent 'selfobject failures' on part of the parents, that is, "a lack of mirroring, a lack of alter-ego support, or an unavailability of idealizable selfobjects", would cause "fragmentation, weakness, or disharmony of the self" (KOHUT, 1983, p. 407).

Deficient mirroring

Maternal interest in and encouragement of the child's grandiose-exhibitionistic expressions together with optimal frustrations of these expressions are required to allow the child to develop a stable self-representation that becomes a reliable source of self-esteem, whereas traumatic or persistent failures on the part of the mother result in a developmental fixation. If the mother's mirroring responses are insufficient, the child will remain "fixated on archaic forms of exhibitionism" (KOHUT, 1977, p. 9). Development would be "stunted by the child's lack of the needed admiring responses from his mother" (KOHUT, 1971, p. 301). A disorder of the self can ensue if, in early childhood, "tentative attempts at standing, walking, running, or swimming led selfobjects to withdraw their attention or become anxious rather than react with pride" (KOHUT, 1983, p. 407). Persistently disregarding or rejecting responses to the child's exhibitionistic and grandiose displays or massive disapproval or rejection by selfobjects endow the child, for the rest of his life, with a 'precarious self' that compulsively seeks to induce the mirroring selfobject responses that he lacked in his childhood, a self that is sensitive to rejection and prone to fragmentation (KOHUT, 1977). Not only would

---

[13] Due to insufficient idealization of the superego during the oedipal period, the patient's "narcissistic equilibrium is safeguarded only through the interest, the responses, and the approval of present-day (i.e., currently active) replicas of the traumatically lost self-object" (KOHUT, 1971, p. 55).

archaic exhibitionism persist, exhibitionistic perversions can arise when, as a result of protracted failure of the selfobject to phase-appropriately mirror the child's grandiose-exhibitionistic behaviour, the 'broad psychological configuration' of "healthy assertiveness vis-à-vis the mirroring self-object" breaks up (Kohut, 1977, p. 172).[14]

Grandiose self

Infantile grandiosity, persisting into adulthood, can cover over a precarious self. While narcissistic-exhibitionistic impulses form the drive aspect of the 'narcissistic self', fantasies of power and greatness form its ideational content (Kohut, 1966). The grandiose self is designed to protect against the fear of abandonment (separation anxiety) and to keep alive the illusion of self-sufficiency and omnipotence, which, on a deeper level, represents the wish for refusion with the omnipotent object. Reliance, into adulthood, on infantile grandiosity is predicated on early, preoedipal fears of abandonment (Miller, 1979). If infantile grandiosity, that is, the grandiosity of the 'narcissistic self', is insufficiently modified in the course of personality development, the adult remains liable to be narcissistically injured and to experience shame and embarrassment, since, due to irrational overestimation of the self, his ambitions are likely to be thwarted (Kohut, 1966). Thus, the success-driven person, who experiences intense 'narcissistic-exhibitionistic tensions', is prone to fail and to experience shame as a result.[15]

Stalled development can resume if, in psychoanalysis, the patient is allowed to develop a 'mirroring transference', in which his infantile exhibitionistic and grandiose self can be expressed safely without fear of rejection (Kohut, 1971). In psychoanalysis, the patient can bring his unconscious grandiose self out of repression; or, in Winnicott's terms, the patient's 'true self' can emerge tentatively from behind his 'false self'. Both Kohut and Winnicott understood that traditional psychoanalytic interpretation of the narcissistic patient's need for approval or for idealization of the analyst is likely to elicit narcissistic rage. Destructiveness and rage arising in the psychoanalytic situation in response to 'empathy failures' from the side of the analyst are "revivals of reactions to empathy failures from the side of the self-objects of childhood" (Kohut, 1977, p. 115). Empathy failures leave the patient feeling abandoned by the analyst; and as the patient withdraws from the narcissistic transference, his grandiose self is repressed again.

---

[14] Even though the child's 'central self structures' can be 'injured' by a 'lack of maternal responsiveness', the self defect can be *compensated* "in relation to the idealized self-object", when the child turns to the idealized father and acquires certain of his abilities (Kohut, 1977, p. 11).

[15] Narcissistic mortification in response to the thwarting of ambitions is defensively replaced by renewed overestimation of the self in fantasy, leading to oscillations in self-esteem (Kohut, 1966).

4.3.8 Overindulgence

When mirroring responses by selfobjects are not combined with 'optimal frustration' of narcissistic needs, personality development is impaired, as was described already by ADLER. ADLER (1938) argued that "whenever a mother is too lavish with her affection and makes behaviour, thought, and action, even speech superfluous for the child, then the child is more readily inclined to develop" a selfish and exploitative attitude; the child "will continually press always to be the centre of attention" (p. 113). Children who are spoilt and pampered develop "an inordinate and insatiable craving for affection" (ADLER, 1927, p. 43). They expect and demand "that their mother should pay attention to them at every possible opportunity" (ADLER, 1938, p. 42).

Pampered children "will develop egoistic, envious, jealous traits to a high degree of intensity" (p. 114); they "will never co-operate", expect everything, and give nothing (ADLER, 1938, p. 115). They will develop a tendency to exploit and oppress others; "[t]heir life becomes bound up in a struggle to keep the affection of others by fair means or foul" (ADLER, 1927, p. 44). A pampered child will "regard it as her right to suppress other people and always be pampered by them, to take and not to give" (ADLER, 1938, p. 114). If, on the other hand, the child is not overindulged and, at the same time, deeply "impressed with the reliability and the partnership of others", then she will be endowed with 'social interest'; she will be able to give and "be inclined for communal life" (ADLER, 1938, p. 113).

Pampered children are not only greedy but also impatient; they lack perseverance and have "a tendency to passionate outbursts" (ADLER, 1938, p. 114). Pampered children are resistive to "any change in a situation that gratifies their wishes" (p. 42). Their "resistant actions and reactions" to any change "achieve their ends" "either actively or passively" (p. 42). Whichever method of resisting change and maintaining conditions conducive to the satisfaction of their craving for affection is successful (is rewarded and thus reinforced), it provides "a model which is followed in later years" (p. 43); it becomes part of the 'life style' of the adult (ADLER, 1938).

4.4 Compliance and approvability

The self, as SULLIVAN (1953) recognized, consists of reflected appraisals from significant others. The child sees himself, and feels about himself, as his parents see and feel about him. The child's self-esteem is "connected with his capacity to avoid doing what the parents do not want him to do" as well as "with his capacity to do what his parents want him to do" (ARIETI, 1970, p. 21). Experiences in infancy, firstly, of anxiety coinciding with the mother's tenseness and forbidding gestures and, secondly, of reward associated with the mother's soothing ministrations lead to the formation of a 'self-dynamism'[16] (SULLIVAN, 1953). The infant's 'bad me' personification, corresponding to a personification of a bad mother, organizes his interpersonal experiences of anxiety, while his 'good me' personification, corresponding to the good mother personification, organizes his interpersonal experiences of reward. Self-dynamism, therefore, consists of manoeuvres that, while 'expending energy', shift the infant from 'bad me' to 'good me' and, concurrently, transform the interpersonal matrix from a threatening or rejecting to an *accepting* and *approving* one. SULLIVAN's (1953) 'self-system', a concept that reflects the central role he assigned to the self in the regulation of social behaviour, emphasizes that the subject's attempts to maintain satisfactory relations with his fellows, that is, to maintain narcissistic homeostasis, are linked to the subject's adherence to "prescribed ways of doing things" (p. 168).

While the 'good self' is a state in which the infant feels accepted (by the 'good object') and narcissistic sustenance is freely available to him, 'true self' and 'false self' refer to predominant, habitual ways of attaining maternal acceptance and upholding the narcissistic homeostasis (they are, in other words, two forms of self-dynamism). The false self *has to be* good and acceptable; the true self *is* good and acceptable, by being oneself, by 'expending energy' effortlessly and *spontaneously*. 'True self', according to WINNICOTT (1960b), refers to an experience of aliveness and spontaneous comfort. An *excessive* need for compliance with maternal wishes or excessive demands to 'entertain' the mother (to provide her with narcissistic gratification) result in the systematic suppression of the true self and adoption by the infant of a 'false self'. The 'false self' is based on compliance, on the imperative need to 'be good'. The mother's 'moral code' sets the infant on a path of developing a 'false' self and, thereby, blocks his normal development, which is to say that adaptation to reality comes at a cost of hiding the 'true self', of suppressing true talents. The 'false self' lives a life that is separated off from the person's 'true self' (WINNICOTT, 1960b, 1971, 1989).

4.4.1 Fear of punishment

Punishment involving exposure to vocal or gestural expressions of threat (aggressive intention movements) from a conspecific is innately aversive. If a stimulus (discrete or contextual) is associated with such punishment, then this stimulus becomes a conditioned, *fear*-inducing stimulus. Exposure to a context in which parental punishment was incurred evokes in the child a 'fear of punishment' (RADO, 1956). This fear of punishment "exerts a restraining influence upon his activities" (p. 224). The (contextualized) recollection of exposure to a punishing or threatening gesture or vocalization (which

---

[16] SULLIVAN's (1953) concept of 'dynamism', in general, refers to an *enduring pattern* of energy transformation.

may involve "the inner reproduction of the original auditory experience", a voice saying 'don't do it!' [p. 226]), too, may act as a conditioned fear stimulus, with the effect of restraining the child's behaviour and defeating his temptation. With progressive 'automatization', the fear of punishment becomes the 'fear of conscience' (p. 225). The faintest recollection of disapproval has, by then, become self-criticism; and parental restraint has turned into self-restraint (RADO, 1956). In a parallel development, parents "reward the child's obedience with loving care" (p. 224) and praise. With progressive 'automatization', parental reward becomes "the self-reward of self-respect and rising moral pride" (p. 225). These mechanisms, shaping obedience, continue to work into adulthood "as fear of social punishment, and as rising self-respect and pride in social recognition" (RADO, 1956, p. 224).

4.4.2 Conditionality of love

FREUD (1930) thought that the child's motivation for yielding to parental commands and expectations and for foregoing the satisfaction of his drives is to be found in his helplessness and dependence on his parents for survival. For this reason, the child fears to lose the love of his parents. The child learns that what is 'bad' is whatever causes him to be threatened with the loss of parental love (FREUD, 1930). Losing the love of someone on whom one is dependent is evolutionarily tantamount to one's annihilation. *It is the fundamental dependence of the child on the mother that renders us, for the rest of our lives, fearful of losing the approbation of our social surround and that makes us work towards establishing and maintaining that approbation, whereby the approval or recognition we obtain from others is essentially equivalent to the love of the mother.* In abstract terms, by gaining recognition and approval from our environment, we secure for ourselves the love of the omnipotent object.

> The small child loses self-esteem when he loses love and attains it when he regains love. That is what makes children *educable*. They need supplies of affection so badly that they are ready to renounce other satisfactions if rewards of affection are promised or if withdrawal of affection is threatened. The promise of necessary narcissistic supplies of affection under the condition of obedience and the threat of withdrawal of these supplies if the conditions are not fulfilled are the weapons of any authority ...
> (FENICHEL, 1946, p. 41)

Early self-esteem depends on the *receipt* of external narcissistic supplies (praise and affection) (FENICHEL, 1946). Narcissistic supplies are accessible under certain conditions; and the child has to adapt to, and to learn to control, these conditions. Obedience, that is, fulfilment of parental demands and expectations, raises self-esteem, precisely insofar as it creates or maintains conditions conducive to receiving narcissistic supplies from the parents. The need to maintain conditions favourable to receiving narcissistic supplies leads to the formation of the superego. As the superego forms, the child becomes less dependent on narcissistic supplies "from the outside" (FENICHEL, 1946, p. 41). The superego becomes the provider of narcissistic supplies in the sense that the child becomes *less obviously* concerned with the satisfaction of his narcissistic needs. The child obeys rules, adheres to norms, and meets expectations, without anybody suspecting that it is the need for praise and affection (and ultimately for safety) that motivates his behaviour.

> The superego is the heir of the parents not only as a source of threats and punishments but also as a source of protection and as a provider of reassuring love. Being on good or bad terms with one's superego becomes as important as being on good or bad terms with one's parents previously was. ... Self-esteem is no longer regulated by approval or rejection by external objects, but rather by the feeling of having done or not having done the right thing.
>
> (FENICHEL, 1946, pp. 105–6)

Parents *spoil* their child if they provide him with narcissistic gratification unconditionally. If the child "is allowed to express his impulses in anti-social ways", that is, if he can act on his impulses in inappropriate ways without consistently incurring punishment or *withdrawal of love*, then he "has little motive to develop those restraints on impulse that are embodied in the super-ego" (FLUGEL, 1945, p. 192). If parents do not force on their child "some restraint on the free expression of egoistic desires", then the child fails to develop an adequate superego, as he will not learn that "renunciation of immediate gratification is often a necessary preliminary to approval" (FLUGEL, 1945, p. 193). For the child to develop an adequate superego, narcissistic gratification (approval) has to be consistently contingent on his renouncing the immediate gratification of aggressive, sexual, or other 'instinctual' desires.[17]

4.4.3 Protomorality

ARLOW (1989) argued that "concepts of right and wrong, good and bad, have their origin in an affectively laden set of very early object relations that have only the most distant connection to morality" (p. 152). The child, when practising his motor skills, will "look to his mother for a complementary, confirmatory response" (p. 151). The mother's expression of

---

[17] Children, on the other hand, who are treated excessively harshly by their parents, who are not rewarded by love in return for good behaviour, and who, in fact, can do nothing to procure their parents' love, will also fail to develop a superego. There will be no inducement for them to restrain their impulses, because such restraint brings them no approval (FLUGEL, 1945, p. 193). Similarly to spoiled children, these children can become delinquent, but they can be reeducated by rewarding them consistently with love and approval for efforts at restraint.

pleasure provides the child with "the primordial experience of approval", of being approved, "which soon becomes transformed in a sense of doing the right thing" (p. 151). ARLOW (1989) emphasized that "the most ordinary, most commonplace steps in development become the subject of expressions of approval and/or disapproval" (p. 151). Every act the child performs "becomes for the child fraught with a sense of judgment, approval, or disapproval" (p. 151).[18] What the mother approves becomes good, and what she disapproves becomes bad. Pleasurable experiences of having done the 'right thing' and the unpleasure associated with having been 'bad' "become the dynamic background against which later, more highly developed concepts of good and evil are examined and processed" (ARLOW, 1989, p. 152).

In Freudian theory, "the demands of morality and respect" are linked with "the anxiety of losing the love of the object" (LEBOVICI, 1989, p. 423). Desire is sacrificed and impulses are controlled; and such sacrifice and control are "the means of assuring oneself of the persistence of parental love" (p. 424). Self-control is "intended to avoid separation and the anxiety which its fear causes in the infant from the moment he is aware of the maternal object's continuity of existence" (LEBOVICI, 1989, p. 429). Self-control is related to the control of selfobjects, of narcissistically invested objects, of objects that provide love and approval and that thereby maintain self-esteem, inner harmony, and safety. LEBOVICI (1989) suggested that "the vicissitudes of narcissistic investments" "cannot be overlooked" in the precocious foundations of morality (p. 425).

Internalization of parental expectations, demands, and prohibitions means that activation of "a *mental representation* of the adult authority-love object" is sufficient to encourage or suppress the child's actions (ARLOW, 1989, p. 153). What the child thinks of is "the mother's potential affective response to his behaviour" (p. 153). Anticipation of a negative affective reaction from the mother (based on activation of a 'traumatic' memory), that is, entertainment of "the possibility of pain from the threatened loss of the mother's love and the fear of punishment by her", suppresses the wish and inhibits action (p. 153).[19] While the preoedipal

---

[18] The mother's confirmatory responses are affective as well as verbal. The child learns to "connect his pleasurable perception of the mother's positive reactions to the spoken words she customarily exclaims under those circumstances" (e.g., "good boy") (ARLOW, 1989, p. 151).

[19] Another step in the development of the preoedipal child's morality is reached when "the child takes into consideration the pain, both physical and psychological, that his behavior (and wishes) may occasion in others" (ARLOW, 1989, p. 154). 'Compassionate identification' involves "a transient identification in conscious and/or unconscious fantasy with the 'other'" (p. 154). When the child can feel pain *on behalf of* the other (with whom he is transiently identified), he can develop "the capacity to feel sorry, to feel remorse" (ARLOW, 1989, p. 154).

child's "protomorality is dominated by the fundamental potential catastrophes of childhood, namely, fear of the loss of the object's love and fear of punishment", "true morality becomes possible" "with the disappearance of the need for a conscious awareness of the moral imperative" (ARLOW, 1989, p. 155).

What had been experienced as a conflict with other persons has been transformed into an intrapsychic conflict. What was formerly a wish to maintain or reestablish harmonious relations with the important objects now appears as a pursuit of inner harmony, of a freedom of tension experienced as guilt, fear of punishment, and loss of love.

(ARLOW, 1989, p. 155)

4.4.4 Turning aggression against the self

Parents place "taboos on many potential sources of joy and satisfaction" and inflict punishment on the child "at the slightest hint that these taboos may be infringed" (FLUGEL, 1945, p. 76). The child's innate reaction to frustration or punishment inflicted by the parents is anger and revolt. Given that "parents are bound to frustrate their children in some degree", the arousal of "anger and revolt against the frustrating parent figures" is inevitable (p. 77). However, the child's parents "are also persons whom he loves and on whom he is dependent" (p. 36). The child "is compelled to hate those whom also he most loves", a fact that constitutes "man's unique and inevitable tragedy (due to his long period of helpless infancy)" (p. 36). Since the child loves his parents and is dependent on them, his "aggression cannot be fully and freely expressed"; his aggression is frustrated and has to be inhibited (FLUGEL, 1945, p. 77).

... a child represses his hostility against his parents because he is afraid that any expression of it would spoil his relationship to the parents. He is motivated by plain fear that these powerful giants would desert him, withdraw their reassuring benevolence or turn against him.

(HORNEY, 1937, pp. 86–7)

The child's expression of anger against his parents provokes them into acting in retaliation; "they punish him, and withdraw their help, love and approval" (FLUGEL, 1945, p. 36). The child therefore has to learn to displace his aggression. Aggressive impulses against his parents can be redirected and turned against the self, insofar as the parents "are introjected, i.e. are incorporated in the self in the form of the super-ego" (p. 36). Moreover, "the inward recoiling aggression also becomes attached to the super-ego" (p. 36), because the superego – representing the forbidding and punishing parents – "is already endowed with the aggression naturally attributed to them as frustrating agents" (pp. 36–7).[20] Aggression against the parents becomes attached to the part of the superego that "corresponds to the child's picture of the parent[s] as ... harsh, forbidding, terrifying, and punishing being[s]" (as contrasted with the part of the superego that corresponds to the picture of them as "loving, helping, and protecting" [and thus narcissistically gratifying] beings) (p. 76). Thus, "the sadism of these authorities and the sado-masochistic relation in which we stand to them in our external life [are] mirrored in the relation between the super-ego and the ego in our internal life" (p. 38) (wherein the sadism of the superego complements the [moral] masochism of the ego) (FLUGEL, 1945).

4.4.5 Oedipus complex

In the developmental constellation of the Oedipus complex, the boy unconsciously sees his father as a competitor for the affection of his mother and so, out of fear of the father's retaliatory aggression (punishment), he has to suppress his libidinous impulses towards his mother. FREUD (1923) considered the ego ideal to be "the heir of the Oedipus complex" (p. 36). He argued that the ego ideal arises when the boy identifies with his father in an attempt to resolve or repress the Oedipus complex. Dealing with an unconscious 'dread of castration' by the father (fear of punishment for unrestrained libidinal impulses), the boy takes his father as a model. Attitudes and standards of the father, and later those of other authority figures, are internalized. Through this unconscious identification with his father, the boy preserves his object relation to his mother. A similar development occurs in girls. The repression of the Oedipus complex, that is, the repression of libidinal desires for the opposite-sex parent, was thought to be responsible for "the interruption of libidinal development by the latency period" (FREUD, 1923, p. 35).

The ego ideal defines standards that, if the child lives up to them, allow him to gain narcissistic satisfaction (FREUD, 1914), that is, to restore his sense of wellbeing (SANDLER). When performing in accordance with the standards defined by the ego ideal (even when acting exhibitionistically in accordance with these standards), the child can elicit his mother's smiling response and thereby control her presence in his unconscious fantasy (ROTHSTEIN, 1979). Behaviour in accordance with moral standards is *likely* to be approved by parents or other external authorities, which means that it *is* positively approved internally by the superego (in the sense of a smiling response from the omnipotent object). Praise and approval, or the confident *expectation* thereof, sustain the person's self-representation; and this self-representation will bear the mark of the superego (MILROD, 1972).

---

[20] There is, in other words, "a collaboration between the aggression from outside (or from the corresponding introjected moral authority) and the recoil of the person's own aggressiveness" (FLUGEL, 1945, p. 80).

According to self psychology, the child experiences an upsurge of assertiveness and affectionateness in the oedipal phase of development. The developmental need of the oedipal child is to be affirmed in his self-assertiveness and affectionateness. The task of the parents is to fulfil phase-specific mirroring and idealizing selfobject functions for the child. The child's affection towards the heterogenital parent has to be mirrored appropriately; and the child's admiration of, and striving to merge with, the homogenital parent has to be permitted and supported appropriately, too. If the child has a loving parent whom he can admire and respect, he will identify with the parent and *accept oedipal limits* on the expression of his drives. If parents do not fulfil these requirements, the child will be vulnerable to experiencing intense castration anxiety.

Pathological distortion

Distortions in self–selfobject relationships (i.e., pathogenic experiences with selfobjects) in the oedipal *phase* lead to the pathological conflicts that characterize, according to KOHUT (1983), the 'Oedipus *complex*'. The Oedipus complex is a "pathological distortion of the normal stage" (p. 388). In accordance with "Freud's original seduction theory" (p. 389), based on "the stories of parental seduction told by his hysterical patients", KOHUT (1983) argued that "the failures of oedipal selfobjects ... transform the normal upsurge of affectionateness and assertiveness ... into ... infantile sexuality" (p. 390). Characteristics of the Oedipus complex, namely "infantile sexuality and hostile-destructive aggression", "supervene only after the selfobjects have failed to respond to the primary affectionateness and assertiveness of the oedipal-phase self with fondness and pride", because the child's parents "have, on the basis of their own psychopathology, experienced (preconsciously) these emotions of their oedipal child as sexually stimulating and aggressively threatening" (p. 390). Thus, "the object-instinctual drives (and the related conflicts, guilts, and anxieties)" are "only intermediate pathogenic links" between "a more deeply buried selfobject transference that underlies the Oedipus complex" and "the manifestations of the oedipal neuroses" later in life (KOHUT, 1983, p. 389).

4.4.6 Ego identity

Surrounded by such mighty disapproval, the child's original state of naïve self-love is said to be compromised. He looks for models by which to measure himself, and seeks happiness in trying to resemble them. Where he succeeds he achieves *self-esteem*, a not too convincing facsimile of his original narcissism and sense of omnipotence.

(ERIKSON, 1959, p. 191)

FREUD (1914) thought that self-esteem is a derivative of the child's narcissism and omnipotence. ERIKSON (1959) emphasized that realistic self-esteem is more than "a narcissistic corroboration of infantile omnipotence" (p. 194). To begin with, the maternal environment must sustain the "residue of infantile narcissism" "with a love which assures the child that it is good to be alive in the particular social coordinates in which he happens to find himself" (p. 199). Infantile narcissism is shaped and channelled into realistic dimensions by the encouragement the child receives from his social environment for his functional achievements. ERIKSON (1959) pointed to "the many steps in child development which, through the coincidence of physical mastery and cultural meaning, of functional pleasure and social recognition, contribute to a more realistic self-esteem" (p. 194). Later, tangible social recognition is promised "for the acquisition of skills and knowledge during latency" (p. 201). Importantly, "self-esteem grows to be a conviction that the ego is learning effective steps toward a tangible collective future, that it is developing into a defined ego within a social reality" (p. 194). What emerges is a sense of 'ego identity', which is "a subjective experience", "a dynamic fact", and "a group-psychological phenomenon" (p. 194). Ego identity is indissolubly linked with group identity, much as "ego synthesis and social organization" are mutually complementary (p. 198). ERIKSON (1959) suggested that "the self-esteem attached to the ego identity is based on the rudiments of skills and social techniques which assure a gradual coincidence of functional pleasure and actual performance, of ego ideal and social role" (p. 199).

4.5 Compulsiveness versus spontaneity

There appears to have evolved in primates a balance between the innate aversiveness of conspecifics (as communicated by innately recognized hostile expressions) and their attractiveness, that is, between the individual's guardedness and paranoia, on the one hand, and the pleasure and reward he derives from affiliative interactions with them, on the other. Feelings of inferiority and worthlessness instil a sense of vulnerability towards a world that is *innately hostile*, a sense that corresponds to what HORNEY called 'basic anxiety', and that needs to be kept at bay by attaining superiority, in ADLER's sense, that is, by ambitious pursuit of goals and realization of ideals, in KOHUT's sense. Ambitiousness, aim-inhibited exhibitionism, and attainment of superiority or of socially approved ideals all help to maintain the feeling of safety (in SANDLER's sense); and their value for the developing personality structure is the greater the more urgent the need for safety, and the less developed (or more inhibited) the child's courage (assertiveness) and his capacity to make contact with others spontaneously and playfully (i.e., the more his 'social feeling', in ADLER's sense, has been stifled in early development). Affiliative interactions not only have pleasurable potentialities but are also associated with inhibition of intraspecific aggression; they thus generate or perpetuate safety. Repeated frustrations in attempts to make affectionate or playful contact and repeated rejections in early life can lead to deep inhibitions and embed into the personality a strong element of habitually self-directed (FLUGEL) or other-directed aggression, tendencies that would interact with the more or less compulsive pursuit of eminence or dominance (mediating the striving for attention, approval, and acceptance and hence for safety).

4.5.1 Inferiority and striving for superiority

ADLER (1927) noted that "the beginning of every life is fraught with a fairly deep-seated sense of inferiority", a reflection of the infant's "weakness and helplessness" (p. 66). If children feel consistently cherished and loved for who they are (and are not merely approved for their performances) and if they can express affection ('social feeling') without fear of rejection, their sense of inferiority lessens. Children who feel deprived of love and affection early in their lives grow up with a deep sense of 'inferiority'. Persistence or deepening of the sense of inferiority (a sense of insecurity and "battered self-esteem" [p. 74]) is coupled with an excessive desire for recognition, which manifests itself in a "tendency to push oneself into the limelight, to demand parents' attention" (p. 68). Persistent and deep inferiority also leads to a striving for superiority (which then mediates the striving for security) (ADLER, 1927).

Instead of being loved for who they are, children may be treated by their parents "as animated dolls to be played with", "as valuable property", or as "useless freight", which "often leads children to believe they have control over only two things: the pleasure and displeasure" of their parents (ADLER, 1927, p. 67). They then have to constantly evaluate themselves, review the value they have for their parents. The more their 'social feeling' is strangulated in early development, the more preoccupied children become "with themselves and with the impression they make on other people" (p. 66), and the more their life will be dominated by the goal of superiority (as a means of achieving security) (Figure 4.1). They will create 'compensatory devices' that "guide them out of their inferiority" and towards some goal that corresponds to *heightened self-estimation* (superiority) (p. 70). Some children will rely on an "exaggerated drive for power" in order "to assert their mastery over their environment" (p. 72), or they "develop in an antisocial direction in order to achieve their goal", while others "may become perfectly behaved and admirable, with the same goal in view" (ADLER, 1927, p. 44).

ADLER (1927) suggested that self-centredness and the preoccupation with strivings for power and superiority are consequences of inadequate development in earliest childhood of 'social feeling' or the ability to show affection. Affectionate interactions with the parents generate security. If, early in childhood, affectionate interactions with parents are inadequate (if the child does not experience his parents' affectionateness, or if his affectionate approaches are not welcomed or reciprocated), the solicitation of

140 Narcissism and the Self

```
                              Courage
                                 │
                                 ▼
  Need for relatedness ────► Libidinal investments ────► Rejections
         ▲                    ('social interest')
         │  ─                       ▲
         │                          │ ─
  Maturation                        ▼
         │                  Passive attraction of
         │                  narcissistic supplies       Sensitivity to rejection
  Need for merger
  (primary narcissism)
```

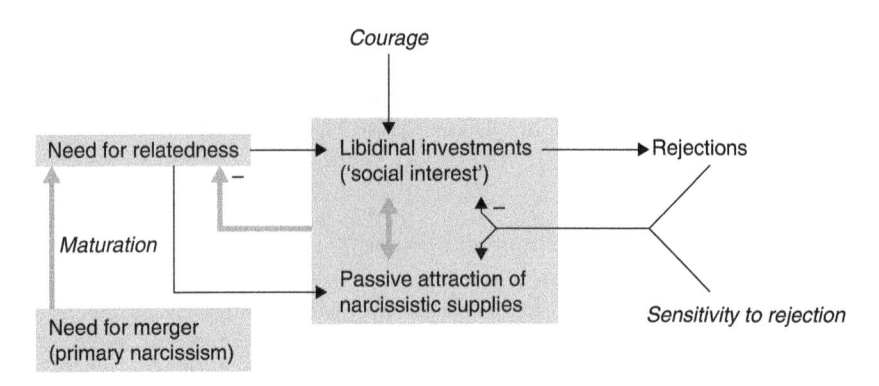

Figure 4.1 Relatedness to the social surround (associated with security) can be achieved spontaneously, via libidinal investments, or more passively, via enhancement of approvability (superiority) and attraction of narcissistic supplies. Courage means confidence in establishing relatedness and attaining security directly via expressions of social interest. Lack of courage (lack of assertiveness) and sensitivity to rejection shift the balance in early development towards mechanisms that involve escape from insecurity and attainment of superiority

parental attention and approval becomes a substitute means for attainment of security (Figure 4.1). A person may be excessively ambitious and vain and demand an extraordinary amount of attention if, in his earliest childhood, his parents' tenderness towards him was not adequately manifested and he missed out on their warmth and affection (pp. 42–3). Children whose upbringing was too strict and who "have come to expect bad experiences" "will be largely preoccupied with the defence of their personal space, desperately anxious to avoid any invasion of territory" (ADLER, 1927, p. 45) (through which they hold on to security).

ADLER (1927) emphasized the social determination of children's ambitiousness and their striving for superiority (grandiosity). He thought that "family upbringing is concerned, for the most part, in spurring on the ambition of children and awakening ideas of grandeur" (p. 63). Children grow up in an environment in which they learn that "the greatest attention is paid to whoever is biggest, best, or most glorious" (p. 63). At the same time, parental rejection or mockery of the child or parental show of preference for a sibling fosters the sense of inferiority. ADLER (1938) thought it to be important that "children should have complete freedom to talk and ask questions"; and he cautioned that laughing at them or mocking them "will injure the sense of contact and may induce reserve, shyness, or some other acute feeling [of] inferiority" (p. 166). Timidity prevents children "from making contact with others" and imbues them with a deep sense of inferiority (ADLER, 1938, p. 167).

4.5.2 Formation of neurotic trends and loss of spontaneous initiative

HORNEY (1939), too, appreciated that, as a result of adverse influences, the "child's spontaneous assertion of his individual initiative, feelings, wishes, opinions is warped" (p. 252). The child loses "the capacity for initiative of his own, wishes of his own, goals of his own" (p. 218); "and he feels the world around him to be potentially hostile" (p. 252). The child becomes "alienated from people" and "afraid of them" (p. 218). 'Neurotic trends' become established if the developing child is alienated from others and from himself. The development of "narcissistic, masochistic or perfectionistic trends" provides a way "out of this fundamental calamity" (p. 218), a solution to the problem of being dependent on a hostile world. Perfectionistic neurotic trends (involving overconformity and pseudoadaptation), in particular, eliminate "manifest conflict with people" (HORNEY, 1939, p. 252).

Perfectionistic trends develop if the child's "own individual self is stunted through his being forced to conform with his parents' expectations" (HORNEY, 1939, p. 218). The growth of the spontaneous individual self is suppressed if righteous parents create "a situation in which the child feels compelled to adopt their standards for the sake of peace" (security) or if the child feels he "should live only for the parents' sake" (p. 91). The child comes to feel that "he is loved for imaginary qualities rather than for his true self" or that "in order to be liked or accepted he must be as others expect him to be" (p. 91). The child is left feeling "too uncertain of his acceptability" (p. 219) and becomes excessively "dependent on the opinion of others" (p. 92). As a result, "the child ceases to have a center of gravity in himself but shifts it entirely to the authorities" (HORNEY, 1939, p. 219).

Factors that foster the development of neurotic trends include "direct blows to the self-esteem, derogatory attitudes of parents who miss no opportunity to make a child feel that he is no good, the parents' preference for other siblings, which undermines his security and makes him concentrate on outshining them" (HORNEY, 1939, p. 92). These factors "impair a child's self-sufficiency, self-reliance and initiative" (p. 92). As a result, the child's "positive emotional ties with others become thin", and "he loses his capacity to love" (p. 90). The child learns to cope with life "by defiantly conforming with the standards" of his parents (perfectionistic trends) or by developing narcissistic or masochistic trends (HORNEY, 1939, p. 92).

4.5.3 Playfulness and ego-syntonicity

Games and the pursuit of playful interests have pleasurable potentialities, and they also have an intrinsic capacity to reduce anxiety, a capacity that seems to be unrelated to social approval. Games help children to achieve mastery of their anxiety (KLEIN, 1932). *Latent* anxiety, the latent "fear of internal dangers" (i.e., of abstract external dangers), "makes itself felt as a continual impulsion to play"; but as soon as anxiety becomes manifest, "it puts a stop to their game" (p. 254). This is in keeping with the "normal impulsion to obtain pleasure from the overcoming of anxiety-situations that are associated with not too much and not too direct (and therefore better apportioned) anxiety" (p. 264). Mastering his anxiety, the child increasingly links his playful interests and achievements with his endeavours to win his parents' approval and recognition. In the latency period, the child finds allayment of his anxiety "in the successful pursuit of his activities in so far as they are made ego-syntonic by the approval of his environment" (KLEIN, 1932, p. 262).

In harmonious development, as opposed to development that establishes neurotic trends (HORNEY) or a compulsive superiority complex (ADLER), spontaneous (playful and affectionate) expressions are not stifled but act in the same direction as (and therefore facilitate) the child's endeavours to win the love and approval of his parents. The child's ability to express himself spontaneously in affectionate interactions helps to render his paranoid anxieties latent and reduces the intensity of his need for approval and his reliance on measures to solicit approval and recognition from his objects. If the child or adolescent can master his latent anxieties in play (or through other activities that have pleasurable potentialities), then he will be less dependent on his objects. His object relations would then not be the sole means of mastering his anxiety (KLEIN, 1932, p. 259).

5
Superego

Parental approval provides the child with narcissistic gratification. Parental approval and criticism and the child's anticipation of these responses give rise to polar opposite affective developments that channel into the formation of the superego, the psychic structure that ensures the propagation of cultural norms of behaviour from one generation to the next. According to SANDLER (1960b), the 'preautonomous superego schema' (precursor of the superego) "functions to indicate to the ego which piece of behavior will evoke the love and admiration of the parents, and which will cause their displeasure, with consequent lowering of the narcissistic level of the self" (p. 38). The function of the superego precursor is to obtain the *parents'* love and to avoid their displeasure. The danger of loss of parental love is, according to RADO (1928), "sufficient to compel formation of the super-ego" (p. 59). The ego submits itself first to parental standards and thence to the standards of the superego "because it is rewarded by love and protection" (NUNBERG, 1955, p. 146) – at first from the parents and then from *introjected* parental objects, that is, from the superego. The 'good object', "whose love the ego desires, is introjected and incorporated" and "raised to the position of the super-ego" (RADO, 1928, p. 60). As NUNBERG (1955) saw it, initially "the impressions of objects are absorbed into the ego", but then "they detach themselves" from the ego and "amalgamate with each other, and thus form an independent structure, the superego" (p. 141). The superego becomes a "psychic agency differentiated from the ego" (p. 140). The superego "stands apart from the ego" and "takes the ego as an object" (NUNBERG, 1955, p. 142). In other words, the superego (like a parent) monitors the self (ego) and judges whether the self is *worthy* of praise (narcissistic gratification) or *deserving* of punishment (disapproval), that is, whether praise or punishment are *likely* to be received from external sources (from parents or other external replicas of the superego) (Figure 5.1).

Once the 'superego proper' has been formed, the "major source of self-esteem is no longer the real parents, but the superego" (containing 'introjects' of the authority of the parents, introjects that are now the "source of narcissistic gratification") (SANDLER, 1960b, p. 38). In consequence of situationally appropriate and socially approved behaviour, "the feeling of being loved is restored by approval of the superego", replicating "the affect experienced by the child when his parents show signs of approval and pleasure at his performance" (p. 39). Likewise, "what was previously experienced as the threat of parental disapproval becomes guilt"; "and an essential component of this affective state is the drop in self-esteem" (SANDLER, 1960b, p. 39). Like self-esteem, guilt (fear of conscience) – a form of anxiety that arises when the individual does not act in accordance with parental or wider social norms – is a manifestation of superego functioning (a manifestation that is sometimes referred to as 'threat of the superego'). Guilt is a "warning signal of impending punishment or loss of love" when however no potentially punishing agent is present (and the role of the punishing agent is played instead by a superego 'introject') (SANDLER, 1960b, p. 38).

In agreement with FREUD, SANDLER (1960b) stressed "the role of narcissism in the development and function of the superego" (p. 43). The superego is formed to protect the child's narcissistic equilibrium; and it comes to do so in a manner that is independent of whether the child's behaviour is actually approved or praised (or disapproved or punished). The influence that the superego continues to exerts over the individual's behaviour "is a reflection of the child's dependence on his real parents as a source of narcissistic gain in the earliest years of life" (SANDLER, 1960b, p. 41). The individual's *self* and his sense of self (and self-esteem) depend on love and approval from the superego, much as the love and care he received earlier in his life from his parents was an essential condition for the survival of *himself*. The narcissistic cathexis of the self (derived from the superego or from others in the social surround and reflective of their attitudes towards the self) is enhanced by adherence to social norms or fulfilment of socially prescribed roles, whereby "the level of narcissistic cathexis of the self" correlates with the individual's "affective state of wellbeing" or 'safety' (SANDLER, 1960b, footnote on p. 35) (i.e., with the degree of protection against others' attacks). If the self, an experiential concept, is "in receipt of regular narcissistic supplies" (and therefore safe), then the 'ego', when considered to be part of the mental apparatus, functions well (SANDLER, 1960b, p. 42), a statement that anticipated KOHUT's self psychology.

5.1 Instinctual life and social reality

Narcissistic cathexis of the self is threatened time and again, as external sources of approval turn into sources of disapproval in consequence of "the interaction of the instinctual life ..., in both its libidinal and aggressive aspects, with the demands and frustrations of the real world" (SANDLER, 1960b, p. 43). The superego plays an important role in the regulation of self-esteem (narcissistic homeostasis), and it does so by promoting or suppressing drive-related (instinctual) impulses in accordance with accepted standards of behaviour. In order to secure the parents' love, the "ego must renounce above all its genital and sadistic impulses, in so far as they are directed against the parents" (RADO, 1928, p. 59). Restrictions on the discharge of instinctive impulses, which are demanded at first by the parents and then by the superego, are accepted by the ego (i.e., the child him*self*) "because it is compensated by narcissistic gratification" (NUNBERG, 1955, p. 147). Sexual, aggressive, and especially exhibitionistic impulses can enhance the narcissistic cathexis of the self and the individual's sense of safety whenever they are expressed in an appropriately modified and 'aim-inhibited' manner. Safety, in turn, when the narcissistic balance has been reestablished, facilitates the expression of libidinal and aggressive impulses vis-à-vis objects. Conversely, in a state of anxiety (or guilt), when there is possible exposure to rejection or punishment, the expression of libidinal and aggressive drives is inhibited. By forming the superego and learning to feel anxious when contemplating or pursuing unacceptable wish fulfilment, even in the absence of critical parents, the child erects "the same obstacle to instinctual expression as existed outside in the shape of the parents" (SANDLER, 1960b, p. 24).[1]

Although it is said that the superego acts as an internal source of love and approval, it only promotes what *would be* approved of, and suppresses what *would be* disapproved of, in an external social context. By modulating drive impulses in accordance with social standards, the superego ensures that the individual *can* receive and confidently expect approval from his social surround, that is, from whichever social agent or formation acts as an external replica of the superego. It is the mere *expectation* of approval (in the knowledge of acting normatively) that can have a beneficial effect on the narcissistic homeostasis. The individual effectively shapes others' attitudes towards himself, that is, their *propensity* to be appreciative or disparaging of the self.[2] The superego reflects the fact that "persons remain influenced in their behavior and self-esteem not only by what they consider correct themselves but also by the consideration of what others may think" (FENICHEL, 1946, p. 107). The superego encapsulates the individual's attitudes towards himself; it is, at the same time, an expression of his expectations of others' approvals or disapprovals of himself, expectations that are inherently uncertain. In the absence of such uncertainty, if "narcissistic support is available in sufficient quantity" from the group or its leader, "the superego may be completely disregarded, and its functions taken over by the group ideals" (SANDLER, 1960b, p. 41). The overarching principle is the individual's "reliance on others as a

---

[1] "The degree to which his hostile wishes cannot find expression" is a reflection of "the degree of severity or even savagery of his superego" (SANDLER, 1960b, p. 39).
[2] The self is constituted by 'what others may think' about oneself (JAMES, 1890; MEAD, 1934; GOFFMAN, 1959).

source of self-esteem" (reliance of the self on acknowledgments and approvals), a reliance that "persists throughout life" (SANDLER, 1960b, p. 42).

The superego is a part of FREUD's mental apparatus but it could also be regarded as an aspect of the world we perceive around us. The superego is embedded, in a sense, in the subjectively perceived social context with its layers of cues indicating which behaviour is acceptable or even desirable and which would be frowned upon. FENICHEL (1946) emphasized the close relationship between superego and outside world. The superego is that part of the mental apparatus that is closest to external reality. The superego is "the inner representative of a certain aspect of the external world", which is to say that "the superego is derived from the introjection of a piece of the external world" (p. 106). The aspect of the external world that is represented by the superego is the sphere of "threat and promise, of punishment and reward" (FENICHEL, 1946, pp. 106–7). The superego not only reflects social reality but also structures the perception of social reality. Once the demanding and prohibiting functions of authority figures have been 'introjected' (acquired), superego functions can be "reprojected, that is, displaced onto newly appearing authority figures" (p. 107). Group formation and the belief in authority, for instance, are based on the reprojection of an introjected authority figure onto external persons (FENICHEL, 1946).

5.1.1 Superego projection

Our sense of morality, of having done the right thing, is closely linked with our narcissistic balance and sense of safety. We are "morally sensitive to our environment", inasmuch as we "are rendered happy by the approval and admiration of those about us" (FLUGEL, 1945, p. 174). FLUGEL (1945) suggested that "the super-ego provides us with the power of self-regulation in a moral sense" (p. 174), which is the power of regulating the narcissistic homeostasis in *relative* independence from external sources of approval. Internal control of our moral sense derives from "external moral control" (p. 174), that is, from the control of our sense of safety by way of soliciting the approbation of parents and other external authority figures. External moral control "is in some respects easier and involves less strain and a lesser expenditure of energy" than "internal control by the super-ego" (p. 174). This explains why there is "a constant temptation to project the super-ego and to find fresh super-ego representatives in the outer world, provided only we can discover external figures that sufficiently resemble the pattern of our super-ego as it has been formed by early introjections" (pp. 174–5). We are thus liable "to find in the outer world masters who will guide our conduct and heroes who will exemplify our ideals, thus affording us some relief from the greater effort of self-regulation" (FLUGEL, 1945, p. 175) (Figure 5.1).

The superego, having taken over the role of our parents, continues to both love and thwart us. Using projection, we "find, or invent, good and bad figures that correspond respectively to what were originally the loving

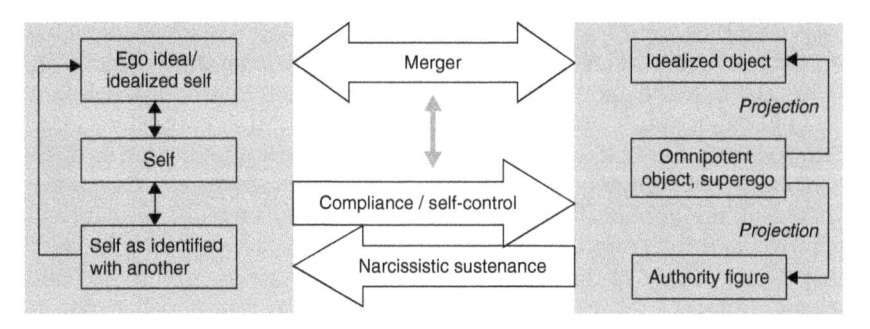

Figure 5.1 The self, in one of its various forms, relates to the superego, in its internal (and largely unconscious) form (the omnipotent object) or in one of its projected forms, by way of compliance (or self-control) in exchange for approval (narcissistic sustenance) or by seeking to merge with it. Merger (as occurs in mania, love, or hypnosis) releases the energy that the self would otherwise have to use for compliance or self-control (involving defence mechanisms)

and thwarting aspects of our parents" (FLUGEL, 1945, p. 60). This process of 'decomposition' plays an important part in religion, politics, and other social and moral fields, as discussed by FLUGEL (1945). The superego is commonly projected upon the leader of a group. A leader, if successful, "does indeed inevitably become to a large extent the object of super-ego projection on the part of his followers" (p. 184). The superego can be projected also upon a group or the country or nation to which we belong. Our country or state "stands in a symbolic relationship to the parent-figures of our infancy" ("as is revealed in the very words 'patriotism', 'motherland', 'fatherland'"), so that "[o]ur earlier loyalty and obedience to the parents are ... very easily transferred to the state" (p. 290). Control by standards of the group or state, that is, control by an external representative of our superego, replaces "control of ourselves through our (internal) superego" (conscience), with the effect of losing the "individual critical power and moral sensibility" (p. 182) of which we may pride ourselves. Indeed, group action implies relaxation of individual responsibility (FLUGEL, 1945).

5.2 Ego ideal

> The possibility of identifying with a father figure and realizing that one is obeying the moral commandments of a super-ego, gives us an inner security that we cannot do without.
>
> (LORENZ, 1973, p. 205)

It is narcissism, according to FREUD (1914), that forces the subject to respect cultural ideas and norms. Libidinal (and aggressive) impulses have to be *repressed* if they come into conflict with the subject's cultural ideas, ideas that the subject recognizes as standards for himself. The subject, by submitting to the claims made upon him by the culture to which he belongs, represses his libidinal impulses, but he *maintains his self-respect*, that is, the narcissistic cathexis of his ego (self) (FREUD, 1914). The subject measures his ego by a *cultural ideal*; and fulfilment of this ideal brings about narcissistic satisfaction.[3] This ideal, the 'ego ideal', is a narcissistic device, the target of the subject's self-love, and the conditioning factor of repression.[4] FREUD (1914) thought that the setting up of the ego ideal – the standard against which the child assesses himself – reflects an attempt by the child to return to the state of primary narcissistic union with the mother (primary narcissism).

NUNBERG (1955) confirmed that the child performs commended actions, and refrains from undesirable ones, not only out of fear of punishment but also in expectation of praise and narcissistic gratification. The child conforms to his ego ideal out of fear *and* out of desire for love. The ego ideal is the shape of the self that is most likely to invite *praise* from the parents and that is, at the same time, least likely to provoke the parents' wrath (NUNBERG, 1955). RADO (1956) spoke of the 'desired self' as the "blueprint for cultural self-realization" (p. 302). Fulfilling a cultural ideal provides narcissistic satisfaction; it enhances self-regard. The pleasurable feeling attained by fulfilment of ideals derives from restoration of infantile 'self-feeling' (RADO, 1956) (i.e., primary narcissism).

FREUD, when elaborating his structural model of the mind, replaced the term 'ego ideal' with the term 'superego'. NUNBERG (1955) differentiated between the two concepts. The ego ideal is aligned with the ego; it stands in a similar relation to the superego as the ego itself. The ego ideal emphasizes the parents' libidinal functions and the role of the mother in particular, whereas the superego is associated more closely with the critical and punishing functions of the parents, the father in particular (NUNBERG, 1955). Thus, the ego ideal is the shape of the self that is likely to attract approval and unlikely to draw criticism from the introjected parental object (superego) or from one of its external representatives.

5.2.1 Idealization and identification

Idealization refers to the emotional overestimation or aggrandizement of a person, group, or some other object. Unacceptable aspects of the object are *denied* in the process of idealization (LAUGHLIN, 1970). Idealization of parents

---

[3] FREUD recognized, as SANDLER (1960b) pointed out, that "the satisfaction provided by the attainment of a cultural ideal is essentially a narcissistic one" (p. 22).

[4] The ego ideal may demand *sublimation* of libidinal impulses, instead of their repression. Sublimation is a method by which the demands of the subject's cultural standards, the demands of the ego ideal, can be met without recourse to repression (FREUD, 1914).

fosters the child's identification with them and, thereby, importantly contributes to character formation. The child seeks to accrue 'emotional satisfaction' through libidinal attachment to the ideal he has created (LAUGHLIN, 1970), which is to say that the child regulates his narcissistic balance by identifying with the idealized object. In particular, such identification may allow the child to participate in the omnipotence he attributes to the object. NUNBERG (1955) thought that the ego ideal is based on identification with the mother. By identifying with the idealized mother, the child participates in her omnipotence. Alternatively, identification with an object (like the father) manifests an unconscious wish to be *liked* like that object, to be liked, that is, *by* the mother (or unconsciously by the omnipotent object). During the oedipal period, the child tends to identify with the parent of the same sex (based on idealization of the same-sex parent), which leads to the resolution of the Oedipus complex, insofar as the child, being identified with the same-sex parent, can satisfy his desire for *attention from* the opposite-sex parent.

The sex of the parent is however not relevant. The ego ideal can be thought of as emerging from the triangular oedipal constellation, in which there is rivalry with a *third person* (typically the father), who is successful in attracting love and approval (narcissistic supplies) from the child's primary object (the mother). At first, the child *imitates* the desirable qualities and attitudes of his rival, but later he may fleetingly imagine himself in the shape of the third person, the shape in which that person was able to obtain praise and affection from the primary object. Through *identification* with the idealized father or, later in life, with a socially successful person or a person of high social status or celebrity status, the child or, later in life, the adult unconsciously aims to gain acceptance, recognition, or approval, and, hence, safety or security (LAUGHLIN, 1970). In the process of identification, one takes over traits, mannerisms, goals, or attitudes of another person. Attributes of the idealized object are "attractive and appealing, and thus are far more readily emulated or taken over" (LAUGHLIN, 1970, p. 130). The attractive and appealing qualities of emulated or adopted attributes relate to the potential of these attributes to act as a magnet for narcissistic supplies.

Persecution

Beginning in the first year of life, the *primitive superego* – a demanding and prohibitive primitive morality – is formed by introjections of 'bad objects' (persecutory objects) (KLEIN, 1940, 1952). Attempting to reconcile Kleinian and Freudian conceptualizations of the superego, KERNBERG (1996) suggested that the superego can operate on an earlier, 'persecutory level' or on a later, 'idealizing level'. The first layer of the superego would consist of "all-bad, "internalized" object relations" (p. 113), while the second layer of the superego "is constituted by the ideal representations of self and others reflecting early childhood ideals that promise the assurance of love and dependency if the child lives up to them" (KERNBERG, 1996, p. 113). Earlier psychoanalysts, such as FREUD (1923) and BERGLER (1952), recognized that, during the oedipal period (when the Freudian superego is formed), *identification* with desirable aspects of the *idealized* same-sex parent provides a defence against the fear of persecution by that same-sex parent (i.e., persecution for desiring the opposite-sex parent). Maintenance of the narcissistic balance, through idealization and identification, has inevitably the effect of avoiding persecution and persecutory anxiety.

5.2.2 Infantile grandiosity and need for merger

BERGLER (1952) emphasized the role of the parents' prohibitions in the formation of the child's ego ideal. Inner prohibitions, established by introjection, substitute the parents' external prohibitions and thereby save the child from repeated punishment. Introjected precepts of the parents and social taboos provide the child with a way of avoiding external conflicts and punishment. Another factor of critical importance in the formation of the ego ideal is, according to BERGLER (1952), the child's 'infantile megalomania', that is, "the child's boasting about what he can do and will do in the future" (p. 13). The ego ideal "enshrines all the grandiose ideas the child has built up in speculating about his own glorious future" (BERGLER, 1952, p. 257). According to self psychology, infantile grandiosity is one of the branches into which primary narcissism differentiates, the other one being the child's need to idealize, and to merge with, an idealized object (KOHUT, 1971). Grandiosity is a means for upholding the narcissistic homeostasis, and so is the ego ideal.

The 'pole of ideals' in KOHUT's bipolar model of the self develops from the infant's need to idealize a selfobject and merge with it (KOHUT, 1977). The 'pole of ideals' can be taken to roughly correspond to the Freudian ego ideal (WALLERSTEIN, 1983; SHANE & SHANE, 1986). By analogy, the 'pole of ambitions', which is developmentally related to the infant's 'grandiose-exhibitionistic urges', would correspond to the 'id' in FREUD's tripartite structural model of the mind. Skills and talents (ascribed to the 'tension arc' connecting the two poles of the self) are roughly comparable to the ego (WALLERSTEIN, 1983; SHANE & SHANE, 1986). Together, ideals (goals), ambitions (the mature expression of grandiosity), and skills define an 'action programme' of the personality that the person strives to realize in the course of his life. In doing so, the person controls the responsiveness of his selfobject surround and his access to narcissistic supplies and thus maintains his self-esteem. KOHUT (1971) thought that one of the functions of the superego is to sustain the person's self-esteem *independently* of selfobjects. In fact, the superego controls the selfobject milieu on a more *abstract* level, compared to the developmentally earlier level at which narcissistic sustenance is solicited and received directly from selfobjects.

ANNIE REICH (1953), too, recognized that the ego ideal is essentially a narcissistic structure; it is formed in childhood for the very purpose of keeping up the child's self-esteem. Having to forgo his own infantile feelings of omnipotence, the child endows his parents with omnipotence. He then desires to become *like* a glorified parent, a desire that will create a constant inner demand on his ego. It is this demand that forms the ego ideal. The ego ideal is tinged with grandiosity as it is based on the wish to identify with a glorified parent. If reality testing is impaired, the wish to be *like* the glorified parent can turn into magic *identification with* the glorified parent. The ego ideal is based on *denial* of the ego's limitations (and of those of the glorified parent) and on a desire to regain infantile omnipotence, although the grandiosity of the ego ideal is gradually modified in normal development (A. REICH, 1953). The formation of the superego (as distinct from the ego ideal) is based, from the outset, on acceptance of and adjustment to reality; the superego represents the internalization of parental commandments and prohibitions, especially of those of the father (A. REICH, 1953; NUNBERG, 1955). In another sense, the superego represents the 'omnipotent object' (derived from the mother) with which the ego seeks to merge by adopting the shape of the ego ideal or by identifying with another desirable object (such as the father).

5.2.3 Ideal self

Feeling loved by the parents increases the narcissistic cathexis of the self (i.e., self-esteem). If, unlike the earlier FREUD, we were to regard the ego strictly as part of the mental apparatus (along with id and superego), then we would have to say that it is the self (or self-representation), not the ego, that is narcissistically cathected (SANDLER, 1960b; HARTMANN, 1964; JACOBSON, 1964). SANDLER et al. (1963) defined the 'ideal self' as the "shape of the self" that, under particular circumstances "and under the influence of particular instinctual impulses of the moment", "would yield the greatest degree of well-being for the child", and "would provide the highest degree of narcissistic gratification" (p. 85). Identification with the 'ideal self' is "based upon the wish to attain "ideal" states previously experienced in reality or in fantasy" (p. 87). By adopting the shape of the 'ideal self' (i.e., conforming to the ego ideal, in FREUD's terms), the child can obtain narcissistic gratification from his parents (secondary narcissism) and experience feelings of triumph and safety. At the same time, the ideal self is the shape of the self that "would minimize the quantity of aggressive discharge on the self" (SANDLER et al., 1963, p. 85).

If the individual fails in his efforts to identify with, or attain the shape of, his ideal self ("the wishful concept of the self"), "then he will suffer the pangs of disappointment, and the affective states associated with lowered self-esteem" (SANDLER et al., 1963, p. 88). The ego, or rather the self, reacts with anxiety if it does not live up to the demands of the ideal self (ego ideal), anxiety being the polar opposite state of narcissistic satisfaction. Anxiety signals a threat of parental disapproval or criticism or that of later authority figures. The ideal self is determined not only "by the child's need to gain the love and approval of his parents or introjects", but also by the need "to avoid their disapproval" (p. 85). The ideal self is therefore "a compromise formation, a compromise between the desired state of instinctual gratification and the need to win the love of, or to avoid punishment from, authority figures, internal or external" (SANDLER et al., 1963, p. 85).

The ideal self changes in personality development. *Regression*, accordingly, can be understood as a return to, or identification with, a previous shape of the 'ideal self' (SANDLER et al., 1963). Mental pain, reemerging time and again whenever the child "experiences discrepancies between actual and ideal states of the self" (JOFFE & SANDLER, 1965, p. 172), can be mastered in an adaptive way. Mastery of mental pain furthers development. In the developmental process of 'individuation', "the wish for past and inappropriate ideal states" of the self is given up, and "new phase-specific reality adapted ideals" are acquired instead (JOFFE & SANDLER, 1965, p. 174).

5.2.4 Ideal object

The 'ego ideal' can be defined systemically (structurally) as "the superego function of holding up moral ideals or standards", in which case the ego ideal has to be distinguished from the "ideal self toward which one aspires" (SCHAFER, 1967, p. 154). The 'ideal self' is a phenomenological concept, a mental content that is largely determined by the systemically defined ego ideal. The ideal self is "the illusory representation of a complete and lasting solution of the problems internal to the ego system and of this system's problems with the id and superego tendencies"; "it is an image and concept of oneself as one would have to be to achieve perfect harmony internally and in relation to the surrounding world" (SCHAFER, 1967, p. 155). As the person approximates the ideal self, he feels secure, because he feels *deserving of love* and care (from an ideal or omnipotent object or from the selfobject surround, in general).

Importantly, the ideal self is linked in the mind with the 'ideal object' (conceived phenomenologically as another mental content), which "is the one that promises full satisfaction without internal or interpersonal disharmony" (SCHAFER, 1967, p. 155). The ideal object is a derivative of the primary parental object, so that the ideal self ultimately expresses a longing for this primary object. In psychoanalytic therapy, the patient may revive his ideal object in the transference, perceiving the analyst as an ideal object or manoeuvring him into adopting this role. The patient needs his "analyst to be perfect for his own narcissistic reasons – to be the protecting and loving mother and father, and someone on whom it is safe to depend" (SCHAFER, 1967, p. 165).

..., the patient re-experiences an infantile ideal in his relation to the analyst. Further, by idealizing the analyst, by playing on his narcissistic needs, the patient also hopes to seduce and manipulate him, while at the same time he is bolstering his own low self-esteem and strengthening his weak feelings of security by warding off his tendencies to devalue the person on whom he is so dependent.

(SCHAFER, 1967, p. 167)

Thought

Ideal selves and ideal objects are organizers of social behaviour; they "are crucial reference points or guidelines for behavior" (SCHAFER, 1967, p. 154). The ideal self "is always ahead of us, in the future, something we hope we may realize but even at best never quite do, just as it is an ideal object that we always search for and never quite find" (pp. 154–5). Ideal selves and objects impact on behaviour, just as goal imagery (outcome simulation) does. Inherent in thought, as SCHAFER (1967) argued, "is a tendency to create ideal images, to stabilize and elaborate them however vaguely and unstably, to search the environment for their counterparts, and to perceive and assess the environment (and the self) in terms of its correspondence to these ideal images" (p. 160). Wishes, including those for safety (narcissistic gratification), create ideal images (goal images), including images of "an ideal self and an ideal object, or, alternatively, a self and object in an ideal wish-fulfilling relationship" (pp. 160–1). SCHAFER (1967) likened this mechanism to FREUD's description of the infant's hallucinatory experience of the object (breast or mother) whenever the infant wants the object as a means to fulfil his wishes and satisfy his needs. Such "hallucinatory wish fulfilment in the absence of the need-satisfying object [is] the model situation in which ideation originates" (SCHAFER, 1967, p. 161).

5.2.5 Self-satisfaction and -dissatisfaction

The 'real self' has "defects and limitations, physical, mental and moral", of which "we become all too painfully aware" (FLUGEL, 1945, p. 35). We compensate the defects and limitations of the 'real self' "by building up in imagination a sort of ideal self, which we would like to attain" (p. 35). This ego ideal is the means by which we win others' praise and avoid their blame, and, as such, it comes to reflect "the traditional code of the society" in which we live (p. 40). We "construct a better and more worthy object" (FLUGEL, 1945, p. 35), worthy of others' approvals and thus better able to satisfy our 'need for approval'. If we are *dissatisfied with our real self*, the ego ideal becomes an alternative object for our narcissism (self-love). A gulf between the real self and the ego ideal evidences, according to FLUGEL (1945), the individual's "primitive narcissism and the degree to which this narcissism has been displaced from the real ego to the ego-ideal" (p. 49). The ego ideal is "an ideal to which our self-love is to some extent directed and with the attainment of which our self-respect and self-approbation are bound up" (p. 45). Narcissistic libido invested in the self (ego), in its real or ideal shape, is interchangeable with narcissistic sustenance actually or potentially attracted to the self, meaning that we can approve of ourselves only insofar as others actually do or potentially can approve of us. Indeed, others' "approbation should reinforce, supplement, or even replace, the approval of our own ego-ideal" (FLUGEL, 1945, p. 174), that is, the self-satisfaction (narcissistic gratification) attained by approximation of our ego ideal.

Failure to live up to the standards of the ego ideal gives rise to a sense of self-dissatisfaction or inferiority, which is "comparable to that induced by arousing the displeasure of the parents", whereas fulfilment of the commands of the ego ideal gives rise to self-satisfaction, comparable to the satisfaction felt by the child in response to his parents' praise (FLUGEL, 1945, p. 53). Self-dissatisfaction entails feelings of unworthiness, unworthiness of others' love and approvals. Self-satisfaction, on the other hand, means that we feel loveworthy and "in possession of a sense of inner harmony, the union between the ego-ideal and the ego reflecting the relation between a parent who is proud of his child and a child who willingly, obediently, and trustfully follows the precept and example of its parent" (FLUGEL, 1945, pp. 53–4). This sense of inner harmony is the state of narcissistic equilibrium or SANDLER's feeling of safety. Self-dissatisfaction is equivalent to lack of safety; and a sense of insecurity will increase our need to actualize our ego ideal. HORNEY, as summarized by FLUGEL (1945), thought that the superego "can more properly be described as a need than an agency", that is, the need to keep up appearances (p. 48). "Part of the self revolts against the necessity of maintaining a façade"; and this necessity "the individual may be glad to cast off as a burden, if only he feels safe in doing so" (FLUGEL, 1945, p. 48).

5.2.6 Mechanisms of defence

Some mechanisms of defence aim "at preventing the ego from falling, or appearing to fall, too far below the standard required by the ideal" (FLUGEL, 1945, p. 69). Reaction formation is one of these mechanisms. It covers egodystonic greed and selfishness ("a crude and avaricious egoism") with "an exaggerated deference or humility", or hides egodystonic aggressiveness underneath "a quasi-obsessive kindliness, friendliness, or humanity", or generates "an excessive concern about some other person's health or welfare to hide unconscious hostility and death wishes against that person" (p. 70). Reaction formation serves "the purposes of the ego-ideal", "inasmuch as it substitutes supposedly desirable and ethical qualities for unrespectable or immoral ones" (p. 70) (i.e., inasmuch as it substitutes approvable for condemnable qualities, qualities that define how far we can become the object of others' approvals or condemnations). Reaction formation not only "restricts and confines the manifestations of the personality" but also gives it "an appearance of spuriousness, hypocrisy, or camouflage" (FLUGEL, 1945, p. 70).[5] 'Restriction of the ego', another mechanism of defence described by ANNA FREUD, similarly serves to reduce "the tensions created by the existence of the ego ideal" (FLUGEL, 1945, p. 69). Restriction of the ego involves an attitude of regarding ourselves "as dabblers, amateurs, dilettanti, or beginners", so as to avert from the ego others' blame, ridicule, or condemnation for our inferior performances (p. 70).

If we are to aim consistently at the highest of which we are capable, we must continually exert ourselves to the utmost. But in so far as we pitch our aspirations to a lower key, we may legitimately and quite realistically console ourselves for the little showing we have made by the thought that we could have done more had we chosen to make the necessary effort.

(FLUGEL, 1945, p. 71)

5.2.7 Superiority and perfectionism

The Freudian superego or, more precisely, the ego ideal corresponds to the 'ideal goal of perfection' in Individual Psychology (ADLER, 1938, p. 34). Human beings strive for perfection or superiority. Children form for themselves a goal of superiority, "a vision of a height lying in the future" (p. 37). The striving for superiority and preeminence often "takes the form of ambition – an ambition that is solely concerned with the individuals themselves" (ADLER, 1938, p. 121). The need to "assert ourselves and prove our superiority" ("our selfish need to dominate and be superior") is, in Adlerian psychology, a fundamental human motive, which however comes to bear especially when "our wounded self-esteem [arouses] in us a sense of injury and outrage at the limitations of our powers" (FLUGEL, 1945, p. 46). When we realize "that in many respects we are not superior but inferior to others, we erect a 'guiding fiction', an ideal corresponding to that which we are not but which we would like to be" (FLUGEL, 1945, p. 46). It is the realization or *fear* of inferiority (a fear that is arguably related to HORNEY's basic anxiety) that urges us to pursue our 'guiding fiction' and strive for superiority. In our striving for superiority, "spurred on by a sense of inferiority" (p. 36), we perpetually compare ourselves with our "unattainable ideal of perfection" (ADLER, 1938, p. 35). In many cases, "the guiding fiction may be one which is sufficiently realistic to constitute a real spur to achievement" (FLUGEL, 1945, p. 47). If the guiding fiction is "too unrealistic to constitute

---

[5] Reaction formation differs from ADLER's concept of 'compensation' for inferiority, which, as pointed out by FLUGEL (1945), has less of a repressive quality and enhances, rather than restricts, the personality.

an incentive to real endeavour", then "the person takes refuge in phantasies, in an attempt to regain in this way his sense of worth" (FLUGEL, 1945, p. 47).

FLUGEL (1945) pointed out that ADLER's insights concerning the influence of an ideal on character formation predate FREUD's (1914) paper *On Narcissism*. What is important to emphasize is that, for ADLER (1938), the goal of perfection and superiority is also a goal of security (p. 59). Superiority engenders safety and safeguards the individual's narcissistic equilibrium; however, attainment or realization of any socially valuable goal or ideal (in KOHUT's sense) has this effect. By aiming for perfection or superiority or by pursuing a socially valuable goal, the individual retreats from insecurity and approaches or attains (albeit temporarily) a state of security (safety). According to the 'law of movement', every act or thought that expresses the individual's 'life style', "every psychic expression represents movement from a 'minus' to a 'plus' situation" (p. 35), that is, from insecurity to security, which often takes the form of movement from inferiority to superiority (ADLER, 1938).

HORNEY's (1939) 'neurotic trends' are safety devices; they are personality structures by way of which the individual obtains *safety*. HORNEY (1939) regarded the Freudian superego "as a safety-device, that is, as a neurotic trend toward perfectionism" (p. 77). The superego can be taken to refer to a particular neurotic trend, to "a special need of the individual"; it is the more or less stringent need to appear perfect, "to keep up appearances of perfection" (p. 216). Persons who "adhere to particularly rigid and high moral standards" and have "a passionate drive toward rectitude and perfection" can be said to have a strong superego (p. 207); or they can be said to have a perfectionistic neurotic trend, a tendency to attain perfection at any price. This "compulsion to appear perfect" pertains "to whatever is valued in a given culture" (p. 217). Characteristics that the person tries to emulate to perfection are "qualities which have impressed him favourably in childhood"; they are traits that he borrowed from persons who had impressed him in his childhood (p. 217). The kind of perfection emphasized by the person also depends on "his actual possibilities to excel" (p. 217). HORNEY (1939) acknowledged that "everyone living in an organized community must keep up appearances" to some extent (p. 216), as "we are all dependent on the regard others have for us" (p. 217). However, the perfectionistic neurotic person "turns altogether into a façade" (p. 217). For him, all that matters is "to measure up to expectations and standards and to fulfill duties" (HORNEY, 1939, p. 217).

False self

The narcissistic (or otherwise neurotic) individual is forced to earn the love of his objects by conducting himself in accordance with a 'false self' (MILLER, 1979). As a child, he was not loved for who he was, but loved only for his achievements and qualities, which have come to constitute his 'false self'.

By maintaining conformity with his 'false self', the narcissistic individual lives up the expectations of his parental introjects (superego). The 'false self', encapsulating the individual's qualities and capacities, which he, as a child, felt his parents admired and *needed*, aims to attain the love of derivatives of the primary objects. The narcissistic individual does not allow himself to really live his own life, to act in accordance with his 'true self', as his only concern is to be accepted and loved by his objects (MILLER, 1979) (i.e., to be narcissistically nourished).

5.2.8 Self-actualization and inner dictates

The neurotic person, according to HORNEY (1950), strives to actualize his mental images of an 'idealized self', which is to say that he has "to prove [his self] in action" and to model himself "into this special kind of perfection prescribed by specific features of his idealized image" (HORNEY, 1950, p. 25). Similarly, the nonneurotic person pursues his life trying to actualize an *ideal* self (SANDLER et al., 1963). The ideal or idealized self – when fleetingly experienced in the realm of imagination – reveals possibilities for interpersonal security (safety) and potential resources of narcissistic supplies. What characterizes such imagery in neurotic persons is "the fantastic nature of their self-glorification" (HORNEY, 1950, p. 32). Moreover, the neurotic person is "bent on actualizing his idealized self"; and, under "the tyrannical inner system" of inner dictates (the "shoulds and taboos"), "he tries to mold himself into a godlike being" (p. 368). It is the intensity of narcissistic need that renders self-imagery fantastic and its actualization maladaptive. Imagery of the idealized self can however be uncoupled from the striving for self-actualization; then imagery of the idealized self would "take the form of imaginary conversations in which others are impressed or put to shame" (HORNEY, 1950, p. 33).

The neurotic person tries to achieve his goals and to actualize his 'idealized self' by making demands on himself, by complying with his 'inner dictates' (representing "a complicated system of shoulds and taboos" [p. 25]) (HORNEY, 1950). Compliance with inner dictates helps the neurotic person to hold on to resources of narcissistic supply and thus to maintain his safety. Inner dictates of the neurotic person are equivalent to moral standards and ideals of the nonneurotic person; however, where moral standards and ideals "have an obligating power over our lives", inner dictates of the neurotic person have a coercive character (p. 73). The more the neurotic person is driven to actualize his idealized self, the more his inner dictates "become the sole motor force moving him, driving him, whipping him into action" (HORNEY, 1950, p. 84). While, for all of us, "there are quick retributions if we do not measure up to expectations", the neurotic person responds to nonfulfilment of ideals with "anxiety, despair, self-condemnation, and self-destructive impulses" (p. 74). Anxiety reactions tend to be fleeting "because the customary defences against anxiety are set going instantaneously"

(p. 74). However, anxiety may result in "an increased need for affection" (p. 74) and a need to "feel wanted" (p. 75). When the person consistently fails to measure up to his inner dictates (or moral standards), he hates and despises himself. Self-criticism reveals the 'tyranny' of inner dictates (HORNEY, 1950). Attitudes towards the tyranny of inner dictates "range between the opposite poles of compliance and rebellion" (HORNEY, 1950, p. 75). Compliance can manifest as self-righteousness. When the person's compliance with his inner dictates and his self-righteousness are externalized, he imposes "his standards upon others" and makes "relentless demands as to *their* perfection" (p. 78). Externalizing his compliance with inner tyranny, the neurotic person tries to "make other people do the 'right' thing", and he does so often "by force" (pp. 84–5). Thus, self-criticism "becomes tenaciously externalized" (HORNEY, 1950, p. 79). Indeed, we enforce norms and laws insofar as these norms and laws are critical to defining our self and realizing our ego ideal, insofar as they mark our rights of access to narcissistic resources.

Externalization

Self-contempt can be externalized, in that one either comes to despise others or comes to feel "that it is others who look down upon oneself" (HORNEY, 1945, p. 118). A person who feels "right and superior" will readily despise others when externalizing his self-contempt, whereas an excessively compliant person, who recriminates himself "for his failure to measure up to his idealized image", tends to feel "that others have no use for him" (p. 118) and look down upon him. It is painful to despise oneself for any weakness; and so is being despised by others, but when self-recriminations are externalized (so that others are seen as despising oneself), "there is always hope of being able to change their attitude" (p. 119). Externalization of self-recriminations can manifest as "an incessant conscious or unconscious fear or expectation that the faults which are intolerable to oneself will infuriate others" (p. 121). Increased compliance is "one of the major consequences of this form of externalization" (p. 121). Alternatively, rage against the self (self-contempt) "may appear as intestinal maladies, headaches, fatigue, and so on" (HORNEY, 1945, pp. 121–2). In those whose hostile tendencies are not inhibited, rage against oneself easily turns into rage at others; "anger is easily thrust outward" (p. 120). Externalized self-hatred "appears either as irritability in general or as a specific irritation directed at the very faults in others that the person hates in himself" (HORNEY, 1945, p. 120).

The idealized image is maintained by way of self-imposed, inner coercion. Inner coercion, that is, compliance with the exacting demands of the idealized self-image, can be externalized "by imposing pressure on others", by "imposing the same standards upon others as those under which the person himself chafes" (HORNEY, 1945, p. 123). At other times, externalization of inner compulsion takes the form of "hypersensitivity to anything in the outside world that even faintly resembles duress" (p. 123). The economic advantage bestowed upon the person by this form of externalization of inner coercion is twofold. He can rebel against his inner constraints when they are externalized and thereby maintain "an illusion of freedom"; and he does not have "to admit the inner coercion" and therefore does not have "to admit that he is not his idealized image" (p. 125) (of which in fact he falls short). He can hold on to his idealized image; and it is his idealized image that holds him (i.e., his self) together (HORNEY, 1945, p. 126), insofar as it is his only means of keeping himself safe (and retaining his narcissistic balance). In general, "externalization replaces inner conflicts with external ones" (p. 130) and, at the same time, allows the person to maintain a socially approved (or desirable) and *protective* illusion about himself, that is, his idealized image (HORNEY, 1945).

5.2.9 Moral masochism

The ego ideal, as was also recognized by BERGLER (1949), is "originally erected to bolster up the child's own threatened narcissism" (p. 47); it is formed "in a compromising attempt of the ego to maintain its supposed omnipotence" (p. 46). As the child's "fictitious omnipotence is severely shaken by the demands of the outer world", and as he is faced with his helplessness, he has "to take to himself the commands of the parents and then disguise this involuntary act as voluntary, in order to preserve his fictitious omnipotence" (p. 46). Introjected parental commands are thus invested with the child's narcissism (p. 46). Henceforth, "every deviation from the self-erected ego-ideal appears in the ego in the form of guilt" (p. 47). Every discrepancy between the ego and the ego ideal, insofar as it cannot be denied, attracts "punishment in the form of guilt" (BERGLER, 1949, p. 107). BERGLER (1949, 1952) argued that it is the 'daimonion' aspect of the superego that "imposes a sentence" ("exacts penance") on the ego (in the form of dissatisfaction, guilt, or depression), whenever the ego does not live up to its ideal.

The ego can counteract the superego's cruelty by engaging in 'psychic masochism' (BERGLER, 1952). 'Psychic masochism' refers to the ego's 'masochistic submission' to the superego's cruelty (submission that has become 'secondarily libidinized'). Psychic masochism can manifest as unconscious craving for injustice ('injustice collecting'). 'Pseudoaggressive behaviour' can be used by the subject to elicit external retaliation, allowing him to feel treated unjustly (BERGLER, 1952) and possibly to blame the 'bad outer world' for his failure to live up to the ego ideal. It may appear that the sense of having been treated unjustly, of being a victim, counteracts the dissatisfaction (and shame) associated with having fallen short of internalized standards. Perhaps, the superego relents its harsh demands as it shows pity for the self.

Moral masochism and self-disparagement – arising whenever the subject cannot measure up to his high ego ideal – may *conceal or split off fantasies of grandiosity*, fantasies that operate as a defence against depression and fears of abandonment (MILLER, 1979). Grandiose fantasies and their compulsive and perfectionist realization represent adaptations to parental expectations – and, later in life, to expectations of parental introjects – that had to be met as a precondition for the receipt of parental love, and that continue to be felt as a precondition with regard to the approval and admiration attainable from present-day authority figures (which are projections of the parental introjects). When anxiety arises in consequence of loss of access to narcissistic sustenance (when the grandiose ego ideal is out of reach), adopting a mode of submission – making oneself feel small, insignificant, helpless, and pitiful – appeases parents or their derivatives who are intent on aggressive rejection and thereby offers access to an alternative source of narcissistic sustenance in the form of pitying acceptance.

5.3 Self-observing function

When an action is contemplated by the self, the action is "subjected to an imaginary audience" (CASHDAN, 1988, p. 50). Critically, the 'imaginary audience', a derivative of early authority figures, communicates approval or disapproval; it signals whether the contemplated action is approved or disapproved of. When imagery is engaged (goal or outcome imagery), the subject may adopt the perspective of the imaginary audience and judge the self; or the self may feel itself to be judged by the audience. Imagery of an imaginary audience expressing imaginary approval or disapproval implies that there is complimentary imagery of a self, of that which is approved or disapproved by the imaginary audience. The self wants to leave a favourable impression on the imaginary audience, so as to ensure its narcissistic balance. The fleeting emotional feeling (anxiety or safety) that is created by this interaction then determines whether the contemplated action is carried out or the goal is pursued. Thus, the superego could be regarded simply as an anticipatory device that shapes behaviour by capitalizing on man's preeminent need for approval and his fear of disapproval (felt as anxiety). It seems that the infant's ability to evoke a reassuring image of his mother during her absence and the related development of his ability to think (BALINT, 1952; BION, 1962) take on a function later in life (the internal generation of substitute approval) that is of major importance for the organization of voluntary or goal-directed behaviour. Evolutionarily, the animal's ability to anticipate the location of a food reward, and to experience incentive arousal in relation to such anticipation, could have been the precursor of the oedipal child's ability to fleetingly anticipate the approving response of his parents. The pursuit of narcissistic supplies, aided by anticipation of narcissistic resources (applause from an imaginary audience), is not unlike the animal's foraging for food when this is guided by intermittent recall of locations of food resources. Foraging for narcissistic sustenance capitalizes on old appetitive behaviour mechanisms. An unceasing need to access and control narcissistic

5.3.1 Anticipatory affects

> At the height of the phallic phase the infantile ego (intimidated by the dread of castration – loss of love) has to renounce its dangerous Oedipus wishes and to secure itself against their recurrence. To do this it forms out of the primary function of self-observation a powerful institution (the super-ego) and develops the capacity for becoming aware of the criticisms of this institution in the form of a dread of conscience.
> (RADO, 1928, p. 52)

Whenever the child feels alone, or whenever he is punished and thus not loved, he experiences a sense of annihilation and low self-esteem. Once the child has acquired the ability to anticipate the future (in imagination), he experiences "states of 'minor annihilations' or small 'diminutions' in self-esteem as a precaution against the possibility of a real and definite loss of narcissistic supplies" (FENICHEL, 1946, p. 388). The superego, even in its early stages of development, serves "to anticipate the probable reactions of the external world to one's behavior" (p. 102) (whereby it has to be underlined that these external reactions, in terms of punishment or praise, are probabilistic). At an early stage of superego development, "a constant watchman" (instituted in the mind "through an act of introjection" of the mother) "signals the approach of possible situations ... that might result in the loss of the mother's affection, or the approach of an occasion to earn the reward of the mother's affection", so that standards and "prohibitions set up by the parents remain effective even in their absence" (p. 102). The 'constant watchman' with which the child identifies is an anticipating section of the ego; and it is this "anticipating ego" that "begins to guard against any action on its part that might result in a loss of the necessary parental love" (FENICHEL, 1946, p. 136).

Self-observation can signal to the ego pleasure (narcissistic gratification) or anxiety (NUNBERG, 1955). The mechanism of self-observation, "which watches all processes within the ego" (p. 193), and which is derived from the praising and criticizing attitudes of parental objects towards the self, can generate anxiety, just as external disapproval can do. When self-observation signals anxiety, the ego is prompted to institute defensive measures, that is, "*to undertake suitable actions in order to return to the state of rest*" (narcissistic equilibrium) (NUNBERG, 1955, p. 149). Minor states of anxiety ('minor annihilations') that establish themselves transiently when anticipating the *probable* response of the external world to the actions one is tempted to carry out (FENICHEL) may not require instatement of defensive measures, insofar as

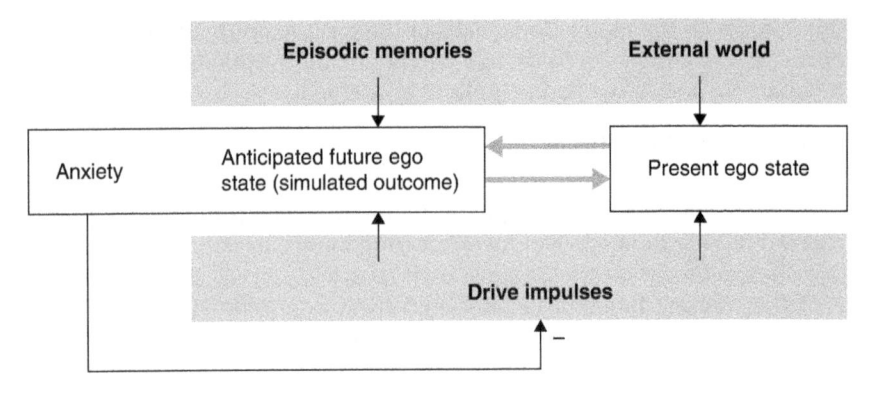

Figure 5.2 Transient anxiety that is associated with, or forms part of, an anticipated ego state inhibits drive impulses. Anticipated ego states are simulated with the aid of episodic memories that may be retrieved insofar as they are associated with aspects of the present ego state

they have the important effect of *inhibiting* drive impulses. Anxiety, which arises when the danger is probabilistic and ill-defined, favours defensive quiescence and behavioural inhibition over drive-related behaviour; and anticipatory capacities conceptualized as superego may draw on this inhibitory function of anxiety (Figure 5.2).

> It is probable that pleasure automatically fosters, and pain inhibits, the instinctual drives. Anxiety is the most important kind of pain working in this way.
>
> (FEDERN, 1952, p. 239)

5.3.2 Choice conflicts and decision making

'Choice conflicts' are conflicts in which the ego has to choose between conflicting alternatives; "the ego is 'in conflict' as to what to do next" (RANGELL, 1969, p. 600). In the decision-making process, the ego permits "a small amount of instinctual discharge to take place experimentally", whereupon "the ego screens the present partial gratification through its filter of past memories, to see whether or not any past traumatic memory is revived, associatively connected with the experimental discharge" (p. 600). Memories are scanned and a psychic trauma that was experienced in the past is sampled tentatively. In other words, an anxiety reaction is brought about (under control of the ego) in a minimal and experimental way (signal anxiety). It is the function of the superego to evaluate the permissibility of the experimental discharge, to judge the utility of the anticipated decision. The ego (i.e., the self) experiences "a signal of anxiety, indicating the danger of punishment or disapproval by the superego, and/or of the external world" (p. 600). Alternatives are considered; and eventually the ego (the self) experiences "a feeling of safety and security" (p. 600), allowing the experimental discharge to be translated into action (RANGELL, 1969).

According to SANDLER and JOFFE (1968), thoughts are concerned with trial *enactments* of drive-related or externally cued wishes ('trial actions'); their purpose is "to assess the feeling signals associated with these trial ideomotor representations" (p. 263). Anxiety is felt (in addition to a reduction in drive tension) in "anticipation of the consequences of overt instinctual activity" (SANDLER & JOFFE, 1969, p. 252), if what is anticipated is punishment or loss of love. Safety would be felt in anticipation of consequences of actions, if what is anticipated is approval or love from authority figures. Brief experience of safety (intact narcissistic cathexis of the self) has a facilitatory effect on instinctual wishes. Problem-solving (decision-making) activity, which "goes on smoothly and extremely rapidly", involves the repetition of previous solutions in trial form, "until one is found or constructed that represents a satisfactory compromise solution so that feelings of drive tension are reduced and the basic feeling state [of safety] maintained within tolerable limits" (SANDLER & JOFFE, 1969, p. 252).

5.3.3 Identification with the ideal self

The 'ideal self' is constructed on the basis of identifications with the parents, although the "ideal, conveyed to the child by the parents, need not be identical with the ideals or behavior of the parents themselves"; it can, rather, represent "the parents' ideal of a desirable and loved child" (SANDLER et al., 1963, p. 86). Ideal self, ideal object, and ideal child "need not necessarily be the same" (p. 86). Nevertheless, by way of identification the child "can transfer some of the libidinal cathexis attached to the object to the ideal self", so that his love for the object "is transformed into secondary narcissism, with resulting potential increase in well-being and self-esteem" (p. 86). In other words, love for the parents becomes love for the self because the self, when identified with the ideal self, also reflects an identification with the loved parents. An ideal self "that is modeled on the object provides a double gain" (p. 85). By complying "with the wishes of authority", the child not only "gains a feeling of being loved", he also "can love and admire himself as he does the object" (SANDLER et al., 1963, p. 85). As he identifies with the parental object, the child feels that he is himself the admired and omnipotent object.

When acting in accordance with the ideal self (ego ideal), the self (not the ego, if 'ego' is taken to represent part of the mental apparatus) can be said to identify with the ideal self. If the ideal self is formed from identifications with parental objects (SANDLER et al., 1963), then this identification, when the self adopts the shape of its ideal, is a reenactment, in abstract form, of the child's earlier identifications with one or the other parent. When the self is identified with the ideal self (ego ideal), the self is experienced, at the same time, as an object to the ideal self (insofar as the ideal self is derived from identifications with parents), much as the child experienced himself as an object for his parents when identifying with them earlier in life (SANDLER, 1960b). This mechanism of the self identifying with the ideal and being an object to the ideal is closely related to the self-observing function of the superego and may explain the shifting of perspectives between ego and superego that occur in states of imagination.

5.3.4 Oscillation between wishing and 'oughtness'

Conscious fantasies are often concerned with our approvability and acceptability to others, to our social surround, and to the unconscious omnipotent object in particular. As we fantasize about ourselves, we see our self from another's perspective, from the perspective of the approving or disapproving omnipotent object or superego. Some of these fantasies appear to unfold on a background of safety, while others are predicated on anxiety. ERIKSON (1950) described how conscious fantasy follows a "seesaw towards and away from a state of relative equilibrium" (p. 171). Some of the time, "stepping out of the confines and possibilities of our circumscribed existence", we fantasize about "things which we wish we could do or wish we had done", and "we imagine how it would have been or how it would be if and when we might come to realize certain fantasises of omnipotent control or of sovereign choice" (p. 171). Interlaced with these grandiose fantasies are irrational worries about having aroused and antagonized others and "thoughts of 'oughtness': what we ought to have done instead of what we did do; what we ought to be doing now in order to undo what we have done; and what we ought to do in the future instead of what we would wish we could do" (ERIKSON, 1950, p. 171). These thoughts of 'oughtness' more clearly manifest the working of the superego.

5.3.5 Oscillating perspective

The superego arises from identifications with parents; such identifications are ego states in which the child "adopts the attitudes of his educators" (FEDERN, 1952, p. 338). These ego states "merge into the superego, which has sharp boundaries toward the 'ego', the latter being only partially influenced by identification" (pp. 338–9). The superego is a state or form of the "ego which had absorbed the parents in itself"; it is derived from a compound representation of the parents that was cathected with 'ego feeling' (p. 315) (and that thus became part of the self), although "the representation of the original persons was repressed" and "only the inhibiting and direction-giving power remained in consciousness"

(FEDERN, 1952, p. 316). The superego, "be it demanding, prohibiting, or permitting, ... always deals in the first place with the ego" (p. 309). Whenever the superego uses "functions of moral evaluation, demand, and rejection" vis-à-vis the ego (p. 312), "the boundary between ego and superego leads to a division in the ego, so that one becomes aware in oneself of that double structure" (p. 313). The boundary between ego and superego is accentuated when there is "strict supervision on the one side" and "intense fear of this supervision on the other" (FEDERN, 1952, p. 314).

The ego is libidinally attached to the superego; and, as "the ego accepts the superego's orders", the superego invests (narcissistic) libido in the ego (FEDERN, 1952, p. 309). Acting in accordance with one's ego ideal is a source of pride or self-esteem, reflecting a strong narcissistic cathexis of the ego (a strong 'ego feeling'). The ego's narcissistic strivings can be satisfied – and 'ego libido' (narcissistic cathexis of the ego) can be increased to the point of "joyful tension" – when "claims on one's own ego" can be fulfilled, that is, when one's ego ideal can be approximated (p. 353). The superego is associated with 'ego feeling' when one adopts the perspective of the superego; "the ego and the superego actually correspond to *two* ego feelings, that is, to *two unities of ego libido*, each homogenous in itself, but not with the other" (pp. 314–15). The torments of self-reproach illustrate that "the ego vacillates between ego and superego in peculiar manner" and that "one cannot simultaneously be ego and superego" (p. 314). One has to lose "the sensation of one's ego before one gains that of one's superego, and vice versa" (FEDERN, 1952, p. 314) (Figure 5.3).

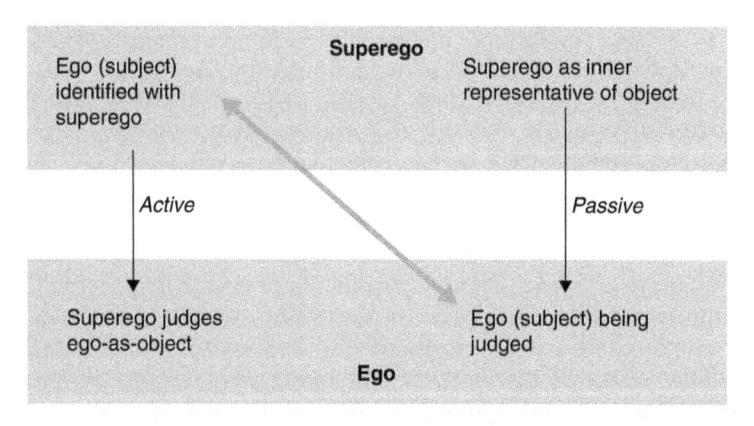

Figure 5.3 Ego feeling oscillates between ego and superego (FEDERN, 1952)

5.4 Drive modulation

> The ego, when it is normal, must accept, and wants to accept, instinctual drives. This acceptance must be modified or refused when the ego is forced to do so by the superego or by the standards which have been set up the by ego itself.
>
> (FEDERN, 1952, p. 239)

Time and again, there is a conflict in the mind between an instinctual wish or impulse (pressing for 'discharge') and "a wish to conform to superego ideals" (SANDLER, 1985, p. 15). Conflict means that gratification of the instinctual wish or impulse (drive impulse) would undermine one's 'safety', in the sense of disrupting one's narcissistic supplies and potentially exposing oneself to hostile and dismissive reactions from others. Intrapsychic conflict – "a conflict between two tendencies of the ego" – leads to the arousal of anxiety, that is, "the arousal of a threat of something unpleasant occurring" (SANDLER, 1985, p. 15), a threat of punishment or rejection. The conflict is intrapsychic because the wish or impulse is followed by a fleeting simulation *in imagery* of the social consequences (outcome) of enactment of the wish or impulse, a simulation that features the adoption, by the inner 'watchman' (FENICHEL) or self-observing agency (NUNBERG), of a critical, disapproving, or rejecting attitude towards the ego (self). It is this attitude that arouses anxiety, which then inhibits the wish or impulse. Drive impulses that can be in conflict with one's need for safety (one's dependence on narcissistic supplies from objects or the superego) and that, if expressed, would expose oneself to disapproval, criticism, or ridicule (or at least to an increased risk thereof) include the wish to love or show affection (libidinal impulses), the impulse to exhibit oneself and attract attention, and aggressive impulses, the latter being employed, in part, for the sake of controlling the object (selfobject) that provides love, approval, or attention (narcissistic supplies).

According to SULLIVAN (1953), "anxiety always interferes with any other tensions with which it coincides", particularly tensions urging the satisfaction of physiological needs. Anxiety opposes 'tensions of needs' and the satisfaction of these needs. Anxiety and related aversive feelings (shame, guilt, disgust) oppose the discharge of instinctual drive impulses; they "tend toward withdrawal from the world", while an instinctual drive that seeks discharge "tends toward the world" (FENICHEL, 1946, p. 140). Anxiety and related aversive feelings are *counterforces* that "seem to be governed by a striving to avoid objects", while the drive pressing for discharge is "governed by its hunger for objects" (p. 140). These are the conflicts that lie at the heart of neurotic symptom formation (FENICHEL, 1946). The readiness with which the sequence impulse-anticipation-anxiety-inhibition operates – and the need for safety (recognition and acknowledgement by the selfobject surround) and the aversiveness of disconnectedness that this implies – may well be an essential ingredient of human nature and form the essential foundation for increasing social complexity and cultural evolution. Disconnectedness (unrelatedness), in turn, is aversive due to (or in keeping with) man's instinctual endowment with intraspecific aggression: man's readily expressed hostility towards those who are different, do not conform, or do not employ one kind or another of appeasing gestures and displays. In the final analysis, as LORENZ (1963) recognized, society is built upon aggression and the fear thereof.

5.4.1 Deflection of aggression

Instinctive (intraspecific) aggression, being incited by any of the frustrations naturally arising in the context of any object relationship, seeks an outlet and would be discharged readily against the frustrating object. However, the child's instinctive aggression against the 'external authority' is in conflict with his fear of its disapproval and his need for its love. It has to be emphasized that the child renounces his aggression against his authority figure not only because of a fear of the authority's disapproval but also "in order to avoid losing its love" (FREUD, 1930, p. 64). Developmentally, "renunciation of the drives, resulting from fear of aggression from the external authority" is supplanted by "the setting up of the internal authority and the renunciation of the drives, resulting from fear of this authority, fear of conscience" (p. 64). The superego takes over the function of disapproval previously fulfilled by external authority figures (FREUD, 1930). Insofar as "the parents block the outlet of the child's aggression toward them", the developing superego, too, "makes it so difficult for the child to feel aggressive toward them" (A. FREUD in SANDLER, 1985, p. 267).

If the child's aggression is inhibited by fear of conscience (fear of the internalized authority), and hence cannot be discharged against external objects, then aggression can be said to recoil against the ego (being redirected against a self-representation acting as a substitute for the object representation). Intrapsychically, the source of aggression is then attributed to the internal authority (superego), so that the aggressive impulse felt against the object turns into aggression by the internal authority against the ego. FREUD (1933) thought that "aggressiveness that has turned back from the external world is bound by the super-ego, and so used against the ego" (p. 141). The superego "is endowed with that part of the child's aggressiveness against its parents for which it can find no discharge outwards on account of its love-fixation and external difficulties" (FREUD, 1933, p. 142). In melancholia, an excessively strong superego "rages against the ego with merciless violence", illustrating how "the destructive component had entrenched itself in the super-ego and turned against the ego" (FREUD, 1923, p. 53).

> It is remarkable that the more a man checks his aggressiveness towards the exterior the more severe – that is aggressive – he becomes in his ego ideal. ... the more a man controls his aggressiveness, the more intense becomes his ideal's inclination to aggressiveness against his ego. It is like a displacement, a turning around upon his ego. But even ordinary

normal morality has a harshly restraining, cruelly prohibiting quality. It is from this, indeed, that the conception arises of a higher being who deals out punishment inexorably.

(FREUD, 1923, p. 54)

Aggression turned against self manifests in unconsciously contrived "self-imposed obstacles and handicaps" or in "self-punishment and self-humiliation" (FLUGEL, 1945, p. 80) (or suicide or attempted suicide). Aggression turned against self is put in the service of morality and plays a role in asceticism, "that apparently wilful and perverse forgoing of the possibilities of pleasure" (p. 88). Self-imposed deprivation (sacrifice) and self-inflicted suffering may be essential to subsequent narcissistic gratification by the loving and protecting part of the superego or by an external representative of the superego. In 'masochistic asceticism', where "there is enjoyment of suffering or renunciation for its own sake" (p. 91), the superego or external moral authority similarly "demands that the ego should suffer in atonement for its guilt" (FLUGEL, 1945, p. 92), whereby this atonement likely represents narcissistic gratification expected from the superego or external authority. Aggression turned against oneself can be coupled with indirect expression of aggression against external persons, so long as the form of this indirect expression is egosyntonic and socially justifiable or acceptable (so long as it does not upset the ego's narcissistic balance).

5.4.2 Momentary awareness of impulse

For there to be conflict in the ego, an instinctual impulse has to "invade the ego in search of gratification, with resulting tension and unpleasure in the ego" (SANDLER, 1985, p. 16). ANNA FREUD confirmed that a threshold, that is, "a certain level of drive intensity" "has to be reached for the ego to take note of the drive" (SANDLER, 1985, p. 17). If instinctual impulses "make hostile incursions into the ego" (SANDLER, 1985, p. 20; A. FREUD, 1937, p. 7), that is, if instinctual impulses cannot be satisfied without attracting a hostile reaction from the superego or social surround, then the ego seeks "to put the instincts permanently out of action by means of appropriate defensive measures, designed to secure its own boundaries" (SANDLER, 1985, p. 20; A. FREUD, 1937, p. 7), designed, in other words, to avoid ego disintegration and 'disintegration anxiety' (KOHUT). Some defences, such as reaction formation, may be employed habitually or automatically, and would thus succeed in avoiding anxiety altogether; however, in many instances, defensive measures would be employed when instinctual wishes, pressing for discharge, "proceed a certain way into the ego" and manifest themselves in form of representations that "would arouse an anxiety signal of some sort" (p. 21). Thus, an instinctual impulse may find an altogether fleeting expression in consciousness, "a momentary awareness" (SANDLER, 1985, p. 23), which then elicits a *minute anxiety signal* and activates the defence (Figure 5.4).

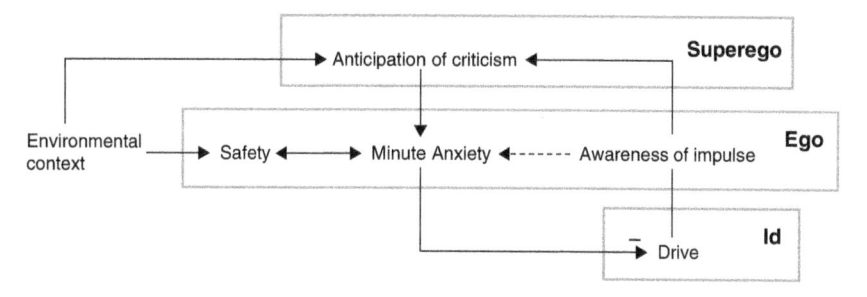

Figure 5.4 Intrusion of a drive impulse into the ego may lead, via anticipation of punishment, to minute anxiety, which, in turn, may inhibit the drive

> ... the ego must constantly be aware of the impulses intruding into it, and assessing them as well as the anxiety or other signals aroused by the instinctual wishes. It must make a judgement about whether it can proceed to be a collaborator, or whether it has to put the wish 'out of action'.
>
> (SANDLER, 1985, p. 21)

> ... in its deeper parts, so to speak, the ego will scan any impulse coming up, will assess it and put a counterforce against it if it does represent a danger. If it is a well-known danger, the ego may automatically take an opposite stance, as in reaction formation, but the process of scanning and sampling has, in my view, to occur over and over again, even though it may proceed extremely quickly. There might be a minute anxiety signal which each time initiates the defense.
>
> (SANDLER, 1985, pp. 23–4)

5.4.3 Anticipation of punishment or reward

The child's "instinctual wishes and impulses" are in conflict with "the frustrating agencies and powers in the external world" (A. FREUD in SANDLER, 1985, p. 274). Prohibitions enforced by the superego are developmentally preceded by the child's anticipatory assessment of the reaction of the external world. It is through anticipation of reactions of external authority figures that the child starts to build up his superego (SANDLER, 1985, pp. 150–1). ANNA FREUD pointed to three stages in the internalization of external conflict: first, "the prohibiting agent has to be actually present"; second, the prohibiting agent "is thought of"; third, "the prohibiting agent is inside" (in SANDLER, 1985, p. 151). The superego, the internalized prohibiting agent, 'condemns' or 'criticizes' the child for his wishes or impulses in the sense that it produces a fleeting anticipation of criticism *without* imagining a particular 'prohibiting agent'. It is the ego which anticipates "that it is going to be punished from some internal or internalized source" (SANDLER, 1985, p. 262). 'Superego anxiety' ('fear of the superego') is "an anxiety the ego experiences in relation to its superego", an "anxiety caused by superego introjects" (p. 261). Superego anxiety is, in other words, an uncertain expectation of punishment exerted by an unspecified, that is, an abstract authority figure; and it is felt by the ego insofar as the attitude of the authority figure is directed towards, and thus defines, the self.

Superego anxiety arises when one *contemplates* (in the realm of imagination) an instinctual wish, which, "in pressing forward for gratification, moves not only toward consciousness, but simultaneously forward to motility and action" (SANDLER, 1985, p. 261). The person who is contemplating or considering is driven to action, yet, in the face of superego anxiety, his drive is aborted or moderated, and his actions are stalled or redirected. By contrast, anticipation of reward in the absence of superego anxiety incentivizes and propels behaviour seeking that reward. The reward that is anticipated may relate not only to the instinctual drive that presses for discharge but also to social approval or recognition; appetitive behaviour would then pursue a twofold aim. Anticipation of approval or recognition alone can incentivize and propel behaviour aiming to attain that reward or, as would commonly be the case, aiming to reach or create a situation in which narcissistic sustenance from an abstract authority can be expected (a situation associated with 'safety'). The superego consists of 'guiding standards' that, if adhered to, lead to feelings of "safety by creating an unconscious illusion of the presence and love of authority figures" and that, if disregarded, lead to feelings of guilt (a special form of anxiety) (SANDLER & JOFFE, 1969, p. 251), possibly, again, by creating an unconscious illusion of the presence and criticism of authority figures (Figure 5.5).

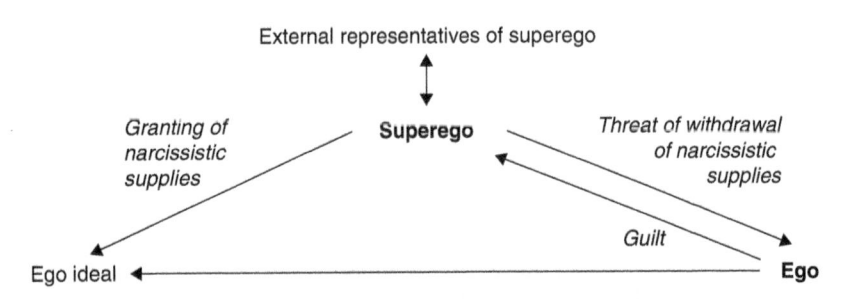

Figure 5.5 When the fear of conscience is felt, the ego transiently occupies a state that *invites* criticism and disapproval. Anxiety may be experienced very briefly, only at the point of consideration, in imagery, of social reactions to the actions one is tempted to take. By refraining from inappropriate drive-related actions, the ego retains a state that better approximates the ideal state ('ego ideal' or 'ideal self'), a state of being that *invites* approval

The need to maintain safety is the overriding regulatory principle in the mental apparatus (SANDLER & JOFFE, 1969). KOHUT, too, realized that safety (responsiveness of the selfobject surround) is the superordinate objective of man's behaviour, and the gratification of instinctual impulses is subordinate. Gratification of instinctual impulses tends to be pursued only if the pursuit does not substantially undermine the subject's safety. Drive impulses are allowed "to proceed if these lead to pleasure, but only if at the same time they do not radically lower the safety level" (SANDLER & JOFFE, 1969, p. 246). The principle of safety (primacy of narcissistic homeostasis) is directly connected with FREUD's reality principle, whereby the perception and anticipation of reality (social repercussions of actions) are structured in accordance with the striving for narcissistic supplies. If, in pursuing an instinctual wish, reality, "as it is known or anticipated by the individual", is disregarded, anxiety arises; whereas taking "present and future reality" into account provides a feeling of safety (SANDLER & JOFFE, 1969, p. 247).

5.4.4 Defence

An instinctual wish (drive impulse) cannot be gratified if its 'incursion into the ego' is associated with conflict (with superego demands) and anxiety (signalling an increased risk of disapproval or criticism from the social environment that is internally represented by the superego). Repression is a basic defence that erases the instinctual wish from awareness and thereby terminates superego anxiety. Related to the repression of instinctual impulses is the inhibition of thought. Thoughts are erased from, or not allowed into, consciousness (and may be converted into hysterical symptoms instead) because of a fear of the superego (superego anxiety). The internal authority (superego) can forbid thought, much as the external authority can forbid speech (SEGAL, 1989b, p. 53). Defences provide a compromise between an instinctual wish (which, pressing for discharge, may express itself fleetingly in an inappropriate thought) and superego prohibitions. Superego anxiety, which, like any other form of anxiety, is "a motive for defense", "starts the defensive process" (SANDLER, 1985, p. 258). The 'ego' (referring here to the part of the mental apparatus) then enlists a defence mechanism in order to ensure that gratification of the instinctual wish can be obtained *safely*, without the prospect of punishment. The ego, while "going along with the id", is "looking for the best way of satisfying the instinctual wish" (SANDLER, 1985, p. 19), so as to avoid disapproval, criticism, or some other hostility, which, if the wish were to be expressed *inappropriately*, would be inflicted upon the *self* by the social environment (or, in an abstract sense, by the superego). The ego (i.e., part of the mental apparatus, not the self) then "controls motility, puts it at the service of the wish, and in this way achieves gratification" (A. FREUD in SANDLER, 1985, p. 262).

Lines of defence

In warding off inner wishes (originating from the 'id'), the superego acts as the 'antihedonistic force' in the personality (BERGLER, 1952). Confronted with an unconscious wish, the superego emits a stop signal, "a signal which is meant to be obeyed, and is obeyed" (p. 22). Repressed wishes ("driven back into the storehouse of the unconscious" [p. 22]) can reemerge "as raw material for dreams or as sublimations (after translation into socially approved functions)" (p. 22). The superego veto prompts the employment of defence mechanisms by the unconscious ego, which is "the factory of inner defenses" (p. 19). The first line of defence is usually warded off by a *second veto from the superego*, leading to the employment of a *secondary defence* by the ego. The secondary defence "is chosen in such a way that it coincides, if only tangentially, with some precept enshrined in the ego ideal" (p. 259) (so that it safeguards the narcissistic homeostasis). It is only the secondary defence that 'appeases' the superego (because it helps to approximate the ego ideal). Thus, "the ego receives attenuated wish-fulfillments, camouflaged with double unconscious defenses" (BERGLER, 1952, p. 22).[6]

5.5 Guilt

> The powerful urge to emulate a teacher only takes effect if one is able to revere him in every respect, but particularly with regard to his ethical standards. What one inherits from such a model are mainly norms of social behaviour, or moral attitudes. The guilt one feels at any infraction of these norms is closely akin to the embarrassment one would feel if one were caught in the reprehensible act by the 'father figure' in question.
>
> (LORENZ, 1973, pp. 203–4)

The superego, developing from idealization of the parents and identification with them, "accounts for the fact that moral conflict and guilt feelings become a natural and fundamental aspect of human behavior" (HARTMANN, 1964, p. 325). The superego criticizes the ego for its failures (involving the mechanism of self-observation [NUNBERG, 1955]); and "the sense of guilt is the perception in the ego answering to this criticism" (FREUD, 1923, p. 53). Guilt, which is "nothing other than a topical variety of anxiety" (FREUD, 1930, p. 72), is felt when "loss of love or castration" is "no longer an external danger" but is *threatened* by "an inner representative" (FENICHEL, 1946, p. 105). The fear of being punished by the superego is ultimately a fear of

---

[6] BERGLER (1952) argued that it is only the secondary defence that produces the patient's neurotic symptom ("only the defense against the defense is shown in the neurotic symptom" [p. 264]).

loss of narcissistic supplies; and such loss increases the risk of being abandoned or annihilated. Actually *being* punished by the superego ("inner punishment performed by the superego") uncovers a deeper anxiety; it "is felt as an extremely painful decrease in self-esteem and in extreme cases as a feeling of annihilation" (p. 105). The actual "cessation of narcissistic supplies which were initially derived from the affection of some external person and later from the superego" gives rise to a "feeling of annihilation" (FENICHEL, 1946, p. 135). The feeling of annihilation may be related to KOHUT's 'disintegration anxiety' and perhaps to *shame*.

Failure to live up to the ego ideal curtails the needed access to narcissistic supplies and causes shame. Shame has been linked to the operation of the ego ideal, while guilt is associated with the punitive function of the superego (MORRISON, 1983). Shame may be in essence a fear of annihilation by the group that arises when one falls short of one's ego ideal, when one is aware of one's *being* ridiculous, inferior, and worthless. Guilt, by contrast, is a fear of punishment (as opposed to annihilation) for having *done* something 'bad' ('wrong') or for considering to act in defiance of social norms (in defiance of expectations of the superego or external authority figures), although what is implicitly feared is also loss of love or approval (from the superego or external authorities). Guilt is experienced when norms or boundaries *have been* transgressed or when prohibitions *have been* ignored. Guilt signifies an *expectation* of punishment by the superego, that is, a fear of retaliation ('castration', as opposed to 'annihilation') by parental introjects (or their external derivatives). Guilt promotes remorse and confession; the guilty individual seeks forgiveness. Guilt engenders reparative and submissive behaviour, which serves to appease the parental introjects (or their external derivatives) and, thus, to maintain access to narcissistic supplies (FENICHEL, 1946; RADO, 1956).

5.5.1 Shame

MORRISON (1983) thought that shame represents a tension between self and ego ideal (i.e., ideal self), a tension that arises whenever the shape of the ego ideal cannot be attained. Shame can also result from a comparison between self and others, whenever a discrepancy is perceived as *inferiority*, as a deficiency of the self. Exposure of one's *defects or failures* to those on whose goodwill one depends is dangerous, in that it can lead one being ridiculed or rejected (or expelled).[7] Shame would then prompt an adaptive response aimed at curtailing the exhibitionism that is inherent in efforts to outshine others and to attract attention, recognition, or praise from authority figures.

---

[7] Human anxiety, as ERIKSON (1950) saw it, is a "fear of invasion by vast and vague forces", of "strangling encirclement" by enemies, and of "devastating loss of face before all-surrounding, mocking audiences" (pp. 365–6).

Shame is indeed rooted in an archaic physiological reaction pattern that is directed against exhibitionism (FENICHEL, 1946, p. 139).

Shame, according to ERIKSON (1950), "supposes that one is completely exposed and conscious of being looked at: in one word, self-conscious" (p. 227). Importantly, while one is aware of being visible to others, one is "not ready to be visible" (p. 227). The sense of visibility is combined with a sense of vulnerability. Hence, one experiences "an impulse to bury one's face, or to sink, right then and there, into the ground" (p. 227). Shame can give rise to defensiveness, an aggressive impulse "to destroy the eyes of the world" (p. 227). Feeling ashamed, the individual "would like to force the world not to look at him, not to notice his exposure" (ERIKSON, 1950, p. 227). Guilt can be a defence against shame. In our civilization, shame "is so early and easily absorbed by guilt" (p. 227). When shame is absorbed by guilt, the sense of vulnerability to attack gives way to a flight to the omnipotent object (superego) combined with self-recrimination as a precondition to being protected by the omnipotent object. As ERIKSON (1950) remarked, "visual shame" is followed by "auditory guilt, which is a sense of badness to be had all by oneself when nobody watches and when everything is quiet – except the voice of the superego" (p. 227).

The neurotic person, according to HORNEY (1937), "builds up a façade of strength" ('persona') in order to "hide how weak and insecure and helpless he feels" (p. 240). He must keep up his *pretences*, "because they represent the bulwark that protects him from his lurking anxiety" (p. 239). Guilt feelings "and their accompanying self-recriminations" (p. 241) are activated in "an attempt to cope with an emerging anxiety" (p. 240). The neurotic person's feelings of guilt are related to, but not identical with, his "haunting fear of being found out or of being disapproved of" (p. 231). Unlike guilt, the state of being found out, when a person feels "honestly regretful or ashamed of something", is *painful*; and it is "more painful still to express the feeling to someone else" (p. 233). Guilty feelings, by contrast, are expressed "very readily" (p. 233). The neurotic person tends to "cover up anxiety with guilt feelings" (p. 235). He is liable to feel "guilty because, as a result of his anxieties, he is even more than others dependent on public opinion" (p. 236). He is more dependent on his 'persona' (idealized self); and more afraid of its collapse (of being 'found out') (HORNEY, 1937).

Shame on behalf of others

A person feels shame on behalf of an other to whom he is close and with whom he identifies (whom he perceives "to be representative of him in some way" [p. 493]) if the other's behaviour does not conform to the norms of the group (MOSES, 1989). He feels "acutely embarrassed and painfully ashamed" by the behaviour or appearance of the other, "as though he himself were being shamed in public" (MOSES, 1989, p. 493). What we may fear unconsciously when we are ashamed on behalf of another is that we will be attacked by and expelled from the group by virtue of association with someone who is regarded as an outcast (so that we ourselves feel the impulse to hide from the group). It can also be said that our self depends on those with whom we identify; and we experience a deflation of self-esteem, and a related sense of increased vulnerability, if those who underpin or bolster our self are rendered valueless in the eyes of the group (or its leader). Our self is similarly deflated when we realize that we do not measure up to our ego ideal, which is in itself a product of identifications with those who we felt, in earlier life, commanded the respect of others or the group. Shame then reflects a discrepancy between ego and ego ideal, or between self and ideal self (MORRISON, 1983; MOSES, 1989).

5.5.2 Fear of loss of love

The sense of guilt, representing fear of the 'internal authority' (superego), derives from the developmentally earlier fear of the 'external authority' (FREUD, 1930). Guilt derives from the fear of punishment (retribution) by the external authority for *having shown* aggression, in particular. The fear of aggression from the external authority is tied up with the fear of loss of love from the external authority ("love being a protection against this punitive aggression") (FREUD, 1930, p. 64). With the establishment of the superego, the child's naturally arising aggressive impulses are inhibited by fear of the 'internal authority'. The child renounces his aggressive impulses so as to not lose the love of the internal authority (and ultimately of external representatives of this internal authority). Feelings of conscience are "states of minor annihilations or small diminutions in self-esteem to warn against the danger of a definite loss of narcissistic supplies, this time from the superego" (FENICHEL, 1946, p. 388) (Figure 5.5).

The child's underlying concern is the "fear of the loss of love" (p. 64), a fear that is relevant because of his fundamental "helplessness and dependence on others" (FREUD, 1930, p. 61). In the final analysis, it is the fear of loss of love that is responsible for "the emergence of conscience and the fateful inevitability of guilt" (FREUD, 1930, p. 68). Proximally, however, what is feared is punishment (aggression) by the external authority, by its internal representative (superego), or by an external replica of this internal representative. The fear of aggression, at the oedipal stage, insofar as external objects are concerned, is predominantly a fear of the father (fear of 'castration'), which is evolutionarily related to the fear of the leader of 'the primal horde'. At the oedipal stage, the child also idealizes the father, suggesting that fear of the leader and idealization of the leader evolved concurrently in primates, emerging jointly in individual development at a time when primate infants become independent from their mothers, although, in humans, the emergence of fear and idealization of the father predates the age of independence by several years (by the period of 'latency').

5.5.3 Conflict resolution

BERGLER (1952) distinguished between two constituents of the superego: the ego ideal and the 'daimonion'. The 'daimonion' – an accumulation of rebounding, self-directed aggression within the superego – "metes out punishment by holding the ego ideal up to the ego" (p. 257). Any discrepancy between the ego and the ego ideal – "between present reality and the bragging of the past" (p. 18), "between the grandiose promises of childhood and the realistic achievements of the adult" (p. 350) – causes dissatisfaction, guilt, and depression. Since such discrepancy is unavoidable, "guilt is unavoidable too" (p. 257). When, on the other hand, the ego acts in accordance with the ego ideal, that is, when the ego achieves a *narcissistic victory* in the form of "external success, acknowledgement, flattery" (p. 305), the 'daimonion' is temporarily silenced. Conscious elation "represents the unconscious ego's elation" at having silenced the daimonion (p. 305). The daimonion is also silenced whenever a defence instituted by the ego "corresponds to one of the precepts enshrined in the ego ideal" (p. 257). In either case, "the ego allies with the ego ideal to achieve temporary immobilization of the Daimonion sector of the superego" (BERGLER, 1952, p. 258).[8]

Assuagement of guilt through others

Individuals look for opportunities to safely discharge their drives; they looks for opportunities to do so in an *egosyntonic* manner, in a way that does not undermine their safety (or weaken their ego). To this effect, they monitor the behaviour of others in the group. A courageous person in the group, who commits an 'initiatory act', "renders a service to the ego" of others and "saves them anxieties and conflicts" (REDL, 1942, pp. 35–6). The 'initiatory act' has a "guilt- and fear-assuaging effect" (p. 60). By doing "first what the others hardly dare to think of doing", the courageous person takes the risk and guilt (risk of punishment) upon himself and "destroys the magic expectation of punishment" for others (REDL, 1942, p. 64).

A person in the group may render a service to the ego of other group members – saving them "the expense of guilt feelings, anxieties, and conflicts" and allowing them to express or to more securely repress "latent undesirable drives" – simply by being 'unconflicted' (a phenomenon REDL [1942] termed 'infectiousness of the unconflicted personality constellation upon the conflicted one') (p. 38). The *insecurity* of the conflicted ego is decreased by adopting "the already fulfilled solution in another person" (p. 65), by emulating the 'unconflicted' person's solution to a conflict between security needs and instinctual impulses. REDL (1942) postulated

---

[8] BERGLER (1952) argued that moods, such as depression or elation, "are the outward reverberation of the dynamic fight between the different parts of the unconscious personality" (p. 305).

that the solution to a conflict in one person tends to be repeated in another person if "the solution for the one really is a solution of approximately the same conflict, similarly organized, in the other" (p. 67).

> The solution will be determined by the type of support the ego is able to obtain in its conflict. If this support tends to be in line with superego wishes, it will successfully manage the unruly drives. If the type of support it is given encourages the satisfaction of the drives, the decision will be in their favor.
> (REDL, 1942, p. 65)

5.5.4 Tension between ego states

> As soon as one's own past behavior no longer has one's own approval, a slight feeling of guilt is experienced, side by side with intellectual self-judgement.
> (FEDERN, 1952, p. 338)

Guilt is a feeling of deserving or expecting punishment from the internalized authority figure (superego); it "is the expression of a condemnation of the ego by its critical agency" (FREUD, 1923, p. 51). The sense of guilt signifies a "tension between the demands of conscience and the actual performances of the ego" (p. 37), which corresponds to a "tension between the ego and the ego ideal" (FREUD, 1923, p. 51). Complex affects, according to FEDERN (1952), "develop as feelings of tension between two ego states" (p. 337), tensions that arise when "the ego meets with itself at drive cathected boundaries" (p. 340). In the case of guilt, the ego is faced with 'inner dissension'; there is tension between the current ego state and an ego state from the past. If the current ego state is identified with the superego, then the tension arises "between the interacting boundaries of the superego and the ego" (p. 339). Guilt, accompanied by self-judgement (superego judgement), is felt when "one's past behavior no longer has one's own approval" (p. 338) (whereby 'one's own approval' is the approval of an authority figure with whom the ego identifies). The 'inner dissension' inherent in the feeling of guilt ultimately finds relief in the "end-state of the need for punishment, the compulsion to confess, to self-condemnation and readiness for atonement" (FEDERN, 1952, p. 338).

5.5.5 Need for absolution

> Fear of conscience elicits conscious restraint, or automatic repression of dangerous thought and desire, and automatic inhibition of dangerous action. Guilty fear, on the other hand, elicits the reparative pattern of

expiatory behavior, a pattern often complicated by rage retroflexed and vented on the self.

(RADO, 1956, p. 245)

Normal guilt feeling contains an "impulsive demand for a chance to make good" (FENICHEL, 1946, p. 103). The child, having been punished by his parents for disobedient behaviour, shows remorse or asks for forgiveness (expiatory behaviour), which prompts his parents "to take him back into their loving care" (RADO, 1956, p. 226). Punishment is experienced as a prerequisite for forgiveness. Guilt is associated with a need for punishment in the expectation of absolution and forgiveness; "the pain of punishment is accepted or even provoked in the hope that after the punishment" the object's *affection* and forgiveness will be forthcoming (FENICHEL, 1946, p. 103). Angry punishment by the object (an external representative of the superego), which – as it is hoped – will be followed by forgiveness, is preferable to "the greater pain of guilt feelings" signalling the prospect of annihilation (FENICHEL, 1946, p. 105).

After the experience that punishment may be a means of achieving forgiveness, a need for punishment actually may develop.

(FENICHEL, 1946, p. 138)

Punishment, which, in the absence of a suitable external authority, may take the form of self-punishment, terminates guilt, as it opens the prospect for forgiveness. The child may seek relief from feelings of guilt ('guilty fear') by self-punishment "for the sake of forgiveness, and the recapturing of the love of the parents, which it entails" (RADO, 1956, p. 226).

The crucial component of guilty fear is retroflexed rage; it is the component which humbles the self most. If this rage becomes once again environment-directed and defiant, the self turns from self-reproach to reproaching the very person he guiltily fears, from expiation to attack: "You are to be blamed (not I)." The self then believes it is acting purely in 'self-defence'. Actually, this is a mechanism of miscarried repair; we call it rage of over guilty fear, or guilty rage.

(RADO, 1956, p. 226)

5.5.6 Need for punishment and its manifestations

FLUGEL (1945) defined guilt as a fear of unpleasant consequences (punishment, withdrawal of love) for not acting in accordance with moral sentiments. Guilt implies wrongdoing, which "is in the last resort a kind of behaviour that hurts other people (physically, mentally, socially)" (in part because, by challenging social conventions and the norms that define others' social positions, we inflict narcissistic injuries on them). Responding to our wrongdoing, others "grow angry and retaliate" (p. 144), that is, they inflict punishment upon ourselves. Unpleasant consequences of which we may be fearful when feeling guilty include "a purely internal sense of sin, unworthiness, or self-dissatisfaction" (FLUGEL, 1945, p. 144), which is, in the last analysis, a sense of vulnerability to others' aggressive, punishing actions.

> Actions that arouse guilt, being actions that hurt others, are therefore also actions that tend to involve us in punishment, and by an inevitable process of conditioning we learn to expect punishment when we feel guilty.
> (FLUGEL, 1945, p. 145)

Importantly, we learn not only to expect punishment but also to anticipate "relief when we have been punished" (FLUGEL, 1945, p. 145). We learn that, after others inflict punishment upon ourselves, "their anger abates, and they tend to regard the incident as closed" (p. 145). External authority figures, or our superego as their internal representative, are "satisfied when punishment has been inflicted"; and their satisfaction is linked to our sense of being accepted again by them (i.e., to our access to the previous source of narcissistic supplies being restored). In this regard, "the relations between the ego and the super-ego mirror those between the child and parent" (FLUGEL, 1945, p. 145). Guilt, apart from being a sate of anxiety, is also "a state of tension, and gives rise to a need for the removal of this tension" (p. 144). The tension that is associated with guilt is a "tension between the ego and the super-ego, which in turn corresponds to tension between child and parent" (p. 145). Given that "in both cases punishment is the natural method of relief" (FLUGEL, 1945, pp. 145–6), there arises the 'need for punishment', a concept originally introduced by FREUD.

Confession can be an expression of the need for punishment. Confession assuages guilt feelings by inducing reproach from moral authorities or self-reproach (FLUGEL, 1945, p. 148), the latter referring to denigration of the ego by the superego. Confession may be "indirect and involuntary", "as with those criminals who unnecessarily provide clues pointing to their guilt" (p. 149). Insofar as the pain inflicted upon us by way of punishment allows us to overcome the burden of guilt, we may bring about this punishment ourselves. Self-punishment is thought to manifest aggressive and destructive tendencies of the superego. Guilty feelings and hence the need for punishment may arise when we fail to live up to the standards of our superego, for instance, when we inappropriately gratify desires or enact impulses (arising from the 'id'). Self-punishment and suffering can be a form of bribery or tribute in order that "the super-ego permits a certain amount of gratification of desire of which it does not approve" (FLUGEL, 1945, p. 158).

We may provoke disasters or hardship for ourselves or suffer somatic or conversion symptoms of neurosis in order to satisfy the need for punishment

(FLUGEL, 1945, p. 155). The search for or creation of situations in which punishment can be suffered may become established in the personality as a habitual method of escaping from guilt, as captured by the concept of 'moral masochism'. Other, generally maladaptive ways of dealing with guilt are denial, rationalization ("in which we endeavour to assuage our guilt by finding a secondary justification for the guilty action"), or projection of guilt ("on to some other party, who is then regarded as responsible, so that we ourselves feel innocent" [and loveworthy]) (p. 150). FLUGEL (1945) proposed that the need for punishment can be satisfied vicariously; it "can be dealt with by the punishment of others" (p. 174). Projecting our own guilt upon others and witnessing their punishment rebalances our 'moral equilibrium', helping us to preserve our own virtue and feel self-satisfied (FLUGEL, 1945, pp. 168–74).

The need for punishment is a function of our sense of security. If we feel relatively secure, we "have little need for punishment and are free to react to frustration vigorously and aggressively" (FLUGEL, 1945, p. 163). If we feel relatively insecure, "we may be liable to feel guilty whenever we enjoy ourselves or express aggression, unless our guilt has been temporarily assuaged by punishment" (p. 163). If we feel a "still greater degree of moral insecurity, any expression of impulse, or even temptation of such expression, may arouse overwhelming guilt, and we feel safe only when we suffer; in this case the need for punishment may be almost insatiable" (p. 163). FLUGEL (1945) thought that "the need for punishment plays a significant and hitherto largely unsuspected rôle" in the maintenance of the "equilibrium between suffering and satisfaction" in the personality (p. 164). Ultimately, the need for punishment contributes to the maintenance of the narcissistic equilibrium, the feeling of safety.

5.5.7 Unconscious guilt

FREUD (1923) distinguished between the conscious sense of guilt (conscience) and unconscious guilt. The conscious sense of guilt is pronounced in melancholia and obsessive neurosis, in which "the ego ideal [i.e., the superego] displays particular severity and often rages against the ego in a cruel fashion" (p. 51). Unconscious guilt may express itself in "as a resistance to recovery" (p. 50); or it may manifest in criminal actions that seem to allow a fastening of "this unconscious sense of guilt on to something real and immediate" (FREUD, 1923, p. 52). According to KERNBERG (1992), superego functions can produce an unconscious sense of guilt whenever unacceptable drives are activated. Behaviourally, this manifests in "a proneness to minor self-defeating behaviors", in "characterological inhibitions and self-imposed restrictions of a full enjoyment of life", or in a "tendency for realistic self-criticism to expand into a general depressive mood" (p. 36). These are minor manifestations of 'moral masochism' that are "an almost ubiquitous correlate of normal integration of superego functions" (p. 36).

Patients who present a syndrome of 'moral masochism' seek out a position of victimhood (without any sexual pleasure involved) in order to appease their unconscious sense of guilt (Kernberg, 1992).

5.5.8 Love and reparation

The need for punishment is thus an expression of guilt, whereby the guilt that gives rise to the need for punishment may be unconscious, as stressed by Klein (1937). There is another, generally constructive method of dealing with (escaping from) conscious or unconscious guilt, that of reparation. By making good the damage inflicted on the object by our wrongdoing or aggression, we assuage our feelings of guilt (Klein, 1937). The need for reparation may be allied with the need for punishment, in that the process of reparation may be arduous and may itself involve suffering (Flugel, 1945).

Klein (1937) drew our attention to the fact that we feel guilty "if we detect in ourselves impulses of hate towards a person we love" (p. 62). She emphasized that aggressive impulses and related feelings of guilt "form part of feelings of love and reinforce and intensify them" (p. 104). Feelings of guilt are, according to Klein (1937), related to the fear of losing the loved person (fear of the death of the loved one) and act as an incentive to making reparation; "feelings of guilt and the drive to make reparation are intimately bound up with the emotion of love" (p. 83). The loved one may be harmed in fantasy, which, too, would lead to feelings of guilt and to an "urge to make sacrifices, in order to help and to put right" the loved one (p. 65). We may "unconsciously feel very guilty" for "the injuries which we did in phantasy", and we would then make good these injuries "in our unconscious phantasy" (p. 68). Klein (1937) argued that "the drive to make reparation can keep at bay the despair arising out of feelings of guilt" (p. 117). The desire to make reparation to objects of our early life is "unconsciously carried over to the new objects of love and interest" (p. 117) (much as our dependence on the primary maternal object is unconsciously carried over to a dependence on later objects). We overcome unconscious feelings of guilt connected with aggressive fantasies by being considerate and helpful to those who stand for earlier objects we had harmed in our unconscious fantasy. Our identifications with others, too, which allow us to share in their happiness, contain an element of guilt and reparation (Klein, 1937).

If "there is little capacity to tolerate frustration", then "aggression, fears and feelings of guilt are very strong" (Klein, 1937, p. 112). Overstrong feelings of guilt impede the "drive to make reparation" (p. 93). Impulses of hatred and "the unconscious sense of guilt to which these give rise" would then seriously inhibit and disturb feelings of love (p. 112). Moreover, "if guilt is too strong, this may lead to a turning away from loved people or even to a rejection of them" (Klein, 1937, p. 83).

6
Self-Experience

STOLOROW (1975) defined narcissism as a *function* that serves to maintain self-esteem. When self-esteem is lowered or threatened, narcissistic activities are called upon to reestablish homeostasis and to restore the cohesiveness of the self-representation (STOLOROW, 1975). HARTMANN (1964) suggested that the ego should be defined by its functions. Accordingly, he proposed that narcissism is "the libidinal cathexis not of the ego but of the self" (p. 127); it is the self, not the ego, that is narcissistically cathected (if we were to regard the ego as structure within the mental apparatus, albeit a structure that is functionally defined). JACOBSON (1964) similarly regarded narcissism as libidinal investment in the self-representation, that is, the investment of libidinal energy, as she saw it, in the self-representation. Like HARTMANN and KOHUT, she treated the ego as an abstract entity, rather than an experiential one. The self, by contrast, is the experiencing subject, as distinct from the surrounding world of objects (JACOBSON, 1964). Perhaps, the self is but a product of narcissism; narcissism is what defines the self and constitutes the self. More precisely, the self is formed by responses of the social surround to the subject's narcissistic-exhibitionistic activities and displays. Exhibitionistic impulses, expressed by the child in an attempt to attain narcissistic supplies, are the developmental precursor of the adult's healthy ambitions, which, when they pursue healthy ideals, shape the self and determine the sense of identity. The self, according to self psychology, is defined by the person's ambitions, his goals and ideals, and his skills and talents (KOHUT & WOLF, 1978). Skills and talents, utilized in ambitious pursuits of goals, are conceptualized to lie on the tension arc that connects the pole of ideals (and goals) with the pole of ambitions (in the bipolar self). The programme of action that is determined by the pattern of ambitions, goals, ideals, skills, and talents operates to maintain self-esteem (narcissistic homeostasis). Victory or defeat, success or failure, encountered as this programme of action unfolds, are accompanied by swings in self-esteem that can be felt as triumph and joy or despair and rage (KOHUT & WOLF, 1978).

Selfobjects are used in the service of the self; they serve the needs of the self; narcissistic needs of the self, to be precise (KOHUT, 1971). Selfobjects maintain the cohesiveness of the self and are hence experienced as part of the self. Selfobjects are required throughout life by narcissistic persons and healthy individuals alike; no one ever becomes independent of them (KOHUT). The individual exerts control over his selfobjects, so as to make them meet his narcissistic needs; and he does so especially when the cohesiveness of his self is threatened. Unresponsiveness of selfobjects (their failure to provide the needed approving or admiring responses) can cause loss of self-esteem and provoke anger, but the healthy individual draws on 'inner structures' to replenish lost self-esteem (i.e., to rebalance the narcissistic homeostasis). The narcissistic person, by contrast, cannot rely on his inner resources for regulating self-esteem; he has to have full control over his selfobject milieu. He maintains intense attachments to his selfobjects; and any experience of loss of control inflicts narcissistic injury and gives rise to intense shame and narcissistic rage. What lies at the heart of any individual's dependence on his selfobject milieu is the evolutionary vestige of vulnerability to others' aggression; by maintaining connectedness to the selfobject milieu, the individual maintains his safety, which is what he experiences as self-cohesion and intact self-esteem. SANDLER's concept of 'safety' goes to the heart of man's narcissistic needs. Although a cohesive self stands for safety, concern with (narcissistic investment in) the self is also a defence utilized when safety is evanescent and anxiety threatens to resurge.

6.1 Constitution of the self

The self, as KOHUT (1971) saw it, is a "comparatively low-level, i.e., comparatively experience-near, psychoanalytic abstraction" (p. xv). Constituents of the 'mental apparatus', namely the ego, id, and superego, by contrast, belong to a higher, experience-distant level of abstraction in psychoanalysis. The self is a content of the 'mental apparatus'; it is "not an agency of the mind" (p. xv). Self-contents vary; they can have the character of grandiosity or inferiority. The self is "cathected with instinctual energy" (p. xv); more precisely, it is cathected with 'narcissistic libido'. Stable *self-esteem* reflects a reliable 'narcissistic cathexis' of the self (KOHUT, 1971). Objects that participate in the regulation of self-esteem, too, are cathected with 'narcissistic libido'. 'Selfobjects' are objects that are cathected with 'narcissistic libido', rather than 'object libido'; they are cathected narcissistically rather than libidinally. Beginning in early childhood, the subject "invests other people with narcissistic cathexes and thus experiences them narcissistically, i.e., as self-objects" (p. 26). Selfobjects are objects that are either used in the service of the self or that are part of the self. Self-esteem depends on the presence of selfobjects, their confirming approval, or their admiration of oneself (KOHUT, 1971).

According to SULLIVAN (1953), the self dynamically depends on, and reveals itself through, the interpersonal situation. The self cannot exist in itself but emerges in the process of interaction with other human beings. More particularly, the self is dynamically built by appropriations and recognitions emanating from those with whom the subject shares the social situation, but also from cues inherent in the situation that signal the availability of narcissistic supplies. Approvals and recognitions foster connectedness and thereby counteract or prevent disintegration anxiety, the very anxiety that accompanies fragmentation of the self (KOHUT). As understood by SULLIVAN (1953), the self is that part of the personality that is central to the experience of anxiety (or, as previously stated by FREUD, the ego is the seat of anxiety). In some sense, however, the self is the antithesis of and a defence against the kind of anxiety that reflects the individual's relative unconnectedness or unrelatedness to the social surround. Insofar as it is an 'inner structure', the self compensates for fluctuations and uncertainties in one's social surround. The self is a source of pain, insofar as it reflects uncertainties of one's connectedness and one's vulnerability to rejection. Perfect relatedness in association with complete certainty and dependency dissolves the self (Figure 6.1). The dynamics of self-depreciation and surrender to dependency in characterological masochism illustrate a general phenomenon: that "abandoning oneself to and losing oneself in something" greater (p. 273), "losing oneself in some great feeling" or in "enthusiasm for a cause" (p. 274), can provide some kind of satisfaction and act as an opiate against pain (HORNEY, 1939, p. 273).

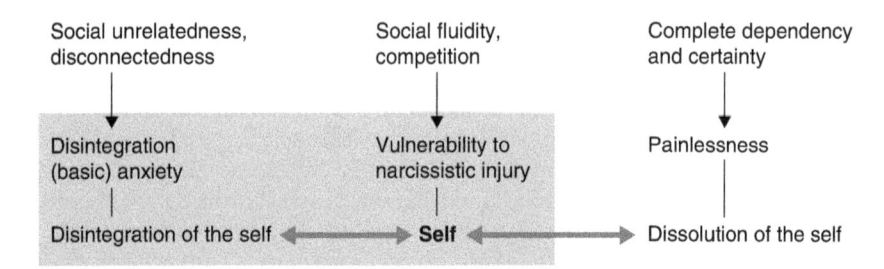

Social unrelatedness, disconnectedness	Social fluidity, competition	Complete dependency and certainty
↓	↓	↓
Disintegration (basic) anxiety	Vulnerability to narcissistic injury	Painlessness
|	|	|
Disintegration of the self ⟵⟶	**Self** ⟵	⟶ Dissolution of the self

Figure 6.1 The self is a defence against anxiety, and it disintegrates if anxiety is overwhelming. On the other hand, the self can also dissolve, freeing the individual form any prospect of narcissistic pain. The individual then loses his individuality and surrenders his 'will' to the leader of a group or the dominant partner in a masochistic relationship

6.1.1 Satisfaction and desire

> Normally, there is no more awareness of the ego than of the air one breathes; only when respiration becomes burdensome is the lack of air recognized.
>
> (FEDERN, 1952, p. 242)

The 'ego', according to FEDERN, is a continuous *mental experience*; it is not a conceptual abstraction. KOHUT used the term 'self' in the same way.[1] The ego, or self, is formed by a specific cathexis, namely narcissistic cathexis (FEDERN, 1952). 'Ego feeling', "the feeling of the ego unit", "is due to one coherent ego cathexis" (p. 222). Ego feeling is based on narcissism, that is, "on the libido directed on to the ego" (p. 45). Narcissism, in other words, is "cathexis of the ego by libido" (p. 284) or "libido employed for ego feeling" (p. 45). The libidinal 'ego cathexis', which constitutes the ego feeling, "appears to be particularly desexualized" (p. 287); "the healthy ego feeling is a pleasurable feeling, but does not have the character of a state of special satisfaction" (p. 288). Ego feeling refers to "enjoyment of one's own self" and to the contentedness with the way in which one performs one's duties (FEDERN, 1952, p. 100).

FLUGEL (1945) suggested that one of the origins of self-experience is the tendency "to identify pleasure with the self and unpleasure with the non-self" (p. 111). Of prime consideration here is the pleasure of narcissistic gratification. Unpleasure, such as in the form of separation anxiety or the pain of rejection, tends to be ascribed to the outer world, presumably in an effort to protect self-feeling (narcissistic homeostasis).[2] The child, in projecting badness onto the object (turning the object into a 'bad' object), is "attempting to re-establish the equations good = self, bad = outer world" (FLUGEL, 1945, p. 116).

> The permanent narcissistic level which is experienced as well-being in the ego feeling is probably relatively high in normal narcissism.
>
> (FEDERN, 1952, p. 356)

Undisturbed ego feeling is the "precondition of all happiness" (p. 38); "happiness is a corollary of ego cathexis" (FEDERN, 1952, p. 111) (i.e., of narcissistic cathexis of the self). FEDERN's concept of undisturbed ego feeling corresponds to SANDLER's concept of 'safety' or 'wellbeing'. Feeling states of safety, happiness, or wellbeing are associated with actual conditions of

---

[1] In fact, FEDERN anticipated self psychology in many ways, although his contributions have remained mostly unacknowledged.

[2] Ego defences operate on this basis.

safety and protection (such as vis-à-vis others' and the group's aggressive potential). FREUD had indeed related narcissistic libido, which FEDERN (1952) thought is responsible for ego feeling, to the 'self-preservative instincts' (p. 289).

Ego feeling can also be regarded as an unsatisfied state, a state of lack of satisfaction, a state of tension. From this perspective, the self is in a state (or the self *is* a state) of perpetual longing born out of narcissistic disequilibrium. This brings us to LACAN's psychoanalytic theory. LACAN (1966) stated that human 'desire' is the desire for recognition (by the other), the desire to be seen and affirmed and to be wanted for one's own sake. Desire is satisfied by winning the other's interest or care, as communicated by the other's interested or caring (or desiring) gaze. The subject can have a sense of integration when he is desired or wanted. Nevertheless, the self, as LACAN (1966) saw it, is a manifestation of desire. It is in the desire to be desired or recognized by the other that the self emerges. Since the desire for the other's desire (to be desired not merely by an other but by an omnipotent other) can never be fully or lastingly satisfied, the Lacanian self is essentially alienated and lacking. Inasmuch as desire is alternately frustrated and satisfied, the self is appearing and disappearing. The self is appearing when it is lacking the other's desiring, approving, and devoted attention; and it is paradoxically disappearing when the other's desire provides the subject with a sense of integration.

6.1.2 Ego boundary

The term 'ego boundary' expresses "the fact that the ego is actually felt to extend as far as the feeling of the unity of the ego contents reaches" (p. 222); ""ego boundary" shall not designate more than the existence of a perception of the extension of our ego feeling" (FEDERN, 1952, p. 285). The term reflects the fact that "everything that belongs to the ego in an actual moment of life" is sharply distinguished "from all the other mental elements and complexes not actually included in the ego" (p. 222); "a person senses where his ego ends, especially when the boundary has just changed" (p. 285). Perceptions of reality stimulate the ego from outside its boundaries, "whereas mere thoughts are inside the ego boundaries and included within the cathexis unity that is the ego" (p. 114). Whatever is "included into the coherent cathexis, which is experienced as ego feeling", is mental; whatever lies outside is experienced as reality. Attention can be directed inside and outside the ego boundary, "without any difficulty in separating them" (FEDERN, 1952, p. 225).

Importantly, aspects of the external world can be cathected with ego feeling. Objects can be cathected with narcissistic libido ('ego libido'), not just with object libido. Secondary narcissism ('ego cathexis') "enters into relationships with the external world and with the object representations", whereby this world and these objects, being cathected with ego libido, are already part of the ego (FEDERN, 1952, p. 326), very much consistent with KOHUT's concept of 'selfobjects'. Objects that are "felt as *belonging to the ego*" satisfy the self-preservative drive (FEDERN, 1952, p. 295), emphasizing again the correspondence between FEDERN's concept of 'ego feeling' and SANDLER's concept of 'safety'. In FEDERN's terms, narcissistically cathected objects are enclosed by the 'ego boundary' (a boundary that itself is cathected with ego libido).[3]

FEDERN (1952) explained his observation of narcissistically cathected objects by pointing out that, in primary narcissism, the ego boundary coincides with the child's entire world, that, "from the beginning, the primary ego feeling also includes the external world" (p. 294). However, "primitive man was forced to detach his ego from the external world and to abandon primary narcissism only laboriously and under the pressure of the frightening external world" (p. 298). In ontogenesis, the ego boundary is withdrawn from external objects "whenever the child experiences disappointments from them, whenever he finds that they are not subservient to his wishes, and whenever he undergoes pain, grief, anxiety, and even fright from them" (p. 299). As ego libido "withdraws from the objects which had been narcissistically cathected", only the object cathexes are left behind (p. 299). Nevertheless, parts of the external world "remain narcissistically cathected and pertaining to the ego" (p. 299); and, even after withdrawal of ego libido has occurred, ego feeling and object libido can fuse again, leading to "a transitory enlargement of the ego boundary" (p. 300). In other words, ego feeling can expand "to cover object representations", so that an object cathexis becomes "a secondary narcissistic one" (FEDERN, 1952, p. 319).

Narcissistic cathexis of an object, turning the object into a selfobject, serves to "strengthen the ego feeling" (FEDERN, 1952, p. 306), and it partially restores the lost state of primary narcissism, a state towards which, according to FREUD (1914), the ego will always try to return in a roundabout way. Importantly, in secondary narcissism, ego feeling is maintained through narcissistic cathexis of objects, which means the *use of objects for the purpose of strengthening the ego feeling*. Fulfilment of narcissistic desires, "the realization of narcissistic attitudes, and the confirmation of narcissistic self-elevation occur through others" (FEDERN, 1952, p. 355); and it is through others that the feeling of safety can be maintained. Anxiety, as the state opposite to wellbeing and undisturbed ego feeling, weakens the ego, it "allows the ego boundaries to become more labile" (FEDERN, 1952, pp. 355–6), a

---

[3] Objects that are not narcissistically cathected any longer and do not contribute to narcissistic sustenance of the ego and maintenance of ego feeling can be experienced as strange or lifeless. FEDERN (1952) thought that "the outer world is estranged when the ego boundary is deprived of its narcissistic cathexis", that is, when "the ego loses its narcissistic boundary cathexis" (p. 46).

statement that anticipated KOHUT's notions of 'disintegration anxiety' and self-fragmentation.

6.1.3 Selfobjects

The self, according to self psychology, is not an agent that initiates actions but a 'structure of self-experience', "a psychological structure through which self-experience acquires cohesion and continuity" (STOLOROW, 1983, p. 291). Infant developmental research suggests that self-experience "is inseparable from experiencing the other" (p. 74), that the self "cannot be experienced without a concomitant complementary experience of the other" (STERN, 1983, p. 73). Self-experiences "can never become free from experiencing the complementary aspect of the other" (p. 73); they "can never even occur unless elicited or maintained by the actions of another" (STERN, 1983, p. 74). Self-awareness arises out of "self-regulating, interactive processes – going on between individual and caregiving environment"; and self-awareness may, in turn, affect these interactions (SANDER, 1983, p. 87). For KOHUT (1977), the self is constituted by "a milieu of empathic self-objects" (p. 249); the 'nuclear self' is formed "by the deeply anchored responsiveness of the self-objects" (p. 100). KOHUT (1983) thought that "the self and its matrix of selfobjects are, in principle, an indivisible unit" (p. 389). Selfobjects are narcissistically experienced objects that serve to maintain self-esteem (KOHUT, 1971). They are distinguished from objects that act as targets for libidinal or aggressive drives; selfobjects are distinguished from "true objects (in the psychoanalytic sense) which are cathected with object-instinctual investments, i.e., objects loved and hated" (KOHUT, 1971, p. 51). Unlike selfobjects, true or 'drive objects' are not experienced as belonging to the self, because they are not what the self is made of, and because they are the targets for drives or wishes that are, in turn, attributed to the initiative of the self.

Selfobjects are experienced by the subject as being under his control and hence as parts of the self, not dissimilarly to how body parts controlled by the subject are experienced as parts of the self (GOLDBERG, 1983). Selfobjects are controlled by the subject in order to maintain self-cohesion and self-esteem (but also to reduce anxiety). The experience of selfobjects as belonging to the self "is based on needs that preserve the integrity of the self" (SHANE & SHANE, 1986, p. 145). These are the narcissistic needs, that is, needs for selfobject responses: the need for mirroring responses from selfobjects and the need to be allowed to merge with an idealized selfobject. Ties to selfobjects are required to "sustain a subjective sense of self-cohesion, self-continuity, and self-esteem" (STOLOROW, 1983, p. 291). Self–selfobject relationships "provide self-confirmation and self-sustenance" (KOHUT, 1983, p. 395). On an archaic level of personality organization, cohesion of the self depends on the actual receipt of narcissistic sustenance; with greater maturity, self-cohesion depends on the *responsiveness* of selfobjects. In order to maintain self-cohesion, mirroring or idealizable selfobjects have to be *available*, which is to say that the selfobject surround has to be experienced as responsive. Selfobject responses or the availability and responsiveness of selfobjects sustain not only the person's self but also his sense of security. Both, cohesive self-experience and the sense of security or safety, can be defined as connectedness to the selfobject milieu. Connectedness to others enhances self-esteem and provides safety.

Interaction with object libido

In narcissistic object relations, the object is influenced (controlled) so as to provide the needed narcissistic gratification. The aim is to feel accepted and approved by the object or *to fuse with the object* and participate in the object's omnipotence (FENICHEL, 1946, p. 84). These are the mirroring and idealizing modes of relating to a selfobject, in KOHUT's terms. Loving care implies an ability to actively consider and understand the loved object. Narcissistic modes of relating hinder empathetic understanding of the other person (KOHUT, 1966), but only if one of these modes predominates. There can be no understanding of the real object, if identification, "feeling oneself in union with the object", is the exclusive aim of the relationship (FENICHEL, 1946, p. 84). In mature object relationships, on the other hand, there "must be a kind of partial and temporary identification for empathic purposes which either exists alongside the object relationship or alternates with it in short intervals" (FENICHEL, 1946, p. 84). Indeed, in healthy persons, narcissistic modes of relating are intertwined with object love and concern for the object.

Although a narcissistically cathected representation of the object (cathexis that strengthens ego feeling, in FEDERN's terms) can be distinguished from an object representation cathected with object libido, ego feeling and the libido invested in an object representation fuse whenever the object acts as selfobject *and* love object. In every psychic occurrence, "the object representation, with its libido cathexis, unites with the narcissistically cathected representations of the same object which pertain permanently to the ego" (FEDERN, 1952, p. 305). Thus, objects can be both the "targets of passionate desire" (STOLOROW, 1986b, p. 273) (drive objects) and selfobjects, from which the self – "a psychological structure ... characterized by varying degrees of cohesion and continuity" (p. 274) – obtains narcissistic sustenance. These are two dimensions of experiencing an object. These dimensions "coexist in any complex object relationship" (p. 275); although one or the other dimension predominates in the object relationship at any one time. For instance, the analyst may supply the patient with narcissistic sustenance whenever he, the analyst, empathically responds to the patient; however, when he fails to do so (when "the selfobject dimension of the transference has become temporarily obliterated or obstructed by what the patient has perceived as actual or impending selfobject failure"), the analyst becomes "a source of painful and conflictual affect states" (STOLOROW, 1986b, p. 276).

6.1.4 Self as another

Human desire, expressed on the symbolic plane, is the desire of a third person with whom the self (the speaking subject) is linked (LACAN, 1966).[4] The Lacanian self, inhabiting the symbolic plane, is *an other*, a model, an ideal. According to RICOEUR (1990), "the selfhood of oneself implies otherness to such an intimate degree that one cannot be thought of without the other, that instead one passes into the other" (p. 3). Taking oneself as another is related to the process of identification with another (the third person). It is through identification with another that we can satisfy our desire (for devotion and care from the omnipotent object). In the oedipal period, the child seeks to ensure access to narcissistic supplies from the mother (thereby to satisfy his desire) by adhering to norms and rules laid down by the father (the third person), and the child does so by identifying with the father, by taking on the father's attributes and traits. It is this identification with another (the third person) that, with the resolution of the Oedipus complex, constitutes the child's sense of self. Following the oedipal period, *we live our lives looking through the eyes of the third person (the father) – or rather through the eyes of the ego ideal representing the introjected father – towards the omnipotent object (a derivative of the mother)*. It is through the resolution of the Oedipus complex that the self is positioned in the symbolic order of language and hence in the symbolic world of culture and social norms (the 'law of the father').

FREUD (1923) had previously considered the ego, that is, the *self*, as a precipitate of former identifications with objects (of abandoned object cathexes). Being identified with an object, the self *is an other*. As a result of identification with the third object in the oedipal period, self and other become, to some extent, interchangeable. Relationships formed with others later in life are often formed between the self-identified-with-another and a derivative of the primary love object. FENICHEL (1946) saw that object relationships are often coupled with identifications that are based on earlier identifications "with the objects of the Oedipus complex" (p. 109). If the self is a precipitate of object identifications, then the self, too, is an object (in contradistinction to the subject). FREUD (1923) did regard the ego, that is, the *self*, as an object. MEAD (1934), too, thought that the self, being essentially another, can be an object to the person himself, so that he can respond to his self as another person may respond to it. Awareness of the self (self-consciousness) may not be essentially different from awareness of

---

[4] The ego, according to LACAN (1966), is a formation of *reflexive* libido and inhabits the plane of 'the imaginary', on which the sense of identity is given by the perceptual 'imago' (the imago being the other to the ego). The 'imaginary' ego has to be distinguished from the speaking subject (the self), which inhabits the plane of 'the symbolic', the plane of desire. All dyadic relations are of an 'imaginary' style; for a relation to become 'symbolic', there has to be a mediating third person (LACAN, 1966).

any object; "consciousness may adopt it as an object to be observed like any other object" (FINK, 1997, p. 86). The self can be regarded "as an external view or image of the subject which is internalized" (FINK, 1997, p. 86). If the self is an object, then it can be cathected (invested) with (narcissistic) libido like any other object.

6.1.5 Internalized object relations

Having internalized the mother, the child is able to invoke an inner vision of her in her absence (BALINT, 1952; BION 1962). As the child increasingly relies on language to engage the mother, he becomes able to engage the inner vision of the mother in conversation. This 'inner dialogue' (CASHDAN, 1988) not only holds the internalized mother in place and keeps her engaged; it also attracts, in imagination, her *benevolent interest and approval*. As the child's interpersonal world expands, "inner dialogues extend beyond the mother to include conversations with a whole host of others" (p. 45). The inner presences of childhood are transformed into a sense of self, so that the child starts conversing with his self. The self, according to CASHDAN (1988), "is the linguistic derivative of internalized relationships that have their beginnings in childhood" (p. 48). In general, relationships that people establish with one another "are instrumental in maintaining a viable sense of self" (p. 55). People's self-esteem, self-worth, and self-regard "describe how they feel about who they are and how they relate to others" (CASHDAN, 1988, p. 47). Both, external and internalized relationships, form and sustain the self, but the internal image of the self, which engages in, *and is engaged in*, inner dialogues, reflects internalized relationships.

> When a person says, "I don't like myself", he may not realize it, but he is indicating that there are figures in his inner world who put him down and actively disparage him.
> (CASHDAN, 1988, p. 48)

KERNBERG (1982a) suggested that interpersonal relationships are enacted in accordance with internal templates of 'self–other experiences'. He called these interactional templates 'bipolar intrapsychic representations'; they consist of an image of the self, an image of the other, and an affective colouring. 'Bipolar intrapsychic representations' are the 'building blocks' of the personality and the mind. They determine not only our relationships but also the ways in which we perceive others in interpersonal situations and the way we think about them. The integrated sense of self is the total sum of self-images contained in bipolar intrapsychic representations. In childhood, the self "evolves gradually from the integration of its component self-representations into a supraordinate structure" (p. 905). The self is "the sum total of self-representations in intimate connection with the sum total of object representations" (KERNBERG, 1982a, p. 900). Self and internalized object representations remain intimately connected because the view one has of oneself is dependent on one's objects. The self representation is dependent on others because "trust in one's self and one's goodness is based upon the confirmation of love from internalized good objects" (KERNBERG, 1976, p. 73).[5]

6.1.6 Façade and self-alienation

There is a *qualitative* difference, according to HORNEY (1939), between normal self-esteem and narcissistic self-aggrandizement (self-inflation). While normal "self-esteem rests on qualities which a person actually possesses", "self-inflation implies presenting to the self and others qualities or achievements for which there is no adequate foundation" (p. 99). Narcissistic striving for self-aggrandizement becomes a feature of the personality "if self-esteem and other qualities pertaining to the individual's spontaneous self are smothered" in childhood (p. 99). Narcissism, as HORNEY (1939) saw it, is an expression "of alienation from the self" (p. 100). Narcissistic persons "lack judgment of their own value base because they have relegated it to others" (p. 98). The narcissistic person tries to obtain admiration from others to compensate for feelings of being unwanted; his behaviour is designed to make others "pay attention to him and admire him", so as to try and overcome his sense of not being loved and respected "for what he is" (p. 93). His security rests on being admired or flattered by others. If his efforts to secure others' admiration fail, or if admiration is "paid to someone else", his deep insecurity is brought back to the surface again (HORNEY, 1939, p. 94).

> While in all of us self-esteem is to some extent dependent upon the estimate of others, in this case nothing but the estimate of others counts.
> (HORNEY, 1939, p. 92)

The 'spontaneous individual self' is warped in neurosis, in general (HORNEY, 1939). The neurotic person is alienated from himself, in that he "has lost his center of gravity in himself and shifted it to the outside world" (p. 189). He, that is, his self, has become excessively dependent on the opinion of others. In neurosis, the person feels dependent upon and, at the same time, helpless towards "a potentially hostile world"; he feels "defenseless in the midst

---

[5] In general, self and object images in bipolar intrapsychic representations are linked by an affect, reflecting the narcissistic, libidinal, or aggressive nature of the relationship. Affects have a cognitive component (along with behavioural, communicative, and autonomic components) (KERNBERG, 1992). The cognitive content always reflects "a relation between an aspect of the patient's self and an aspect of one or another of his object representations" (p. 11). In the context of a particular affect, the subject experiences "an image or representation of the self relating to an image or representation of another person" (KERNBERG, 1992, p. 7).

of danger" (p. 253).[6] The image that "the neurotic is anxious to present to himself and others" "is determined mainly by his fear of disapproval and his craving for distinction" (p. 176). The neurotic person's "need to appear perfect", "to present an infallible façade will conflict with all the trends not fitting into the façade" (p. 192). These are the conflicts of neurosis (HORNEY, 1939).

The neurotic person lacks aliveness; his 'emotional energies' are not available to him (HORNEY, 1945, p. 100). To the extent that his capacities to solicit recognition and love through his spontaneous actions are inhibited, his striving for safety is mediated by his efforts to furnish and present to others an 'idealized image' of himself, an image that, so he believes unconsciously, will attract others' approval, admiration, or affection. To the extent that he is inhibited in his assertive and affectionate capacities, in his abilities to reach out and make contact with others, he is also alienated from his self. He is estranged from himself; and instead of living his own life, he has to "live the life of his image", of his idealized self-image (p. 111). In being overly dependent on an idealized image and in giving others' "evaluation of himself undue importance", "his center of gravity comes to rest more in others than in himself" (p. 151). Inasmuch as he lacks "realistic self-esteem" and inasmuch as he has to derive "unrealistic pride" from an idealized self-image, he feels "like a shadow without weight or substance" (HORNEY, 1945, p. 151). If, in the process of psychoanalysis, realistic self-esteem can be strengthened, the centre of gravity shifts back to the person himself.

> The stronger a person becomes, the less he feels threatened by others. The accrual of strength stems from various sources. His center of gravity, which had been shifted to others, comes to rest within himself; he feels more active and starts to establish his own set of values. He will gradually have more energy available: the energy that had gone into repressing part of himself is released; he becomes less inhibited, less paralyzed by fears, self-contempt, and hopelessness.
>
> (HORNEY, 1945, p. 238)

6.2 Sociological perspectives

The self, according to WILLIAM JAMES (1890) and GEORGE HERBERT MEAD (1934), is a social self. Our selves exists only insofar as others exist and enter into our experience, insofar as others' actions influence our thoughts, feelings, and attitudes (MEAD, 1934). Others' actions influence our thoughts, feelings, and attitudes insofar as they help us redefine our relation to others and our position in a fluctuating social fabric. In a social situation, we *reflect*

---

[6] Confirming that the self serves to inhibit the latent hostility of the social surround.

on our actions and *survey*[7] the results of our actions, that is, the effects that our actions have had on others, especially on their attitudes towards ourselves. We *survey*, according to MEAD (1934), *our selves* with reference to the reactions of others. As FOULKES (1964) noted, the individual gets to know himself "by the effect he has upon others and the picture they form of him" (p. 110). The self is constituted of the attitudes of others towards the self, so that we see ourselves as others see us. The demands of society thereby enter into the construction of the self; social criticism becomes self-criticism. GOFFMAN (1959) not only saw that the self is essentially situationally defined, defined by others' attitudes towards ourselves as they manifest in a particular social situation; he also argued that we actively influence others' attitudes and thereby shape our self-experience by performing a role that is socially acceptable and appropriate to the occasion, a role that reflects expectations of others and of society at large.

6.2.1 Me and I

The self is constituted by the attitudes of particular others towards oneself (MEAD, 1934). The attitude of the 'generalized other' towards oneself encapsulates these particular attitudes. The term 'generalized other' refers to the community or social group that engenders one's self and confers unity (cohesion) to the self. Thus, the self is also constituted "by an organization of the social attitudes of the generalized other or the social group as a whole" (p. 158). MEAD (1934) distinguished between the 'me' and the 'I'. It is the person's 'me' that is constituted by organized sets of attitudes of others towards himself and that represents the demands and expectations of society. The 'I' is, in part, the person's response to these attitudes. The response of the 'I' is determined, in part, by what is captures by the 'me'. The 'I' and the 'me' belong together (one being the response to the other) and jointly constitute the self.[8] The person's response to the social situation – the response that constitutes the 'I' – is inherently unpredictable and thus responsible for the person's sense of freedom and initiative (MEAD, 1934).

The 'me' is the social self, whereas the 'I' is less constrained by society, insofar as it refers to personal desires, wishes, and needs that express themselves spontaneously and creatively. Thus, the person not only gathers others' attitudes towards himself and organizes them into a view of himself (of his self), he also expresses himself *spontaneously* and thereby creatively shapes others' attitudes towards himself (MEAD, 1934). The 'me' is not an entirely passive structure, given that a great part of social behaviour (namely narcissistic behaviour) is guided by, and aims to optimize, others' attitudes

---

[7] Implicating the brain's default mode.
[8] Self-awareness, MEAD (1934) contended, arises from the person's ability to distinguish between 'me' and 'I'.

towards oneself. The distinction between 'me' and 'I' resonates with the distinction drawn by psychoanalytic writers, such as HORNEY and WINNICOTT, between 'false self' and 'true self', with the 'false self' (persona) representing the façade that is maintained for and projected to others, and the 'true self' being the agent of spontaneous assertive and affectionate actions.[9] Similarly, WILHELM REICH spoke of a 'true self', which he thought has to be suppressed and subordinated to the demands of modern society. Most persons possess both true and false selves. A person may act variously in accordance with his true self or false self, his 'I' or 'me', depending on the familiarity or formality of the social situation he occupies and on how certain his position therein is.

6.2.2 Role performance

According to GOFFMAN (1959), individuals perform roles within specific social settings and thereby manage the impressions they create on others. The self, in a first approximation, is an awareness of the multitude of roles played in various social settings; the self is a façade, a character, or a set of characters, performed for audiences. Social performances by individuals involve the monitoring of impressions made upon others (GOFFMAN, 1959). An audience, being impressed in whichever direction by a social performance, imputes a self to the performer; so that the self, at any one time, is also an awareness of the social effect of the performance. The performer seeks to present and realize a self-image that is *acceptable* to others, one that accords with social expectations and conventions relevant to the particular situation. The self, thus defined, is not the initiator of performances; instead, subjective intentions and capabilities are attributed to the self after successful performances. The performer is primarily concerned about whether the audience will credit or discredit his performance, whether he will be accepted or ridiculed. Social performances aim to elicit or maintain others' respect and trust, which, in turn, signify safety for the individual and crystallize into his self-esteem. The self is also related to *symbolically defined* social statuses and positions, as these support the individual's role performances and augment the impression they make on others. Thus, self and identity are constructed in part through the adoption of social positions or functions that are validated by social institutions operating on different levels of society (GOFFMAN, 1959).

---

[9] The 'I' may cover aspects of the false self. It may reflect standards and expectations of society insofar as it says 'I was', 'I am', or 'I will be', as opposed to saying 'I want', 'I need', or 'I will', which are expressions attributable to the true self. The 'my' can be distinguished from the 'I' and 'me'. It expresses the person's narcissistic use of objects; it refers to narcissistic investments in, or selfobject functions of, objects, both animate and inanimate.

Nevertheless, the self is not exclusively defined by roles; individuals are capable of maintaining a distance to the roles they play in various settings. 'Role distance' is related to confidence, competence, and credibility of the self (GOFFMAN, 1959). Normative performances also alternate with expressions of spontaneity and creativity. GOFFMAN (1959) spoke of 'front regions' and 'back regions'. Spontaneous aspects of the personality are suppressed in 'front regions', but in 'back regions', where individuals do not have to worry about the image they project, these aspects of personality can be expressed. It is important to understand where the demarcations lie between front and back regions; for neurotic persons, there may be very few 'back regions'. Moreover, the more a particular culture values appearances, the less scope there will be for back-room behaviour.

6.2.3 Duty

While *wishes* express our spontaneous or true self, *duties* that we assume in accordance with our social position help to define our self-for-others, which is, to some extent, a false self. FLUGEL (1945) suggested that the duty is "originally in a way extraneous to the self" (i.e., egodystonic), but it "becomes adopted by the self"; "it becomes as it were a part of our self, so that its fulfilment becomes at least as much the concern of the self as the fulfilment of a wish" (p. 18). As we grow older (and as our ego identity changes), duties we have taken on "become 'second nature' and almost as spontaneous as wishes" (meaning that "with older people the sharp contrast between wish and duty tends to get obliterated") (FLUGEL, 1945, p. 19). Our willingness to fulfil our duties (and to engage in moral conduct, in general) utilizes "the energy that is always ready to be mobilized on behalf of the self" (p. 25). FLUGEL (1945) explained (with reference to WILLIAM MCDOUGALL) that we make a tendency our own when "we endow it with the interest and value that we attach to the idea of the self as an object with which we are vitally concerned" (p. 25). The fulfilment of a duty is the concern of the self, inasmuch as it is "essential to our mental well-being" (FLUGEL, 1945, p. 18), inasmuch as it helps to uphold our feeling of safety or narcissistic equilibrium. FLUGEL (1945) thought that "one of the central features of the development of the moral life" is that it makes an essential contribution to our mental well-being (p. 18).

6.2.4 Ego identity and collective consciousness

> A strong ego, secured in its identity by a strong society, does not need, and in fact is immune to, any attempt at artificial inflation. ... it tends toward the creation of a strong mutual reinforcement with others in a group ego, which will transmit its will to the next generation.
> (ERIKSON, 1959, pp. 208–9)

ERIKSON (1950, 1959) emphasized that the individual's sense of identity is a group-psychological phenomenon. Ego identity is shaped by membership of a social group and embeddedness in a historical and cultural context. ANZIEU (1987) suggested that the individual has experiences of mental shape (as well as experiences of mental content). The *individual's* mental shape ('psychic envelope') is a protective boundary that retains his sense of identity. The *group*, too, has an envelope that retains its identity. Mental shape ('psychic envelope') is used by ANZIEU (1987) as a bridging concept between individual and group psychology. Group members have an identity through their relationship with the group. Individuals' confused feelings concerning self and identity are resolved by participation in a collective identity. Group members also have a collective consciousness, a collectively experienced illusion, which provides them with their own boundary and identity. Collective consciousness, as a collectively experienced illusion, is necessary for group formation; and it entails the collective imaginative belief that the group operates "like a good, exacting, and giving mother" (ANZIEU, 1975, p. 95). The group is the mother with whom, on the deepest unconscious level, the individual seeks to reunite, restoring the symbiotic (and primary narcissistic) unity between mother and child.

DURKHEIM (1893) described two opposing forces: the inclination to think and act for ourselves and the inclination to think and act like other people. Either "the ideal is to create for ourselves a special, personal image", or, alternatively, our personality disappears and we become a collective being, indistinguishable from others (p. 84). Accordingly, there are two forms of consciousness within us. One comprises states that are "characteristic of us as individuals"; "whilst the other comprises states that are common to the whole of society" (p. 61). These two consciousnesses interpenetrate each other (DURKHEIM, 1893). 'Collective consciousness', that is, the "totality of beliefs and sentiments common to the average members of a society" (pp. 38–9), envelops individual consciousnesses. When this envelopment is total, individuality is zero. Individuals may be less absorbed in the life of the collective, providing them with space for individuality and initiative. DURKHEIM (1893) emphasized that individual life emerged from collective life; personal individuality "developed from within a pre-existing social environment", and "it necessarily bears its stamp" (p. 221). The individual, in seemingly becoming autonomous, remains intimately linked to the collective; individual psychology is derived from, and can only be understood on the basis of, group psychology.[10]

---

[10] DURKHEIM (1893) likened the individual personality, participating in society's division of labour, to "an organ or part of an organ that has its own definite function, but that cannot, without running a mortal risk, separate itself from the rest of the organism" (p. 221). The division of labour produces a sense of alienation when individuals feel a lack of contact with one another or with the collective as a whole (DURKHEIM, 1893).

6.2.5 Affirmation of identity

Religious, philosophical, or political beliefs "constitute a vital part of a man's sense of his own identity" (Storr, 1968, p. 54). We obtain reassurance and *security* from other people who "think and feel exactly like ourselves", whereby "the more insecure we are, the more we look for this kind of affirmation of our own identities" (p. 54). The person who feels insecure within himself "will look for people with whom he can identify himself in order to affirm his own identity" (p. 56). Relationships between people are often "based upon identification and mutual reassurance", as can be observed in organizations and associations (Storr, 1968, p. 57). Identification with others means dependence; "and dependence means vulnerability to attack from those upon whom one is dependent" (p. 56). A difference in beliefs and opinions between oneself and the person with whom one identifies will be felt as an attack. The expression by others of beliefs and opinions that diverge from one's own beliefs and opinions is felt as a threat to one's inner security and, hence, produces offensive aggression, often with the apparent aim of asserting one's beliefs and opinions. Ultimately, however, aggression in these situations serves to preserve or reestablish one's identity (Storr, 1968). Others are manipulated, through more or less overtly aggressive means, into supporting one's identity and, hence, one's self-esteem. One's identity (being a source of self-esteem) is established and defended in a manner that is not dissimilar to the role played by aggression in territoriality.

Most of us are dependent on "recurrent affirmation of our value as lovable human beings" (Storr, 1968, p. 70). Having acquired in childhood "an inner source of self-esteem derived from parental love" (p. 70), we will constantly renew our "sense of value through loving and being loved" (p. 69). The belief in our masculinity or femininity "is a fundamental part of human identity" and a basic source of self-esteem (p. 68). Persons who, due to emotional difficulties in their childhood, are uncertain "that, as man or woman, they are both able to love and be loved" (p. 68), may "translate their disappointment into creative work"; or they may, "by feverish competition in the world of power, achieve wealth and status" (p. 69). Their "achievements which single them out from their fellows" (p. 69) provide an alternative, albeit less secure, source of self-esteem. Persons, who "possess no inner sense of self-esteem", however successful they may be in life, "will remain intensely vulnerable to failure, rejection or disappointment" (Storr, 1968, p. 78).

6.2.6 Self as a narrative or theory

The self, in the sense of ego feeling, is constructed in social situations through one's role performance. The image of the self, on the other hand, is constructed through recollection of one's past. The self constructs its own image and organizes its own history by selective remembering (GREENWALD, 1980). The self is, in a sense, a 'personal historian', as it engages not only in mnemonic preservation but also in retrospective invention (falsification) of its own history. Mnemonic biases are applied in the creation of personal history, aiming to maximize the *survivability of the self*. Egocentricity, one of these biases, construes the self as the reason of, and a target for, others' actions. 'Beneffectance', another mnemonic bias, means that the self accepts credit for successful outcomes; the self is so constructed that it become the "origin of good effects" (p. 605). People are inclined to see themselves (i.e., regard their selves) as the cause of good effects, yet they regard themselves (i.e., their selves) "reluctantly as the origin of ill effects" (p. 605). 'Vicarious beneffectance' means that the self readily shares in the good results or victories of others and distances itself from defeats; and it is in this spirit that the self is remembered. Siding with the winners, the self bathes in others' glory (enhancing its narcissistic cathexis). Another bias is 'cognitive conservatism'; it refers to the inclination to justify one's actions and decisions retrospectively. Thus, knowledge about oneself, and hence the image of one's self, is structured and organized in self-focused, self-aggrandizing, and self-justifying processes (GREENWALD, 1980).

In GREENWALD's (1980) model, the self is indistinguishable from the process that gives rise to it. The self is its own creation. One could however say that it is not the self that creates its own image; the self *is* the image, and it is constructed by narcissism, by the need to maintain connectedness, inclusion, and safety. The image of the self constructed in one's mind expresses one's need for safety; and as we create, and cling to, an illusion of safety, we create ourselves. EPSTEIN (1973) argued that the self is but a self-theory; the self "is a theory that the individual has unwittingly constructed about himself as an experiencing, functioning individual" (p. 407). Individuals have theories about themselves; and these theories *are* their selves. Although the self image is but a theory, it is a theory that plays in important regulatory function. It sets the framework for forthcoming interactions with others. It informs the individual about his safety; it sets the appropriate level of anxiety prior to engaging with others; and it regulates whether and how 'instinctual drives' should be expressed in any particular social situation.

6.3 Vulnerability of the self

Defence mechanisms that modify the behavioural expression of an 'instinctual drive', so as to safeguard or fortify external sources of narcissistic sustenance, can be distinguished from defences that repress an instinctual wish (drive impulse) or that change its appearance in consciousness alone; no interaction needs to take place. Anxiety arises before an *unacceptable* impulse that seeks satisfaction and moves upwards towards consciousness can reach full consciousness (A. FREUD in SANDLER, 1985, p. 240). Anxiety arises if a libidinal or aggressive impulse, pressing for 'discharge' and reaching consciousness, is in conflict with one's striving for safety, that is, one's need for protection against aggression from without. Anxiety, signalling a "threat arising from outside" (SANDLER, 1985, p. 17), then implements a defensive manoeuvre.

> If, as the impulse proceeds, there is a signal of danger, then his psychic apparatus is activated to apply the appropriate psychological structures in order to change the content of the realm of experience into a form that is safer, even if it means giving up direct instinctual gratifications.
> (SANDLER & JOFFE, 1969, p. 246)

We defend not only against intrusive wishes (arising from the 'id') but also against "painful reality" (p. 19), again insofar as reality is in conflict with our striving for safety (SANDLER, 1985), for a state in which we are unlikely to be attacked by the group or authority figures. Why can the mere awareness of an inacceptable impulse, deed, or personality characteristic give rise to anxiety? The ego seems to deal with inacceptable impulses and thoughts about deplorable past deeds or unflattering personality characteristics as if these were visible to others. *They are, of course, visible, in a sense, to the superego, the internal representative of authority figures.*

Defence mechanisms of repression and projection also illustrate the proposition that the self is a precious attractor of others' approving and affirming gestures. There is an unfaltering striving to enhance one's self-worth as a proxy for one's *access* to narcissistic supplies and for one's connectedness to the selfobject surround. An inacceptable impulse bestows an undesirable property upon the self, thereby lowering self-worth and increasing one's perceived vulnerability to rejection and conspecific attack. It is this increased vulnerability of the self that is experienced as anxiety or guilt. Repressing or projecting the inacceptable impulse immediately raises self-esteem and decreases anxiety.

6.3.1 Self-serving bias

The Freudian 'unconscious' does not include *mechanisms* that we deem to be unconscious. The unconscious, as a system, contains only those elements that have the *potential to be conscious* and that were, in the past, part of consciousness, but that have been suppressed by social influences and the desire to be accepted and not to be disapproved by others. *Defence reactions skew the content of conscious experience* and, thereby, regulate self-esteem (MOORE, 1926). Consciously, the person tends to overestimate himself. The person's overestimation "tends to stay at the conscious level", while "the underestimation, because of its unfavourable character, is readily repressed to the depth of the unconscious" (p. 175).[11] It is the "system of defense reactions" that guards "against the realization of our own defects" (p. 174). Consciousness of oneself (one's self) and self-esteem (including neurotic pride) are intricately liked with the operation of repression. We have "an instinctive tendency ... to keep others from talking about anything in our life which we look upon as shameful or disgraceful"; and "we do not like to think about such incidents ourselves" (p. 211). Events, "especially those involving wounded pride", "are at once glossed over with excuses" (MOORE, 1926, p. 211).

> With some, their personal self-esteem is so hedged in with a system of defense reactions that nothing seems capable of disturbing it. Their ignorant blunders, imperfections, sins, are promptly excused and all blame shifted on to the shoulders of others. Murmurings of a self-accusation are promptly suppressed and securely confined in the dungeons of the subconscious. With others, the least shadow of failure or disappointment brings on a depression, deprives them of all self-confidence, robs them of energy, takes away their desire and hope to do and accomplish.
> (MOORE, 1926, p. 174)

6.3.2 Self-system

The essential undesirability of being anxious corresponds to the essential desirability of being acceptable to others (of being 'good-me') (SULLIVAN, 1953). The self is closely related to the experience of anxiety as well as to the receipt, or lack of receipt, of external appraisals. The 'self-system' is formed "on the basis of reflected appraisals from others and the learning of roles which one undertook to live" (SULLIVAN, 1953, p. 17). The self-system constitutes "all the defenses that are built to cope with these appraisals and their distortions" (ARIETI, 1973, p. 126). The way in which one sees oneself "is controlled by the self-system", whereby the self-system "manipulates the content of consciousness depending on the prevailing level of anxiety" (CHRZANOWSKI, 1973, p. 143). The self is perhaps but "the content of consciousness within the framework of a person's socialization, acculturation, and his formative relational patterning" (p. 133); it is "more or less

---

[11] The dynamic unconscious contains "unacceptable states of self-awareness" (KERNBERG, 1982b, p. 12). These are states (memories or insights) that are *unacceptable* to oneself because they are unacceptable to one's authority figures; they are *repressed* because they would undermine the self (disrupt the narcissistic homeostasis). It is the mechanism of repression that "leads to the formation of the dynamic unconscious in a broad sense, and to the id as an organized mental structure in a narrower one" (KERNBERG, 1982b, p. 12). If repression fails, "contents of the id appear in consciousness in split-off or mutually dissociated ego states" (reactivation of the developmentally earlier mechanism of 'ego splitting') (KERNBERG, 1982b, p. 5).

coterminous with the information directly available to the individual" (CHRZANOWSKI, 1973, p. 134). The self-system is engaged during the pursuit of "every general need that a person has" (SULLIVAN, 1953, p. 166).

The origin of the self-system can be said to rest on the irrational character of culture or, more specifically, society. Were it not for the fact that a great many prescribed ways of doing things have to be lived up to, in order that one shall maintain workable, profitable, satisfactory relations with his fellows; or, were the prescriptions for the types of behavior in carrying on relations with one's fellows perfectly rational – then, for all I know, there would not be evolved, in the course of becoming a person, anything like the sort of self-system that we always encounter.

(SULLIVAN, 1953, p. 168)

The self-system acts as a "vigilant guardian against the experience of crippling anxiety" (CHRZANOWSKI, 1973, p. 142). Interpersonal experiences that deprive the person of appraisals and lower his self-esteem give rise to anxiety; and lowered self-esteem precipitates 'security operations' (some of which are self-defeating) (SULLIVAN, 1953). The self-system responds to, or prevents reexposure to, interpersonal situations that provoke anxiety, including situations that remind the infant of the mother's 'forbidding gestures'. If the person goes "through a whole series of consistent failures of what we call security operations", "self-system activity will come in *more* readily at the faint hint of anxiety-provoking situations" (SULLIVAN, 1953, p. 191). The 'self-system' and its 'security operations', notions of interpersonal psychoanalysis, resemble the classical notions of ego and its defences. The defence against anxiety is one of the key *functions* of the ego (HARTMANN, 1964). Defence mechanisms are at the disposal of the ego, if 'ego' is conceived as part of the mental apparatus; and they serve to protect the ego, if 'ego' means 'self'. Defence mechanisms, according to ARIETI (1970), are "devices to protect the self or the self-image" (p. 25). They are devices that bring about "feelings, ideas, and strategic forms of behavior that make the self-image acceptable or at least less unacceptable" (ARIETI, 1970, p. 25) to the person's social surround.

6.3.3 Repression

Repression is an escape response to painful thought and feeling (RADO, 1956). Similarly to other pain-related behaviours, repression effects a "riddance from painful thought and feeling" (RADO, 1956, p. 244). Thoughts, wishes, urges, and feelings that are consciously intolerable to oneself are reassigned to a deeper layer of the psyche, the Freudian 'unconscious'. The unconscious can be considered as a "repository for much that is painful in fantasy, ideation, or experience" (LAUGHLIN, 1970, p. 358). Inaccessible to conscious recall, the repressed material remains active and potent. The repressed material continues to seek expression in indirect ways through behaviour and ideation (FREUD, 1915, 1920). Repression, as FREUD (1915) emphasized, "interferes only with the relation of the instinctual representative to *one* psychical system, namely, to that of the conscious"; "repression does not hinder the instinctual representative from continuing to exist in the unconscious, from organizing itself further, putting out derivatives and establishing connections" (p. 149). The instinctual wish "is withdrawn by repression from conscious influence" but "proliferates in the dark, as it were, and takes on extreme forms of expression" (FREUD, 1915, p. 149).

An impulse that is about to be repressed has come "near enough to consciousness to arouse anxiety but not near enough to be perceived" (A. FREUD in SANDLER, 1985, p. 243). Anxiety is the active force that brings about repression (LAUGHLIN, 1970, p. 359). Anxiety also signals to the ego the threat of 'derepression' and calls into operation other defences as reinforcements of repression (p. 359). Repression, as a basic process, is a "prerequisite to the elaboration of the other ego defenses" (LAUGHLIN, 1970, p. 359). Not infrequently, a third line of defence is required to deal with intolerable aspects of ideation or behaviour that attempt to express the repressed material indirectly (BERGLER, 1952).

> A primitive wish or the content associated with it may be fully inhibited (repressed) or may be absorbed into a thought or action that seems ... nonthreatening, and that can then be allowed to proceed to discharge in consciousness or action.
> (SANDLER & JOFFE, 1968, p. 261)

Instinctual impulses that are expressed relatively freely in consciousness have, as a rule, been modified by defences; "they have been modified so that they are ego syntonic" and "acceptable to the ego in free association" (SANDLER, 1985, p. 38), that is, their expression in action *would* be acceptable to, and would not be criticized by, others, or it would be approved of by others.[12] What is reduced or prevented in each case, be it repression or modification of an impulse, is anxiety or another form of 'unpleasure', as it captures the risk of being attacked or criticized, which, in turn, is inversely related to the stability of one's narcissistic resources and one's connectedness to the selfobject milieu.

6.3.4 Displaced action

Instinctual wishes give rise to *ideas* in consciousness, but they tend to do so only if these ideas are egosyntonic. An idea is repressed (relegated to the dynamic unconscious), if it is "incompatible with the main body of a

---

[12] The feeling that others can have access to one's thoughts is enshrined in the very experience of one's self.

patient's socially and consciously acceptable ideas" (G. KLEIN, 1967, p. 86) (with ideas that constitute the patient's identity and are relevant to his need to be *accepted* or approved, or to be *acceptable* or approvable). The repressed idea (or the instinctual wish that gave rise to it) produces an action tendency. The repressed idea acts by priming representations of objects or events that can gratify the instinctual wish; and once such objects or events are encountered, they "become encoded in respect to their relevance to the wish" (G. KLEIN, 1967, p. 111). Actions can ensue and gratification of the wish can be achieved, "while the person fails to comprehend what his good feeling really refers to" (p. 111). As G. KLEIN (1967) pointed out, an "action instigated by a repressed idea is often characterized by its apparent absence of intentionality" (p. 111). Repressive (displaced) actions are associated with "failures to comprehend connections, e.g., not seeing causal links" (unawareness of the significance of actions), "gaps of awareness or attentional failures" (perceptual scotomata), and "diversionary behavior that helps evade or reduce painful affect" (p. 112). Repressive action can be blocked by further defences or take the form of trains of "purely intellectualizing thought" (G. KLEIN, 1967, p. 112).

6.3.5 Projection

Projection directs outwardly and attributes to others aspects of one's own disclaimed and personally objectionable character traits, attitudes, motives, and desires.

(LAUGHLIN, 1970, p. 228)

Projection refers to the imputation to another of disapproved and thus consciously disowned feelings and motives (LAUGHLIN, 1970, p. 221). Conflict and anxiety can be avoided by ascribing to another one's burdensome responsibility, guilt, or anger (LAUGHLIN, 1970, p. 220). As ANNA FREUD put it, projection effects "an immediate warding off of a feeling of responsibility, of guilt, of a punishable action" (in SANDLER, 1985, p. 58).[13] SANDLER (1985) distinguished between projection and externalization by pointing out that, in projection, the unwanted *impulse* that has been attributed to another person is "felt as coming back against the person himself" (p. 136). An aggressive impulse, for instance, would, as a result of projection, be felt "as an aggressive act or intention coming back at the subject from someone else" (p. 57). In externalization, aspects of the self-representation are similarly attributed

---

[13] Projection, like identification, operates on "a background of empathy"; empathy provides "the unconscious framework for the projection" (SANDLER, 1985, p. 146). Projection and 'secondary identification' "are opposite sides of the same coin", and where one exists the other must exist too, "because in identification an attribute of the object is taken over into one's own self-representation, and in projection the reverse occurs" (SANDLER, 1985, p. 436).

to others, but there is no "turning back of the wish or impulses against oneself" (SANDLER, 1985, p. 137).

Others' attitudes that are critical of ourselves (others' disapprovals) are anxiety-provoking; they tend not to be accepted by or attributed to the self. We tend not to "recognize traits about ourselves that have personally and socially handicapping consequences" (LAUGHLIN, 1970, p. 224). Externalization and projection enable us to remain blind to undesirable traits and impulses and thereby avoid feelings of vulnerability to social disapproval and hostility (and hence avoid anxiety). Socially inacceptable traits and impulses are disowned insofar as they would decrease our acceptability in the eyes of others (and hence decrease our safety). They can be disowned by being allocated to and perceived in others instead ('externalized'), so that our hostility (which may be increased in the context of our insecurity, resulting from a dim awareness of our unacceptable qualities and attitudes) can find an outlet, a justifiable target. By way of projection, we secure "a substitute and more tolerable target for [our] resentment, accusations, and recriminations" (LAUGHLIN, 1970, p. 228).

Any awareness of having unacceptable attitudes or impulses invites *self-criticism*, yet self-critical feelings tend to be projected. Self-critical feelings about unacceptable attitudes and feelings of self-condemnation for failed responsibilities may be intolerable and are then projected onto others (LAUGHLIN, 1970, p. 228). They turn into beliefs that one is being criticized unjustly by others, beliefs that justify one's own aggression against others. Evidence "or what may be interpreted (or perhaps rather misinterpreted) as such by the individual" serves to "reinforce the projected image of hostility and persecution" (LAUGHLIN, 1970, p. 231). In general, evidence in support of one's self-appraisal, prejudiced beliefs, projections, and paranoid system is "eagerly seized upon" (p. 231). Delusions of persecution, in which the individual elaborates beliefs of being hated and plotted against, are the most malignant manifestations of projection. Projection serves as psychodynamic "basis for most of the paranoid delusions in schizophrenia" (LAUGHLIN, 1970, p. 232).

6.3.6 Denial

Denial is a primitive defence mechanism that is closely related to repression. Denial concerns consciously intolerable facts, usually facts about oneself (LAUGHLIN, 1970). Denial, as an unconsciously operating defence mechanism, is a failure (of the ego) to perceive "something significant that for one reason or another is unwelcome" (SANDLER, 1985, p. 246). It is a withdrawal of attention from, or an avoidance to look at, "something painful or threatening" in the external world (SANDLER, 1985, p. 246). The aim of denial, as of any other defence mechanism, is *to secure the ego*, to prevent it from experiencing painful affects. Denial can do away with a disagreeable reality that would give rise to anxiety, feelings of inadequacy, or narcissistic injury;

something that has happened in the external world is "declared not to have happened" (A. FREUD in SANDLER, 1985, p. 528).

Aspects of reality are denied in order to ward off *disapproval*, combat insecurity, and prevent anxiety (LAUGHLIN, 1970, p. 59). Disability or symptoms of illness may be denied because of "personal embarrassment or self-critical attitudes, or because of unpleasant social connotations" (p. 69). For the same reason, one may deny the presence of terminal illness, alcoholism and its effects, drug addiction, physical handicap, or age and the effects of aging. Denial serves to maintain or enhance one's self-image and to gloss over low self-confidence. Denial allows oneself to sees *one's self* and "one's behaviour and standards as compatible with those of society" (LAUGHLIN, 1970, p. 65). Denial fosters an unconscious sense of invulnerability (omnipotence). The possibility of death is often denied, as is the possibility of external danger. Similarly, one's dependence on others can be denied, as is characteristically the case in mania. Dependence entails vulnerability (of the self), and both can be denied. Denial of the loss of a love object is part of the mourning process (LAUGHLIN, 1970).

Children often use denial to "try to push aside the impending or actual loss of a love object" (SANDLER, 1985, p. 526). Fantasy involves denial of reality. Fantasy may be a way of "restoring the child's narcissistic supplies, restoring his well-being" (p. 341). It is particularly easy for children to use denial, because "denial is a most useful mechanism" in the "here and now", and children "never take the long-term view" (A. FREUD in SANDLER, 1985, p. 351). Children easily transition "between fantasy and reality, between denial and realization", whereas the adult who uses denial "has to do it very firmly" (p. 353). Attesting to the effective defence afforded by denial of reality, it can be "terribly difficult to convince somebody of something which they have denied" (A. FREUD in SANDLER, 1985, p. 350).

6.3.7 Rationalization

Socially unacceptable wishes or motives are consciously repugnant and intolerable for the self; so they have to be repressed. Alternatively, the ego attempts to justify socially unacceptable impulses, needs, feelings, or motives. Through rationalization, one justifies one's behaviour (to oneself and others) and gains "increased acceptance, primarily from oneself, but also by others" (LAUGHLIN, 1970, pp. 251–2). Rationalization illustrates the "dependence on others' opinion for one's self-esteem" (p. 264). One uses rationalization "to save face" and "to avoid being forced to make ego-deflating admissions" (LAUGHLIN, 1970, p. 273). Envy, for instance, "is often personally and socially disapproved and therefore must be 'covered over' or concealed" (p. 254). Given that "people tend to look down on feelings of envy", there "are often considerable pressures toward disowning this feeling" (p. 254). Rationalization then devises an explanation for one's behaviour that "is likely more socially and personally acceptable" (p. 254). Failure to attain social approval through the pursuit of a socially valuable goal causes injury to self-esteem, unless we "try and make that goal seem less worthwhile and attractive" (p. 259). Devaluation of an unattained or unobtainable goal is an important function of rationalization; we use rationalization to devalue material possessions that are beyond reach (LAUGHLIN, 1970).

> Rationalization is an unconscious endeavor to provide the ego with plausible, acceptable, and rational reasons for actions and motives. In this way, appeasement of the conscience or superego and society is sought. Rationalization is often employed to maintain or enhance one's self-esteem.
>
> (LAUGHLIN, 1970, p. 259)

By finding "extenuating circumstances for one's own lapses, failures, weaknesses, failings, or unacceptable behavior" or "supplying an acceptable motive in place of one which would ordinarily appear irrational or unacceptable" (LAUGHLIN, 1970, p. 274), one tries to maintain one's self-esteem; however, rationalization "tends to modify one's realistic self-evaluation" (LAUGHLIN, 1970, p. 264) and can amount to self-deception. Rationalization is closely related to denial. Either mechanism helps us to maintain self-esteem and ward off anxiety, allowing us to shape the perception of our social environment and self in ways that reduce our sense of vulnerability and protect our access to narcissistic supplies. Ultimately, these mechanisms, insofar as they involve self-deception, may fail, resulting in increased anxiety and more urgent use of defences and eventually leading to serious psychopathology.

Idealized image

HORNEY (1945) defined rationalization "as self-deception by reasoning" (p. 135). Rationalization supports the 'idealized image' that neurotic persons have of themselves (an omnipotent or perfectionistic view of themselves); "discrepancies between the actual self and the image must be reasoned out of existence" (p. 135). Rationalization supports "neurotic attempts to create artificial harmony" (p. 135). If there are factors that are in conflict with the person's idealized image or "predominant attitude" (an attitude of compliance or superiority, for instance), "factors that would bring the conflict into sight", then these can be "either minimized or so remodeled as to fit in with" the idealized image or the predominant attitude (HORNEY, 1945). Thus, the person's narcissistic balance, insofar as it depends on the idealized image of himself, can be maintained.

6.4 Self-enhancement through identification

MONEY-KYRLE (1961) suggested that "our everyday reasoning about our fellows is anthropomorphic and based on identification" (p. 17). When observing others and their behaviour, "inferences about them" rest ultimately on our "sense of being partially identified with them" (pp. 22–3). Then, there is the capacity to see the self from another's point of view. This is related to "the capacity to be self-conscious, that is, to observe as from outside the 'psychic self' in its relation to its objects" (p. 78). The capacity to observes the self is based on "the power to identify with other people, and so to perceive the world, with the self in it, from their point of view" (MONEY-KYRLE, p. 78).

The self featuring in fantasy life is narcissistically invested, most notably so in megalomanic or exhibitionistic fantasies. Such fantasies are not usually communicated because others' reactions would produce shame in the subject. Grandiose fantasies are often tolerated only at the margins of consciousness. Grandiose fantasies fulfil protective functions, preventing disintegration anxieties or shame concerning an insufficiently established self. In fantasies about oneself, but also in actual interactions, one often plays an adopted role. Thus, one can be identified with an other (such as a successful competitor *for the attention* of a derivative of the primary maternal object [omnipotent object]) and, at the same time, see oneself through the eyes of an other (of a derivative of the primary maternal object).

6.4.1 Identification with an admired object

Identification, in the most common sense of the term, refers to the fusing of a representation of oneself with that of an object. SANDLER (1960b) defined identification as "a process of modifying the self-schema on the basis of a present or past perception of an object" (p. 35). One sees oneself as another, usually an admirable or enviable person. According to FEDERN (1952), identification with an object involves narcissistic cathexis of the object (cathexis with 'ego feeling' or 'narcissistic libido') and extension of ego boundaries ("so that they now include the other person within themselves" [p. 350]). The purpose of identification is to harness the narcissistic supplies available to the object and to thereby enhance one's own self-esteem and wellbeing. A child, identifying with a parent, "feels not only fearless and protected, but also of increased bodily size and freed from the experience of the weakness of his ego" (FEDERN, 1952, p. 350). Identification with and imitation of an object is one of the techniques[14] used by the child in an attempt to restore the primary state of narcissism, the feeling of being loved (SANDLER, 1960b, p. 35). When the child, as a result of identification with the object, feels "the same as the admired and idealized object", "some of

---

[14] Compliance with the demands of the parents being the other notable technique.

the libidinal cathexis of the object is transferred to the self"; "the child feels loved and obtains an inner state of well-being" (p. 36). In other words, "the esteem in which the omnipotent and admired object is held is duplicated in the self and gives rise to self-esteem" (p. 36). Identificatory and imitative behaviour of the child "is further reinforced by the love, approval, and praise of the real object" (SANDLER, 1960b, p. 36).

Conversely, parents can derive narcissistic satisfaction from identification with their children. By identifying with their children, parents can *be at the centre of attention* once more (FREUD, 1914). Parents can, through their children, renew their claims to privileges, which they had to give up early in their lives. Parents can relive their aspirations for power or possessions through their children, that is, by identification with them (FREUD, 1914).

Adolescents have the tendency to identify with many others. The adolescent assimilates himself "as much as possible to the person who at the moment occupies a central place in his affection" (A. FREUD, 1937, p. 168). ANNA FREUD pointed out that "many adolescents actually copy and learn to act like the people they admire" (in SANDLER, 1985, p. 514). Such identifications are fleeting and changeable, aiming to present oneself as a "pleasing person" to whoever one meets, and giving the impression of a 'false self' (SANDLER, 1985, p. 515). Identifications with objects for the purpose of attaining narcissistic supplies change the subject's self-representation; and it may be in this sense that we can understand FREUD's famous phrase that the ego is the precipitate of abandoned object cathexes (p. 115). Even though an object cathexis can be abandoned, one's "admiration, affection, and esteem for the object", with which one identified, "can be transferred to the self, adding to secondary narcissism" (SANDLER, 1985, p. 116).

6.4.2 Altruism

In a form of altruism described by ANNA FREUD (1937), forbidden instinctual wishes are projected onto other people with whom the person identifies. The person "seeks out the wishes in the outside world to represent his own wishes" (A. FREUD in SANDLER, 1985, p. 442). He takes a friendly interest in other people and thereby gratifies his impulses through them (A. FREUD, 1937, p. 126). Thus, through observation and identification, 'vicarious pleasure' can be obtained. Parents may realize their exhibitionistic wishes and ambitions through their children's achievements. Even though the person, that is, his superego, would be critical of his impulses, such as exhibitionistic ones, he "is not critical of the fulfillment so long as it is not his own person involved" (A. FREUD in SANDLER, 1985, p. 442). Usually the person with whom the altruist identifies, and who can better fulfil his wishes, has once been envied (A. FREUD, 1937, p. 131). Unless such identification takes place, the person onto whom the altruist transfers his instinctual wishes (such as exhibitionistic impulses) would be "envied enormously". Thus, altruistic identification is "an escape from envy"; "it's another way of solving the situation in which somebody has what one hasn't got" (A. Freud in Sandler, 1985, p. 443).

To understand how instinctual wishes can get gratification via a proxy, how there can be "a reduction in instinctual pressure through a substitute representation", Sandler (1985) proposed that "[t]here must be an unconscious fantasy in which the object is equated with the self, and this must happen in a way in which there can actually be adequate gratification", so that "the perception of something happening gives the gratification" (p. 455). He thought that "the implications for our theory of drive gratification are tremendous" (Sandler, 1985, p. 455). What affords gratification of narcissistic needs is the perception of others praising the person with whom one is identified, much as perception of approbation directed towards oneself would gratify one's exhibitionistic impulses and ambitions, if expressed in action.

The life of the object, onto whom the altruist displaces his wishes, may become more precious than his own. On the other hand, the altruist may use aggression to control the object with whom he identifies; he may be "bossy, because the urge that is usually behind the fulfillment of one's own wishes is now placed behind the fulfillment of the wishes of the other person" (A. Freud in Sandler, 1985, p. 444). So, the process of obtaining vicarious pleasure also "liberates, or creates an outlet for, the aggression", given that securing the fulfilment of nonaggressive instinctual wishes is one of the uses of aggression. Moreover, "with the altruism, you can fight for somebody else's fulfillment of the wish with the same aggression, with the same energy" (p. 450). Thus, altruism provides a justifiable outlet for aggressive impulses, a way of expressing aggression that is not accompanied by guilt (A. Freud in Sandler, 1985, p. 451).

6.4.3 Identification with the aggressor

Identification with the aggressor, another defence mechanism described by Anna Freud (1937), necessarily involves "a reversal of roles with the attacker" (Sandler, 1985, p. 398). Through impersonation of and identification with an aggressor, the child "transforms himself from the person threatened into the person who makes the threat" (A. Freud, 1937, p. 113). Appropriation of qualities of a powerful authority figure serves "to bolster up the self" and defends against feelings of helplessness or impotence (A. Freud in Sandler, 1985, p. 149). The mechanism of identification with the aggressor contributes to superego formation, in that the child identifies with the parental threat of punishment and thereby internalizes parental criticisms (A. Freud, 1937).

Identification with the superego introject

Once the superego has become established, identification with the aggressor can take "the form of identification with the superego introject" (Sandler, 1985, p. 390), allowing "people who have very strong guilt feelings" to "identify with their superego introjects and attack others for the very things they feel guilty about" (SANDLER, 1985, p. 391). By identifying with a superego introject (the introjected parental authority), the child, and later the adult, can adopt a critical and moralizing attitude towards another person. When the child identifies "with the critical aspects of his superego", he projects, at the same time, "his self-imago onto another" (SANDLER, 1960b, p. 41). This mechanism effects a defence against feelings of guilt associated with unacceptable wishes and explains why "those who most vocally proclaim moral precepts are often those who feel most guilty about their own unconscious wish to do what they criticize in others" (SANDLER, 1960b, p. 41).

6.4.4 Omnipotent fantasy

FENICHEL (1946) distinguished between "creative fantasy, which prepares some later action, and daydreaming fantasy, the refuge for wishes that cannot be fulfilled" (p. 50). Daydreaming fantasy ("magical pictorial daydreaming") "becomes a real substitute for action in the state of "introversion", when 'small' movements accompanying fantasy become intense enough to bring discharge" (FENICHEL, 1946, p. 50). Daydreaming fantasy "keeps to the secondary process", but "in so many ways it approaches the primary process and permits the instinctual demands" (A. FREUD in SANDLER, 1985, p. 281). It is perhaps only when one feels connected with reality, when one is ready to interact with real objects and is potentially or actually in the focus of their attention, that one has to use defences to modify instinctual impulses whenever they are about to enter consciousness. It is only then that even minimal expressions of instinctual impulses ('micro-expressions') can influence one's evaluation by real objects. In daydream fantasy, exhibitionistic impulses can be expressed (and narcissistic needs be met) without risk of rejection and narcissistic injury.

In daydreams, a lowered narcissistic cathexis of the self, that is, diminished self-esteem, can be restored (SANDLER & NAGERA, 1963). Daydreams often feature the person of the daydreamer himself; and experiences involving the daydreamer often have a narcissistic emphasis (FEDERN, 1952).[15] Exhibitionistic fantasies during daydreams indulge in self-flattery. Wishes that are fulfilled in fantasy are often *ambitious* ones. Imaginary, wish-fulfilling situations are created in which the person sees himself playing "a central and often heroic role" (SANDLER & NAGERA, 1963, p. 91). The ego featuring in daydreaming fantasies may be omnipotent and invulnerable, precisely insofar as the person wishes to be seen as such by others, by those who, at other times, can pose a threat to the ego. Importantly, "the ego figure of

---

[15] Daydreaming not only serves ego exaltation but also provides an outlet for the expression of the person's object-libidinal interests. FEDERN (1952) recognized that "phantasies of love, greatness, and ambition ... always unite contents and goals that are clearly narcissistic and those that are directed toward the object" (pp. 357–8).

these phantasies has arisen through identification with persons in whom the desired claims are fulfilled" (FEDERN, 1952, p. 358).

Narcissistic gratification and defence against narcissistic hurt are major factors in children's fantasies (SANDLER, 1985, p. 347). Narcissistic reverie can be a pathological form of self-esteem regulation when it "indulges in timeless sham events, actually substituting for the present" (FEDERN, 1952, p. 360). Narcissistic patients are preoccupied with omnipotent and megalomanic fantasies. Fantasies that aim at self-aggrandizement are based on primitive *identifications* with idealizable infantile objects (A. REICH, 1960). Alternatively, narcissistic patients identify with an archaic ego ideal. In narcissistic fantasies, the 'inner yardstick', that is, the ego ideal, becomes an hypercathected image of the self that magically fulfils the patient's excessive need for approval (A. REICH, 1960).

6.5 Paying attention to oneself

If we are at ease in a familiar social situation, then we act spontaneously and genuinely, since we expect with confidence others' positive reactions towards us. In other words, we have healthy self-esteem or self-confidence, confidence, that is, in our ability to elicit positive social reactions towards ourselves by way of our spontaneous affectionate, playful, or assertive expressions. We are not conscious in these situations of an image of ourselves (although we have a sense of self-cohesion). If, on the other hand, we are in a novel or formal social situation, in which others take note of us, we feel subliminally anxious and are compelled to act in accordance with social expectations or to play a role that fits the occasion (GOFFMAN), whereby our social performance may be *incentivized* by an image of ourselves as an object of others' approval, an image that is equivalent to or derived from our ego ideal. The self-image, having evolved as an anticipatory vision of reassuring or approving responses towards us, can in itself act as a security device. We can transiently feel safe by fantasizing ourselves as someone who would command others' attention and approval. We can consider and cherish our idealized self (ego ideal) in fantasy for as long as we do not expose ourselves to a social situation or for as long as we do not feel compelled by others, in a social situation, to react, that is, for as long as we are not acted upon and can remain detached from others. We may try to remain aloof, sustaining the state of detachment in various ways, in order to prolong this form of self-securing, self-deceptive imagery (Figure 6.2).

In an anxiety-provoking or formal situation, we may also closely observe ourselves as if through the eyes of those on whose opinion we depend. We may concurrently perform an act or play a role *and* observe ourselves doing so. We would then go beyond monitoring others' reactions to our performance; we would look at our performance (and at our self as the performer) through the eyes of authority figures (or the superego as their

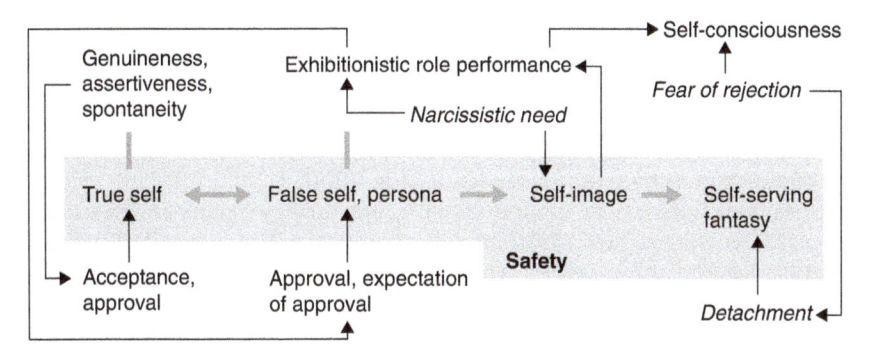

Figure 6.2 Self-feeling (in the form of true or false self) is a measure of safety; and self-imagery (whether fleeting or sustained) is a safety device. Self-consciousness arises when the conflict between exhibitionistic-narcissistic strivings and fear of rejection (between wanting to be seen and not wanting to be seen [LAING]) is acute, when attention-seeking performance occurs in the context of pronounced anxiety

internal representative). We may look at ourselves, and be conscious of ourselves, so as to readily detect any shortcoming or sign of weakness and so to guard against any potential attack. Such self-consciousness is a form of self-observation, one that is associated with *active engagement* in a social situation. This contrasts with self-observation in *detached* states of daydreaming (for the purpose of self-aggrandizement or, if more adaptive, the planning of ambitious pursuits and self-realization) (Figure 6.2).

Internal self-images picture one's self to oneself. The self can be viewed by oneself (internally, in imagination), if the viewing self is identified with another, or if the viewing self is the superego, which in itself is a product of identifications. FEDERN (1952) pointed out that "by a unique paradox the individual is conscious of the ego"; "the ego is at once subject and object" (p. 185). The ego, when it is "defined as subject", that is, as the self, regards and "feels this 'ego' as object" (p. 106). FEDERN (1952) understood that "a good part of secondary narcissism has such *representations of the ego*, one's thoughts about one's ego, as its object" (p. 310). The narcissistic relation of the ego to itself, the meeting of the ego "with itself time and again in innumerable relationships", is to be distinguished from primary narcissism, where there is "not yet a *directing* of the libido toward oneself" (FEDERN, 1952, p. 312).

6.5.1 Self-observation as a social phenomenon

There is "a special faculty which, as it where, sees and hears inside" (p. 139), so that "what has been perceived" *by the ego itself* is often observed by another "faculty of the ego and is either approved or disapproved" (NUNBERG, 1955, p. 135). Self-observation serves "to regulate the course of pleasure and unpleasure feelings" (p. 136). Self-observation "stems from the external world, from the power of the parents or their substitutes" (p. 139); it has its origin in the child regarding "the person who takes care of him as a source of pleasure" (approval), at one time, "and at another as a cause of pain" (disapproval) (Nunberg, 1955, p. 138). The self-observing faculty "exercises a selective, inhibiting, criticizing influence upon the intentions, wishes, and impulses of the individual", and thereby "gains an irresistible power over the ego" (p. 139). The self-observing faculty forms the basis of conscience and the superego. The self-observing faculty is situated in the 'system preconscious'; it becomes conscious only infrequently, such as in form of self-criticism (p. 139). However, even self-reproaches are only "more or less conscious"; the individual directs criticism against himself "almost without noticing it" (Nunberg, 1955, p. 140).

The superego, once it has been established, can give rise to experiences of self-observation, to reinstatements of a self-observing authority. In the process of self-supervision, "the ego might well feel itself to be the object of supervision by the superego" (Federn, 1952, p. 310). Affirming and criticizing functions can "have the self as object", so that "the ego feels itself as an object of such self-preoccupation" (p. 310). Considering oneself from the perspective of a *benevolent* abstract authority enhances 'ego feeling' (or self-esteem as a manifestation of undisturbed ego feeling). Self-observation occurs not only in narcissistic daydreaming but also in fantasy that is "slanted more and more toward real tasks, interests, relations, desires, and activities" (Federn, 1952, p. 358), which, too, express exhibitionistic impulses and satisfy narcissistic needs.

Schilder (1976) argued that the thoughts we have about ourselves are "what others have thought about us" (p. 540). The knowledge we have of our actions and thinking contains within itself "the attitude of others to our actions and thinking" (p. 545); it "is a product of the social relations to the group" (p. 540). We do not only *know about* but can actually observe our own actions and psychic processes; and "we observe ourselves in the same way that we have been observed by others, especially by the parents" (p. 545). Self-observation (self-consciousness), too, "is a social phenomenon" (p. 540); it is an act "of a social character" (p. 545). Self-observation is based "on the introjection of the admiring mother, a distinct part of the superego" (Schilder, 1976, p. 541) (the omnipotent object).

Schilder (1976) suggested that "we study the psychology of the body image ... in connection with the reactions of others to our body" (p. 547). If blushing can be regarded as an "expression of the oversocialization of the body image", then excessive consciousness of one's own thoughts (self-consciousness concerning one's thinking) would be an "oversocialization of the thinking process" (p. 547). Such oversocialization can be ascribed to narcissism (Schilder, 1976), to an excessive concern with the reflection of one's body, actions, and thinking in the eyes of others, including in the inner eye of the superego. The narcissistic function of self-observation can be seen even in masochistic self-reproaches. In states of depression, the patient, if he is excessively self-conscious, may observe himself "in order to punish himself" and to thereby "get reassurance of love from the superego and the parents from whom it is derived" (SCHILDER, 1976, p. 541).

6.5.2 Self-consciousness

Self-consciousness, according to ANNIE REICH (1960), describes an accentuated state of awareness of one's own self, a hypercathexis of the self. Accentuated awareness of one's self corresponds to an assumption that others are paying excessive attention to oneself. The self-conscious person, in an attempt to compensate for feelings of inadequacy, insufficiency, or impotence, longs to be the object of others' approving or admiring attention (REICH, 1960). Others' attention towards himself is contained in his own awareness of and concentration upon his self (hypercathexis of the self). The self-conscious person does not perform activities for their own sake but for the purpose of attracting attention; his actions are but an expression of exhibitionism. As he attempts to attract others' positive attention towards himself (i.e., upon his self), he cannot but feel that their attention is actually focused on him in a negative way, because he realizes that they can discern the warded-off inadequacy behind his *false front* (REICH, 1960).[16]

Self-consciousness is "an awareness of oneself as an object of someone else's observation" (LAING, 1960, p. 113). It is an expression of exhibitionism, of one's *need to be seen*. Self-consciousness is associated with anxiety. *Frightening* experiences of self-consciousness arise if tendencies of excessive exhibitionism, for which one was punished in childhood, have not been curtailed or cannot be suppressed (KOHUT, 1971). In self-consciousness, "the preoccupation with being seeable may be condensed with the idea of the mental self being penetrable, and vulnerable" (LAING, 1960, p. 113) to others' criticism or ridicule. One needs to be seen in order to belong; but the self-conscious person is "frightened that he will look a fool, or that other people will think he wants to show off" (LAING, 1960, p. 114).

> In a world full of danger, to be a potentially seeable object is to be constantly exposed to danger. Self-consciousness, then, may be the apprehensive awareness of oneself as potentially exposed to danger by the simple fact of being visible to others.
>
> (LAING, 1960, p. 117)

---

[16] The 'false self', which the child adopts in excessive compliance with maternal wishes (based on an overriding need for 'being good'), is not unrelated to the self-observing function of the ego (WINNICOTT, 1989).

Paranoia

In patients with schizophrenia or neurosis, self-consciousness is a frequent experience, and self-observation accompanies most aspects of social life. Self-consciousness, which arises in consequence of attempts to increase the cathexis of the self and ward off feelings of inadequacy, can be the first step towards paranoia (REICH, 1960). In paranoia, rejecting and critical aspects of self-observation are projected. Identification with the internal authority figure gives way to disidentification: a separation into a persecuted self and a persecuting external agency. In delusions of being watched, "the observing faculty is projected upon people who are everywhere, who spy on the patient, lie in wait for him, see and know everything he is thinking and wishing" (NUNBERG, 1955, p. 137). The patient with paranoia thus "becomes conscious of his own observing and criticizing faculty through projection" (p. 137). His observing and criticizing faculty reappears as persecutors in the external world (p. 138). Hallucinatory voices utter "words which come form the patient's early childhood and which were used by persons with whom he had libidinal relations"; they "express the criticism of the parent or the parent surrogate" (NUNBERG, 1955, p. 139).[17]

6.5.3 Self-pity and inconsolability

Loss and deprivation can "produce an internal situation that necessitates consolation" (WEINSHEL, 1989, p. 63). Loss, deprivation, frustration, rejection, or pain can also bring about a state of inconsolability. The inconsolable person is resolutely and stubbornly determined not to give up his misery. He stimulates in others attempts to alleviate his unhappiness or unpleasure, only to let these attempts fall flat or reject them with hostility. Inconsolability is related to self-pity (WEINSHEL, 1989).

Self-pity is a self-soothing, self-comforting response to an injury to the self (a narcissistic injury inflicted by a rejection or expression of dislike by an important selfobject) (WILSON, 1985). Self-pity involves a "special combination of pain and pleasure in which the self-representation is hypercathected with libidinal energy" (MILROD, 1972). Self-pity was described by MILROD (1972) as a "a narcissistic orgy, tinged with masochism" (p. 507). The self-pitying person, in his pain, can savour a "unique bittersweet gratification", the gratification of comfort and consolation (MILROD, 1972, p. 507). The person's self-concept, at a time of self-pity, is that of an innocent victim. The soothing and comforting object is experienced within the self, so that both subject and object are within the self (WILSON, 1985).

---

[17] Paranoia is also "an attempt at freeing oneself from the tormenting conscience" (NUNBERG, 1955, p. 140). As FREUD (1914) had recognized, hallucinatory voices commenting on and criticizing the patient's actions (third-person verbal hallucinations) reproduce the evolution of conscience regressively.

The self-pitying response is thought to be a derivative of the soothing response of the mother or caretaker to the distressed infant vocalizing an appeal for help (WILSON, 1985). If a soothing and empathetic response from a needed selfobject, such as the mother, is not forthcoming, despite the subject's appeal, self-pity may set in. Individuals prone to a self-pitying response to a narcissistic injury are 'narcissistically vulnerable', sensitive to rejection. The narcissistic wound tends to be inflicted by a needed selfobject, a person who is vitally important but who fails to show empathy. Self-pity allows the narcissistically injured person to recover selfobject connectedness (reconnect with a needed selfobject) by accessing "a new form of empathy ... that of the self taking itself as its own selfobject" (pp. 187–8). There may be, within the self-pitying response, "a component of self-righteousness that registers as a complaint against the person who has triggered the reaction" (WILSON, 1985, p. 188).

7
Character Defences

ADLER (1938) conceptualized "character as a guiding-line for the goal of superiority" (p. 165). Character, according to ADLER (1927), comprises "the tools used by the total personality in acquiring recognition and significance" (p. 135). The striving for recognition can "take many different forms, and every human being approaches the problem of their personal significance in an individual way" (ADLER, 1927, p. 137). Strivings for recognition and significance express narcissistic needs. Structures built up in the personality serve to channel and modify the expression of narcissistic demands (KOHUT, 1971). All character defences have a narcissistic function, in that they serve to protect self-esteem (KERNBERG, 1970). WILHELM REICH (1928, 1929) thought that a person's character is his 'narcissistic protection mechanism' ('narcissistic protection apparatus'). The ego and the character defences at its disposal develop "on the basis of the primary narcissism which serves self-preservation" (p. 127). Through his character, the person "satisfies a good part of his libido in the narcissistic relation of his ego to his ego-ideal" (REICH, 1929, p. 130). The ego, that is the self, is narcissistically cathected (HARTMANN, 1964) whenever the ego ideal is approximated.

The need to maintain safety (i.e., narcissistic homeostasis) is the overriding regulatory principle of the mental apparatus (SANDLER & JOFFE, 1969). Self psychology speaks of the motivational *primacy* of self-experience (KOHUT, 1977; STOLOROW, 1983). The personality is organized around the principle of having to avoid or counteract "feelings of inner deadness, self-fragmentation, and self-loss", that is, "to maintain a sense of self-cohesion in the face of threats of self-disintegration" (STOLOROW, 1983, p. 288). The 'action program' of the personality is defined by ambitions, ideals (goals), and skills (KOHUT, 1977, 1984). By realizing this 'action program', the person controls the responsiveness of his selfobject surround (the availability of selfobject responses) and maintains his narcissistic homeostasis (and safety). There are less mature, more archaic strategies of regulating the narcissistic homeostasis and maintaining self-cohesion. Unless the bipolar self, consisting of the pole of ambitions, the pole of ideals, and the tension arc of skills and talents (in-between the two poles), has been firmly established in childhood, archaic forms of self–selfobject ties prevail; and the person remains inordinately addicted to praise and admiration. The infantile wish or demand for parental approval or admiration – for something on which the cohesion of his self depends – then persists unabated throughout life.

Character types "whose conflicts are centered around their need for narcissistic supplies" (narcissistic character types) can be "contrasted to types with genuine object-libidinal conflicts" (FENICHEL, 1946, p. 479). Narcissistic persons have excessive narcissistic needs and are overly dependent on approval from outside, usually because their libidinal object relations are weak (ANNIE REICH, 1960). These persons are excessively focused on the good opinion of others, which they strive to secure in more or less mature ways. In general, weakness of libidinal object relations is correlated with less mature (more archaic) ways of regulating narcissistic homeostasis. ADLER (1927) contrasted 'social feeling' (which can be defined as the capacity to make libidinal investments in objects) with the striving for recognition and superiority (self-aggrandizement through the narcissistic use of objects). If a person's 'social feeling' is sufficiently developed, then his goal of superiority does not appear overtly; "it grows in secret and hides behind an acceptable façade" (p. 138). In persons with a "great degree of social feeling", there is only a "muted striving for personal power and prestige", whereas in those with little social feeling, behaviour "is predominantly selfish, ambitious, and useful only in creating a sense of superiority" (ADLER, 1927, p. 149). Persons with little social feeling are always "preoccupied with the question of what other people think about them and with the impression that they make on the world"; they pursue their goal of power and superiority "with great intensity and violence" and "live their lives in the expectation of great triumphs" (p. 157). Some persons approach "their goal of superiority by direct attack", whereas others become "cowardly and timid", pursuing "their goal of recognition and power" along various detours (ADLER, 1927, p. 143).

7.1 Primitive modes of attracting attention

The self of a person offers itself to others' view through its "wanting to be admired and confirmed" (KOHUT, 1977, p. 151); others' accepting and approving responses, in turn, provide narcissistic sustenance to the self, that is, they enhance self-esteem. The need for acceptance and approval, met by 'mirroring selfobjects', originates in child's healthy grandiosity and exhibitionism. "The psychologically healthy adult continues to need", and to induce, "the mirroring of the self by self-objects", much as "he continues to need targets for his idealization" (KOHUT, 1977, p. 188). If we are to remain free of anxiety, we have to manipulate our environment into supplying selfobject experiences (sustenance for the self); and we do so mostly in situationally appropriate and culturally sanctioned ways. High anxiety and imminent 'self-fragmentation' may bring about desperate attempts to provoke the environment into supplying selfobject experiences; desperate solicitations (of narcissistic supplies) in the form of bragging or arrogance cause antagonistic reverberations that worsen the individual's anxiety and suffering (WOLF, 1988). If others' acceptance and approval of ourselves is not forthcoming, we experience "a lowering of self-esteem in ourselves, and, feeling narcissistically injured, we react to it with depression and/or rage" (KOHUT, 1977, p. 188).

Our dependence on experiencing others' acceptance and approval may be more or less pronounced and expressed in more or less socially appropriate ways. If exhibitionistic urges did not mature into healthy ambitions in the course of personality development – if, in other words, sources of narcissistic supplies continue to be controlled on a concrete (rather than abstract) level – and if, at the same time, the capacity for libidinal investments and genuine object relations ('social feeling' [ADLER]) is decreased (as it was stifled in childhood), then self-esteem and self-cohesion remain highly dependent on the explicit receipt of praise, approval, and attention. The feeling of security ('safety') then depends on actually being approved by others. Greater insecurity (inferiority, inadequacy) (which, in turn, is correlated with lack of 'social feeling') is associated with greater need for explicit approval and acknowledgment.

'Mirror-hungry personalities', described by KOHUT and WOLF (1978), are *compelled* to display themselves (drawing on more or less primitive exhibitionistic methods) in order to attract the attention of others and thereby counteract their weakness of self-esteem and overcome their sense of worthlessness (inferiority). They are "impelled to display themselves to evoke the attention of others, who through their admiring responses will perhaps counteract the experience of worthlessness" (WOLF, 1988, p. 78). Mirror-hungry personalities will only ever achieve temporary relief, and they continue to search for new selfobjects whose recognition and appraisal they can induce (KOHUT & WOLF, 1978). Outright 'attention seeking' is contrasted with more indirect or mature and culturally sanctioned methods of self-esteem regulation, which are ubiquitous but used more *compulsively* and with greater urgency again by persons with deep-seated feelings of inferiority (reflecting a lack of 'social feeling' or a lack of genuineness and spontaneity at the heart of the personality). Thus, feelings of inferiority "may be covered up by compensating needs for self-aggrandizement, by a compulsive propensity ... to impress others and one's self with all sorts of attributes that lend prestige in our culture" (HORNEY, 1937, p. 37).

7.1.1 Craving and clinging

The need to be approved or loved by others can take the form of "an indiscriminate hunger for appreciation or affection" (HORNEY, 1937, p. 36).

Dependence on others' approval or affection is excessive in neurotic persons, attesting to their inner insecurity. The neurotic person "reaches out desperately for any kind of affection for the sake of reassurance"; he "needs another's affection for the sake of reassurance against anxiety" (p. 109) (whereby he may "feel entitled to demand special attention" [p. 143]). Inner insecurity can manifest as constant requests for company, an incapacity to be alone, and a tendency to cling to a significant other. Finding himself unable to be alone, the neurotic person would *insist* on the other's presence (cling to the other person); then, reassurance would be "supplied by the fact that the other is available" (HORNEY, 1937, p. 118). The greater the person's insecurity (and 'basic anxiety'), the more desperate and inflexible are his attention-seeking and clinging behaviours.

The 'craving personality' type (corresponding to dependent personality disorder) is characterized by an excessively clinging, needy, and demanding attitude towards objects that are derivatives of the primary, 'omnipotent object' (BURSTEN, 1973).[1] Clinging is a 'mode of narcissistic repair' that aims to reestablish narcissistic symbiosis (and that is related to the proximity-seeking behaviour by which infants overcome their separation anxiety). Craving personalities act as though they are constantly expecting to be disappointed by their object; and disappointments frequently do occur. Narcissistic injury stimulates aggression, which, when it is mixed with 'libidinal elements', manifests as sulking. At the same time, sulking contains an element of grandiosity. Concealed behind the clinging and demanding behaviour of craving narcissists, there is a core of grandiosity (the grandiose self), which gives them a sense of entitlement, makes them feel that they have a right to demand attention and care (BURSTEN, 1973).

'Oral characters', according to FENICHEL (1946), "are fixated on the level of ego development at which their original omnipotence was already lost and they were striving to get it back" (p. 509). They need objects "as pacifiers, protectors, bringers of supplies" (p. 509). 'Oral characters' try to influence their objects by force or ingratiation, to make them furnish narcissistic supplies. Along the way, they may become enmeshed in a vicious circle, in that "the very act of asking for the supplies makes them afraid of the intensity of their asking; thus they need more supplies, and thus they become more fearful" (FENICHEL, 1946, p. 509).

---

[1] In craving personalities, compared to other narcissistic personality types, the archaic omnipotent object has been internalized less firmly. Narcissistic personalities of other types have achieved greater internalization of the omnipotent object, affording them an internalized source of approval. Nevertheless, other narcissists can adopt a state of craving (when they become clinging and demanding) at times of physical illness or when drunk (BURSTEN, 1973).

7.1.2 Pseudovitality

KOHUT (1977) thought that "empathy failure from the side of the self-objects – due to narcissistic disturbances of the self-objects" – can lead to "defects in the self" (p. 87). 'Defensive structures' serve to cover over the primary defect (acquired in childhood) "in the psychological structure of the self" (p. 3).[2] An example of a 'defensive structure' is a person's tendency "to be overly enthusiastic, dramatic, and excessively intense" when responding "to everyday events", "often to the embarrassment of those around" him (p. 5). What lies behind such 'pseudovitality' is "low self-esteem and depression – a deep sense of uncared-for worthlessness and rejection, an incessant hunger for response, a yearning for reassurance" (p. 5). Similarly, "an intense devotion to romanticized cultural – esthetic, religious, political, etc. – aims" (romanticized ideals that feature in "an excited, overly enthusiastic, hyperidealistic adolescence devoid of meaningful interpersonal attachments" and that "do not recede into the background when the individual reaches adulthood") (pp. 5–6) is an attempt to cover over the primary defect of the self (KOHUT, 1977).[3]

7.1.3 Regression

Regression is "the return to a lower form of functioning" (A. FREUD in SANDLER, 1985, p. 117). Regression typically aims towards a state of 'infantile dependence' ('regression to dependence') (WINNICOTT, 1989). Regression is "a dependency-seeking process" (LAUGHLIN, 1970, p. 338). The position towards which the ego retreats is one of greater *dependence* and *safety*, "a more protected and less exposed position" (p. 322). It is often a passive position. The individual seeks to obtain "acceptance, love, and security" by adopting an earlier, often infantile mode of gratification (LAUGHLIN, 1970, p. 322).[4] Infantile dependence can be reestablished, if the *environment* meets the individual's dependency needs, if a new 'environmental provision' offers reliable care and thus allows for greater dependency (WINNICOTT, 1989).

Regression is an "efficient way for the whole personality to adapt to an intolerably difficult situation"; it "is a way of avoiding intolerable stress" (A. FREUD in SANDLER, 1985, p. 117). Regression, as a personality defence,

---

[2] 'Compensatory structures', by contrast, offset a defect in one of the two poles of the self "through the strengthening of the other pole", so that, for instance, "a weakness in the area of exhibitionism and ambitions is compensated for by the self-esteem provided by the pursuit of ideals" (KOHUT, 1977, p. 4).

[3] Psychoanalytic work can penetrate defensive structures, leading to exposure of the primary defect in the self. Having been exposed, the defect can be "filled out" "via working through and transmuting internalization" (KOHUT, 1977, p. 4).

[4] While, in regression, the ego reverts "to an earlier and less mature level of adjustment and development" (p. 320), 'fixation' refers to an arrest or cessation of personality development (LAUGHLIN, 1970).

may be employed at times of physical or emotional illness or in response to overwhelming stress, when the individual's attempts to cope with his environment consistently fail (LAUGHLIN, 1970). Regression is a "response to overwhelming unconscious needs for safety and security" (p. 322), whereby an "individual weakness of ego organization" is a precondition for regression (p. 334). Retreating from "danger, anxiety, stress, and responsibility", the ego "stabilizes itself on an earlier, simpler level" of functioning (p. 322) (representing a safer era). The individual reverts "to the position in development which is 'remembered' (unconsciously of course) as providing him the most gratification" (p. 331). Regression may be facilitated by psychogenic recapitulation (unconscious readoption) of physical symptoms[5] that were associated with a serious or prolonged illness in early life (LAUGHLIN, 1970).

> At times there is psychic reversion to a childhood period which was significant because of illness. This can represent an important era of gratification because of the extra care, attention, and love received at such times. Parental worry and concern over health also come to be valued by the child, especially when acceptance or love are lacking.
> (LAUGHLIN, 1970, pp. 331–2)

7.1.4 Illness behaviour and appeal to pity

Illness allows people to satisfy their "desire for someone constantly to shower attendance on them" (ADLER, 1927, p. 164). Children and adults, "having once tasted the concern their relatives show for their health", may "use their illness to hijack their family's attention" and thereby "feel their power growing" ('sickness complex') (ADLER, 1927, p. 164). The neurotic person may seek to obtain approval or affection "by appealing to pity", "by a dramatic demonstration of his complaints", or "by involving himself in a disastrous situation which compels our assistance" (HORNEY, 1937, p. 141). Similarly, children "may either want to be consoled for some complaint or may try to extort attention by unconsciously developing a situation terrifying to the parents, such as an inability to eat or to urinate" (HORNEY, 1937, p. 142).

Those who readily display symptoms of anxiety express in this way their need for "someone to pay attention to them at all times" (ADLER, 1927, p. 218). Some people use anxiety as a "device to compel someone to be close to them and take care of them" (p. 192). Those who strive for superiority as a way of restoring security (and connectedness) will feel anxious whenever "their sense of superiority is threatened" (p. 191); "[t]heir scream of anxiety" serves to link (connect) them "with the world again", in that it ensures that "someone hurries up to them", so that "[t]hey are no longer alone

---

[5] Fatigue states and neurasthenia may be manifestations of regression.

and forgotten" (ADLER, 1927, p. 191). Similarly, grief may be expressed by grief-stricken individuals in an attempt to influence "the attitude of those around them" (p. 216). They "find their position alleviated by the way others hurry to help them, sympathize with them, support them, encourage them" (p. 216). For the same reason, "childish bad habits" may be maintained into adulthood (p. 201). These habits are "directed towards gaining attention from the adult world", but *unconsciously* they are designed to ensure that the mother (omnipotent object) pays constant attention (ADLER, 1927, p. 201).

Secondary gain

Not only physical but also depressive and other mental illness provides 'secondary gain', in that patients attain "attention, sympathy, love, solace, affection, and protection" through their symptoms and illness-related behaviours (LAUGHLIN, 1970, p. 342). Secondary gain, which "consists in getting attention by being sick" (FENICHEL, 1946, p. 461), plays an important role in maintaining illness. Illness is "frequently perceived as a right to privileges" (coupled with the loss of responsibilities); it bestows economic advantages "by provoking pity, attention, love, the granting of narcissistic supplies" (p. 461). Illness behaviour may persist insofar as it manifests a "longing for the time of childhood when one was taken care of" (p. 461), and insofar as it allows a "regression to childhood times, when one was still protected" (p. 462). What is often reactivated at times of illness is a "need of a sign of parental affection and of assurance against abandonment" (p. 461). The expression of this need through illness "may in turn arouse guilt feelings, creating secondary conflicts and vicious circles" (FENICHEL, 1946, p. 461).

7.1.5 Masochistic submission

Masochism involves 'introjection' of a hated or disappointing object into the self or ego. Through introjection of the hated object, the person can redirect unacceptable and consciously disowned hostile impulses against his self. The self or ego, identified with the hated object, is a 'safer' target (less hazardous scapegoat) for intolerable aggressive impulses (LAUGHLIN, 1970), because, when aggression is self-directed, it does not jeopardize narcissistic supplies. MASSERMAN (1968), doubting that a desire for pain or suffering lies at the heart of masochism, considered whether "patterns of conduct usually interpreted as 'masochistic' are essentially not 'self-punitive', but instead rooted in expectations of previously available rewards through temporarily strenuous or even hurtful behavior" (p. 206). These may be narcissistic rewards in the form of the object's affection or care.

Masochistic behaviour is acquired because, "in spite of the pain created by it, it leads to a heightening of the level of safety feeling" (SANDLER & JOFFE, 1968, footnote on p. 262), that is, to an increase in the narcissistic cathexis of the self. Masochism is related to exhibitionism, an instinctual means of obtaining narcissistic supplies. Masochistic persons "derive pleasure from exhibiting their misery" (FENICHEL, 1946, p. 363). Exhibition of weakness (helplessness) is evolutionarily related to appeasement of an aggressive opponent and to solicitation of maternal care. The attitude of masochistic persons is one of total *submission* and *ingratiation*; they seek humiliation and failure in order to gain forgiveness (and hence acceptance) from a severe superego (pp. 363–4). Masochism has not only a demonstrative but also a provocative dimension. Through masochistic behaviour, which "has an accusing, blackmailing tone", masochistic persons "attempt to force their objects to give love or affection" (p. 363). Sacrificing and humiliating themselves, they "try to enforce their privileges and protection from the omnipotent persons" (FENICHEL, 1946, p. 365).

7.2 Identification

FREUD and his followers have justly pointed to the fact that one often wants to take the place of an admired love object and may express such a wish, of which one is not aware, by assuming some characteristics of the other. This is called identification, which is an imitation that does not take place in the full light of consciousness. One may identify oneself with a person because one wishes to be like this person and potentially receive whatever the other person does (SCHILDER, 1951, p. 273).

We may try to control how other persons see us and react to us by adjusting our gestures, our bodily postures, our verbalizations, and the like; and we may do so even when we are not directly interacting with others. Unconsciously, we would thereby adopt the role of another person who we remember (unconsciously) as having been effective in attracting narcissistic supplies. When identifying with a successful or admired person, the subject takes over desirable traits, attitudes, or mannerisms in order to secure *acceptance*, love, recognition, and security (LAUGHLIN, 1970). In most instances, identification is "motivated by deep basic needs for acceptance, approval, and love" (p. 135), that is, by desires for "acceptance or love from the object" (LAUGHLIN, 1970, p. 146). Alternatively, we may adopt features of (identify with) our 'idealized self' (HORNEY) or present the façade of a 'false self' (WINNICOTT), although these self-representations, like the ego ideal, are themselves the product of past identifications with objects.

7.2.1 Idealization and merger

Idealization as a defence mechanism may deal with a hidden dissatisfaction with one's own ego (LAUGHLIN, 1970). Idealization of an object also aids identification with it, which, insofar as the idealized object is a derivative or replica of the primary object, may satisfy primitive needs for merger with the omnipotent object (return to the primary narcissistic state). The need to idealize an object (and merge with it) is one of the two branches of secondary narcissism (into which primary narcissism differentiates) (KOHUT, 1971). 'Ideal-hungry personalities' search for selfobjects whose wealth or prestige they can admire or whom they can admire for their power or attractiveness (KOHUT & WOLF, 1978). Ideal-hungry personalities need "selfobjects to whom they can look up and by whom they can feel accepted" (WOLF, 1988, p. 73). Ideal-hungry personalities feel worthwhile only if they are in the company of such selfobjects (or for as long as they can relate to such selfobjects). If they perceive any defect in their ideal, as they will do in consequence of the persistent defect in their own self, then they will search for new idealizable objects (KOHUT & WOLF, 1978).

In alterego experiences, one feels an essential sameness or likeness with somebody else. 'Alterego personalities' seek to relate to an object who can confirm their own appearance, values, or opinions (KOHUT & WOLF, 1978). Alterego personalities search for and attach themselves to a selfobject whose values and appearance allow them to confirm the existence of similar attributes of their own self, that is, to *confirm their self*. However, no selfobject completely lives up to their expectations in this regard, so they will look for one replacement after another (KOHUT & WOLF, 1978). Finally, 'merger-hungry personalities' need to merge with, and closely control, a mirroring or idealized selfobject or an alterego. Merger-hungry persons need the presence of a person whom they can experience as their own self; they have difficulties distinguishing their own thoughts and feelings from those of their selfobject. Merger-hungry persons are unable to tolerate the other's independence or even absence (KOHUT & WOLF, 1978).

7.2.2 Love and subservience

The state of being in love revives the object relation that prevailed prior to the development of the distinction between self and object. Being in love means feeling *at one* with someone, being completely identified with the other person, and also losing the sense of self. Tender love, the "enigmatic wish of lovers to embrace each other", and sexual intercourse "represent *narcissistic attempts at restitution of unity*", that is, attempts at "negation of the feeling of separation, incompleteness, basically, of the lesion in narcissism" (BERGLER, 1949, p. 48). The complete fusion of self and object revives early feelings of omnipotence. The longing for omnipotence (infantile megalomanic longings) may not have been outgrown or can be revived *regressively* (A. REICH, 1953). The longing or fantasy of becoming one with an omnipotent object may reflect a primitive attachment to the mother that has never been fully relinquished. Alternatively, by regression to a primitive form of object relationship in which there is no differentiation between self and object, inferiority feelings can be undone. Identification with a stronger or idealized partner, the feeling of oneness with him, provides narcissistic gain for the 'subservient woman' and compensates her feelings of inferiority (A. REICH, 1953).

BERGLER (1949) argued that, in romantic love, the lover's ego ideal is projected on the beloved person. The lover attempts to "rid himself of the constant reproach of not having achieved the high-pitched demands of his own ego ideal" (i.e., to rid himself of feelings of guilt) by first projecting "*his ego-ideal on the beloved object*" and then reintrojecting "the projected object" (p. 48). In this process, the object is overvalued and idealized (i.e., the object takes on the ideal shape of the self) and "is tinged with narcissistic libido" (p. 48). Reintrojection of the beloved and overvalued object (i.e., identification with it) "has the purpose of restoring the narcissistic unity of the personality" (BERGLER, 1949, p. 48). Idealization of the object can be based on externalization of the individual's own ego ideal, as recognized also by A. REICH (1953). All greatness is ceded to the object, so as to allow the individual to achieve, by way of identification, unity with her ego ideal, the admired object she herself longs to be. Identification with her ego ideal then allows for fusion with the omnipotent parental object (in unconscious fantasy).

In some women, as argued by A. REICH (1953), the externalized ego ideal is of the *paternal* type. These women may have had to renounce, during their earlier development, character traits that proved incompatible with their femininity. They came to love these traits in male objects, instead. These woman admire men for masculine qualities, which they were unable to develop for themselves in adolescence. They love men who represent their own former ego identifications (A. REICH, 1953). The love object cannot usually live up to the grandiosity of the woman's narcissistic demand; hence the image of the object must me overinflated (idealized). The object's failure to live up to the woman's expectations would incite her hostility; however, aggression against the love object is warded off and transformed into masochistic behaviour. By way of masochistic subservience, the individual holds on to the omnipotent object at any cost (A. REICH, 1953).

7.2.3 Acting a part

Identification with and enactment of a role allows for socially acceptable (sublimated) expression of exhibitionistic impulses. The tendency to adopt the role of another is particularly evident in persons with a 'hysterical structure' of character (SCHULTZ-HENKE, 1951). Histrionic behaviour, characterized by self-dramatization, pretentiousness, and insincerity, allows the person to defensively ingratiate himself with others "in order not to realize that he believes himself to be unlovable" (SCHAFER, 1976, p. 327). Likeable and enviable characters featured in cultural media provide plenty of scope for identifications. There are persons whose speech is full of jargon, who "sound like cheap novels", and who "think and act according to the clichés of the tabloids and movies" (ADLER, 1927, p. 204).

Schizoid persons experience difficulty "over expressing emotion in a social context" (p. 15), especially "over giving in the emotional sense"

(FAIRBAIRN, 1952, p. 14). They are, however, "able to express quite a lot of feeling and to make what appear to be quite impressive social contacts" by "playing a role or acting an adopted part" (p. 16). What lies behind the tendency of schizoid persons to adopt or play roles – and what generally motivates many artistic and other socially constructive activities – is exhibitionism. Exhibitionistic pursuits of the artistic kind provide a "means of expression without involving direct social contact" (FAIRBAIRN, 1952, p. 16).

7.3 Detachment

An attachment is severed in order to avoid psychic pain and in order to neutralize or prevent anxieties of separation, abandonment, or loss of love. 'Characterological detachment' involves an active movement away from relationships and a 'freezing' of the capacity for relatedness (SCHECTER, 1978). Characterological detachment, formed on the basis of fearful anticipation of psychic pain, especially the fear of being abandoned, is a relatively stable system of defences that protects against psyche pain arising in consequence of abandonment or loss of love. Characterological detachment in adults parallels detachment in children (active avoidance of the mother), which, as described by BOWLBY (1973), follows the initial stages of 'angry protest' and 'despair' in response to separation from the mother. Transitory detachment is a component of the process of mourning in adults. In schizoid persons, there is a particularly severe and enduring detachment from relationships that has its roots in infancy. Lasting detachment, due to a lingering fear of the painful effects of separations, hinders the formation of new attachments. Nevertheless, there remains in schizoid persons an often strong desire to emerge from the state of detachment and form new attachments (SCHECTER, 1978). Characterological detachment can be accompanied by periodic regressions to fusion with internal objects (symbiotic fantasies), aiming "to fill the extreme isolation of the very detached person" (SCHECTER, 1978, p. 83).

Schizoid persons are withdrawn, introverted, and self-sufficient, while maintaining an often secret sense of superiority (SCHECTER, 1978). Schizoid persons keep themselves "at a safe emotional distance from others ... via emotional coldness", whereas paranoid personalities distance themselves from others "via hostility and suspiciousness" (KOHUT, 1977, p. 192). Defensive organizations of both schizoid and paranoid personalities involve distancing. Traumatic selfobject experiences in early life lead to a reliance, later in life, on schizoid mechanisms to keep involvement with others' shallow or paranoid mechanisms to surround oneself "with an aura of hostility and suspicion that will keep noxious selfobjects at bay" (WOLF, 1988, p. 68). Traumatic selfobject experiences, empathy failures by selfobjects, and narcissistic injuries disrupt the cohesiveness of the self (insofar as the integrity of self depends upon the empathic responsiveness of selfobjects) (KOHUT) and undermine the sense of safety or wellbeing (SANDLER). Maintaining "a safe emotional distance from others" protects "against the danger of incurring a permanent or protracted breakup, enfeeblement, or serious distortion of the self" (KOHUT, 1977, p. 192) (it protects against 'disintegration anxiety').

In some narcissistic personalities, the central concern is to keep away from the ego anything that can diminish it. Narcissism in these personalities impresses as self-contentment and inaccessibility, a tendency to not concern themselves about others (FREUD, 1914). The narcissistic person, who "is constantly preoccupied with inflating his ego", "does it not primarily for the sake of self-love, but for the sake of protecting himself against a feeling of insignificance and humiliation, or, in positive terms, for the sake of repairing a crushed self-esteem" (HORNEY, 1937, p. 172). He needs "to be infallible and wonderful in his own eyes", since any "shortcoming, whether recognized as such or only felt dimly, is considered a humiliation" (p. 172) (it arouses 'basic anxiety'). Internalization of his quest for prestige and infallibility presupposes that the narcissistic person has to remain distant in his relations with others (HORNEY, 1937). In people who withdraw from society, who "do not look other people in the eye" or "refuse to greet others", ADLER (1927) saw "an undercurrent of ambition and vanity", of striving for superiority and glory, in that they "attempt to raise themselves above others by accentuating the differences between themselves and the rest of society", although "the most they can gain is an imaginary glory" (pp. 188–9).

7.3.1 Aloneness

Detachment is continuous with the adaptive state of aloneness. Aloneness (the absence of an external object) is associated with creativity (BALINT, 1968). Aloneness is a balanced state of 'being'. It is the experiential opposite of reacting; reacting disrupts the balance of 'being' (WINNICOTT, 1960a). The infant's developing capacity to be alone in the presence of the mother is a precursor of the mature capacity to seek out and enjoy a relationship solely with oneself (WINNICOTT, 1958). Aloneness, as opposed to loneliness, presupposes the internal presence of an other. The mature capacity to be alone depends on the presence of a good object in psychic reality (an internalized good object). The capacity to be alone and enjoy one's own company rests on the successful transformation, in early development, of the objective world into the subjective. The subjective sense of self is a derivative of objective others. The subjective self is never alone, according to WINNICOTT (1958), because inner life is populated by good objects with which the self is in relationship (internal object relations).

7.3.2 Fantasy

> If they fail to reach a superior position in real life, they continue to hope that they will do so, and lead a secret life of phantasy in which they imagine that they are so powerful as to be invulnerable.
>
> (STORR, 1968, p. 83)

Approval, acceptance, and love may be sought not only "externally in the social context from others" but also "from internal aspects of oneself" (LAUGHLIN, 1970, p. 18). Fantasy in the form of daydreaming is directed by unconscious forces that aim for substitute gratification or wish fulfilment. Firstly, daydreaming fantasy often provides narcissistic gratification (FEDERN, 1952; SANDLER & NAGERA, 1963). The objective then is self-glorification. Secondly, in face of external dangers, fantasy as an 'ego aid' enables retreat into self-absorption. Fantasy is "a potent means for the avoidance of conflict" (LAUGHLIN, 1970, p. 119). It may provide an unrealistic 'emotional aura' within which realistic action is avoided. Thirdly, fantasy may help to resolve emotional conflict, such as by blocking or aiding partial expression of rage. Fantasies about revenge restrain action, in that they "serve as caution or break to oneself" (LAUGHLIN, 1970, p. 116).

Daydreaming is predominantly 'pure pleasure thinking', a manifestation of the 'id' (p. 218), which means that the superego does not intervene in day dreams (FLUGEL, 1945). FLUGEL (1945) thought that "the well-preserved distinction between reality and phantasy serves in some way to keep this reserved field free from super-ego interference – for quite a number of our phantasies would probably incur lively super-ego opposition if we attempted to put them into practice" (p. 218). In night dreams, by contrast, the superego exercises a vigorous influence, perhaps "because the distinction between reality (albeit here an hallucinatory reality) and phantasy has been lost in sleep" (FLUGEL, 1945, p. 223).

The content of fantasy, whether it is concerned with narcissistic gratification or revenge, is usually not revealed to others and hence not even fully acknowledged to oneself. Its revelation outside a nonjudgmental therapeutic context is *unsafe*, because such revelation would invite others' judgement or criticism; and internally full awareness of the content would provoke judgement by the superego (the internal representative of critical objects). The manifest content of fantasy can be viewed "as the outward shadowy reflection of more potent and meaningful underlying *unconscious* material" (LAUGHLIN, 1970, p. 117). The latent content and significance of fantasy is referred to as 'unconscious fantasy'. Fantasy can be fleeting or even instantaneous, its emergence being rapidly and automatically repressed. Fleeting fantasies that hardly reach conscious awareness can also be regarded as 'unconscious fantasies'. The nearly instantaneous 'repression' of fantasies serves defensive purposes (LAUGHLIN, 1970).

7.3.3 Intellectualization

Neurotic detachment functions "to keep major conflicts out of operation" (Horney, 1945, p. 95), although "the compulsive cravings for closeness as well as aggressive domination" remain active under the surface and "keep harassing if not paralyzing their carrier" (p. 95). Detachment also helps to moderate inhibitions that lie at the heart of any neurosis (inhibitions concerning affectionateness, assertiveness, and spontaneity). By keeping himself "at a safe distance from others", the detached person "can release and express a host of feelings", including creative feelings, and express them in a manner that is "not directly connected with human relationships" (p. 83). In the context of neurosis in general, "detachment will provide the best chance of expressing what creative ability there is" (p. 90). Detachment is also associated with intellectualization. Inasmuch as emotions have to be checked, "emphasis will be placed upon intelligence", with an expectation that "everything can be solved by sheer power of reasoning" (Horney, 1945, p. 85).

Intellectualization is a manifestation of preoccupation with the inner world (Fairbairn, 1952). Preoccupation with the inner world and overvaluation of thought are related to difficulties experienced by schizoid individuals in expressing their libidinal tendencies naturally towards other people and making emotional contact with them. Individuals with a schizoid tendency substitute intellectual solutions of their emotional problems for "attempts to achieve a practical solution" within the sphere of "relationships with others in the outer world" (p. 20). Individuals with a schizoid tendency "are often more inclined to construct intellectual systems of an elaborate kind than to develop emotional relationships with others on a human basis" (p. 21). Their attempts to circumvent their difficulty over emotional relationships are directed "towards attainment within the intellectual sphere" (Fairbairn, 1952, p. 23).

Schizoid persons concentrate "their often considerable libidinal resources on pursuits which minimize human contact (such as interest and work in the area of aesthetics; or the study of abstract, theoretical topics)" (Kohut, 1971, p. 12). They can thus increase their approvability, affirm their inner grandiosity, and attract narcissistic supplies. Detachment and grandiosity are two facets of the same phenomenon. Schizoid individuals tend "to look down from their intellectual retreats upon common humanity" (Fairbairn, 1952, p. 21). Schizoid individuals have "a sense of inner superiority", "even when, as is commonly the case, this is largely unconscious" (p. 22). Their attitude of superiority or omnipotence may be "concealed under a superficial attitude of inferiority or humility; and it may be consciously cherished as a precious secret" (p. 7). Similarly, their attitude of isolation and detachment "may be masked by a façade of sociability" (Fairbairn, 1952, p. 7).

7.3.4 Religiosity

God is an incarnation of the omnipotent object with which the individual unconsciously wishes to remerge. God is the superego projected into the heavens; and our relationship with God is that of our ego with the superego. Gods are 'supernatural providers' (not unlike the primary maternal object, from which the superego is derived) who "must be appeased by prayer and self-torture" (ERIKSON, 1950, p. 225). Religions "abound with efforts at atonement which try to make up for vague deeds against a maternal matrix" (ERIKSON, 1950, p. 225). If our relationships with God represents our striving for reunion with the primary maternal object, then the ego ideal is the shape we feel we ought to adapt in order to be acceptable to and accepted by our God. ADLER (1938) thought that "the idea of God really embraces the movement towards perfection as a goal, and that, as a concrete goal, it best corresponds to the obscure yearning of human beings to reach perfection" (p. 199).

> It is easy to show that the ego ideal answers to everything that is expected of the higher nature of man. As a substitute for a longing for the father, it contains the germ from which all religions have evolved.
> (FREUD, 1923, p. 37)

Religious faith has a defensive purpose. JAMES (1890) pointed out that whenever the verdict of others goes against me, "I am always inwardly strengthened in my course and steeled against the loss of my actual social self by the thought of other and better possible social judges" (p. 315). The seeking of divine approval is but a form of 'social self-seeking', the longing for social approval; and inasmuch as social self-seeking is at times compulsive, we give in to an impulse to pray when we feel unprotected or misunderstood.

> The impulse to pray is a necessary consequence of the fact that whilst the innermost of the empirical selves of a man is a Self of the social sort, it yet can find its only adequate Socius in an ideal world.
> (JAMES, 1890, p. 316)

The humblest outcast on this earth can feel himself to be real and valid by means of this higher recognition. On the other hand, for most of us, a world with no such inner refuge when the outer social self failed and dropped from us would be the abyss of horror (JAMES, 1890, p. 316).

God provides narcissistic sustenance in the form of 'higher recognition' or divine approval. In taking on the protective function originally fulfilled by the primary object, God answers to man's self-preservative drive ('ego instinct'). As, in the course of cultural evolution, ancient kinship structures disintegrated and social structures became more fluid, the patriarchal leader (the original developmental derivative of the primary maternal object) lost his importance and God became a substitute anchor of stability, a reliable compass for social conduct and thus a determinant for the individual's safety and sense of self. Now, God and religion are themselves under threat of extinction. For those who are insecure or ill-equipped and who are readily marginalized, the demise of religion can only mean greater vulnerability of the self and more desperate self-seeking in the face of disintegration anxiety ('the abyss of horror' [JAMES]).

ADLER (1927) remarked that "individuals who have suffered a mental breakdown" and who "withdraw from other human beings" may "engage in personal conversation with God" or "consider themselves close to God", who they feel is "concerned personally with the worshippers' well-being" (p. 177). There are those who believe that God "is responsible for their every action", who seem to believe that "the dear Lord has nothing else to do but to be occupied with their troubles and pay a great deal of attention to them" (p. 211). By engaging with, or being close to, God, people "can easily achieve a sense of magical greatness" (ADLER, 1927, p. 177), a sense that approximates the omnipotence associated with primary narcissism.

Fate

Our belief in God in many ways resembles our belief in fate. Both God and fate are projections of the superego that regulate our sense of safety. Punishment by parent figures, by their internal representative (the superego), or "by those more shadowy external influences", such as fate or luck, which "we at bottom also tend to identify with the parents", "will cause us fear in so far as we feel ourselves weak and dependent on these figures" (FLUGEL, 1945, p. 161). Being delivered a blow by fate is equivalent to the withdrawal of parental love and care. "When fate delivers us a blow", "we may be overcome by the same sense of loneliness and helplessness that we experienced in early years if we imagined our parents had forsaken us" (p. 161). When, however, "fate 'smiles' upon us", we feel as though we are "'basking' in the approval of the parents" (FLUGEL, 1945, p. 161).

7.3.5 Gambling

> Gambling, in its essence, is a provocation of fate, which is forced to make its decision for or against the individual. Luck means a promise of protection (and of narcissistic supplies) … But what is more important is that the typical gambler consciously or unconsciously believes in his right to ask for special protection from fate. His gambling is an attempt to compel fate in a magical way to do its 'duty'; …
>
> (FENICHEL, 1946, p. 372)

The neurotic gambler has "strong yearnings for omnipotence", yet he also has "the feeling that he is omnipotent" (GREENSON, 1947, p. 7). His belief in his omnipotence is "shaky" and "full of doubts", so that he "seeks a sign from Fate" or from the Gods that will confirm his omnipotence (p. 7). His gambling aims to challenge fate or the Gods to confirm his omnipotence, "to calm his grave doubts" concerning his omnipotence (p. 7). The neurotic gambler "wants to convince himself that he is lucky, i.e., omnipotent" (p. 7). The omnipotence that the neurotic gambler longs for, and "unconsciously is attempting to recapture", stems from the infant's "feeling of unlimited omnipotence" (GREENSON, 1947, p. 7), the 'oceanic feeling' experienced by the infant in a state of union with the mother (FENICHEL, 1946, p. 39). The neurotic gambler's thinking and actions "have a strikingly animistic, superstitious, and magical quality" (p. 7), consistent with the regressive character of neurotic gambling. GREENSON (1947) argued that "the neurotic gambler has regressed to infantile longings for omnipotence", that "strong longings for omnipotence and oceanic feelings are evidence of a failure of the ego to maintain a mature level" (p. 9).

Winning produces transitory euphoria (a feeling of triumph), which is a derivative of the infant's oceanic feeling (GREENSON, 1947). Luck in gambling unconsciously means that the gambler has been accepted by God, the representative of the father, so that he can share in God's, that is, the father's, omnipotence (p. 8). Perhaps, the gambler feels accepted, on a more basic level, by the omnipotent object, the internal derivative of the primary maternal object. Winning produces feelings of triumph, "because it represents reunion with the omnipotent one" (p. 10). In euphoric states, ego and superego are united; there is a minimum of tension between ego and superego (GREENSON, 1947, p. 12). Insofar as the ego refers to the self and the superego stands for the omnipotent object, winning instils omnipotence into the self and elevates the self to a level at which it can fuse with the omnipotent object.

Thus, neurotic gambling expresses a need for being accepted, a need for security. The neurotic gambler has an urgent need for security; he "is a personality on the brink of a severe depression" (GREENSON, 1947, p. 8). Losing means being abandoned and produces depression. The neurotic gambler's inability to stop gambling stems from his inability to "bear the feeling of abandonment and depression" that arises when he loses (p. 10). Nevertheless, the neurotic gambler also has a need to lose, which can be explained as unconscious guilt feeling and unconscious need for punishment (and need for concomitant absolution or expiation). Punishment in the form of losing "is a lesser evil than the terrifying punishment of castration or total loss of love" (GREENSON, 1947, p. 11).

7.3.6 Self-sufficiency

Some neurotic persons are determined not to get emotionally involved with others; they tend to get along with others only superficially. The detached person avoids "any close and lasting relation", as it "would be bound to jeopardize his detachment" and need for distance from others (HORNEY,

1945, p. 85). Anything that threatens his self-sufficiency and anything that amounts to a "threat of dependence will cause him to withdraw emotionally" (p. 84). In psychoanalysis, although the patient may be "interested in observing himself" and "fascinated by ... the intricate processes going on within him" (p. 86), he keeps "his relationship to the analyst and to the whole analytical process away from him – not to let the analysis touch him in any way" (p. 87); and he "abominates being urged or 'forced' in a direction he has not foreseen" (HORNEY, 1945, p. 86). The neurotic trend for detachment or independence "manifests itself in a hypersensitivity to everything in any way resembling coercion, influence, obligation" (p. 77). Long-term obligations are avoided inasmuch as emotional attachment is avoided. Others' expectations towards the person, even timetables, "constitute a threat" and make him feel "uneasy and rebellious" (p. 78). Others' "advice is felt as domination and meets with resistance even when it coincides with his own wishes" (p. 78). The detached person "will conform outwardly in order to avoid friction, but in his own mind he stubbornly rejects all conventional rules and standards" (HORNEY, 1945, p. 78).

> These ordinarily quiet and rational persons may freeze with rage or become actually abusive if their aloofness and independence are threatened. Positive panic may be induced at the thought of joining any movement or professional group where real participation and not merely payment of dues is required. If they do become involved they may thrash about blindly to extricate themselves.
>
> (HORNEY, 1945, p. 88)

Detached persons have the "capacity to look at themselves with a kind of objective interest" (HORNEY, 1945, p. 74). When looking at themselves, they may see themselves as a superior or uniquely significant being who is bound to attract others' approval or admiration without having to establish direct contact with and reach out to them. The need for detachment is closely linked with the need to feel superior or uniquely significant, which, in turn, is manifested in the person's "fantasies of a future when he would accomplish exceptional things" (HORNEY, 1945, p. 79). Feelings and fantasies of superiority presuppose detachment; detachment facilitates these feelings and fantasies, and may be maintained for this purpose. While the 'compliant type' of neurotic personality craves for, and tries to induce in various ways, others' acceptance and affection (and while the 'aggressive type' induces others recognition and thereby attains a sense of safety), the detached type seeks to maintain his self-esteem and safety by *feeling* superior or unique (HORNEY, 1945). Feelings and fantasies of superiority and unique significance are detached means of regulating self-esteem and approximating safety. If superiority breaks down, then detachment is not maintained, and acceptance and affection need to be solicited urgently by direct interpersonal means.

When the detached person's feeling of superiority is temporally shattered, whether by a concrete failure or an increase of inner conflicts, he will be unable to stand solitude and may reach out frantically for affection and protection.

(HORNEY, 1945, p. 79)

The detached person's remoteness is "an over-all protection to which he must tenaciously cling and which he must defend at whatever cost" (HORNEY, 1945, p. 92). Detachment is a precondition for safety or, more precisely, for the neurotic trends that aim at safety. Neurotic trends that are associated with detachment, such as the striving for superiority, "give the individual a feeling of security as long as they function"; "conversely, anxiety is aroused when they fail to function" (p. 91). When, in the course of psychoanalysis, "detachment begins to crumble, [then] the patient not only becomes diffusely apprehensive but directly and indirectly expresses definite fears": such as "a fear of becoming submerged in the amorphous mass of human beings", a "fear of being helplessly exposed to the coercion and exploitation of aggressive persons" (a realization of "utter defenselessness"), or a fear of going insane (HORNEY, 1945, p. 93).

Detachment, when it is the predominant trend in a personality, "renders a person ... helpless in any realistic dealing with life" (HORNEY, 1945, p. 92). The detached person is clearly estranged from others; however, the estrangement from others that the detached person experiences "is no greater than that of other neurotics" (pp. 73–4), such as the compliant or aggressive neurotic. Estrangement from others "is only an indication that that human relationships are disturbed", which "is the case in all neuroses" (p. 74). The three neurotic attitudes described by HORNEY (1945), namely neurotic compliance ('moving toward people'), aggressiveness ('moving against people'), and detachment ('moving away from people'), are not exclusively characteristic of neurosis and not necessarily associated with estrangement. These are basic attitudes towards others that do have their positive, adaptive value; "all three attitudes are not only desirable but necessary for our development as human beings" (HORNEY, 1945, p. 89).

In moving toward people the person tries to create for himself a friendly relation to his world. In moving against people he equips himself for survival in a competitive society. In moving away from people he hopes to attain a certain integrity and serenity.

(HORNEY, 1945, p. 89)

7.3.7 Infidelity

There is, according to KLEIN (1937), a tendency to give up an overly strong attachment. The fear of the death of the attachment object drives the person (or child) to lessen his attachment (p. 92). The person (or child) is driven away from the attachment object (the maternal object or a later derivative of it) because dependency "gives rise to the fear of losing this all-important person" (p. 91). The fear of dependency plays a role in "the process of displacing love ... from one's mother to other people and things" (KLEIN, 1937, p. 91). Infidelity, "the repeated turning away from a (loved) object", "partly springs from the fear of dependence" and from "the dread of the death of loved people" (p. 86). Infidelity is a defence against this dread. While some people are driven by "a great dread of the death of the loved person" to rejecting the object "or to stifling and denying love", others are "driven from one person to another", whereby each love object stands for their mother (KLEIN, 1937, p. 86).

> ... through his attitude towards women an unconscious compromise finds expression. By deserting and rejecting some women he unconsciously turns away from his mother, saves her from his dangerous desires and frees himself from his painful dependence on her, and by turning to other women and giving them pleasure and love he is in his unconscious mind retaining the loved mother or re-creating her.
> (KLEIN, 1937, p. 86)

7.4 Compliance

Anxiety arises when one feels unrelated to the selfobject surround, when one is not anchored in the social position one claims or does not enjoy the social status one expects. It is then that, evolutionarily, the danger of attack from others arises. Social position or status essentially demarcates one's access to narcissistic supplies in complex social configurations. Compliance with traditions and rites protects against anxiety, because it prevents oneself from being dislodged from or deprived of one's position or status. For the same reason, compliance also preserves one's self-esteem and protects one's access to narcissistic supplies. Compliance is a derivative of submission; one submits to the social law and order and to the expectations and demands of those who are in a position of authority. Submissive and appeasement gestures, when expressed towards others, have the effect of inhibiting their innate aggressiveness and thereby increasing the likelihood that they will display caring and attentive gestures (provide narcissistic supplies) in return.

7.4.1 Submissiveness

We adopt authoritative ideas and conventional opinions with varying degrees of readiness and conviction. In persons with hysterical or compulsive character pathology, there may be a greater "readiness to defer to authoritative opinion, to accept ideas and eventually 'believe' them, or rather to think that one believes them" (SHAPIRO, 2000, p. 41). In general, conventional ideas "are not genuinely believed, but they cannot be dismissed without great anxiety" (SHAPIRO, 2000, p. 41).

> Authoritative, even rigid, rules of many kinds are convenient for living. They make reflection unnecessary and save energy. They are not followed out of deep conviction, but out of vague acceptance, often not quite acceptance of their usefulness, but of their authority; it is inconvenient to consider them thoughtfully. ... Many rules – perhaps religious rules, various customs and traditions – we follow simply because it feels wrong or, again, would require inconvenient reflection to do otherwise.
> (SHAPIRO, 2000, pp. 51–2)

Some people "consider it an honour to appear submissive"; they can be seen "bending forward in the presence of others, listening carefully to everyone's words, not so much to weigh and consider them, but rather to carry out their commands and to echo and reaffirm their sentiments" (ADLER, 1927, p. 206). The submissive person complies "with the potential wishes of all persons" and avoids "everything that might arouse resentment" (HORNEY, 1937, p. 97). Compliance, which "may take the form of not daring to disagree with or to criticize the other person, of showing nothing but devotion, admiration and docility" (pp. 119–20), may be the price one has to pay for securing others' affection or approval. Submissive or complying attitudes and behaviours "serve the purpose of securing reassurance by affection" (p. 97). The 'complying attitude' is incompatible with, and behaviourally opposed to, an attitude of assertion or dominance; the 'complying attitude' extinguishes "not only aggressive impulses but all tendencies toward self-assertion" (HORNEY, 1937, p. 120).

7.4.2 Inconspicuousness

Compliance implies submission *to the group*, much as basic anxiety has its evolutionary roots in the fear of becoming the target of joint aggression by the group. Compliance is associated with inconspicuousness, and both have the effect of inhibiting intraspecific aggression in other members of the group.

> Indeed, considered biologically, the very fact of being visible exposes an animal to the risk of attack from its enemies, and no animal is without enemies. Being visible is therefore a basic biological risk; being invisible is a basic biological defence. We all employ some form of camouflage.
> (LAING, 1960, p. 117)

One needs to be seen in order to have any hope of belonging or being connected to the social surround, but being seen is potentially dangerous. Defences employed against the "many anxieties about being obvious, being out of the ordinary, being distinctive, drawing attention to oneself" – in essence representing fears of attack by others and rejection by the group – "so often consist in attempts to merge with the human landscape, to make it as difficult as possible for anyone to see in what way one differs from anyone else" (LAING, 1960, p. 118). According to LAING (1960), one's 'false self' or 'persona' is constructed from compliance with others' social expectations and is designed to keep in check one's fears of aggression. One's 'false self' or 'persona' is one's "identity-for-others", an identity that arises "in compliance with the intentions or expectations" of the social environment (LAING, 1960, p. 105).

One of the aspects of the compliance of the false self that is most clear is the fear implied by this compliance. The fear in it is evident, for why else would anyone act, not according to his intentions, but according to another person's? Hatred is also necessarily present, for what else is the adequate object of hatred except that which endangers one's self? However the anxiety to which the self is subject precludes the possibility of a direct revelation of its hatred, except ... in psychosis.

(LAING, 1960, p. 106)

7.4.3 Controlled self-definition

Conformists "keep busy judging how closely they approximate common features of the surrounding world"; their conscious experience is focused on "what goes on around them and how to fit into it unobtrusively" (SCHAFER, 1997, p. 28). Conformists are prone to experience embarrassment and shame "whenever they judge that the have lapsed from being acceptably expectable and unremarkable" (p. 29). Shame "is the main affect signal by which they regulate their conduct and conscious experience" (SCHAFER, 1997, p. 29). The ready experience of shame betrays a heightened sense of vulnerability (weak self-esteem).

Extreme conformity is associated with remoteness in interpersonal relationships and in psychotherapy; extreme conformists are "rigidly defended" (p. 30) and "do their damnedest to remain disengaged" from their therapist (SCHAFER, 1997, p. 31). Extreme conformists "constantly try to put an end to spontaneous, unrehearsed, unscrutinized expressions of feeling" (p. 29). Their "intolerance of ambiguity and pain ... precludes emotional commitment to individualized others and sets severe limitations on the sense of aliveness" (p. 29). The incapacity to spontaneously reach out to others gives rise to a weak, fragmentation-prone sense of self. Extreme conformity is "built over fragmented selves and objects" (SCHAFER, 1997, p. 29).[6]

---

[6] Excessive repression of spontaneous feelings also means that emotional "difficulties are expressed mostly psychosomatically" (SCHAFER, 1997, p. 30).

What underlies "the maintenance of iron control of the self and others, including the therapist", is "a sense of omnipotence" (SCHAFER, 1997, p. 32). The sense of omnipotence compensates the conformist's weak self-esteem. The role of omnipotence is particularly evident in those who show *negative conformism*, that is, extreme individualism. The extreme individualist defines his self "by what it must not be" (p. 32); his "goal is the construction of oppositeness as a steady state" (p. 33). The extreme individualist is so concerned with defining his self by way of oppositeness, originality, imaginativeness, and freedom that his poses impress "as parodies or mere gestures of imaginativeness and freedom" (p. 33), and his "subjectivity will be considered theatrical and shallow" (p. 33). Like the extreme conformist, the extreme individualist "is self-defining under severe constraints" (p. 33); and, like the extreme conformist, he does so in order to counteract the "fragmentation of self and objects" (SCHAFER, 1997, p. 33). The extreme conformist has a narcissistic ethos (p. 30); extreme individualists, too, "live in a predominantly narcissistic internal ethos" (p. 33). The narcissistic organization of the personality of extreme individualists is complemented by their omnipotence. Lacking in self-confidence, extreme individualists have to "maintain their illusions of omnipotence", which they do in part by not allowing themselves "to respect tradition" (SCHAFER, 1997, p. 33).

The self that is defined by conformity or individualism is a 'false self', in WINNICOTT's sense. The false self, aiming to prevent or conceal self-fragmentation, is a narcissistic formation. Genuineness, aliveness, and vitality define the 'true self'. "Genuineness in human existence is always at risk", as SCHAFER (1997) pointed out, and so is true identity (p. 34). To the extent that the true self is at risk (i.e., to the extent that one is oversensitive to pain and rejection), the self is a 'false self', a self that is built on compliance (even negative compliance). The false self, that is, one's excessive compliance with social expectations and demands, is associated with an excessive concern about others' perception of oneself. Extreme conformists "live with a fear of discovery" (SCHAFER, 1997, p. 29), a fear that partly expresses itself in self-consciousness. The fear of discovery also pertains to concealed grandiosity. The greater one's sensitivity to pain and humiliation, the more the true self is driven into the background, and the greater is one's reliance on the false self, and the greater is also the role of latent grandiosity and fantasies of omnipotence in the regulation of narcissistic equilibrium.

7.4.4 Humour

Humour is "the ability at rare moments to play with and to reflect fearlessly on the strange customs and institutions by which man must find self-realization" (ERIKSON, 1950, p. 365). Humour allows us to gain respite from the ceaseless need, when in a social situation, to define our self and maintain narcissistic supplies. Humour entails a decathexis of the 'narcissistic self'; it is a way of achieving mastery over the exhibitionistic demands of the 'narcissistic self' (KOHUT, 1966).[7] In humour, the ego, adopting the perspective of the superego and looking down upon itself (back upon the ego), "sees its own unimportance, with a consequent indifference to its own extinction" (FLUGEL, 1945, p. 181). What produces a sense of exaltation is the sudden relief of the pressure to conform to the demands of the superego, brought about by a sudden insight into the absurdity of these demands. Absurdity of demands implies unimportance of whatever the ego does to appease the superego as well as, perhaps, unimportance of the approval provided by the superego (or by one of its external representatives) and consequent independence from the superego.[8]

7.5 Enhancement of approvability

> Man's need for the society of his fellows is of course no simple manifestation, and every single element and every mechanism in his psychology will be found to contribute to it; but it is probably true that where this instinct is strongly developed it represents more particularly the need to collect and accumulate a specially large measure of love, support and so security, which will be available as a perpetual reserve to be drawn upon at need. ... Thus by collecting goodness all round them, which they can dip into at any moment, they re-create for themselves (by their unconscious phantasy-attitude) a kind of substitute mother's breast which is always at their disposal and never frustrates or fails them.
> (RIVIERE, 1937, p. 24)

The actual receipt of approval needs to be distinguished from an individual's approvability, that is, his access to narcissistic resources. Actual receipt of approval or praise not only enhances self-esteem but also reinforces the individual's behaviour aimed at returning to the situation or state in which approval or praise was experienced. Characterological adaptation can be regarded as an abstract form of place preference learning; social strategies characteristic for the personality are acquired through the reinforcing effects of narcissistic sustenance. Many characterological devices and defence mechanisms enhance wellbeing and safety (SANDLER), ego feeling (FEDERN), or narcissistic cathexis of the self by way of increasing or maintaining the individual's approvability, his *attractiveness* for narcissistic supplies. Narcissistic cathexis of the self is enhanced effortlessly and sustainably in successful, powerful, or rich individuals who are generally highly regarded (or envied)

---

[7] Whereas sarcasm entails a hypercathexis of the omnipotent self (KOHUT, 1966).

[8] Swearing similarly produces pleasure and a "sense of power"; "when we swear we enjoy a 'sudden glory' that is derived from a temporary overthrow and defiance of our super-ego, and of the social authorities from which our super-ego is derived" (FLUGEL, 1945, p. 143).

by others. Individuals *work* towards attainment of success, prestige, or power precisely because the attainment of such attributes guarantees access to narcissistic resources in society. There is a difference between approvability briefly maintained in the individual's fantasy and actual approvability achieved in reality, between schizoid grandiosity (associated with detachment) and genuine success, the latter being associated with genuine safety and healthy pride. However, not every increase in approvability achieved vis-à-vis objects in the real world is sustained or adaptive. Approvability in reality can be maintained at great cost or ineffectively through false compliance and enactment of a false self (HORNEY). Lying is a maladaptive and often counterproductive way of increasing one's approvability temporarily in real interpersonal situations.

7.5.1 Self-seeking

> It is his image in the eyes of his own 'set', which exalts or condemns him as he conforms or not to certain requirements that may not be made of one in another walk of life.
> (JAMES, 1890, pp. 294–5)

JAMES (1890) proposed that "a man's Social Self is the recognition which he gets from his mates" (p. 293). 'Social self-seeking' is the behaviour that manoeuvres others into adopting a stance, directed towards oneself, of approving recognition or positive regard. Self-feeling, in the form of self-satisfaction (self-esteem) or self-despair, reflects "one's actual success or failure, and the good or bad actual position one holds in the world" (p. 306). The individual controls his self-regard by influencing the "thoughts in other men's minds", the "images other men have framed of" him (JAMES, 1890, p. 321). These thoughts and images are concerned with the individual's approvability, his social standing and achievements; and, in order to effect favourable thoughts and images in the minds of others, the individual has to act in accordance with the standards of his community, much as he had to perform in accordance with parental standards when, as a child, he wished to be well regarded (narcissistically nourished) by his parents.

> Those images of me in the minds of other men are, it is true, things outside of me, whose changes I perceive just as I perceive any other outward change. ... when I perceive my image in your mind to have changed for the worse, something in me ... contracted, and collapsed. ... Is not the condition of this thing inside of me the proper object of my egoistic concern, of my self-regard?
> (JAMES, 1890, pp. 321–2)

JAMES (1890) contended that "self-seeking is the outcome of simple instinctive propensity" (p. 320). The 'social self', the recognition one gets from others, depends on one's material property, so that instinctive seeking of recognition from others can manifest as 'instinctive' collection of property. The instinctive desire for admiring recognition, as JAMES (1890) saw it, organizes all aspects of social behaviour; even "the places and things I know enlarge my Self in a sort of metaphoric social way" (p. 308); and "much that commonly passes for spiritual self-seeking in this narrow sense is only material and social self-seeking beyond the grave" (p. 309). In order to succeed in one's striving for recognition, one has to compete with others, much as one had to compete with siblings or the other parent in one's longing to be at the centre of the primary object's attention.

> I must not be a failure, is the very loudest of the voices that clamor in each of our breasts: let fail who may, I at least must succeed.
> (JAMES, 1890, p. 318)

7.5.2 Ego interests

The ego, according to HARTMANN (1964), "is defined by its functions" (p. 114). 'Ego functions', including the mechanisms of defence, centre on the organism's adaptation to reality; and development of the ego proceeds "in the direction of an ever closer adjustment to reality" (p. 82). 'Ego tendencies' have aims that "center around values (ethical values, values of truth, religious values, etc.)" (p. 136). 'Ego interests' are "a special set of tendencies", having aims that "center around one's own person (self)" (p. 136). Ego interests, representing "only one set of ego functions" (p. 138), are "concerned with social status, influence, professional success, wealth, comfort, and so forth" (p. 64). Unlike the mechanisms of defence, "ego interests are hardly ever unconscious in the technical sense" (p. 136). Many ego functions, including the ego interests (such as strivings for wealth or social prestige), work with neutralized instinctual energy (derived from 'id tendencies') (HARTMANN, 1964), whereby neutralization of the exhibitionistic instinct likely plays a prominent role in ego interests. Man's "highest achievements" (art, science, religion) can be considered to "have their origin in libidinal tendencies" (HARTMANN, 1964, p. 217), particularly libidinal tendencies of the narcissistic type, tendencies that regulate self-esteem. HARTMANN (1964) understood that ego interests also have a 'defensive character'; they are "an attempt to deny inner conflicts and to protect oneself from fear" (p. 65).

7.5.3 Sublimation

> ... sublimation is a bargain. There is the wish to keep as much as possible of the original pleasure and to avoid as much as possible feelings of prohibition, disapproval, or guilt.
> (A. FREUD in SANDLER, 1985, p. 173)

Classical psychoanalytic theory is concerned with defences against anxiety that would arise in association with the expression of an instinctual wish. The main purpose of sublimation is to allow for the *safe* expression of an instinctual wish; it safeguards the expression of the wish. Sublimation is at the service of the instinctual wish, as "behind every sublimation there is, at some level, an unconscious fantasy gratification of the instinctual wish" (SANDLER, 1985, p. 167). Sublimation prevents anxiety because it implements acceptable "ways for securing gratification of otherwise unacceptable unconscious desires and wishes" (LAUGHLIN, 1970, p. 300). Many activities, including sports, involve socially acceptable gratification of aggressive impulses or of the wish to dominate (the need for omnipotent control). Other sublimations, such as performances of arts or music, are motivated by, and provide gratification for, exhibitionistic impulses (SANDLER, 1985). The idea that instinctual impulses can be "deflected and redirected" (LAUGHLIN, 1970, p. 303) and, through sublimation, obtain a "welcome and constructive external expression" (p. 298) is related to HARTMANN's concept of neutralization. Through sublimation, "inner libidinal energy becomes outwardly expressed as nonlibidinal", and "the energy of aggression ... becomes expressed in outwardly nonaggressive terms" (LAUGHLIN, 1970, p. 299). Thus, nonsexual activities secure the satisfaction of the sexual instinct, while nonaggressive activities secure the gratification of the aggressive drive. The greater the modification of the instinctual impulse, the greater would be the potential of an activity derived from this impulse to attract approval, whereas "closeness to the direct instinctual aims would be the reason for disapproval" (A. FREUD in SANDLER, 1985, p. 170).

> Essentially, then, sublimation means disguising or transforming the activity in such a way that it is socially acceptable or acceptable to the superego, and as a result there is in the activity an absence of direct instinctual gratification.
> (SANDLER, 1985, p. 171)

Sublimation, according to LAUGHLIN (1970), "may be viewed as the diverting of purely instinctual energy and purpose toward aims which society looks upon with greater favor, and which are therefore also more acceptable to the ego or self" (p. 312). An activity is acceptable to the self, that is, ego-syntonic (and not objected by the superego), insofar as it strengthens the secondary narcissistic cathexis of the ego or self. Sublimation not only enables the safe expression of instinctual impulses (preventing disapproval and anxiety, which the unrestrained expression of instinctual impulses would provoke); it importantly serves narcissistic needs. Sublimated expression of instinctual wishes is positively welcomed and approved by society. SANDLER (1985) recognized that sublimations, "including artistic activities, have as much to do with self-esteem as they have to do with the drives, although developmentally one might be able to argue that they are drive derivatives" (p. 175). Considering skills and sublimations, "one has to ask whether or not the gratification is a narcissistic one rather than a more direct instinctual one" (SANDLER, 1985, p. 179). The 'defence mechanism' of sublimation may be motivated more by the need to enhance self-esteem and less by an imperative to avoid conflict between drive impulses and prohibitions of external reality. In sublimation, instinctual drives cooperate with, or even serve, the need for acceptance and approval and the need to maintain one's narcissistic balance. Instinctual drives "secure disguised outward expression and constructive utilization through their unconscious diversion into approved and useful pathways" (LAUGHLIN, 1970, p. 297). Sublimated methods of drive expression and substitute aims for drives "must of necessity have the acceptance of society" (p. 313); they "must be ways which are acceptable socially" (LAUGHLIN, 1970, p. 314). Methods and aims are acceptable to society precisely inasmuch as they compliment the self or ego, because the self is constructed from and depends on others' appraisals.

FREUD (1923) thought that, in the process of sublimation, object libido (erotic object choice) is transformed into *narcissistic libido* and thus into a modification of the ego. Sublimation strengthens the ego or self by ensuring access to narcissistic supplies. Sublimation contributes to ego strength, and it evidences ego strength; sublimated activity is, in a sense, the opposite of a neurotic symptom (BERNFELD, 1922). Nevertheless, sublimation can have a defensive purpose and contribute to symptom formation. Anxiety, against which defences are erected, is the polar opposite of narcissistic equilibrium. Narcissistic equilibrium safeguards against aggression (and criticism) from without, a danger that GLOVER (1931) understood to be reflected in *social anxiety*. GLOVER (1931) argued that sublimations, such as cultural activities, can develop in a context of social anxiety or guilt; they may be reactions to "a mixture of social anxiety with displaced guilt" (p. 151). Sublimated activities, when forming "part of larger psychic formations resembling symptoms" (p. 149), allow individuals to remain inconspicuous and avert others' aggression or criticism. Sublimations would then be motivated by a "desire not to be found out" (p. 151) (as worthless or inferior). Individuals may be "clinging to a thin façade of cultural preoccupation in order to escape detection and criticism" (p. 151) and thus to reduce their social anxiety. Sublimations that are accompanied by anxiety and anxious preoccupation can be allied with obsessional neuroses. Sublimations can in some cases be regarded as 'extended phobias', insofar as "the spontaneously disappearing phobias of earlier life" may "reassemble and organize themselves in association with sublimated activities", thereby forming defensive structures (symptoms) that "'hold' anxiety better" (GLOVER, 1931, p. 151).

7.5.4 Reaction formation

Reaction formation can be defined "as the development of a pattern of attitudes and reactions" that hinders "the expression of contrary impulses" (LAUGHLIN, 1970, p. 281). Reaction formation bolsters or reinforces the defence mechanism of repression; reaction formation operates "in an attempt to keep repressed such inclinations as are consciously disowned" (p. 288). Impulses that are modified by way of reaction formation, and that are hence repressed, are "particularly those which are ultimately aggressive-hostile and sexual in nature" (LAUGHLIN, 1970, p. 294). In reaction formation, the ego adopts an *attitude* that is opposite to what needs to be repressed. Identification is a component of this defence mechanism. In reaction formation, there is "at the same time an identification with an attitude of the parent or of some other authority figure", "an attitude which is opposed to the impulse or to the affect concerned" (SANDLER, 1985, p. 102). The aim of reaction formation is "to keep an opposite part unconscious or repressed", so that, for instance, overconcern for everyone's safety would *conceal* "bad wishes toward the object" (A. FREUD in SANDLER, 1985, p. 222). Reaction formation "extends from the original objects for whose sake it was erected to a general attitude to other people" (pp. 221–2). A reaction formation "is part of the character and personality", whereas "sublimation is much more an activity", an activity that safely expresses an instinctual impulse (A. FREUD in SANDLER, 1985, p. 174).

Nevertheless, both reaction formations and sublimations contribute to the formation of characterological armour (REICH, 1928, 1929). REICH (1929) pointed out that, while reaction formation is "cramped and compulsive", sublimation is "free and flowing" (p. 141). When activity that represents a reaction formation is interrupted, "restlessness will appear sooner or later which may increase to irritability or even anxiety", whereas sublimation-related work can be interrupted "for quite a while" (REICH, 1929, p. 141). In reaction formation, "the interest is focused on the action itself", as it helps to keep an instinctual wish repressed, whereas, in sublimation, "the emphasis is on the effect of the action" (p. 141). Reaction formation involves "a reversal of the direction of the instinct", whereas, in sublimation, "the instinct is simply taken over by the ego and diverted to a different goal" (p. 141). Generally, "reactive achievements are less successful socially than sublimated ones" (REICH, 1929, p. 141), meaning that they are less effective in attracting social approval. Ultimately, however, both reaction formations and sublimations improve the individual's adaptation to his culture; they ensure that he is accepted and approved by others.

Instinctive impulses are repressed by way of adopting an opposite attitude because their expression would be *dangerous*. Through the adoption of "reactive patterns of excessive kindness, fairness, morality, and idealism, humans seek to protect themselves against the dangers resulting if they were to follow their inner impulses of anger, sex, or rage" (LAUGHLIN, 1970, pp. 287–8). The dangers for the person are others' disapprovals and criticisms; for the ego, the state of danger equals anxiety. Conversely, by adopting reactive patterns, the person "seeks to avert anxiety" and to ensure that he is the subject of others' approving gestures and favourable opinions. The person adopts socially acceptable attitudes and develops socially acceptable goals and character traits so as to ensure his "self-evaluation is maintained and enforced" (LAUGHLIN, 1970, p. 288).

7.5.5 Ego restriction

The ego may not reenter a situation in which an unpleasurable affect is likely to be aroused. The ego may simply "refuse to encounter the dangerous external situation at all" (A. FREUD, 1937, p. 93). The ego could move along alternative routes; and "we don't know how many of our moves in life are really avoidance of situations which we dread" (A. FREUD in SANDLER, 1985, p. 214). A child may avoid an activity in which he is inferior, that is, in which his performance compares unfavourably with that of others. What is avoided defensively is "an unpleasant realization of inferiority" (SANDLER, 1985, p. 356).[9] In some cases, a competitive activity may be avoided despite one's superiority because of "fear of the aggression which might arise from the envy of competitors" (p. 356). The ego of the child is thus restricted in its development; but, in contrast to *neurotic inhibition*, the ego usually develops an interest in another activity, one in which the child feels himself to be superior (p. 355). In neurotic inhibition, "there is a constant struggle against an instinctual wish, with the expenditure of much energy", preventing the translation of a forbidden impulse into action (SANDLER, 1985, p. 357). In neurotic inhibition, "the wish survives, even if it cannot be put into action and cannot be fulfilled", whereas in ego restriction, the wish is fulfilled in another activity (A. FREUD in SANDLER, 1985, p. 367).

Ego restriction has to be distinguished also from *phobic avoidance*. What is avoided in phobic avoidance "is an inner situation, an inner urge, which is projected outward, displaced outward, and then avoided in the external world" (A. FREUD in SANDLER, 1985, p. 360). The dangerous inner wish has to recur constantly; it "has to stay alive in order for the phobic avoidance to be there" and for the feared situation to be avoided time and again (p. 360). In ego restriction, unlike phobic avoidance, "there is no fear left" (A. FREUD in SANDLER, 1985, p. 362); "the person does not need to be preoccupied with the danger all the time" (SANDLER, 1985, p. 362). Ego restrictions in themselves are not pathological; they account for some of the individual personality differences. However, if activities that produce unpleasure or anxiety cannot be avoided, if "protection against anxiety through restriction of the ego" is lost, then a neurosis may be precipitated (SANDLER, 1985, p. 358).

7.5.6 Compensation

Through the defence mechanism of compensation, the individual seeks to offset, or make up for, actual or imagined deficiencies in his "physical, intellectual, or emotional endowment" (or to offset "almost any aspect of

---

[9] A neurotic person, having experienced an embarrassing or humiliating incident, similarly avoids "an activity because it might hurt his pride" (p. 107); having experienced a humiliation and painful injury to his pride, he avoids "to take the risk of exposing [his] pride" (HORNEY, 1950, p. 108).

failure" in his "personal attributes or experiences") (LAUGHLIN, 1970, p. 26). Compensation "may be the result of actual inferiorities, deficiencies, and losses, or it may follow purely subjective and even quite unrealistic feelings of this nature" (p. 25). Loss of physical ability through illness may call forth compensatory phenomena. Strivings for power and prestige may be compensations for physical weakness or feelings of inferiority; athletic skills or scholastic achievements may compensate for perceived or actual personal deficiencies. The defence mechanism of compensation is closely related to ADLER's (1938, 1965) notions of 'inferiority complex' and the striving for superiority. Striving for superiority is an enduring character trait that importantly shapes personality development. Compensation, on the other hand, is an ego defence; it operates outside conscious awareness, although, in some cases, compensation is "achieved primarily through conscious efforts" (LAUGHLIN, 1970, p. 24). Compensation is motivated by "inner needs to secure ego reenforcement" (p. 18), that is, by "inner needs for acceptance and love" (p. 25). Compensation reflects conscious and unconscious desires to attain "approval, acceptance, or love" from others (p. 18); compensation aims "to secure recognition, attention, or self-esteem" (LAUGHLIN, 1970, p. 25).[10]

7.5.7 Ambition

The ego ideal, an aspect of the self, can be likened to positive life aims and goals of mastery (reviewed in SANDLER et al., 1963). In KOHUT's model, the ideals or goals, which we long to attain, form one pole of the 'bipolar self', the other pole being formed by our ambitions, the developmental continuation of exhibitionistic urges of the 'narcissistic self' (KOHUT, 1966). Driven by our ambitions, we seek to reach our goals and live up to our ideals. The bipolar self includes "an intermediate area – the executive functions (talents, skills) needed for the realization of the patterns of the basic ambitions and basic ideals that were laid down in the two polar areas" (KOHUT, 1977, p. 49). The 'tension arc' "that establishes itself between the two poles of the self" facilitates the interaction between the ambitions by which a person is "driven" and the ideals by which he is "led" in his basic pursuits (p. 180). As a consequence of normal development (or successful psychoanalytic treatment of a narcissistic personality disorder), the person's nuclear self, consisting of "nuclear ambitions and ideals in cooperation with certain groups of talents and skills", becomes "sufficiently strengthened and consolidated to be able to function as a more or less self-propelling, self-directed, and self-sustaining unit which provides a central purpose to his personality and gives a sense

---

[10] Grandiose delusions are pathological overcompensations. Confabulations in Korsakoff's syndrome (the filling-in of memory gaps by imaginary experiences that are relayed as though they are factual) can be regarded, in part, as a compensatory phenomenon and, in part, as a type of rationalization (LAUGHLIN, 1970).

of meaning to his life" (p. 139) and enables "optimal productivity and creativeness of the personality" (KOHUT, 1977, p. 158). Narcissism participates in creative activity, acting as a spur towards fame and acclaim (KOHUT, 1966). Narcissism prompts the scientist or artist towards the communication of his work. Moreover, the scientist or artist invests his work and surroundings, insofar as they are significant to his work, with narcissistic-idealizing libido, thereby expanding his narcissistic experience to parts of the world (attributing selfobject functions to parts of the world), in the same way as objects can be cathected with narcissistic libido and thereby included in the self. Idealization, as a form of investment of narcissistic libido, is evidenced by the scientist or artist thinking very highly of his work. The scientist's or artist's work, having been invested with narcissistic libido, acts as a 'transitional object', mediating his ability to sustain his narcissistic balance by safeguarding sources of approval (KOHUT, 1966).

7.5.8 Striving for superiority

Feelings of inferiority, which are equivalent to poor self-esteem, can be the consequence of selfobject failures in early childhood or of objective deficiencies that marginalize the child in his peer group. Feelings of inferiority produce a state of stress that demands action; feelings of inferiority generate compensatory movements towards feelings of superiority (ADLER, 1927, 1965). The individual tries to rid himself of feelings of inferiority by changing the situation he faces, sometimes by changing the perception of the situation he faces to the point of self-deception (ADLER, 1965). Every neurotic person, according to ADLER, has an 'inferiority complex'. Enduring feelings of inferiority determine the neurotic person's life choices in terms of a pathway to power, prestige, or possessions. Once the goal of superiority has been defined, all the habits and behaviours of the person will be consistent with that goal. These efforts will only be partially successful, insofar as feelings of inferiority will continue to constitute the undercurrent of the neurotic person's psychological makeup (ADLER, 1965). Although ambitious and superior behaviours often conceal underlying feelings of inferiority, the 'striving for superiority' or 'will to power' is an important motive of social behaviour in general, whether or not this striving constitutes part of an 'inferiority complex'.

Ambition, according to ADLER (1927), conceals vanity. The "ceaseless striving for the acquisition of worldly goods" and "the heaping up of possessions" are merely forms of vanity that allow individuals "to come close to possessing the power of an enchanter" (p. 178); "individuals who spend their lives chasing after gold are spurred on merely by their vain desire for God-like power" (ADLER, 1927, p. 178) (omnipotence). Greed is closely related to ambition, vanity, and envy. Like vanity and envy, greed tends to be seen in those who are reluctant "to give pleasure to other people" (p. 183) (narcissists), although, similarly to envy, traces of it can be seen in "[a]lmost everyone in today's civilization" (p. 183). Greed, like envy, is an objectionable characteristic; and so it is often concealed "behind an exaggerated generosity, which amounts to nothing more than the giving of alms" (p. 183) (reaction formation). At the same time, "through gestures of generosity" one bolsters "one's self-esteem at the expense of others" (ADLER, 1927, p. 183).

ADLER (1965) recognized that 'striving for superiority' is based upon or recruits the instinct of aggression. Aggression in the service of 'striving for superiority' is generally not destructive; however, aggression can manifest as anger, rage, or hatred when the person's progress towards his goal of superiority is frustrated or when his underlying inferiority is uncovered (and when shame is felt). STORR (1968) pointed out that schizoid persons, who avoid close relationships for fear of abandonment or rejection, have "a strong desire for power and superiority, combined with an inner feeling of vulnerability and weakness" (p. 83). Schizoid persons feel "attacked and humiliated" by any criticism; and their defeat in competitive striving may produce "extreme and vindictive rage" (STORR, 1968, p. 86).

7.5.9 Achievements and possessions

> The questions as to who is bigger and who can do or not do this or that, and to whom – these questions fill the adult's inner life far beyond the necessities and the desirabilities which he understands and for which he plans.
>
> (ERIKSON, 1950, p. 364)

ERIKSON (1950), too, understood that the child's sense of smallness (his sense of helplessness and vulnerability) lives on in the adult's latent anxieties and apprehensions; the child's sense of smallness forms an ineradicable substratum in the mind of the adult (p. 364). The adult's "triumphs will be measured against this smallness, his defeats will substantiate it" (p. 364). The adult's sense of achievement, too, has its infantile roots in the sense of smallness and related dangers. The adult's sense of achievement is in part an expression of his remaining "ready to expect from some enemy ... in the outer world that which, in fact, endangers him from within: ... his own sense of smallness" (p. 365). Achievements compensate the adult's ineradicable sense of smallness and calm his latent anxiety, much as, earlier in life, maternal care compensated the child's smallness and soothed his anxieties, so that ultimately the adult's achievements are concerned with preventing a "sudden loss of attentive care" (ERIKSON, 1950, p. 368).

> The longing or greed for good things can relate to any and every imaginable kind of good – material possessions, bodily or mental gifts, advantages and privileges; but, beside the actual gratification they may bring, in the depths of our minds they all ultimately signify one thing. They stand as proofs to us, if we get them, that we are ourselves good, and so

are worthy of love, or respect and honour, in return. Thus they serve as proofs and insurances against our fears of the emptiness inside ourselves, or of our evil impulses which make us feel bad and full of badness to ourselves and others. They also defend us against our fear of the retaliation, punishment or retribution which may be carried out against us by others, whether in material or in moral ways, or in our affections and love-relations. One great reason why a loss of any kind can be so painful is that unconsciously it represents the converse idea, that we are being exposed as unworthy of good things, and so our deepest fears are realised.
(RIVIERE, 1937, p. 27)

Persons can enhance their self-regard by whatever they achieve or possess; and they can do so also by fulfilment of their ego ideal (FREUD, 1914) (whereby achievements and possessions have a beneficial effect on self-esteem insofar as they function also as attributes of the culturally determined ego ideal). In personality development, whatever has been found to augment self-esteem "has an encouraging effect and is therefore sought by persons who are fighting anxiety" (FENICHEL, 1946, p. 479) (Figure 7.1). In "trying to overcome and to deny their anxiety", narcissistic persons are "absolutely governed by a need to collect reassurances against supposed dangers" (p. 479). They may do so on a 'primitive' level "by collecting narcissistic supplies, affection, confirmation, power, prestige" (whereby what yields power and prestige is determined by cultural conditions); or they may do so on a more mature level "by collecting approval from their superego" (FENICHEL, 1946, p. 479). Narcissistic persons, being incapable of genuine attachment and libidinal involvement, excessively rely on the self-esteem-regulating function of achievements and possessions (FREUD, 1914). Narcissistic persons can reach their goal of self-aggrandizement through

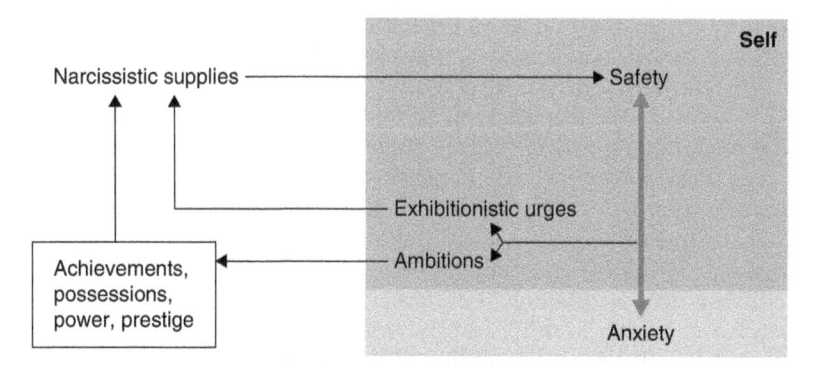

Figure 7.1 Ambitions, the mature derivative of infantile exhibitionistic impulses, are directed at the acquisition of means of attracting narcissistic supplies

achievements, if they are endowed with special physical or intellectual capacities (REICH, 1960) (KOHUT's 'talents'). Achievements and possessions can be regarded as remnants of the primitive sense of *omnipotence* that have been corroborated by experience. Absence of achievements or possessions can amount to a realization of *impotence* and be a source of feelings of inferiority (FREUD, 1914).

7.5.10 Search for glory

HORNEY (1937) emphasized in her discussion of the 'neurotic personality' that the "striving for power serves as a protection against the danger of feeling or being regarded as insignificant" (p. 166). By exerting power, gaining prestige, or piling up possessions, one achieves greater security and independence and hence protects oneself against 'basic anxiety'. Having power, prestige, or possessions also guards against the possibility of being hurt by others (HORNEY, 1937) (narcissistically hurt). While "the normal striving for power" protects against anxiety, "neurotic striving for power … is borne out of anxiety … and feelings of inferiority" (p. 163). In neurotic persons, strivings for power and possessions "are highly charged with emotion" (p. 180). The neurotic person's striving for power and possessions is the more compulsive, the more it is determined by anxiety. Power, prestige, and possessions may provide reassurance against anxiety by "fortifying one's own position" (HORNEY, 1937, p. 162), that is, one's social position. One's social position not only enshrines one's rights of access to narcissistic supplies but also facilitates one's control over others, over their readiness to emit submissive, approving, or affectionate signals towards oneself.

Idealized self

HORNEY (1950), like KOHUT, understood the interaction in the personality between ambition and ideals. The striving for recognition and approval is guided by an ideal: an image of oneself occupying a position or playing a role that is desirable in society and attracts others' attention and approval. The 'drive towards external success' and 'search for glory' – reflecting "the need to actualize the idealized self" – "are by necessity compulsive" (p. 38) in the neurotic person, yet healthy ambitions aiming to actualize an ideal self (ego ideal) have a driven character (the quality of an urge), too. Self-realization, that is, healthy striving for success ("the live forces of the real self" that "urge one toward self-realization" [p. 38]), and neurotic ambition (the search for glory) are similar, "because they have a common root in specific human potentialities" (HORNEY, 1950, p. 37). The neurotic person's search for glory, his wanting to actualize his idealized self-image, is more compulsive, in that he *must* actualize his idealized self "lest he incur anxiety, feel torn by conflicts, be overwhelmed by guilt feelings, feel rejected by others" (p. 29). The search for glory can be "a most powerful drive"; it can be "like a demoniacal obsession" (HORNEY, 1950, p. 31). Another difference is that the neurotic person's "glow of elation over the favourable reception of some work done, over a victory won, over any sign of recognition or admiration ... does not last" (p. 30). The neurotic person's "relentless chase after more prestige, more money, ... keeps going, with hardly any satisfaction or respite" (HORNEY, 1950, p. 30).

The capacity of imagination is at the service of both healthy striving for success and neurotic search for glory. An ideal to be realized or a goal to be attained has to be imagined, that is, the future shape of the self has to be imagined; however, in the neurotic person's search for glory, 'checks on imagination' tend to malfunction (HORNEY, 1950, p. 35). Actualization of the idealized self by the neurotic person (but not by the healthy one) involves falsification of reality. The neurotic person "is aversive to checking with evidence when it comes to his particular illusions about himself"; "he disregards evidence which he does not choose to see" in a great number of ways (p. 36). He fails "to recognize limitations to what he expects of himself and believes [is] possible to attain" (p. 36). The neurotic person "must shove aside the checks" on imagination because the "need to actualize his idealized image is so imperative" (HORNEY, 1950, p. 36).

7.5.11 Pretence and deception

> He *must* come out victorious in any argument, regardless of where the truth lies. ... The compulsiveness of the neurotic person's need for indiscriminate supremacy makes him indifferent to truth, whether concerning himself, others, or facts.
>
> (HORNEY, 1950, p. 30)

The quest for prestige is related to "a stringent need to impress others, to be admired and respected" (HORNEY, 1937, p. 171). If "self-esteem rests on being admired", then it "shrinks to nothing" when admiration cannot be elicited (p. 172). Neurotic persons, in order to bolster their prestige and maintain their self-esteem, "have to be able to talk about the latest books and plays, and to know prominent people" (p. 172). Neurotic persons "have to know everything better than anyone else"; they "want to be right all the time, and are irritated at being proved wrong, even if only in an insignificant detail" (HORNEY, 1937, p. 168). When a neurotic person with perfectionistic trends "is confronted with a question he cannot answer, he will pretend to know it at any price"; "he will juggle merely formalistically with scientific terms, methods and theories" (HORNEY, 1939, p. 216). ADLER (1927) described as 'schoolroom behaviour' the tendency of some individuals to assume "the role of the all-knowing one, appearing to understand everything immediately or seeking to pigeon-hole everything according to predetermined rules and formulae" (p. 205). What underlies this tendency is the "seeking of a good school report" (p. 204) (a sign of approval) whenever the individual finds himself "in a situation in which schoolroom behaviour would be appropriate" (ADLER, 1927, p. 205).

Lies serve to "ascribe some great achievements to the self of the liar" (KOHUT, 1971, p. 110). Lying, as a symptom of narcissistic personality disturbance, "may be due to the pressure of the grandiose self" (pp. 109–10). Alternatively, "the persistent demand of the grandiose self" may force the ego "to respond with unusual performance" (p. 112). Narcissistic persons may struggle "valiantly to live up to the assertions of the grandiose self concept on which they have become fixated" (KOHUT, 1971, p. 112).

7.6 Aggressive strategies of narcissistic control

Much of social behaviour is designed to elicit supportive and companionable interactions (HEARD & LAKE, 1986), if necessary by exerting pressure on others. We may become hostile if we do not receive the expected effective support or companionship. Then, hostile aggression is a defensive strategy "to handle fear concerning survival" (HEARD & LAKE, 1986, p. 436). This is the most elementary fear, a fear of disintegration or annihilation, a *basic anxiety* that shades into pain. People feel hurt when the attention or approval they solicit is not forthcoming. Distress arises "when a companion or supportgiver fails to recognise or acknowledge a request for supportive or companionable interaction, or having recognised it, devalues or rejects it" (HEARD & LAKE, 1986, p. 435). Persons with a neurotic disposition may experience an "inordinately sharp sting of disappointment" when their secret expectation of a return for the favours or generosity they have shown is not fulfilled (HORNEY, 1937, p. 143). A rebuff "not only throws them back on their basic anxiety", it also "arouses a tremendous rage" (p. 135). A rebuff "may stimulate outbreaks of hostility or result in a complete withdrawal of all feelings, so that they are cold and unresponsive" (p. 136). Hostility, incited when efforts to obtain approval or affection are frustrated or rejected, can manifest as irritability, spitefulness, or vindictiveness. Hostility of neurotic persons whose "self-esteem has been wounded by humiliation" may take "the form of a desire to humiliate others" (p. 178). In most instances, "rebuff may have been so slight as to escape conscious awareness", and, therefore, "the connection between feeling rebuffed and feeling irritated remains unconscious" (HORNEY, 1937, p. 136). Apart from rebuff, a challenge to one's social position (corresponding, in territorial animals, to an intrusion into one's territory) can cause an angry reaction (offensive aggression). In either case, the threat that provokes anger is a threat to the self.

7.6.1 Defiance and stubbornness

Defiance, according to ROTHSTEIN (1979), represents a wish to experience victory over a frustrating parent, over an object that does not meet the child's narcissistic needs. It is an attempt by the child to force the object to be more loving and available, to be like the gratifying parent he remembers from earlier years; it is the child's attempt to recapture his original omnipotence, his lost sense of control over the maternal smile, that is, over narcissistic supplies (ROTHSTEIN, 1979). At the same time, defiance allows the child to indulge in omnipotent narcissistic self-preoccupation, thereby partially restoring his narcissistic balance in fantasy. Defiance is related to stubbornness. Stubbornness, too, is a passive type of aggressiveness (FENICHEL, 1946, p. 279). Stubborn persons provoke others to be unjust, so that they can see themselves as "being treated unfairly" and, hence, attain "a feeling of moral superiority which is needed to increase their self-esteem" (p. 279). Stubborn persons are forever engaged in a "struggle for the maintenance or the restoration of self-esteem"; they are "filled with narcissistic needs, whose gratification is required to contradict some anxiety or guilt feeling" (FENICHEL, 1946, pp. 279–80).

7.6.2 Jealousy

Persons who are inclined to feeling jealous "are not able to love but need the feeling of being loved" (FENICHEL, 1946, p. 391). They have an intense fear over loss of love, especially insofar as "this loss means a diminution of their self-esteem" (p. 512). They are dependent on their objects for the gratification of their narcissistic needs (narcissistic dependence), but are nevertheless unable to commit to their objects (insofar as their object choice is of the narcissistic type). Their longing for another object, for a more secure source of narcissistic supplies, produces jealousy "on a projective basis; their longing for another partner is projected", so that they believe that it is their partner, not they themselves, who is "looking for a new object" (p. 391). Such projection is reinforced by the special intolerance of jealous persons to a loss of love and a related special sensitivity to signs of their object's unfaithfulness. To the actual loss of love, jealous persons react with depression and aggressiveness (FENICHEL, 1946, p. 512).

ADLER (1927) regarded jealousy as "the sister of ambition" (p. 178) and as "an especially well-marked form of the striving for power" (p. 180). Jealous individuals "bind their partner with chains of love"; they "build a wall around their loved one" (ADLER, 1927, p. 180). The jealous individual feels he has an *exclusive claim* to the object's attention and love. He is sensitive to and concerned about lapses in his object's attentiveness; and such lapses have to be punished, so they would not happen again. Jealousy "may be recognized in mistrust and the setting up of traps for others, in critical sizing-up of other people"; and it can express itself "in energetic obstinacy", in "[s]poiling the enjoyment of others, senseless opposition, the restriction of others' freedom and their consequent subjugation" (ADLER, 1927, p. 180).

Jealousy involves hostility against the attachment object, the external representative of the omnipotent object. Feelings of envy, by comparison, are concerned with a perceived rival (the third person in a triangular constellation) competing with oneself for an external object's devotion (or, unconsciously, for attention from the omnipotent object). Envy arises when the other's qualities are perceived as being more *attractive* than one's own, when the other is perceived as being more worthy of attention and praise from the derivative of the primary object (or from the internalized omnipotent object). Both envy and jealousy are played out in relation to one's striving to maintain an exclusive object relation (in reality or unconscious fantasy); they are accompanied by aggressive impulses directed at perceived obstacles to this striving.

7.6.3 Envy

The phenomenon of envy, as ADLER (1927) saw it, is inseparable from ambition, vanity, and the "striving for power and domination" (p. 180). Ambitious people "spend their time in measuring the success of others" (against their own successes) and in occupying themselves "with what others have accomplished" (p. 181). If ambitious people cannot achieve superiority over others, they become envious, being "interested solely in taking things away from other people, in depriving them and putting them down" (p. 182). Thus, "individuals who are unable to satisfy their own vanity are often to be found striving to prevent others from enjoying their own lives to the full" (ADLER, 1927, p. 158). People who are consumed with envy tend to be those "who are not concerned about making themselves useful to others" (p. 183) (they are narcissists, in that they lack 'social feeling'). They may be considered as antisocial personalities to the extent that they are not moved "one whit" by the "fact that their actions cause suffering to others"; they may even "take pleasure in their neighbours' pain" (ADLER, 1927, p. 183).

Envy is the feeling of resentment or hostility towards the good qualities or abilities of another person. An attempt or desire to spoil these qualities is fundamental to envy; the envious person is interested in taking something away from the other person (JOSEPH, 1986). In more extreme cases, an envious person cannot bear to face another person's success. He cannot even bear when another person gives something good to him; and he is unable to experience gratitude. Excessively envious people are also unable to feel enjoyment since good experiences are accompanied by a nagging feeling that they could get more or someone else has got better or that there is something wrong with it. Excessive envy prevents the person from having warm and trusting relationships. As a consequence, the envious person is likely to remain insecure, giving rise, in a vicious circle, to an increase in his envy towards others (JOSEPH, 1986).

Defences

Persons employ defences against unpleasant (because inacceptable and *disapproved*) feelings of envy as soon as these feelings arise. The envious person may try, for instance, to regard the envied person as inferior or else idealize him. This would render the envied person (in the eyes of the envious person) as either not enviable after all or being on a pedestal and out of reach (JOSEPH, 1986). Idealization of the envied person (such as the leader of a group) would make comparisons irrelevant (SPILLIUS, 1993). Idealization is linked with identification; and identification with the envied person and introjection of the envied person's good qualities allows the envious person to feel he possesses these good qualities (SPILLIUS, 1993). Another defence against envy is to devalue *oneself*, again in an attempt to increase the gap between oneself and the envied person – a defence that is related to masochism (JOSEPH, 1986).

The envious person may project his envy so that others appear envious and destructive (SPILLIUS, 1993). A related defence is to stir up feelings of envy in other people by making them aware of one's own outstanding qualities or capacities (JOSEPH, 1986). Some envious people restrict contact with others and avoid situations that can stimulate feelings of envy. Competitiveness is a more adaptive defence against feelings of envy; in acquiring superior qualities or capacities (in terms of power, prestige, or possessions), the person aims to prevent feelings of envy towards others (JOSEPH, 1986). Where, in spite of strong ambitions, we fail to obtain social status, possessions, or prestige, "and where disappointment is incessant and the struggle unending" (p. 311), we may protect our self by denying the value of others (looking upon them with indifference or "chill negation, if not positive hate") and denying that the goods we fail to obtain "are goods at all" (JAMES, 1890, p. 312).

7.6.4 Prejudice

Our habits of living, our habits of feeling and thinking and doing are largely governed by prejudice. So are our traditional virtues, our apocryphal precepts, our cherished 'principles of conduct'.

(BURROW, 1949, p. 31)

Our compliance with social norms and commonly held expectations inhibits others' offensively aggressive tendencies, while our active endorsement and propagation of social prejudices and 'principles of conduct' expresses our own offensive aggressiveness. BURROW (1949) spoke of a "monstrous *social mood* of systematized prejudice and absolutism", a "social mood begotten of partitive feeling, or affect"; and it became clear to him that "this impervious mood of competitive affectivity or prejudice", "whether manifesting itself singly or collectively", "was of one cloth throughout the entire social structure" (p. 52).

> The difference between the partitive response of the animal and the partitive response of man is that man's symbolic or partitive reaction has become socially or interrelationally systematized throughout the organism of the species. This systematization, as I have said, is represented

subjectively in the pseudo-identity each of us reflexly impersonates as the "I" or 'I'-persona – a constellation of affects and prejudices ...
(BURROW, 1949, p. 140)

Our status or position in the social hierarchy is a major determinant of our seemingly private self-image ('I'-persona') and of our self-regard. Self-regard or self-love ('amour propre') reflects the confident expectation of others' positive appraisals of ourselves, an expectation that rests, in part, on cultural symbols signifying our social position or status. We use offensive (intraspecific) aggression to control others' appraisals of and respect for ourselves, mostly indirectly through the defence of our social position and the advancement of our status. Social position or status can be regarded as an abstract 'social territory' that governs our *access* to narcissistic supplies and that is defined in terms of norms, rights, and traditions commonly accepted in our culture. Therefore, we use offensive aggression (in its 'neutralized' form) to the effect of upholding these norms, rights, and traditions; we are prejudiced.

In our social relationships we seem ever at pains to preserve what is known as our *amour propre*, our mental and social 'right' or prestige. ... The measures we adopt for its protection and security now operate automatically among us. These measures are both defensive and offensive. The defensive mechanism is seen in one's effort to achieve credits, to be thought approvingly of, to be 'somebody'. The offensive aspect of the mechanism is shown in the tendency to disparage others, to indulge in personal criticism and irritation towards them. Thus one shows a reflex readiness to uphold at all costs this affective image he calls his 'character'. ... one insists upon preserving at all times this social image of his 'right', his 'character' or prestige, and by the same token he belittles the rights and deprecates the prestige of others. We demand our rights with special virulence when the rights of others conflict our own magnified self-image, when the opinions or the prejudices of others are not sympathetic to our own and so do not contribute to sustain our *amour propre* or private prerogative.
(BURROW, 1949, p. 39)

7.6.5 Sense of entitlement

The sense of entitlement refers to one's thinking of oneself as an exception, as having special rights, as being entitled to break the law (MOSES, 1989). The conscious sense of entitlement derives from the child's demand for "the total, undivided attention of the mother" (p. 485). Feelings of entitlement are part of the child's sense of omnipotence. Gradually, children give up their sense of entitlement, along with their omnipotence. Nevertheless, the sense of entitlement persists in ameliorated form into adult life; it then "consists of making demands which are appropriately one's right" (p. 486). The sense of entitlement can be excessive; yet it can be, at the same time, unconscious, being hidden "behind a cloak of marked modesty" (p. 486). The sense of entitlement tends to be excessive in persons who believe that they were subjected in their earlier life to unjust deprivation and suffering. Excessive entitlement is a feature of the narcissistic personality (MOSES, 1989).

The person with an excessive sense of entitlement "holds tenaciously to the conviction that his behavior is correct, appropriate, and adequate" (MOSES, 1989, p. 489). He would "not entertain doubts or experience shame" (p. 489). Any challenge to his entitlement, to "his view of himself as someone with rights of special entitlement", can lead to "self-righteous indignation" (p. 492) and "the righteous rage of entitlement" (p. 488). Shame and the sense of entitlement "do not consciously exist at the same time" (p. 484). What seems to coexist instead with entitlement is shamelessness. The sense of entitlement and shame "are in some way opposite sides of the same coin" (p. 484). Both the sense of entitlement and shame are narcissistic phenomena; both are "closely related to the self, to narcissistic proclivities" (MOSES, 1989, p. 483).

7.6.6 Bossing attitude and rightness

The striving for power, prestige, or possessions serves "as a channel through which repressed hostility can be discharged" (HORNEY, 1937, p. 166). When hostility is repressed and channelled in this way, "the person has not the remotest idea that he is hostile" (p. 66). Neurotic striving for power "does not necessarily appear openly as hostility toward others" when it is "disguised in socially valuable or humanistic forms" (p. 174). Nevertheless, insofar as hostility is concealed in activities such as "giving advice" or "taking the initiative or lead", "the other persons ... will feel it and react either with submissiveness or with opposition" (p. 174). Hostility that was hitherto "pressed into civilized forms" can break out more overtly, if the neurotic person does not succeed in having his own way (p. 174). The neurotic person can show a "plain anger reaction to a lack of compliance" with his wishes and expectations (p. 169) or react angrily to others' failure to follow his advice (HORNEY, 1937).

Neurotic persons are prone to have a bossing attitude, of which they may not be aware (HORNEY, 1937, p. 169). HORNEY (1945) observed that "a combination of predominant aggressive trends and detachment is the most fertile soil for the development of rigid rightness; and the nearer to the surface the aggression, the more militant the rightness" (p. 138). The 'aggressive type' of neurotic personality "seems to have an unusual capacity for definite opinions"; "his opinions will often have a dogmatic or even fanatic character" (HORNEY, 1945, p. 170).

In the striving for power or possessions, whether neurotic or not, "a certain amount of hostility may be discharged in a non-destructive way" (HORNEY, 1937, pp. 174–5). Aggressiveness invested in the attainment and cementation of a position of power (or any other socially desirable asset) becomes manifest when one's position is under threat. The main difference between neurotic and nonneurotic persons may lie in the readiness with which a social situation is perceived as a threat to one's position and rightful access to narcissistic resources (and hence as a threat to one's self). Thus, the bossing attitude and irritability of neurotic persons may be due to their tendency to *interpret* seemingly innocuous situations as evidence that they are unwanted, excluded, or rejected (HORNEY, 1937).[11]

7.6.7 Depreciative and critical attitude

ADLER (1927) observed that people who are afflicted with a deep inner insecurity (inferiority) – because they "are unable to form real friendships" (p. 198) (i.e., they lack 'social feeling') – not only engage in compensatory striving for superiority but also have a tendency to judge, criticize, and ridicule anything; "[t]hey are dissatisfied with everything" (p. 162). Their sharp and critical manner, an expression of their 'social hostility', allows them "to gain a feeling of superiority by degrading other people" ('depreciation complex') (p. 163). Their tendency to degrade others is associated with their insistence on being always right. They "go to great lengths to prove themselves right" and to prove others to be in the wrong (ADLER, 1927, p. 198).

The 'paranoid type' of narcissistic personality is characterized by argumentativeness and litigiousness (BURSTEN, 1973). Paranoid narcissistic persons have a need to reunite with a powerful and nourishing object, not unlike other narcissistic persons. Argumentativeness, critical suspiciousness, and jealousy reflect a sense of disappointment (rationalized narcissistic injury) or betrayal when narcissistic union (with the omnipotent object) cannot be attained. Argumentativeness, critical suspiciousness, and jealousy also comprise a 'mode of narcissistic repair'; these attitudes and behaviours betray a need to be the 'special selected one' in the eyes of the omnipotent object (BURSTEN, 1973). Inadequacy (inferiority), which renders the person *unacceptable in the eyes of the omnipotent object*, and related shame are counteracted by way of externalizations and projections. The paranoid narcissist constantly looks for shameful conduct in others, so as to affirm

---

[11] Despite their sensitivity to rebuff or challenge, neurotic persons "often are incapable of defending themselves against attack" (p. 38) or of expressing anger in situations when this is warranted (Horney, 1937). The neurotic person, "knowing how hurt and vindictive he feels when humiliated, is instinctively afraid of similar reactions in others" (Horney, 1937, p. 179).

and support his projections. If others can be experienced as inadequate and shameful, the paranoid person feels more acceptable again to the omnipotent object with which he seeks to reunite (BURSTEN, 1973). Projective identification can be a defence against shame and is a method of controlling self-esteem. Projective identification, that is, "forcible projection of bad aspects of the self", allows for the "perception of one's own vice in others", after first forcing them "to display it actively" (MONEY-KYRLE, 1961, p. 98). Projective identification has "the aim of getting rid of depressed parts of the self", namely the "sense of inferiority, of being despised as useless" (MONEY-KYRLE, 1961, p. 99).

Paranoid narcissists easily become disenchanted with their allies (BURSTEN, 1973). They have a destructive tendency to betray their former allies; they do so by finding new allies and inducing them to hurt or ruin their former allies. 'Paranoid criticism' and devaluation of former allies support the paranoid narcissist's projections of his shameful self, while, through his search for new alliances, he pursues his aim of reuniting with a source of power (an instance of the omnipotent object) (BURSTEN, 1973).

7.6.8 Aggressive competitiveness

According to ADLER (1927), "angry individuals are those who are striving for superiority" or recognition by overtly aggressive means; their striving "degenerates into real power-madness" (p. 213). Angry individuals, too, lack 'social feeling' and hence are burdened with feelings of inferiority; and "their striving for power is rooted in their feeling of inferiority" (p. 215). The purpose of anger "is the rapid and forceful destruction of every obstacle in the way of the angered person" (p. 213). Angry individuals tend to "respond with violent outbursts to the slightest occurrence that might distract from their sense of power" or might impede their "striving for power and domination" (p. 213), although most nonneurotic persons will "remember how they have won back their prestige or got their own way through an occasional outburst of fury" (p. 214). Angry individuals (similarly to BURSTEN's paranoid narcissists) are distrustful; "they are continually on guard in case anyone comes too close to them or does not value them highly enough" (ADLER, 1927, p. 214).

'Phallic narcissistic personalities', in BURSTEN's (1973) classification, achieve 'narcissistic repair' (defence against shame associated with being weak or insignificant) by means of *arrogance*, aggressive competitiveness, and pseudomasculinity. Their need to be admired reflects their wish to effect reunion with the omnipotent object (to satisfy their narcissistic needs). They are prone to take risks, feeling they will be miraculously saved, and engage in acts of bravery for the sake of self-glorification. Phallic narcissists (and manipulative narcissists) have a relatively firm sense of self, reflecting their greater degree of individuation. They have more successfully internalized their sources of approval, whereas 'craving narcissists' depend on an almost continuous presence of their object. While the reliance of phallic narcissists on their omnipotent object is hidden in internalized structures, their grandiose self (the counterpart of the omnipotent object) is manifest in their ambition and competitiveness (Bursten, 1973).

7.6.9 Manipulativeness

The 'manipulative type' of narcissistic personality (related to antisocial personality disorder) is characterized by manipulativeness and propensities for deception (lying), superficial relationships, and contempt for others (Bursten, 1973). Manipulative personalities experience little guilt. Their 'mode of narcissistic repair', allowing them to overcome inner feelings of worthlessness, involves *deception* and aggressive competition aimed at defeating others. By defeating others, the manipulative personality proves his superiority and hence his acceptability to the omnipotent object with which he seeks to reunite. Good manipulators can 'size up a situation', while engaging in 'trial identifications', and use the information thus ascertained to influence others, to move them around in such a way that their own narcissistic wishes will be gratified (Bursten, 1973).

The expression towards others of 'social feeling', that is, of affection and concern, is not always genuine. Vain (narcissistic) persons "who would like to rule others must first catch them in order to bind them to themselves" (Adler, 1927, p. 173). They may show an attitude of "amiability, friendliness or approachability" in order to lull others "into a sense of security" and use them (narcissistically) so as to "maintain their personal superiority" (p. 173). They would however proceed to aggressively control those who they have bound to themselves, thus removing their veil of apparent amiability (Adler, 1927, p. 173).

Manipulations for the sake of restoring the narcissistic equilibrium can involve indirect expressions of hostility. For instance, a neurotic person may use a traumatic experience or injury he suffered as a "basis for demands" for sympathetic treatment, while expressing his hostility through an "appeal to justice" (p. 144); he "may arouse feelings of guilt or obligation in order that his own demands may seem just" (Horney, 1937, p. 144). His injury or illness may be used implicitly as an accusation, as "a kind of living reproach, intended to arouse guilt feeling" in others and to make them "willing to devote" all their *attention* to him (p. 144). Neurotic persons "may be willing to pay the price of suffering", "because in that way they are able to express accusations and demands without being aware of doing so, and hence are able to retain their feeling of righteousness" (pp. 145–6). A neurotic person may resort to more overt expression of hostility, that is, "threats as a strategy for obtaining affection", threatening to commit acts such as "ruining a reputation or doing some violence to another or to himself" (Horney, 1937, p. 146).

7.6.10 Criminal aggressiveness

> We have reasons to believe that in human life, activity and aggression alternate in cycles with passivity and submission.
> (SCHILDER, 1951, p. 209)

An important aim of activity and aggression is "to be the master of the fate of objects" (SCHILDER, 1951, p. 213). SCHILDER (1951) argued that "aggressive action takes place when the individual feels restricted in his power to achieve an adequate mastery of the situation" (p. 219). Inability to control objects or the situation – when the individual feels that a passive role has been forced upon him – may provoke a reaction of aggression and criminal behaviour. SCHILDER (1951) regarded the aggressive criminal action as "a protest against passivity and enforced submission" (p. 218). Acts of aggression ("especially with a gun") help the individual to restore his "threatened masculinity" (p. 214), that is, to assert his capacity to control his fate and environment and, at the same time, to restore his self-esteem (narcissistic homeostasis). Through the criminal act, the "aggressive criminal restores his prestige" (p. 218). Inability to control one's fate or environment (helplessness) is accompanied by feelings of inferiority and insecurity. Feelings of inferiority and insecurity, which SCHILDER (1951) found to be present in all but one of the aggressive criminals he studied, may increase dispositions to perceive a threat and/or to react to a threat with counteraggression. Aggressive criminals often explained their aggressive action with reference to "real or imaginary minor aggression of another"; or they felt that their "action was a counteraction against the aggressiveness of others" (p. 215). Feelings of inferiority and the resulting heightened need for approval predispose to criminal behaviour in conjunction with cultural factors, because an "aggressive impulse has a much greater chance of becoming criminal action when the criminal action can reckon with open or tacit approval of those social factors which play a part in the ego formation" (SCHILDER, 1951, p. 217).

> Criminal aggressiveness in our cases was almost invariably reactive in its nature. It was a reaction to an immediate situation and to a situation in childhood. Since cultural influences connect passivity and submission with femininity and activity and aggression with masculinity, the assault becomes a symbol for masculinity regained.
> (SCHILDER, 1951, p. 215)

8
Psychopathology

Ontogenetically, the self is formed in the matrix of the child's selfobject environment (in a process of 'transmuting internalization') (KOHUT & WOLF, 1978). The 'nuclear self' of the child crystallizes in this matrix if his mirroring and idealizing needs are *realistically* gratified by his selfobjects, and if the child is also exposed to minor, nontraumatic failures of the responses of his selfobjects. If the child's mirroring and idealizing needs are not responded to sufficiently, a stable structure of the self cannot emerge; the child's dependence on his selfobjects cannot be replaced by functions that are normally adopted by the self as it matures (i.e., by endopsychic self-esteem-regulating structures). Persistent failure of the parents to respond to the child's existence and assertiveness with effective mirroring can cause lasting enfeeblement of the self. Persistent failure of the parents to allow the child to experience merger with one of them acting as an idealized object, too, has this effect (KOHUT & WOLF, 1978).

> The understimulation due to parental remoteness that is a pathogenic factor in disorders of the self is a manifestation of a disorder of the self in the parent. In many instances, the parents of those who suffer from disorders of the self are quite manifestly walled off from their children, and it is thus easy to see that they deprive them of empathic mirroring and of a responsive target for their idealizing need.
> (KOHUT, 1977, p. 274)

Narcissistic object choice can stabilize a weak self-representation, whereby narcissistically chosen objects act as substitutes for a defective self, that is, for a defective endopsychic self-esteem-regulating structure (KOHUT, 1966, 1971). Weakness of self and narcissistic measures aimed at its stabilization can have pathological consequences. Primary disturbances of the self, caused by persistent failures of selfobjects in early development, can be divided into four groups (KOHUT & WOLF, 1978). Firstly, serious and protracted damage to the self, damage that *is not* covered over by defensive structures, leads to psychosis. Secondly, serious and protracted damage of the self that *is* covered over by complex defences gives rise to 'borderline states'. Thirdly, less severe damage with temporary enfeeblement of the self can be covered over by perverse, delinquent, or addictive behaviours, giving rise to a narcissistic *behaviour* disorder, whereas, fourthly, in the narcissistic *personality* disorders, temporary enfeeblement of the self produces hypochondria, depression, and hypersensitivity to slights (KOHUT & WOLF, 1978). In the narcissistic behaviour disorders, fragile self-esteem can be protected from further damage "through perverse, delinquent, or addictive behavior" (p. 69), whereas, in chronic depression, the patient may have "no expectation of any real interest in him from anybody" (WOLF, 1988, p. 71).

> The intense suffering associated with pathology of the self impellingly motivates toward amelioration by forcing the environment to yield the required comfort-giving experiences. Intensity of need combined with expectation of rebuff causes deep shame. Stridently expressed demands may alternate with total suppression of them. Demands, whether expressed in fantasy or in behavior, whether they are related to grandiosity or to being accepted by idealized figures, are not derived from the normal healthy self-assertive narcissism of childhood, but from the fragments of archaic selfobject needs or from the defences against them.
> (WOLF, 1988, p. 74)

8.1 Narcissistic personality disturbance

Patients with a narcissistic personality disturbance are handicapped by an "inability to regulate self-esteem and to maintain it at normal levels" (KOHUT, 1971, p. 20). Narcissistic patients have an "intense hunger for a powerful external supplier of self-esteem and other forms of emotional sustenance in the narcissistic realm" (p. 17). Narcissistic patients tend to be "vain, boastful, and intemperately assertive with regard to their grandiose claims" (p. 178). Their narcissistic displays are designed to elicit 'narcissistic sustenance' from others in the form of approving, mirroring, and echoing responses. When forming a relationship (such as in the process of psychoanalysis), the narcissistic patient engages the object only insofar as it satisfies his needs in the area of 'narcissistic requirements'; he "acknowledges the object only as a source of approval, praise, and empathic participation" (p. 174). The narcissistic person may cover his extreme neediness in the area of 'narcissistic requirements' "by a display of independence and self-sufficiency" (KOHUT, 1971, p. 293). Related to the shallowness of his relationships and his proneness to feelings of envy, the narcissistic person feels unable to give with joy or to receive with gratitude (SPILLIUS, 1993).

The self of the narcissistic person is, according to KERNBERG, an empty and hungry one. The narcissistic person lacks a sense of full involvement in life.

His life is an ongoing preparation for the next moment, an eternal waiting for the moment when real life and true love can begin (BROMBERG, 1983). The narcissistic patient experiences "a chronic sense of dullness and passivity"; however, "in consequence of having received external praise or of having had the benefit of interest from the environment", he "feels suddenly alive and happy" and, for a short period of time, "has a sense of deep and lively participation in the world" (KOHUT, 1971, p. 17). Unavoidable narcissistic injury, in form of "rebuff, the absence of expected approval, the environment's lack of interest in the patient, and the like, will soon bring about the former state of depletion" (p. 17). At signs of disapproval of him or of loss of interest in him, the narcissistic patient may "become fist enraged and then cold, haughty, and isolated" (KOHUT, 1971, p. 58).

Undue craving for admiration, which is characteristic of narcissistic individuals, contrasts with healthy ambition (KOHUT), that is, healthy striving to be valued by others, a striving that supports healthy self-esteem (HORNEY, 1939). Undue craving for admiration is associated with concealed self-inflation or self-aggrandizement. Any revelation to others of one's infantile grandiosity and persistent exhibitionism can provoke shame and anxiety (KOHUT, 1971). Admitting to others, and even to oneself, the grandiosity that determines one's goals and life projects – and the exhibitionism and the relentless need to validate the grandiose self that underpin one's actions – would imply the momentary collapse of one's self. Such admission or insight would reveal one's worthlessness and inferiority underneath. Depression experienced by narcissistic individuals when their grandiosity breaks down is unlike the depression experienced by those who mourn the loss of an object. In narcissistic individuals, a depletion or loss of self gives rise to an empty depression, a 'depression without guilt' (KOHUT, 1977; MILLER, 1979).

8.1.1 Disturbed object relationships

Narcissistic personalities are extremely self-centred and show a high degree of self-references in interactions with other people (KERNBERG, 1970). Narcissistic personalities have a highly inflated concept of themselves and, at the same time, an extraordinary need for approval from others. These *disturbances of self-regard* are connected with specific *disturbances in object relationships*. The narcissistic personality is involved with others only insofar as narcissistic use can be made of them. Others are used as sources of approval and admiration reflected back on to the narcissistic person; or others are idealized and admired, so that their admired qualities can be owned by the narcissistic person. Thus, the narcissistic person treats others only as an *extension of himself* (KERNBERG, 1970), as selfobjects. What is distinctly lacking in pathological narcissism is the capacity to genuinely care for, take interest in (be curious about), love, or become involved with others. Accordingly, there is an incapacity to experience separation anxiety or mourn over the loss of an object, along with an incapacity to feel guilt (KERNBERG, 1970, 1974).

ADLER (1927) recognized that vanity, when it is excessive, "cannot co-exist with concern for our fellow human beings" ('social feeling') (p. 159). HORNEY (1939) thought that the egocentricity of narcissistic individuals *detracts* them from real interest in others (p. 100). FREUD (1920), too, supposed that narcissism drains object libido. However, it is more likely that lack of real interest in others (pervasive inhibition of object libido, of 'social feeling' or interest), due to rejections experienced in early childhood, is the primary problem in narcissistic disorders. Narcissistic individuals have a decreased capacity to love, rendering their emotional ties with others tenuous. As a consequence, individuals with a narcissistic disorder do not have effortless access to resources of narcissistic supplies. Because of deep-seated fears of rejection, individuals with a narcissistic disorder *cannot* attain narcissistic sustenance (and maintain their self-esteem) effortlessly through love relations or genuine care for objects (true object-libidinal investments). Their self-esteem, and hence their safety, can be maintained only by way of self-aggrandizement, narcissistic object choice, and exhibitionistic efforts to attain approval and admiration from others. In other words, self-esteem may be weak because, primarily, object relations are weak; and self-inflation, narcissistic object choice, and excessive exhibitionism are compensatory methods of bolstering weak self-esteem, and thus attaining safety and preventing annihilation.

8.1.2 Methods of self-aggrandizement

In HORNEY's (1939) view, narcissism should "be described as essentially self-inflation" (p. 89). The 'narcissistic trend', that is, the neurotic trend towards self-inflation (self-aggrandizement), is, according to HORNEY, *one* of the mechanisms by which the personality attains *safety*. The tendency to aggrandize oneself and to appear "unduly significant to oneself" cannot be separated from the craving for "undue admiration from others" (p. 90). For the narcissistic person, "safety rests on being appreciated and admired"; "the vital danger" for him "is that of losing caste" (p. 198). He becomes anxious "if he finds himself in an environment that does not recognize him" (HORNEY, 1939, p. 198). Not being recognized or respected increases one's vulnerability to be attacked by conspecifics and is hence anxiety-provoking; not being recognized implies a danger of being abandoned or annihilated by the primal horde.

Self-aggrandizement allows the narcissistic person to escape "the painful feeling of nothingness by molding himself in fancy into something outstanding" (HORNEY, 1939, p. 92). The narcissistic person may have "an inarticulate feeling of his own significance"; or "he indulges in an active conscious play of fantasy – thinking of himself as a prince, a genius, a president, a general, an explorer" (p. 92). These "notions of himself become a substitute for his undermined self-esteem" (p. 93). By way of self-aggrandizement, he consoles himself "for not being loved and appreciated" (HORNEY, 1939, p. 93) (i.e., for not having been genuinely loved as a child).

Self-aggrandizement is often an objective of artistic and work-related activities. HORNEY (1939) pointed out that "striving for admiration may be a powerful motor toward achievement, or toward developing qualities which are socially desirable or which make a person lovable, but it involves the danger that everything will be done with both eyes on the effect it has on others" (p. 94). The danger is that "superficiality, showmanship, opportunism will choke productivity" (p. 94). Whether self-aggrandizement "is pursued in reality or only in the realm of fantasy" depends on "the extent to which the individual's spirit has been broken" (p. 97). In the schizoid personality, the narcissistic trend is "combined with a tendency to withdraw from people" (HORNEY, 1939, p. 97), hence grandiose fantasy plays a prominent role in the schizoid personality.

Presumptuousness and arrogance

A compromise between active pursuit and pursuit in fantasy of the "phantom of admiration" (p. 97) can be reached in form of narcissistic expectations (HORNEY, 1939). The narcissistic person develops expectations that the world owes him devotion or glory, and that "devotion or glory can be obtained without effort and initiative of his own" (p. 95). He expects to "be recognized as a genius without having to give evidence of it by actual work" or that women will fall in love with him and "should single him out without his actively doing anything about it" (p. 95). These expectations are determined by and compensate for the narcissistic person's lack of "spontaneity, originality and initiative", a lack that has arisen "because of his fear of people" (p. 95). Inasmuch as "his inner activity" has been paralyzed, he insists "that fulfillment of his wishes should come from others" (p. 95). The narcissistic person's "illusions about himself, and his peculiar kind of expectations of others, are bound to make him vulnerable", leading to an "increasing impairment of human relationships" and to him being "driven ... to take refuge in his illusions" (HORNEY, 1939, p. 96).

Arrogance is often recognized as such and so has adverse social consequences; it leads to "occasional clashes with others" and alienates the person from people, which "only drives him deeper into his neurosis" (HORNEY, 1945, p. 178). Arrogance can be conspicuous, or it can be "hidden behind overmodesty and apologetic behaviour", depending on "the measure of available aggression" in the personality (or, rather, on the person's capacity to express aggression overtly). If arrogance is conspicuous, the "person openly demands special prerogatives"; if it is hidden, "he is hurt if they are not spontaneously given to him" (p. 167). Hidden arrogance entails "the apparent contradiction between self-recrimination, with its apologetic attitude, and the inner irritation at any criticism or neglect from outside" (HORNEY, 1945, p. 168).

8.1.3 Grandiose self-image and unattainable ego ideal

'Narcissistic libido', which is normally invested in selfobjects (narcissistically used objects), may be "tied to the unrealistic unconscious or disavowed grandiose fantasies and to the crude exhibitionism of the split-off and/or repressed grandiose self" (KOHUT, 1971, p. 144). HORNEY (1939), like KOHUT, saw that self-aggrandizement in fantasy is a consequence of disturbed relationships in early childhood. An early fear of closeness to objects and a defensive avoidance of object relationships are of central importance in the psychopathology of narcissistic character disorder. The fear of closeness causes the formation of a precocious sense of self and a tendency to indulge in omnipotent or grandiose fantasies (MODELL, 1975). It is a 'precocious separation' from the mother – due to disillusionment with her or an awareness of her unreliability – that leads to the precocious internalization of the self, to the formation of a fragile sense of self that needs to be supported by fantasies of omnipotence and grandiosity (MODELL, 1975). The illusion of self-sufficiency or omnipotence, entertained in fantasy, compensates for the narcissistic patient's enduring fear of closeness and the associated deep-seated conviction of his worthlessness. However, projection of an inflated, grandiose image of the self into the future may prompt or incentivize inappropriate or maladaptive actions. Self-inflation thus leads to painful humiliations in human relations, and the resulting grievances and hostility further impair human relations (HORNEY, 1939).

Preoccupation in fantasy with ideas of omnipotence and greatness provides temporary relief from the craving for approval; however, narcissistic persons depend on others to validate their megalomanic ideas if they want to enhance their precarious self-esteem in a more sustained manner. By conforming with high moral standards, as represented by their ego ideal (ideal self), narcissistic patients can obtain others' admiration or approval and, at the same time, avoid attacks to which they fear they would be subjected if they were not to act in accordance with their ego ideal (KERNBERG, 1970). Most other persons feel the need to conform and to live up to an ego ideal. What distinguishes narcissistic persons from most others is their almost exclusive reliance on this mechanism for self-esteem regulation.[1] Another difference is that the ego ideal of narcissistic personalities has grandiose proportions and is hence out of reach, whereas that of other persons is more attainable (KERNBERG, 1970). Ultimately, narcissistic persons may not be

---

[1] Again, narcissistic persons are convinced (unconsciously) that they are unlovable, that their attempts to establish libidinal contact with others will be rejected. As a consequence, their narcissistic homeostasis cannot be supported by object-libidinal investments.

able to maintain their narcissistic balance other than in grandiose fantasy. Internally, they may withdraw from social life as effectively as those with a severe schizoid character (KERNBERG, 1970).

Fusion with an ideal object

The 'pathological grandiose self' can be projected onto an unavailable love object, "with an effort to establish a relationship that unconsciously would confirm the stability of the patient's own grandiosity" (KERNBERG, 1992, p. 43). Through pathological infatuation, the narcissistic patient seeks to acquire for himself the idealized object's attributes of physical attractiveness, wealth, prestige, or power (KERNBERG, 1992). These attributes would confirm the patient's own attractiveness and enhance his approvability in the eyes of the omnipotent object (and thus his self-esteem). In general, narcissistic patients admire themselves and identify themselves with their ideal self-image (grandiose ego ideal) not only in order to deny dependency on external objects but also in order to be loved in unconscious fantasy by an ideal object (KERNBERG, 1970). Being loved by an ideal object (the omnipotent object or benevolent aspects of the superego) allows for fusion with it.[2]

Narcissistic personalities of all types harbour and express (unconscious) fantasies not only about a grandiose self but also about an 'omnipotent object' (BURSTEN, 1973). Narcissistic persons aim to achieve reunion with the 'omnipotent object' (corresponding to KOHUT's 'idealized parent imago'); and they do so by living up to the values they had internalized in childhood from their families (ego ideal). The self has to be grandiose, that is, perfect in terms of its values, in order to be acceptable to and accepted by the omnipotent object. Shortcomings and weaknesses, as judged against those internalized values, are a source of shame and a threat to the objective of reunion with the omnipotent object (BURSTEN, 1973).

8.1.4 Vanity

ADLER (1927) acknowledged that "every human being is vain to some degree" (p. 157) (and that "it is impossible to divorce ourselves entirely from a certain degree of vanity" [p. 159]).[3] Those who can be characterized as vain greedily seek public acclaim; they always try to be at centre stage in their social circle, "to be constantly in the limelight" (p. 161). They have a

---

[2] For fusions to occur in the narcissistic personality, self and object have to have been sufficiently differentiated from each other in early development. A certain degree of ego integration has to have occurred, providing for adequate social adaptation overall, in contrast to the splitting of the self that is characteristic of borderline personality disorder (KERNBERG, 1974).

[3] ADLER (1927) thought that vanity is a product of culture, that it flourished in "thousands of years of tradition", and that, in modern society, "there is no longer any place for the strivings of personal vanity" (p. 163).

haughty attitude; their "vanity is evident in their every attitude, their dress, their way of speaking" (p. 160). They feel under a "terrible duty of appearing clever and superior at all times" (p. 171). Vain persons "want to be more important and successful than anyone else in the world, and this goal is the direct result of their feeling of inadequacy", of their having "little sense of their own worth" (p. 161). Vain persons "do not care what weapons they use in their fight for superiority" (p. 160); they attempt "to maintain their feeling of superiority at all costs" (ADLER, 1927, p. 159).

ADLER (1927) pointed out that "exhibitions of vanity are not considered good form" (p. 157); "people who demand special treatment are usually either antagonized or ridiculed" (p. 162). Therefore, vain people attempt "to shield their vanity from any insult" (p. 159). Insofar as they "realize how they are estranging themselves from society", they have to "make every attempt to camouflage the overt signs of their vanity" (which they may do by "dressing sloppily and neglecting their appearance in order to indicate that they are not vain") (p. 160). They may give the appearance of not wishing to be in the limelight of social gatherings by "[t]urning down invitations, coming late, or obliging their host to coax and flatter them into coming" (p. 161). Vanity has to be disguised; and "there is a type of modesty that is essentially vanity in disguise" (p. 157). If the striving for superiority is outbalanced by fear of ridicule (as may be the case in schizoid or schizotypal personalities), the insecure person may "withdraw timidly and lead an isolated or eccentric existence", while maintaining his "fiction of greatness" in fantasy (ADLER, 1927, p. 162).

Vain persons always have "grave doubts surrounding their ability to achieve the victories their vanity seems to demand" (ADLER, 1927, p. 160). These doubts, alternating with self-love, are reflected in their self-preoccupation. Vanity makes people "think constantly either of themselves, or of other people's opinions of them" (ADLER, 1927, p. 157). Vain persons "are concerned solely with their reputation with other people", yet they "cannot get along with anyone" (p. 159). Vanity is "a cause of permanent unhappiness to many human beings" (p. 159). Vanity, often manifesting as ambition, "makes people constantly dissatisfied, and robs them of their rest and sleep" (p. 169); it "robs them of all true happiness" (p. 171). Vain, ambitious, and "acquisitive people are usually discontented, being occupied solely with the thought of what they must still achieve, still possess, in order to be happy" (ADLER, 1927, p. 172).

8.1.5 Screen character

'Screen memories' serve a screening function for more severe traumatic memories; they ensure successful repression of more severe traumatic memories. Similarly, a 'screen identity', featuring pleasing or approvable aspects of the self, serves to maintain in repression a more painful self-image; it thereby helps to maintain the person's 'psychic equilibrium' (GREENSON,

1958, p. 118). 'Screen characters', that is, patients who feel the need to use a 'screen identity', "are unduly concerned with their social standing and long to be accepted, popular, and entertaining" (p. 113) (so as to uphold their narcissistic equilibrium). They adopt a new, likable self-image in an attempt to deny another, insecure image of the self. Thus, when they like another person, they take over character traits of that person. They frequently change jobs or careers and may even change their names or undergo plastic surgery. Screen characters have "difficulty in maintaining a consistent and integrated self image" (p. 121); they show "striking incongruities in their self images" (p. 122). They have multiple self images, often displaying "a markedly different set of character traits at work and at home, with their family or with strangers"; and "the entire analysis may be isolated from the rest of their lives or important segments of their lives may remain outside of the analysis for years at a time" (GREENSON, 1958, p. 114).

Screen characters have a self-image that "is many years younger than their chronological age"; and, "[t]hough they dread old age, death is unreal to them", as "they tend to believe in their immortality" (GREENSON, 1958, p. 121). They have "feelings of omnipotence and expansiveness" and secretly believe "that they are God's favorite and that they are pursued by good fortune" (p. 121). Accordingly, they tend to maintain the fantasy of being the analyst's favourite. Patients with a screen character, when in psychoanalytic treatment, "keenly need to feel understood" (p. 113), yet "[t]hey tend to exaggerate to the point of lying" (p. 113). They are not only sensitive and empathic ("qualities they use for ingratiation" [p. 113]) but also impressionable and suggestible (GREENSON, 1958).

Patients with a screen character have a perpetual hunger to find new objects and new experiences that help them to deny their insecurity and satisfy their narcissistic and libidinal needs, whereby objects are often chosen "on a narcissistic basis" (GREENSON, 1958, p. 131). Owing to their hunger for objects, they quickly and intensely relate to other people; and they tend to split objects into good and bad ones, there being "no coexistence, no simultaneity, of love and hatred toward the object" (GREENSON, 1958, p. 124).

> The object they love is different from the object they hate. They resemble a little child who loves the good mother and hates the bad mother; and these are quite separate people for the child. These patients apparently do not have the capacity to fuse the loved and hated object into a single object.
> (GREENSON, 1958, p. 124)

In their childhood, these patients were exposed to open marital discord (GREENSON, 1958). The parents of these patients had contempt for each other and for each other's values. Their parents used to openly disagree on what is right and wrong, good and bad. This "made for a heterogeneous and unstable superego development" (p. 129). Moreover, in their childhood, these patients were deprived of their mother's love, yet there were periods in their life when they were favoured by one of their parents, preferred by one of their parents to the marriage partner. These narcissistic gratifications were responsible, according to GREENSON (1958), for fixations at the developmental level at which they occurred. Unreliable but real gratifications in their childhood are responsible for their hunger for objects and their optimism (GREENSON, 1958). It is perhaps the combination of early deprivation and unreliable gratifications that sets these patients apart from those with borderline personality disorder. GREENSON (1958) thought that the screen characters he described had a disorder of the self-image (an identity disorder), or, in today's terms, a narcissistic personality disorder; but he also acknowledged similarities with 'borderline cases' and with DEUTSCH's (1942) 'as if' personalities.

8.1.6 False self

FEDERN (1952) observed that "a greeting or a hand-shake" can be extended narcissistically or "with mere object cathexis" (p. 328). The narcissistic nature of an interaction, that is, the intrusion of a "more narcissistically cathected ego boundary", is often betrayed by "little 'symptomatic mannerisms'" (that "are multiplied and intensified in a very characteristic way"), by the "cadence of inflection and accentuation" of an individual's voice, or by "a mere slowing-down of the pronunciation" (p. 328). The "speaker wishes to 'represent'" something (FEDERN, 1952, p. 328), something that allows him *to be held esteem and to feel safe. Increased* narcissism can manifest in affects or emotional displays that are "full of self-pity, pathos or self-flattery and obvious self-aggrandizement – affects which may be covered up by compensatory opposite affects but will be noticeable nevertheless" (p. 333). By contrast, "strong participation in one's own experiences, affirmation of one's own affective reactions, and satisfaction with one's own personality" are the normal "narcissistic countercathexes to the multitude of object libidinal attachments" (FEDERN, 1952, p. 342).

> The fact that an individual acts out his experiences excessively in a narcissistic manner may betray a kind of ego weakness – in fact, paradoxically, it may indicate a lack of normal narcissistic countercathexes. In addition, such behavior frequently is the continuation of the general behavior of the parents toward the little child who was not permitted to develop, nor to experience his development, naïvely. This behavior of the environment is perpetuated, not only in the superego, but also in the ego in the form of self-observation.
> (FEDERN, 1952, p. 343)

In patients with a presumptive narcissistic disorder, the 'true self' (an experience of aliveness and spontaneous comfort) hides behind a 'false self' (WINNICOTT, 1965). Through the false self, the patient maintains a false compliance with external demands. The false self operates defensively, protecting the individual against threatened annihilation. The false self arises in consequence of early failures in the infant's 'holding environment', of failures of the 'not-good-enough' mother to respond to the infant's grandiosity and omnipotent expressions. When in analysis, the patient's true self emerges from behind his false self, he becomes extremely dependent on the analyst. The analyst must not obstruct the regression of the self, if therapy is to succeed in strengthening the self and reestablishing the predominance of the true self (WINNICOTT, 1965).

8.1.7 Shame and humiliation

Patients with a narcissistic personality disturbance, due to a fixation on childhood grandiosity and exhibitionism, are easily hurt and offended (KOHUT, 1971). Situations that normally arouse anxiety, apprehension, and worry elicit immoderate and intense upset and "temporary paralysis of psychic functions" (p. 230). Expecting "to shine" in a social situation and "anticipating acclaim in his fantasies" (p. 230), the narcissistic patient readily experiences shame or pain, if acclaim is not forthcoming or a rejection has occurred. The narcissistic patient is "flooded with shame and anxiety" when he recalls a situation in which he "told a joke which turned out to be out of place" or "talked too much about himself in company" (p. 230). He then experiences "painful embarrassment" and "anger that the act that has been committed cannot be undone" (KOHUT, 1971, p. 231).

> The narcissistic patient tends to react to the memory of a *faux pas* with excessive shame and self-rejection. His mind returns again and again to the painful moment, in an attempt to eradicate the reality of the incident by magical means, i.e. to undo it. Simultaneously the patient may angrily wish to do away with himself in order to wipe out the tormenting memory in this fashion.
>
> (KOHUT, 1971, p. 231)

KOHUT (1971) established that the patient's "old grandiosity and exhibitionism" (stemming from his childhood) lie "in the center of these reactions" (p. 232). Strong exhibitionistic impulses, pressing for unmodulated discharge, are counteracted by shame. The "damming up of primitive forms of narcissistic-exhibitionistic libido" is responsible for a "heightened tendency to hypochondriacal preoccupation, self-consciousness, shame, and embarrassment" (p. 144). Although narcissistic patients are readily "overwhelmed by shame", they are not easily "swayed by guilt feelings (they are not inclined to react unduly to the pressure exerted by their idealized superego)" (KOHUT, 1971, p. 232).

Shame is the counterpart of the grandiose self and of grandiose fantasies about the self. Shame is experienced when the narcissistic person feels *unacceptable to the omnipotent object* (BURSTEN, 1973). If the person's behaviour reveals itself to others as exhibitionistically driven, as pursuing a grandiose aim, and as being calculated to attract the attention of (and effect a reunion with) an omnipotent object, then the illusion of grandiosity collapses. Once the façade, feverishly maintained by ambitious or vain behaviour, has become transparent for others, the person suddenly feels inferior and worthless, not worthy of being accepted by the omnipotent object. He feels vulnerable, expecting to become a target of others' disgust and hostility and to be aggressively rejected from the community; he feels disconnected and about to be annihilated ('disintegration anxiety'). Anxiety encountered in the analysis of narcissistic personality disorders represents a "fear of loss of contact with reality and fear of permanent isolation through the experience of unrealistic grandiosity"; it involves "frightening experiences of shame and self-consciousness through the intrusion of exhibitionistic libido" (KOHUT, 1971, p. 153).

Self-deflation and self-dejection

Shifts from grandiosity and megalomanic elation to feelings of worthlessness and hopelessness or hypochondriacal anxiety are precipitated by the slightest disappointments (REICH, 1960). When grandiosity collapses, intolerable feelings of annihilation ensue, and the narcissistic patient redirects aggression, *formerly applied to competition*, against his dejected self (he hates himself) (REICH, 1960). Patients with malignant narcissism may resort to self-mutilating behaviour or show suicidal tendencies "when their pathological grandiosity is challenged, resulting in their experiencing a traumatic sense of humiliation or defeat" (KERNBERG, 1992, p. 40). Identification, in fantasy, with an archaic ego ideal or identification with an idealized object, in the greatness of which the patient can participate, may shift the patient out of self-deflation and anxiety back to self-inflation and elation (REICH, 1960). The regulation of self-esteem does not stabilize; self-esteem continues to oscillate, if the archaic character of the ego ideal has persisted into adulthood (REICH, 1960).

8.1.8 Envy

Narcissistic persons continuously search for prestige, wealth, and power; and they do so in an aggressively competitive fashion. At the same time, narcissistic personalities experience chronic, intense envy of other people who have things they do not have (KERNBERG, 1970, 1974). In most individuals, envy is mostly unconscious; when a patient in analysis becomes aware of his envy, intense guilt is aroused (SPILLIUS, 1993). Such 'ego-dystonic envy' can be distinguished from 'impenitent envy': some patients are conscious of their envy without experiencing guilt. Impenitent envy is more obvious to the outside observer and is seen in patients with narcissistic personality disorder. Impenitent envy – which is often accompanied by feelings of legitimate *grievance* against and *blame* of others – defends against a sense of loss that would arise if one were to realize that one cannot attain a good object. Feelings of grievance and blame provide a similar defence. As SPILLIUS (1993) pointed out, "feeling perpetual grievance and blame, however miserable, is less painful than mourning the loss of the relationship one wishes one had had". The envious and narcissistic patient unconsciously mourns not only the "loss of the ideal parents" he wishes he had had (feeling deprived of "the love and attention" he wishes he had had) but also the "loss of the ideal self" he would like to have been. The narcissistic patient unconsciously assumes he is profoundly unlovable and inferior but, as a defence, projects these qualities onto others in order to feel lovable and superior (in order to maintain his illusion of grandiosity) (SPILLIUS, 1993).

KERNBERG (1974) thought that narcissistic persons use idealization and omnipotent control of their objects, devaluation of their objects, and narcissistic withdrawal (characterological isolation) as defences against their envy. Narcissistic patients would devalue their external objects and destroy their sources of love and gratification, thereby repeating pathological devaluation of parental images, in order to eliminate the source of their envy (KERNBERG, 1974). Idealization and omnipotent control or devaluation and depreciation of the analyst, as well as efforts to hold on to a grandiose self, can be revealed in psychoanalysis as defences against intense envy or contempt. KERNBERG (1974) argued that KOHUT's approach neglects the significance of envy and, therefore, the crucial role of conflicts around aggression (around contempt, greediness, and hatred) in the psychopathology of narcissistic personality disorder. However, it is possible that envy (like greed) is as much a consequence of an excessive reliance (for purposes of regulation of self-esteem) on others' approval and admiration as are the need to exert omnipotent control and the tendency (if such control cannot be exerted) to withdraw into grandiose fantasy (an excessive reliance that is due, in turn, to a deeper incapacity to form meaningful emotional relationships with external objects and a deeper conviction of unworthiness and unlovability). Inasmuch as narcissistic sustenance has to be extracted from selfobjects by omnipotently controlling them, the narcissistic person finds himself in aggressive competition with others who he believes pursue the same objective. Competitors have to be outperformed or subdued *or their achievements have to be spoilt*, if the narcissistic person wants to keep under his control resources of narcissistic sustenance.[4]

---

[4] Of course, feelings of envy and hatred cannot be tolerated easily and call forth the use of defences (some of which may be more easily accessible than others from within a particular personality structure and would thus contribute to its narcissistic stabilization).

8.1.9 Destructiveness

The narcissistic ego has to deny its dependence on real objects, depreciate its objects, and exert 'tyrannical mastery' over them in all situations (RIVIERE, 1936). Omnipotence, which concerns the ego's omnipotent denial of its dependence on its objects and its omnipotent control over them ('manic attitude'), allows the narcissistic patient to attain *security* and defend against 'depressive anxieties'. The narcissistic patient defends against his depressive anxieties (avoids experiencing the depressive position) by controlling his objects (using them as selfobjects), yet his destructiveness adds, in a vicious circle, to his inability to establish real object relations. Narcissistic patients have been destructive towards their objects all their life for which they unconsciously fear analysis will bring them punishment (RIVIERE, 1936).

> All the injuries he ever did them in thought or deed arose from his 'selfishness', from being too greedy, and too envious of them, not generous and willing enough to allow them what they had, whether of oral, anal or genital pleasure – from not loving *them* enough, in fact. In his mind every one of these acts and thoughts of selfishness and injury to others has to be reversed, to be made good, by sacrifices on his own part, before he can even be sure that his own life is secure – much less begin to think about being well and happy himself.
>
> (RIVIERE, 1936, pp. 315–16)

> His egoistic self-seeking attitude corresponds accurately enough to one side of things in his unconscious mind – to the hatred, cruelty and callousness there; and it represents his fears for his own ego if the love for his objects became too strong. We all fear the dependence of love to some extent.
>
> (RIVIERE, 1936 p. 318)

For the patient with 'malignant narcissism', object relations "contain the seeds for an attack by the omnipotent cruel object" (KERNBERG, 1992, p. 82) (the internalized sadistic parental object). Because real dependence (on real objects) is fearfully avoided (inasmuch as the pain of rejection is avoided), objects (acting as selfobjects) have to be controlled for the sake of the ego (i.e., to maintain the cohesiveness of the self), and controlled they are aggressively. Objects are forced to provide narcissistic sustenance, punished for their failure to do so, and destroyed in the process. *As 'tyrannical mastery' is exerted over them, the narcissistic patient controls his self-esteem concurrently by identifying with the 'cruel tyrant' or by rendering himself acceptable (in his unconscious fantasy) to the cruel tyrant (who is an omnipotent object on whom the patient depends).* KERNBERG (1992) linked the narcissistic patient's apparent need to destroy anything good that may come from contact with objects to the "unconscious identification with the originally hated – and needed – object" (p. 25).

Rage and sadism

According to KOHUT (1977), the rage to which narcissistic patients are prone reflects "the lack of control over the self-object" (p. 262). Their rage is a "regressive transformation of the self's assertiveness" mobilized by a narcissistic injury, an injury that they incur when their "germinally displayed exhibitionism" or their "cautiously offered tendrils" of idealization are rejected ('empathy failures', e.g., in the psychoanalytic situation) (KOHUT, 1977, p. 259). While narcissistic *personality* disorder entails hypersensitivity to slights (and thus a disposition to narcissistic rage), narcissistic *behaviour* disorders manifest "as perversion, delinquency, or addiction" (KOHUT, 1977, p. 193). In patients with a narcissistic *behaviour* disorder, who are usually men, "the primary defect – the diseased unmirrored self – is covered over by promiscuous and sadistic *behavior* toward women", whereas, in patients with narcissistic personality disorder, the defect is covered over by fantasies (p. 193). Disturbed behaviour or fantasies "are only *one* step removed from the underlying defect in self-esteem" (p. 195). Defensive promiscuity is an attempt to raise self-esteem. The sadism of patients with narcissistic behaviour disorder "toward women is motivated by the need to force the mirroring self-object's response to them" (KOHUT, 1977, p. 194).

8.1.10 Transference

Psychic structure, the mature structure of the bipolar self, is accrued in consequence of 'optimal frustrations' of developmental mirroring and idealizing needs (KOHUT, 1977, 1984). Traumatic disruptions of self–selfobject relationships in childhood "or insufficient availability of those emotional nutriments in the self–selfobject matrix" (p. 360) lead to *deficits* in psychic structure and secondary conflicts and defences (ORNSTEIN, 1983). Defensive structures "develop to cover over the void, to fill in the defects" (p. 362). Defensive structures are secondary elaborations of deficit; they obscure the deficit, which nevertheless "powerfully emerges in the transference" (p. 362), as mirroring and idealizing needs "clamor for belated recognition" (ORNSTEIN, 1983, p. 361). In the psychoanalytic therapy setting, archaic selfobject transferences (narcissistic transferences) revive the link between the defective self and its archaic selfobject. Selfobject transferences are archaic patterns of interaction that aim to support a vulnerable and fragmentation-prone self. It is "the not yet structuralized part of the psyche" that "would manifest itself in a cohesive selfobject transference, in which the issues of self-regulation would be paramount" (ORNSTEIN, 1983, p. 373).

Narcissistic transferences (selfobject transferences), representing the revival in the context of therapy of key developmental phases of childhood, are diagnostic of narcissistic personality problems. The narcissistic transferences fall, according to KOHUT (1971), into two categories. Firstly, the 'mirroring transference', an expression of archaic mirroring needs, betrays an early derailment in the developmental line emanating from the 'grandiose self'. The mirroring transference activates the 'grandiose self' that seeks confirming attention and admiration from the analyst.[5] Secondly, in the 'idealizing transference', the patient, in an effort to support his self-esteem, maintains an attachment to (and merger with) an idealized, omnipotent object (the analyst).[6]

The narcissistic patient relies on his archaic idealizing and mirroring ties for his self-esteem regulation and the preservation of his sense of self-cohesion and self-continuity. In psychoanalysis, the patient focuses on the selfobject functions of his analyst "because of certain thwarted developmental needs of the self" (Kohut, 1983, p. 391). He has to control his analyst, acting as a selfobject (that is, as an extension of the patient's self), in order to protect the cohesion of his self. Failures, on part of the analyst, to serve as a mirroring or idealizable selfobject lead to narcissistic rage or withdrawal into haughty isolation. Minor empathy failures, on the other hand, can serve as 'optimal frustrations'. Kohut (1977) emphasized the importance of recognizing that the transference established in psychoanalysis by a patient with a narcissistic character disorder represents "the reactivated attempt to build a cohesive self by means of the empathic response of the self-object" (p. 262). Through reactivation, in the selfobject transference, of "the needs of a self that had been thwarted in childhood" and through repeated exposure of these needs to optimal frustrations, the patient can acquire "the reliable ability to sustain his self with the aid of selfobject resources available

---

[5] In the mirror transference, the analyst is coerced by the patient into making echoing, approving, and confirming gestures and remarks (Kohut, 1971). The patient *demands* from the analyst "an echo and a confirmation of his greatness and an approving response to his exhibitionism" (p. 123); and he controls the analyst (mirroring selfobject) to this effect. The "listening, perceiving, and echoing-mirroring presence of the analyst" serves to maintain the cohesiveness of the patient's self (p. 125). Mobilization of the 'grandiose self' in the mirror transference means that the patient can reveal "his infantile fantasies of exhibitionistic grandeur" (p. 148) and "cathect a reactivated grandiose self with narcissistic libido" (p. 128). When the mirror transference has been established, the patient elaborates recurrent themes of being special, being unique, or being precious, themes that appear "to be the nodal point of a host of frightening, shameful, and isolating narcissistic fantasies" (Kohut, 1971, p. 150).

[6] An idealizing transference ('archaic type') can arise on a developmental background of early disappointments in the idealized mother, disappointments that occurred at a "period when the idealized mother imago [was] still completely merged with that of the self" (Kohut, 1971, p. 55). Alternatively, an idealizing transference ('oedipal type') can establish itself in consequence of a developmental fixation at the preoedipal or oedipal period, that is, before the *ultimate internalization* of the idealized object, "i.e., before the consolidation of the idealization of the superego" (p. 54). In other words, a person is "forever attempting to achieve a union with the idealized object" (e.g., in form of the analyst), if there was "insufficient idealization of the superego" (Kohut, 1971, p. 55).

in his adult surroundings" (KOHUT, 1984, p. 77). Predictable availability of empathic responses from the selfobject milieu provides the opportunity for the acquisition of "the sense of the continuity of the self in time" and "the capacity for self-soothing" (KOHUT, 1984, p. 65).

8.1.11 Resistance

In the setting of psychoanalytic treatment, the patient's character reveals itself in his "manner of speech, the way in which he looks at the analyst and greets him, the way he lies on the couch, the inflection of his voice, the measure of his conventional politeness", as well as in "the manner in which the patient keeps silence or indulges in sterile repetition" (REICH, 1928, p. 112). 'Character analysis' is concerned with the analysis of resistances that establish themselves in psychoanalytic treatment; it entails a consistent effort to highlight and interpret the patient's character resistances, helping him, in the first place, to gain "an objective attitude towards his character and an analytic interest in it" (REICH, 1928, p. 120). Excessive politeness and punctiliousness may point to a hidden resistance to go along with psychoanalytic treatment. Similarly, patients with "a cold, haughty demeanour towards the analyst" (p. 114) or "with an inward smile for everything and everybody" (p. 113), patients who never cease "to doubt everything or to pretend acceptance or inwardly to ridicule everything" (p. 116), or those who talk in a "bombastic manner or in technical terms" or "speak in carefully chosen words or in a confused manner" (p. 121) keep up "an impenetrable wall" (p. 121). They avoid genuine experiencing of emotions, especially the experiencing of anxiety; they resist true insight and change, because true insight and change would be accompanied by *unbearable anxiety*. Character analysis eventually "gives rise to violent emotional outbursts" on part of the patient (REICH, 1928, p. 122), outbursts that likely represent reactions to narcissistic injuries.[7]

In psychoanalytic therapy, the narcissistic patient consciously or unconsciously refuses to freely associate; he maintains a flow of carefully selected and arranged material, which is calculated to deceive the analyst (RIVIERE, 1936). He accepts no alternative point of view or anything that he has not already said himself, except with lip service. The patient denies the value of everything the analyst says and implicitly claims to supersede the analyst and do the analytic work better himself. The patient manages to *control* the analyst and the analytic situation in a way that is masked very cleverly and often not apparent to the analyst. Under a mask of feigned compliance, superficial politeness, and intellectual rationalization, he remains *self-satisfied* and defiant. Such deceptiveness is characteristic of the 'manic defence'; it is

---

[7] It is when aggressive impulses make their appearance, when the blocking of affects has been overcome, that the patient is deemed to be analyzable (REICH, 1928).

a cover for the narcissistic patient's attempts of securing exclusive control (RIVIERE, 1936).

The narcissistic patient is determined to keep the upper hand in the analytic situation and resists any progress in treatment for fear that the analyst will gain power over him (RIVIERE, 1936) (and for fear that he will become genuinely dependent on the analyst). If he were to freely associate, admit to his failings, or develop a positive transference (in which the analyst is treated, in accordance with an early object relation, as a separate person, as a representative of a parental object), he would expose himself to the analyst's mercies. The patient cannot endure any praise of progress, and any partial solution or insight produces an exacerbation of symptoms. This is the 'negative therapeutic reaction' seen in patients with a narcissistic type of character. These patients do not wish to change or get well, but need to preserve things as they are. They do so because of an inherent assumption that there can only be change in one direction if their *equilibrium* is upset, namely for the worse (RIVIERE, 1936).

Self-psychological approach

In patients with a narcissistic personality disorder, "the self has not been solidly established", which means that the "cohesion and firmness" of the self "depend on the presence of a self-object (on the development of a self-object transference)" (KOHUT, 1977, p. 137). The self, in these patients, "responds to the loss of the self-object with simple enfeeblement, various regressions, and fragmentation" (p. 137) or with "uncontrollable rage" (p. 138). Resistances arising in psychoanalytic therapy of patients with narcissistic disorders "are motivated by disintegration anxiety"; they are "the activities of the archaic nuclear self, which does not want to re-expose itself to the devastating narcissistic injury of finding its basic mirroring and idealizing needs unresponded to" (p. 136). What is operating here is an "avoidance of the mortification of being re-exposed to the narcissistic injuries of childhood (disintegration anxiety)" (p. 137), whereas what motivates resistances arising in psychoanalytic treatment of patients with oedipal neuroses, and what these patients are trying to avoid, is a "fear of punishment (castration anxiety)" concerning "incestuous drive wishes" (KOHUT, 1977, p. 137).

In self psychology, defence mechanisms and personality manoeuvres are governed by the 'principle of self-preservation'. Defence mechanisms, such as social withdrawal and adoption of a stance of superiority ('superior isolation'), and resistances that emerge in therapy serve to protect the self against 'destruction and invasion' (KOHUT, 1984). They are, in general, 'healthy psychic activities' that serve 'the basic ends of the self'; they constitute 'valuable moves to safeguard the self'. The analyst must consider the patient's defences and resistances in terms of their role in maintaining the integrity of the patient's self. Even though self-development may have been thwarted in childhood, due to deficiencies in maternal or paternal selfobject relationships, it can be remobilized in later life. *Defences and resistances are valuable in protecting a weak or defective self*, allowing it to grow again under favourable circumstances in the future (KOHUT, 1984, pp. 222–35).

8.2 Borderline personality disorder

Borderline personality disorder, like narcissistic personality disorder, develops from a failure in the early maternal environment (in the first two years of the infant's life). The core disturbance in borderline conditions, the lack of integration of good and bad images of self and objects, is often a consequence of high levels of parental rejection and hostility experienced in childhood. From a self-psychological perspective, the cohesiveness of the self is severely impaired in borderline conditions; nuclear narcissistic structures are liable to break up. The constant threat of inner fragmentation differentiates borderline conditions from narcissistic personality disorder. In narcissistic personality disorder, but also in schizoid conditions and other disorders of the self, the self is precarious, yet more stable, so that it can be bolstered defensively and threats to self-esteem can be countered by increased efforts to use objects as selfobjects or achieve narcissistic hypercathexis of the self through self-deception or inner fantasy. Borderline patients, in contrast to narcissistic patients, do not attempt to maintain an illusion of self-sufficiency and instead show an intense hunger for objects (MODELL, 1975). In borderline personality disorder, narcissistic needs are met by way of idealization and participation in the omnipotence of an idealized object, whereas narcissistic patients rely predominantly on their grandiose self (as the counterpart to and attractor of the omnipotent object), maintaining it either by self-deception and fantasy or by forcing mirroring responses from their selfobject milieu.

8.2.1 Fixation in the paranoid-schizoid position

KLEIN (1940, 1946) described how, in the paranoid-schizoid developmental position, the infant's feelings of frustration are split off and projected onto the object, which is then experienced as 'bad' or persecutory. As a defence against 'depressive anxiety' (fear of loss of object), the infant reverts to the paranoid-schizoid position, because paranoid fears, that is, fears of the object's hostility, are more bearable than the fear of abandonment. If the depressive position is not successfully 'worked through' in infanthood, then, later in life, the ego readily regresses to the paranoid-schizoid position, in which paranoid (persecutory) fears prevail. Fixation on the paranoid level of development has the defensive effect of preventing the emergence of depression and guilt; however, persecutory fears continue to disturb the ego's ability to establish representations of 'good' objects *inside* (KLEIN, 1940, 1946; ROSENFELD, 1965). Patients who are fixated in the paranoid-schizoid position have not retained a good internal relationship with their primary object and remain unable to integrate and internally repair loved objects. Since object representations, self-representations, and representations of relations between self and objects are essentially interchangeable concepts (KERNBERG, 1982a), not having retained good *internal* relationships is equivalent to an insecure sense of self.

The infant's failure to progress to the depressive position, in which a stable 'internal object relation' (i.e., a representation of a *secure* relation between infant and mother) can be established, may be due to unpredictability of the mother's attitudes and responses or to the fact that the infant mistrusts the mother early on. Lack of good internal objects can be compensated, and fragmentation of the self can be prevented, by an *external* object that takes the role of the primary maternal object. Idealization of an object and merger with it satisfy primitive narcissistic needs (KOHUT) and thus provide safety. Patients who are fixated in the paranoid-schizoid position continuously search for the 'ideal object' and can therefore never be quite satisfied with the responses or responsiveness of real objects (MAIN, 1957). Objects regularly turn out not to be 'ideal', leading to the recurrence of paranoid anxieties and the perception of previously idealized objects as persecutory or 'all-bad'. Alternation between paranoid anxieties and idealizations is conceptualized as the 'splitting' of objects into all-bad and ideal ones (MAIN, 1957).

Patients who are fixated in the paranoid-schizoid position deal with frustrations by turning away form their objects "with intense hostility, leaving [them] entirely bad and persecuting and turning to secondary objects as entirely good, or rather idealised"; however, "the primary persecutory anxiety soon re-asserts itself and even the secondary objects soon turn bad" (ROSENFELD, 1965, p. 204). There is an impulse to punish bad objects, which, too, is a vestige of the infant's relationship to the mother. In the context of mother and infant, hostility against the inattentive mother acts as a "forceful reminder" that helps to ensure that she "would not err again" (BOWLBY, 1973, p. 247). Indeed, aggressive behaviours directed by the patient who is fixated in the paranoid-schizoid position against a previously idealized person can be seen as "sophisticated versions of the signals an infant uses to dominate his mother and bring her to help him" (MAIN, 1957). Other aspects of the patient's behaviour, including her efforts to make another person feel important and omnipotent ('ideal') or to cause the person to compete with others for the honour of being the patient's favourite, are designed, too, to create an *exclusive relationship with somebody who would take responsibility for her and meet all her needs* (MAIN, 1957).

8.2.2 Idealization and identification

ANNIE REICH (1953) described a pattern of sudden overvaluations of love objects followed by sudden devaluations, a pattern that is displayed by women who failed to develop real object relationships in their childhood and who can relate to external objects only by way of a primitive form of identification. Overvaluation of the object is associated with the taking over of the object's personality and interests and the development of a deep dependence on the object. By taking over the idealized object's personality and interests, the woman identifies with him; she thus shares in the object's grandeur and feels great and wonderful herself. Developmentally, primitive identifications predate object love. The women described by ANNIE REICH (1953) were fixated on a level of 'primary identifications' (immature ego identifications), fleeting identifications that became the basis of narcissistic object choice. They made these 'primary identifications' with their objects (involving superficial imitations) as a substitute for real object love and real object relations (REICH, 1953). Similarly, 'as if' personalities, described by HELENE DEUTSCH (1942), established relationships more on the basis of a primitive form of identification than on the basis of love. By way of superficial imitations, reminiscent of the child's tendency to imitate, 'as if' personalities adopted the identity of their partner.[8]

Identification with the love object may not be a reenactment of the infant's identification *with* the primary object but an attempt to be pleasing and acceptable *to* the primary object (and to thus achieve merger with the primary object indirectly). This can be achieved by identification with an externalized ego ideal. The value of the love object, with whom the woman identifies, would then consist in the value it has for the internalized omnipotent object. The woman that emerges from ANNIE REICH's (1953) description readily glorifies, and identifies with, anyone whose worth is recognized *by other people*. Appreciation of the object and hence the value of the object for the self are completely dependent on outside judgement. Any minor criticisms of the object by a third person causes the narcissistic overvaluation of the object to break down; the object is suddenly devalued and identification with it is relinquished. Devaluation of the object and relinquishment of identification with it are associated with a sudden drop in self-esteem and hostility towards the abandoned object (REICH, 1953). *Devaluation of the object with which the woman is identified is tantamount to a devaluation of and injury to the self.*

The woman then turns to a new object, which is again rapidly idealized and identified with, only to be devalued and abandoned some time thereafter (REICH, 1953). Poor self-esteem has to be restored time and again by way of narcissistic object choice. Rapid identifications provide some narcissistic compensation for narcissistic injuries sustained in childhood; they provide a temporary substitute for lacking real object relationships.

---

[8] DEUTSCH's (1942) 'as if' characters were schizoid personalities who lacked genuine object relationships and readily took on anyone's characteristics and affect, since they were themselves empty and had no character of their own.

ANNIE REICH (1953) found that underneath this pattern of relating to objects lies a deep distortion of the woman's early relationship with her mother, which in turn was caused by excessive narcissistic traits of the mother herself. The mother's overconcern with the child's ability to make an impression on other people and the mother's use of her child for her own exhibitionistic purposes were coupled with excessive critical evaluation by the mother of the child's appearance and superficial behaviour, producing in the child an intense feeling of insufficiency (REICH, 1953). As a counterpoint to the feeling of insufficiency, the child forms an overcathected, grandiose ego ideal, representing the child's desire to be liked by the mother. Being identified with her ego ideal, the woman becomes, in her unconscious mind, lovable for the primary maternal object (omnipotent object).

8.2.3 Self-harm

In patients with histrionic or borderline personality disorder, self-destructive behaviour, emerging at times of intense rage, "frequently represents an unconscious effort to reestablish control over the environment by evoking guilt feelings in others" (KERNBERG, 1992, p. 40). Others' guilt justifies feelings of victimhood; what is unconsciously expected is others' remorse and asking for forgiveness. In essence, self-destructive behaviour is a way of regaining control over the selfobject milieu.

8.3 Schizoid personality disorder

Schizoid personality features include overvaluation of thought processes (intellectualization), preoccupation with inner reality, an attitude of isolation and detachment, the repression of affect, a sense of difference from others, and an attitude of omnipotence or superiority (which can be conscious or unconscious) (FAIRBAIRN, 1952). The attitude of superiority, maintained by schizoid individuals, "is based upon an orientation towards internalized objects", while their attitude in relation to objects in the outer world is one of inferiority (pp. 50–1). Schizoid individuals have difficulty in expressing their feelings naturally towards other people, finding it difficult to act "naturally and spontaneously" (FAIRBAIRN, 1952, p. 20) (i.e., their 'social feeling' [Adler] is inhibited). They have "learned to distance themselves from others in order to avoid the specific danger of exposing themselves to a narcissistic injury" (p. 12); their distancing is a consequence of "the correct assessment of their narcissistic vulnerability" (KOHUT, 1971, p. 12). Individuals with schizoid personality problems gained the conviction, early in life, that "their mother did not really love them and value them" (FAIRBAIRN, 1952, p. 23). The mother failed "to convince her child by spontaneous and genuine expressions of affection that she herself loves him as a person" (p. 13). As a consequence, "the child tends to transfer his relationships with his objects to the realm of inner reality"; his "objects tend to belong to the inner rather than to the outer world" (FAIRBAIRN, 1952, p. 18). Insofar as contact with external objects is avoided, the narcissistically cathected, defensively grandiose self has to be sustained by internal objects.

8.3.1 Fear of rejection

Despite his detachment, the schizoid individual "longs deep down to love and be loved" (FAIRBAIRN, 1952, p. 26). Patients with schizoid or schizophrenic conditions experience a "perpetual conflict between the wish for human contact" and "the danger of excessive closeness" (REISER, 1986, p. 232). These patients are unable to use selfobjects to maintain their narcissistic equilibrium, so that "they are forever at risk and forever alone" (p. 232), forever left to defend against their anxiety by way of schizoid or psychotic defences. However, "sooner or later the dreadful loneliness catches up and drives the schizophrenic patient to seek human contact, despite the risks" (REISER, 1986, p. 232), only to expose him to renewed rejection and to reinforce his withdrawal and loneliness. The schizoid individual's fear of rejection and his anxiety over the threat, posed by rejection, to his ego renders his libidinal attitude "highly self-preservative and narcissistic" (p. 23). While loving his self (sustaining his secret grandiose self), he knows, with regard to the object world, that "he can only permit himself to love and be loved from afar off" (FAIRBAIRN, 1952, p. 26). The persistent fear of rejection (of empathy failure by an unresponsive selfobject) is responsible for the compulsion experienced by the schizoid individual to keep his objects at a distance and explains the inhibition of his spontaneous impulses to love them and to induce in them a caring attitude towards himself.

8.3.2 Withdrawal into fantasy

Again, schizoid personalities "are unable to endure any narcissistic injury" (FENICHEL, 1946, p. 532) and readily "react to frustrations with partial loss of object cathexes" and withdrawal into a state of "primary and omnipotent narcissism", a state in which they see themselves as independent of other people (p. 531). Schizoid fantasies feature a grandiose self that does not have to depend on objects; *or they produce a temporary elevation in the worth of the self in the eyes of an unconsciously fantasized omnipotent object*. In general, the fantasized self does not exist in itself but has to be in a relationship with an internal object, although this relationship may not be explicit in consciousness. The schizoid individual is compelled to compensate his lack of satisfactory relationships with external objects by turning to relationships with internalized objects.[9] As his 'libido' is withdrawn from external objects, "it is directed towards internalized objects", so that it is in the "inner reality

---

[9] The individual's relationship with an internalized object can be compulsive, as illustrated by the phenomenon of schizoid infatuation (FAIRBAIRN, 1952).

that the values of the schizoid individual are to be found" (FAIRBAIRN, 1952, p. 50). Excessive libidinization (overvaluation) of internalized objects is an aspect of narcissism; "and such narcissism is specially characteristic of the schizoid individual" (p. 50). Individuals with a schizoid tendency build up the libidinal value of their objects in the inner world, and "they tend to identify themselves very strongly with their internal objects" (FAIRBAIRN, 1952, p. 18). Identification with internalized libidinal objects, coupled with a sense of *"secrete* possession" of these objects, leads to "a narcissistic inflation of the ego" and a secret sense of superiority (p. 22). Secret possession of internalized objects causes "the individual to feel that he is 'different' from other people – even if not, as often happens, actually exceptional or unique" (p. 22). The need for secrecy is partly "determined by fear of the loss of internalized objects which appear infinitely precious (even as precious as life itself)" (FAIRBAIRN, 1952, p. 22).

8.3.3 Concealed hostility

Insofar as contact can be made, schizoid individuals tend to treat their objects "as means of satisfying their own requirements rather than as persons possessing inherent value" (FAIRBAIRN, 1952, p. 13) (as selfobjects). Objects that are *incorporated into the self* (selfobjects) yet perceived as part of the external world have to be controlled compulsively, if the individual is unable to form mature object relationships (if he has not progressed to 'mature dependence'). The individual who is fixated, for whatever reason, on the infantile attitude of 'taking' ('infantile dependence') resorts to exhibitionism, masochism, or sadism (FAIRBAIRN, 1952) as compulsive methods for controlling selfobjects ('incorporated objects'). This is the situation particularly in patients with a *narcissistic personality disorder.* Narcissistic injuries and frustrated longings for love engender anger or rage, not unlike frustrations of other kinds. *Schizoid* persons "necessarily encounter many frustrations", so that "they are always filled with unconscious hostilities", hostilities that are warded off (due to their pervasive inhibition) and "supplanted by patterned behavior, by vacant smiles or by other catatonoid attitudes" (FENICHEL, 1946, p. 532).

8.4 Neurotic personality organization

The 'neurotic personality' discussed by KAREN HORNEY (1937, 1950) has many features of the 'disorders of self' with which KOHUT was concerned. Neurotic persons have an incapacity for love; they cannot *show* care or affection *to others,* for they "may become extremely afraid of incurring obligations" (HORNEY, 1937, p. 143). However, they need affection and reassurance *from others,* whereby "the primary feeling is the need for reassurance" (HORNEY, 1937, p. 109). The need to love and *to be* affectionate is captured by ADLER'S (1927, 1938) concept of 'social interest' ('social feeling'). Neurotic persons are deficient in 'social interest', yet their need for approval from others is particularly high. 'Social interest' refers to the individual's ability to be caring towards others, an ability that provides for more sustainable relatedness to others. Social interest involves 'courage' (ADLER) or 'assertiveness' (KOHUT). Neurotic persons lack courage; they have a "hesitant attitude towards the tasks of life" (ADLER, 1938, p. 122). Lack of courage is associated with fear of rejection and with a sense of inferiority. For neurotic persons, relatedness has to be ensured by passive means, by enhancing their preeminence or superiority and thus *attracting* others' approvals.

Neurosis, in Adlerian psychology, is the outcome of "attempts to preserve the patient from the full consequences of his real or supposed inferiority" (FLUGEL, 1945, p. 47). Feelings of inferiority and attempts to compensate for inferiority, by attaining superiority or conforming to moral ideals, lie at the heart of neurosis. Psychoanalysts, by contrast, would, according to FLUGEL (1945), regard feelings of inferiority more likely as "the consequence than the cause of moral ideals, since failure to achieve the goals set by the ideal almost inevitably brings in its train a sense of guilt and unworthiness" (p. 47). FLUGEL (1945) pointed out that the "setting of too high a standard for one's own self", that is, a great "distance between the real self and the ego-ideal", is apt to cause misery and feelings of dissatisfaction and inferiority (p. 49).

8.4.1 Superiority complex

The sense of insecurity experienced by neurotic persons "leads to a violent struggle for a state of repose and security" (ADLER, 1938, p. 121). In their struggle for security, they aim to restore a "sense of great personal worth", a sense of superiority (p. 130). Neurotic persons have, from childhood onwards, avoided "tasks that might, so they fear, if they fail them, injure their self-esteem and interfere with their struggle for personal superiority, their struggle to be first" (p. 130). Hence, their "sphere of activity ... does not extend very far; it is much more restricted than that of a more normal person" (ADLER, 1938, p. 122). The 'superiority complex' is "the superstructure that disguises" the inferiority complex (p. 95). In those who feel insecure and struggle to attain security (i.e., narcissistic equilibrium), the striving for superiority and preeminence "takes the form of ambition" (a self-centred ambition), and it occasionally "takes other forms, such a greed, avarice, envy, and jealousy" (p. 121). The 'superiority complex' manifests itself "in the bearing, character-traits, and thinking of individuals conscious of their own super-human gifts and abilities", in "vanities in connection with personal appearance", in "arrogance, exuberant emotion, snobbism, boastfulness, a tyrannical nature, nagging, a tendency to disparage", "an inclination to fawn upon prominent people or domineer over people who are weak, ill or of diminutive stature" (p. 94). The "sense of inferiority which finds conclusion in a superiority complex" may be evidenced by "heightened affects", such as "desire for revenge, grief, enthusiasm, habitually loud laughter", or by behaviours such as "averting one's gaze on meeting other people, directing the conversation to one's own self, habitual excitement over trivial happenings" (ADLER, 1938, p. 94).

8.4.2 Inhibition and self-restraint

Neurotic inhibitions, concerning healthy exhibitionistic, self-assertive, and affectionate tendencies, lie at the heart of the neurotic person's weak self-esteem. Exhibitionistic, self-assertive, and affectionate tendencies cannot be expressed in the presence of a deep-seated fear of rejection. Neurotic persons are extremely vulnerable to disregard, humiliation, and ridicule (HORNEY, 1945). Owing to "the ghastly prospect of ridicule", "they do not dare to make themselves attractive, to try to impress, to seek a better position" (to be healthily exhibitionistic or ambitious, in KOHUT's terms) and "do not dare to approach people who seem superior to them in any way" (p. 152). The 'aggressive type' of neurotic personality may at first seem less inhibited, as he is able to "assert his wishes", "give orders, express anger, defend himself" (p. 68). However, he does have crippling inhibitions concerning "his capacity for friendship, love, affection, sympathetic understanding, disinterested enjoyment" (HORNEY, 1945, p. 68). Neurotic phenomena are the result of these inhibitions, consequential poor self-esteem, and the compensatory need to present an agreeable (approvable) persona.

> If someone wants to be friendly but at the same time resents the idea because he feels it to be ingratiating, he will be stilted; if he wants to ask for something but also feels he should command it, he will be ungracious; if he wants to assert himself but also to comply, he will be hesitant; if he wants to make contact with people but anticipates rejection, he will be shy; ...
>
> (HORNEY, 1945, p. 159)

Persons who are "held together merely by their idealized image" exercise excessive self-control in an attempt "to check all spontaneity" (HORNEY, 1945, p. 136). They exert will power, consciously or unconsciously, to keep under control impulses that are disruptive to or in conflict with their idealized self-image, whereby "the greatest degree of energy is directed toward the control of rage" (p. 137). Such self-control is compulsive. When control is not exerted "in the most rigid way", panic arises; and such "panic may appear as a fear of insanity, which clearly indicates that the function of control is to ward off the danger of being split apart" (HORNEY, 1945, p. 137).

Although neurotic persons are inhibited, especially in novel social situations, there are, nevertheless, "the few occasions when they can relax, feel at ease, and be spontaneous", when their 'inner strain' is released (HORNEY, 1945, p. 160). There may also be occasions when persons who are not considered to be neurotic feel not at ease and are not spontaneous, when they have to exert self-restraint and project a socially agreeable persona, suggesting that neurotic dynamics are not fundamentally different from processes in the healthy or well-adapted personality and that the 'idealized image' (also conceptualized as 'ego ideal') is generally part of the human condition (although its importance in the structure of the personality differs between neurotic and nonneurotic persons).

> As we know, it is not in the actual structure of his mind that the normal man differs from the neurotic, but in the quantitative factors at work.
> (KLEIN, 1932, p. 201)

8.4.3 Neurotic pride

The neurotic person has an imperative "need to be proud of himself" (HORNEY, 1950, p. 93). Excessive dependence on external narcissistic supplies is what characterizes 'neurotic pride', as opposed to healthy self-esteem. The neurotic person has "a total dependence on others for self-evaluation"; his self-esteem "rises or falls with the attitudes of others toward him" (p. 137). Feeling "at bottom unwanted", the neurotic person "is easily hurt" and "needs incessant confirmation of his value" (p. 86). Any "lack of genuine warmth and interest" gives him "the feeling of being unloved and unworthy – or at any rate of not being worth anything unless he is something he is not" (p. 87). The neurotic person has a compulsive need to actualize an 'idealized self', thereby attaining a state of glory and perfection. He is subject to a "compulsive drive for worldly glory through success, power, and triumph" (HORNEY, 1950, p. 368), precisely insofar as worldly glory would compensate for an inner insecurity (inferiority [ADLER]). Not only does the neurotic patient fear "failure, disgrace, ridicule", but he is afraid of "all that falls short of glory and perfection"; he "is afraid of not performing as superbly as his exacting shoulds demand, and therefore fears that his pride will be hurt" (HORNEY, 1950, p. 101). If he "wields power and influence and is supported by praise and deference", he "may feel strong and significant" (p. 86). However, "in a strange environment", where "this support is lacking", his "feelings of elation collapse easily" (HORNEY, 1950, p. 86).

Neurotic pride, according to HORNEY (1950), "rests on the attributes which a person arrogates to himself in his imagination, on all those belonging to his particular idealized image" (p. 90). Neurotic pride would be less fleeting, and elation more sustained, if the neurotic person's glorified version of himself could be actualized through accumulation of power, prestige, or possessions. Work of intellect and imagination would be required to transform the virtues of the idealized self into assets of which the neurotic person can be proud (HORNEY, 1950). Neurotic pride may rest on compulsive compliance with external standards, allowing the person to "feel that he is a moral wonder to be proud of" (p. 93). The neurotic person's pride can thus be invested outside of himself, invested in possessions he accumulates or moral standards with which he complies, although "work of intellect and imagination" may still be needed for "maintaining the private fictitious world through rationalizations, justifications, externalizations, reconciling irreconcilables – in short, through finding ways to make things appear different from what they are" (HORNEY, 1950, p. 91).

8.4.4 Idealized image

The neurotic person's self-confidence is weak because it had been crushed early in his life, or because conditions indispensable for the formation of healthy self-esteem were absent (HORNEY, 1945). The neurotic person feels weak "in a world peopled with enemies ready to cheat, humiliate, enslave, and defeat him" (p. 101). In his "search for something that will make him feel better, more worthy than others" (p. 101), he creates his idealized image. The idealized image serves to enhance self-esteem; it "substitutes for realistic self-confidence and realistic pride" (HORNEY, 1945, p. 100). The idealized image reflects the neurotic person's need for superiority or preeminence; it excludes everything that is regarded as a shortcoming and that would increase his sense of vulnerability to rejection or humiliation. The idealized image blends out conflicts; shortcomings that "would confront him with his conflicts" are excluded (p. 104). Recognition of shortcomings would be in conflict with an attitude of superiority; they would jeopardize "the artificial harmony he has established" (HORNEY, 1945, p. 104) (the narcissistic balance). The neurotic person is not aware that he is idealizing himself, but whatever he does, he must not allow his idealized image to be undermined.

> But if he allows it to be undermined he is immediately threatened with the prospect of facing all his weaknesses, with no title to special claims, a comparatively insignificant figure or even – in his own eyes – a contemptible one. More terrifying still, he is faced with his conflicts and the hideous fear of being torn to pieces.
> (HORNEY, 1945, p. 109)

> Any questioning or criticism from outside, any awareness of his own failure to measure up to the image, any real insight into the forces operating within him can make it explode or crumble. He must restrict his life lest he be exposed to such dangers. He must avoid situations in which he would not be admired or recognized.
> (HORNEY, 1945, p. 110)

The idealized image can be constructed and maintained in two principal ways: in fantasy (in an attitude of detachment) or through arrogant ('narcissistic') or perfectionistic behaviour (Figure 8.1). With regard to the second way, the neurotic person conducts his life so that his idealized image remains intact, either in that he avoids situations that could confront him with his shortcomings or in that he generates, or exposes himself to, situations that strengthen his idealized image. To the extent that he has to involve others in the maintenance of his idealized image, "[h]e is dependent upon endless affirmation from others in the form of approval, admiration, flattery – none of which, however, can give him any more than temporary reassurance" (HORNEY, 1945, p. 110). Even when the idealized image can be actualized in some situations, self-deception may play a role. The *narcissistic (arrogant)* neurotic person identifies himself with his idealized image, so that – being his own image – he feels "as wonderful and ideal", whereby he has to *presume* that others do regard him as wonderful and ideal; whereas the *perfectionistic* neurotic person "may stand on tiptoe to try and measure up to its demands" (the demands of the idealized image) (p. 112). Sometimes, a neurotic person "may switch from an apparently unreserved self-adoration to perfectionism" (HORNEY, 1945, p. 113).

Dynamic function

The neurotic person tries to convince himself unconsciously that "he *is* his idealized image" (HORNEY, 1945, p. 98); he does not have to become it. On some level, however, he realizes that there is a gap between is actual self

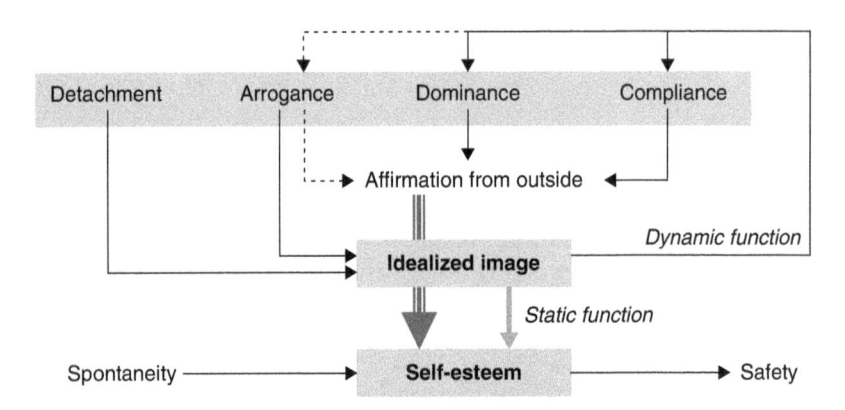

Figure 8.1 Dynamic and static functions of the idealized image. Incentivizing the solicitation from others of affirmation and approval, the idealized image plays a dynamic role in neurotic compliance and dominance. Owing to its static function, the idealized image replenishes self-esteem (or neurotic pride) in a state of detachment. In regulating self-esteem, the idealized image compensates for the neurotic person's lack of genuineness and spontaneity

and the idealized image. This realization gives rise to "incessant attempts to bridge the gap and whip himself into perfection" (p. 98). This is not dissimilar from the function of genuine or 'authentic ideals' of nonneurotic persons, which HORNEY (1945) distinguished from the idealized image of neurotics. Authentic ideals, she pointed out, "have a dynamic quality; they arouse an incentive to approximate them; they are an indispensable and valuable force for growth and development" (HORNEY, 1945, p. 98).[10] The idealized self-image of neurotic persons is unrealistic and so cannot be approximated readily. Hence a grandiose self-image tends to be associated with an attitude of detachment; and hence the idealized image in neurosis often "has a static quality" (HORNEY, 1945, p. 98). The weaker the person's self-esteem and the more dependent he is on outside affirmation and recognition, the more unrealistic is his self-image, and the greater has to be his detachment. The grandiose ideas of psychotic and hence severely detached patients are the most extreme forms of the idealized image.

8.4.5 Self-contempt and self-recriminations

Low self-esteem (a deep-seated sense of worthlessness, of being unacceptable to others) results in compulsive pursuit of *"the attention, regard, appreciation, admiration, or love of others"* (HORNEY, 1950, p. 136). The neurotic person believes that he can be appreciated or loved only for his performances, so he has to outperform others who he unconsciously believes compete with him for access to external narcissistic supplies. The neurotic person's pride "demands that he *should* be superior to everybody and everything" (HORNEY, 1950, p. 134). Competitive attainment of narcissistic supplies is mediated by actualization of a grandiose or idealized self. Idealizing his self in imagination and attempting to actualize the self thus idealized, the neurotic person is bound to fail and, therefore, to hate his actual being (for not being able to "make himself over into something he is not") (HORNEY, 1950, p. 374). Narcissistic deprivation and frustration in the pursuit of narcissistic resources arouse anger that cannot be expressed. The aggressive energy used for competition (in its neutralized form) is then rechannelled against the self.

This is what HORNEY (1950) thought lies at the heart of neurosis: The more a person idealizes himself (and the more he is thus *alienated from his real self*), the more he hates and despises himself "for being as he is" (p. 373). The neurotic process "is a process of abandoning the real self for an idealized one; of trying to actualize this pseudoself instead of our given

---

[10] HORNEY (1945) equated her notion of the 'idealized image' with FREUD's 'ego ideal'. She thought that the ego ideal, too, is a purely neurotic phenomenon; however, FREUD not only introduced the ego ideal "into the theory of neurosis" (HORNEY, 1945, p. 99) but also ascribed to it normal developmental functions that resemble those of HORNEY's (1945) 'authentic ideals'.

human potentials; of a destructive warfare between the two selves" (p. 376). Self-hate, as Horney (1950) thought, "makes visible a rift in the personality that started with the creation of an idealized self" (p. 112).

Hatred of the real self, arising whenever "we are driven to reach beyond ourselves" (p. 114), manifests in "relentless demands on self, merciless self-accusations, self-contempt, self-frustrations, self-tormenting, and self-destruction" (Horney, 1950, p. 117). Witnessing others' superior skills or shining qualities "must call forth a self-destructive berating", too (p. 134). As the neurotic person is "eaten up by self-doubts" (p. 145), he recoils from competition. Tormenting himself in imagination, he engages "in endless and inconclusive inner dialogues, in which [he] tries to defend himself against his own self-accusations" (p. 145).[11] In self-tormenting, the person "is always both the torturer and the tortured", and "he derives satisfaction from being degraded as well as from degrading himself" (Horney, 1950, p. 148) (accessing an alternative, albeit internal and fleeting source of narcissistic gratification) (Figure 8.2).

Face-saving function

When expressed openly, self-recriminations are an attempt to prevent others from making recriminations; they are a "strategy of warding off reproaches (p. 241); they are an attempt "to appease others" and "to elicit reassurance" (Horney, 1939, p. 240). Self-recriminations that accompany

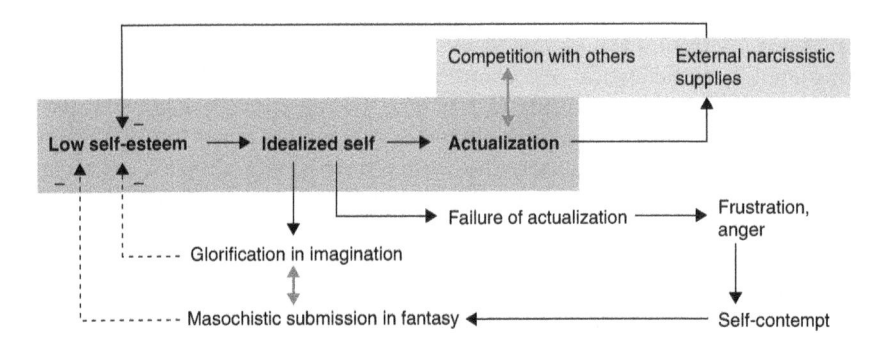

Figure 8.2 Regulation of self-esteem in neurosis. Actualization of the idealized self corresponds, in Kohut's model, to the attainment of goals or ideals through ambitions

---

[11] The neurotic person's self-recriminations can take the form of preoccupations "for hours about what he has said, what the other person has said, what he might have said, what effect his words had" and "endless pondering over what he should have said, done, or omitted doing" (Horney, 1939, p. 233). The person may "be angry at himself for having forgotten to mention a point which would have put him in a good light" (Horney, 1939, p. 239)

feelings of guilt "invite positive reassurance, by provoking reassuring statements to the contrary" (Horney, 1937, p. 242). The neurotic person has a "tendency to seek and find fault within himself" (p. 249) and feel guilty accordingly (Horney, 1937). However, neurotic self-recriminations avoid, with great certainty, "what are actually the weak points" and serve, in fact, the function of preventing the person "from facing any real deficiencies" (Horney, 1939, p. 245).[12] Self-recriminations "are a face-saving device", in that they provide the neurotic person with "reassurance that he is not so bad after all and that his very qualms of conscience make him better than others" (Horney, 1939, p. 245). Self-recriminations, even "when no outside person is involved", enhance the neurotic person's "self-respect, for they imply that he has such a keen moral judgment that he reproaches himself for faults which others overlook" (Horney, 1937, p. 242). Guilt feelings, in the context of which self-recriminations occur, "are felt as a virtue because they prove to the individual his high sensitivity toward moral requirements" (Horney, 1939, p. 220).

8.4.6 Neurotic claims

As the neurotic person strives to turn himself into his idealized image, as he works to actualize the glorified image of his self and "to mold himself into a supreme being" (p. 64), he asserts exceptional rights for himself and makes unreasonable demands ('claims') on others (Horney, 1950). Being driven and compelled to actualize his idealized self, the neurotic patient is "liable to expect an unreasonable amount from others"; he is liable to make claims on others, to the fulfilment of which he feels entitled (p. 370). The neurotic person feels "entitled to be treated by others, or by fate, in accord with his grandiose notions about himself"; he "feels entitled to special attention, consideration, deference on part of others" (p. 41), "entitled never to be criticized, doubted, or questioned" (p. 43), "entitled to everything that is important to him" (p. 42). What, for the healthy person, would be an understandable wish or need turns into a grandiose 'claim', a sense of entitlement to have one's needs met (Horney, 1950). If the neurotic person's grandiose claims are not satisfied or duly respected, if others do not "cater to his illusions", he experiences a deep sense of unfairness (p. 41), and he can become "furiously indignant" (p. 42). Nonfulfilment of a grandiose claim "is felt as an unfair frustration, as an offense about which we have a right to feel indignant" (p. 42). The more compelling the need to actualize the idealized self, the more intense is the reaction to frustration. Severe reactions to frustration "are indicated by the terror of doom and disgrace", by panic, despair, or "rage at self and others" (Horney, 1950, p. 31).

---

[12] Interestingly, the "person who accuses himself so abundantly is furious if others criticize him in the slightest way" (Horney, 1939, p. 241).

> Considering all the energies invested in justifying the claims, and in asserting them, we cannot but expect intense *reactions to their frustrations*. There are undercurrents of fear, but the prevailing response is anger or even rage. This anger is of a peculiar kind. Since the claims are subjectively felt as fair and just, the frustrations are experienced as unfair and unjust. The ensuing anger has therefore the character of a righteous indignation. The person feels, in other words, not only angry but the right to be angry – a feeling which is vigorously defended in analysis.
> (HORNEY, 1950, pp. 55–6)

Besides the neurotic person's sense of entitlement, his insistence on his exceptional rights, and his taking benefits "accruing from laws or regulations ... for granted" (HORNEY, 1950, p. 44), he also adopts fictitious rights. In accordance with his tendency to deceive himself about his position in the world, he tends to adopt "a right, a title, which in reality does not exist" (HORNEY, 1950, p. 42). The person's rights, whether adopted, claimed, or fictitious, demarcate his access to sources of narcissistic supplies; and these rights are defended in much the same way as a territory is defended against intrusions.

8.4.7 Irresponsibility and undependability

Neurotic persons "often cannot commit themselves to a feeling or opinion about another person"; they often cannot take "a stand in accordance with the objective merits of a person, idea, or cause"; however, they "are readily swayed – unconsciously bribed, as it were – by the lure of greater affection, greater prestige, recognition, power" (HORNEY, 1945, pp. 168–9). They rationalize as fairness their inability to make up their mind or take a stand, whereby such fairness can in itself be "a compulsory part of the idealized image" (HORNEY, 1945, p. 169). A related moral problem is the inability to take responsibility for oneself, to acknowledge to oneself and others one's intentions and "be willing to take the consequences" of one's actions (p. 171). The neurotic person, when faced with the consequences of his actions, "often tries to wiggle out by denying, forgetting, belittling, ... feeling misunderstood" or placing responsibility on others (p. 171). Recognizing the consequences of his actions and assuming responsibility for them would shatter his "hidden feeling of omnipotence" (p. 172). His idealized image "does not permit of the possibility of being wrong", so "he must falsify matters and ascribe the adverse consequences to someone else" (HORNEY, 1945, p. 173).

8.4.8 Vindictiveness

'Neurotic trends' are structures of the personality concerned with attainment of 'safety' (HORNEY, 1939). Aggressiveness can be regarded as a neurotic trend, but "only if a neurotic's feeling of safety rests on being aggressive" (p. 77).

Aggressiveness as a neurotic trend contains elements of vindictiveness, enviousness, and sadism. Compulsory adherence to inner standards and insistence on grandiose claims (both being related to actualization of the idealized self-image) are associated with righteousness and vindictiveness, the desire "to triumph vindictively over others" (Horney, 1939, p. 222). Feeling wronged, the neurotic person becomes vindictive and insists on retribution. Then, the 'search for glory', incentivized by the idealized self-image, becomes a striving for 'vindictive triumph' (Horney, 1950). The vindictive element in the neurotic person's search for glory is related to (and, as self psychology would suggest, a *disintegration product* of) the normal assertiveness woven into competitive pursuits of socially acceptable goals and into one's insistence on others' compliance with norms and rules that define one's self.

> The vindictive person, who may ruin others with insatiable claims, tries through hardhitting accusations to enforce their compliance.
> (Horney, 1950, p. 55)

The neurotic person, having raised "his needs to the dignity of claims" (p. 63), responds with indignation and hostility to any frustration of his needs (Horney, 1950). If his claims are frustrated by another person, "that person suddenly becomes untrustworthy, nasty, cruel, contemptible" (p. 56). Feeling wronged, the neurotic person ponders "the hateful qualities of somebody" and "feels the impulse to get back at others" (p. 57). If however the expression of anger or hostility is precluded by the situation and socially inacceptable, then "one will have to exaggerate the wrong done; one will then inadvertently build up a case against the offender that looks logic tight" (p. 56). If anger can still not be expressed, the wronged neurotic person becomes despondent or plunges "into misery and self-pity" (p. 57); or his anger may appear in psychosomatic symptoms (p. 56). Then, his suffering would become "the medium to express reproaches" (Horney, 1950, p. 57).

Horney (1950) saw vindictive elements in grandiose claims when these "are made with reference to past frustration or suffering" (p. 51), when an injury suffered is stressed (p. 55). Overemphasis on justice when making grandiose claims can be "a camouflage for vindictiveness" (p. 55). The idea of injustice then stands out in the person's consciousness, while the vindictive aspect of his search for glory (and pursuit of safety) is hidden (Horney, 1950) (because it is socially unacceptable and hence egodystonic).

Sadism

The sadistic person is more than just vindictive in a reactive sense. By degrading others, he "gives himself a feeling of superiority" (Horney, 1945, p. 206). He "gains a stimulating feeling of power over them" (p. 206); and his "feeling of strength and pride" reinforces "his unconscious feeling of omnipotence" (p. 207). His triumphant "elation at being able to do with others as he pleases" thus "lessens his own sense of barrenness" and "obscures his own hopeless defeat" (p. 207). Sadism, as a neurotic trend, is a defence against deep-seated inferiority. The sadistic person "seeks to alleviate his own misery" "by making others miserable" (p. 206). His hope is that, "if others are as defeated and degraded as he is, his own misery is tempered" (HORNEY, 1945, p. 202).

> The sadistic impulses may be expressed merely in derogatory thoughts concerning the mistakes and shortcomings of others. But the impulse is to tell others how stupid, worthless and contemptible they are and to make them feel like dust; the impulse is to strike them with righteous indignation from the height of one's own infallibility.
> (HORNEY, 1939, p. 220)

The sadistic person's misery reflects his self-contempt; however, his self-contempt remains unconscious as he externalizes this by blaming, berating, and humiliating others (HORNEY, 1945). Sadism is both a defence against self-contempt and "an outgrowth of hopelessness" (p. 206). Self-contempt, too, is a manifestation of hopelessness; "and the self-contempt grows more violent and merciless the more hopeless [the person] becomes" (p. 204). Hopeless despair breeds recklessness. Feeling "beyond repair and beyond forgiveness", the neurotic "develops the recklessness of a person who has nothing to lose" (p. 204). Feeling "excluded and doomed", he "runs amok, venting his rage at others in blind vindictiveness" (HORNEY, 1945, p. 206).

8.4.9 Envy

Grandiose claims are crippling in their effect; they are responsible for "chronic smoldering envy and discontent" (HORNEY, 1950, p. 47). The neurotic person, whose self-esteem depends on his power, possessions, or prestige, enters "a miserable state" when "he fails to have the one advantage in which another person surpasses him" (HORNEY, 1937, p. 183). He experiences a similar sense of humiliation when he has to "give someone credit for something" (p. 196). This sense of humiliation incites anger, whereby "hostility usually takes the form of a tendency to deprive others" (p. 180). The tendency to deprive others – or more generally the "impulse to defeat or frustrate the efforts of others" (p. 193) – is "accompanied by an emotional attitude of begrudging envy", although most of us "will feel some envy if others have certain advantages we should like to have ourselves" (HORNEY, 1937, p. 182). The neurotic person devalues others' achievements and thereby "succeeds in assuaging his envy and discharging his resentment" (HORNEY, 1945, p. 203).

Others' happiness and "their 'naïve' expectations of pleasure and joy" irritate the neurotic person (HORNEY, 1945, pp. 201–2). Begrudging envy together with an impulse to "trample on the joy of others" (p. 202), "to frustrate and to crush the spirit of others" (p. 202) arise in him when he sees others "love, create, enjoy, feel healthy and at ease, belong somewhere" (HORNEY, 1945, p. 201). The neurotic person also tends to underestimate "what he has himself", depriving himself of the ability "to enjoy and appreciate the possibilities for happiness that are available" (HORNEY, 1937, p. 183). Associated with the neurotic person's "tendency to deprive and exploit" others is "an anxiety that he will be cheated or exploited by others"; he has "a perpetual fear that someone will take advantage of him, that money or ideas will be stolen from him" (p. 185). Whenever he *feels* cheated, exploited, or deprived by others, a "disproportionate amount of anger is discharged", suggesting that there has been a projection of his "own abusing tendencies on others" (HORNEY, 1937, p. 186).

8.4.10 Fear of retaliation

If the outside world is felt to be hostile, if one feels helpless toward it, then taking any risk of annoying people seems sheer recklessness. For the neurotic the danger appears all the greater, and the more his feeling of safety is based on the affection of others the more he is afraid of losing that affection. ... Hence he feels that annoying them involves the danger of a final break; he expects to be dropped altogether, to be definitely spurned or hated.

(HORNEY, 1937, p. 252)

In a competitive environment, power, prestige, or possessions can be acquired only at the cost of defeat of competitors. A person's anxiety reflects, in part, a fear that others "will want just as intensely to defeat him"; it reflects "a fear of retaliation for the ruthless pursuit of ambition" (HORNEY, 1937, p. 207). The neurotic person is "anxious about hurting others", since he "automatically assumes that others will feel just as much hurt and vindictive after a defeat as he does himself" (p. 196). He feels that "once he has shown an interest in success he is surrounded by a horde of persecuting enemies, who lie in wait to crush him at every sign of weakness or failure" (p. 211). They wait for him to make a mistake. He fears that "others will gloat over a failure" (p. 211) and that he will be "the object of disrespect or ridicule" (p. 224). The neurotic person's "fear of the begrudging envy of others" is associated with a fear "of the loss of their affection" (p. 214). The neurotic person is thus caught in a conflict between "an excessive desire to be loved by everyone" and "an aggressive striving for a 'no one but I' dominance" (HORNEY, 1937, p. 208).

Basic anxiety – reflecting feelings of insignificance, helplessness, and insecurity – pushes the person "into enhanced efforts to be more successful and more invincible" (p. 208); anxiety impels him "to strive for and attain more and more strength and power in order to be safe" (HORNEY, 1937, p. 268). At the same time, anxiety – engendered by an expectation of retaliation – results in an inhibition towards competition; the neurotic person 'recoils' from competition. The fear of disapproval and retaliation produces a "lack of spontaneous self-assertion" (p. 250). This leaves the neurotic person with "difficulties in criticizing and making accusations" (Horney, 1937, p. 250). The neurotic person "is afraid of people", and – insofar as "he must present a rational front" and maintain the semblance of perfection – "he is prevented from feeling or venting any grievance" (Horney, 1939, p. 242). The fear of accusing or reproaching others "is another factor instrumental in engendering self-reproaches" (p. 241). Self-recriminations are a means of checking and rechannelling piled-up "bitter reproaches against others" (p. 242); reproaches are shifted from others to oneself (Horney, 1939).

8.4.11 Timidity

The neurotic person covers up a "feeling of intrinsic weakness" ("a deep feeling of insignificance or rather of nothingness") (Horney, 1937, p. 267) with a grandiose and fragile façade or 'persona'. The neurotic person is also "excessively afraid of or hypersensitive to being disapproved of, criticized, accused, found out" (p. 235); "he cannot help believing that others will despise him ... if they find out about his weaknesses" (p. 240). For him, "even a minute disagreement is equivalent to a criticism" (p. 243). Incurring "a defeat in competition" or merely being criticized ("having to realize a definite weakness or shortcoming") is "unbearable" for a person who has "high-flung notions of his uniqueness" (Horney, 1937, p. 265). There are at least two strategies of protecting the self against further criticism and recurring pain of rejection. Firstly, increased sensitivity to rejection can "result in a complete withdrawal of all feelings", manifesting in an attitude of coldness and unresponsiveness (p. 136). The person has "to become emotionally detached from people so that nothing will hurt or disappoint" him (Horney, 1937, p. 99). Emotional withdrawal helps to protect the grandiose persona but also increases vulnerability to criticism. Secondly, submissiveness and inhibition of assertiveness (timidity) are designed to reduce the risk of further exposure to rebuff, although ultimately they perpetuate the sense of inferiority (Figure 8.3).

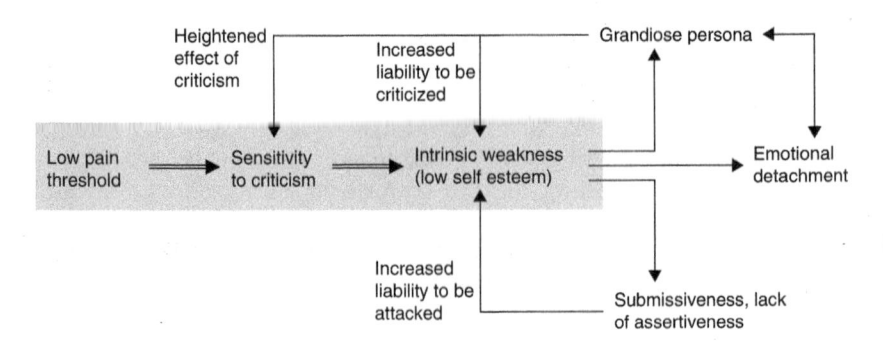

Figure 8.3 Two of the vicious circles afflicting the neurotic person

Neurotic persons try to be *modest* and avoid being conspicuous "by sticking to conventional standards, staying out of the limelight, being no different from others" (HORNEY, 1937, p. 213). The fear of rejection or rebuff "may lead to a series of severe inhibitions falling in the category of timidity" (p. 137). Neurotic persons may "have inhibitions about expressing their wishes or asking for something, about doing something in their own interest, expressing an opinion or warranted criticism, ordering someone, selecting the people they wish to associate with, making contacts with people" (pp. 37–8). Orders "will be given in an apologetic, ineffectual manner" (p. 57). Their "anxiety concerning the hostility of others" renders them "afraid of success" (p. 214) and prevents them from pursing their demands and ambitions. Directly or indirectly, "[t]he fear of rebuff is thus a grave handicap to the wish for affection" and need for approval (HORNEY, 1937, p. 137).

8.4.12 Perfectionism

Perfectionistic persons "are dependent on other's opinions about them", and "[t]heir feelings, thoughts and actions are determined by what they feel is expected of them" (HORNEY, 1939, p. 215). Their façade of rightness and perfection is "a pretense for the benefit of others as well as themselves" (p. 216). For a neurotic person with perfectionistic trends, what is more important than perfection is the "to maintain the *appearance* of perfection" (p. 215). The person's efforts are "directed toward a 'pretense' of perfection and infallibility" (p. 216). The perfectionistic neurotic person's "strivings for perfection lack genuineness"; his "pursuit of moral goals is too formalistic" and has a "hypocritical character" (p. 213). His standards do coincide with approved standards and moral norms but "they only ape the gestures of moral norms" (p. 230). For the neurotic person with perfectionistic trends, moral standards "mean nothing more than keeping up the appearance of morality" (HORNEY, 1939, p. 230).

The perfectionistic neurotic person "gains a feeling of superiority" through his compulsory "adherence to inner standards" (HORNEY, 1939, p. 220). Even though "his security rests on an automatic conformance with what he believes others expect of him", "he is anxious to hide from himself the fact and the extent of his dependency" (pp. 250–1). The perfectionistic neurotic person "secures the semblance of independence" and acquires "the right to be left alone" (p. 219). The neurotic person's "overconformity to standards or to expectations" puts him "beyond reproach and attack" (HORNEY, 1939, p. 220).

Moral standards have been adopted "under stress of fear for the sake of peace" (HORNEY, 1939, p. 231). The *safety* of the perfectionistic person "rests on measuring up to his particular standards" (p. 198); his security is solely "rooted in his subjection to rules and to what is expected of him" (p. 226). The anxiety against which he defends himself is an anxiety that "conjures up the danger of condemnation, which is as vital a menace to the perfectionistic type as is desertion to the masochistic type" (p. 198). If safety rests on the operation of perfectionistic trends alone, "then to make a mistake provokes the danger of being exposed to ridicule, contempt and humiliation" (p. 225). The Freudian concept of 'fear of the superego' was explained by HORNEY (1939) as an anxiety that is associated with the possibility "of making any mistake, of recognizing any shortcoming or of anticipating any failure" (p. 224). It is "a fear of being unmasked", a "fear of being found out in all his pretenses", a "diffuse fear that one day he will be unmasked as a swindler, that one day the others will detect that he is not really generous or altruistic but is really egocentric and egoistic, or that he is really interested not in his work but only in his own glory", or that one day "his bluff of "knowing it all" would be called" (HORNEY, 1939, p. 224).

GREENSON (1973) linked the neurotic striving for perfection with feelings of inferiority and the longing to fuse with a perfect (omnipotent) object. The quest for perfection arises in those personalities who carry "inside themselves, from childhood on, the feeling of not having been loved sufficiently" (p. 487). They are "haunted by the dread of being found unlovable"; their "wish to be loved and to be found lovable is opposed by *unconscious* harsh and unrealistic self-criticism" (p. 487). By attaining perfection, these persons seek to return to an emotional state in which they "feel a joyous sense of losing their self-boundaries and flowing into, or merging, and becoming one with another person or being – like God, Fate, or Nature" (GREENSON, 1973, p. 485).

> They yearn for a constant loving mother they never had and create an *idealized* mother who is unattainable because of their sense of internal badness. They continue to hope for some special form of approval, acceptance, or union with this perfect mother who never existed in real life.
> (GREENSON, 1973, p. 487)

Rebellion against new expectations

The striving to be perfect (the need to excel in ambitious pursuits) is coupled with a reluctance to meet new expectations. The perfectionistic neurotic person tends to rebel "against everything that is expected of him" (HORNEY, 1939, p. 222). Any piece of work, insofar as it becomes "an obligation that must be fulfilled", "will precipitate a passive resistance against doing it" (p. 223). The person will be drawn "between a hectic drive toward accomplishing something perfect and an unwillingness to work at all" (p. 223). It is a strain to have to accomplish something perfect; and, insofar as "every undertaking must be unassailably right", "the possibility of committing an error arouses anxiety" (HORNEY, 1939, p. 223).

8.4.13 Obsessionality

KLEIN (1932) thought that "anxiety belonging to the early danger-situations" is "closely associated with the beginnings of obsessions and obsessional neuroses" (p. 231). Order and cleanliness are reaction formations against an anxiety associated with the child's earliest danger situations, that is, danger situations arising from primitive superego pressures. The severe superego featuring in obsessional neurosis "is no other than the unmodified, terrifying super-ego belonging to early stages of the child's development" (p. 229). Obsessive acts serve the purpose of mastering superego anxiety (KLEIN, 1932, p. 231). Anxiety, being allied with uncertainty, "gives rise to an obsessive desire for knowledge" (p. 231). Moreover, the individual seeks to overcome doubt and uncertainty, and hence anxiety, "by being over-precise" (p. 231). Anxiety, or rather the uncertainty that is inherent in it, gives rise to "inclinations towards exactness and order and towards the observance of certain rules and rituals" (KLEIN, 1932, p. 231).

FREUD showed that obsessional neurosis is one of the equivalents of taboo in modern society. Similarly to the tension and anxiety experienced by primitive man when not complying with a taboo, the patient with obsessional neurosis "feels strain and worry whenever the compulsive ceremonial is not carried out" (FLUGEL, 1945, p. 136). Infringement of a taboo precipitates aggression from others against oneself. Similarly, in obsessional neurosis, primitive superego pressures may symbolize diffuse fears of aggression potentially being unleashed by authority figures or the group. These fears arise when one is not included in a network of mutual appeasement and reassurance, a network that has to be actively controlled by each individual. KERNBERG (1992) stated that obsessive-compulsive patients seek "to control and dominate others to feel protected against threatening outbreaks of aggressive rebelliousness and chaos in others" (p. 29). In patients with obsessive-compulsive personality disorder, "inordinate aggression has been neutralized by its absorption into a well-integrated, but excessively sadistic superego, leading to the perfectionism, self-doubts, and chronic need to control the environment as well as the self that are characteristic of this personality disorder" (KERNBERG, 1996, p. 125).

Precariousness of the self

The obsessional person always watches out for danger; he "has to be ready to avoid any danger from the world outside and to parry, like a fencer in a duel, any possible attack from others"; "the dangers he fears are dangers seen from the perspective of pessimism and distrust; the attacks he fears often have to do with blame and rejection" (SCHACHTEL, 1973, p. 45). The obsessional person is prepared for a battle with others, whereby his "readiness to fight about logical points and his search for the right rules are intensely emotional" (p. 46). He is ready "to detect any fault or mistake in them; but he must be equally or even more on the alert and watchful about himself, about any fault or mistake in himself" (p. 45); "he has to be irreproachable, so that he be spared the painful and repressed possibility of feeling unacceptable" (SCHACHTEL, 1973, p. 46). Thus, the obsessional person's fear of attack from others is related to a repressed sense of being unacceptable, of being not worthy of others' approval or love, as reflected in his precarious sense of self. The obsessive person may isolate his sense of precariousness from its source in the interpersonal sphere "and experience it primarily in relation to the world in general, to daily routines, to things, to technicalities of their work, and in such well-known phenomena as excessive preoccupation with orderliness, exactness, and the like" (SCHACHTEL, 1973, p. 45).

> But even where it is consciously related to people, it is often isolated from its real source and experienced mostly with regard to minute questions of etiquette and similar details of behavior, both in the other person and in the self. The real source of the uncertainty, precariousness, and doubt in the obsessive-compulsive's life ... is to be found in his pervasive confusion whether the other person and the world in general are friendly or hostile, accepting and approving or rejecting and blaming.
> (SCHACHTEL, 1973, pp. 45–6)

8.5 Moral masochism

Masochism, according to HORNEY (1937), refers to a tendency to submerge oneself "in feelings of helplessness, unhappiness and unworthiness" (p. 264). A masochistic person "unconsciously exaggerates his weakness and he tenaciously insists on being weak" (p. 268). This submergence in misery is a strategy for coercing others to fulfil his wishes. The person with masochistic tendencies uses suffering and helplessness as "means of obtaining affection, help, control" (pp. 263–4). Unconsciously, he wishes to "be completely taken care of" (p. 269). At the same time, his suffering and helplessness allow him to express "accusations against others in a disguised but effective way" and "to evade all demands others might make on him" (HORNEY, 1937, p. 264). Moreover, masochism is a strategy for alleviating the *pain* of loss or rejection. Such "aggravating experience loses some of its reality" when the person submerges "himself in a general feeling of misery or unworthiness" (p. 265). Abandoning his "self to excessive suffering" narcotizes the pain of rejection or loss (p. 265). The aim of the masochistic person "is not suffering itself but a relinquishment of the self" (p. 280). The masochistic attitude transforms deep feelings of insecurity and vulnerability into "a feeling of being in the power of others" (p. 267). The common denominator of masochistic fantasies "is a feeling of being putty in the master's hand, of being devoid of all will, of all power, of being absolutely subjected to another's domination" (p. 274). Submergence in misery produces "satisfaction by losing the self in something greater, by dissolving the individuality, by getting rid of the self with its doubts" (HORNEY, 1937, p. 270).

Masochistic trends, that is, tendencies towards self-disparagement, constitute one of the strategies by which the personality obtains safety (HORNEY, 1939). Masochistic trends represent "a special way of gaining safety" (p. 249). The masochistic person attains safety by way of *dependency* and *unobtrusiveness*. The tendency towards self-minimizing, self-belittling, or self-deflation provides a special kind of security, "the security of unobtrusiveness" (p. 254). Unobtrusiveness can be maintained, for instance, by expressing views in an apologetic way or wearing inconspicuous clothes. The masochistic person recoils from self-assertion; the need for unobtrusiveness makes him afraid of success. Moreover, "when he dwindles to nothing in his own estimation, the categories of success and failure, superiority and inferiority cease to exist" (p. 273). Unobtrusiveness facilitates dependency on others, and it is through dependency (and merger with an omnipotent object) that the masochistic person gains safety. The life of the masochistic person is automatically arranged in accordance with this tendency towards unobtrusiveness (p. 255). His unobtrusiveness may be "carried to such extremes as losing himself entirely in 'love' or in a sacrifice, losing his identity, losing his dignity, submerging his individuality in self-depreciation" (HORNEY, 1939, p. 271).

The masochistic person "feels that he is incapable of living without the presence, benevolence, love, friendship of another person" (HORNEY, 1939, p. 251). He expects to receive "love, success, prestige, care, protection" from a partner (p. 251). The masochistic person allays his anxiety and gains reassurance by thrusting himself "on the mercy of someone", "[b]y submerging his own individuality entirely and by merging with the partner" (p. 253). Clinging to his partner, he is insatiable for signs of affection and interest (p. 252). In the masochistic person's mind, "the process often takes on the appearance of loyalty, devotion or great love" (p. 253). The masochistic person adores the partner's strength, much as any person who shows courage or "dares to be openly aggressive or assertive" inspires "at least secret adoration" (p. 258). However, the masochistic person, like other neurotic persons, is incapable "to give active spontaneous affection to others"; "he cannot afford to have spontaneous feelings for them concerning their interests, their needs, their happiness" (HORNEY, 1939, p. 270).

8.5.1 Control through helplessness and suffering

Besides unobtrusiveness, the display of helplessness is a way of fostering a dependent relationship (HORNEY, 1939). The masochistic person displays his helplessness and "exaggerates his misery and needs for the strategic purpose of getting what he wants" (p. 261). The masochistic person expresses his wishes in the form of "a desperate cry for help" and thereby puts others "under a stringent moral obligation" (p. 261). The display of helplessness and misery not only exerts pressure on others but also serves to justify his demands, allowing him to feel "entitled to demand help" (p. 262). Sooner or later, however, "persons around him become tired of this type of entreaty", "take his misery for granted", and "are no longer spurred to action" (Horney, 1939, p. 261).

The masochistic person reacts with hostility to disappointments, "to the slightest sign of disregard or neglect" (Horney, 1939, p. 259); and "he is bound to become disappointed and resentful" "because of his excessive expectations of his partner" (p. 271). The masochistic person "is or feels humiliated and suppressed, and in his heart he makes others responsible for his suffering" (p. 263). The masochistic personality structure "is fertile soil for sadistic trends" (p. 264). If masochistic trends are "combined with an imperative need for power and control", then "the masochistic person exerts control ... by his very suffering and helplessness" (Horney, 1939, p. 268). He may "live in a helpless dependence and at the same time exert a tyranny over others by means of his weakness" (Horney, 1937, p. 277). Others will submit "because they are afraid that if they do not there will be an upheaval of some kind" (such as despair or functional disorders) (Horney, 1939, p. 268).

8.5.2 Inverted sadism

If a person fears his sadistic impulses, in part due to a fear of retaliation, then "he leans over backward to keep them from being revealed to himself or others" (Horney, 1945, p. 211). "He will shun everything that resembles assertion, aggression, or hostility and as a result will be profoundly and diffusely inhibited"; he will be "incapable of giving any order" or of "assuming a position of responsibility or leadership" (p. 211). The person with inverted sadism will not dare "to express any wish" or even "have a wish" (p. 211). "He will be overanxious not to disappoint" other people; he will "avoid anything that could conceivably hurt their feelings or in any way humiliate them" (p. 212). Even though he thinks "he is really fond of people", "he has very little feeling for them at all"; he harbours "unconscious contempt for others, superficially attributed to their lower moral standards" (Horney, 1945, p. 214).

> In the case of a conflict between self-effacing tendencies and a need for triumph, all the cramping inhibitions inherent in inverted sadism must be understood. The patient must see how he responds to every self-effacing move with self-contempt, and with rage at the person before whom he cringes; and how, on the other hand, he responds to every attempt to triumph over someone with horror of himself and a fear of retaliation.
> (Horney, 1945, p. 234)

The inverted sadist "may sometimes put up with sadistic behavior directed at himself" (Horney, 1945, p. 214). He may even put himself "in the way of exploitation" (p. 215) and indulge "in feeling victimized" (p. 214), as he seeks and relishes "an opportunity to live out his own sadistic impulses through someone else", while, at the same time, feeling "innocent and morally indignant" (p. 215). Developmentally, the inverted sadist, having been "crushed into submission in childhood", initially developed 'compliant trends' and later in life "took refuge in detachment" (p. 213); but, as "his need for affection became so desperate", "he became hopeless and developed sadistic trends", which however, as "his need for people was so insistent", had to be repressed and inverted (HORNEY, 1945, p. 213).

8.5.3 Depressive-masochistic personality disorder

Patients with severe masochistic personality pathology grow up with a sense that any object relationship renders them vulnerable to attack by their object (KERNBERG, 1992). They learn that total submission to the cruel and powerful object "is the only condition for survival" (p. 49) (i.e., for their safety). Submission and suffering become essential conditions for object relations later in life. Patients with 'depressive-masochistic personality disorder' show an "overdependency on support, love, and acceptance from others" (narcissistic needs); they often go "far out of their way to obtain sympathy and love" (p. 37). These patients also "show an abnormal vulnerability to being disappointed by others" (p. 38). They can obtain "narcissistic gratification from the sense of being unjustly treated and thus implicitly morally superior to the object" (KERNBERG, 1992, p. 48). Although patients with depressive-masochistic personality disorder have "difficulties in the expression of aggression", they may resort to "attacks on those they need and feel rejected by, followed by depression and abject, submissive, and/or compliant behavior" (KERNBERG, 1992, p. 38).

> The sense of being rejected and mistreated in reaction to relatively minor slights may lead these patients to unconscious behaviors geared to making the objects of their love feel guilty. A chain reaction is set up of heightened demandingness, feelings of rejection, and an unconscious tendency to try to make others feel guilty; consequent actual rejection from others may spiral into severe problems in intimate relations and may also trigger depression connected to loss of love.
> (KERNBERG, 1992, p. 37)

Patients with depressive-masochistic personality disorder (moral masochism) are exposed to excessive superego pressures (KERNBERG, 1992). They are responsible and reliable persons but "tend to judge themselves harshly and to set extremely high standards for themselves", failing which they may become depressed. They can "show harshness in their judgement of others, a harshness that may be tinged with justified indignation" (p. 37). Hatred of others, arising from "identification with a strict and punitive superego", may take the form of "justified indignation" or "aggressive assertion of idiosyncratic but well-rationalized systems of morality" (KERNBERG, 1992, p. 24).

The punitive superego of patients with depressive-masochistic personality disorder also predisposes them to guilt feelings and self-defeating behaviours. Their punitive superego "reflects an unconscious need to suffer as an expiation for guilt feelings" (KERNBERG, 1996, p. 126).

8.5.4 Injustice collection

During the earliest, 'oral' phase of development, the child lives in a fantasy of self-sufficiency and magic omnipotence. The child believes that the wish fulfilments produced by his mother are the result of his own omnipotence (BERGLER, 1949). An inevitable "long and protracted series of disappointments" (p. 2) – in the form of maternal refusals of the child's wishes or delays in his wish fulfilment – causes a "gradual collapse of autarchic fantasies" (p. 3). Every refusal inflicts a narcissistic wound and provokes the child's fury. The child's anger is directed against "mother, later father – both people with a halo" (BERGLER, 1949, p. 3). Aggression against the parent is followed by expectation of retribution and, later, feelings of guilt. Guilt can be overcome by solicitation of parental punishment and, with it, of parental forgiveness. Received punishment is likely followed by parental forgiveness if the punishable offence can be minimized in the eyes of the parent (and hence neurotic patients unconsciously always plead guilty to the 'lesser offence' [BERGLER, 1949, 1952]). Forgiveness and acceptance back into the parent's loving care are even more likely if the punishment can be portrayed (in fantasy or reality) as excessive, as unwarranted, as an injustice (and hence neurotic patients are 'injustice collectors' [BERGLER, 1949, 1952]). Parental remorse and acceptance back into the parent's loving care are fantasized in the detached state of self-pity. The self feels unjustly punished and victimized and then pities it*self*; that is, the self, as identified with the omnipotent (parental) object, pities the narcissistically injured self. By feeling oneself as the object of the omnipotent object's pity, the narcissistic balance is restored.

In 'psychic masochism', a phenomenon regarded by BERGLER (1949) as reflective of 'oral regression' and central to the dynamics of neurosis, the patient provokes the anger of a derivative of the parental object (of "some substitute of my pre-oedipal mother-image" [p. 5]) *in order to feel unjustly treated, victimized, excluded, rejected*. This then enables withdrawal into the state of self-pity. The other's aggression may be elicited and experienced as pleasurable by the patient precisely because it provides narcissistic gratification. The need to manoeuvre another person into a mode of aggressive behaviour (i.e., the need to enact an abusive internal object relation) may reflect the patient's dependence on or attachment to "the 'bad mother' who *refuses*" (BERGLER, 1949, p. 199) (or who may only ever have shown love to the child whenever she felt guilty about her own aggression towards him). Another consequence of the unconscious creation *or misuse* of situations in which the patient feels that he is rejected or his wishes are refused is the sense of *righteous indignation*. Righteous indignation is involved with *self*-defensive ('ego-strengthening') 'pseudoaggression' (p. 5) (i.e., with 'neurotic aggression', "the typical fury of the unjustly treated person" [p. 6]). Righteous indignation and pseudoaggression are followed by or alternate with masochistic self-pity. 'Injustice collectors' have a tendency to *construct or imagine* a situation "in which somebody was unjust and refusing" to them, so that they can pity themselves (enjoying 'psychic masochistic pleasure') and revel "in fury and anger from their arsenal of 'righteous indignation', seemingly in self-defense" (BERGLER, 1949, p. 7).

Psychic masochism also designates striving towards a position of passivity and submissiveness vis-à-vis the omnipotent and, in some cases, cruel object. Submissiveness and infantile passivity have an inhibitory effect on parental aggression and promote parental care-giving behaviour, leading to the receipt of parental care, evolutionarily related to the receipt of narcissistic nourishment. BERGLER (1949) did suspect that "*passively* endured experiences" are actively repeated "for *the purpose of restoring a lesion in narcissism*" (p. 15); and he emphasized the link between psychic masochism and 'oral regression', that is, regression to a state of *passive* receipt of oral nourishment associated with a sense of autarchic omnipotence. He thought that "*there is only one basic neurosis and that neurosis is oral in genesis*" (p. 38). Nosologic entities that seem to be based on regression to the later, anal and phallic, phases reactivate these developmental phases insofar as they "*are but rescue – and survival attempts from the oral danger*" (p. 39), the fundamental danger implicit in the child's passivity and helplessness (the danger faced by the child as unconscious fantasies of omnipotence gradually collapse). If the child's developmental escape from passivity remains incomplete, then "neurosis is inevitable" (BERGLER, 1949, p. 40) and the adult's intrapsychic functioning readily regresses to the oral, anal, or phallic levels of development.

> ... we can state that man's whole psychic life is a desperate attempt to *escape from passivity*. That passivity was biologically, because of the helplessness of the child, most pronounced in the first months of life – on the oral stage. Hence my conviction that there is only *one* neurosis, the oral one, but many rescue stations. These different rescue stations correspond to the many nosologic groups subsumed as results of regression to anal and phallic phases.
>
> (BERGLER, 1949, pp. 60–1)

8.6 Symptom neuroses

> ... we cannot grasp the significance of any symptomatic disorder without an understanding of its fundamental human basis.
>
> (HORNEY, 1945, p. 154)

According to early Freudian theory, conflicts that lie at the heart of simpler neuroses occur between the need for 'pleasure' (i.e., the need to express sexual or aggressive instinctual impulses) and the need for self-preservation ('ego instinct') (HENDRICK, 1958, p. 139). The self-preservative need is the same as the need for narcissistic nourishment (others' love, care, or appraisals), that is, for connectedness to the self-object milieu. Neurotic symptoms are compromise formations between instinctual wish fulfilment (pleasure principle) and the need to preserve safety and avoid anxiety; they are solutions to conflicts, just like many defences are (SANDLER, 1985). Neurotic symptoms are "very carefully constructed as last-line measures when the defenses fail" (p. 539). They serve the same function as defence mechanisms: avoidance of anxiety and preservation of wellbeing (safety) (SANDLER, 1985, p. 539). Yet, neurotic symptoms would not be called 'symptoms' if they did not "also cause pain and loss" (A. FREUD in SANDLER, 1985, p. 539). Defensive activity in itself "should not lead toward symptom formation" (A. FREUD in SANDLER, 1985, p. 539).

Many neurotic symptoms express childhood conflictual wishes (BRENNER, 1989), often wishes for love and care that are in conflict with fears of punishment for expressing *demands* for love and care. Hysterical (conversion) symptoms, for instance, may be a compromise between the patient's wish to force others to provide special love and care (the love and care the patient did not receive in her childhood) and a wish to punish herself for having such wishes (BRENNER, 1989), that is, an internalized fear of parental punishment coupled with an expectation of expiation. Neurotic symptoms tend to appear whenever "something in the present has activated the childhood instinctual conflict of which the symptom is a result"; then, "the past has become active in the present as a neurotic symptom" (BRENNER, 1989, p. 86).

Unlike patients with a disorder of self, patients with a 'structural neurosis' "had been overstimulated as children"; "they had been involved in the emotional life of their parents to a degree that overtaxed the capacity of their immature personality organization" (KOHUT, 1977, p. 256).[13] The "greatest terror" faced by patients with 'structural neuroses' is not 'disintegration anxiety' but 'castration anxiety'; and their "most compelling objective" is not "the establishment of self-cohesion" but the solution of conflict (p. 281). KOHUT (1983, 1984) later thought that selfobject failures in childhood are the ultimate cause of all psychopathology, not only of narcissistic disturbances.

According to the 'principle of self-preservation', the subject must maintain his ties to his selfobjects if he is to preserve the integrity of his self (BRANDCHAFT, 1985). This imperative can be in conflict with other, internal or

---

[13] "The overstimulation due to parental overcloseness that is a decisive factor in the genesis of structural disturbance is a manifestation of a structural neurosis in the parent, an acting out of a neurotic conflict with the aid of the child" (KOHUT, 1977, p. 273).

external, demands. All psychological conflicts are ultimately concerned with preservation of the integrity of the self and self-esteem regulation. In the child, conflicts "center around the ... basic needs for mirroring responses and for connectedness to idealized sources of comfort and strength" (STOLOROW, 1985, p. 194). Defence mechanisms have the function of preserving the self, that is, preserving the subject's perception of connectedness to the selfobject milieu (safety). To this end, they resolve conflicts with instinctual drives.

Neurotic conflicts and "a varied mixture of defensive or characteristic expressive patterns ... cover or convey ... the dominant underlying disturbance" (P. TOLPIN, 1986, p. 103), namely a deficit in supporting structures of the self, that is, a deficit in autonomous regulation of self-esteem. Conflicts experienced by patients with neuroses "have their origin in deficits in the supporting structures of the self", deficits that "have arisen from the cumulative trauma of failures within the child–parent selfobject milieu" (MARKSON & THOMSON, 1986, p. 39). Selfobject failure (i.e., the failure of selfobjects to meet the child's needs for narcissistic sustenance) and the conflict of drives "are indissolubly interrelated" (p. 274); the formation of psychic conflict "always takes place in ... contexts ... of selfobject failure" (STOLOROW, 1986b, p. 275).

8.6.1 Superego conflict

Neurosis represents a conflict between "guilt-laden instinctual wishes" (p. 161) and "the fear of being abandoned, the fear of loss of love, and the fear of punishment" (ARLOW, 1989, p. 160). This fear is the origin of moral judgements "directed against the self" (p. 161) (the superego being an internalization of anticipation of parental punishment). The patient (adopting the perspective of his superego) harshly judges himself; and, as a consequence, his *self* "has to suffer pain or experience inhibition" (ARLOW, 1989, p. 161). Ultimately, neurosis represents a conflict between instinctual wishes and the desire for love of internalized objects (superego), on whom the *self* and the sense of inner harmony (narcissistic equilibrium) depend. It is, as ARLOW (1989) stated, the "quest for inner harmony that brings patients to treatment" (p. 155).

> Beyond the primitive fear of being punished in a retaliatory way for his own hostile and forbidden impulses lies the individual's wish to regain, in his mind, the lost or disrupted harmonious relationship to those internalized object representations whose good will and love at one time represented the difference between life and death.
> (ARLOW, 1989, p. 160)

STOLOROW (1985) suggested that "superego and superego conflict originate in the child's perceptions of what is required of him to maintain the selfobject ties that are vital to his well-being" (p. 195). Often, one of the requirements is that the child has "to serve significant selfobject functions for his parents" (p. 195), functions that are more or less essential to *their* wellbeing and that may conflict with the child's "phase-appropriate strivings for individualized selfhood" and greater self-demarcation (phase-appropriate strivings that may be misconstrued by his parents as deliberately cruel and destructive towards them) (STOLOROW, 1985, p. 196). Persons may be unable to control their selfobject milieu joyfully or assertively due to a fear of rejection or hostile retaliation. Demands for narcissistic supplies then have to be made indirectly or passively, even passive-aggressively. Defence patterns, and the "concealed rage that is a regular part" of these patterns, are "methods of self-stabilization" (P. TOLPIN, 1986, p. 104).

The overriding need to maintain the narcissistic equilibrium (and to *defend* the self or ego against anxiety) keeps assertive and libidinal drives suppressed or forces them through more indirect channels, channels that are controlled by the superego. Alternatively, demands for narcissistic supplies have to be foregone in order to allow the expression of instinctual drives. Loss of love from the superego and consequential depression, unhappiness, or self-disintegration can be anticipated when drive-related behaviour is not curtailed. In neurotic patients, the superego allows gratification of inner wishes "in exchange for the bribe of depression, unhappiness and self-damage" (BERGLER, 1952, p. 23).

8.6.2 Inhibition and gigantic claims

Inhibition, the holding back of a drive entering into consciousness or action, is a common forestage of neurotic symptom formation (A. FREUD in SANDLER, 1985, p. 534). Drive inhibition forms the 'core' of any neurosis, according to SCHULTZ-HENKE (1951). The assertive or aggressive drive and the drive to express and expand oneself ('urethral drive') underpin strivings for social recognition and approval and for dominance and superiority; and either of these drives, or the libidinal drive (expressing tenderness and affection), may be inhibited pervasively in the neurotic personality structure. Under adverse circumstances in early development, spontaneous expression, by the child, of one of these drives or needs may be met repeatedly with rejection; or the drive may be satisfied only under stringent conditions (of obedience) or in an unpredictable or uncertain way (SCHULTZ-HENKE, 1951). Conditionality and uncertainty of maternal responses amount to 'harshness', which, if paired with hypersensitiveness (to punishment) or hyperactivity on part of the child, lead to an intensification of inhibitions that normally accompany any experience of drive or need. Inhibition of the assertive drive manifests in an inability to be self-assertive and a reluctance to assume a dominant and recognized social position. Inhibition of the expansive ('urethral') drive manifests in difficulties to show off or be impulsive without concern. Inhibition of abilities to induce appraising and cherishing (caring) behaviours in others towards oneself – behaviours that *confirm one's worth and security* – afflict many neurotic patients (SCHULTZ-HENKE, 1951). As

MONEY-KYRLE (1961) saw it, much of neurotic behaviour consists in ineffectual efforts to solicit others' praise or acknowledgement.

Inhibited drives remain latently active in terms of their potential to flow into conscious phenomena whenever this seems acceptable and tolerable to the subject (in 'tempting situations') (SCHULTZ-HENKE, 1951). Then, suppressed drives produce neurotic psychic phenomena and dispose to neurotic behaviours. These neurotic experiences and behaviours form the 'shell' of any neurosis. In addition, excessive inhibitions, born out of conflictual situations in childhood, lead to feelings of inferiority, which, in turn, foster reaction formations and overcompensations in the form of 'gigantic claims' (important constituents of the 'shell' of neurosis) (SCHULTZ-HENKE, 1951). 'Gigantic claims', being *conscious residuals or traces of suppressed experiences of drive or need* (experiences that were more fully expressed prior to their suppression in childhood), can be actualized in behaviour, which is when they would encounter resistance and punishment from the world (Figure 8.4). As a result, the relevant drive or need is suppressed further; and expectations in the form of gigantic claims are driven back to the margins of consciousness (SCHULTZ-HENKE, 1951).

8.6.3 Defeat and disillusionment

Neurotic persons, and to a lesser extent nonneurotic persons, "cling fast to their security", "which keeps them from being driven on towards defeat" (ADLER, 1938, p. 131). Lack of appreciation or a defeat or disappointment experienced in the realms of society, occupation, or love ("the three great problems of life" [p. 101]), that is, a setback "in accordance with the law of movement" (such as loss of property or employment) (p. 102), can be experienced as a 'shock' (a psychological trauma and, more particularly, a narcissistic injury). A shock can cause a "lasting sense of disappointment"

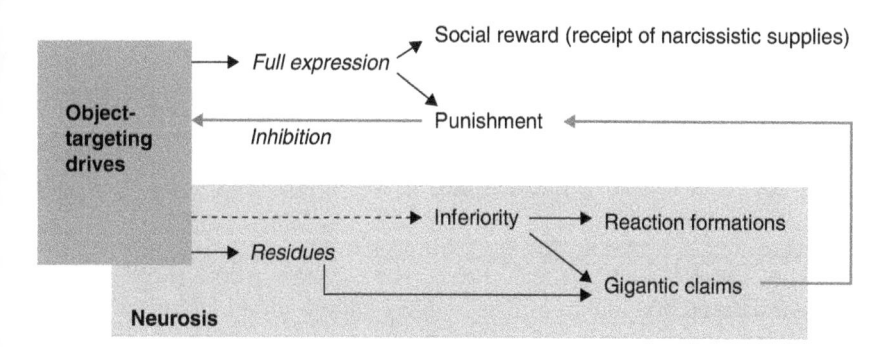

Figure 8.4 Inhibited and ineffectual approach to objects leads to narcissistic deficits and feelings of inferiority, which are overcompensated by gigantic claims, which, if translated into actions, expose to further punishment and reinforce inhibitions

and a "fear of fresh disappointments and defeats" (ADLER, 1938, p. 100). Having experienced shock and been defeated (and having glimpsed their sense of worthlessness), neurotic persons may remain in a state of "fear of being unmasked in all their worthlessness" (p. 125). Neurotic persons "are standing before a deep abyss and are afraid of being pushed into it – i.e. afraid that their worthlessness is going to be revealed" (p. 125). Insofar as they are "in danger of having their worthlessness revealed", they "cannot be induced to take a single step forwards" (ADLER, 1938, p. 125). If the shock "develops into a chronic condition", the person "suspiciously avoids all personal intimacy" (p. 123); "after being rejected once", he makes "no further advances" (p. 124). Disillusionment, owing to the persistence of a state of shock, brings the person "to a position of isolation" (p. 124). Persistent "shyness and embarrassment" prevent the person "from coming into closer contact with others" (ADLER, 1938, p. 123).

ADLER (1938) thought that what is of central importance in neurosis is "the hypersensitivity of the neurotic person" (p. 120). Hypersensitivity renders the neurotic person vulnerable to experiencing 'shock' (Figure 8.5). Some people have, and have had from their childhood, "a high degree of susceptibility to shock" (p. 102). A person is prone to experiencing shock (narcissistic injury), and he is more likely to remain in this state, if "he advances only on condition of being successful in everything he attempts", and if he "has not acquired a sufficient degree of co-operative ability" (p. 124). The effects of shock are "less for the courageous than for the cowardly", and they "are greater for people who have been badly prepared" in their earliest childhood, who did not develop their social interest because they were pampered or neglected (ADLER, 1938, p. 128).

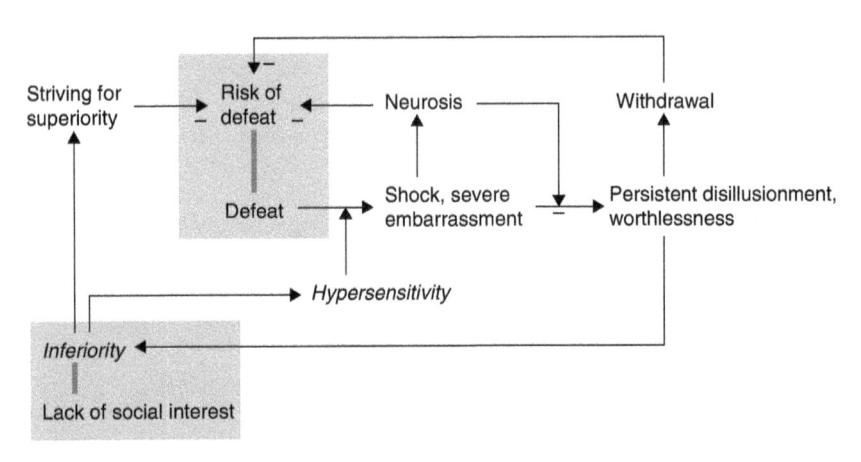

Figure 8.5 Role of hypersensitivity (to rejection) and shock (narcissistic injury) in ADLER's model of neurosis. Hypersensitivity to rejection is "an expression of the feeling of inferiority" (ADLER, 1938, p. 121)

Neurotic patients protect themselves "from the collapse of their self-esteem and pride" "by intensifying the physical and psychical shock-symptoms that have resulted from the impact of a problem that threatened them with defeat" (ADLER, 1938, p. 130). In their neurosis, patients automatically and unknowingly exploit "symptoms resulting from the effects of a shock" (p. 135), whereby it "is more feasible for those who have a great dread of losing prestige" to exploit the symptoms of shock in this way (p. 135). Neurotic persons "prefer their present suffering to the greater ones they would experience were they to appear defeated" and were they to "have their worthlessness revealed" (pp. 124–5). Neurotic persons hold on to their symptoms and neurotic suffering because "they are more afraid of something else: of being proved worthless"; they are afraid that "the sinister secret – the fact that they are worthless – might come to light" (ADLER, 1938, p. 125).

8.6.4 Social fears and social neurosis

Stuttering when speaking in public, erythrophobia, stage fright, and other social fears are "built on the basis of inhibited exhibitionistic impulses" (FENICHEL, 1946, p. 316). When speaking in public or "in the presence of persons of authority", "the reaction of the audience is needed for a reassurance against castration anxiety or as a satisfaction of some narcissistic need";[14] however, the orator may feel that it is unacceptable to seek reassurance in this way, or he may fear that his performance could "actually bring about [his] castration" (p. 316). Anticipation of "serious consequences from a failure" would result in inhibition of exhibitionism, manifesting in *stuttering* (FENICHEL, 1946, p. 316). Similarly, *agoraphobia*, the fear of open streets, represents an unconscious fear that the subject will be rejected for exhibiting himself. Erythrophobia and stage fright are based on an unconscious "idea that what is done to protect the person's self-esteem against danger may result in the opposite, in his complete annihilation" (FENICHEL, 1946, p. 201).[15]

Social anxiety disorder, which is characterized by "constant fear of being criticized, ostracized, or punished", is related to "the child's fear of castration or loss of love and the adult's bad conscience" (FENICHEL, 1946, p. 518). The danger feared by the patient with social neurosis is, according to SCHILDER (1951), indistinct. When the patient becomes sure of the hostility of others, or when he blames others, rather than himself, social anxiety disappears and outspoken paranoia emerges. Erythrophobia and stammering are related to (but not identical with) social neurosis (SCHILDER, 1951).

---

[14] Public speaking has the aim of "magically influencing an audience by means of omnipotent words" (FENICHEL, 1946, p. 316).

[15] In the closely related fear of examinations, "an authority, an external representative of the superego, is about to decide whether one is accepted and permitted to participate in certain privileges, that is, to obtain the narcissistic supplies, or whether one is rejected and sentenced to isolation and narcissistic hunger" (FENICHEL, 1946, p. 201).

The fear of being seen or observed by others and a resulting paranoid attitude play a greater part in erythrophobia than in social neurosis. In stammering, the patient's counteraggression comes into the foreground; whereby speech "becomes the weapon which the patient would like to use" (p. 90). In social neurosis, symptoms of shaking, sweating, and dryness of mouth as well as the giving way of the voice serve to deny (unconsciously) that aggressive action (including 'oral aggression') is intended; instead, "the superiority of the other person is acknowledged" (p. 93). Inhibition of social conduct, a characteristic feature of social anxiety, occurs especially "in the presence of specific persons socially or professionally superior" (SCHILDER, 1951, p. 77).

> He wants everybody's admiration and appreciation. Sensitiveness and irritability may follow, and harmless remarks may provoke the full impression of complete rejection. A reactive hostile reaction follows in some cases, but this is comparatively rare. The symptoms will multiply in proportion to the number of individuals present. Persons who otherwise do not show symptoms of this type when faced by an audience may show symptoms of stage fright in which the speech phenomena and forgetting or inability to think clearly are outstanding.
> (SCHILDER, 1951, p. 93)

> In many cases the shyness leads to a more or less complete blocking. The patient may be unable to clearly formulate any thoughts and may remain silent against his will. The patient may also prefer to remain silent instead of saying banal and unimportant things.
> (SCHILDER, 1951, p. 77)

The longing for love (narcissism) and fear of loss of love are of paramount importance in the pathogenesis and psychodynamics of social anxiety disorder ('social neurosis') (SCHILDER, 1951). Normally, the individual's self-appreciation or self-love (self-admiration) is dependent not only upon "a continuous stream of appreciation coming from other human beings" (p. 91) but also "upon the appreciation given by early love objects" (p. 94). The child "builds up the consciousness of itself by the love and appreciation it gets from its surroundings" (SCHILDER, 1951, p. 91) (i.e., he builds up good internal objects acting as internal sources of self-esteem). If, due to adverse infantile experiences (selfobject failures, in KOHUT's terminology), "demands for self-appreciation" are heightened, "the amount of appreciation offered in social contacts will become insufficient" (SCHILDER, 1951, p. 91). Social neurosis first manifests at the time of puberty, "when the individual demands not only social but also sexual recognition and finds that he cannot get them in full measure" (p. 92). As the socially anxious individual "becomes dependent upon the social surroundings which take the place of the parents", his "exaggerated infantile demands concerning recognition in the widest sense are no longer satisfied" (SCHILDER, 1951, p. 92).

> Self-appreciation can only be sustained when supported by the continuous approval of others. The appreciation of others becomes insufficient in this respect when the individual demands from himself an extraordinarily high degree of self-admiration and self-love.
> (SCHILDER, 1951, p. 94)

Socially anxious individuals, "whose self-esteem still depends on their getting external supplies", are unable to "endure a state of not being loved" or of being regarded with indifference; they "long to be loved", but "their fear of losing the affection of others is so great that they even fear losing an affection they never had" (FENICHEL, 1946, p. 519). The patient with social neurosis has "the ideal of having poise and social grace" (SCHILDER, 1951, p. 93). He has strong wishes for beauty or intelligence and harbours a "fear of an impairment of attractiveness or narcissism of a high degree" (p. 82). He is concerned that others might consider him unattractive or intellectually inferior; and his concerns about inferiority are often increased as a result of his inadequacy in social situations. He may avoid all situations in which he "has to meet other persons and especially groups" (p. 78), yet even when social contact is avoided, "the patient is usually surrounded by an imaginary society in which he lives intensely" (SCHILDER, 1951, p. 93).

Socially anxious individuals, in order to make their social environment well disposed towards them (i.e., control their selfobject milieu), have to be constantly submissive and energetically suppress all aggressive strivings (FENICHEL, 1946, p. 520). Patients with social neurosis are unable to control or dominate others (fearing their retaliation). Due to their inhibitions, patients also find it difficult to actively solicit appreciation or affection from others. SCHILDER (1951) noted that the position adopted by these patients in social situations is a passive one. In childhood, they may have been "pushed into a passive position" by their "parents' strictness and aggressiveness" (SCHILDER, 1951, p. 91).

8.6.5 Compulsions

The ambivalence that "plays such a decisive part in obsessional (compulsive) neurosis" (p. 50) betrays, as BERGLER (1949) proposed, a "constant fight between *active-progressive*, and *passive-regressive* tendencies" (p. 49). Obsessional ambivalence is a state of "being drawn towards inner passivity and fighting against it with 'autarchic' fantasies" (p. 58). The obsessional neurotic seeks to autarchically preserve his narcissism "[b]y changing the role of the passively victimized into that of the active bearer of a doubt" ("some 'activity'!") (p. 58). Magical thought, too, supports autarchic fantasies. The obsessional neurotic confirms his "omnipotence of thought" by effecting "guided miracles" (p. 57). It appears to him that "an external fate" enacts "his own omnipotence"; his observations provide "proof that he is beloved by fate, and therefore has power over it" (p. 58). He thus attains "narcissistic gratification" (BERGLER, 1949, p. 58).

According to BERGLER (1949), 'pseudoaggressiveness' ('neurotic aggression') is used "as a defence against the inner passivity of these patients"; "their exaggerated aggressiveness conceals the very opposite attitude" (p. 74). Their pseudoaggression (neurotic aggression) covers "but deeper repressed psychic masochism" (p. 77); it is "often used to provoke 'masochistic pleasure' expected from enemy's retaliation" (BERGLER, 1949, p. 78). 'Psychic masochism', which is associated with 'oral regression' and passivity, provides a means for counteracting the superego's cruelty (BERGLER, 1952). There is another way of keeping an excessively severe and demanding superego at bay. BERGLER (1949) referred to ALEXANDER who pointed out that the ego attains independence and breaks off "its moral dependence on the superego" (p. 54) by reducing the demands of the superego ad absurdum, that is, "by means of arousing the superego to unjust demands" (p. 54) ("by teasing the superego" [p. 58]). Compulsive behaviours have to be crude in order to effectively reduce the demands of the superego ad absurdum. The obsessional neurotic not only defends "against a too strict superego" but also attains "great narcissistic gratification" "by means of this obsessional check-mating of the superego" (BERGLER, 1949, p. 55).

8.6.6 Hypochondriasis

SCHILDER (1976) regarded narcissistic libido as "the libido directed toward one's own body" (p. 14). FEDERN's (1952) position, by contrast, is that narcissistic libido is invested in objects, which however, if they satisfy narcissistic libido, are not true objects, but selfobjects, in KOHUT's terminology. Hypochondriasis is classically considered as overcathexis of an organ with narcissistic libido. SCHILDER (1976) pointed out that the part of the body that produces the hypochondriac's symptoms is often the one "that was given particular attention by love objects" (p. 42). Bearing in mind also that the hypochondriac's symptoms may reflect similar symptoms that "have been seen in a love object", SCHILDER (1976) concluded that "the hypochondriac organ is an organ that has been and still is in particular lively contact with the surroundings" (p. 42). Thus, hypochondriasis may be linked with narcissism insofar as hypochondriacal symptoms express frustrations in the control of selfobjects and aid solicitation of narcissistic sustenance.

Hypochondriasis can be regarded as a 'state of heightened narcissistic-exhibitionistic tension', which arises when discharge of exhibitionistic impulses is incomplete or aberrant (due to insufficient modification of the 'narcissistic self' in early personality development) (KOHUT, 1966). The failure to relieve narcissistic tensions, to control selfobjects and meet narcissistic needs, is tantamount to diffuse anxiety. Diffuse anxiety that accompanies self-fragmentation (disintegration anxiety) at times of impending separation from a selfobject, such as the analyst, flows into hypochondriacal worries, preoccupations with "various physical sensations" and "minor physical defects" (KOHUT, 1977, pp. 155–6). Patients with a narcissistic personality disorder respond to minor disappointments or rebuffs with profound anxiety; a feeling of fragmentation of the body arises, resulting in hypochondriacal worries about health (KOHUT & WOLF, 1978). If, subsequently to having suffered a narcissistic injury, the patient senses the analyst's empathic attention, these worries disappear, and the patient feels whole and self-accepting again (KOHUT & WOLF, 1978).

8.6.7 Alexithymia and somatization

Patients with psychosomatic disorders often show "a paucity of affective description and intrapsychic awareness", "a deficiency in usage of affective words", called alexithymia (RICKLES, 1986, p. 214). These patients "describe their lives in pragmatic, functional terms without reference to emotion, fantasy, and intrapsychic or interpersonal meaning" (p. 214). They tend to use "pronouns such as 'it', 'one', or even 'you' ... instead of 'I'", and bodily parts are not owned but referred to impersonally (p. 215).[16] Patients with alexithymia "relate to others in rather rigid, emotionally stunted, nonempathic ways"; their "capacity for empathic experiencing of objects" is missing (RICKLES, 1986, p. 215).

There are similarities between alexithymia and narcissistic personality disorders (RICKLES, 1986). In both alexithymia and narcissistic personality disorders, "dependency on others for maintenance of psychological and/or psychophysiological equilibrium" is *consciously* denied (p. 213). Patients with narcissistic disorders, when they experience self-fragmentation and anxiety, are prone to hypochondria; alexithymia predisposes to 'psychosomatic breakdown' (somatization) under similar conditions. In patients with alexithymia, somatization is a common response to narcissistic injury; "the characteristic hypersensitivity of narcissistic personality disorders to personal slights, humiliations, and disappointments is not expressed in the usual way but is channeled into nonverbal, somatised behavior" (p. 215). Alexithymia can be regarded as "a self disorder that utilizes development of somatic symptoms as a major mode of dealing with permanent or temporary enfeeblement of the self" (p. 220). Psychophysiological regression, "in which somatisation of affect is a major mode of response", is coupled with "demands for dependency" (RICKLES, 1986, p. 219).

Patients with psychosomatic disorders, as well as those with narcissistic disorders, suffer from "a deficiency in self care and self-soothing"; they

---

[16] Moreover, there is "an absence of daydreams and fantasy"; and these patients "seldom remember their dreams" (RICKLES, 1986, pp. 214–15).

presume that "such caretaking activities are the providence of the primal maternal object and she alone" (RICKLES, 1986, p. 216). These patients remain dependent "on others or selfobjects to carry out soothing and self-esteem regulating functions" (p. 218). They may have experienced, in their childhood, "individuation of their body from the mother" with "intense annihilation anxiety", possibly as a reflection of their mother having felt "threatened by the child investing soothing capability into the teddy bear or blanket" (WINNICOTT's [1953] 'transitional object') (RICKLES, 1986, p. 217).

8.6.8 Conversions and dissociations

Drive impulses arouse anxiety insofar as they are socially inacceptable and hence consciously unbearable, that is, insofar as they threaten the narcissistic homeostasis and the integrity of the self (i.e., insofar as they are in *conflict* with the 'principle of self-preservation'). Intolerable (egodystonic) impulses or ideas can be 'converted' into behavioural, functional, or somatic symptoms (LAUGHLIN, 1970). Transforming an inacceptable and consciously unbearable impulse or idea into a conversion symptom renders the impulse or idea innocuous (egosyntonic). The purpose of conversion is to allay anxiety and to secure some resolution of or relief from unconscious conflict. Conversion allows "the return to consciousness of elements of the conflict ... in a converted and disguised form" (p. 51). Conversion symptoms "allow some measure of disguised external expression" and hence partial gratification of disowned impulses (p. 31). Conversion symptoms *convey a message*, in that they express unconscious impulses and resulting conflicts in symbolic form.[17] While the 'primary gain' associated with conversion is the defence against anxiety (and hence maintenance of self-esteem), there may be a 'secondary gain' for the patient in terms of material advantage or fulfilment of dependency needs (LAUGHLIN, 1970) (affording a *secondary increase* in self-esteem).

Consciously disowned impulses and unconscious conflict over them can be transmuted, for instance, into loss of sensory or motor function (LAUGHLIN, 1970). Paralysis of a limb, loss of the ability to speak (aphonia), functional loss of vision, and other neurological symptoms may be intended to express an intolerable impulse in a consciously more tolerable form and "to secure a position of dependency" at the same time (p. 43). Similarly, in somatoform disorders, hostility can be converted into headaches and other somatic symptoms, whereby *emotional* pain is concurrently converted into the experience of *bodily* pain. Finally, consciously disowned impulses can be

---

[17] Elucidation, in psychotherapy, of the unconscious meaning of the symptom "results in the surrender of the symptom, as it becomes more patently an inappropriate means of attempted solution" of unconscious conflict (p. 36). Maintenance of the patient's self-esteem is a necessary prerequisite for the gradual relinquishing of conversion symptoms through therapy (LAUGHLIN, 1970).

converted into symbolic *behaviour* and thus expressed in a consciously more acceptable form, again allowing for a partial resolution of emotional conflict over them. 'Behavioural conversion' is the expression of intrapsychic conflict in the form of 'acting out' (neurotic behaviour). Patients who 'act out' "may express significant hostile or loving feelings in some self-concealed and disguised form of outward action" (p. 39). Behavioural conversion may be motivated by "inner insecurity, and inferiority and by the need for approval and love" (LAUGHLIN, 1970, p. 41).

8.7 Depression

Mourning is a reaction to object loss. A person in mourning may psychically prolong the existence of the object and even cling to the object through 'hallucinatory wishful psychosis' (FREUD, 1917). Melancholia, too, is a reaction to object loss, but, in contrast to mourning, object loss is hidden from consciousness, that is, the loss is unknown to the patient. Both conditions have in common a temporary loss of the capacity to adopt a new object of love. Melancholia differs from mourning, in that a *lowering of self-regard* is present in the former but not the latter condition (FREUD, 1917). Moreover, instead of there being "shame in front of other people", the melancholic shows "an almost opposite trait of insistent communicativeness which finds satisfaction in self-exposure" (p. 247). The melancholic patient exposes himself to others as "morally despicable"; he "vilifies himself and expects to be cast out and punished"; he "abases himself before everyone" (FREUD, 1917). The patient not only feels worthless but crucially presents himself as such. Through submissiveness, in displaying his worthlessness, the patient unconsciously hopes to redeem himself and become *worthy* again of others' love and attention (narcissistic sustenance). Furthermore, in consequence of an identification of the patient's ego with the lost object, the patient *unconsciously* punishes the lost object when he *consciously* depreciates himself. Ambivalence and hate come into operation and make this substitutive object suffer, thereby taking revenge on the original object (FREUD, 1917).

Melancholia breaks out after "an object cathected with libido has been lost", or "after *a disappointment in love* in the broadest sense of the word" has been suffered (NUNBERG, 1955, p. 143). A person is likely to become melancholic following the loss of love, if he is "very narcissistic", being unable to "endure the injury to his self-esteem", and if he has "an excessively severe superego" (p. 143). It is because of the person's ambivalence towards his objects (as characteristically associated with narcissistic object choice) and because of his disposition to 'narcissistic identification' (absorption of the object into the ego) that he gives up (and condemns) the object and, at the same time, identifies with it (NUNBERG, 1955). The excessively severe superego directs its aggression "against the formerly loved person, with whom the ego of the melancholic has become one through identification" (p. 143). This manifests as self-reproaches (NUNBERG, 1955).[18]

8.7.1 Loss of self-esteem

Narcissistic supplies are needed to regulate self-esteem. In persons whose object choice is of a narcissistic type, object loss or loss of another vital source of narcissistic sustenance (a source of love, admiration, approval) precipitates a fall in self-esteem. NUNBERG (1955) reported to "have seen melancholia set in after professional disappointments or after the patient had had to give up an aim to which he had devoted his entire life" (p. 144). A person can become melancholic in response to such disappointments (injuries to his narcissism or self-esteem), if he "has, on the whole, loose object relations", so that "the demands of his ideals are exaggerated" (NUNBERG, 1955, p. 144). In those who are prone to narcissistic object choice, self-esteem tends to be weak, and overvalued ideals or pursuits fulfil a vital function in regulating their narcissistic homeostasis.

RADO (1928) thought that the most striking feature of depressive conditions is "the fall in self-esteem and self-satisfaction" (p. 48). FENICHEL (1946), too, argued that loss of self-esteem plays a central role in depression (p. 391). A person is at risk of becoming depressed if he "is fixated on the state where his self-esteem is regulated by external supplies" (or he may become depressed when his "guilt feelings motivate him to regress to this state") (p. 387). Narcissistic supplies, "which the patient had hoped would secure or even enhance his self-esteem", are lost in consequence of "failures, loss of prestige, loss of money", the assignment of a task that would "make him more aware of his "inferiority", or "a disappointment in love or the death of a love partner" (pp. 390–1). Loss of self-esteem, due to a loss of external narcissistic supplies (or "due to a loss of internal supplies from the superego" – in consequence of loss of prestige or money) (FENICHEL, 1946, p. 391), precipitates depression. The clinical picture that unfolds, depression, can be described "as a great despairing cry for love" (RADO, 1956, p. 46), for narcissistic nourishment.

Critically, what can bring about depression (melancholia) is not just loss of an object but also "a reduction in the person's apparent loveworthiness" (FLUGEL, 1945, p. 95) (self-esteem). If depression is caused by a reduction in loveworthiness, the patient loses narcissistic supplies not from a concrete object (being a derivative of the primary maternal object) but from the superego or its external representatives (whereby the superego is in itself a derivative of the primary maternal object). Loss of love from the superego

---

[18] Self-reproaches and self-accusations are also characteristic of compulsive neurosis; however, the compulsive neurotic, "despite his pronounced ambivalence, never completely gives up his object" (NUNBERG, 1955, p. 144).

is linked with failure to meet the standards of the ego ideal. Melancholia can be regarded as an extreme and pathological case of self-dissatisfaction that arises when standards of the ego ideal cannot be met (FLUGEL, 1945), when the self does not live up to the expectations of the inner representative of the parents, when the self is not worthy any longer of the approval of the superego *and is inescapably subject to its disapproval.* Correspondingly, the patient suffering from melancholia "often accuses himself of many and unpardonable crimes, while the 'voice of conscience' may be heard by him in the form of hallucinated words of reproach or abuse whispered in his ear" (p. 54). It is the superego that, by way of projection, "appears as the accusing voice" (FLUGEL, 1945, p. 55).

8.7.2 Precarious self

At the heart of melancholia, there is an incapacity for love (for making libidinal investments in objects). Object choice by persons predisposed to melancholia "conforms to the narcissistic type" (FREUD, 1917). In other words, "passive narcissistic aims prevail in their object-relations" (RADO, 1928, p. 49). Persons predisposed to melancholic depression are "unable to love actively"; they "passively need to be loved" (p. 387); they "need the feeling of being loved" (and, without it, they "lose their very existence") (FENICHEL, 1946, p. 391). Persons predisposed to depression "have not attained to the level of independence where self-esteem has its foundation in the subject's own achievements", so that they remain "wholly reliant and dependent on other people for maintaining their self-esteem" (RADO, 1928, pp. 48–9). They increase their self-respect predominantly by "attracting to themselves narcissistic gratification from *without*" (p. 49). Persons predisposed to depression feel secure "only when they feel themselves loved, esteemed, supported and encouraged"; "their self-esteem largely depends on whether they do or do not meet with approbation and recognition" (p. 49). Persons predisposed to depression "are never weary of courting the favour" of their objects "and seeking for evidences of love from them" (RADO, 1928, p. 49). Being dependent on their objects for their narcissistic needs, they nevertheless "tend to change objects frequently because no object is able to provide the necessary satisfaction" (FENICHEL, 1946, p. 387).

MILLER (1979) reported that patients who suffered from depression were often exposed in their childhood to insecure mothers or mothers who themselves suffered from depression. The insecurity of these mothers meant that they (the mothers) had to use their children for the purpose of making themselves feel valued; they had to use their children to satisfy their own narcissistic needs. Other patients with depression were brought up in families that were excessively concerned with their prestige established and maintained in their communities though conformity and outstanding achievements (MILLER, 1979). If children are not loved for who they are, but if, instead, they are admired or approved by their parents only for their qualities or performances, especially for those qualities or performances that allow their parents to feel valued themselves or to be highly regarded in their communities, then the self-esteem of these children remains dependent on others' admiration and approval throughout their lives. They experience a *loss of self* later in life when others' admiration or approval cannot be obtained. Loss or disintegration of the self, in turn, can lead to depression characterized by feelings of emptiness, futility, and loneliness (MILLER, 1979).

> People who are liable to severe depressive reactions find difficulty in personal relations because they are ultimately looking for something which they should have had in infancy from their mothers, and which it is impossible for them to obtain in an adult relationship. ... They hate those whom they love since they cannot get from them what they really need, and since they dare not to show this hate for fear of losing even that which they have, they turn it inwards against themselves in self-torment and despair.
>
> (STORR, 1968, pp. 80–1)

8.7.3 Concealed grandiosity

Grandiosity is a defence against and the counterpart of depression; depression, as a manifestation of the loss of self, is constantly lurking behind grandiosity (MILLER, 1979). Grandiosity is an expression of excessive dependence on others' admiration, reflecting the persistence of primitive needs for mirroring and for being seen and understood by the maternal object and, ultimately, reflecting the persistence of fears of abandonment. The grandiose individual feels compelled to fulfil the expectations of the introjected mother, lest he sees himself as a failure and faces abandonment by the disappointed mother. Depression ensues when grandiosity breaks down, when sources of narcissistic supplies have dried up. Analysts often discern unconscious or split-off grandiosity behind their patients' depression (MILLER, 1979). Once grandiosity has been reestablished, the patient emerges from depression; however, he may continue to cycle through alternating phases of grandiosity and depression. The risk of depression can be reduced, if the grandiose individual can maintain an illusion of constant attention and admiration from his selfobjects by continuous outstanding achievements attributable to his brilliance or excessive perfectionism. On a deeper level, both grandiosity and outstanding achievements salvage the illusion of availability of the primary selfobject (MILLER, 1979).

JOFFE and SANDLER (1965) regarded depression as a reaction to psychic pain, to pain that is caused by a discrepancy between the actual self and the 'ideal self', which, in those prone to depression, is often a grandiose self. Such discrepancy signals a danger of loss of love, of narcissistic impoverishment of the self. The 'ideal self' reflects early expectations, towards the child, of the

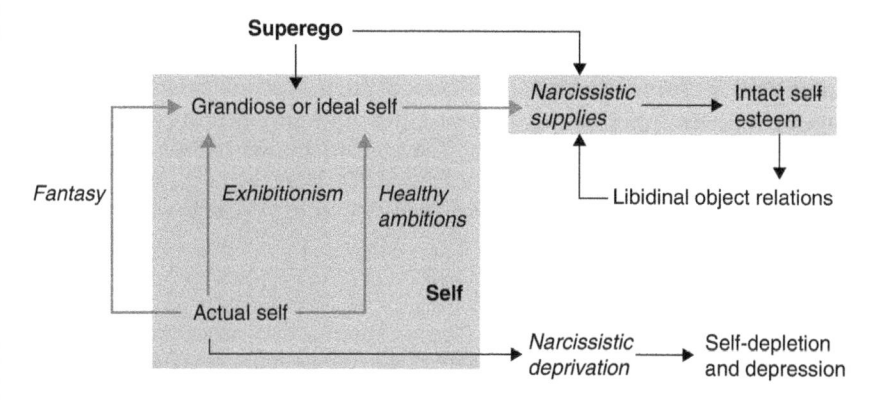

```
                Superego ─────────┐
                    │             ↓
        ┌──→ Grandiose or ideal self ──→  Narcissistic ────→ Intact self
        │        ↑         ↑              supplies            esteem
        │        │         │                 ↑                  │
Fantasy │   Exhibitionism  Healthy           └── Libidinal object relations
        │                  ambitions
        │        ↑
        │        │         Self
        └── Actual self ────┐
                            └─────────→  Narcissistic ────→ Self-depletion
                                         deprivation        and depression
```

Figure 8.6 Intact self-esteem and confident expectation of narcissistic supplies can be established, firstly, in consequence of healthy (libidinal) object relations or, secondly, through attainment, in fantasy or reality, of the 'ideal self'. Only the second mechanism is available to those who are prone to depression (whose object choice tends to be narcissistic)

primary objects, on whose approval and love the child's sense of wellbeing depended. Wellbeing is experienced when the actual self measures up to the 'ideal self', when exhibitionistic performances meet the expectations of the omnipotent object. Conversely, when the actual self does not live up to the standards of the ideal self, especially when these standards are defined by a grandiose self, pain and depression ensue, unless grandiosity can attract narcissistic supplies in fantasy (Figure 8.6). What protects against depression is authentic self-esteem, that is, self-esteem that is not based on the possession of admirable qualities, on qualities that tend to be embellished in grandiose fantasy (MILLER, 1979).

8.7.4 Hopelessness

Hopelessness expresses a lack of hope of ever becoming worthy of others' praise and affections without having to put up pretences; it is a lack of hope of ever being able to gain others' recognition or affection by one's spontaneous actions, by simply being oneself. Hopelessness is related to the despair of not being one's true self (HORNEY, 1945, p. 183). Hopelessness has "its deepest roots in the despair of ever being wholehearted and undivided" (i.e., of always remaining entangled in conflicts and divided between the true self and an idealized image). Attempts at the solution of neurotic conflicts fail and "increasingly alienate the person from himself" (p. 184), increasingly make him live the life of his idealized image. Hopelessness increases in consequence of inevitable failures in the "hopeless enterprise of trying to measure up to the idealized image", "when the patient becomes aware that he is far from being the uniquely perfect person he sees in his imagination"

(p. 184). Realization by the patient of his worthlessness, when it cannot be externalized or covered up with deeper entanglement in conflicts, causes manifest hopelessness, lack of hope of "ever attaining anything, whether in love or in work" (p. 184). Any minor failure or harmless critical remark, if "it proves his general unworthiness", "may set him worrying or brooding" and "plunge him into a depression" (p. 179). Hopelessness, according to HORNEY (1945), "is the deeper source from which the depressions emanate" (p. 188).[19]

8.7.5 Narcissistic object control

Patients with depression *unconsciously* experience a sense of failure in relation to one particular person in their immediate environment: the 'dominant other' (ARIETI, 1973). The dominant other could be regarded as a derivative of the unconscious omnipotent object. The 'dominant other', with whom the patient "is in a relation of dependency", "is symbolic of the mother, as she appeared to the patient in very early childhood" (ARIETI, 1973, p. 129) (it is also an external replica of the superego). The depressed patient "is always afraid of losing or of having already lost what she needs from this dominant figure: love, affection, praise, admiration, approval, a precious supply of intangible things that only he can give" (ARIETI, 1973, p. 129). Persons who are prone to depression (or those who have learned in childhood that to be good and accepted is to be weak and helpless) respond to threats or anxiety by placing significant others in a care-taking role. The patient who is severely depressed forces others to take over basic care-taking functions by being unable to perform basic tasks of self-maintenance. Others in the patient's environment are "drawn into a relationship in which they are asked to provide things that only a mother could reasonably be asked to provide" (CASHDAN, 1988, p. 63). 'Projective identification of dependency', which may be reinforced by statements of suicidal intent, is used to reconstitute the early infant–caregiver relationship. On the other hand, depression can arise if projective identifications aiming to induce care-giving behaviour in others and to thereby maintain self-esteem are frustrated (CASHDAN, 1988). Then, more desperate means are required to induce care-giving responses in others and restore self-esteem.

Depression has defensive and manipulative aspects; it "is a complex way of simultaneously acting angrily, fearfully, self-punitively, even protectively or lovingly" (SCHAFER, 1976, p. 349). The depressed patient is "attempting in these and other ways to regulate both self-esteem and relationships with others" (p. 350). He protects "loved ones from directly destructive actions"

---

[19] Pervasive hopelessness can manifest as "easy discouragement in the face of difficulty" or "ready emergence of suicidal thoughts – with or without affect" (HORNEY, 1945, p. 181). Hopelessness in neurosis may be "deeply buried" (HORNEY, 1945, p. 180). Neurosis is latent depression.

and interacts with them "lovingly" insofar as they support his "precarious self-esteem" and provide him with narcissistic sustenance (p. 350); and he interacts "with them hatefully, even to the extent of wishing them dead, insofar as they do not relate to [him] in the way [he] desire[s]" (p. 350). When *reproaching himself*, the patient is "simultaneously reproaching these others as well, so that secretly it is [his] esteem for them as well as self-esteem that is at stake" (SCHAFER, 1976, p. 350).

The patient reproaches himself for not having attained the parental ideal, which, in childhood, granted him access to parental approval (and, later, that of the superego). Depression arises when self-esteem cannot be maintained, because expectations of the 'dominant other', which were internalized in childhood (as parental ideals), have not been lived up to (ARIETI, 1973). Failing to meet the expectations of the 'dominant other', "the patient feels deprived of love, affection, admiration" (p. 129). At the same time, he feels "guilty for not having met these expectations"; and this "guilt confers to the depression the particular self-blaming aspect" (ARIETI, 1973, p. 129).

Claiming depression

ARIETI (1973) differentiated between 'self-blaming depression' (characterized by prominent self-accusations and guilt feelings) and 'claiming depression'. In 'claiming depression', the patient's symptoms seem to signify his *need for pity* and an expectation for *and demand on* others to relieve his suffering. Even the suicidal attempt or statement is an appeal to others and an attempt to attribute to others a power to prevent his death. The person who is prone to 'claiming depression' "did not necessarily try to obtain gratification or fulfilment through her own efforts", but obtained gratification and fulfilment "by receiving support, praise, admiration from others, especially from the dominant other" (ARIETI, 1973, p. 130). The person prone to 'blaming depression', by contrast, is more concerned with meeting internalized expectations of the 'dominant other'. The person prone to 'claiming depression' "is not able to transform an important part of the interpersonal into the intrapsychic" (p. 130). Therefore, she "must depend on interpersonal contacts for gratification"; and even if she praises herself, she would do so "only after she has been admired by others" (p. 130). Thus, the patient suffering from 'claiming depression' "needs an external agent from whom to extract praise and approval" (ARIETI, 1973, p. 130). Ultimately, both conceptualizations, self-blaming depression and claiming depression, highlight the underlying narcissistic vulnerability.

Aggression

Persons who are predisposed to depression tend to show "an intensely strong craving for narcissistic gratification and a very considerable narcissistic intolerance", in that "even to trivial offences and disappointments they immediately react with a fall in their self-esteem" (RADO, 1928, p. 48). When suffering a narcissistic injury, they "recover their self-respect only in complete dependence on their love-objects" (p. 49). They control their object with "tenacity"; they accept their object's devoted love "with a sublime nonchalance, as a matter of course, and become more and more domineering and autocratic, displaying an increasingly unbridled egoism, until their attitude becomes one of full-blown tyranny" (p. 49). Ultimately, "they react with embittered vehemence ... to the threat of withdrawal of love and ... feel the final loss of the object of their tormenting love to be the greatest injustice in the world" (RADO, 1928, p. 49).

If a person who is disposed to depression cannot satisfy his narcissistic needs and becomes fearful about "being abandoned by the superego" (the omnipotent object) (p. 389), then "his self-esteem diminishes to a danger point" (p. 387), and, in relation to the external object world, he makes "desperate attempts to force an object to give the vitally necessary supplies" (FENICHEL, 1946, p. 389). He may react to the frustration of his narcissistic needs with aggression. Neurotically depressed patients, and even those who are psychotically depressed, are prone to accuse their objects of not loving them and to behave aggressively towards them (p. 392). Alternatively, they may try and get vital narcissistic supplies by way of ingratiation and submissiveness. Condensation of aggressiveness and ingratiation (or submissiveness) lies at the heart of many depressive attitudes (p. 387). Patients frequently "try to captivate their objects in a way characteristic for masochistic characters, by demonstrating their misery and by accusing the objects of having brought about this misery, and by enforcing and even blackmailing their objects for affection" (p. 391). Despite their submissive and ingratiating attitude, these patients are "actually often successful in dominating [their] environment" (FENICHEL, 1946, p. 392).

8.7.6 Self-contempt

Having realized that the patient with melancholia, but not the person in mourning, characteristically depreciates himself, FREUD (1917) was "faced with a contradiction that represents a problem which is hard to solve": "The analogy with mourning led us to conclude that he had suffered a loss in regard to an object; what he tells us points to a loss in regard to his ego" (p. 247). Firstly, FREUD (1917) reasoned, self-depreciation manifests a split in the ego. It is the patient's 'critical agency', his conscience, that is "split off from the ego"; the critical agency sets itself above the ego, critically judging it. Secondly, the patient's self-reproaches are not "applicable to the patient himself, but ... with insignificant modifications they do fit someone else, someone whom the patient loves or has loved or should love"; they are "reproaches against a loved object which have been shifted away from it to the patient's own ego" (p. 248). What has taken place in the melancholic patient is a reversal to a primitive form of object relation, to identification, which is the first way in which the ego "picks out an object" (FREUD, 1917). The lost or disappointing object has been 'introjected' and *become identified with the ego*, so that the painful experience of loss can be avoided; however, hostility originally felt for the object is now directed against the ego (and attributed to the critical agency), explaining the characteristic self-reproaches of the melancholic (FREUD, 1917) (Figure 8.7).

The choice of a love object in those prone to melancholia is made on a narcissistic basis (FREUD, 1917). Object cathexis on a narcissistic basis is readily abandoned and regresses to *narcissistic identification with the object*. Object relationships established by those who are prone to melancholia are characterized by *ambivalence* towards the object (insofar as the object is narcissistically controlled and not loved in its own right). Those prone to melancholia have a greater intolerance for disappointments and react more readily with bitterness and anger to *withdrawal of love*. In melancholia, reproaches against the lost object are transformed into reproaches against the self. As a result of introjection (which is "the opposite of the defense mechanisms of projection") reproachable characteristics of the object are now "perceived in one's own ego instead" (FENICHEL, 1946, p. 397). The superego punishes the ego for these reproachable characteristics. The superego, which is another introjected object, turns against the ego-identified-with-the-object "with the same rage that this ego previously used in its struggle with the object" (FENICHEL, 1946, p. 393).

RADO (1928) found that the patient's self-reproaches, remorseful contrition, and confessions of guilt ("because by his aggressive attitude he has himself to blame for the loss of the object") may give way again to hostility directed against the object ("which has already shown its force in the

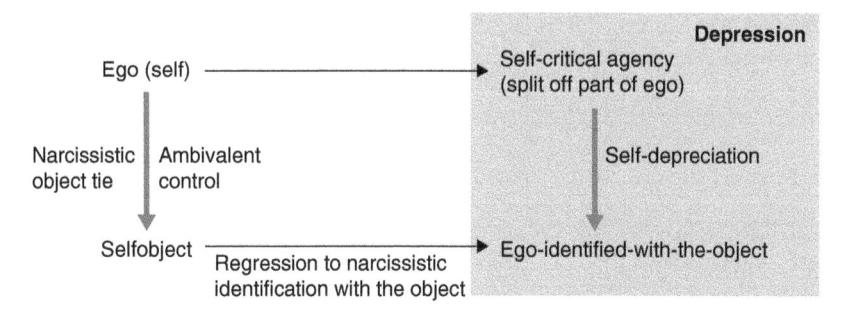

Figure 8.7 Self-reproaches are reproaches shifted away from the lost or disappointing object and directed at the patient's own ego (self), which has become identified with the object. A narcissistic style of object-relatedness is a precondition for melancholia

ambivalent character of the love-relation") (p. 55).[20] The patient comes to believe (unconsciously) "that the object alone was to blame" (p. 55). The constellation then reverts back to the one in which the ego "is thrust into the place of the hated object" (p. 56), so that "the super-ego visits upon the ego all the fury which the ego would otherwise have been capable of visiting upon the object" (p. 55); the ego "submits to the role of the object, takes upon itself the whole guilt of the object and suffers without resistance the cruelties of the super-ego" (RADO, 1928, p. 56).

According to MONEY-KYRLE (1961), self-reproaches and the sense of worthlessness that accompany depression may relate, firstly, "to a sense of incapacity for love" ("despair about not being able to love") and reflect, secondly, "complaints, probably unjust ones, directed at external figures – originally his parents – who are now felt to have been 'introjected' as part of himself, and to be, as it were, living on in him in a crushed and despairing state" (p. 20). Self-reproaches are derivatives of feelings of ambivalence felt towards early objects whose love could not be attained consistently. Self-reproaches may be an overshoot of a healthy form of aggression that is employed for the purpose of controlling the receipt of attention and care from the primary attachment figure. The patient undergoing psychoanalysis will uncover behind his sense of worthlessness "'memories in feeling' of the like way in which, in phantasy, he attacked his parents – as, at a still more primitive level, he attacked parental 'part-objects'", whereupon "his sense of worthlessness is replaced by conscious regret for the harm he has done to these people – at a still more primitive level also to 'part-objects' – and a desire somehow to make amends" (MONEY-KYRLE, 1961, pp. 20–1).

8.7.7 Contrition and expiation

The patient's indignant rebellion against the loss of his object or against the irrevocable loss of the object's love fails; and contrition is his reaction to this failure (RADO, 1928). The patient does penance and engages in remorseful self-punishment; his ego "begs for forgiveness and endeavours in this way to win back the lost object" (p. 50). However, "instead of procuring the pardon and love of his object, he tries to secure those of his super-ego" (p. 50). Thus, the patient's "struggle for the love of his object" is transferred "to a different stage"; his "narcissistic desire to be loved" is "carried over to his relation

---

[20] Depression is associated with a general increase in irritability and aggressiveness, whereby excessive aggression is partly redirected against the self (in the form of self-blame and self-denigration) – so as to not increase the patient's contemptibility in the eyes of others or the superego (which would further disrupt his narcissistic balance) – and partly spills over into aggression against others. As long as the form and context in which aggression is expressed externally renders this aggression justifiable to the self (egosyntonic) and more or less socially acceptable, it is unlikely to further unsettle the melancholic's narcissistic balance.

with his super-ego" (p. 50). This is what Rado (1928) described as "a narcissistic flight from the object-relation to that with the super-ego" (p. 50). In melancholia, there is a "regression from an object-relation to a narcissistic substitute for it" (p. 47), that is, from a relationship with an external object that is narcissistically controlled to an internal relationship with the super-ego (omnipotent object). Thus, the ego, in a state of depression, depreciates itself in order to get assurances of love and appreciation from the superego, the derivative of the parents. In severe depression, the ego "submits to the cruellest torments, to the very point of self-destruction, in order thus to regain the blissful situation of being loved" (Rado, 1956, p. 46).

In the patient's childhood, his "self-esteem depended entirely on his parents' love" (Rado, 1928, p. 50). As a child, he would have understood – "at times when he was naughty and his parents were very angry" – that "he had only to pay the penalty and to ask for forgiveness, in order to be reconciled to them" (pp. 50–1). He would have learned – from the link between his offending behaviour and the punishment and then forgiveness received from his parents – that "he might do penance of his own accord and punish himself, in order quickly to win his parents' forgiveness" (p. 51). Reproducing "within his mind the punishments anticipated from his parents", he unconsciously hoped to win his parents' love (p. 51). After further development, "the active reproduction of parental punishment" ceased "to have reference in the conscious mind to the parents themselves"; expiation was henceforth sought from "the super-ego, which is their internal mental representative" (p. 51) (and which acts as an internal source of narcissistic sustenance). In melancholia, "self-punishment takes place in the hope of absolution", of final forgiveness and acceptance; however, here, the patient's "longing for love", his narcissistic craving, "remains unsatisfied" (Rado, 1928, p. 51).

Reparation

The notion of forgiveness following contrition is related to Klein's concept of reparation. *Mourning* the loss of a loved object (as opposed to *melancholia*) is associated with reactivation of (regression to) the infantile 'depressive position', wherein loss of the primary object was feared and guilt was experienced towards it.[21] The mourner has to *work through the depressive position* again to achieve what he had previously achieved in infancy: integration and repair of the lost object internally (Klein, 1940). In the process of mourning, the lost love object as well as the mourner's primary objects are *internally* repaired (reintrojected as good internal objects). This allows

---

[21] Aspects of the paranoid-schizoid developmental position, too, are reactivated. Fears of persecution come to life again; objects that would have been established securely in infancy turn into persecutors again (Klein, 1940).

for *trust* in external objects to be gradually regained and the connection with the external world to be reestablished (KLEIN, 1940) (whereby external objects act as replicas of internally repaired internal objects). As internal objects are repaired and trust in external objects is reestablished, the self becomes more secure again.

According to RADO (1928), the deepest *fixation* point in the melancholic disposition is the *infant's experience of a threatened loss of love*. This statement corresponds to KLEIN's notion that individuals who are prone to melancholia did not resolve the depressive position in their infanthood. KLEIN (1940) saw the origins of melancholia in a failure by the infant to establish good (trusted) internal objects (corresponding, in self-psychological terms, to *a failure to establish a secure self*). If the infantile depressive position had not been worked through successfully and internal objects were not securely established, lost objects cannot be repaired successfully later in life.[22] In those who are predisposed to melancholia (depression), the ability to *trust* objects and to securely depend on them (for their love) may never have developed, resulting in an insecure sense of self and compensatory pathological narcissism.

8.8 Mania

Every person's mood oscillates between states of elation (hyperthymic states) and states of depression (hypothymic states) (LORENZ, 1973). The pathological exaggeration of this oscillation can be seen in the alternating phases of mania and melancholia in manic-depressive illness (bipolar affective disorder). The normal fluctuation between hypothymic and hyperthymic states is "a biologically necessary process which reflects a search, on the one hand for potential dangers, and on the other for opportunities that we can exploit to our own advantage" (p. 239). If a hypothymic state arises after a personal loss, the individual is "acutely alert to the new dangers which are sure to arise from his changed situation" (p. 239). In a hyperthymic state that arises following a personal gain or success, "it is very sensible to look for ways to profit from [the] good fortune" (p. 240). Physical hyperactivity that accompanies the state of elation enables the individual to take advantage of new opportunities (LORENZ, 1973). There is another, a social dimension to these oscillation between hyperthymic and hypothymic states.

According to MONEY-KYRLE (1961), a person may "seem to oscillate, if only to a small degree, between paranoid, depressive and manic phases" (p. 19). Firstly, in a paranoid mood, the person sees himself as "unfairly kept back by the envious intrigues of his inferiors"; or he may see himself as "surrounded

---

[22] Not being able to depend on good internal objects, those prone to melancholia readily feel persecuted by objects who they regard as bad (i.e., they readily regress to the paranoid-schizoid position) (KLEIN, 1940).

by false friends who do not care for him but only want his money" (p. 19). Secondly, in a depressive mood, the person "feels himself to be rightly despised as altogether worthless" (p. 19). Thirdly, in a manic mood or mood of "confident elation", the person "takes it for granted that he is justly liked and admired by everyone" (MONEY-KYRLE, 1961, p. 19). These moods reflect the degree to which the individual is accepted (and liked) or disliked (and potentially aggressed) by others in the group. These moods are ultimately linked with competition between group members for attention of the leader. Such competition is mediated by the acquisition and defence of a ranking position within the group or, in more abstract social formations, by acquisition of possessions or prestige, whereby either encapsulates the individual's potential to receive positive attention from the leader or, in the case of abstract social formations, unconsciously from the superego (omnipotent object).

8.8.1 Approximation of the ego ideal

Acquisition of a material object can enlarge the person's self-image and instil feelings of optimism and enthusiasm (GREENSON, 1962). Possession of an idealized material object "brings with it a feeling of being joined with it, a feeling of incorporating it, identifying with it, and making it part of the self" (p. 174) (a selfobject). The idealized possession is a projection of the ego ideal; it represents "an idealized aspect of the self" (p. 174). Material objects that evoke enthusiasm are "in accord with one's conscious ideals" (p. 175). When the self-image approximates the ego ideal (owing to acquisition of the idealized object and concomitant enlargement of the self), temporary fusion of ego (self) and superego can be achieved. This fusion is responsible for feelings of elation. The person who is *enthused* by virtue of possessing an idealized material object feels richer and grander and closer to God, literally inspired by God (GREENSON, 1962, p. 175).

Similarly, in hypomania and mania, there is a fusion of the ego with the superego; one however that is maintained by *internal aggrandizement of the self*, in *denial* of external reality (GREENSON, 1962). Mania can be regarded as an extreme and pathological case of self-satisfaction, which arises when standards of the ego ideal have been emulated, when the self feels itself in union with the superego (FLUGEL, 1945). In manic states and in enthusiasm, the fusion of ego and 'superego' (in the sense of a union of the self with the omnipotent object) liberates instinctual energy by doing away with the *tension* between ego and superego and forcing the 'superego' (in the sense of the critical agency) to temporarily give up its functions (GREENSON, 1962, p. 180).[23] It is the union of the ego (having adopted the shape of the

---

[23] Even though "reason is overthrown with the superego", "a manic behavior may be rationalized or idealized as fulfilling some ideal purpose", attesting, in some cases, to "the continued effectiveness of the superego" (FENICHEL, 1946, p. 410).

ego ideal) with the superego that "brings a sense of power and harmony" (FLUGEL, 1945, p. 55), a sense of *narcissistic* harmony.

At "the centre of all manic phenomena" is "an immense increase in self-esteem" (FENICHEL, 1946, p. 407). Mania seems to be a gross exaggeration of more normal swings ("experienced by everyone in some degree") into states of superiority and love-worthiness (FLUGEL, 1945, p. 56). In states of relative inferiority and worthlessness (low self-esteem), there is *tension* between the ego and the superego, the ego needing to be ambitious or utilize defences in order to lift itself up in the eyes of the superego. There is expenditure of energy.

Neurotic enthusiasm

GREENSON (1962) pointed out that "enthusiasm is a temporary state of mind"; "[w]hen it is prolonged, it is likely to be neurotic or a hypomania" (p. 172). Neurotic enthusiasm "is prolonged to ward off some other painful underlying state" (p. 176). Enthusiasm is neurotic "when enthusiastic reactions become a character trait, a habitual, chronic response", and when these reactions are "not as selective and the occasions which evoke enthusiasm are less worthy" (p. 182). In all of these states – in normal enthusiasm, neurotic enthusiasm, and hypomanic elation – "there is the feeling of being joined to something wonderful" (p. 179). *Denial* is an important defence mechanism in mania and hypomania; and it plays a role in normal and neurotic enthusiasm, too. To idealize an enthusiasm-producing (material) object, a degree of denial is necessary. In neurotic enthusiasm, there is greater reliance on denial for the purpose of achieving idealization of the object (GREENSON, 1962).

Intoxication

In states of mild alcoholic intoxication, people experience euphoria and a "sense of freedom and relief", which can be attributed "to a temporary partial paralysis of the super-ego" (FLUGEL, 1945, p. 204). States of drug or alcohol intoxication can also been regarded as states of merger between ego and superego and likened to the oceanic feeling associated with the primary narcissistic state of fusion with the mother (RADO). How can we reconcile these accounts? In the first instance, we regard the superego as the critical agency, while, in the second instance, the superego represents the omnipotent object. Relaxation of superego standards and self-satisfaction (aggrandizement of the ego) would both act to reduce the tension between ego and superego and thus help to bring about the merger of the ego with the superego or omnipotent object (the inner representative of the primary maternal object).

8.8.2 Release of inhibitions

The merger of the ego with the superego in mania represents a repetition of the infantile experience of fusion with the mother ("the faithful, intra-psychic repetition of the experience of that fusing with the mother that takes place during the drinking at her breast") (RADO, 1928, p. 54). In mania, "the omnipotence of primary narcissism" is reenacted, and a state is created that resembles "the original pleasure principle under whose operation impulses were yielded to, whenever they arose, without any consideration of reality" (FENICHEL, 1946, p. 410).

As, with the onset of mania, "the tension between the superego and ego" is "released abruptly", inhibitions are abandoned, so that "the freed impulses as well as the energies, which hitherto had been bound in the efforts to restrain these impulses, now flow out, using any available discharge" (FENICHEL, 1946, p. 407). Patients express their potentialities without inhibitions; their activities are intensified, and they "are hungry for objects" (p. 407). Narcissistic supplies become freely available, and "a total narcissistic victory is at hand", "so that the primary narcissistic omnipotence is more or less regained", manifesting as "extreme self-love" (p. 407). Projection of self-love reinforces the feeling of being "loved and admired by everybody" (FENICHEL, 1946, p. 410).

8.8.3 Lack of good internal objects

KLEIN (1940) thought that the immense increase in self-esteem in patients with mania is defensively motivated: manic defences are a way of preventing depressive feelings of loss and guilt. If the depressive position was not overcome in early childhood, then any loss of an external object in later life – either as a result of ambivalent attack on the object or actual loss – reawakens early 'depressive anxieties' about losing the *good internal object* (the counterpart of a secure self). Depressive anxieties – acting as a reminder of the 'damage' done to one's internal object – can be avoided by means of manic defences. Manic defences avoid depressive anxieties in part by *denying* dependency on internal and external objects (KLEIN, 1940). Denial of dependency offsets depression and prevents grief arising from the loss of an *irreplaceable* object (the loss of an internal or external regulator of self-esteem), a loss that in mania is unconsciously mourned (KLEIN, 1940).

Using mechanisms characteristic for the paranoid-schizoid position, the manic patient keeps at bay feelings of pining and mourning and, instead, experiences feelings of *triumph, contempt,* and *control* (SEGAL, 1973). Triumph is the denial of concern for the object. Contempt involves devaluation of the object. Control of the object fosters denial of dependence (SEGAL, 1973). Persecutory fears strengthen manic mechanisms of defence. Manic defences entail a need to constantly observe and check on bad objects, so that inner bad and persecutory objects can be manically subordinated. Superiority over and humiliation of one's object provides sadistic satisfaction, but the triumph delays the working-through of mourning. While the object is treated with contempt, controlled, and triumphed over, reparative activities cannot be carried out. Instead, attacks on the object increase its destruction, "thereby deepening depressive anxieties and making the underlying depressive situation increasingly hopeless and persecutory" (SEGAL, 1973).

8.8.4 Manic attitude and defence

The narcissistic person depends on objects, like everybody else, but he cannot maintain object relations *in reality*; so he has establish and control them *internally* (RIVIERE, 1936). His 'manic attitude' relates to his omnipotent denial of his dependence on objects and omnipotent control of his objects. The narcissistic patient depreciates his objects and exerts 'tyrannical mastery' over them in all situations (RIVIERE, 1936). Objects that are *depreciated* (i.e., have no value over and above their value for the ego in terms of the ego's safety or integrity) and that are tightly *controlled* are selfobjects (KOHUT); they are, in a sense, introjected objects, objects that belong to the ego (self).

The narcissistic person is unconsciously convinced that any lessening of control over his objects will reawaken his 'depressive anxieties' (RIVIERE, 1936). In the 'depressive position', the patient gains insight into the lack of *real* object relations (believing unconsciously that he has destroyed his objects) and hence into his fundamental loneliness. His internal objects have been destroyed and there is no one to love or feed him (to sustain his narcissistic balance). The narcissistic patient is always close to being aware that he lacks real object relations, and his omnipotent defences are an attempt to avoid the pain and depression that this insight brings (RIVIERE, 1936).

> For his object-relations are not to real people, his object-relations are all within himself; his inner world is *all* the world to him. Whatever he does for his objects he does for himself as well; if only he could do it! and in *mania* he thinks he *can*. So it is the overwhelming importance of the inner world of his emotional relations that makes him in real life so egocentric, asocial, self-seeking – so fantastic!
>
> (RIVIERE, 1936, p. 318)

RIVIERE (1936) argued that manic and narcissistic resistances in therapy are a defence against a more or less unconscious depressive situation that needs to be uncovered in therapy. Patients with narcissistic character resistance are highly sensitive to experiencing anxiety and become easily mortified (narcissistically injured); their depressive position is stronger because their unconscious reality is more unbearable than that of others. Their sense of failure and inability to remedy matters is greater. Analysis is about realizing this despair and uncovering the depression underneath their manic defence (RIVIERE, 1936). The inaccessibility of narcissistic patients in analysis and their resistance to forming a 'positive transference' are expressions of their omnipotent denial of real object relations; these are expressions of their dependence on *internal objects* (selfobjects) that serve the purpose of sustaining their narcissistic balance and precarious self-esteem, of helping them to realize their longing to return to the state of primary narcissism.

> ... it is *the love for his internal objects*, which lies behind and produces the unbearable guilt and pain, the need to sacrifice his life for theirs, and so the prospect of death, that makes this resistance so stubborn. And we can counter this resistance only by unearthing this love and so the guilt with it. ... What is underneath is a *love* (a craving for absolute bliss in complete union with a perfect object for ever and ever), and this love is bound up with an uncontrollable and insupportable fury of disappointment, ...
> (RIVIERE, 1936, p. 319)

8.9 Psychosis

> The case histories of many schizophrenics emphasize that the patients had shown some signs of peculiarity from early on in life and were never able to express strong feelings. There had been a tendency to turn away from the outside world at the least provocation.
> (ROSENFELD, 1965, p. 167)

Schizoid individuals and patients with schizophrenia long for human relatedness, but, for them, social situations are terrifying. Their means of achieving relatedness (assertiveness and exhibitionism) are inhibited. The schizoid individual longs for "'a moment of recognition'" (p. 122) (and, unconsciously, "for complete union" [p. 97]); however, "of this very longing he is terrified" (LAING, 1960, p. 97). Giving in to this longing means exposure to the possibility of rejection. Participation in life is possible "but only in the face of intense anxiety" (p. 95). The schizoid individual "feels more 'vulnerable', more liable to be exposed by the look of another person" (p. 79). His "heightened sense of being always seen, or at any rate of being always potentially seeable", an exaggerated self-consciousness, has a tormenting quality and is of a "compulsive nature" (p. 113). While visibility raises the prospect of rejection, invisibility is dreaded, too, as it associated with 'ontological insecurity' and existential annihilation. The schizoid individual's "fear of being invisible, of disappearing, is closely associated with the fear of his mother disappearing" (LAING, 1960, p. 125).

> The 'self-conscious' person is caught in a dilemma. He may *need* to be seen and recognised, in order to maintain his sense of realness and identity. Yet, at the same time, the other represents a threat to his identity and reality.
> (LAING, 1960, pp. 121–2)

> He is constantly drawing attention to himself, and at the same time drawing attention *away* from his self. His behaviour is compulsive. All his thoughts are occupied with being seen. His longing is to be known. But this is also what is most dreaded.
>
> (LAING, 1960, pp. 122–3)

This dilemma is faced by patients with schizophrenia, too. Their concern with being unacceptable is related to experiences of rejection early in life. ARIETI (1973) suggested that adverse experiences of early childhood (giving rise to the 'original' self-image) are repressed but can be reactivated later in life when the patient comes to feel "that the segment of the world that is important to him finds him unacceptable", and when he realizes "that as long as he lives he will be unacceptable to others" (p. 126). As the patient realizes that he does not fit in and is alone, he experiences a state of panic (SULLIVAN, 1953); he "now sees himself as totally defeated, without any worth and possibility of redemption" (ARIETI, 1973, p. 127). The patient "partially removes the influence of the conceptual interpersonal world that has afflicted the recent injuries" by adopting new forms of cognition, by transforming "the intrapsychic danger into an external or interpersonal one" (ARIETI, 1973, p. 127). Once psychosis has established itself, aggressiveness, which was previously inhibited, can be expressed, being targeted at those who frustrate the patient's longing for human relatedness and have a competitive advantage in the struggle for narcissistic supplies.

> If the patient contrasts his own inner emptiness, worthlessness, coldness, desolation, dryness, with the abundance, worth, warmth, companionship that he may yet believe to be elsewhere …, there is evoked a welter of conflicting emotions, from a desperate *longing* and yearning for what others have and he lacks, to frantic *envy* and hatred of all that is theirs and not his, or a desire to destroy all the goodness, freshness, richness in the world.
>
> (LAING, 1960, p. 96)

8.9.1 Inner self

The schizoid individual, "in order to be safe from the persistent threat and danger from the world, has cut [himself] off from direct relatedness with others" (LAING, 1960, pp. 149–50). To avoid the danger of rejection implicit in participation in social life and to achieve, at the same time, some relief from the urge to relate to others and to reunite with a derivative of the primary object, the schizoid individual withdraws into fantasy and constructs an 'inner self'. From the 'false self' or persona, which is the "identity-for-others", arising "in compliance with [others'] intentions or expectations" (p. 105), he separates a secrete 'inner self', with which he is occupied in fantasy (LAING, 1960).

In phantasy, the self can be anyone, anywhere, do anything, have everything. It is thus omnipotent and completely free – but only in phantasy. Once commit itself to any real project and it suffers agonies of humiliation – not necessarily for any failure, but simply because it has to subject itself to necessity and contingency. It is omnipotent and free only in phantasy. The more this phantastic omnipotence and freedom are indulged, the more weak, helpless and fettered it becomes in actuality. The illusion of omnipotence and freedom can be sustained only within the magic circle of its own shut-up-ness in phantasy.

(LAING, 1960, pp. 88–9)

In an attempt to preserve the compensatory 'inner self' from "destruction from outer sources", the schizoid individual has to eliminate "any direct access from without to this 'inner' self" (LAING, 1960, p. 152). However, "what was designed in the first instance as a guard or barrier to prevent disruptive impingements on the self, can become the walls of a prison from which the self cannot escape" (LAING, 1960, p. 150). The withdrawal into an omnipotent inner self, manifesting as oddity, further compounds the struggle for relatedness.

8.9.2 Ego weakness

KOHUT (1977) thought that schizophrenia, similarly to narcissistic personality disorder, is a form of "the pathology of the fragmented self" (p. 243) that arises as a consequence of "the emotional distance of the self-objects" of childhood (p. 257). Schizophrenia is associated with a diminution or "weakness of the ego" (although schizoid defence mechanisms can, to some extent, effect an "exaggeration of ego feeling") (FEDERN, 1952, p. 105). In psychotic states, the ego suffers from "feebleness of cathexis" (p. 114) (narcissistic cathexis of the self is weak). Ego weakness, or "loss of cathexis of ego boundaries" (p. 118), constitutes "the main damage" in psychosis (p. 166). Anticipating positions of self psychology, FEDERN (1952) stated that "the primary schizophrenic process appears to be a functional deficiency, or even exhaustion, of ego cathexis" (p. 134). Schizophrenia, in other words, "is always due to a deficiency of ego cathexis" (p. 228). By contrast, patients with neuroses typically have an intact ego. Thus, "psychosis is due to a decreased ego cathexis, while neurosis leaves the ego cathexis itself intact or increased and only disturbs the various functions of a still intact ego" (FEDERN, 1952, p. 212).

8.9.3 Psychoanalytic treatment of schizophrenia

The goal of psychoanalysis of psychotic patients is "to restore lost cathexes to the psychotic ego" (FEDERN, 1952, p. 169). The ego has to be "re-established within its normal boundaries, sufficiently invested with mental cathexis", in order to prevent "any increase in psychotic disorganization" (p. 149). In the therapeutic process, the analyst has to foster re-repression, rather than making repressed material conscious; and resistances are not to be broken down but have to be reestablished (p. 136). Similarly, if latent schizophrenia is suspected in a patient with hysterical or obsessional neurosis, care must be taken not to cure the neurosis, as it may be the patient's "most important self-defence against schizophrenia" (FEDERN, 1952, p. 177).

Psychoanalytic treatment of patients with psychosis hinges on fostering continuous support through a positive transference. The analyst must abstain "from resolving the positive transference" (FEDERN, 1952, p. 178). Thus, according to FEDERN (1952), "transferences have to be managed differently" (p. 136).

> One wins the normal transference of the psychotic by sincerity, kindness, and understanding. ... One must avoid blame, severe admonition, any smiling superiority, and especially any lie.
> (FEDERN, 1952, p. 141)

> In order to establish the patient's transference, the analyst must avoid the slightest sign of depreciation or underestimation, and must give full recognition to the patient's right to have his personality respected.
> (FEDERN, 1952, pp. 141–2)

FEDERN (1952) realized that mothers of psychotic patients tend to suffer from "strong narcissism", which opposes the "devotion without hesitation" that is part of the "instinctual behavior pattern" of normal motherhood (pp. 144–5). In KOHUT's terminology, exposure to selfobject failures at an early developmental stage leads to lasting enfeeblement of the self.[24]

> Gertrud Schwing found that every schizophrene craves transference to a new mother. All schizophrenes, she discovered, did not have true mothers, because their mothers themselves had never had true mothers in their infancies. What was always thought to be an increase of the hereditary factor from generation to generation has frequently been found to be recurring deficiency in the infantile libido conditions.
> (FEDERN, 1952, p. 144)

---

[24] FEDERN (1952) observed that when a psychotic patient is nursed by his own mother, the relationship "becomes too possessive, and regresses easily to incest" (p. 145), resonating with KOHUT's findings that oedipal conflicts have their root in earlier deficiencies in mirroring functions of the maternal selfobject.

8.9.4 Depersonalization

In depersonalization, the outer world of objects is experienced as dreamlike or unreal or dead. At the same time, patients experience "themselves and their thinking as automatic and mechanical" (SCHILDER, 1976, p. 43). While experiences of *thought passivity* and *delusions of control* are of pathognomonic significance, depersonalization can be one of the early symptoms of schizophrenia. Depersonalization phenomena can also occur in depression. SCHILDER (1976) saw in depersonalization phenomena the patient's withdrawal from the world coupled with "an incipient tendency to destroy the world and oneself" (p. 43). The patient "no longer dares to fully experience his own body and the world" and "gives up both of them", but he "retains his full interest in merely observing his incapacity", adopting – as "the destroyer" of the world and himself – the stance of "the supreme observer" (p. 43). Self-observation is thus part of depersonalization (SCHILDER, 1976).

It can now be understood more fully how self-consciousness and depersonalization are related to each other, and which role excessive self-consciousness plays in schizophrenia. While, through depersonalization and derealization (estrangement), the ego withdraws narcissistic cathexes from the world (from a world that refuses to meet the patient's narcissistic needs), through self-observation the ego sets itself above its narcissistic needs. As a 'supreme observer', the ego concurrently achieves reunion with the omnipotent object (superego).

8.9.5 Obsessions and catatonia

Individuals with a paranoid character structure "are highly sensitive to slights, or disrespect, alert to the possibility of humiliation" (SHAPIRO, 2000, p. 86). The suspicious person, like the obsessive one, is biased "toward an assumption of threat"; for him, "an error of underestimating the possibility of threat is far more serious than its overestimation" (p. 114). Like the obsessive person, the suspicious person, "must not allow himself to be caught off guard"; and "he must not allow himself to believe he is safe" (p. 114). The paranoid delusion is similar to obsessive rumination, in that both are born out of an increased concern with the possibility of humiliation (and ultimately of the self's [oneself's] destruction). SHAPIRO (2000) suggested that the paranoid delusion resembles "an extreme form of obsession"; it is, "in its general quality", "an anxious preoccupying idea stripped of realistic proportion" (p. 85).

Severe obsessions and compulsions can be a precursor to paranoid or catatonic schizophrenia (SHAPIRO, 2000). In the case of catatonic schizophrenia, obsessive doubts and indecision may be so severe that the patient finds himself immobilized when faced with a decision; catatonic immobilization or "stupor, in fact, seems in important respects to be a direct continuation and intensification of certain kinds of obsessive experience"; it "seems specifically to reflect a radically exaggerated obsessional hesitancy, indecision, and precautionary concern" (p. 149). In catatonic schizophrenia, behavioural inhibition may generalize to all volitional actions, whereas, in the obsessive person, "indecision and its inhibition of action are usually limited to particular occasions when consciousness of personal choice is unavoidable" (SHAPIRO, 2000, p. 151).

8.9.6 Paranoid delusions

All ideas and conclusions are 'felt' as certain. False certainty is to the paranoiac what false reality is to the schizophrenic.

(FEDERN, 1952, p. 232)

Denial of external reality is a primitive defence against conflict and anxiety and as such often enters into the development of delusions (LAUGHLIN, 1970, p. 57). Projection of hostile impulses, too, operates in most of the paranoid and persecutory delusions (pp. 230–2). The patient wishes to harm his objects but cannot do so for fear of retaliation, hence he expects to be harmed by them instead (LAUGHLIN, 1970). Avoidance of guilt stabilizes paranoid delusions. Aggressive impulses against the object, which would normally cause guilt (which, in turn, would have to be assuaged strenuously by reparation or by expression of the need for punishment), can be projected onto supposed persecutors (FLUGEL, 1945).

Denial and Projection are often the basis of delusional jealousy and belief in persecution. In these psychotic manifestations, it is often a basic sense of guilt which the person is unable to tolerate, and against which he calls into play ego defenses of Denial and Projection.

(LAUGHLIN, 1970, p. 69)

FREUD (1914) thought that paranoia is frequently caused by an injury to the ego, "by a frustration of satisfaction within the sphere of the ego ideal". The narcissistic injury has to be undone. In paranoia, the patient obtains an increase in his narcissistic supplies "because he becomes the center of attention" (SANDLER, 1985, p. 142). Attesting to the economic benefit afforded to the patient, 'paranoid indifference' may accompany the paranoid delusion (LAUGHLIN, 1970, p. 234). ADLER (1927) pointed out that some individuals seem "to be proud of their ill-luck, as if some supernatural power had caused it" (p. 210). In acting "as though some sinister deity is singling them out for persecution", they show their vanity; "vanity is at work when such individuals feel that all hostile powers are intent on wreaking vengeance upon them" (p. 210). "Being especially unlucky is one way of feeling important" (ADLER, 1927, p. 210).

During the prepsychotic stages, the patient had, so to say, protected the world from blame and had to a large extent considered himself responsible for his defeat. Now he externalizes again this feeling. No longer does he accuse himself. The accusation comes from the external world. The voices accuse him of being a spy, a murderer, a traitor, a homosexual. These developments are defensive, though they do not seem so. As painful as it is to be accused by others, it is not so unpleasant as to accuse oneself. Moreover, the patient feels falsely accused. Thus, the projected accusation is not injurious to the self-esteem. On the contrary, in comparison with his prepsychotic state, the patient experiences a rise in his self-esteem, often accompanied by a feeling of martyrdom. The really accused person now is not the patient but the persecutor, who is accused of persecuting the patient.

(ARIETI, 1973, p. 127)

8.9.7 Delusions of grandeur

When a child loses his sense of omnipotence, he strives to merge with his parental objects, who he now believes to be omnipotent, although he tries to cling on to his own omnipotence at first. Patients prone to psychosis "react to any narcissistic hurt in later life in the same way that they attempted to react to their first hurt, namely, to the realization that they are not omnipotent": they simply *deny* their loss of omnipotence (making use of the defence mechanism of denial) (FENICHEL, 1946, p. 420). Thus, the objective world "disappears again" (p. 420), and, in a state of isolation and narcissistic aloofness, such a patient may "overcompensate all narcissistic hurts by developing a still higher opinion of himself" (p. 421). If there is concurrently a loss of reality testing, his narcissistic daydreams, in which he feels himself as "being more wonderful than any object", become delusions of grandeur (FENICHEL, 1946, p. 421).

Megalomania is an "extreme example of pathological over-evaluation of the self" (HENDRICK, 1958, p. 119). Acutely psychotic patients wish to be in the public eye, in the centre of world-wide *attention*; they wish to be *acclaimed* for possessing supernatural powers (ADLER, 1965). They need attention and acclaim to sustain their self and prevent it from fragmentation. Patients with paranoid schizophrenia "attempt to maintain self-esteem by grandiose phantasies" and delusions; and even persecutory delusions serve the maintenance of self-esteem: the persecuted patient experiences himself as "a person of consequence" insofar as he has become "the subject of widespread attention, even if this be malicious" (STORR, 1968, p. 95).

Psychotic patients may not only have grandiose *opinions* of themselves (and entertain grandiose fantasies about themselves), they may also identify themselves with, *and act as though they were*, a well-known person of grandiose stature (thereby harnessing narcissistic resources available to that person). The megalomanic patient, "who proclaims that he is Lincoln, Christ, or Napoleon", "actually *feels* himself to be greatest and most important of human specimens" (HENDRICK, 1958, p. 119). A patient's psychotic identification (such as with Napoleon or Christ) is associated with "glaring inconsistencies and incongruities in his behaviour or role, of which the patient is seemingly unaware" (LAUGHLIN, 1970, p. 157).

9
Interpersonal and Social Dynamics

Social group behaviour in humans and other species comprises successive impulses of "aggression, fear, protection-seeking and renewed aggressiveness", impulses that mostly express themselves in ritualized form (LORENZ, 1963, p. 55). LORENZ (1973) thought that "the tension between opposing rituals, such as those of threatening and those of appeasement" results in "a unitary integrated system" that is characterized by high rigidity (p. 213). Cultural ritualization of intraspecific aggression plays a particular role in humans. Curtailed and culturally ritualized intraspecific aggression is, according to LORENZ (1963), an important constituent of social manners and customs and lies at the heart of social ambition, competitiveness, enthusiasm for a cause, envy, and the use of status symbols. Curtailed aggression underpins self-respect and finds expression in "the sublimest artistic or scientific creation" and in the "specifically human faculty" of laughter (LORENZ, 1963, p. 269).

FREUD (1933) acknowledged that civilization and cultural achievements are founded upon aggressive as well as sexual impulses – the very impulses that "are inhibited by society" (p. 143), whereby inhibition (and modification) of aggression, in particular, is achieved by the "setting up of the super-ego, which makes the dangerous aggressive impulses its own" (p. 143). Others' aggression towards oneself (and symbolically that of the superego towards the ego) is *disinhibited* by one's nonconformity, one's failure to control one's own aggressive or sexual impulses. The fear of others' aggression is counteracted by one's conformity and the display of culturally or phylogenetically ritualized appeasement gestures and by one's perception of their appeasing effect on others (or it is overcome by offensively aggressively induced submission in others). Healthy narcissism can be taken to refer to all behaviours that cause others to display appeasing (or submissive) gestures towards oneself, all behaviours that produce a sense of safety in oneself (i.e., maintain one's narcissistic homeostasis) through the perception of others' approvals, approbation, or recognition of oneself.

Burrow (1949) recognized that the "disposition of an individual to exercise projective control over others [is] coupled with a reciprocal subservience on the part of his listeners" (p. 4). At the heart of all social interactions, individuals "approve and are approved of" and "disapprove and are disapproved of"; "society is composed exclusively of these two complemental reactions" (Burrow, 1949, p. 5).[1]

> By virtue of this authoritarian give-and-take that now characterizes man's interrelational level of behaviour, there is to-day early imbued in him – in us all – a dichotomous attitude of servile dependence upon other people on the one hand, and of vindictive repudiation of them on the other. The social fabric of human relations is now shot through with this dualistic factor of personal attraction and repulsion. This bipolar reaction is universal. Our mental world is divided between those towards whom we feel kindly disposed, and those towards whom we feel unkindly disposed. People with whom we agree, or who agree with us, are those for whom we feel affection, while people with whom we do not agree, or who do not agree with us, are those with whom we do not share our affections.
> (Burrow, 1949, pp. 4–5)

Our safety within the group and our access to narcissistic resources are regulated by our social status or ranking position in the group, which we have to maintain dynamically through appropriately targeted assertive (offensively aggressive) and submissive gestures. While competing for social status, in an attempt to maintain in unconscious fantasy our relationship with the primary care giver (omnipotent object), we have to conform to the norms of society in order to *avoid* being driven into social disconnectedness or unrelatedness (which unconsciously stands for maternal separation) and becoming the victim of collective punishment.

9.1 Safety in interactions and relationships

Relationship with an object is the context in which narcissistic needs are satisfied, in which another person's appeasing and affirmative (*self*-affirmative) affect signals are received and can be solicited. In defining the context for affective exchange, the individual projects his self or object representation onto the other person, "while enacting the reciprocal object or self representation" (Kernberg, 1996, p. 127). Thus, an 'internal object relation' is actualized, that is, a "significant past object relation" is recapitulated (Kernberg,

---

[1] Burrow (1949) believed that this dichotomy is entirely socially conditioned, that it is acquired in childhood development as a result of exposure to parental and societal attitudes that have been reinforced in cultural evolution.

1992, p. 11). An early object relation is recapitulated insofar as it was associated with safety and the receipt of narcissistic sustenance (in the form of the object's attention or approving or submissive signals).

Object relationships serve to keep in check 'basic anxiety' (HORNEY), prevent 'fears of annihilation', and maintain, at the same time, self-esteem and cohesive self-experience. The same could be said about relationships with groups and organizations. Anxiety, even when experienced dimly, or the prospect of safety motivates us to adjust our behaviour and influence our social surround to the effect of ensuring our connectedness to the environment and regaining the safety that is implicit in this connectedness. Connectedness means more than being in the presence of others. We need to receive appeasing and reassuring signals, *or we need to confidently expect them*, in order to feel connected. We are safe as long as we are *accepted* and *recognized* by others. The need to maintain safety impels us not to deviate from norms of the group. As long as we conform, and as long as we protect our identity and position within the group, we are protected against an evolutionarily significant but nowadays often hypothetical harm: ejection from or annihilation by the primal horde.

9.1.1 Role relationships

All object relations from childhood on represent attempts at repeating an early object relation. In any relationship, the other person is unconsciously manipulated into behaving in a way that is consistent with an early object relation. An early object relation is revived by imposing a particular role on the other person and adopting a complementary role for oneself, so as to replicate the 'role relationship' that characterized the early object relation (SANDLER, 1976). Partners in relationships unconsciously assign roles to each other and induce each other to respond in certain ways (SANDLER & SANDLER, 1978). These mutual manipulations are motivated by the need to restore feelings of wellbeing or safety, and thus to avoid psychic pain. The imposition of a role relationship is a means for reexperiencing the safety associated with an early object relation. The aim may be to reexperience the exclusivity of the *primary object's interest and devotion* in the present situation involving a derivative of the primary object. The precise form of 'role relationships' imposed on interactions with present-day objects is determined by early childhood experiences, although what is enacted in object relationships from childhood on are not only infantile role relationships but also the defensive role relationships constructed on to them later in life (SANDLER, 1976; SANDLER & SANDLER, 1978). The mutual assignment of roles to each other is related to the defence mechanism of 'projective identification'.

9.1.2 Projective identification

'Projective identification', a concept introduced by MELANIE KLEIN, is a way of making the object take on intolerable feelings that the subject tries to evade.[2] BION (1962) distinguished between projective identification as a means to evade frustration or anxiety and 'realistic projective identification', the latter forming a basis for communication. Such communication however also serves the movement away from anxiety and towards safety. Projective identification is, in a sense, a mechanism through which a role relationship and thus a context of safety is imposed on an interpersonal situation; it is a mechanism that is employed whenever anxiety is felt or whenever the imperative arises to attain safety. Projective identification (in its normal or pathological form) "involves the behavioral and emotional manipulation of others" (CASHDAN, 1988, p. 56).

> ... the recurrent pressure on the analyst to join the patient in the partial enactment of archaic, often disturbed and disturbing object relationships is one of the most interesting and puzzling phenomena we encounter.
> (FELDMAN, 1997, p. 238)

In the psychoanalytic setting, the patient impinges, by way of projective identification, on the analyst's feeling, thinking, and acting (FELDMAN, 1997). The patient's verbal and nonverbal communication influences the analyst's state of mind in such a way that the analyst's behaviour and attitude gratify the patient's need to reexperience an archaic object relation. Thus, projective identification serves a transference function. If there is a discrepancy between the patient's unconscious fantasy of an archaic object relationship and the actual relationship in the analytic situation, then the patient experiences distress and is driven to exert conscious and unconscious pressure on the analyst to try and make the analyst enact elements of the archaic object relationship. The patient does not relent (in his use of projective identification) until he has evidence that the analyst's experience and behaviour correspond to his unconscious fantasy (FELDMAN, 1997).

> ... it seems to serve a reassuring function if what is enacted in the external world corresponds in some measure with an object relationship that is unconsciously present. The alternative, when [the patient] is confronted with the discrepancy between the two, is painful and threatening.
> (FELDMAN, 1997, pp. 238–9)

The analyst's attitude and behaviour, if they are congruous with the patient's projected fantasy, would ultimately *gratify* the patient's need for safety. The analyst would *reassure* the patient. This may be a reciprocal process; and in

---

[2] Specifically, projective identification is a way of evacuating anxiety into the object (whereby the object, sensing the subject's anxiety by way of 'primary identification', may either "retain a balanced outlook" or become "prey to the anxiety") (BION, 1959).

their collusion, both the patient and the analyst would feel *safe* and comfortable, impeding the progress of analytic work (FELDMAN, 1997).

9.1.3 Submission, ingratiation, and dominance

A key dynamic in projective identification is the *induction* that underlies it. Individuals who rely on projective identification engage in subtle but nonetheless powerful manipulations to induce those about them to behave in prescribed ways. It is as if one individual forces another to play a role in the enactment of that person's internal drama – one involving early object relationships.

(CASHDAN, 1988, p. 56)

The term 'projective identification' is often reserved for pathological forms of manipulative interaction, in which "there is usually only one person who reaps the benefits so that ultimately the other party feels used" (CASHDAN, 1988, p. 58). Normal variations of projective identification allow us to ensure that significant others in our life remain bound to us. The projector may, and in pathological instances generally does, employ hidden or covert threats designed to keep the recipient in the relationship. Different forms of projective identification are associated with different patterns of communication and metacommunication. Firstly, in the 'projective identification of dependency', the projector, signalling helplessness, displays help-seeking or submissive behaviours. 'Projective identification of dependency' induces care-taking behaviour in the recipient of the projection (investing the target of the projection with care-taking powers) and, if successful, recreates a caretaker–child relationship (CASHDAN, 1988).

A person who engages in a projective identification of dependency may be fortunate enough to stumble across someone whose life desire is to take care of people. If, on the other hand, the target offers resistance, the projector may experience anxiety, depression, rage, and other 'symptoms' attesting to what amounts to projective failure. These are the people who most often end up seeking help.

(CASHDAN, 1988, p. 77)

Secondly, in the 'projective identification of power', the recipient is forced to take a subservient role (CASHDAN, 1988). The projector makes efforts "to convince the target that he or she needs to be cared for and looked after" (p. 66). A person prone to using 'projective identification of power' may have learned in childhood that "feelings of competence and self-worth can be achieved only if he controls what takes place about him" (p. 68). Inducing others to feel incompetent or inadequate ensures that the person will not be abandoned by them (CASHDAN, 1988). Thirdly, in the 'projective identification of ingratiation', the projector makes sacrifices, thereby provoking an other to be grateful or appreciative. The target of the projection is made (induced) to feel that he owes something to the projector. A person prone to using 'projective identification of ingratiation' may have learned in childhood that his intrinsic worth lies in his ability to be useful to his caretakers; he may have learned that he needs to do things for those who care for him in order to be *loved and appreciated* (CASHDAN, 1988).

> We all want to believe that we are worthwhile human beings and to know that those closest to us feel we are worth being with. Persons who relate through projective identification of ingratiation have little faith that this is the way the world works. They do not really believe that other human beings, even their own family members, really love them for what they are. They are convinced that they need to ingratiate themselves to ensure that they will be wanted. And to make sure this happens, they establish relationships in such a way that others feel indebted to them.
> (CASHDAN, 1988, p. 76)

9.1.4 Transference and transference neurosis

> It has always surprised us that the forgotten and repressed experiences of early childhood should reproduce themselves in dreams and reactions during analytic treatment, especially in reactions involved in the transference, ...
> (FREUD, 1933, p. 138)

'Transference' refers to "all those impulses experienced by the patient in his relation with the analyst which are not newly created by the objective analytic situation but have their source in early – indeed, the very earliest – object relations and are now merely revived under the influence of the repetition compulsion" (ANNA FREUD, 1937, p. 27). SIGMUND FREUD discovered that, in analysis, the patient is compelled to repeat forgotten (repressed) events of his childhood as contemporary experience. The emergence of the patient's *repressed* material in the process of psychoanalysis – the manifestation of this material in the patient's behaviour towards and relationship with the analyst – is called 'transference neurosis'. Patients in psychoanalysis repeat "unwanted situations and painful emotions in the transference and revive them with great ingenuity"; "they contrive once more to feel themselves scorned, to oblige the physician to speak severely to them and treat them coldly"; or "they discover appropriate objects for their jealousy", objects that are of interest to the analyst (FREUD, 1920, p. 21). The patient undergoing psychoanalysis not only repeats aspects of his past relationships within the present analytic relationship but also avoids to consciously 'remember' these aspects. The task of the analyst is to help the patient "to recognize that what appears to be reality is in fact only a reflection of a forgotten past" (p. 19) – a recognition the patient will 'resist' (FREUD, 1920).

Transference involves unconscious attempts, on part of the patient, to *manipulate* the analyst into a reenactment of an early object relation. If the patient's manipulations are successful, the analyst takes on a 'transference role' (SANDLER, 1976). Successful stimulation in the analyst of a mental state that corresponds to the transference role he is meant to play depends on the patient's "ability to perceive, assess and play on the analyst's personality" (CAPER, 1995). Transference manipulations or provocations may be accepted by the analyst, if the analyst is disposed in that direction ('role responsiveness') (SANDLER, 1976). The 'role relationship' transferred onto the analytic setting consists of a role in which the patient casts himself and a complementary role for the analyst. Interaction between patient and analyst is determined not only by the internal role relationship that the patient tries to impose but also by the analyst's response to this imposition (countertransference) and, to some extent, by the analyst's unconscious attempts to impose his own role relationship on the interaction (in accordance with his own early object relations). SANDLER (1976) suggested that the analyst's actions and responses to the patient are a compromise between his own tendencies and his acceptance of the role into which he has been manoeuvred by the patient.

Thus, transference arises when one person treats another in a relationship as though the latter person were a reincarnation of a significant object from the former person's early life. In the context of psychoanalytic treatment, for instance, the patient may put the analyst in the place of his father. The transference is stronger when the patient's ability to differentiate between the past and the present, between the analyst as a reincarnation of an earlier object and the analyst as a real person, is impaired, which it is when the pressure of "repressed impulses" that "seek expression in derivatives" is high (FENICHEL, 1946, p. 30). Again, the analyst is not merely *perceived* as a representative of the patient's past. The patient would, in addition, "attempt to manipulate or to provoke the analyst to react in a particular way, attempting to *make him behave* in the present in the way in which the patient's infantile objects were seen (or fantasised) to behave in the past" (SANDLER et al., 1969, p. 267). Transference neurosis, being an intensification of the transference, arises if "the patient's major conflicts become centered around the person of the analyst" (p. 267). Establishment of a transference provides a means by which the patient's internal conflicts can be turned into "external battles with the analyst" (SANDLER et al., 1969, p. 274).[3]

---

[3] Internal battles include those between the ego and superego. When a transference has established itself, the analyst is identified with the patient's superego (so that the analyst is perceived as relating to the patient in the same way that the superego relates to the ego). Conversely, the patient may identify with his own superego, allowing him to gain "a feeling of virtue" when accusing the analyst of "an impulse of one sort or

Discovery of a secure self

Countertransference can be understood as arising through the patient's projective identification (CARPY, 1989). The patient uses projective identification to split off parts of his self and project them onto the analyst. The patient induces in the analyst a state of mind (anxiety or anger) that is similar to the one he attempts to eliminate in himself (CARPY, 1989). Projective identification is intended to produce a reaction; the analyst will be compelled by the feelings induced in him (anxiety or anger) to act out. Acting out by the analyst can manifest in subtle ways such as the wording, tone, and content of interpretations given to the patient. In trying not to act out, the analyst can help to bring about psychic change in the patient, as the patient gradually realizes that he can rely on the analyst's devotion and concern. The patient sees that he is "affecting the analyst and inducing strong feelings in him", yet, at the same time, he observes the analyst "attempting to deal with these feelings" (CARPY, 1989, p. 292).

> ... it is the *inevitable* partial acting out of the countertransference which allows the patient to see that the analyst is being affected by what is projected, is struggling to tolerate it, and, if the analysis is to be effective, is managing sufficiently to maintain his analytic stance without grossly acting out. ... it is through this process that the patient is able gradually to re-introject the previously-intolerable aspects of himself that are involved. He is also able to introject the capacity to tolerate them which he has observed in the analyst.
>
> (CARPY, 1989, p. 292)

This is reminiscent of BION's (1962) description of how the mother acts as a container for the infant's bad projections. The infant who experiences his mother as tolerating these projections will be able to tolerate his own anxieties. The infant receives "its frightened personality back again, but in a form that it can tolerate" (BION, 1962). The gradual introjection of the *tolerating* analyst leads to, as CARPY (1989) put it, the "patient's discovery of aspects of himself". The patient may discover a *self that is secure in the knowledge of being accepted for who he is*; and he thereby forms an image of himself as being worthy of others' interest and concern ('true self').

Change can be brought about by frustrating, in a nontraumatic manner, the patient's attempts to use the analyst as an object into which he projects split-off uncomfortable aspects of his personality.[4] If the feelings evoked in

---

another", an impulse that is really the patient's own and that, if recognized by the patient as his own, would lead to intolerable feelings of guilt (SANDLER et al., 1969, p. 277).

[4] In terms of object relations theory.

the analyst represent the patient's unconscious material, then a 'mutative interpretation' (derived from the analyst's understanding of his countertransference reaction) aims at undoing the patient's splitting and projection (CAPER, 1995). In making a 'mutative interpretation', the analyst adopts a "policy of non-cooperation with the splitting and projection that the patient depends on" (for his safety), a policy that can "jeopardise his good relationship with the patient". The anxiety that the analyst feels when he is about to make a 'mutative interpretation' (CAPER, 1995) and that he evokes in the patient by making such an interpretation is a testimony to the safety-procuring effects of reenactments of early role-relationships and of collaborations with the patient in this regard. Containment by the analyst of the patient's anxiety, provoked by 'mutative interpretations', allows the patient to rely less on projective identification, while introjection of the tolerating analyst strengthens the self and increases its autonomy.[5]

9.1.5 Defining the situation

In a social situation, the individual controls others' conduct and their attitudes towards himself, giving them an "impression that will lead them to act in accordance with his plan" (GOFFMAN, 1959, p. 4). The individual expresses himself "in a given way solely in order to give the kind of impression to others that is likely to evoke from them a specific response he is concerned to obtain" (p. 6), a response that supports his self-esteem. In effect, he shapes ('defines') the situation in such a way that it renders him in a favourable light. In seeking to define the situation in a self-supportive manner, the individual has to take into account a multitude of cues, such as others' posture, speech patterns, facial expressions, and bodily gestures as well as cues relating to others' social status. Control is exerted not only through what is being said but also through expressions of "the more theatrical and contextual kind, the non-verbal, presumably unintentional kind, whether this communication is purposely engineered or not" (GOFFMAN, 1959, p. 4).

Others will "themselves effectively project a definition of the situation by virtue of their response to the individual", whereby "the definitions of the situation projected by several different participants are sufficiently attuned to one another" (GOFFMAN, 1959, p. 9). "Together the participants contribute to a single over-all definition of the situation", aiming, at the same time, to avoid "an open conflict of definitions of the situation" (pp. 9–10). In reaching what GOFFMAN (1959) called a 'working consensus', "participants must be careful to agree not to disagree on the proper tone of voice, vocabulary, and degree of seriousness in which all arguments are to be phrased" (p. 10).

---

[5] In self psychology, the analyst's minor, nontraumatic empathy failures ('optimal frustrations') are important for advancing the formation of autonomic *self-sustaining* structures in the patient.

354 Narcissism and the Self

The situation thus established or defined provides an optimal solution to the problem of maximizing the narcissistic gain (safety) for each participant.

So much, if not all, of our social interchange consists in saying the 'right' thing to the 'right' person at the 'right' time.

(BURROW, 1949, p. 285)

While the individual projects his definition of the situation and expresses himself accordingly, disruptive events can occur, "which contradict, discredit, or otherwise throw doubt upon this projection", with the effect that "the individual whose presentation has been discredited may feel ashamed while the others present may feel hostile" (GOFFMAN, 1959, p. 12). Each individual manages to avoid experiencing shame and becoming the target for others' hostility inasmuch as he, *through his 'performance'*, wins others' recognition or respect (narcissistic sustenance) or consolidates or improves his social position (through which he controls access to narcissistic resources, unconsciously his proximity to the omnipotent object) (Figure 9.1). Performers tend to "offer their observers an impression that is idealized" (p. 35) in the interest of 'upward mobility'; and, in pursuit of their "desire for a place close to the sacred center of the common values of the society" (p. 36), their performance has to reflect "the officially accredited values of the society" (GOFFMAN, 1959, p. 35).

9.1.6 Self-relevance of others

That each one of the different personalities we imagine as belonging to other people reflects, as in a mirror, something in ourselves may seem an

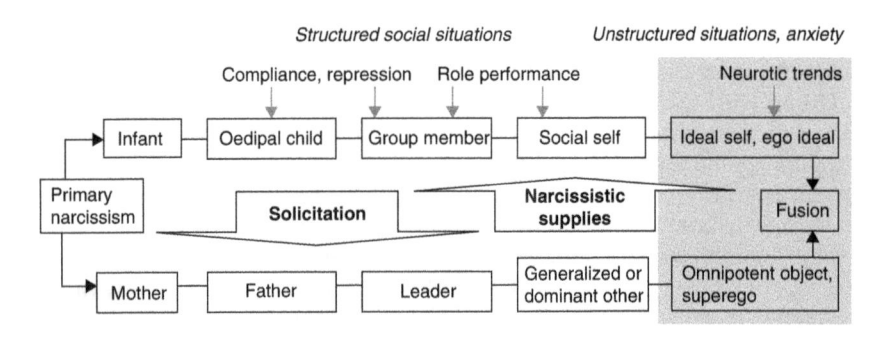

Figure 9.1 Relationship between 'social self' (JAMES) (shaped by role performance [GOFFMAN]) and 'ideal self' (shaped by 'neurotic trends' [HORNEY]), on the one hand, and 'generalized other' (GERTH & MILLS, 1954), 'dominant other' (ARIETI, 1973), 'omnipotent object' (e.g., BURSTEN, 1973), and superego, on the other. In unstructured or anxiety-provoking social situations, the derivative of the primary object (mother) is abstract and generally hidden from conscious awareness ('omnipotent object', 'superego')

improbable, as well as an unwelcome, proposition. ... For we are seldom dispassionate observers, and, for the most part, are interested in seeing only such aspects of them as concern their relation to ourselves.
(MONEY-KYRLE, 1961, p. 87)

The way in which we perceive others serves our self. Our perception of affects and sentiments in others serves "ego-centric interests" (MONEY-KYRLE, 1961, p. 87). We "infer in others such qualities as enable us to classify them into three main groups: friends, chosen enemies and what for want of a better name I will call necessary adjuncts" (p. 87). We populate "our outer world with these three types of person", and we have been doing so since early childhood, so that "the new friends, chosen enemies and necessary adjuncts we find, or imagine that we find, are to a great extent replicas of old ones – projections not only of aspects of ourselves, but re-projections of former personalities, as they were rightly or wrongly conceived by us to be, which have been absorbed into our inner world" (MONEY-KYRLE, 1961, p. 87).

A friend "is someone admitted to be like ourselves", someone with whom we share a "common trait or interest that establishes the bond" (MONEY-KYRLE, 1961, p. 88). The purpose of a friend is to "enlarge some aspect of our ego, making it stronger and less vulnerable in a potentially hostile world" (p. 88). A 'necessary adjunct' contains something we have lost – something we can regain "by attaching ourselves to someone who has, or seems to have it" (p. 90). We find in an 'necessary adjunct' "what was needed to 'complete' the self" (p. 90). Finally, a 'chosen enemy' is "someone whom we dislike because he seems to possess a trait we unconsciously dislike in ourselves" (p. 88). We usually have a trait that, if expressed or acknowledged, would render us "unworthy, unwanted and unloved (and so in danger of annihilation)" (p. 88); and in order to remain free of this trait (i.e., to repress it and thus avoid feeling worthless or inferior), we "must have an external depository" for it – someone "whom we can despise for real defects" (which we exaggerate but do not invent) (MONEY-KYRLE, 1961, p. 89).

MONEY-KYRLE (1961) realized that "much of our behaviour consists of attempts to manipulate our fellows by communicating with them" (p. 95). We manipulate our fellows with regard to the roles we envisage them to play for our self (and hence for our narcissistic equilibrium). In this process, we "equate persons in our current lives with persons who were important to us in infancy" and "react to their current representatives, often most inappropriately, as to 'good' or 'bad' parents or siblings" (p. 96). Our "compulsion to control and mould others in this way", to forcibly enact our projections (using what KLEIN called 'projective identification'), to "try, not merely to find, but to create friends, enemies and, above all, 'necessary adjuncts'", derives its impetus from "a desperate irrational anxiety" (MONEY-KYRLE, 1961, p. 97).

In all such cases, it is ultimately with the survival of something with which we have identified ourselves that we are concerned, if only in a remote way.

(MONEY-KYRLE, 1961, pp. 95–6)

9.1.7 Selection of friends

Our sense of self ('self-image') "at any given time is a reflection of the appraisals of others as modified by our previously developed self" (GERTH & MILLS, 1954, p. 85). The person's sense of self is built "on the basis of a long sequence of previous appraisals and expectations which others have presented to him" (p. 85). Our behaviour in social situations is aimed at gaining these appraisals and thereby enhancing our sense of self. It is "our eagerness to be well thought of by those who matter to us most" that influences our behaviour towards them (p. 91). This tendency of self-enhancement comes to bear in the selection of friends. The person tends to "to select and pay attention to those others who confirm this self-image, or who offer him a self-conception which is even more favorable and attractive than the one he possesses" (GERTH & MILLS, 1954, p. 86). 'Significant others' "are those to whom the person pays attention and whose appraisals are reflected in his self-appraisals" (p. 95). The person limits "his significant others to those who thus confirm his prized self-image" (p. 86). Significant others who are selected by the person for the purpose of confirming his self-esteem were called by GERTH and MILLS (1954) 'confirming others'.

> This principle leads the person to ignore, if he can, others who do not appreciate his prized or aspired-to self-image, or who debunk his image or restrain the development of it. A circle of friends is typically made up of those who further, or who at least allow the other persons to retain, their respective self-images. ... One avoids as best he can the enemies of the self-images one prizes. The cumulative selection of those persons who are significant for the self is thus in the direction of confirming persons, ...
>
> (GERTH & MILLS, 1954, p. 86)

Generalized other

The 'generalized other' is a more abstract concept; it "is composed of an integration of appraisals and values of the significant, and especially the authoritative, others of the person" (GERTH & MILLS, 1954, p. 95). The person can be appraised by "others who are not immediately present" (p. 95); he "may re-experience and use in evaluating his own self-image" past appraisals by significant others, past appraisals that have been deposited and integrated into the 'generalized other' (p. 95). In the 'generalized other', the past appraisals of many significant others – including appraisals "of later others which are more appropriate to [the person's] adult roles" – "are organized into a pattern" (p. 97). The content of the 'generalized other' changes as "new appraisals are added to older ones, and older ones are dropped or excluded from awareness" (p. 98), whereby the appraisals that matter most are the ones expressed by those "who are authoritatively significant to the person" (GERTH & MILLS, 1954, p. 96). The 'generalized other', approving the person and enhancing his self-esteem whenever his actions are in line with authoritative sanctions, is not unlike the Freudian superego (Figure 9.1).

9.1.8 Relationship with God

God, according to FLUGEL (1945), "represents our parents and our super-ego" (p. 167); and our attitude to God is determined by our attitude to our parents early in life. The superego, formed by introjection of our parents, can be projected out again. We project the internal superego onto the external figure of God, who "is in some ways the most suitable of all figures for projection of the super-ego" (p. 186). God is "a divine parent of whose power and infallibility" we can feel assured (p. 186); God is "the perfect loving parent" (p. 187). Religion gratifies "the wish for a protecting, kindly, omnipotent, and omniscient parent" (p. 225). FLUGEL (1945) explained that "in the idea of God we are able to recapture that sense of reliance on an all-good, all-wise parent which we enjoyed in our early years and which, we had regretfully come to realize, could not be permanently and completely satisfied in reference to any purely human figure" (p. 262).

We feel safe in the presence of "an omnipotent Creator who watches over us lovingly" (FLUGEL, 1945, p. 268). This sense of safety is intensified in the experience of religious exaltation, much as healthy self-esteem is on a continuum with neurotic pride and manic elation. Religious exaltation, as FLUGEL (1945) saw it, arises "from a sense of unity with the divine, a unity that seems to correspond psychologically to some condition of fusion between the ego and the super-ego" (p. 262). The raising of the worshipper to the level of his God in states of religious exaltation corresponds to "the ego being somehow raised to the position of the superego, the child to that of the parent" (p. 270). In ecstatic religious experience, the ego loses "its petty individuality" (p. 186) as it merges with the divine representative of the superego. When we are "'in tune with the infinite'", our separation anxiety is completely alleviated, and we "enjoy a sense of bliss and harmony" (FLUGEL, 1945, p. 186), which arguably recapitulates the oceanic sense of wellbeing associated with primary narcissism.

Suffering

Thus, in our relationship with God, we can "enjoy a continuation of the protection and guidance that was given to us by our parents in our infancy" (FLUGEL, 1945, p. 268). Any external representative of the superego, including God, has loving and protecting as well as frustrating and punishing aspects. The ambivalence in our attitude to God is a reflection of the ambivalence in our attitude to our parents and our earthly rulers, who act as sources of approval and as sources of disapproval or punishment. Gods are therefore commonly portrayed "as punishing, malignant beings as well as helpful ones" (FLUGEL, 1945, p. 187). When religions try to reconcile "the all-powerfulness and all-lovingness of God" with the existence of evil (p. 187), they draw inspiration from our often unconscious 'need for punishment'. Temptation by a forbidden impulse or commitment of a sin arouses in us a need to subject ourselves to punishment, so that we can regain the good will and love of our God, much as this dynamic was played out earlier in our life in the relationship with our parents. We hope that "divine justice will recompense us amply for the sufferings we have endured" (and open for us "the prospect of an eternity of bliss") (p. 268), much as a child hopes that, through his acceptance of punishment and endurance of suffering, he will be taken back into his parents' loving care (FLUGEL, 1945).[6]

Not only is the notion of God predicated on our need for punishment and suffering; suffering increases our need for God. Indeed, "men have most need of God when they feel themselves most helpless in the face of evil", even though "the very existence of this evil might seem to belie the divine love" (FLUGEL, 1945, p. 268). Evil and suffering create "so great a need for superhuman help that men will cling all the more desperately to the belief in such a love" (pp. 268–9). The helplessness that is associated with suffering and hardship "naturally induces a tendency to regression to the infantile position when we were dependent upon our early parents" (FLUGEL, 1945, p. 269).

9.1.9 Love

The lover experiences exaltation in the presence of his beloved object. The lover is in a state of joyful and satisfying surrender and experiences an expansion of his personality (FLUGEL, 1945). The beloved object narcissistically nourishes the lover, similarly to how the child feels safe and joyful in the presence of the loving and caring parent, who is the developmental precursor of the loving and helping aspects of the superego. FLUGEL (1945) suggested that, in the state of love (similarly to the state of hypnosis), the superego is projected onto the beloved object. Working through the beloved object, the superego acts "to embrace, attract, and elevate the ego" (p. 179). The projected superego has the power "to exercise a sthenic and elevating effect upon the ego, to raise the ego to its own level and there to undergo in some respects a fusion with it" (FLUGEL, 1945, p. 180) (Figure 9.1).

---

[6] In religious asceticism, the worshipper "inflicts suffering directly on himself to appease or pay homage to his God", while in sacrifice, "the worshipper suffers indirectly by depriving himself of something valuable and offering it to his God" (FLUGEL, 1945, p. 261). The sacrifice of a divine victim, in expectation of moral redemption, is an indirect expression of the need for punishment, wherein "this punishment is suffered vicariously by a scapegoat" (FLUGEL, 1945, p. 167).

Inhibitions are reduced and conflicts are overcome in the presence of the external figure on whom the loving and caring aspects of the superego have been projected (FLUGEL, 1945). Energy – that was hitherto invested into the adaptive or defensive maintenance of the ego as an object that, in the eyes of the superego (omnipotent object), is worthy of approval and acceptance – is freed. When fusion with the superego has been achieved, strenuous efforts aimed at attracting and retaining the attention and love of the superego become superfluous. Thus, in the presence of a loving and caring person who acts as an external representative of the superego, the person experiences "greater freedom and availability of mental energy" (FLUGEL, 1945, p. 180).

9.1.10 Trust and identification

MELANIE KLEIN (1937) described how features of old relationships with our parents, namely our attitude to them and their attitude to us, enter into our adult relationships. We may enter into a relationship with someone who has a parental attitude towards ourselves, so that this person could satisfy our earliest wishes for gratifications from a parent (p. 69), including wishes for "reassurance and security" (p. 76). The trust, protection, and admiration we experience in an adult relationship are not unlike the trust, protection, and admiration we experienced in childhood. The trust, protection, and help we direct at our partner are based on identification with a trusting, protecting, and helpful parent from our own childhood. Both partners in an adult relationship may alternately or simultaneously take the place of a parent (adopting a stance of giving) and put the other into the role of a parent. Under favourable conditions, the relationship for both partners "will be felt as a happy re-creation of their early family lives" (KLEIN, 1937, p. 74).

It seems a paradoxical fact that, in a way, fulfilment of many infantile wishes is possible only when the individual has grown up. In the happy relationship of grown-up people the early wish to have one's mother or father all to oneself is still unconsciously active.

(KLEIN, 1937, p. 75)

When partners in a relationship become parents themselves, they identify with their own helpful, wise, and reassuring parents when relating to their children (KLEIN, 1937). Both partners, identifying with one of their own parents when relating to their children, recreate their own "early family situation"; "and therefore the whole circle of reassurance and security will be wider still, through the relation of the man and woman to their children" (p. 76). The father, identifying with his own good father, expresses protective feelings towards his children. Moreover, when he is identified with his own children, "he shares in his mind their enjoyments" (p. 82); and he also shares "the maternal pleasure of his wife" (p. 81). The mother, by emulating the way her own mother related to her, loves her children and keeps her love prepared for them, so that she "feels unconsciously that she affords them security" (KLEIN, 1937, p. 80).

> In this situation, the mother has identified herself fully with her own helpful mother, whose protective influence has never ceased to function in her mind. At the same time she is also identified with her own children: she is, in her phantasy, as it were, again a child, and shares with her children the possession of a good and helpful mother. The unconscious minds of the children very often correspond to the mother's unconscious mind, and whether or not they make much use of this store of love prepared for them, they often gain great inner support and comfort through the knowledge that this love exists.
> (KLEIN, 1937, pp. 80–1)

Trust is associated with the ability to *give* and *protect* ('social feeling'), to make libidinal investments in objects. Trust in others is essential for secure self-esteem, for a sense of self that does not fluctuate readily in relation to the social situation. Trust moderates, but never abolishes, the need to manipulate others and the social situation for the sake of defining the self and maintaining safety. Both trust (the ability to give) and narcissism (the need to take) contribute to safety in healthy relationships.

> The capacity to give and take emotionally is one essential for true friendship. Here, elements of early situations are expressed in adult ways. Protection, help and advice were first afforded to us by our mothers. If we grow up emotionally and become self-sufficient, we shall not be too dependent upon maternal support and comfort, but the wish to receive them when painful and difficult situations arise will remain until we die. In our relation to a friend we may at times receive and give some of a mother's care and love. A successful blending of a mother-attitude and a daughter-attitude seems to be one of the conditions for an emotionally rich feminine personality and for the capacity for friendship.
> (KLEIN, 1937, p. 100)

9.2 Competition and conformity

> Our seemingly non-homogenous society with apparently great latitude in behavior consists of a mixture in space of different groups which in themselves are not less homogenous than primitive tribes.
> (SCHILDER, 1951, p. 289)

FREUD (1930) believed that "multitudes of human beings are libidinally bound to one another"; and – although "man's natural aggressive drive" seems to oppose the "programme of civilisation" (p. 58) – "contention and competition" between human beings are "indispensable" to civilization (p. 49). FREUD emphasized the link between repression of the destructive drive and progress of culture. The more advanced a culture, the more individuals have to exercise self-restraint in suppressing their violent and destructive tendencies. Aggression is however not repressed completely; it is expressed culturally constructively through the control and domination of others (FREUD, 1930) and the defence of one's social position. Cultural ritualization has converted aggressive tendencies into competitive sports and competitive strivings for power, possessions, and prestige (LORENZ, 1963, 1973; EIBL-EIBESFELDT, 1970). In competitive strivings, aggression "is to a great extent neutralized" (EIBL-EIBESFELDT, 1970, p. 217). RADO (1956) pointed out that "competition is adaptive only to the extent to which it *improves cooperation*; ruthless competition tends to destroy the group" (p. 342).

Whether in sports or other walks of life, we ultimately compete for narcissistic resources, for proximity to the leader the group (the developmental successor of the primary maternal object) or, in more complex social formations, for proximity to the abstract 'sacred centre' (GOFFMAN) of society (which is represented internally by the omnipotent object or superego). Our relationship with the group or its leader or with society at large is importantly a replication of the securing relationship with our primary love object; and it is in this sense that 'human beings are libidinally bound to one another'.

9.2.1 Ranking order

Intraspecific aggression fulfils three functions: the balanced distribution of animals of the same species over the available environment, selection of the strongest in a group by rival fight, and protection of the young (LORENZ, 1963). Mutual repulsion of individuals of the same species prevents overcrowding and exhaustion of nutritional resources and thus fulfils an important survival function for the species. While territorial animals use intraspecific aggression to prevent others from exploiting the resources of their territory, gregarious animals – whose survival depends more on membership of a group or herd – may have come to use aggression for the defence of their position in the group, a position which, like a territory, would determine their access to resources.

Ranking order is an important principle of organization of social life in higher vertebrates (LORENZ, 1963). Ranking order tends to ensure that older, more experienced animals remain in charge of the group and provide templates for imitative learning by younger, less experienced members of the group. As a result, individual experience and learning came to play an increasing role in the evolution of higher vertebrates (LORENZ, 1963, p. 42). Ranking order implies that "every individual in the society knows which one is stronger and which weaker than itself, so that everyone can retreat from the stronger and expect submission from the weaker" (p. 40). Ranking order limits fighting between members of the society, although it also has the consequence that "there is always particularly high tension between individuals who hold immediately adjoining positions in the ranking order" (Lorenz, 1963, p. 41).

9.2.2 Norms and rites

Phylogenetically evolved (innate) patterns of social behaviour are interrelated with cultural tradition (Lorenz, 1963, 1973). All patterns of verbal communication and displays of emotion in all cultures have traditional (cultural) ritualized elements superimposed upon innate components. Both phylogenetic and cultural ritualization serve to curb man's aggressive tendencies (Lorenz, 1963, 1973). Norms of social behaviour developed by cultural ritualization started to play an important role "when invention of tools was beginning to upset the equilibrium of phylogenetically evolved patterns of social behaviour" (p. 249), the "equilibrium between the ability and the inhibition to kill" (Lorenz, 1963, p. 242). Culturally evolved social norms, as expressed in customs and taboos as well as religious prescriptions and laws, function "like a supporting skeleton in human cultures" (Lorenz, 1963, p. 258).

Aggression in the group is absorbed and suppressed, in part, by members' adherence to "an average rule of conduct" (Schilder, 1951, p. 288). Conformity guarantees "to all members a reasonable security in getting the essentials of life – food, protection and sex gratification" (p. 288). However, complete conformity is impossible, "and the individual will always fight against conformity created by others" (Schilder, 1951, pp. 289–90). We cannot but infringe on social norms when trying to improve our social standing (and thus be closer to the sacred centre of society), so that "in all our interpersonal relationships", manifest "conformity and manifest defection are at loggerheads" (Burrow, 1949, p. 303).

Although cultural rituals and norms inhibit aggression between members of the group, there remains the potential for aggression stored up in the group to be released against the individual who deviates from the group's rituals and norms. Any "deviation from a group's characteristic manners and mannerisms" elicits overt aggression, which "forces all its members into a strictly uniform observance of these norms of social behaviour" (Lorenz, 1963, p. 76). The "nonconformist is discriminated against as an outsider" (Lorenz, 1963).

> The ganging up against an individual diverging from the social norms characteristic of a group, and the group's enthusiastic readiness to defend these social norms and rites, are both good illustrations of the way in which culturally determined conditioned stimulus situations release activities which are fundamentally instinctive.
>
> (Lorenz, 1963, p. 251)

As SCHILDER (1951) recognized, "human beings are continually afraid of the hostility of the others"; and "one function of society is to relieve human beings of the fear of mutual hostility and to divert the hostility toward outside groups" (p. 272). FREUD (1930), too, saw that binding "a large number of people together in love" requires that "others are left out as targets for aggression" (p. 50). Insofar as it is "clearly not easy for people to forgo the satisfaction of their tendency to aggression", they have to have an "outlet in the form of hostility to outsiders" (p. 50). Moreover, aggression against outsiders has the effect of "facilitating solidarity within the community" (FREUD, 1930, p. 51).

> Therefore a religion, even if it calls itself the religion of love, must be hard and unloving to those who do not belong to it. Fundamentally indeed every religion is in this same way a religion of love for all those whom it embraces; while cruelty and intolerance towards those who do not belong to it are natural to every religion.
> (FREUD, 1921, p. 51)

9.2.3 Substitutes of taboo

Taboo is a primitive social institution that limits the freedom of action. As civilization advances, the function of the taboo, namely the repression of instinctual impulses and desires, is taken over by the superego (FLUGEL, 1945, p. 133). The individual superego institutes individual repression of the forces of the id. In the form of conscience, it restrains man "from many antisocial actions to which his instincts and desires would naturally prompt him" (p. 133). 'Rational restraint' on part of the individual and the law are other equivalents and substitutes of taboo; the law "must be reckoned as a most important social institution that takes over the function of taboo, with on the whole a great increase in rationality" (p. 134). The law codifies social disapproval contingent upon its infringement (FLUGEL, 1945). Conventions and good manners, too, are equivalents of taboo, yet they are highly variable across society and readily change over time. Here again, the need for "social approval and the desire for conformity are the chief influences at work" (p. 139). Similarly to the disregard of a taboo, failure to comply with conventions or good manners calls forth "social disapproval or contempt", but here (in contradistinction to the law) "social disapproval is not codified" (p. 136). In anticipation of others' disapproval or contempt, failure to observe the sanctioned limits of "permissible action, opinion, and language" (p. 137) produces embarrassment or "feelings of guilty discomfort"; "and these feelings are very similar to those aroused by the infringement of more primitive and permanent taboos" (FLUGEL, 1945, p. 139).

The taboo loses its function in civilized society because "civilized society is far les homogenous than primitive society, exhibiting as it does a far greater variation in aims, ideals, habits, and traditions", "which inevitably subjects the growing individual to conflicting influences from which the younger members of primitive communities are free" (FLUGEL, 1945, p. 133). This diversity and the resulting "greater tendency to mental conflict" are responsible not only for the decline of taboos (and the ascendency of the superego) but also for the prevalence of neurosis among civilized people (p. 133). The repression of desire is an essential factor in neurosis, as it is in the taboo. FLUGEL (1945) thought that "individual neurosis is the price that society has to pay for the greater diversity of thought and outlook that is a characteristic of civilization" (as opposed to primitive society) (p. 133). Inasmuch as the individual superego replaces communal taboos in civilized society, the self arises as the internal counterpart to the superego, and so does the neurosis in which the self gets entangled.

9.2.4 Possessions and prestige

Society neutralizes mutual hostility and puts rivalries "into a definite form which is no longer dangerous" (SCHILDER, 1951, p. 287). Aggressive tendencies are diverted "toward work and toward nature" (as well as "toward the outside enemy") (SCHILDER, 1951, p. 276). Aggression is channelled into socially acceptable outlets, such as *work* concerned with the advancement of one's power, prestige, and possessions. Power, prestige, and possessions "have to be acquired by ... competitive struggle with others" (HORNEY, 1937, p. 188). The quest for power, prestige, and possessions – as a way of gaining "protection against helplessness and against insignificance" (p. 171) – is deeply embedded in Western culture (HORNEY, 1937). Power, prestige, and possessions mark one's narcissistic resources and *enshrine one's safety*. Insofar as power status, prestige, and possessions have a narcissistic (selfobject) function (i.e., insofar as they are narcissistically cathected), any implicit challenge to them is aggressively defended. Then neutralized aggression invested into maintaining, in various abstract ways, one's access to narcissistic resources becomes overt.

The human 'urge to dominate' "prompts us to aspire to positions of eminence and esteem" (HASS, 1968, p. 138) – positions that *impress* others, that is, induce in them a respectful or submissive attitude (*an attitude that narcissistically nourishes the eminent person*). A "pleasurable sense of power" is associated with impressing other people "with the attainment of superior positions, titles, decorations, and marks of distinction" (p. 205). Behaviour motivated by the 'desire to impress' has two objectives. Firstly, it impresses a prospective mate. Secondly, "among creatures which live in groups", it "demonstrates the individual's standing within the group" (HASS, 1968, p. 179).

Man enhances his ability to impress "with the aid of handsome clothing, jewellery, and the like" (thereby influencing "receptive mechanisms in fellow members of the species") (HASS, 1968, p. 182). Man surrounds himself with possessions and symbols designed to "accentuate the impression he makes on others and intensify his pleasurable sense of power", whereby "the desire to acquire them increases his willingness to work" (p. 183). The instinctively motivated "striving for success, esteem, and power, for social acceptance and standing, for recognition, superiority, and admiration" deeply influences man's behaviour towards other people (p. 179). It "influences the course of conversations and negotiations" and "hounds a man into the recesses of his imagination" (p. 179). Failure in this striving has "a particularly corrosive effect"; it breeds "contempt and repudiation on the part of others" (Hass, 1968, p. 179).

> To be vanquished or inferior, to be condescended to, to be mocked, ignored, or looked at askance by others – all these things provoke unpleasant tensions against which we are comparatively powerless. If people work far harder than is necessary just to maintain life and security, if they are ruled by a restless impulse to improve their lot, the underlying motive is often that of the urge to impress.
>
> (Hass, 1968, p. 179)

9.2.5 Enforcement of conformity

The individual's narcissistic "self-assertion" is assured so long as others respect his territory, his rightful access to narcissistic resources, his relative position in a network of narcissistic exchange. The rules and customs against which the individual defines his self, his position, and his access to narcissistic resources are themselves narcissistically cathected. Therefore, others' challenge to these rules and customs, others' nonconformity is threatening; it inflicts a narcissistic injury upon the compliant individual. Others' "divergence" from norms of the group is felt by the compliant individual as though it "involved a criticism" of himself. This is the "source" of man's "hatred". Hatred emerges time and again at different points in an abstract social network that, due to the variability of the conformity of its members (and due to changes in its composition), undergoes deformations of its settled shape. In the settled group, the "aversion" towards others, "this intolerance vanishes" temporarily. Aggression is inhibited so long as everybody conforms (words in quotation marks taken from Freud, 1921, pp. 55–6).

> Once we see evil in someone else it becomes possible and may seem necessary to let loose pent-up aggression against that person. It is here that the large part played in life by condemnation of others, criticism, denunciation, and intolerance generally, comes in. What we cannot tolerate in ourselves we are not likely to tolerate in others. In so condemning others we can obtain gratification, too, both directly from discharging our aggressive impulses, and from the reassurance obtained that we ourselves conform to and uphold the standards of rightness and perfection. ... This

very important expression of aggressive impulses in civilised life is seen in countess everyday situations ...

(RIVIERE, 1937, p. 38)

Others' conformity (their submission to the norms of society) inhibits our aggression, because it signals their *respect* for our social position, the position by which we define our identity (self) and through which we maintain our safety. Others' nonconformity not only represents a challenge to our identity (self), and hence invokes within us an offensively aggressive response, it also provides an opportunity for the *release* of aggression, insofar as the expression of aggression is socially acceptable in situations involving others' infractions of norms. Aggression thus invoked deters others from future norm violations, and hence critically contributes to the upholding of norms. Our insistence on others' conformity, our sensitivity to others' infractions of norms, and our own conformity reflect both our instinctive readiness for aggression and a fear of becoming the target of others' aggression (Figure 9.2).

9.2.6 Therapeutic groups

Individuals wish to be *accepted* by members of their group. In therapeutic groups, too, members experience a "fear of being left out or not being accepted" (PARLOFF, 1968, p. 503). Mutual acceptance increases the self-esteem of members; members feel secure as a result of others' acceptance. Group therapy "provides more opportunity than individual treatment does for experiencing wholesome, loving feelings, sympathy and positive relatedness", although "patients in groups occasionally treat each other with harshness and cruelty" (PARLOFF, 1968, p. 504). The group 'focal conflict', which

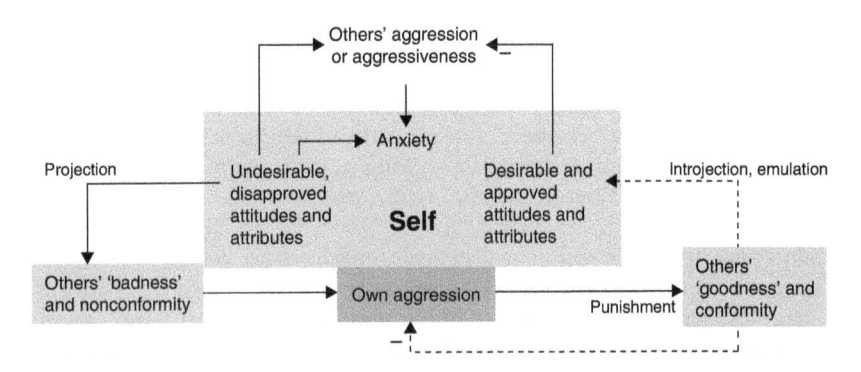

Figure 9.2 Projection and introjection are ways of defending against feelings of anxiety that reflect vulnerability to others' attack. One's own angry expressions, elicited by others' nonconformity or badness, are aversive to others and so help to enforce social norms

finds expression in the various verbalizations and behaviours of patients in a group therapy session, is often between the need to be a member of the group (need for dependency or wish to trust others) and the fear of others (fear of revealing oneself to others [and the shame associated with it] or fear of being hurt or betrayed by other group members) (WHITMAN & STOCK, 1958).

When a new therapy group commences, the main feeling among members is anxiety and the need to find and retain a role in the group (DE BOARD, 1978). The questions that arise in each member's mind are: will I dominate others in the group or will I face the group's hostility? Consciously or unconsciously, the question 'who dominates whom' is on all members' minds (DE BOARD, 1978). The group "stimulates each member to adopt a particular role which corresponds to his own way of defending himself against unconscious fears" (PARLOFF, 1968, p. 517). For example, one member's striving for dominance is complemented and supported by the submissiveness of another. Members must deal with the opportunity of controlling others and with the possibility of being controlled by others. Moreover, the therapeutic group setting engenders intense rivalries for the therapist's attention and *approval* (PARLOFF, 1968). Members try to ascertain the group's rules and regulations and conform with the leader's wishes and expectations. Most of the behaviour exhibited will be that which has gained approval from authority figures in the past (DE BOARD, 1978).

The behaviour of group members is a function of the phase of group development (AGAZARIAN & PETERS, 1981). In the second phase of the development of a therapy group, members tend to challenge other members of the group. Aggressive behaviour ('aggressive dependence behaviour') "induces the conformity of other members to the leader's imagined or real leadership" (p. 135). Members "look to certain members for support and alliance, to others for contention and disagreement" (p. 135). Competitive subgroups scapegoat each other or a particular member (AGAZARIAN & PETERS, 1981). The group is unconsciously on the lookout for scapegoats. The group may be angry with its leader "but not daring to attack him directly or to show open hostility, will relieve and displace its emotion and fury onto one of themselves, usually a weak or absent member" (scapegoat) (FOULKES, 1964, p. 113).

Later, the emphasis in group dynamics shifts to nonconformity and rebellion against the leader's (therapist's) rules (AGAZARIAN & PETERS, 1981). The "projections on the leader turn 'bad', and the leader is seen either as malevolent" or incompetent (p. 136). The leader becomes an 'object of rage'. Questions are asked that cannot be answered to the group's satisfaction and that are, in fact, an act of power ('confrontation questions'); what the group wants is not an answer but to control the leader. The group consolidates in their power struggle with the leader. Scapegoating "becomes a unifying group force that unites the members against the leader" (p. 136); and, however the group raises the 'authority issue', "the effect is to continue to build a strong family feeling among the members" (p. 137). At this point, the "group as a whole provides surrogate ego support for all members", while the leader is left to experience *annihilation* anxiety, a state of terror (AGAZARIAN & PETERS, 1981, p. 138).

9.2.7 Social monitoring and alliance formation

Competition for resources involves the discouragement and aggressive control of competitors. In primates, another method of coordinating social groups can be observed: individuals monitor each other's movements and overt expressions of attention (MOYNIHAN, 1998). Competition for access to resources is regulated "by facilitating, even ensuring, that associates can monitor one another's activities", so that no individual "is likely to get much of a head start in exploiting a resource when and if its companions are watching with interest at the time" (MOYNIHAN, 1998, p. 100). Individuals monitor each other's adherence to norms and their progression or downfall in the ranking order but also others' potential for collaboration and formation of alliances. Indeed, dominant status in primate societies is determined not by aggressiveness alone. Status will be withheld from a purely aggressive animal (EIBL-EIBESFELDT, 1970). In various species of monkeys, "the ability of a male to make friendships with others is a prerequisite for a high ranking status" (p. 83). It is often the especially friendly male "that knows how to win the sympathies of the others" (p. 83).[7] Other factors determining the attainment of status in groups of apes and some monkeys are the individual's age and experience (EIBL-EIBESFELDT, 1970).

9.3 Group cohesion

FOULKES (1964) spoke of the individual's need "to be understood by and related to the group", a need that prevails "in spite of impulses to withdraw" (p. 109). There exists in each individual, according to EZRIEL (1950), an "unconscious dynamic source, a need, which sets up a tension" that "tries to find relief through his establishing a certain kind of relationship between himself" and another person or the social environment, in general (p. 111). These relationships express the individual's "unconscious fantasies about his relations with unconscious objects" (p. 111). As all members of a group attempt to transfer their unconscious object relations to objects in their present environment, a 'common denominator' establishes itself. The group structure is "the result of the individual contributions of all group members working upon one another" (EZRIEL, 1950, p. 146).

The group structure can be conceptualized on different levels of abstraction (FOULKES, 1964). On the 'projective level', relationship patterns in the

---

[7] A positive correlation between aggressiveness and status is however seen in monkeys living in "cramped conditions of zoo life" (EIBL-EIBESFELDT, 1970, p. 84).

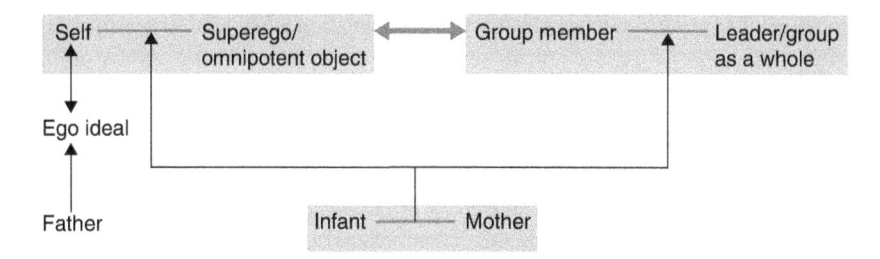

Figure 9.3 Relationship between self and group. The self aims to provide the safety evolutionarily associated with membership of a cohesive group and ontogenetically experienced in symbiosis with the mother. As such, the self remains unconsciously bound to the superego (omnipotent object). In addition, the self is constituted as 'an other' through resolution of the Oedipus complex (LACAN)

group represent inner object relations. On the 'transference level', the leader represents the mother or father, and the other members represent the siblings. The group is a symbolic family with the leader as a parent, especially in the early stages of group formation (FOULKES, 1964). In the setting of group analysis, "the connection between the leader of the group and single members of the group is particularly strong, whereas the bond between the members of the group is otherwise comparatively weak" (SCHILDER, 1951, p. 287). The analyst, as the leader of the group, "represents father and mother", and so "the importance of family ties" becomes apparent (SCHILDER, 1951, p. 287). On a deep level of understanding, attachment to the group as a whole is an attachment to the mother. The group, satisfying individuals' needs for belonging and protection, is, on a deep level, "the symbolic representation of a nurturing mother" (SCHEIDLINGER, 1964, p. 218).

In a cohesive group, the self becomes obsolete; this is why the self of group members can be said to merge with the group. Self, ego ideal, and superego are psychological structures that compensate for the sense of separateness that pervades social situations that are not characterized by tight cohesion. *Self, ego ideal, and superego regulate the individual's narcissistic balance outside the most primitive group processes* (Figure 9.3). Membership of a group that functions on a basic-assumption level (BION, 1952) provides a more primitive way of narcissistic gratification. Narcissistic gratification of group membership finds its starkest expression in what KERNBERG (1998)[8] called "the spirit of the mob, which satisfies every member's need to overcome a sense of separateness by participating in a common, powerfully self-righteous, emotionally laden movement forward" (p. 72). Already DURKHEIM (1893) saw that people can be brought together in a primitive way by sharing their states of consciousness. When participating in a collective

---

[8] With reference to ELIAS CANETTI's *Crowds and Power*.

reaction to someone's wrongdoing, people lose their individuality, and their individual consciousnesses (and identities) merge into the 'collective consciousness' (DURKHEIM, 1893).

9.3.1 Dependency

The need for group membership is, on a deep level, "the wish for reunion with a nurturing mother" (SCHEIDLINGER, 1964, p. 229). The human need to belong to and identify with a group "represents a covert wish for restoring an earlier state of unconflicted well-being inherent in the exclusive union with mother" (p. 218), "the original state of unconflicted well-being represented in the earliest infant–mother tie" (SCHEIDLINGER, 1964, p. 224). The unconscious identification of the group entity with the mother explains "the strong need to be 'at one' with a group" (WHITMAN & STOCK, 1958, p. 183, footnote 4). Identification (union) with the mother, implying a state of unconflicted wellbeing, precedes developmentally the formation of a *relationship with* the mother, a relationships that is based on recognition of the separateness of the object. Identification is an earlier and more primitive form of involvement with an other; and hence, there is in group formation a regression from object choice to narcissistic identification, as proposed by FREUD (1921).

> ... as part of this narcissistic orientation, objects are sought out primarily as instruments for the purpose of relieving inner tension. Insofar as transference reactions involve the unconscious reliving of powerful feelings of love and hate akin to more advanced stages of object relationships, these tend to emerge somewhat later, *after* group formation has taken hold.
>
> (SCHEIDLINGER, 1968, p. 250)

'Basic assumptions', which are unspoken assumptions that are tacitly accepted by all members of a group, influence and direct the activity of the group (BION, 1952, 1961). A common basic assumption shared by members of a group is that "the group exists in order to be sustained by a leader on whom it depends for nourishment, material and spiritual, and protection" (BION, 1952, p. 78). The leader in the basic-assumption group of 'dependency' is a symbol of the protecting, sustaining, and gratifying parent. Members behave as if they are inadequate, immature, and helpless, whereas the leader is endowed with god-like qualities of wisdom, knowledge, and power. Through their behaviour, members underscore their "desperate need for an omniscient and omnipotent leader" (PARLOFF, 1968, pp. 514–15). Their behaviour is designed to *induce* the leader to fulfil their dependency needs. When the leader fails to live up to the group's expectations, the group reacts with disappointment, rejection, and hostility towards the leader (BION, 1952, 1961).

Individuals experience heightened anxiety and readily engage in 'dependence behaviour' when they enter a therapy group (AGAZARIAN & PETERS,

1981). In the process of group formation, there is commonly an initial dependency phase, involving "a regression of the group members to a dependent state in relation to a leader" (SCHEIDLINGER, 1968, p. 241). The regression that members of a therapy group undergo in its formative phase is a regression to the dependent wish to be *nurtured* and cared for by the leader. In the process of group formation, "group members in a shared fantasy appear to seek nurture and support from a magical parent-leader" (p. 245). Members have a wish to merge with the leader. Fantasized gratification of the wish for union with the leader generates euphoria and contentment (SCHEIDLINGER, 1968).

9.3.2 Anxiety

Separation anxiety and the dread of abandonment motivate proximity seeking and group membership. EIBL-EIBESFELDT (1970) discerned two principal roots of sociability in vertebrates: flight motivation and parental care. Group formation motivated by the 'flight drive' is very old and derived from the tendency of the child to go to his mother when in danger (EIBL-EIBESFELDT, 1970, p. 119). Insofar as the proximity of conspecifics has been associated, in the course of evolution, with security, conspecifics act as a 'goal-in-flight', a goal that is approached at times of anxiety. Given that the same motivational process underlies the seeking of shelter and the retreat to places of high familiarity and predictability ('home'), conspecifics and their congregations can be said to have 'home valency' (EIBL-EIBESFELDT, 1970).

In humans (and other primates), the coming together of individuals activates their potential for 'primitive aggression' and arouses in them 'intense anxieties' (KERNBERG, 1998). Group cohesion defends against paranoid (persecutory) anxiety, the fear of becoming the target of others' aggression or that of the group as a whole. Separation from the group is anxiety-provoking, but so is opposition to the group; and either is anxiously avoided (FREUD, 1921, p. 83). JAQUES (1955) thought that the need to defend against 'psychotic anxiety' is a major factor binding individuals into groups and organizations. Social life in groups and organizations affords collective support for members' defences against psychotic (persecutory) anxiety (JAQUES, 1955). Aggression is, at the same time, channelled into "exercise of power in organisational and institutional life" (KERNBERG, 1998, p. 71). BION, too, thought that belonging to the group and the 'basic assumptions' that underlie members' behaviour are defences against psychotic anxiety; they keep in check members' fears that primitive aggression will emerge. Psychotic or paranoid anxiety spontaneously arising in a novel or unstructured social situation precipitates the regression and identification phenomena that are associated with group formation, including the merging of the individual's identity with that of the group.

Social behaviour that adheres to accepted norms and social expectations guides us to a situation of safety. We have an innate disposition to obedience

(EIBL-EIBESFELDT, 1970). Every person has "the need, motivated by fear, to know where one stands" within the social order (p. 164). Even a subordinate position in the dominance hierarchy guards against anxiety, and, for this reason, "human beings submit to the cruel ruler and give him their allegiance" (p. 164). When the overriding need is for security, adoption of a subordinate position is preferable to a higher but uncertain position. Social order guards against anxiety because it allows individuals to reenact a parent–child relationship: "the dominant individual acts in a fatherly manner and the subordinate in a childishly dependent manner" (p. 164). Parental care (in the context of which infants enjoy *protection*) is one of the roots of sociability, the other being 'flight motivation' (EIBL-EIBESFELDT, 1970).

> Our own desire for order has its roots in flight motivation. Order means orientation in time and space and indeed not only in relation to events outside our species. It also gives us a sense of security if we can tell in advance what other people will do, and if we know what we should do. Even a small child will ask firmly what it should and should not do: in this way it acquires social orientation and with this a sense of security.
>
> (EIBL-EIBESFELDT, 1970, p. 164)

9.3.3 Identification with the leader

FREUD (1921) stated that "a group is clearly held together by a power of some kind: and to what power could this feat be better ascribed than to Eros, who holds together everything in the world" (p. 40). Libidinal ties between members of a group and their leader are in part narcissistic ties, concerned with the idea of being *loved* or *accepted* by the leader, who is an omnipotent object and developmentally continuous with the primary maternal object (Figure 9.1). Each group member has the (unconscious) belief or illusion that he is individually loved by the leader. The leader of the group is the object of each group member's attention. This is combined with admiration (idealization) of the leader by each group member (FREUD, 1921). Thus, attainment of narcissistic sustenance (receipt of love) from the leader is coupled with idealization of the leader, just as idealization of the parent imago in early childhood is a narcissistic phenomenon (KOHUT).

Having established that "libidinal ties are what characterize a group" (p. 54), FREUD (1921) argued that, in libidinal relationships that constitute the group, "object choice has regressed to identification", that is, to "the earliest and original form of emotional tie" in which the ego "assumes the characteristics of the object" (p. 64). Members of a group show heightened suggestibility and readiness for mutual identification and identification with the leader (FREUD, 1921). In their adoration of the leader, members identify with him. Feeling loved by and adoration of the leader are two aspects of identification with the leader, an identification that approximates the infant's experience of omnipotent union with the mother.

While in some groups, members' conduct is determined predominantly by the fear of loss of approval from a patriarchal leader (corresponding to 'fear of the superego'), individuals in other groups are more motivated by a desire to emulate their leader (REDL, 1942). In the process of emulating the leader, they identify with him. Members may base their 'ego ideal' ("the other part of their superego" [p. 25]) on their leader, in that "they start wishing to become the type of person he is" (REDL, 1942, p. 26). Identification with the leader of a group has deep roots in primate evolution. It can be observed in other primates, such as macaques. As maternal bonds are broken, between the sixth and the seventh months of an infant's life, adult male leaders of the troop take over the care of male infants. In this context, male infants appear to adopt the personality traits of their mentor (reviewed in MACHADO & BACHEVALIER, 2003).

9.3.4 Omnipotence of the leader

Approval- or attention-seeking behaviour is not randomly directed in the social context; not uncharacteristically, we seek to be "treated kindly by a person who is powerful and influential" (HORNEY, 1937, p. 110). We seek gratification by way of soliciting love, praise, admiration, or approval from the 'dominant other', a derivative of the primary love object (ARIETI, 1973). The need for approval from the 'dominant other' motivates group membership. In seeking attention or approval from a powerful and influential leader, we enter into competitive relationships with each other. Our sense of self marks our closeness to the leader, to the source of narcissistic gratification. On the other hand, we lose our sense of self and gain a sense of safety by identifying with the leader and participating in his omnipotence. What lies at the heart of group dynamics in either case is our need for an omnipotent leader, a derivative of the primary parental object, consistent with the parental care origin of groups.

The omnipotence of the person chosen to be the leader may be projected onto him by those who need an omnipotent leader (FENICHEL, 1946). To facilitate their identification with the chosen object, and to thus enable their "participation in the projected omnipotence" (p. 510), the "object is to be induced to take over characteristics of the ego ideal" (p. 511). The object has to be influenced "by force, by ingratiation, and by every magical means" to "behave in a special manner corresponding to the subject's ideal" (p. 510). This mechanism, too, is not only used for the sake of narcissistic gratification "but also as a defence against anxiety" (FENICHEL, 1946, p. 511).

Through approximation of our ego ideal, we unconsciously seek acceptance by the superego (the omnipotent object). The leader can also be regarded as an external representative of the superego (which, in turn, is the internal representative of the parental object). The leader of the group to which we belong "is par excellence the figure on whom our super-ego is projected" (FLUGEL, 1945, p. 184).[9] Our attitude to the leader is an ambivalent one, similarly to the attitude "of the child to its parent or the ego to the super-ego" (p. 184). The hostile element in our attitude to the leader "may be repressed" but is "liable to break out if the leader's success or prestige should decline" (FLUGEL, 1945, p. 184).

> With all human representatives of the super-ego we are liable in some degree to a repetition of the disappointment that we suffered when we realized the limitations of our own original parents.
> (FLUGEL, 1945, p. 186)

A courageous person ('hero'), who commits an act others do not dare to consider, is admired by them and readily becomes their leader (REDL, 1942). Some persons may be chosen as leader because they seem omniscient and omnipotent; they seem to be *independent* and not to need external narcissistic supplies. Introverted personalities "have succeeded more or less in regaining the security of primary narcissism" (FENICHEL, 1946, p. 510). An introverted person who manifests 'omnipotent behaviour' and "seems to be especially 'independent'" is readily admired by others; "he exerts an especially fascinating effect" on those with dependant personalities ("who need magical helpers") (p. 510). He attracts 'followers' who, "united in their common fascination" for him, "struggle for permission to participate in the 'omnipotent' narcissist's power" (FENICHEL, 1946, p. 510).[10]

9.3.5 Submission to the leader

Members of the group feel secure and sheltered in the presence of their leader; however, "behind the happy security felt in his presence there is a nagging fear of its loss" (REDL, 1942, p. 24). Members feel anxious if they are not sure of the leader's approval, especially if the leader is of a patriarchal type (REDL, 1942). Members feel secure for as long as they behave in accordance with the code of the patriarchal leader.[11] To be accepted by the leader

---

[9] As members of the group substitute their leader for their superego, "a splitting of the superego takes place, and as a member of the group the individual accepts moral standards that as a private person he would reject" (HARTMANN, 1964, p. 51).

[10] Although introverted personalities see themselves as "independent of real objects", they can become "very dependent again whenever external events ... make them doubt their omnipotence" (FENICHEL, 1946, p. 510). They may then need to participate in the omnipotence of another person and "identify themselves with this person so as to enjoy the feeling of being loved by themselves" (FENICHEL, 1946, p. 511).

[11] Insofar as members act in accordance with the code of the leader ('central person'), their superego can be said to "incorporate the superego – conscience – of the central person" (REDL, 1942, p. 24).

is a requirement for happiness, and members are "ready to pay for it by conscientious output of work" (REDL, 1942, p. 25). Members have to *repress* or modulate their 'instinctual drives' (aggression, sexuality) if they want to be spared the wrath of the leader and be assured of his love and approval.[12] The modulation of members' conduct in deference to the wishes or demands of the leader has to be recognized as narcissistic, because the aim of such modulation is to attain safety (wellbeing or narcissistic equilibrium). Outside the hierarchical group context, the individual exercises *self*-restraint when repressing his instinctual drives for the purpose of maintaining his safety. Self-restraint does not depend on the presence of a patriarch or leader. The leader has been replaced by the self-observing and self-critical agency, the superego.

Hypnosis

Hypnosis illustrates the innate potential of humans for submissiveness to the group leader (FREUD, 1921). Human beings have a "habit of accepting authority without testing it" and are "capable of such submission that [they] can fall victim to anyone who poses as the possessor of special powers" (ADLER, 1927, p. 64). Hypnosis is based on this principle, on the capacity of human beings to show "servile obedience" (p. 65). The 'critical faculties' of the hypnotized subject "are completely paralyzed" as he "becomes, so to speak, the tool of the hypnotist, an organ functioning at his or her command" (p. 64). Individuals who "are exceptionally susceptible to suggestion or hypnosis" are those who always overvalue the other person's opinions and therefore undervalue their own (ADLER, 1927, p. 65).

Hypnosis illustrates the principle of projection of the superego (FLUGEL, 1945). The hypnotized person is highly suggestible insofar as he has projected his superego onto the hypnotist. This projection is accompanied by regression to an infantile level of functioning characterized by a high degree of trust in and obedience to a parental figure (FLUGEL, 1945).

9.3.6 Identification with the group as a whole

The individual's relationship with the group as a whole is characterized by identification with the group as a whole. Identification with the group, too, counterbalances the competition between group members for exclusive attention from the leader (symbolizing a nurturing parent). Identification with the group means that each individual regards the group as part of his self. As a result of the individual's identification with the group, "he reacts to the attributes of the group as if these attributes were also his own"

---

[12] Under certain circumstances, instinctual impulses are readily expressed. For instance, when the group is faced by an external threat (BION's basic assumption of 'fight or flight'), individuals are freed, as FREUD (1921) remarked, from the repression of their aggressive impulses.

(SCHEIDLINGER, 1964, p. 223). Identification (feeling at one) with an admired object or with a group has the effect of raising self-esteem (i.e., narcissistic ego feeling). Identification with the group entity "promotes an individual sense of belonging, of enhanced self-esteem, and of ego identity" (p. 226). By way of identification with the group entity, members experience an emotional state that is a derivative of the state of unconflicted wellbeing implicit in the exclusive union with the preoedipal mother (SCHEIDLINGER, 1964). Identification with the group entity is facilitated by idealization of the group. Alternatively, idealization of the group, especially the feeling aspect of such idealization, can be seen as manifestation of the sense of belonging to the group and of restored narcissistic equilibrium.

FEDERN (1952) stated that in groups narcissistic cathexis, by each individual, of a common object (the group or its leader) and the extension of each individual's ego boundaries "to a common identification" serves to "provide the individuals with a much desired strong support" (p. 345). Identification with a group or its leader can effect a partial reversal to primary narcissism, that is, "the primary narcissistic cathexis unity ... may be renewed at the occasion of the expansion of the ego boundaries into the group ego" (FEDERN, 1952, p. 350). In the terminology of self psychology, the group or its leader fulfils a vital selfobject function, meeting one's need for narcissistic sustenance. The 'psychological image' of the organization one joins "can serve as an idealizable selfobject – a source of pride in belonging to it – and may also provide a self-confirming selfobject experience" (WOLF, 1988, pp. 47–8).

Dissolution of the self

The merging of the individual in a group is accompanied by the loss of the sense of individual separateness. FREUD (1921) observed that in a group the individual loses his distinctiveness. In the group, the individual relinquishes his otherwise preciously guarded individuality. BION (1952) specified that individuals lack distinctiveness when they are members of a group that operates in line with one of the basic assumptions. He thought that the loss of the individual's distinctiveness "is a phenomenon indistinguishable from depersonalization" (BION, 1952, p. 105). Belonging to or feeling part of a group implies a "giving up of some aspect of the individual's self" (SCHEIDLINGER, 1964, p. 220). It entails the giving up of an element of the self *to the group* (SCHEIDLINGER, 1964). One could say that the self becomes dissolved in the group as it becomes equated (identified) with the group. The self, as a narcissistically cathected defensive structure, dissolves as ego boundaries extend across the group.

The satisfaction of breaking "through the shell of individuality" (HORNEY, 1937, p. 274) and losing oneself in something greater is evident in the masochistic attitude as well as in normal phenomena such as love and "enthusiasm for a cause" (p. 272). By surrendering our self to a common cause, "we feel at one with a greater whole"; by losing our self, we "can become at one with God or nature" (p. 273). The individual overcomes his limitations and his sense of isolation by "dissolving the self in something greater, by becoming part of a greater entity" (HORNEY, 1937, p. 273).[13] It is the self as a defensive structure that dissolves, while pride or self-esteem (in the sense of narcissistic satisfaction) increases. Group formation thus involves a regression, both ontogenetically and culturally, from self-concern and individual distinctiveness to submergence in the group, a submergence that effortlessly meets each group member's narcissistic needs. The self outside the context of group membership is an alternative, historically more recent safety devise. The self is a modern, individualistic detour to the state of wellbeing (safety). *In overcoming separateness and disconnectedness, narcissism forms the self, much as narcissism is at work when individuals merge with the group or crowd.*

Equality among members

Members of the group compete for an exclusive tie with the leader. Through identification with the leader, group members overcome their rivalries with each other and their envious attitudes towards each other (FREUD, 1921). Competition between members is also counterbalanced by insistence on equality among members and by identification of members with each other. Identification of group members with each other – arising in consequence of the perception of shared qualities or common interests or ideals – fosters mutual bonds between group members (FREUD, 1921). FREUD (1921) thought that it is the common tie to the leader in particular that allows members to feel united, to identify with each other and have a group identity (group self). Identification of group members with each other allows individuals to love each other, so that these identifications form the basis for 'group libido', the "libido aroused under group formational conditions" (REDL, 1942, p. 50).

9.3.7 Joint aggression

As primates living in closed groups we are disposed to close our ranks in danger. Common defence or common aggression establish an exceptionally strong bond. This is true of primitive peoples and there is no question but that we follow the same pattern. Groups are even united by ritualized mock battles (football etc.).

(EIBL-EIBESFELDT, 1970, p. 161)

---

[13] The self may dissolve transiently in *dyadic* situations involving empathic understanding. KOHUT (1966) noted that the phylogenetic prototype of empathic understanding is the "involuntary trancelike condition which occurs in those who become submerged in an excited mob".

Release of collective aggression towards a common enemy unites the group. In the 'social defensive reaction', a common threat "welds gregarious creatures into a fighting unit", "a phenomenon exhaustively studied in rhesus monkeys, baboons, and howling monkeys" (Hass, 1968, p. 197). Alliances or bonds of friendship can be created by forming a common front of aggressive behaviour towards a third party in the form of an outside group or an outsider in the group (Hass, 1968). Freud (1921), too, recognized that shared hatred of an outsider or outside institution fosters group cohesion. Scapegoats, towards whom members of a group jointly discharge their aggression, serve to increase cohesion of the group (Eibl-Eibesfeldt, 1970). Being an outsider or scapegoat is highly aversive and anxiogenic, as much as adherence to social norms and *recognition* by the group are reassuring. Narcissism is the mechanism that counters the fear of annihilation (disintegration anxiety), which is evolutionarily related to the imperative of not becoming the target of an 'expulsion reaction'.

Laughter

Laughter is an 'expressive movement' of aggressive *intent* and has "a strongly infectious quality" (Hass, 1968, p. 127). Laughter evolved from mobbing behaviour, the rhythmic emission of threat sounds by a group of apes or monkeys (Eibl-Eibesfeldt, 1970). In primates, concerted threats directed at an enemy or outsider are "accompanied by a rhythmical emission of sounds strongly reminiscent of human laughter" (Hass, 1968, p. 127). Importantly, it is often "the spectacle of others' misfortune and the agreeable realization that we have been spared the thing that has befallen them" that compels us to laugh (p. 126). Joint mockery, implicit in human laughter, is related to animal behaviour effecting the expulsion of outsiders (nonconformists) from the group (Hass, 1968).

> Joint derision is related to the expulsion reaction commonly observed in animals, which is usually elicited by malformation or, in more general terms, by the quality of being different, physically or behaviourally, from the group. The result of this reaction is that the outsider is not only expelled but in certain circumstances killed.
> (Hass, 1968, pp. 126–7)

Hass (1968) observed that "laughter within a closed group is more likely to excite an outsider's annoyance, especially if he is ignorant of its cause, because he assumes it to be directed at himself" (p. 127).

> The person who is laughed at experiences the laughter as aggressive. But the people laughing together feel themselves to be bound together via this ritualized 'mobbing'.
> (Eibl-Eibesfeldt, 1970, p. 162)

Concerted laughter and its evolutionary precursor, the 'expulsion reaction', not only "afford an opportunity of working off pent-up aggression" but also "lead to the forming of united fronts" (Hass, 1968, p. 127). Laughter has a cohesive effect (Eibl-Eibesfeldt, 1970); joint laughter strengthens the pact between individuals and cements the bond within the group (Hass, 1968).

9.3.8 Enthusiasm

Enthusiasm is a special form of elation; unlike feelings of bliss, enthusiasm is associated with increased *activity*, whereby this activity tends to be realistic and adaptive (Greenson, 1962). Enthusiasm, while containing "some element of play", "lends itself frequently to adaptive, constructive, and even creative actions" (p. 173). Enthusiasm is a temporary state of mind characterized by "a great abundance of energy" that flows into "a plethora of enterprise, talk, gregariousness, and imagination" (p. 180). Enthusiasm, similarly to humour, "makes the ego's defenses unnecessary", so that "[t]he energy which has been used for defense can now be utilized for enthusiasm" (Greenson, 1962, p. 180).[14]

The person filled with enthusiasm is generous and has urgent or compelling "wish to share with others" (Greenson, 1962, p. 172). Enthusiasm is contagious. "One cannot remain enthusiastic alone"; "one needs cohorts, accomplices", as with laughter (p. 172). Others "have to be converted to enthusiasm or else the enthusiasm is endangered" (p. 172). When enthusiasm spreads, "there is the feeling of joining and being a member of a group – a feeling of belonging" (p. 172). Those, however, who do not share in others' enthusiasm "often have a feeling of being left out, cheated – of not belonging"; or they may respond with envy (p. 172). Like other group phenomena, enthusiasm involves a partial regression in the state of mind of those who take part (Greenson, 1962). "People who are prone to evoke enthusiasm often become leaders" (p. 173); the ability to incite enthusiasm in others is an important characteristic of leaders (Greenson, 1962).

9.4 Self-culture

Primate phylogenesis arranged that the infant's 'primary narcissism' is replaced, in the course of individual development, by firm relatedness to a relatively small and stable social network. Tightly organized communities supported by a traditional value system are not compatible with modern civilization, so that increasingly primary narcissism is being replaced, in individual development, by narcissistic hypercathexis of the self

---

[14] Hypomania and mania are pathological forms of enthusiasm, characterized by prolonged elation as well as unproductive and maladaptive hyperactivity. In hypomania, compared to normal enthusiasm, "one sees more agitation and less accomplishment" (Greenson, 1962, p. 181).

(preoccupation with the self and its values). Modern society is characterized by liberalism and the destruction of traditional morality and institutions (LORENZ, 1963, 1973), on the one hand, and by competitive individualism and a culture of celebrity, on the other. Consequences include a growing existential insecurity and a desire to achieve visibility as much as possible. Security can be reclaimed by seeing one's glorious self reflected in others' admiration or by attaching oneself to persons of great power and prestige (LASCH, 1979). Happiness is pursued, in Western society, "to the dead end of a narcissistic pre-occupation with the self" (LASCH, 1979). Excessive narcissistic investment in the self, expressed as an increased concern with the self, is what gives individuals a measure of transitory security in a world in which social networks are fragmenting and traditional value systems are being undermined.

9.4.1 Self-evaluation

DANZIGER (1997) understood that "individuals learn how important the good opinion of others is to their welfare and therefore seek to influence the good opinion by appropriate conduct" (p. 144). The self reflects others' approval or disapproval of one's conduct; it is 'the core of a monitoring mechanism' and 'an object of social control' (DANZIGER, 1997). The self dynamically emerges in the social context, but, under shifting conditions, the self is uncertain. The loss of traditional social distinctions and the loosening of common standards has resulted in greater uncertainties in the evaluation of self-worth (and greater instability of self-esteem), while, at the same time, "the normative pressure on individuals to engage in self-assessment is stronger than ever" (DANZIGER, 1997). Individuals are constantly assessing their own worth, while they are "actively engaged in maximising the flow of approval from others" (DANZIGER, 1997).

> If individuals are no longer bound by rigidly circumscribed conventions, they are free to maneuver among different patterns of conduct, always intent on choosing the alternative that promises the best return from others and from one's reflected self-esteem.
> (DANZIGER, 1997, p. 146)

Already JAMES (1890) realized that individuals evaluate themselves differently in different social situations (according to different standards or expectations that apply to these situations), which led him to conclude that "a man has as many social selves as there are individuals who recognise him and carry an image of him in their mind" (p. 294). GERGEN (1977), too, saw that one's concept of oneself changes in accordance with "messages received from others concerning one's worth" (one's ability to attract approval) and that self-esteem is "inextricably linked to the social context". Therefore, "the stability of self-esteem is importantly dependent on the consistency of the social environment". Self-worth and the sense of personal identity are dependent on the type of social milieu to which one is exposed and the qualities of "those available for comparison" (Gergen, 1977).

> One's identity in general, and self-evaluation in particular, thus seem importantly wedded to social circumstance. As the social environment shifts its definition of the individual, self-definition may be altered accordingly.
> (Gergen, 1977, pp. 376–7)

Personal identity does not represent "a unified core of self-relevant experience"; and self-esteem has little to do with an "essential core level of self-evaluation" (Gergen, 1977). There is no source in which to look for "true knowledge of self"; self-conceptualization remains an "arbitrary process", and self-knowledge can only ever be "constructed anew" (Gergen, 1977). Nevertheless, people concern themselves with abstract ideas about their self and believe they possess a degree of self-knowledge that is independent from the social context. Uncertainty and instability of self-evaluation in varying social contexts can be balanced by self-imagery and self-deception, in which the self is anchored to approvals from unconscious inner objects or from oneself (self-observation).

> The objectified self that persons now harbour within them is above all an object of approval and disapproval, both by others and by the person herself. This self is always conceived as an object of variable worth, and therefore the desire to raise or maintain its worth comes to be regarded as an identifiable human motive.
> (Danziger, 1997, p. 145)

9.4.2 Self-actualization

As transience of social relationships became a pervasive feature of modern Western society, personal identity ceased to be embedded firmly in the local community and culture. Social networks in modern society are vulnerable to disruption or termination, which, according to Baumeister (1997), gave rise to the belief that the self is "a hidden entity that exists inside the person" and that is independent of community and culture (p. 195). Self-esteem – being a "private measure of one's suitability for interpersonal relationships" and for inclusion into social groups or networks (a measure that is based on one's acceptable and approvable performances and characteristics) – became a matter of concern for oneself (p. 206). With social relationships having become temporary and unstable, the need became paramount to have an attractive, likable, and competent self, a self that serves as a means of gaining access to groups, attracting partners, and retaining relationships (as "a tool to attract and retain social ties to other people") (Baumeister, 1997, pp. 205–6).

Social pressure to construct and maintain a highly attractive, competent, and successful self that is worthy of admiration by others is a continuous source of stress; and a crisis may ensue if something happens that casts the self in a less desirable light (BAUMEISTER, 1997). People in modern Western society are constantly vigilant against potential threats to their positive self-image, so that self-awareness is often "tinged with worry or stress" and takes on "an aversive aspect" (BAUMEISTER, 1997). People engage in self-seeking (aiming to disentangle pervasive trends towards self-deception) and self-actualization. Decisions in life are made with regard to the benefits they bestow upon the self. In seeking to actualize their self and thereby supply their life (self) with value, people can draw on new social opportunities and the greater scope for choices offered by modern society (BAUMEISTER, 1997).

> Our culture has come to regard the process of choice as often involving looking inside oneself to discover the correct attitude or nature of one's inner self, which is then presumed to be a basis for making correct choices.
>
> (BAUMEISTER, 1997, p. 198)

As Western society gradually weakened or undermined its value basis in tradition, family, and religion, a 'value gap' arose, an "important cultural response" to which was "to transform the self into a major value base" (BAUMEISTER, 1997, p. 200). The cult of self-actualization is enshrined in modern society. Modern society "must motivate people to work by mobilising the self as a relevant, potent value base" (p. 201). Work serves as a "vital means of glorifying and fulfilling the self", counteracting the sense of insecurity implicit in the fragmentation of traditional social networks and the loss of traditional value systems (BAUMEISTER, 1997).

> [T]he careerist aims to accumulate a record of promotions, achievements, and honors that will reflect favourably on the self. Hence people work very hard at things they personally may care rather little about in order to gain respect and esteem through their achievements. The value that drives them is the value placed on the self.
>
> (BAUMEISTER, 1997, p. 201)

Consumerism

Not only is the transformation of the self into a 'major value base' a consequence of socioeconomic processes in Western society, economic processes depend upon individuals needing to actualize their self and to use their self as a basis for making economic decisions (BAUMEISTER, 1997). Advertising, an important means of stimulating consumer demand and self-indulgence, exploits the fragility and impermanence of modern selfhood and is a critical component of modern economic processes. Through advertising, "the individual is constantly offered aids to happiness", but "he has little time to reflect whether such aids bring him genuine and lasting contentment" (HASS, 1968, p. 184).

9.4.3 Risk awareness

GIDDENS (1991) conceptualized 'reflexive self-consciousness' as the counterpart of risk. Assessment of risks emanating from technological progress has become, he thought, a dominant mode of subjective experience in modernity. The growing concern with risk in modern society goes hand in hand with the loss of sense of social belonging, as recognized by GIDDENS (1991); however, ontological insecurity in modernity is *not* the product of risks born out of technological progress; but, on the contrary, risk awareness, risk aversion, and 'reflexive self-consciousness' are manifestations of (and defences against) ontological insecurity arising from social fragmentation. In other words, selfhood has become a 'reflexive project' in modernity only to the extent that traditional sources of *collective identity* (the traditional narrative of collective beings [ERIKSON]) have been lost. GIDDENS (1991) recognized that the 'reflexive self' emerges inasmuch as the individual is 'freed' from the restraints of traditional society, yet concerns about risk (and defensive entanglement in rationalizing debates about risk) cannot be seen as evidence for a liberation or emancipation of the self. What the self has not become in modernity is an *agent* capable of making rational decisions. Decisions apparently made *by* the self are made instead *for* the self, for the sake of its integrity; they are made by unconscious forces that defend against ontological insecurity, aiming to ameliorate the 'aversive aspect' (BAUMEISTER) of self-awareness.

9.4.4 Emotional emptiness

LASCH (1979) argued that selfhood in modern consumer society has degenerated to an excessive preoccupation with self-image and personal appearance, inasmuch as selfhood has retreated from involvement with others. Preoccupations with attractiveness and style presuppose and entrench emotional detachment from others. Persons in modern capitalist culture tend to be driven by superficial ambitions and are also burdened by a sense of entitlement and feelings of emptiness. This whole constellation is known as narcissistic personality organization (LASCH, 1979).

The prevalence of narcissistic personality disturbances can only increase in a culture that has undermined the patriarchal family, that continues to destroy old traditions and traditional community ties, and that thereby breeds insecurity and renders individuals' sense of self or identity weak and fragile (LASCH, 1979). The decline of the patriarchal family affects children's development. In particular, children do not progress through the Oedipus complex as they did previously, leading to a failure to internalize parental restrictions and to emulate normative standards of their culture; yet emulation of cultural standards plays an important role in the maintenance of self-esteem. Children growing up under these circumstances remain depleted of self-worth and driven by omnipotent fantasies (LASCH, 1979).

Consumerism is an important part of the 'culture of narcissism' (LASCH, 1979). It provides individuals with temporary and superficial escapes from feelings of emptiness. Being unable to form caring relationships, narcissistic persons fill their emotional voids and enhance their feelings of self-worth by way of excessive consumption of goods (LASCH, 1979), goods that are advertised for their very potential to enhance feelings of self-worth.

9.4.5 Psychopathological vulnerability

FREUD (1930) could not endorse the "enthusiastic prejudice" that the path of civilization "will necessarily lead us to heights of perfection hitherto undreamt of", but, with regard to mankind's "cultural endeavour", he felt more inclined to conclude that "the whole effort is not worth the trouble and can only result in a state of affairs that the individual is bound to find intolerable" (p. 81). MISHAN (1967) realized that "despite periods of sustained economic growth and increasing prosperity all social statistics indicate a growing sense of malaise and unfulfilment". He warned that "despite the abundance of man-made goods produced by continued growth", the net effect of economic growth "on human heath and happiness could be adverse and possible disastrous" (MISHAN, 1967, p. 9).

GREENSON (1958) observed that, across the first half of the twentieth century, character disorders became more frequent, especially disorders in which "the pathology seems to be centered around a defective formation of the self image, an identity disorder" (p. 111), with patients struggling to establish their self-image or self-representation. While 'disorders of the self' (narcissistic disorders) appear to have become more prevalent, presentations with conversion hysteria and obsessive-compulsive rituals have become less frequent (WOLF, 1988). KOHUT (1977) explained "the gradual decrease of structural disorders" and "the simultaneously occurring gradual increase in disorders of the self" (p. 277) with reference to "a shift of the leading psychological problem of Western man from the area of guilt-ridden overstimulation and conflict to that of inner emptiness, isolation, and unfulfillment" (p. 291).

WOLF (1988) suspected that "changing patterns in psychological symptomatology" reflect a historical shift in child rearing patterns, a shift from excessive repression of sexuality to the breakdown of the extended family and changing social expectations towards women, resulting in a relative scarcity of appropriate selfobject experiences in early life (p. 25). In recent times, the tendency has been for children to feel "uncared for and unresponded to", pointing to a lack of self-sustaining and self-supporting selfobject experiences in early life (WOLF, 1988).

10
Conclusion

The critical importance of narcissistic needs and narcissistic sustenance will have become apparent by now. What needs to be borne in mind is that narcissistic sustenance is by no means homogenous and its evolutionary origins are likely to be manifold. Narcissistic sustenance can take the form of acceptance or recognition by the object or by the group; or it can take the form of attention, respect, approval, admiration, or love received from the object; or it can be attained through participation in the object's omnipotence. Whatever the form of narcissistic sustenance, the effect for the subject who receives it consists in the renewal of the feeling of safety.

Firstly, narcissistic behaviour is an extension of evolutionarily older proximity-seeking behaviour ('attachment behaviour' in the narrow sense). The emotional state that accompanies proximity seeking is separation anxiety (BOWLBY).

Secondly, the need to attract attention from the primary object or from one of its developmental derivatives is central to narcissistic behaviour. Attention-seeking behaviour performed in the context of exposure to others serves to overcome a derivative of separation anxiety, the anxiety that is inherent in realizing one's separateness from the object (ROTHSTEIN) or unrelatedness to the social surround, although this form of anxiety is likely to be closely related to 'stranger anxiety' (social anxiety), representing fears of others' aggression.

Thirdly, an evident lack of hostility in the object's attitude towards oneself constitutes a form of narcissistic sustenance. The need to pacify (appease) the object (to inhibit the object's aggression) would have arisen as a counterpart to the evolution of intraspecific (offensive) aggression (LORENZ). Appeasement gestures, including their culturally ritualized versions (social mannerisms and greetings), are likely derived from signals that originally served to maintain the mother–infant bond and then also the partner bond in spite of the repulsive effect of intraspecific aggression. In addition, submissive displays used to *terminate* intraspecific disputes about resources, territory, or status could have evolved into behaviours that effect the *inhibition* of others' intraspecific aggression in all kinds of social situations, possibly by signalling submission to the leader of a group and adherence to the norms arbitrarily defined and imposed by the leader (or, in more fluid social constellations, by the 'dominant other' [ARIETI, 1973]). Compliance with social norms avoids punishment by the leader or 'dominant other' (i.e., it defends against 'castration anxiety'). Failure to comply with social norms implicitly challenges others' position or dominance rank in the group and hence disinhibits their innate aggressiveness. This may lead to one's punishment and subordination, followed by renewed acceptance by the leader or the group, or to one's expulsion from the group ('expulsion reaction'). Expulsion from the group may be feared when one completely fails to negotiate the group's ranking system, when one is thoroughly unacceptable to the group or leader (and when one was unacceptable to the primary maternal object). The emotional state that then arises (usually on a background of deep-seated feelings of inferiority [ADLER]) is paranoid or persecutory anxiety, one of MELANIE KLEIN's central concerns.[1]

Fourthly, the subject can attain narcissistic gratification, and keep his own paranoid anxieties at bay, by inducing the object to adopt a submissive or respectful stance. The assertiveness that is implicit in narcissistic behaviour is probably derived from intraspecific (offensive) aggression, which was originally used for competition. Access to narcissistic resources, more generally, is controlled in a manner that is not dissimilar to the way in which access to other resources (as defined, for instance, by territory or ranking position) is controlled. Offensive hostility may be employed in an effort to secure another's commitment to oneself (BOWLBY); or it may help to bring about another's submission and accession to one's demands or the reinstatement of one's rights (and thus indirectly the reinstatement of one's narcissistic resources) (Figure 10.1).[2]

Fifthly, we have a need for approval (FLUGEL). Approval-seeking behaviour involves grandiose and exhibitionistic displays. What is sought is *positive* attention from the object; and positive attention, in the form of approval and admiration, is rewarding for the subject.[3] The object's positive attention, elicited by the subject's grandiose and exhibitionistic displays, involves libidinal signals communicated back to the subject ('gleam in the mother's eye'). This is the process that KOHUT called 'mirroring'. Narcissistic supplies,

---

[1] This type of anxiety is treated in HORNEY's and KOHUT's writings as 'basic anxiety' and 'disintegration anxiety', respectively.

[2] The principle of subordinating others for the purpose of attaining safety is starkly illustrated by attitudes and behaviours subsumed under the term 'sadism'.

[3] The reward associated with experiencing others' approving or caring displays may reinforce appetitive behaviour that establishes and maintains one's relatedness to the social surround.

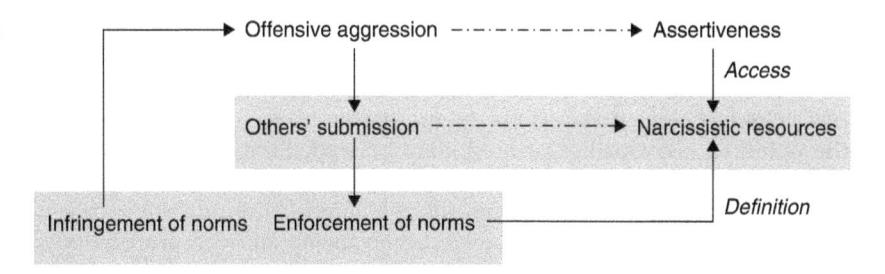

```
                    ┌──▶ Offensive aggression  ────────▶ Assertiveness
                    │              │                          │ Access
                    │              ▼                          ▼
                    │    Others' submission  ────────▶ Narcissistic resources
                    │              │                          ▲
                    │              ▼                          │ Definition
         Infringement of norms  Enforcement of norms  ────────┘
```

Figure 10.1 Offensive (territorial aggression) is evolutionarily continuous with assertiveness that accompanies attention-seeking and exhibitionistic behaviour. Insistence on one's rights and induction of compliance in others secures one's access to narcissistic resources. Attention of the defeated and submissive individual to the victor in an agonistic confrontation represents another form of narcissistic gratification

in the form of others' benevolent interest and affectionate signals, are evolutionarily linked to the mother's care for and devotion to her infant. This form of narcissistic sustenance is thus directly related to true parental care, in which the offspring is not merely protected against predators but also fed and groomed (and socially stimulated).

Sixthly, we have a need for tenderness and affection (SULLIVAN, BALINT). Affectionate behaviours are derivatives of maternal care-giving behaviours (e.g., grooming) that have ceased to be concerned primarily with the infant's physical welfare (e.g., delousing). Appeasement and conformity generate a safe context for the expression of exhibitionistic and affectionate impulses; and unless exhibitionistic and affectionate behaviours are interwoven with appeasing and normative behaviours, they invite an aggressive response from others.[4]

Seventhly, there is the need to retain a good relationships with the object (by way of loving the object and repairing any damage done to the object [KLEIN]), contrasted with the fear of losing the object's love. Object love constitutes a postnarcissistic source of safety (FENICHEL).

Eighthly, the idealizing transference described by KOHUT involves the sending of libidinal (care-giving) signals under the assumption that the self will receive narcissistic nourishment in return. When idealizing an object, the underlying unconscious fantasy (unconscious assumption) is that self and object *are* merged. Idealization of the object entails identification with the object and provides a direct avenue for the return to the state of primary narcissism, which is ultimately the concern of mature object relations, too.

---

[4] Extreme submissiveness for the purpose of attaining safety is called masochism, which can indeed provide a context within which sexual impulses are expressed.

Gratification of narcissistic needs is associated with safety, much as anxiety is associated with danger, the danger of being attacked by predators (upon being separated from or abandoned by the mother or group) or the danger of being attacked by the mother or group (in either case, with the potential consequence of annihilation). Appetitive social behaviour is so organized that it *moves* the subject away from anxiety, which signals a high probability of being attacked, towards safety, towards a state, that is, in which narcissistic supplies are readily available and the probability of being attacked is low. This recurrent movement, adjusting time and again to naturally occurring perturbations in the selfobject surround, is what fuels defensive and character structures and imparts on the ego or personality its apparent intentionality and goal-directedness (ADLER). Narcissism can be defined as this very tendency, automatically expressed following any perturbation, to escape from dangerousness and gravitate to safety. Moreover, narcissism constantly recreates the ego (self), if the ego were to be seen as a distillate of the potential of the social environment to provide narcissistic sustenance, that is, if 'ego feeling' (FEDERN) or self-esteem could be regarded as the antithesis of anxiety.

Safety or social relatedness can be regarded as an envelope (a general situational context) under which affectionate and approving interactions can take place (unconsciously, on LACAN's imaginary plane). Safety is developmentally associated with the context of maternal proximity and maternal responsiveness, the context in which the infant not only receives care and attention but can exchange affectionate gestures with the mother. Situations that are created ('defined' [GOFFMAN, 1959]) in the course of day-to-day interactions often unconsciously signify proximity and responsiveness of an authority figure (the 'dominant other' [ARIETI, 1973]) who is a derivative of the primary object. In relationships, partners unconsciously assign roles to each other and induce each other to respond in certain ways (SANDLER & SANDLER, 1978), replicating patterns of interaction first experienced in childhood. These role relationships are a vehicle for the attainment of a state of safety (SANDLER, 1960a). The individual's relationships to social groups and society at large are developmental continuations of early object relations, too (SCHEIDLINGER, 1964, 1968). The (perceived) social environment, in general, is the product of appetitive behaviour aimed at maintaining safety; and, as such, it is developmentally continuous with the proximity and responsiveness of the primary object.

The self encapsulates a sense of acceptance and recognition by others, a sense of how one is regarded or valued by others. The self reflects one's relatedness to the social surround (or acceptance by the 'dominant other'), that is, one's potential to be approved or liked by others as well as the effectiveness of one's attitudes and behaviours geared towards inhibiting others' aggressive potential (by means of conformity). The ego ideal, when it is adopted or emulated by the self, refers to a sense of being worthy of approval and praise from authority figures, a sense that arises when acting in accordance with their expectations. One identifies with role models, unconsciously emulating them, in order to please authority figures and thus feel safe. Whether one simply *is and acts oneself* ('true self') or emulates an ideal (possibly neurotically, in the sense of a 'false self'), one remains connected in unconscious fantasy to the primary object, the primary guarantor of safety. When narcissistic supplies are readily obtainable from the social surround, that is, when the social situation is experienced as safe, self-esteem and pride are experienced as emanating from the social surround (which then unconsciously represents the primary object), whereas the self as an internal image depends on interest paid by and approbation received from imaginary objects (imaginary representatives of internal objects). The movement to safety, when it takes place in fantasy, when it entails imagery of a safe situation, creates the self as an internal image, a self that is visible to and therefore approvable by an imaginary social surround (CASHDAN, 1988) (although this social surround does not tend to be clearly visualized in imagery or fantasies concerning oneself).

When thinking about oneself, one intermittently adopts someone else's perspective. The self is, by virtue of this identification with an other, looking at itself; the self is an object to itself (FEDERN). The self is 'split' between the ego that observes and the ego that is observed, often between the ego identified with the superego (the observing ego) and the ego ideal, which in itself is based on identifications. This split occurs whenever an image of the self is formed (whenever one thinks about and pays attention to oneself). Feeling the need to be accepted or approved by a derivative of the primary object (the 'dominant other'), one briefly adopts the perspective of the superego (the omnipotent object, the internalized primary object), so as to consider, from this perspective, one's (the ego's) lovability or worthiness of approval. Imagery of the ego ideal, that is, of an ideal or idealized self,[5] entails (or alternates with) an *anticipation*, on part of the self (ego), of approval from the internalized primary object (omnipotent object). The ego ideal (ideal self), *turned by anticipated approval into an incentive image*, may act as a goal that guides appetitive behaviour concerned with improving one's approvability (Figure 10.2). The ego ideal, which, is constituted and reshaped by way of imitating successful objects encountered in the course of development (in the oedipal period and beyond), is a goal to be attained

---

[5] If we regard the ego ideal strictly as an internal (unconscious) representation, then what one experiences in fantasy or imagination is a reprojection of the ego ideal, namely the 'ideal self' (SANDLER) or 'idealized self' (HORNEY).

390 Narcissism and the Self

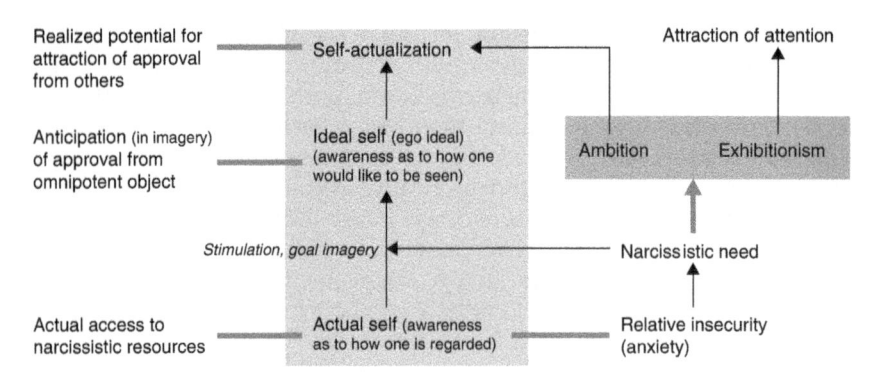

```
Realized potential for                                           Attraction of attention
attraction of approval  ─── Self-actualization ◄───┐                      ▲
from others                          ▲             │                      │
                                     │             │                      │
Anticipation (in imagery)   Ideal self (ego ideal) │                      │
of approval from         ── (awareness as to how one ─── Ambition    Exhibitionism
omnipotent object           would like to be seen)                   
                                     ▲                                ▲
                                     │                                │
            Stimulation, goal imagery ◄─────────────────── Narcissistic need
                                                                      ▲
                                                                      │
Actual access to          Actual self (awareness              Relative insecurity
narcissistic resources ── as to how one is regarded) ──────── (anxiety)
```

Figure 10.2 The ego ideal or ideal self acts, similarly to an incentive cue, as a goal for safety-directed appetitive behaviour. Appetitive behaviour aims to turn the self (being a measure of the security of narcissistic supplies in the situation that one faces) into an idealized self (self-actualization). The driving impetus behind ambition is the same as that behind exhibitionism (KOHUT)

(an ideal to be realized) by more mature narcissistic strivings ('ambitions' [KOHUT]).[6]

The position one attains in a social hierarchy is defined by distance to the leader (and, on a deeper level, by proximity to the internal omnipotent object). Interactions with others in the group serve to confirm dominance relationships or alliances and are often competitive in nature, competitively aiming to attract approval from the leader ('dominant other') who acts as the external representative (projection) of the superego for each member. These interactions often take place within the context of a goal defined by the leader. Participation in work towards a common goal overcomes rivalries and accrues credit from the leader.[7] Being integrated into a cohesive group and identified with a common cause is associated with regression in superego development (FREUD) and surrender of the self (HORNEY), suggesting that both superego and self-experience are adaptations to living in social formations that are less well defined, not clearly centred on a leader, and

---

[6] This is the process that HORNEY (1950) described as 'actualization' of the 'idealized image' or idealized self. The starting point of self-actualization can be a state of anxiety, in which one feels disconnected from the social surround and deprived of narcissistic supplies and hence insecure. Appetitive behaviour, acquired as a result of successes in previous ambitious and self-actualizing pursuits, then creates a situation in which narcissistic supplies are available, and it creates, at the same time, a self that can confidently expect narcissistic gratification in that situation.

[7] The leader in this process fosters his sense of independence, which may be but a defence against insight into his own dependence on his primary object (related to the 'manic defence' [KLEIN]).

not strongly united in the pursuit of a common goal. It is when the group's aggressive potential is not clearly bound to an external objective that the need arises to guard oneself against aggression from within the group; and it is then that the need to appease others and ensure oneself of their benevolence is felt most clearly. It is then that the self may be engaged in efforts to enhance its approvability, to attain an ideal state (ego ideal), and to be accepted by the superego.[8]

---

[8] Whenever the self *is* recognized and approved or feels desirable or *approvable*, the individual would unconsciously feel acceptable to the superego or omnipotent object (and unconsciously *expect* to be reunited with it). Being approved by or approvable to a derivative of the primary object (an external replica of an internal object) means that, in unconscious fantasy, the self is accepted by the superego or omnipotent object. In realizing the ideal self (emulating the ego ideal), the self ultimately aims for acceptance by the omnipotent object (whereby being accepted by the omnipotent object is a condition for the return to primary narcissism, to a reunion with the primary object). Although the self can transform itself into an ideal through self-actualization (in interaction with the world of external objects), it can do so also through self-glorification in conscious phantasy (narcissistic hypercathexis of the image of the self), involving interaction with an imaginary representative of the omnipotent object.

References

ADLER, A. (1927/1998). *Understanding Human Nature*. Oxford: Oneworld Publications.
ADLER, A. (1938/1998). *Social Interest*. Oxford: Oneworld Publications.
ADLER, A. (1965). *Superiority and Social Interest: A Collection of Later Writings* (H.L. Ansbacher & R.R. Ansbacher, eds). London: Routledge and Kegan Paul.
AGAZARIAN, Y. & PETERS, R. (1981/2004). *The Visible and Invisible Group*. London: Karnac.
ANZIEU, D. (1975/1984). *The Group and the Unconscious*. London: Routledge and Kegan Paul.
ANZIEU, D. (1987/1990). *Psychic Envelopes*. London: Karnac.
ARIETI, S. (1970). The structural and psychodynamic role of cognition in the human psyche. In: S. Arieti (ed.), *The World Biennial of Psychiatry and Psychotherapy* (Vol. 1, pp. 3–34). New York: Basic Books.
ARIETI, S. (1973). The interpersonal and the intrapsychic in severe psychopathology. In: E.G. Witenberg (ed.), *Interpersonal Explorations in Psychoanalysis: New Directions in Theory and Practice* (pp. 120–131). New York: Basic Books.
ARLOW, J.A. (1989). Psychoanalysis and the quest for morality. In: H.P. Blum, E.M. Weinshel, & F.R. Rodman (eds), *The Psychoanalytic Core: Essays in Honor of Leo Rangell, M.D.* (pp. 147–166). Madison, Connecticut: International Universities Press.
BALINT, M. (1952). *Primary Love and Psycho-Analytic Technique*. London: The Hogarth Press.
BALINT, M. (1968). *The Basic Fault*. London: Tavistock Publications.
BAUMEISTER, R.F. (1997). The self and society: Changes, problems, and opportunities. In: R.D. Ashmore & L. Jussim (eds), *Self and Identity: Fundamental Issues* (pp. 191–217). New York: Oxford University Press.
BENJAMIN, L.S. (1996). An interpersonal theory of personality disorders. In: J.F. Clarkin & M.F. Lenzenweger (eds), *Major Theories of Personality Disorder* (pp. 141–220). New York: Guilford Press.
BERGLER, E. (1949). *The Basic Neurosis: Oral Regression and Psychic Masochism*. New York: Grune & Stratton.
BERGLER, E. (1952). *The Superego: Unconscious Conscience*. New York: Grune & Stratton.
BERKOWITZ, L. (1989). Laboratory experiments in the study of aggression. In: J. Archer & K. Browne (eds), *Human Aggression: Naturalistic Approaches*. London: Routledge.
BERNFELD, S. (1922). Bemerkungen über "Sublimierung". *Imago* 8: 333–344.
BION, W.R. (1952/1980). Group dynamics: A re-view. In: S. Scheidlinger (ed.), *Psychoanalytic Group Dynamics: Basic Readings* (pp. 77–107). New York: International Universities Press.
BION, W.R. (1959). Attacks on linking. *International Journal of Psychoanalysis* 40: 308–315.
BION, W.R. (1961). *Experiences in Groups*. London: Tavistock Publications.
BION, W.R. (1962). The psycho-analytic study of thinking: II. A theory of thinking. *International Journal of Psychoanalysis* 43: 306–310.
BLANCHARD, D.C. & BLANCHARD, R.J. (1989). Experimental animal models of aggression: what do they say about human behaviour. In: J. Archer & K. Browne (eds), *Human Aggression: Naturalistic Approaches*. London: Routledge.
BOWLBY, J. (1958). The nature of the child's tie to his mother. *International Journal of Psychoanalysis* 39: 350–373.

BOWLBY, J. (1973). *Separation: Anxiety and Anger.* New York: Basic Books.
BOWLBY, J. (1977). The making and breaking of affectional bonds. *British Journal of Psychiatry* 130: 201–210.
BOWLBY, J. (1988). *A Secure Base: Clinical Applications of Attachment Theory.* London: Routledge.
BOWLBY, J. (1989). Psychoanalysis as a natural science. In: J. Sandler (ed.), *Dimensions of Psychoanalysis* (pp. 99–121). Madison, Connecticut: International Universities Press.
BRANDCHAFT, B. (1985). Resistance and defense: An intersubjective view. In: A. Goldberg (ed.), *Progress in Self Psychology* (Vol. 1, pp. 88–96). New York: Guilford Press.
BRANDCHAFT, B. (1986). British object relations theory and self psychology. In: A. Goldberg (ed.), *Progress in Self Psychology* (Vol. 2, pp. 245–272). New York: Guilford Press.
BRENNER, C. (1989). Some remarks on the analysis of dreams and of neurotic symptoms. In: H.P. Blum, E.M. Weinshel, & F.R. Rodman (eds), *The Psychoanalytic Core: Essays in Honor of Leo Rangell, M.D.* (pp. 71–87). Madison, Connecticut: International Universities Press.
BROMBERG, P.M. (1983). The mirror and the mask: On narcissism and psychoanalytic growth. *Contemporary Psychoanalysis* 19: 359–387.
BURROW, T. (1949). *The Neurosis of Man.* London: Routledge & Kegan Paul.
BURSTEN, B. (1973). Some narcissistic personality types. *International Journal of Psychoanalysis* 54: 287–300.
CAPER, R. (1995). On the difficulty of making a mutative interpretation. *International Journal of Psychoanalysis* 76: 91–101.
CARPY, D.C. (1989). Tolerating the countertransference: a mutative process. *International Journal of Psychoanalysis* 70: 285–294.
CASHDAN, S. (1988). *Object Relations Therapy: Using the Relationship.* New York: W.W. Norton & Company.
CHRZANOWSKI, G. (1973). Implications of interpersonal theory. In: E.G. Witenberg (ed.), *Interpersonal Explorations in Psychoanalysis: New Directions in Theory and Practice* (pp. 132–146). New York: Basic Books.
CURTIS, H.C. (1986). Rejoinder. In: A. Goldberg (ed.), *Progress in Self Psychology* (Vol. 2, pp. 50–59). New York: The Guilford Press.
DANZIGER, K. (1997). The historical formation of selves. In: R.D. Ashmore & L. Jussim (eds), *Self and Identity: Fundamental Issues* (pp. 137–157). New York: Oxford University Press.
DE BOARD, R. (1978). *The Psychoanalysis of Organisations.* London: Tavistock Publications.
DEUTSCH, H. (1942). Some forms of emotional disturbance and their relationship to schizophrenia. *Psychoanalytic Quarterly* 11: 301–321.
DURKHEIM, É. (1893/1984). *The Division of Labour in Society* (tr. W.D. Halls). London: Macmillan.
EIBL-EIBESFELDT, I. (1970/1971). *Love and Hate: On the Natural History of Basic Behaviour Patterns.* London: Methuen & Co.
EPSTEIN, S. (1973). The self-concept revisited: Or a theory of a theory. *American Psychologist* 28: 404–416.
ERIKSON, E.H. (1950/1977). *Childhood and Society.* London: Paladin Grafton Books.
ERIKSON, E.H. (1959/1980). Ego development and historical change. In: S. Scheidlinger (ed.), *Psychoanalytic Group Dynamics: Basic Readings* (pp. 189–212). New York: International Universities Press.
EZRIEL, H. (1950/1980). A psychoanalytic approach to group treatment. In: S. Scheidlinger (ed.), *Psychoanalytic Group Dynamics: Basic Readings* (pp. 109–146). New York: International Universities Press.

FAIRBAIRN, W.R.D. (1952). *Psychoanalytic Studies of the Personality*. London: Routledge & Kegan Paul.
FEDERN, P. (1952). *Ego Psychology and the Psychoses* (ed., E. Weiss). New York: Basic Books.
FELDMAN, M. (1997). Projective identification: the analyst's involvement. *International Journal of Psychoanalysis* 78: 227–241.
FELDMAN, R., GREENBAUM, C.W., & YIRMIYA, N. (1999). Mother-infant affect synchrony as an antecedent of the emergence of self-control. *Developmental Psychology* 35: 223–231.
FENICHEL, O. (1946). *The Psychoanalytic Theory of Neurosis*. London: Routledge & Kegan Paul.
FERGUSON, M.J. & BARGH, J.A. (2004). How social perception can automatically influence behavior. *Trends in Cognitive Sciences* 8: 33–39.
FINK, B. (1997). *A Clinical Introduction to Lacanian Psychoanalysis: Theory and Technique*. Cambridge, MA: Harvard University Press.
FLUGEL, J.C. (1945). *Man, Morals and Society*. London: Duckworth.
FOULKES, S.H. (1964). *Therapeutic Group Analysis*. London: George Allen & Unwin.
FREUD, A. (1937/1966). *The Ego and the Mechanisms of Defense*. New York: International Universities Press.
FREUD, S. (1905/1953). Three essays on the theory of sexuality. In: J. Strachey (ed.), *Standard Edition of the Complete Psychological Works of Sigmund Freud* (Vol. 7, pp. 135–243). London: The Hogarth Press.
FREUD, S. (1914/1957). On narcissism: An introduction. In: J. Strachey (ed.), *The Standard Edition of the Complete Psychological Works of Sigmund Freud* (Vol. 14, pp. 67–102). London: The Hogarth Press.
FREUD, S. (1915/1957). Repression. In: J. Strachey (ed.), *The Standard Edition of the Complete Psychological Works of Sigmund Freud* (Vol. 14, pp. 146–158). London: The Hogarth Press.
FREUD, S. (1916–17/1922). *Introductory Lectures on Psycho-Analysis* (tr., J. Riviere). London: George Allen & Unwin.
FREUD, S. (1917/1957). Mourning and melancholia. In: J. Strachey (ed.), *The Standard Edition of the Complete Psychological Works of Sigmund Freud* (Vol. 14, pp. 237–258). London: The Hogarth Press.
FREUD, S. (1920/1955). Beyond the pleasure principle. In: J. Strachey (ed.), *The Standard Edition of the Complete Psychological Works of Sigmund Freud* (Vol. 18, pp. 7–64). London: The Hogarth Press.
FREUD, S. (1921/1922). *Group Psychology and the Analysis of the Ego* (tr., J. Strachey). London: The Hogarth Press.
FREUD, S. (1923/1961). The ego and the id. In: J. Strachey (ed.), *The Standard Edition of the Complete Psychological Works of Sigmund Freud* (Vol. 19, pp. 12–66). London: The Hogarth Press.
FREUD, S. (1930/2002). *Civilisation and Its Discontents* (tr., D. McLintock). London: Penguin.
FREUD, S. (1933/1967). *New Introductory Lectures on Psycho-Analysis* (tr., W.J.H. Sprott). London: The Hogarth Press.
GARROD, S. & PICKERING, M.J. (2004). Why is conversation so easy? *Trends in Cognitive Sciences* 8: 8–11.
GERGEN, K.J. (1977). The social construction of self-knowledge. In: T. Mischel (ed.), *The Self: Psychological and Philosophical Issues* (pp. 372–385). Oxford, England: Blackwell.
GERTH, H. & MILLS, C.W. (1954). *Character and Social Structure: The Psychology of Social Institutions*. London: Routledge & Kegan Paul.

GIDDENS, A. (1991). *Modernity and Self-Identity: Self and Society in the Late Modern Age.* Cambridge: Polity Press.
GLOVER, E. (1931/1956). Sublimation, substitution and social anxiety. In: E. Glover, *On the Early Development of Mind* (pp. 130–160). London: Imago Publishing Company.
GOFFMAN, E. (1959). *The Presentation of Self in Everyday Life.* New York: Anchor Books/Doubleday.
GOLDBERG, A. (1983). Self psychology and alternative perspectives on internalization. In: J.D. Lichtenberg & S. Kaplan (eds), *Reflections on Self Psychology* (pp. 297–312). Hillsdale, New Jersey: The Analytic Press.
GOODMAN, G. (2002). *The Internal World and Attachment.* Hillsdale, New Jersey: The Analytic Press.
GREENSON, R.R. (1947/1978). On gambling. In: R.R. Greenson (ed.), *Explorations in Psychoanalysis* (pp. 1–15). New York: International Universities Press.
GREENSON, R.R. (1958/1978). On screen defenses, screen hunger, and screen identity. In: R.R. Greenson (ed.), *Explorations in Psychoanalysis* (pp. 111–132). New York: International Universities Press.
GREENSON, R.R. (1962/1978). On enthusiasm. In: R.R. Greenson (ed.), *Explorations in Psychoanalysis* (pp. 171–189). New York: International Universities Press.
GREENSON, R.R. (1973/1978). The personal meaning of perfection. In: R.R. Greenson (ed.), *Explorations in Psychoanalysis* (pp. 479–490). New York: International Universities Press.
GREENWALD, A. (1980). The totalitarian ego: Fabrication and revision of personal history. *American Psychologist* 35: 603–618.
HARTMANN, H. (1964). *Essays on Ego Psychology: Selected Problems in Psychoanalytic Theory.* London: The Hogarth Press.
HASS, H. (1968/1970). *The Human Animal: The Mystery of Man's Behaviour.* London: Hodder and Stoughton.
HEARD, D.H. & LAKE, B. (1986). The attachment dynamic in adult life. *British Journal of Psychiatry* 149: 430–438.
HENDRICK, I. (1958). *Facts and Theories of Psychoanalysis*, 3rd edition. New York: Alfred A. Knopf.
HORNEY, K. (1937). *The Neurotic Personality of our Time.* New York: W.W. Norton & Company.
HORNEY, K. (1939). *New Ways in Psychoanalysis.* New York: W.W. Norton & Company.
HORNEY, K. (1945/1992). *Our Inner Conflicts.* New York: W.W. Norton & Company.
HORNEY, K. (1950/1991). *Neurosis and Human Growth: The Struggle Toward Self-Realization.* New York: W.W. Norton & Company.
IZARD, C. (1994). Innate and universal facial expressions: evidence from developmental and cross-cultural research. *Psychological Bulletin* 115: 288–299.
JACOBSON, E. (1964). *The Self and the Object World.* New York: International Universities Press.
JAMES, W. (1890). *The Principles of Psychology*, Vol. 1. New York: Holt.
JAQUES, E. (1955). Social systems as a defence against persecutory and depressive anxiety. In: M. Klein, P. Heimann, & R. Money-Kyrle (eds), *New Directions in Psycho-Analysis* (pp. 478–498). New York: Basic Books.
JOFFE, W.G. & SANDLER, J. (1965/1987). Pain, depression, and individuation. In: J. Sandler (ed.), *From Safety to Superego: Selected Papers of Joseph Sandler* (pp. 154–179). New York: Guilford Press.
JOFFE, W.G. & SANDLER, J. (1967/1987). On disorders of narcissism. In: J. Sandler (ed.), *From Safety to Superego: Selected Papers of Joseph Sandler* (pp. 180–190). New York: Guilford Press.

JOFFE, W.G. & SANDLER, J. (1968/1987). Adaptation, affects, and the representational world. In: J. Sandler (ed.), *From Safety to Superego: Selected Papers of Joseph Sandler* (pp. 221–234). New York: Guilford Press.

JOSEPH, B. (1986). Envy in everyday life. *Psychoanalytic Psychotherapy* 2: 13–22.

KERNBERG, O.F. (1970). Factors in the psychoanalytic treatment of narcissistic personalities. *Journal of the American Psychoanalytic Association* 18: 51–85.

KERNBERG, O.F. (1974). Further contributions to the treatment of narcissistic personalities. *International Journal of Psychoanalysis* 55: 215–240.

KERNBERG, O.F. (1976). *Object Relations Theory and Clinical Psychoanalysis*. New York: Jason Aronson.

KERNBERG, O.F. (1982a). Self, ego, affects, and drives. *Journal of the American Psychoanalytic Association* 30: 893–917.

KERNBERG, O.F. (1982b/1987). The dynamic unconscious and the self. In: R. Stern (ed.), *Theories of the Unconscious and Theories of the Self* (pp. 3–25). Hillsdale, New Jersey: Analytic Press.

KERNBERG, O.F. (1992). *Aggression in Personality Disorders and Perversions*. New Haven, Connecticut: Yale University Press.

KERNBERG, O.F. (1996). A psychoanalytic theory of personality disorders. In: J.F. Clarkin & M.F. Lenzenweger (eds), *Major Theories of Personality Disorder* (pp. 106–140). New York: Guilford Press.

KERNBERG, O.F. (1998/2002). The couch at sea. In: R.D. Hinshelwood & M. Chiesa (eds), *Organisations, Anxieties and Defences: Towards a Psychoanalytic Social Psychology* (pp. 65–76). London: Whurr Publishers.

KLEIN, G.S. (1967). Peremptory ideation: Structure and force in motivated ideas. In: R.R. Holt (ed.), *Motives and Thought: Psychoanalytic Essays in Honour of David Rapaport* (pp. 80–128). New York: International Universities Press.

KLEIN, M. (1932/1937). *The Psycho-Analysis of Children*. London: The Hogarth Press & The Institute of Psycho-Analysis.

KLEIN, M. (1937). Love, Guilt and Reparation. In: M. Klein & J. Riviere (eds), *Love, Hate and Reparation* (pp. 57–119) (Psycho-Analytical Epitomes No. 2). London: The Hogarth Press and the Institute of Psycho-Analysis.

KLEIN, M. (1940/1948). Mourning and its relation to manic depressive states. In: M. Klein (ed.), *Contributions to Psycho-Analysis, 1921–1945*. London: Hogarth.

KLEIN, M. (1946/1952). Notes on some schizoid mechanisms. In: M. Klein, P. Heimann, S. Isaacs, & J. Riviere (eds), *Developments in Psycho-Analysis* (pp. 292–320). London: The Hogarth Press.

KOHUT, H. (1966). Forms and transformations of narcissism. *Journal of the American Psychoanalytic Association* 14: 243–272.

KOHUT, H. (1971). *The Analysis of the Self: A Systematic Approach to the Psychoanalytic Treatment of Narcissistic Personality Disorders*. New York: International Universities Press.

KOHUT, H. (1976). Creativeness, charisma, group psychology. In: P. Ornstein (ed.), *The Search for the Self* (Vol. 2). New York: International Universities Press.

KOHUT, H. (1977). *The Restoration of the Self*. New York: International Universities Press.

KOHUT, H. (1983). Selected problems of self psychological theory. In: J.D. Lichtenberg & S. Kaplan (eds), *Reflections on Self Psychology* (pp. 387–416). Hillsdale, New Jersey: The Analytic Press.

KOHUT, H. (1984). *How Does Analysis Cure?*, ed. A. Goldberg with P. Stepansky. Chicago & London: The University of Chicago Press.

KOHUT, H. & WOLF, E.S. (1978). The disorders of the self and their treatment: An outline. *International Journal of Psychoanalysis* 59: 413–425.

KOJÉVE, A. (1947/1980). *Introduction to the Reading of Hegel* (tr., J. Nichols). Ithaca, New York: Cornell University Press.
LACAN, J. (1966/2002). *Écrits: A Selection* (tr., B. Fink). New York: W.W. Norton & Company.
LAING, R.D. (1960). *The Divided Self*. London: Tavistock Publications.
LASCH, C. (1979). *The Culture of Narcissism: American Life in an Age of Diminishing Expectations*. New York: W.W. Norton & Company.
LAUGHLIN, H.P. (1970). *The Ego and Its Defences*. New York: Appleton-Century-Crofts.
LEBOVICI, S. (1989). Precocious aspects of the formation of morality. In: H.P. Blum, E.M. Weinshel, & F.R. Rodman (eds), *The Psychoanalytic Core: Essays in Honor of Leo Rangell, M.D.* (pp. 421–434). Madison, Connecticut: International Universities Press.
LORENZ, K. (1935/1957). Companionship in bird life. In: C.H. Schiller (ed.), *Instinctive Behavior: The Development of a Modern Concept* (pp. 83–128). New York: International Universities Press.
LORENZ, K. (1937/1957). The nature of instinct. In: C.H. Schiller (ed.), *Instinctive Behavior: The Development of a Modern Concept* (pp. 129–175). New York: International Universities Press.
LORENZ, K. (1939/1957). Comparative study of behavior. In: C. H. Schiller (ed.), *Instinctive Behavior: The Development of a Modern Concept* (pp. 239–263). New York: International Universities Press.
LORENZ, K. (1952/1957). The past twelve years in the comparative study of behavior. In: C.H. Schiller (ed.), *Instinctive Behavior: The Development of a Modern Concept* (pp. 288–310). New York: International Universities Press.
LORENZ, K. (1963/2002). *On Aggression*. London: Routledge.
LORENZ, K. (1973/1977). *Behind the Mirror: A Search for a Natural History of Human Knowledge*. London: Methuen & Co.
MACHADO, C.J. & BACHEVALIER, J. (2003). Non-human primate models of childhood psychopathology: the promise and the limitations. *Journal of Child Psychology and Psychiatry* 44: 64–87.
MAHLER, M.S. (1967). On human symbiosis and the vicissitudes of individuation. *Journal of the American Psychoanalytic Association* 15: 740–763.
MAHLER, M.S. (1968). *On Human Symbiosis and the Vicissitudes of Individuation*. New York: International Universities Press.
MAHLER, M.S. (1972). On the first three subphases of the separation-individuation process. *International Journal of Psychoanalysis* 53: 333–338.
MAHLER, M.S., PINE, F., & BERGMAN, A. (1975). *The Psychological Birth of the Human Infant*. New York: Basic Books.
MAIN, T. (1957). The ailment. *British Journal of Medical Psychology* 30: 129–145.
MARKSON, E. & THOMSON, P.G. (1986). The relationship between psychoanalytic concepts of conflict and deficit. In: A. Goldberg (ed.), *Progress in Self Psychology* (Vol. 2, pp. 31–40). New York: Guilford Press.
MASSERMAN, J.H. (1968). The biodynamic roots of psychoanalysis. In: J. Marmor (ed.), *Modern Psychoanalysis: New Directions and Perspectives* (pp. 189–224). New York: Basic Books.
MCCLUSKEY, U. (2002). The dynamics of attachment and systems-centered group psychotherapy. *Group Dynamics: Theory, Research, and Practice* 6: 131–142.
MCDOUGALL, W. (1924). *An Outline of Psychology*, 2nd edition. London: Methuen & Co.
MEAD, G.H. (1934). *Mind, Self, and Society: From the Standpoint of a Social Behaviorist* (ed., C.W. Morris). Chicago: The University of Chicago Press.

MILLER, A. (1979). Depression and grandiosity as related forms of narcissistic disturbances. *International Journal of Psychoanalysis* 60: 61–67.
MILLER, N.E. (1948). Studies of fear as an acquirable drive: I. Fear as motivation and fear-reduction as reinforcement in the learning of new responses. *Journal of Experimental Psychology* 38: 89–101.
MILROD, D. (1972). Self-pity, self-comforting, and the superego. *The Psychoanalytic Study of the Child* 27: 505–528.
MISHAN, E.J. (1967). *The Costs of Economic Growth*. London: Penguin.
MODELL, A.H. (1975). A narcissistic defence against affects and the illusion of self-sufficiency. *International Journal of Psychoanalysis* 56: 275–282.
MONEY-KYRLE, R.E. (1961/1978). *Man's Picture of his World: A Psycho-analytic Study*. London: Duckworth.
MOORE, T.V. (1926). *Dynamic Psychology: An Introduction to Modern Psychological Theory and Practice*. Philadelphia: Lippincott.
MORRISON, A.P. (1983). Shame, ideal self, and narcissism. *Contemporary Psychoanalysis* 19: 295–318.
MOSES, R. (1989). Shame and entitlement: Their relation to political process. In: H.P. Blum, E.M. Weinshel, & F.R. Rodman (eds), *The Psychoanalytic Core: Essays in Honor of Leo Rangell, M.D.* (pp. 421–434). Madison, Connecticut: International Universities Press.
MOWRER, O.H. & LAMOREAUX, R.R. (1946). Fear as an intervening variable in avoidance conditioning. *Journal of Comparative Psychology* 29: 29–50.
MOYNIHAN, M.H. (1998). *The Social Regulation of Competition and Aggression in Animals*. Washington: Smithsonian Institution Press.
NUNBERG, H. (1955). *Principles of Psychoanalysis*. New York: International Universities Press.
ORNSTEIN, P. (1983). Discussion of papers by Drs. Goldberg, Stolorow, and Wallerstein. In: J.D. Lichtenberg & S. Kaplan (eds), *Reflections on Self Psychology* (pp. 339–384). Hillsdale, New Jersey: The Analytic Press.
PARLOFF, M.B. (1968). Analytic group psychotherapy. In: J. Marmor (ed.), *Modern Psychoanalysis: New Directions and Perspectives* (pp. 492–531). New York: Basic Books.
PRETZER, J.L & BECK, A. (1996). A cognitive theory of personality disorders. In: J.F. Clarkin & M.F. Lenzenweger (Eds), *Major Theories of Personality Disorder* (pp. 36–105). New York: Guilford Press.
RADO, S. (1928/1956). The problem of melancholia. In: *Psychoanalysis of Behavior: Collected Papers* (pp. 47–63). New York: Grune & Stratton.
RADO, S. (1956). *Psychoanalysis of Behavior: Collected Papers*. New York: Grune & Stratton.
RANGELL, L. (1954). The psychology of poise: With a special elaboration on the psychic significance of the snout or perioral region. *International Journal of Psychoanalysis* 35: 313–333.
RANGELL, L. (1969). Choice-conflict and the decision-making function of the ego: A psychoanalytic contribution to decision theory. *International Journal of Psychoanalysis* 50: 599–602.
REDDY, V. (2003). On being the object of attention: Implications for self-other consciousness. *Trends in Cognitive Sciences* 7: 397–402.
REDL, F. (1942/1980). Group emotion and leadership. In: S. Scheidlinger (ed.), *Psychoanalytic Group Dynamics: Basic Readings* (pp. 15–68). New York: International Universities Press.
REICH, A. (1953). Narcissistic object choice in women. *Journal of the American Psychoanalytic Association* 1: 22–44.

REICH, A. (1960). Pathologic forms of self-esteem regulation. *The Psychoanalytic Study of the Child* 15: 215–232.
REICH, W. (1928/1950). On character analysis. In: R. Fliess (ed.), *The Psychoanalytic Reader: An Anthology of Essential Papers with Critical Introductions* (pp. 106–123). London: The Hogarth Press.
REICH, W. (1929/1950). The genital character and the neurotic character. In: R. Fliess (ed.), *The Psychoanalytic Reader: An Anthology of Essential Papers with Critical Introductions* (pp. 124–144). London: The Hogarth Press.
REISER, D.E. (1986). Self psychology and the problem of suicide. In: A. Goldberg (ed.), *Progress in Self Psychology* (Vol. 2, pp. 227–241). New York: Guilford Press.
RICOEUR, P. (1990/1992). *Oneself as Another* (tr. K. Blamey). Chicago: The University of Chicago Press.
RICKLES, W.H. (1986). Self psychology and somatization: An integration with alexithymia. In: A. Goldberg (ed.), *Progress in Self Psychology* (Vol. 2, pp. 212–226). New York: Guilford Press.
RIVIERE, J. (1936). A contribution to the analysis of the negative therapeutic reaction. *International Journal of Psychoanalysis* 17: 304–320.
RIVIERE, J. (1937). Hate, greed and aggression. In: M. Klein & J. Riviere (eds), *Love, Hate and Reparation* (pp. 3–53) (Psychoanalytic Epitomes No. 2). London: The Hogarth Press and the Institute of Psycho-Analysis.
ROSENFELD, H.A. (1965). *Psychotic States: A Psychoanalytical Approach*. London: Maresfield Reprints.
ROTHSTEIN, A. (1979). The theory of narcissism: An object-relations perspective. *The Psychoanalytic Review* 66: 35–47.
SANDER, L.W. (1983). To begin with – reflections on ontogeny. In: J.D. Lichtenberg & S. Kaplan (eds), *Reflections on Self Psychology* (pp. 85–104). Hillsdale, New Jersey: The Analytic Press.
SANDLER, J. (1960a/1987). The background of safety. In: J. Sandler (ed.), *From Safety to Superego: Selected Papers of Joseph Sandler* (pp. 1–8). New York: Guilford Press. [originally published in: *International Journal of Psychoanalysis* 41: 352–356]
SANDLER, J. (1960b/1987). The concept of superego. In: J. Sandler (ed.), *From Safety to Superego: Selected Papers of Joseph Sandler* (pp. 17–44). New York: Guilford Press.
SANDLER, J. (1972/1987). The role of affects in psychoanalytic theory. In: J. Sandler (ed.), *From Safety to Superego: Selected Papers of Joseph Sandler* (pp. 285–297). New York: Guilford Press.
SANDLER, J. (1976). Countertransference and role-responsiveness. *International Review of Psychoanalysis* 3: 43–47.
SANDLER, J. (1985). *The Analysis of Defense*, With A. Freud. New York: International Universities Press.
SANDLER, J. (1989a). Unconscious wishes and human relationships. In: J. Sandler (ed.), *Dimensions of Psychoanalysis* (pp. 65–81). Madison, Connecticut: International Universities Press.
SANDLER, J. (1989b). The id – or the child within? In: J. Sandler (ed.), *Dimensions of Psychoanalysis* (pp. 219–239). Madison, Connecticut: International Universities Press.
SANDLER, J. & JOFFE, W.G. (1966/1987). On sublimation. In: J. Sandler (ed.), *From Safety to Superego: Selected Papers of Joseph Sandler* (pp. 191–207). New York: Guilford Press.
SANDLER, J. & JOFFE, W.G. (1968/1987). Psychoanalytic psychology and learning theory. In: J. Sandler (ed.), *From Safety to Superego: Selected Papers of Joseph Sandler* (pp. 255–263). New York: Guilford Press.

SANDLER, J. & JOFFE, W.G. (1969/1987). Toward a basic psychoanalytic model. In: J. Sandler (ed.), *From Safety to Superego: Selected Papers of Joseph Sandler* (pp. 235–254). New York: Guilford Press.

SANDLER, J. & NAGERA, H. (1963/1987). The metapsychology of fantasy. In: J. Sandler (ed.), *From Safety to Superego: Selected Papers of Joseph Sandler* (pp. 90–120). New York: Guilford Press.

SANDLER, J. & SANDLER, A.-M. (1978). On the development of object relations and affects. *International Journal of Psychoanalysis* 59: 285–296.

SANDLER, J., HOLDER, A., & MEERS, D. (1963/1987). Ego ideal and ideal self. In: J. Sandler (ed.), *From Safety to Superego: Selected Papers of Joseph Sandler* (pp. 73–89). New York: Guilford Press.

SANDLER, J., HOLDER, A., KAWENOKA-BERGER, M., KENNEDY, H., & NEURATH, L. (1969/1987). Theoretical and clinical aspects of transference. In: J. Sandler (ed.), *From Safety to Superego: Selected Papers of Joseph Sandler* (pp. 264–284). New York: Guilford Press.

SCHACHTEL, E.G. [1973]. On attention, selective inattention, and experience: an inquiry into attention as an attitude. In: E.G. Witenberg (ed.), *Interpersonal Explorations in Psychoanalysis: New Directions in Theory and Practice* (pp. 40–66). New York: Basic Books.

SCHAFER, R. (1967). Ideals, the ego ideal, and the ideal self. In: R.R. Holt (ed.), *Motives and Thought: Psychoanalytic Essays in Honour of David Rapaport* (pp. 131–174). New York: International Universities Press.

SCHAFER, R. (1976). *A New Language for Psychoanalysis*. New Haven, Connecticut: Yale University Press.

SCHAFER, R. (1997). Conformity and individualism. In: E.R. Shapiro (ed.), *The Inner World in the Outer World* (pp. 27–42). New Haven, Connecticut: Yale University Press.

SCHECTER, D.E. (1973). On the emergence of human relatedness. In: E.G. Witenberg (ed.), *Interpersonal Explorations in Psychoanalysis: New Directions in Theory and Practice*, (pp. 17–39). New York: Basic Books.

SCHECTER, D.E. (1978). Attachment, detachment, and psychoanalytic therapy. In: E.G. Witenberg (ed.), *Interpersonal Psychoanalysis: New Directions* (pp. 81–104). New York: Gardner Press.

SCHEIDLINGER, S. (1964/1980). Identification, the sense of belonging and of identity in small groups. In: S. Scheidlinger (ed.), *Psychoanalytic Group Dynamics: Basic Readings* (pp. 213–231). New York: International Universities Press.

SCHEIDLINGER, S. (1968/1980). The concept of regression in group psychotherapy. In: S. Scheidlinger (ed.), *Psychoanalytic Group Dynamics: Basic Readings* (pp. 233–254). New York: International Universities Press.

SCHILDER, P. (1951). *Psychoanalysis, Man, and Society*. New York: W.W. Norton & Company.

SCHILDER, P. (1976). *On Psychoses* (ed. L. Bender). New York: International Universities Press.

SCHULTZ-HENKE, H. (1951/1988). *Lehrbuch der Analytischen Psychotherapie*. Stuttgart: Georg Thieme Verlag.

SEGAL, H. (1973). *Introduction to the Work of Melanie Klein*. London: Hogarth Press.

SEGAL, H. (1989a/1997). The Oedipus complex today. In: J. Steiner (ed.), *Hanna Segal: Psychoanalysis, Literature and War: Papers 1975–1995*. London: Routledge.

SEGAL, H. (1989b). Psychoanalysis and freedom of thought. In: J. Sandler (ed.), *Dimensions of Psychoanalysis* (pp. 51–63). Madison, Connecticut: International Universities Press.

SHANE, M. & SHANE, E. (1986). Self change and development in the analysis of an adolescent patient: The use of a combined model with a developmental orientation and approach. In: A. Goldberg (ed.), *Progress in Self Psychology* (Vol. 2, pp. 142–160). New York: Guilford Press.
SHAPIRO, D. (2000). *Dynamics of Character*. New York: Basic Books.
SILVERMAN, D.K. (1991). Attachment patterns and Freudian theory: An integrative proposal. *Psychoanalytic Psychology* 8: 169–193.
SPILLIUS, E.B. (1993). Varieties of envious experience. *International Journal of Psychoanalysis* 74: 1199–1212.
STERN, D.N. (1983). The early development of schemas of self, other, and "self with other". In: J.D. Lichtenberg & S. Kaplan (eds), *Reflections on Self Psychology* (pp. 49–84). Hillsdale, New Jersey: The Analytic Press.
STERN, D.N. (1985). *The Interpersonal World of the Infant: A View from Psychoanalysis and Developmental Psychology*. New York: Basic Books.
STOLOROW, R.D. (1975). Toward a functional definition of narcissism. *International Journal of Psychoanalysis* 56: 179–185.
STOLOROW, R.D. (1983). Self psychology – a structural psychology. In: J.D. Lichtenberg & S. Kaplan (eds), *Reflections on Self Psychology* (pp. 287–296). Hillsdale, New Jersey: The Analytic Press.
STOLOROW, R.D. (1985). Toward a pure psychology of inner conflict. In: A. Goldberg (ed.), *Progress in Self Psychology* (Vol. 1, pp. 193–201). New York: Guilford Press.
STOLOROW, R.D. (1986a). Beyond dogma in psychoanalysis. In: A. Goldberg (ed.), *Progress in Self Psychology* (Vol. 2, pp. 41–49). New York: Guilford Press.
STOLOROW, R.D. (1986b). On experiencing an object: A multidimensional perspective. In: A. Goldberg (ed.), *Progress in Self Psychology* (Vol. 2, pp. 273–279). New York: Guilford Press.
STORR, A. (1968). *Human Aggression*. New York: Atheneum.
SULLIVAN, H.S. (1953). *The Interpersonal Theory of Psychiatry*. New York: W.W. Norton & Company.
THORNDIKE, E.L. (1911). *Animal Intelligence*. New York: Macmillan.
TOLPIN, M. (1986). The self and its selfobjects: A different baby. In: A. Goldberg (ed.), *Progress in Self Psychology* (Vol. 2, pp. 115–128). New York: Guilford Press.
TOLPIN, P.H. (1986). What makes for effective analysis? In: A. Goldberg (ed.), *Progress in Self Psychology* (Vol. 2, pp. 95–105). New York: Guilford Press.
WAELDER, R. (1960). *Basic Theory of Psychoanalysis*. New York: International Universities Press.
WALLERSTEIN, R.S. (1983). Self psychology and classical psychoanalytic psychotherapy: The nature of their relationship. In: A. Goldberg (ed.), *The Future of Psychoanalysis* (pp. 19–63). New York: International Universities Press.
WEINSHEL, E.M. (1989). On inconsolability. In: H.P. Blum, E.M. Weinshel, & F.R. Rodman (eds), *The Psychoanalytic Core: Essays in Honor of Leo Rangell, M.D.* (pp. 45–69). Madison, Connecticut: International Universities Press.
WHITMAN, R.M. & STOCK, D. (1958/1980). The group focal conflict. In: S. Scheidlinger (ed.), *Psychoanalytic Group Dynamics: Basic Readings* (pp. 173–188). New York: International Universities Press.
WILSON, S.L. (1985). The self-pity response: A reconsideration. In: A. Goldberg (ed.), *Progress in Self Psychology* (Vol. 1, pp. 178–190). New York: Guilford Press.
WINNICOTT, D.W. (1953). Transitional objects and transitional phenomena. *International Journal of Psychoanalysis* 34: 89–97.

WINNICOTT, D.W. (1958/1965). The capacity to be alone. In: D.W. Winnicott (ed.), *The Maturational Processes and the Facilitating Environment* (pp. 29–36). New York: International Universities Press.

WINNICOTT, D.W. (1960a/1965). The theory of parent-infant relationship. In: D.W. Winnicott (ed.), *The Maturational Processes and the Facilitating Environment* (pp. 37–55). New York: International Universities Press.

WINNICOTT, D.W. (1960b/1965). Ego distortion in terms of true and false self. In: D.W. Winnicott (ed.), *The Maturational Processes and the Facilitating Environment* (pp. 140–152). New York: International Universities Press.

WINNICOTT, D.W. (1962/1965). Ego integration in child development. In: D.W. Winnicott, *The Maturational Processes and the Facilitating Environment* (pp. 56–63). New York: International Universities Press.

WINNICOTT, D.W. (1963/1965). From dependence to independence in the development of the individual. In: D.W. Winnicott (ed.), *The Maturational Processes and the Facilitating Environment* (pp. 83–99). New York: International Universities Press.

WINNICOTT, D.W. (1969). The theory of the parent-infant relationship. *International Journal of Psychoanalysis* 50: 711–717.

WINNICOTT, D.W. (1971). *Playing and Reality*. London: Routledge.

WINNICOTT, D.W. (1989). *Psycho-Analytic Explorations* (C. Winnicott, R. Shepherd, & M. Davis., eds). Cambridge, MA: Harvard University Press.

WOLF, E. (1988). *Treating the Self: Elements of Clinical Self Psychology*. New York: Guilford Press.

YOUNG, P.T. (1959). The role of affective processes in learning and motivation. *Psychological Review* 66: 104–125.

Index

affection (affectionate interactions, affectionateness) 13, 33–6, 38, 40, 49, 52, 65, 68–9, 80, 95, 110–11, 130, 132–3, 136–7, 139–40, 142, 166, 178, 193, 220–1, 223–5, 251–2, 262, 287, 289, 299, 304–5, 317, 325–8, 346, 387–8
alexithymia 319
aloneness 229
altruism 209–10
ambition 56, 82, 102, 121–3, 126, 128–9, 140, 150, 155, 182, 209–11, 218, 220, 229, 248–9, 251–2, 255–7, 262, 288, 299, 301, 345, 383, 390
ambitiousness 35, 70, 73, 138, 140, *see also* ambition
annihilation (fear or threat of) 19, 53, 55, 57, 59, 97, 132, 161, 173, 175, 178, 254, 274–5, 315, 320, 337, 347, 355, 368, 378
antisocial personality disorder 262, 263
appeasement 23–7, 29, 38, 85, 225, 237, 303, 345, 385, 387
assertiveness 21–3, 73, 85, 91–2, 97–8, 123–4, 129, 137–8, 264, 278, 288, 297, 300, 386–7
attachment 33, 38, 46–8, 50, 63–4, 94–5, 112, 117–20, 228, 369
attunement 33, 68, 111
avoidance learning 19, 74–5, 77–8

basic anxiety 51–3, 64, 82–3, 138, 229, 252, 254, 299, 347, *see also* disintegration anxiety
begging 26, 38
bereavement 95, *see also* mourning
bond formation (bonding) 24–6, 28, 38
borderline personality disorder 270, 273, 282, 284–5
bossing attitude 259–60
bowing 28–9

castration anxiety (fear of castration) 53–6, 136–7, 161, 172–3, 175, 234, 281, 310, 315, 386
clinging 33, 36–7, 113, 125, 220–1, 305

coercion 22–3, 235–6
communication 15–16, 31, 34, 38, 110, 348–9, 353, 362, *see also* conversation, language
compensation 81, 155, 247–8, 284, 313
competition 15, 55, 81, 101, 198, 275–6, 293–4, 299–300, 333, 360–1, 368, 277, *see also* competitiveness
competitiveness 257, 261–2, 345
compliance 18, 34, 109, 130–1, 147, 157–8, 236–40, 257, 291–2, 297, 386–7, *see also* conformity, obedience
compulsions 71, 87, 156, 158, 177, 286, 317, 341, 355, *see also* obsessions
compulsiveness 138, 253, *see also* compulsion
conformity 19–20, 85, 239–40, 301, 345, 360–3, 365–7, 387–8, *see also* compliance, obedience
consumerism 382, 384
contempt 16–18, 262, 276, 297–8, 306, 335, 363, 365, *see also* hatred
cooperation 100, 361, *see also* social interest
countertransference 351–3
conversation 31–2, 68–9, 365, *see also* communication, language
conversion 179, 310, 320–1, 384
courage, courageous 91, 138, 140, 176, 288, 305, 314, 374
cries 35, 37, *see also* separation cries
criminality 179–80, 263
criticism 54, 56, 58, 84–5, 143, 148, 152, 161, 166, 169–72, 194, 203, 205, 210–11, 214–16, 230, 238, 245–6, 250, 258, 260–1, 269, 284, 291, 295, 300–1, *see also* disapproval, self-criticism
crying 33, 36, 46, *see also* cries
customs 238, 240, 345, 362, 365, *see also* norms, tradition

deception 253–4, 262, *see also* self-deception
decision making 76, 162–3

403

404 Index

defence mechanisms (mechanisms of defence, ego defences)   3–4, 20–1, 40, 44, 56–61, 73–4, 77–8, 84–5, 101, 116, 154–5, 157, 168, 171–2, 176, 183–5, 199–200, 202–7, 210–12, 218, 222, 225, 228, 238, 241, 243–4, 245–8, 256–8, 261, 265, 276, 278, 280–2, 286, 298, 310–2, 320, 324, 334–6, 339–40, 342–3, 371, 374
defeat   23, 29, 99, 182, 199, 250, 262, 275, 291, 298–300, 313–15, 338, 343, 387, *see also* self-defeating behaviour
deference   154, 290, 295, 375, *see also* respect
defiance   241, 254–5
delusions of grandeur   71, 248, 343, *see also* grandiosity
denial   45, 61, 96, 151, 180, 205–7, 277, 333–6, 342–3
depression   100–1, 159, 176, 215, 234, 265–6, 307, 312, 321–32, 335–6, *see also* melancholia
depressive anxiety   5, 116, 282
depressive position   5, 115–16, 277, 282–3, 331–2, 335–6
desire (Lacanian)   67–8, 149, 185–6
despair   157, 181–2, 228, 242, 295, 298, 322, 324–5, 330, 336
detachment   71, 212, 228–9, 231, 234–6, 259, 285–6, 292–3, 307, 383
disappointment   56, 98, 121, 151, 187, 198, 201, 221, 254, 257, 260, 275, 306, 308, 313–14, 319, 321–2, 327, 329, 337, 370, 374, *see also* narcissistic injury
disapproval   13–14, 53–4, 66, 84–5, 128, 132, 134, 143–5, 152, 160–1, 166–7, 170–171, 205–6, 243–4, 246, 323, 363, 380–1, *see also* criticism
disgust   16–17, 56–8, 275
disintegration anxiety   52–3, 55–6, 69, 97–8, 168, 173, 184, 188, 208, 218, 229, 233, 254, 275, 281, 310, 319, 324, 378
displacement   54, 67, 71, 135, 146, 153, 167, 203–4, 210, 237, 245, 247, 367
disrespect   18, 98, 299, 341, *see also* slights
dissociation   320, *see also* conversion
distrust   16, 18, 93, 261, 303
depersonalization   341, 376
dominance (dominance rank, dominance hierarchy)   17, 19, 20, 25, 29, 31, 139, 238, 292, 299, 312, 349, 367, 372, 386, 390, *see also* superiority
duty   196

ego boundary   186–7, 208, 273, 339, 376
ego defences   *see* defence mechanisms
ego feeling   164–5, 185–7, 189, 214
ego functions   21, 59, 70, 84, 243
ego identity   117, 137–8, 196–7, 376
ego instincts   59, 62–3, 232, 310
ego interests   243
ego restriction   61, 247
embarrassment   56–7, 129, 172, 206, 222, 239, 274, 314, 363, *see also* shame
empathy, empathy failures   22, 53, 103, 107, 109, 114, 129, 204, 217, 222, 228, 279, 286, 353
entitlement (sense of)   221, 258–9, 295–6, 383
enthusiasm   184, 289, 333–4, 345, 376, 379
envy   206, 209, 247, 249–50, 255–7, 265, 275–6, 298–9, 379
euphoria   234, 334, 371, *see also* oceanic feeling
exhibitionism   35, 39–40, 56–7, 92, 121–3, 128–9, 138, 173–4, 215, 219, 224, 228, 266–7, 269, 274, 278–9, 287, 315, 390
expiation (expiatory behaviour)   178, 234, 308, 310, 330–1, *see also* repentance, need for punishment

facade   70, 83, 92–3, 154, 156, 174, 192–3, 195, 219, 225, 231, 245, 275, 300–1, *see also* false self
false self   92, 109, 129, 131, 156–7, 195–6, 209, 215, 225, 239–40, 242, 273–4, 338, *see also* facade
fate   233–4, 263, 295, 302, 318
familiarity   24–5, 27, 195, 371
fear of castration   *see* castration anxiety
fear of punishment   78, 131–2, 134–6, 148, 173, 175, 281, 311, *see also* castration anxiety, persecutory anxiety
fear of retaliation   51, 173, 251, 299, 306, 312, 317, 342, *see also* fear of punishment
fear of strangers (stranger anxiety)   27, 50–1, 64

feeding 15, 26, 36, 38–9, 68
forgiveness 173, 178, 225, 285, 298, 308, 330–1

gambling 233–234
genuineness 220, 240, 301, see also spontaneity, true self
glory 83, 93, 199, 229, 241, 252–3, 268, 290, 297, 302, see also pride
God 66, 232–4, 249, 302, 333, 357–8, 370, 377, see also religion
grandiosity 55–6, 113, 121–3, 129, 150–1, 159, 183, 219, 221, 227, 231, 240, 242, 265–6, 269–70, 274–6, 324–5
grandiose delusion see delusions of grandeur
gratitude 41, 256, 265
greed 93, 130, 154, 249–50, 270, 276–277, 288
greeting 28–30, 37, 39, 273
gregariousness 26–7, 36, 46–7, 361, 378–9
grooming 19, 26, 39
group cohesion 368–9, 371, 378
group identity 138, 375–7
guilt 54, 58, 67, 89–90, 99–100, 144, 159, 170, 172–81, 200, 210–11, 234, 262, 266–7, 274–5, 282, 285, 295, 307–8, 311, 327, 329–31, 335, 342, 363, 384

hatred 20, 22–3, 181, 239, 250, 272, 276–7, 307, 338, 365, 378, see also contempt
helplessness 26, 35, 37–8, 41, 51–2, 56, 58–9, 100–1, 112, 132, 135, 139, 159–60, 174–5, 192, 210, 225, 233, 236, 250, 263, 299, 304–6, 309, 326, 339, 349, 358, 364, 370
hierarchy 258, 372, 390
hopelessness 73, 101, 193, 275, 298, 325–6
humiliation 56–7, 73, 99, 168, 225, 229, 240, 247, 254, 269, 274–5, 289, 291, 298, 302, 319, 335, 339, 341, see also shame
humility 57, 154, 231, see also modesty
humour 40, 240–1, 379, see also laughter
hypnosis 147, 358, 375
hypochondria 53, 265, 274–5, 318–19, see also somatization
hypomania 333–4, 379, see also mania

idealization 71, 103, 121–2, 126–8, 148–50, 175, 225, 227, 249, 257, 276, 279, 282–3, 334, 372, 376
idealized image (idealized self-image) 57, 70, 72–3, 157–9, 193, 207, 252–3, 289–93, 295–7, 325, 390
ideal self 98, 101, 151–3, 157, 163–4, 173, 175, 252, 270, 276, 324–5, 389–90, see also idealized image
identity 18, 20, 109, 137–8, 182, 195–8, 239–40, 271–3, 284, 337–8, 366, 376–7, 381, 383
illness behaviour 223–4
imagination 77, 81, 85, 153, 157, 161, 164, 170, 191, 213, 253, 290–1, 293–4, 325, 365, 379
imitation 51, 106, 111, 119, 208, 225, 284
infantile dependence 105, 115, 222, 287
infantilism 26, 38
infatuation 270, 286
infidelity 236–7
inferiority 56, 71, 81–3, 87, 91, 138–40, 154–6, 173, 183, 220, 226, 231, 247–50, 252, 260–1, 263, 285, 288, 298, 300, 302, 305, 313–4, 317, 321–2, 386
ingratiation 28, 221, 225, 227, 272, 289, 328, 349–50, 373
injustice, injustice collection 22, 159, 297, 308–9, 328
inner coercion 158–9
inner dialogue 157, 191, 233, 294
intellectualization 231, 285
internal working models 119–20
introjection 66, 114, 116–17, 119, 127, 146, 149–50, 161, 214, 224, 227, 257, 329, 352–3, 357, 366

jealousy 255–6, 260, 288, 342

language 68–9, 110, 190–1, see also communication, conversation
laughter 19, 28, 40, 57, 289, 345, 378–9
leader (of a group) 85, 88, 145, 147, 175, 232, 306, 333, 361, 367–77, 379, 386, 390
liberalism 380, see also consumerism, modernity
loneliness 25, 47, 49–50, 54, 72, 229, 233, 286, 336

mania 89, 206, 332–6, 379
manic defence 280, 335–6, 390
masochism (psychic, moral or characterological) 34, 136, 159, 180–1, 184, 216, 224–5, 257, 287, 304, 307–9, 318, 387
mechanisms of defence *see* defence mechanisms
mirror stage 110
megalomania 71, 88, 150, 343, *see also* grandiosity
melancholia 167, 180, 321–3, 328–9, 331–2, *see also* depression
modernity 383, *see also* consumerism, liberalism
modesty 57, 259, 268, 271
mood 16, 26–7, 31, 42, 176, 180, 257, 332–3
mourning 206, 228, 276, 321, 328, 331, 335

narcissistic cathexis of the self 70–1, 86–7, 96, 101, 144–5, 148, 151, 163, 165, 183, 185, 199, 211, 224, 241, 244, 339
narcissistic object cathexis (narcissistic object relation or choice) 55, 84–7, 115, 183, 187, 189, 208, 267, 284, 321–2, 326, 341, 376
narcissistic injury 22, 53, 70, 86, 97–8, 183–4, 205, 211, 216–17, 221, 260, 266, 278, 281, 285–6, 313–14, 319, 328, 342, 365
need for punishment 99–100, 177–81, 234, 342, 358
neurotic claims 295
neurotic trends 82–3, 92, 141–2, 156, 235–6, 267, 296–8, 354
neutralization 20–2, 243–4
nodding 28–9

obedience 132, 147, 312, 371, 375, *see also* conformity, compliance
obsessions (obsessive symptoms or neurosis) 100, 154, 180, 245, 253, 303–4, 317–18, 340–2, *see also* compulsions
oceanic feeling 105, 113, 234, 334, 357
oedipal period 127–8, 149–50, 190, 279
Oedipus complex 68, 136–7, 149, 190, 383, *see also* oedipal period
omnipotence 71, 104–6, 108–9, 113–14, 126, 129, 137–8, 149, 151, 159, 221, 226, 233–4, 240, 252, 255, 258, 269, 272, 277, 282, 285, 296–7, 308–9, 317–8, 335, 339, 343, 373–4, 385, *see also* superiority
outcome simulation 153
outsider 19, 362–3, 378, *see also* scapegoat

pain of loss 70, 96, 304
pain of rejection 185, 277, 300, 304
paranoia, paranoid delusion 27, 138, 205, 216, 315, 341–2
paranoid anxiety *see* persecutory anxiety
paranoid personality / character 99, 228, 341
paranoid-schizoid position 5, 116, 282–3, 332, 335
persecutory anxiety (fear of persecution) 56, 59, 115–16, 149–50, 205, 216, 282, 299, 331–2, 335–6, 342–3, 371, 386
persona 174, 195, 239, 258, 289–90, 300, 338, *see also* false self, facade
playfulness 110–11, 141, *see also* spontaneity
pleasure principle 68, 79, 84, 310, 335
possessions 18, 67–8, 207, 209, 249–52, 257, 259–60, 290–1, 298–9, 333, 361, 364
prejudice 205, 257–8
prestige 67, 100, 219–20, 226, 229, 242–3, 248–9, 251–3, 257–9, 261, 263, 270, 275, 290, 296, 298–9, 305, 315, 322–3, 333, 361, 364, 374, 380
pride 39, 98–9, 128, 132, 137, 147, 165, 193, 201, 242, 247, 290–3, 297, 315, 357, 376–7
primary narcissism 62, 74, 80, 89, 102, 104–6, 121, 126, 148, 150, 187, 213, 218, 235, 357, 374, 376, 379
projection 84, 108, 115–16, 146–7, 200, 204–5, 216, 233, 255, 260–1, 342, 349–50, 352–5, 375
projective identification 261, 326, 347–50, 352–3, 355
poise 70, 317
psychotaxis 77–8

rationalization 180, 206–7, 248, 286, 280, 291
reaction formation 154–5, 168–9, 245–6, 250, 303, 313
reality principle 68, 84–5, 171

Index 407

reassurance 13, 37, 40, 49, 51–2, 62, 65, 70, 72, 80, 83, 85, 94–5, 100, 117, 120, 133, 135, 160, 198, 212, 215, 221–2, 238, 251–2, 287, 292, 294–5, 305, 315, 348, 359, 365
rebuff 49, 254, 260, 265–6, 300–1, 319, see also narcissistic injury
religion, religiosity 51, 147, 198, 232–3, 238, 243, 357–8, 362–3, 382, see also God
regression 84, 152, 222–4, 226, 308–9, 318–19, 331, 358, 370–1, 375, 377, 379, 390
reinforcement learning 13, 44, 72, 74–6
reparation 89–90, 99–100, 181, 331, 342
repentance 99–100, see also expiation
repetition compulsion (compulsion to repeat) 79, 350
repression 61, 63, 84, 93, 96, 136, 148, 171, 200–3, 245, 271, 361, 363–4, 375
respect 20, 73, 97, 134, 137, 147, 175, 195, 258, 267, 341, 354, 364–6, 382
retaliation 98–9, 135, 159, 318, see also fear of retaliation
revenge 23, 95, 97, 99, 230, 289, 321
reverie 108, 212
ridicule 19, 39, 55–7, 84, 155, 166, 173, 195, 215, 260, 271, 280, 289–90, 299, 302, see also humiliation
righteousness (self-righteousness) 22, 158, 217, 262, 297
rightness 259, 301, 365
ritualization 15, 28–30, 345, 361–2
role performance 92, 194–6, 198, 212–13, 353–4

sadism 136, 278, 287, 297–8, 306–7, 335, 386
secondary gain 224, 320
scapegoat 224, 358, 367, 378, see also outsider
schizoid personality 108, 268, 284–6
schizophrenia 71, 108, 205, 216, 237–43
self-absorption 230, see also self-glorification
self-actualization 157, 381–2, 390
self-consciousness 190, 213–16, 274–5, 337, 341, 383, see also self-observation
self-contempt (self-hate) 158, 193, 293–4, 298, 306, 328, see also self-recrimination

self-criticism 132, 158, 180, 194, 205, 214, 302, 315, 365
self-deception 207, 249, 282, 292, 381–2
self-defeating behaviour 180, 202, 308
self-denigration 330, see also self-contempt
self-glorification 157, 230, 261, 391
self-hate, self-hatred see self-contempt
self-imagery 157, 213, 381, see also idealized image, self-observation
selfishness 72, 83, 89, 130, 154–5, 219, 277
self-observation 124, 161, 172, 213–16, 273, 341, 381, see also self-consciousness
self-pity 216–17, 273, 297, 308–9
self-recrimination 158, 174, 268, 293–5, 300, see also self-contempt
self-regard 85–6, 148, 191, 242, 251, 258, 266, see also self-respect
self-regulating other 120
self-respect 40, 87, 132, 148, 154, 295, 323, 328, 345, see also self-regard
self-restraint 132, 289–90, 361, 375
self-seeking (social) 61, 232–3, 242–3, 277, 336, 382, see also self-actualization
self-system 131, 201–2
separation anxiety, separation distress 33, 48–50, 54, 63–4, 95, 112–13, 118, 123, 125, 129, 185, 221, 266, 357, 371
separation cries 13, 35
shame 39–40, 56–8, 70, 97, 121, 129, 157, 173–5, 208, 239, 259–61, 265–6, 274–5, 321, 354, see also embarrassment
slights 265, 278, 307, 319, 341, see also narcissistic injury
smile, smiling 27–8, 33, 35–6, 38, 42, 51, 102, 123, 125, 136, 233, 255, 280, 287, 340
social interest (social feeling) 40–1, 83, 90–2, 110, 130, 138–40, 219–20, 256, 260–2, 267, 287–8, 314
social norms 19–21, 27, 59, 98, 133, 143–4, 147, 158, 172–4, 178, 190, 257–8, 297, 301, 346–7, 362, 365–6, 368, 371, 378, 386–7, see also customs, tradition
social orientation 372

social status 17, 23, 29, 55, 68, 82, 100, 149, 195, 198, 237, 243, 257–8, 345–6, 353, 364, 368
somatization (somatic symptoms) 179, 239, 297, 319–20, *see also* hypochondria
splitting 116, 201, 270, 283, 353, 374
spontaneity 73, 92, 109, 138, 196, 220, 231, 268, 289, 292, *see also* true self
sublimation 39, 84–5, 148, 243–6
submission 14, 18, 20–4, 29, 31, 159–60, 224–5, 237–8, 263, 307, 349, 362, 366, 374–5, 386
submissiveness 34, 52, 237, 259, 300, 309, 321, 328, 367, 375
superiority 81–3, 91, 138–40, 155–6, 218–19, 223, 228–9, 231, 235–6, 247–50, 255–6, 260–2, 271, 281, 285, 287–8, 291, 297, 301, 305, 312, *see also* omnipotence
swearing 241

taboo 59, 135, 150, 157, 303, 362–4
tenderness (tender interactions) 49, 89, 100, 110, 140, 226, 312, 387
timidity 46, 140, 300–1

tradition 28, 51, 153, 237–8, 240, 257–8, 270, 362, 364, 379–80, 382–3, *see also* customs, norms
transference 55, 81, 129, 137, 152, 189, 278–9, 281, 336, 340, 348, 350–1, 369–70
transitional object 36, 249, 320
transmuting internalization 103, 124, 222, 264
triumph 99, 105, 151, 182, 219, 234, 250, 290, 297, 306, 335
true self 92, 109, 129, 131, 141, 157, 195–6, 240, 273–4, 325, *see also* spontaneity, genuineness
trust 25, 116–17, 121, 192, 195, 332, 359–60, 375

vanity 39–40, 82, 229, 249, 256, 267, 270–1, 342
vindictiveness 20, 93, 99, 250, 254, 260, 296–8, 346

wealth 198, 226, 243, 270, 275, *see also* possessions
worthlessness 101, 138, 173, 220, 222, 245, 262, 266, 269, 275, 293, 314–15, 321, 326, 330, 333–4, 338, 355, *see also* inferiority

Printed and bound by CPI Group (UK) Ltd, Croydon, CR0 4YY